31ST EDITION

Two year
olds of
2015

31ST EDITION

Two year olds of 2015

STEVE TAPLIN

Foreword by Tom Dascombe

Raceform

Published in 2015 by Raceform
27 Kingfisher Court, Hambridge Road, Newbury, Berkshire, RG14 5SJ

ISBN: 978-1-909471-99-3

Designed by Fiona Pike

Printed and bound in the UK by CPI Group (UK) Ltd, Croydon CR0 4YY

Contents

Foreword

I was delighted when Steve asked me if I would write the foreword for his excellent *Two Year Olds of 2015*. Since I started training I have had the pleasure to be included in his book and I have found it to be a valuable asset, especially in the early season two-year-old races.

When it comes to Chester in May I like to read what the trainers say about their Lily Agnes entries as this is a race that is dear to me. It is also interesting to go back over time and see what you have written about your own horses. It is good to see that my description of Brown Panther in the spring of 2010 reads: 'A big, strong colt and a really nice horse'. Unfortunately I have also made plenty of mistakes but we will gloss over those!

Steve travels around all over the British Isles interviewing trainers about their horses and the fact that so many are delighted to help him produce his wonderful book is only testament to Steve's enthusiasm and the lack of intrusion that he brings with himself. He has a knack of seeing the excitement in a trainer's face when they talk about a two-year-old that they really like and his list of Fifty to Follow is usually very informative. Getting the views of agents as well as the trainers is a very good idea such as Ivawood's description in last year's book: 'he reminds them of Toronado'.

I hope that you find *Two Year Olds of 2015* as invaluable as I am sure to.

Tom Dascombe

Introduction

Welcome to the latest edition of 'Two-Year-Olds', a book intended to highlight the best of this year's two-year-olds in England and Ireland.

It was fitting for me to ask Tom Dascombe to write the foreword this year. Not only is he an excellent trainer of two-year-olds but Manor House Stables is probably the closest Flat racing yard to my home. A wonderful training establishment it is too, being an ultra-modern complex in the heart of the beautiful Cheshire countryside. The yard is owned jointly by Michael Owen and Andrew Black, but of course Tom trains for a wide number of owners and how they all must enjoy their visits to see the horses there.

My Living Legend Racing Partnership had a great year in 2014. It was the best we've had for seven years and we even managed to achieve that rarity for racing in England – a profit! Mick Channon trained two horses for us and they both won, including Kickboxer. A tough, genuine sprinter, he was rated 109 in Timeform's brilliant 'Racehorses' annual. He's now with Godolphin. Our two horses for 2015 are also trained by Mick Channon – the sprinter Chilworth Icon and the 2-y-o colt Breslin.

My visits to the trainers this spring included a trip to Saeed bin Suroor's yard in Newmarket to get acquainted with his assistant Tony Howarth. I thoroughly enjoyed talking to Tony and it turns out that we're both Manchester United fans, so of course we're both hoping for a change in fortunes for the Red Devils. Tony was actually born and bred in Newton Heath, which was the birthplace of our team. If you see me around this year sporting a smart Godolphin jacket, you'll know where it came from!

Also in Newmarket I had a nice surprise waiting for me at William Haggas's yard. After mentioning his 'Bargain Buy', a Tamayuz filly, William immediately rang the owner, Sheikh Rashid, to ask if we could call the filly just that – Bargain Buy – and he got the thumbs up. So that made my day!

Each spring I begin by feeling a bit daunted at the prospect of arranging interviews with 70 – 80 trainers (about 40 of them in person and the rest on the telephone), in little more than three weeks. However, that feeling gradually disappears because it never ceases to surprise and delight me that so many trainers welcome me every year and are very keen to share their knowledge and enthusiasm for their young horses. I know they enjoy seeing their team of two-year-olds in the book and reading the comments from other trainers.

Pedigree enthusiasts are likely drool over many a two-year-old in the book, but just to point to two in particular take a look at this duo. Michael Halford's filly 'Pirquet' (a Sea The Stars filly out of a half-sister to Kingman) and Aidan O'Brien's enticingly named 'Coolmore' (a Galileo full sister to two of Aidan's Group 1 winners).

As always there are a number of 'horses to follow' lists, such as the sections 'Fifty To Follow' and the 'Bloodstock Experts Mark Your Card'. These are always useful for those who want to follow a select number of horses. The 'Bloodstock Experts' always do well and last year was no exception with 41 individual winners of 64 races including the champion two-year-old filly Tiggy Wiggy. That total represents the best effort by the 'experts' in all the years they've been advising us!

As usual, the two-year-olds in the book are listed under their trainers and my aim is to choose those horses most likely to be winners. You'll notice a 'star rating' for each of the two-year-olds, so take note in particular of those with three stars or more. There are no star ratings for those two-year-olds without any comments from the trainer.

I think to give them a rating just based on the pedigree is too speculative.

The following is a rough guide to my description of the ability of family members mentioned in the pedigree assessment of every two-year-old, based upon professional ratings. Please note that these descriptions are standard throughout the book in the vast majority of cases, but there are instances where I rely upon my own judgement of each horse's rating.

Below 60 = moderate
60 – 69 = modest
70 – 79 = fair
80 – 89 = quite useful
90 – 99 = fairly useful
100 – 107 = useful
108 – 112 = very useful
113 – 117 = smart
118 – 122 = very smart
123 – 127 = high-class
128 – 134 = top-class
135 and above = outstanding

To make it easier to find a specific horse the book is comprehensively indexed. So you'll find an index of the horses, their dams and their sires.

The book is divided into the following sections:

- Fifty To Follow.
- Ten to Follow in Ireland.
- Star Two-Year-Olds. This system gives an instant appraisal of the regard in which a horse is held. Those horses awarded the maximum of five stars are listed here.
- Bloodstock Experts Mark Your Card. Bloodstock agents and stud managers suggest potentially smart two-year-olds bought or raised by them.
- Bargain Buys. A list of relatively cheaply bought two-year-olds the trainers feel will turn out to be good deals.
- Two-Year-Olds of 2015. The main section of the book, with each two-year-old listed under the trainer. T*rainers' comments (when given) are in italics after the pedigree assessments*. Readers should bear in mind that all the trainers' comments come from my interviews, which took part in late March and early April.
- Stallion Reference, detailing the racing and stud careers of sires with two-year-old representatives in the book.
- Stallion Index.
- Racing Trends. An analysis of some juvenile events that regularly highlight the stars of the future. It includes a list of three-year-olds to follow this season.
- Index of Two-Year-Olds.
- Index of Dams.

Inevitably there are some unnamed horses in the book, but please access my website www.stevetaplin.co.uk throughout the season for updates on those horses named after the book was published.

Researched and compiled by
Steve Taplin BA (Hons).

Fifty to Follow

An elite selection of two-year-olds, highly thought of by their trainers.

ANCIENT ASTRONAUT
b.c. Kodiac – Tatora (Selkirk).
"His half-brother Tariq was a good winner for Peter Chapple-Hyam and this horse wouldn't be dissimilar to him. He'll come into his own over six and seven furlongs in mid-summer. Should be one to follow". John Quinn.

BIG AMIGO (IRE)
b.c. Bahamian Bounty – Goldamour (Fasliyev). *"A big colt and a lovely animal, he finds it all easy. A good-moving horse for six furlongs in the middle of May. If he proves good enough we'll go to Ascot".* Tom Dascombe.

BROROCCO
b.c. Shirocco – Lady Brora (Dashing Blade). *"A very nice horse and very similar to his brother Elm Park at this stage last year. It wouldn't surprise me if he was running in some good races in the autumn. He looks pretty nice".* Andrew Balding.

BY THE LAW
b.c. New Approach – Walk On Bye (Danehill Dancer). *"A nice, strong individual that shows some natural speed. He should be out in the early part of the season".* Charlie Appleby.

CATCHMENT
b.f. Oasis Dream – Mirror Lake (Dubai Destination). *"A lovely filly, she looks a 2-y-o runner and is doing some nice work at the moment, so hopefully we'll see her out in May. She's a lovely individual and a five/six furlong 2-y-o".* Amanda Perrett.

CINDERS (IRE)
b.f. Lilbourne Lad – The Fairies Did It (Elusive Quality). *"She goes quite well, she's got a bit of size to her and we quite like the look of her. She'll be our sharpest filly and should be racing by May or June".* Hughie Morrison.

COOL SILK BOY
b.c. Big Bad Bob – Kheleyf's Silver (Kheleyf). *"A half-brother to Tiggy Wiggy, this is a strong, good-sized horse, pretty precocious but with scope as well. We really like him and would love to think he could be a Norfolk Stakes 2-y-o".* James Given.

DUBAI FASHION (IRE)
b.f. Dubawi – Oriental Fashion (Marju). *"An attractive filly with lots of scope, a good action and a good temperament to go with it. Very straightforward, she's very nice I think".* Saeed bin Suroor.

DUTCH HEIRESS
b.f. Dutch Art – Regal Heiress (Pivotal). *"A tall filly, but she's more precocious than you'd think. She's always cantered nicely and has grown since she came here. Looks a 2-y-o".* Sir Mark Prescott.

EGLANTYNE DREAM (FR)
b.f. Oasis Dream – Bright Morning (USA) (Storm Cat). *"Likely to be one of our first 2-y-o runners, not very big, very athletic and bred to be speedy. Quite nippy at the moment, she'll be a 2-y-o in April or May".* Roger Charlton.

EMERALD BAY
b.f. Kyllachy – Bahia Emerald (Bahamian Bounty). *"A sharp filly, she wants fast ground which is unlike most by this sire and she'll be out in April or May. Very keen to please, she's not very big but strong and definitely quick".* William Haggas.

FIRST RATE
b.c. Kyllachy – Hooray (Invincible Spirit). *"This colt goes well...a strong, well-matured horse that should be out in May or June over six furlongs".* Roger Varian.

FRESH ARUGULA (IRE)
b.c. Fast Company – Temecula (High Chaparral). *"He's a lovely horse. He's got the speed for five furlongs but will probably want further, he's tall, muscular and has a great attitude".* Tom Dascombe.

GADWA
b.f. Oasis Dream – Lady Of Everest (Montjeu). *"She's just as nice as her sister Lady Of Dubai was at this stage. She's likeable, goes well and I suspect she'll be out in June or July".* Luca Cumani.

GALE SONG
b.f. Invincible Spirit – Please Sing (Royal Applause). *"A very nice filly, hugely athletic and does everything easy at this stage...A very likeable filly from a good family, she's got plenty of speed".* Ed Walker.

GIFTED MASTER (IRE)
b.c. Kodiac – Shobobb (Shamardal). *"I think he might be very smart. He's one of those horses who, from the word go, has given the impression he's done it all before. I'll be disappointed if he's not better than average".* Hugo Palmer.

GOLDEN HELLO (IRE)
b.c. Zebedee – Your Opinion (Xaar). *"Probably our sharpest colt, he does everything very easily. The riders really like him and he hasn't been off the bridle yet. It's a fast family and he's one for five/six furlongs".* Michael Bell.

GOLDENFIELD (IRE)
b.c. Footstepsinthesand – Society Gal (Gulch). *"A big, strong, well-made colt...there's plenty of quality about him. He has the right sort of temperament and he's a lovely, capable, big-moving horse that should be wheeled out mid-summer".* Olly Stevens.

HILLSIDE DREAM (IRE)
b.f. Dream Ahead – Knapton Hill (Zamindar). *"She wants a few stars adding to her name, she goes very nicely. A medium-sized, strong, imposing filly who is working well".* James Tate.

ICE AGE (IRE)
b.c. Frozen Power – Incendio (Siberian Express). *"A lovely horse, he's very racy and he'll be a six furlong 2-y-o...I'd say he'll be racing in May and he's a really nice colt".* Eve Johnson Houghton.

JERSEY BREEZE
gr.f. Dark Angel – Sixfields Flyer (Desert Style). *"Yes, she's smashing – she's got to be in the book. We haven't really done much speed work but what bits we've done she shows plenty. Everything is nice about her".* Mick Channon.

JUSTICE ANGEL (IRE)
gr.f. Dark Angel – Malaica (Roi Grande). *"A lovely, very quick filly, she'll be a nice 2-y-o and one to watch out for".* David Elsworth.

KING COLE (USA)
ch.c. Scat Daddy – Volver (Danehill Dancer). *"I really like this horse, he covers the ground really well. He looks more than capable and once we start working him I think he'll show us he's got an engine".* Robert Cowell.

KING OF DREAMS
ch.c. Dream Ahead – Complexion (Hurricane Run). *"A lovely horse, he really wants to get on with everything in a nice, professional way. I'm very pleased with him and he's very similar to his sire in the way he carries himself and the way he stands up".* David Simcock.

LUANG PRABANG (IRE)
b.f. Invincible Spirit – Sauvage (Sri Pekan). *"A nice filly, much taller now than at the sales, but she's an athletic filly and she should be a summer 2-y-o over seven furlongs. She's one I have a bit of time for".* Chris Wall.

MAGICAL PATH (IRE)
gr.f. Zebedee – Road To Reality (Indian Danehill). *"I see her as a June type 2-y-o. She's grown quite a lot and is staggeringly athletic, really strong and I like everything I've seen of her".* Hugo Palmer.

MAXIMIAN (IRE)
ch.c. Shamardal – Via Milano (Singspiel). *"A good looking colt, he's showing natural speed and he'll be ready to run early".* Charlie Appleby.

MAY ROSE (IRE)
b.f. Lawman – Rose De France (Diktat). *"A smart filly and a great mover, she's got plenty of class, won't be early but she's very correct and strong, so she could be anything".* Marco Botti.

MISS MONEYPENNY
b.f. Kodiac – Pearly Brooks (Efisio). *"I love the page, Kodiac above Efisio, and she looks to have all the toughness that her pedigree should impart. We should have a bit of sport with her over five and six furlongs".* Ralph Beckett.

MODELLO
b.f. Intikhab – Precious Citizen (Proud Citizen). *"Bigger, stronger and more relaxed than her good half-sister Bronze Maquette. She's been showing me stacks...I'm very pleased with what I've seen so far".* Gary Moore.

OH THIS IS US (IRE)
b.c. Acclamation – Shamwari Lodge (Hawk Wing). *"Out of a mare we trained who was very good, this colt goes well. A typical Acclamation, he pleases and does everything on the bridle".* Richard Hannon.

PARAFIN YOUNG
ch.c. Cape Blanco – Hasty (Invincible Spirit). *"He's well put together, the mare was quite quick and I like him a lot...if I've got one for the Chesham it might be him".* Peter Chapple-Hyam.

POINT OF WOODS
b.c. Showcasing – Romantic Myth (Mind Games). *"He's all speed and we're just starting to crank him up now. He's doing well, five or six furlongs will suit him and he's a nice horse".* Ralph Beckett.

PREDILECTION (USA)
b.c. First Defence – Summer Shower (Sadler's Wells). *"He's an early 2-y-o type you should put in the book. He's doing well and should be worth keeping an eye on during the first half of the season".* John Gosden.

RAAQY (IRE)
gr.f. Dubawi – Natagora (Divine Light). *"A quality filly with plenty of scope. Being by Dubawi she should give the dam a real chance of breeding a proper horse".* Barry Hills.

RED SPECTRE
b.c. Kyllachy – Just Devine (Montjeu). *"The most expensive yearling I bought, a half-brother to Code Red and he's by one of my favourite sires in Kyllachy. Potentially one of my star horses".* Willie Muir.

RING OF TRUTH
b.f. Royal Applause – Spinning Top (Alzao). *"She shows loads of speed, everyone who rides her likes her and although it's early days you could be forgiven for thinking she's a possible Queen Mary filly".* Richard Hannon.

SAHREEJ (IRE)
gr.c. Zebedee – Petite Boulangere (Namid). *"He's ready to run now. He's done all his prep work and everybody likes him. Well put together, he's got plenty of speed and he may well be our first 2-y-o winner".* Charlie Hills.

SANTE (IRE)
b.f. Dream Ahead – Zeiting (Zieten). *"A good horse! She looks like a 3-y-o already, very mature, well-grown and with a great attitude...she shows us a very good level of ability and could be Royal Ascot material".* Jamie Osborne.

SEPAL (USA)
b.f. Afleet Alex – Faraway Flower (Distant View). *"This is a really nice filly. She'll be a six/seven furlong 2-y-o, just needs to strengthen up a bit, but she's a lovely filly".* Charlie Hills.

SHALAA (IRE)
b.c. Invincible Spirit – Ghurra (War Chant). *"A grand colt, he's a good mover with a good attitude. He's done a bit of work already, goes nicely and is the type I'd like to have out before the end of April".* John Gosden.

SHINE LIKEADIAMOND
ch.f. Atlantic Sport – Solmorin (Fraam). *"All the family win, this filly goes really well and looks like a 2-y-o but she's got a bit of size about her too. An absolute smasher"*. Mick Channon.

STRONG CHALLENGE
ch.c. Exceed And Excel – Miss Brief (Brief Truce). *"A nice, precocious type who is showing a lot of speed...he'll go into fast work to see if he's going to be an early runner. All being well he may even be our first two-year-old runner"*. Saeed bin Suroor.

SWIRRAL EDGE
b.f. Hellvelyn – Pizzarra (Shamardal). *"A very nice filly. Well put-together, she'll be running soon and looks the part. It's a fast family and she's inherited that speed"*. David Brown.

TETRADRACHM
b.c. Holy Roman Emperor – Dahlia's Krissy (Kris S). *"He's going very well, he's a good-sized horse, has a good mind and is an attractive colt with a touch of quality. Everything about him is nice"*. David Lanigan.

THE LILLSTER
b.f. Kodiac – Wind Surf (Lil's Lad). *"A strong filly, she's quite big but she'll be a 2-y-o alright. She has a lot of quality and the speed for five furlongs in May. She'd be my pick at the moment"*. David Lanigan.

VROOM
ch.c. Poet's Voice – Shivaree (Rahy). *"A very sharp little horse. He's done two pieces of work already, he'll be out very early and I'm really pleased with the way he's going...he's got a beautiful action so he wouldn't want soft ground"*. Charlie Fellowes.

WARRIOR SONG (USA)
b.f. Harlan's Holiday – More Oats Please (Smart Strike). *"A half-sister to our 2-y-o Grade 1 winner from last year Peace And War and she's very similar to her. I really like her, she's got bags of quality"*. Olly Stevens.

WAR WHISPER (IRE) ****
b.c. Royal Applause – Featherweight (Fantastic Light). *"A nice big colt, he goes well, we like him and he could be a Royal Ascot 2-y-o"*. Richard Hannon.

UNNAMED
b.f. Hellvelyn – Talampaya (Elusive Quality). *"A very big, very strong filly... if she wasn't so big she'd almost be running now. We'll give her a bit more time and she should be one to follow"*. Henry Candy.

Ten to Follow in Ireland

AASHEQ (IRE)
b.c. Dubawi – Beach Bunny (High Chaparral). *"A lovely colt, we like him a lot. One for July/August over seven furlongs, he's a strong, powerful horse".* Dermot Weld.

ARGENTERO
ch.c. Zoffany – Frabjous (Pivotal). *"A grand, straightforward colt, he's done everything we've asked of him and he'll be out sooner rather than later. We like him and he'll win his maiden".* Ger Lyons.

COOLMORE
b.f. Galileo – You'resothrilling (Storm Cat). A full sister to two Group 1 winners (the dam's first two foals) and given the huge endorsement of carrying the name of the world famous Coolmore Stud. She has plenty to live up to, so look out for her. Trained by Aidan O'Brien.

CRY ME A RIVER (IRE)
b.f. Danehill Dancer – River Flow (Affirmed). *"She goes nicely, we'll probably set her off at six furlongs and she's a big, strong, mature filly. She goes well".* Tommy Stack.

MUNAASHID (USA)
b.br.c. Lonhro – Freefourracing (French Deputy). *"A very nice colt that came from Goffs Sales, he looks a 2-y-o and he'll be out around June/July. I like this horse".* Dermot Weld.

REDDOT DANCER (IRE)
b.c. Danehill Dancer – Roselyn (Efisio). *"A beautiful, big horse, he does everything easily and has a good action. He's got a good attitude and he'll make a 2-y-o in the second half of the year".* Michael Halford.

ROCKAWAY VALLEY (IRE)
b.c. Holy Roman Emperor – Sharapova (Elusive Quality). *"He's sharp and could be running in May. A medium-sized, good-moving colt with a good attitude, he has a bit of quality I think".* Jessie Harrington.

STAR OF KINGS
b.f. Sea The Stars – Kocooning (King's Best). *"A particularly nice filly, she'll make a 2-y-o and she comes from quite a fast family. A lovely looker, she's lengthy, a beautiful mover and a perfect representative of the sire's stock. She'll be out in June".* John Oxx.

SPIRIT GLANCE
b.f. Invincible Spirit – Gonfilia (Big Shuffle). *"A sharp type of filly, she's done everything well so far and should be one of our first fillies to run. She's very straightforward, does everything nicely and is one to start at six furlongs".* Michael Halford.

SUFOOF (IRE)
b.f. Acclamation – Walayef (Danzig). *"We like her a lot, she should be racing in May and the family are better off going six furlongs than five. I think she'll make a nice 2-y-o, she's very strong and looks like a 3-y-o now".* Kevin Prendergast.

Star Two-Year-Olds

The stars placed along the side of each two-year-old in the main section of the book give the reader an instant appraisal of the regard in which they are held. The highest rating a horse can attain is five stars.

Bear in mind that some of the 'Five Star' horses will be at their peak as three-year-olds, so you should definitely keep an eye on them next year as well. Last year the high-class filly and Group 1 Moyglare Stud Stakes winner Cursory Glance was in this list.

The five-star two-year-olds of 2015 are listed below for quick reference.

b.f. Elusive Quality – Causeway Lass	Charlie Appleby
VISCOUNT BARFIELD	Andrew Balding
DESERT HAZE	Ralph Beckett
MOST CELEBRATED	Saeed bin Suroor
NAJM KABIR	Saeed bin Suroor
b.c. Champs Elysees – Dahama	Marco Botti
SUBOTAL	Luca Cumani
DASHING APPROACH	David Elsworth
MIDDLEMAN ❧	John Gosden
SOVEREIGN PARADE	John Gosden
LAPILLI	William Haggas
MUZDAWAJ	William Haggas
GREAT PAGE	Richard Hannon
MANAAFIDH	Richard Hannon
DARK CRESCENT	Charlie Hills
b.c. Lope De Vega – Danielli	Hugo Palmer
ZHUI FENG	Amanda Perrett
BEBHINN	Kevin Prendergast
SHOW AYA	Olly Stevens
AMAZEMENT	James Tate
AGHAANY	Roger Varian
TRUE SOLITAIRE	Dermot Weld

The Bloodstock Experts Mark Your Card

Each year the number of winners from this section seems to increase. Last year the Experts found 41 winners of 64 races which was the best total yet, compared to the previous best of 39 of 58 in 2014. The message is clear – you should take very careful note of the following selections.

The stakes winners pinpointed last year were Baitha Alga, Beacon, Ivawood, Mind Of Madness, Muhaarar, Osaila and Tiggy Wiggy. Amazing!

The experts who selected two individual winners apiece last year were Charlie Gordon-Watson, Harry Herbert's Al Shaqab picks (the Group winners Baitha Alga & Osaila), Luke Lillingston, David Redvers (including the Listed winner Mind Of Madness), Chris Richardson, Ed Sackville and Peter Stanley.

With three winners apiece were Malcolm Bastard (including the breeze-up horse and Group 3 winner New Providence), Alistair Donald, Ross Doyle (whose picks included the Group 1 Cheveley Park winner Tiggy Wiggy), Harry Herbert's Highclere picks (they included the Flying Childers winner Beacon) and Amanda Skiffington (including the dual Group 2 winner Ivawood).

Angus Gold only had five selections but, impressively, four of them won including the Gimcrack winner Muhaarar.

I'm going to declare the Top Tipster award a draw between Ross Doyle, Harry Herbert and Angus Gold. From a small selection Ross picked another Champion in Tiggy Wiggy (after selecting Toormore in 2014). Angus got four winners from five including the Gimcrack victor. Harry had plenty of picks between the Highclere and Al Shaqab camps, but they were certainly inspired because they included three Group winners!

Remember, most of the two-year-olds selected here can be found in the main section of the book listed under their trainers and highlighted by the symbol ♠

MALCOLM BASTARD

'I've dealt with well over 100 of this year's 2-y-o's, breaking them in, prepping them for the sales or pre-training them etc. Here's a selection of really nice ones, some of which I still have but will be sending them out to their trainers shortly'.

ELJEEMI (IRE)
b.c. Shamardal – Arthur's Girl. A nice, strong colt that moves well, he has a good temperament and he's been in steady work with us. Due to go to William Haggas.

GALA
b.f. Galileo – Misk. She's one for the back-end of the season but she's big and strong. For a filly of her size and at this time of the year, everything she's doing makes her look good. She'll be going to John Gosden.

HENRY CROFT
b.c. Dubawi – Karen's Caper. A big, strong colt, like a lot of Dubawi's he doesn't have the best action but he's very powerful and he could be anything as a 3-y-o. He'll be going to John Gosden.

PURE VANITY.
b.f. New Approach – Miss Pinkerton. Not over-big, but she has a lot of quality and moves nicely. She gets to the top of the gallop easily and is more than likely an autumn filly. She's nice. Roger Charlton.

RAINBOW LIGHT (USA)
b.f. Tapit – Rainbow View (Dynaformer). A gorgeous filly belonging to Mr Strawbridge that came to us in February from America. The dam was a champion 2-y-o. This filly was

just broken and riding when she arrived and we've been fairly quiet with her, just giving her foundation work. She's just gorgeous to look at, seriously strong, a nice medium-size and a very good action cantering. I'd like to think she could be a very good horse. She's going to go to John Gosden.

UNNAMED

b.f. Galileo – Baraka. She's only been in steady work with us but she just looks above average for what we're doing with her. William Haggas.

UNNAMED

b.c. Fastnet Rock – Crystal Maze. A very nice half-brother to the French Group 1 winner Okavango. He'll be a back-end colt but he goes really well and he's very strong. He moves well and we like him a lot. John Gosden.

UNNAMED

b.c. Oasis Dream – Independence. We sold him the other day at the Tattersalls Craven Breeze Up to John Ferguson for 250,000 Gns. He's a really nice colt with a nice action when he's galloping and a lot of pace. He should be very nice come the autumn and hopefully a good horse as a 3-y-o.

UNNAMED

ch.c. Eskendereya – La Capella. An absolutely gorgeous colt to look at. He's strong, a nice medium size and has very clean limbs. I expect he'll start at seven furlongs but I'm hoping he could be very nice. I sold him at the Craven Breeze Up to Blandford Bloodstock for 90,000 Gns.

UNNAMED

b.c. Shamardal – Multicolour Wave. He looks a quality horse and I assume he'll be a late summer 2-y-o. He stands 16 hands, he's strong and the stallion is doing phenomenally well. He's a good actioned colt and gives us all the right vibes. John Gosden.

UNNAMED

c. Hat Trick – Promptly. A good-looking colt, 15.3 hands, he has a laid-back action. I know the family well and he could be a nice colt in the autumn and a nice 3-y-o. He's going to Sir Michael Stoute.

ALISTAIR DONALD
DARK SIEGE

b.c. Iffraaj – Green Poppy (Green Desert). He cost 115,000 Gns from Tattersalls Book 2. A very athletic, no nonsense horse, he does everything very well. Should be ready around June over 6/7f. Ed Walker.

LITTLE VOICE

b.f. Scat Daddy – Excelente. €160,000 from Goffs Orby. A very speedy looking filly with a nice pedigree and a great hind end. Doing everything very well and will be ready in May. Charlie Hills.

SHANGHAI GLORY

ch.c. Exceed And Excel – Hecuba. €115,000 from Goffs Orby. He was my favourite yearling last year and never expected to be able to afford him. He has a very fast pedigree and will hopefully be another Cotai Glory for the same owners. Should be running in May over 5f. Charlie Hills.

SHOW AYA

ch.f. Showcasing – Mimiteh. 27,000 Gns. Doncaster Premier Sale. She's a strong, stocky, sprinting filly. Reports are very good and she'll be ready in May. Olly Stevens.

TRIKINGDOM

b.c. Showcasing – Spritzeria. 65,000 Gns. Tattersalls Book 2. A strong, typical Showcasing, bred to be fast. He'll be ready by mid-summer over 6f. Ed Walker.

PETER DOYLE
ARCTIC ANGEL (IRE)

b.c. Dark Angel – Charlene Lacy. A sharp sort by another favourite sire, hopefully he won't keep us waiting. Dean Ivory.

HUMPHREY BOGART

b.c. Tagula – Hazarama. A nice colt by a favoured sire, he has developed well and we're looking forward to his debut. Richard Hannon.

SUNSET DREAM

b.f. Acclamation – Oasis Sunset. This is a gorgeous filly by the outstanding Acclamation and the updates are encouraging. Richard Hannon.

ZHUI FENG (IRE)

b.c. Invincible Spirit – Es Que. A real nice horse with a tremendous walk and a pedigree to match. Amanda Perrett.

ROSS DOYLE

GREAT PAGE

b.f. Roderic O'Connor – Areeda. We purchased her at the Tattersalls Ireland September yearling sale for Middleham Park Racing. We thought she was the best mover in the sale and very good looking as well. She is a nice, medium-sized filly with plenty of strength in the right places and by a first season sire we like. Richard Hannon.

OH THIS IS US

b.c. Acclamation – Shamwari Lodge. We purchased him at the Goffs Orby yearling sale for Team Wallop. This fella is a very sharp looking horse out of a very good race mare, Shamwari Lodge, who we also bought as a yearling. He looks like he won't take too long to come to hand. Richard Hannon.

PREMIER CURRENCY

b.c. Elusive Pimpernel – Zeena. We purchased him at the DBS Premier yearling sale for William Drew. He is a very mature colt with plenty of size and a great mover as well. The stallion's stock kept catching our eye at the sales and this fella was the nicest one we saw at the sales by him. Richard Hannon.

TAQWAA

ch.c. Iffraaj – Hallowed Park. Purchased at the Tattersalls Newmarket yearling sale Book 2 for Shadwell Stud. He is a very classy individual, very good looking and a great mover by a very decent sire that can get very good horses. Richard Hannon.

WILL EDMEADES

CLIFF EDGE

b.c. Canford Cliffs – That's My Style. A really nice colt, he was purchased at DBS Premier for Thurloe and was, in my view, an eye-catching individual from the first crop of his sire. His dam, by Dalakhani, did not win until she was four, but this colt looks as if he will be a mid season two year old. With Roger Varian.

PORT PARADISE

gr.g. Paco Boy – Yacht Woman. A nice, scopey sort bought from Tattersalls Book 3 for a client of William Jarvis. His dam was a stakes winner in Italy and her first foal won twice at 2 in France. Off games with sore shins at present, but his trainer likes him. William Jarvis.

REMEMBER ME

b.f. Acclamation – Forgotten Me. Typical of her sire, this well named filly came from Tattersalls Book 2 for Thurloe Thoroughbreds. A very good mover with a great outlook, she is from an unraced half sister to two Listed winners, so she has a fair page. Hughie Morrison is sweet on her.

TAILWIND

b.c. Dubawi – Time Saved. With an even cleverer name than the previous 2-y-o in my list, this tough looking colt was raised and grazed here at Fair Winter Farm. From Day 1 he has been an outstanding individual, very typical of his prolific sire and from a successful cross. He narrowly failed to achieve our valuation in Tattersalls Book 1 - probably because he was the first Dubawi in a sale which did not wake up until Day 2 - and is in training with Roger Varian.

TOM GOFF

GINGER JOE

ch.c. Medicean – Susi Wong. The pick of our Doncaster purchases for me. A really sharp Medicean colt purchased alongside Peter Chapple-Hyam. We've both always had a bit of luck with the sire and the dam has produced three black type performers to date and he is out of a Selkirk mare which we both love. He cost £32,000 from Brendan Holland's Grove Stud, Ireland and looks very sharp at the moment. Peter Chapple-Hyam.

LULWORTH (IRE)

b.c. Canford Cliffs – Aitch. A really nice colt bought with James Toller at Tattersalls October Book 3 for 22,000gns. I bought the half brother by Yeats a few years back and he showed plenty of ability but sadly split a pastern badly on his second start and had to be put down. This fellow is a lot sharper and has loads of quality from Luke Barry's Manister

House Stud, Ireland. I would be hopeful that he'd make into a nice July time type with a tail wind. James Toller.

UNNAMED
b.c. Rip Van Winkle – Chehalis Sunset. We bought this colt at Tattersalls October Book 2 for the not meagre sum of 260,000 Gns for Mrs Mary Slack and John Gosden. Bred by Clairemont Stud in Hampshire, he is the most beautiful colt and a really lovely mover. I love the stallion and would be very hopeful about this colt's prospects long term although it's obviously very early days. John Gosden.

UNNAMED
b.c. Starspangledbanner – Donna Giovanna. This colt was a real star and we gave 105,000 Gns for him at Tattersalls. He doesn't have a massive page but is what I would call a proper two-year-old racehorse individual who we all loved from Drumachon Stud, Ireland. He seems relatively sharp and I would like to think he might be a June/July two-year-old with a bit of luck on his side. John Gosden.

ANGUS GOLD
DHAROOS (IRE)
ch.c. New Approach – Cailiocht. This is another horse we bought as a foal who seems to have a very good temperament and looks a good sort. I hope he will be a nice horse from mid-summer onwards. John Gosden.

ELRONAQ
b.c. Invincible Spirit – Cartimandua. We bought this horse as a foal and he has always been a good sort to me. I don't think he'll be particularly early, but hopefully he'll be a nice horse from mid-summer onwards. Charlie Hills.

MUJAMALA (IRE)
b.f. Exceed And Excel – Habaayib. She is the second foal of a mare who won the Albany at Ascot and was second in the Cherry Hinton. A sharp looking filly, the trainer says she shows plenty of speed so far. Ed Dunlop.

RAAQY.
gr.f. Dubawi – Natagora. This is the fourth and much the nicest foal out of Natagora who was

the champion two year old filly and trained on to win the 1000 Guineas. She is a lovely type of filly who could be pretty nice in the second part of the season. Barry Hills.

TABARRAK (IRE)
b.c. Acclamation – Bahati. We paid plenty of money for this horse at Doncaster Sales and he looks a really good sort of Acclamation to me. I believe the Hannon team like him so far. Richard Hannon.

CHARLIE GORDON-WATSON
This is quite a cross section of selections ranging from 22,000 Gns to 550,000 Gns. It will be interesting to see if Poet's Voice gets mid-season two-year-olds, but reports are positive. I would expect the John Gosden trained Shalaa to be the earliest. Perhaps I'm playing safe with two by Oasis Dream and Invincible Spirit. I am very fortunate that I buy horses for the most talented of trainers.

ALDAIR
b.c. Pastoral Pursuits – Tremelo Pointe. 22,000 Gns. Richard Hannon.

CHESTER STREET
b.c. Invincible Spirit – Expressive. 70,000 Gns. Roger Charlton.

MELABI (IRE)
b.c. Oasis Dream – Briolette. 250,000Y. William Haggas.

POET'S WORD (IRE)
b.c. Poet's Voice – Whirly Bird. 300,000 Gns. Sir Michael Stoute.

SHALAA (IRE)
b.c. Invincible Spirit – Ghurra. 170,000 Gns. John Gosden.

VROOM
ch.c. Poet's Voice – Shivaree. 45,000 Gns. Charlie Fellowes.

UNNAMED
gr.c. Oasis Dream – Warling (Montjeu). 550,000 Gns. John Gosden.

ED HARPER
BARRON'S LAD
ch.c. Compton Place – Dance Away. A £50,000 purchase at DBS, he's a small colt with a very big walk. He caught the eye of many good judges at Doncaster and he should be precocious. David Barron.

EXCESSABLE
ch.c. Sakhee's Secret – Kummel Excess. Bought for £6,000 at DBS, this colt was always very powerful with very strong hind quarters even as a young foal. I think he was well bought by Tim Easterby.

EXIST
b.f. Exceed and Excel – Harryana. A 180,000gns half-sister to Temple Meads, she looks like a sharp early 2-y-o. The ideal 'Queen Mary' type of filly. John Gosden.

TREVOR HARRIS
GALE SONG
b.f. Invincible Spirit – Please Sing. We bought her as a foal at Tattersalls in 2013 for 120,000 gns and she's a half-sister to the three year old Dubawi colt Four Seasons, who has won five races already including the three year old Mile Championship at Lingfield. Please Sing won the Group 2 Cherry Hinton and the mare has made a good start. She should be a two year old but not early and she'll be out around July. Ed Walker

LUCKY LOT
b.f. Exceed and Excel – Sweetie Time. She was sold as a yearling at Arqana in August to Anthony Stroud for 165,000 euros. Her dam was a Listed placed two year old winner and this is her first foal. She looks a ready-made two year old and hopefully will be out before the middle of the season. Simon Crisford.

LUGANO
b.c. Galileo – Swiss Lake. He was sold at Tattersalls Book 1 for 250,000 gns. He is a big colt, with plenty of scope. Most of the family have been precocious early two year old types but this colt will take longer, however he could be out at the end of the summer. He is a half-brother to the Group 3 winners Swiss Spirit and Swiss Diva, triple Listed winner Swiss

Dream and Coventry Stakes runner up Swiss Franc. Sir Mark Prescott.

UNNAMED
b.f. Dream Ahead – Flanders. A good looking, strong filly we bought from Tattersalls Book 1 sale for 400,000 gns. She is a half-sister to the European three year old Group 1 winning sprinter G-Force and to the dam of French Guineas winner Flotilla. Although she'll be a sprinter, she'll probably not be out until the middle of the summer and should be one for the second half of the season. William Haggas.

HARRY HERBERT
Here are a few thoughts on Highclere and Al Shaqab two year olds:

HIGHCLERE
AUXILIARY
b.g. Fast Company – Lady Xara. We gelded this cracking son of Fast Company because he was getting to be rather interested in the ladies. He has come through that operation very well and is back in full exercise. He could be making his debut in May and is one that I really like despite the early gelding. William Haggas.

FOUNDATION
ch.c. Zoffany – Roystonea. This is an outstanding son of first season sire Zoffany and is one of those colts that really takes your breath away. He gets to the top of Warren Hill with the minimum of fuss and should be on everyone's Highclere two year old short list! John Gosden.

PLANTATION
b.c. Invincible Spirit – Matula. This is a neat, racy colt who is finding it all very easy and he just could be our first two year old runner this season. He is not the biggest but is one of those that really elevates himself with a rider on board and I will be disappointed if he isn't capable of winning races this season. Roger Varian.

PROSECUTE
b.c. Lawman – Dissitation. This colt looks very strong and well balanced and is one of those who gets to the top of Warren Hill with the

greatest of ease. He could easily by making his debut when the first 7f maidens come along. David Simcock.

RAUCOUS
b.c. Dream Ahead – Shyrl. I really like this son of first season sire Dream Ahead. He is a very strong quartered colt who is finding it all very easy and I know that William regards him as one of his more precocious two year olds. He is one of ours that just could make up into a Royal Ascot prospect. William Haggas.

TORMENT
gr.c. Dark Angel – Selkirk Sky. A very strong and well balanced son of Dark Angel who moves beautifully. I see him as a mid-summer starter and from what we have seen so far he possesses a wonderful temperament. Richard Hannon.

AL SHAQAB
DHEBAN (IRE)
gr.c. Exceed And Excel - Comeback Queen. This is a cracking two year old in the making who really catches the eye when out in Richard's string. He has a great action and could make up into a Royal Ascot prospect. Richard Hannon.

ELTEZAM (IRE)
b.c. Kodiac – Tymora. This is a real tank of a colt and is another that catches the eye out in the string. He has a great action and holds himself in the manner of a decent colt in the making. Richard Hannon.

FASHAAK (IRE)
b.c. Starspangledbanner – Szabo. This colt reminds me of The Wow Signal and hopefully he will be good enough to follow in his footsteps! He is very strong and seems to find it all very easy at the moment. Richard Hannon.

MELABI (IRE)
b.c. Oasis Dream – Briolette. This is a neat, strong, precocious looking son of Oasis Dream who reminds me of a two year old we had at Highclere called Gusto who was by the same sire. I would be disappointed if he can't make an impact this season and he just could be precocious enough to run before Royal Ascot. William Haggas.

SHALAA (IRE)
b.c. Invincible Spirit – Ghurra. I love this colt and he looks to be a really precocious sort who could be making his debut in May. John Gosden.

UNNAMED
b.c. Shamardal – Multicolour Wave. We have a few Shamardal two year olds who are all lovely horses but this one looks as though he will be the most precocious. He finds it all very easy and should be making his mark in the second half of the season. John Gosden.

UNNAMED
ch.c. New Approach – Waadat. This is a cracking son of New Approach who looks as though he will be strong enough to make into a summer two year old. Watching him recently I was very taken with the ease with which he went up Warren Hill. Luca Cumani.

UNNAMED
b.c. Champs Elysees – Dahama. This is an absolute beauty who also boasts a wonderful pedigree being a half brother to Al Thakhira. He has much more scope than his sister but he still looks strong enough to be making his mark by mid-summer. Marco Botti.

RICHARD KNIGHT
ANCIENT ASTRONAUT
b.c. Kodiac – Tatora. I purchased this colt twice as I bought him as a foal to pinhook and then purchased him with the Quinn's as a yearling in Book 1. He was a very athletic colt and I am told he is expected to make into a nice summer 2-y-o. John Quinn.

ARTISANDRA (FR)
ch.f. Mastercraftsman – Kezia. Purchased for €60,000 from the Arqana Yearling sale with William and she was a scopey, good moving filly. I am told that she moves well and William is very happy with her. William Knight.

LEARNING CURVE (IRE)
b.c. Monsieur Bond – Existentialist. Purchased for £65,000 from Doncaster Premier sale with

the Quinn's and he was a tough, sharp looking colt. I am told he moves well and will be out in May time. John Quinn.

SPIRIT OF ZEBEDEE (IRE)
gr.c. Zebedee colt ex Sampers. Purchased for €60,000 from Tattersalls Ireland with the Quinn's and he was a strong, powerful colt who looked every inch a 2-y-o. I am told he moves well, is tough and likeable. John Quinn.

UNNAMED
b.c. Approve – Miznapp. Purchased for €47,000 from Goffs with the Quinn's and he was a tall, good-looking, good moving colt. I am told he is a 6f/7f horse who has always done his work easily. John Quinn.

UNNAMED
b.c. Lilbourne Lad – Elizabelle. Purchased for 34,000gns in the Tattersalls December sale with William having loved him when I first saw him in Tattersalls Ireland where he had to be withdrawn on the day of the sale having got cast. He looked a sharp 2-y-o and I am told that he is coming along well. William Knight.

LUKE LILLINGSTON
ARGENTERO
ch.c. Zoffany – Frabjous. We pinhooked him from Tattersalls December to Doncaster and was a colt we really liked through the year. He is in the right hands and I believe is creating a good early impression. Ger Lyons.

LOVE ON THE ROCKS (IRE)
ch.f. Exceed And Excel – My Love Thomas. A strong , well balanced and really fast looking filly. Her dam is a daughter of Flanders and is a half sister to G Force so she is bred to fly. Early reports are encouraging . Charlie Hills.

STEEL OF MADRID (IRE)
b.c. Lope De Vega – Bibury. A colt who really improved in the latter stages of last year. He took the eye of the Doyle / Hannon team and is now in the right place to be another good runner for his sire. Richard Hannon.

STROKE OF MIDNIGHT (IRE)
br.f. Dark Angel – Timbre. We bought her at Fairyhouse for Kennet Valley Thoroughbreds.

By a very reliable stallion and with high class fillies Calando and Diminuendo as her second and third dams she received an encouraging entry in the Weatherbys Super Sprint, suggesting that she will not take too long . Richard Hannon.

TI AMO (IRE)
f. Holy Roman Emperor – Became. When we bought this filly at the Goffs Sportsmans sale we wondered if she was big enough . She has developed out of all proportion and being out a Giants Causeway mare from a decent US family she is starting to show some of the potential her pedigree would suggest. John Joseph Murphy.

JOHNNY MCKEEVER
PRINCESS KODIA (IRE)
b.f. Kodiac – Pixie's Blue. She cost £20,000 from Doncaster Premier. A really sharp, speedy sort and hopefully a Royal Ascot type for this prolific sire. Brian Meehan.

UNNAMED
b.c. Acclamation – Fritta Mista. He cost 47,000gns from Tattersalls Book 2. He's an own brother to the very useful Montecchio and a half to Sans Reward who I also bought for Brian and was a decent two year old in his own right. Brian Meehan.

UNNAMED
b.c. High Chaparral – Diarra Angel. He cost 35,000gns from Tattersalls December. Probably not the earliest, but he should make into a very nice horse come the Autumn. Hugo Palmer.

UNNAMED
b.f. Mastercraftsman – Dama'a. A 35,000gns purchase from Tattersalls Book 2. Another by a prolific sire who looks every inch a smart two year old in the making. Hugo Palmer.

DAVID MCGREAVY
TRANSPENNINE STAR
gr.g. Mount Nelson – Brave Mave. I bought him as a foal and he was 'stolen' at the saes by a very good judge. He may need the summer on his back but he's a very good prospect. Michael Dods.

UNNAMED

b.f. Acclamation – Musical Bar. A really sweet filly of great quality who shows lots of potential and should win this year before going on to a higher level. Noel Quinlan.

UNNAMED

b.f. Invincible Spirit – Bratislava. An all-quality filly with a superb outlook. She should blossom through the summer and prove top-class in the autumn. William Haggas.

KIRSTEN RAUSING
ALAMODE

ch.f. Sir Percy – Almamia (Hernando). More forward than her pedigree would at first glance suggest, this filly should win at two. Marcus Tregoning.

CLEAR CUT

b.c. Acclamation – Claiomh Solais (Galileo). A €300,000 Goffs Orby yearling, bred by Lanwades and Mrs J.S.Bolger. An athletic, forward sort, in very good hands; should be seen out by early Summer. His winning dam was also fourth in the Irish 1,000 Guineas and is an own sister to Group winners Cuis Ghaire and Scintilulla. Jim Bolger.

GALAPIAT

b.c. Galileo – Lady Jane Digby. Unsold at Tattersalls Oct Sales Book One, this colt is subject of very favourable reports from his master trainer, and is expected to appear in public by mid-season. His dam won a German Group One and is three-parts sister to multiple Group Three winner Gateman, their unraced dam being a half sister to European Champion Sprinter Polish Patriot. Andre Fabre.

HOT TO THE TOUCH

gr.f. Aussie Rules – Heat of the Night. A filly with quite some speed. Her sire had 21 individual 2-y-o winners in 2014, her dam was a Listed winner over 8f at 3. She is pleasing her Group 1 (Fiesolana, by Aussie Rules) trainer. W. McCreery – Ireland.

IN THE CITY

ch.c. Exceed and Excel – Soft Morning. A 100,000 gns purchase from Tattersalls October Book One. A sturdy, sprinty-looking

colt from a very good Lanwades family. His dam was a Listed winner at 3 in Deauville. William Haggas.

MS GILLARD

b.f. Aussie Rules – Oval Office. A forward sort and a half-sister to the Group (at 2) winner Glass Office and the useful Captain Morley. Her sire had 21 individual 2-y-o winners in 2014, her dam was unbeaten in her only two starts in a career shortened by injury. David Simcock.

ZANJABEEL

b.c. Aussie Rules – Grain Only. A 210,000 gns purchase from Tattersalls October Book Two. A lovely colt, with much athletic prowess and presence. A half-brother to the Group 3 winner Caravan Rolls On, this colt will not need staying distances but should be seen to advantage when the 7f races commence. His sire had 21 individual 2-y-o winners in 2014. Simon Crisford.

UNNAMED

gr.c. Archipenko – Albanova (Alzao). Unsold at Tattersalls Oct Sales Book One, this colt is now much admired. He should be out by early Autumn. His dam won her only start at two, and went on to win three Gr 1's and a Horse of the Year title in Germany. David Simcock.

BRUCE RAYMOND
ACROSS THE STARS

b.c. Sea The Stars – Victoria Cross. A lovely horse with a great action. Should be out around September time. Sir Michael Stoute.

ADHAM

b.c. Dream Ahead – Leopard Creek. This 2-y-o gallops well. Will be early. James Tate.

AMAZEMENT

ch.c. Lope De Vega – Aglow. A big, strong colt with loads of quality. Should be early. James Tate.

BALLET CONCERTO

b.c. Dansili – Ballet Ballon. A good looking colt, he'll make a 2-y-o by mid-season. Sir Michael Stoute.

UNNAMED
b.c. Manduro – Krynica. A well-balanced, quality colt and the pick of Clive's two-year-olds. Clive Brittain.

DAVID REDVERS
CAPE ORFORD
ch.c. Cape Blanco – Latte. A $200,000 yearling purchase from Keeneland. A lovely looking colt who we're very pleased with so far. Michael Bell.

GWENDOLYN (GER)
b.f. Invincible Spirit – Golden Whip. A 60,000Gns yearling purchase from Tattersalls. An attractive racy filly who will hopefully be quite forward. Roger Varian.

NEW HOPE
b.c. Exceed and Excel – Great Hope. A €375,000 yearling purchase from Goffs, he's a smart, quality colt we're very excited about. Kevin Ryan.

RESTIVE
b.c. Rip Van Winkle – I Hearyou Knocking. This colt cost £110,000 yearling purchase from DBS. He's a very nice colt. Ger Lyons.

WAR QUEEN
b.f. Acclamation – New Deal. €67,000 yearling purchase from Tattersalls Ireland. A particularly nice physical and a full sister to New Pearl, who we had previously. David Brown.

UNNAMED
b.f. Hellvelyn – Talampaya. A 50,000 gns yearling purchase from Tattersalls, this filly is a strong precocious type who is going nicely. Henry Candy.

CHRIS RICHARDSON
DANCING YEARS
ch.f. Iffraaj – Daganya. Her dam was a Listed winner and Group placed in the Group 2 Big Shuffle Flying Five and is a full sister to the talented Snaefell, so all speed. Cost €175,000. Richard Fahey.

EMERALD BAY
b.f. Kyllachy – Bahia Emerald. Her dam was a dual winner and is a half sister to Vital Statistics, who won The EBF Dick Poole Stakes and who was third in the Princess Margaret Stakes Group 3 at Ascot. William Haggas.

EXIST
b.f. Exceed and Excel – Harryana. A half sister to the precocious Temple Meads, winner of the Dubai Duty Free Mill Reef Stakes Group 2. Cost 180,000 Guineas – she looks a sharp prospect. John Gosden.

QUEEN'S TRUST
b.f. Dansili – Queen's Best. This filly may not be that precocious, but she is a lovely mover. Out of a mare who won the Winter Hill Stakes Group 3 and who was placed second in the Blandford Stakes Group 2; it is only a matter of time before the mare produces a filly of similar talent. Sir Michael Stoute.

ED SACKVILLE
CHARLOTTE ROYALE (IRE)
gr.f. Zoffany – Lady Gray. This is a big scopey filly who is really beginning to fill out and look the part. I imagine she will start off over six. The trainer has an exceptional record with De La Warr Racing's two-year-olds over the last couple of years so lets hope this filly continues the run. Richard Hannon.

UNNAMED
ch.c. Exceed And Excel – Hill Welcome. A big, imposing colt I actually saw on the farm in the springtime. I loved him then and so was delighted to be able to buy him at Donny. Both Tom and I have been lucky with the stallion. Tom Dascombe.

UNNAMED
b.f. Kodiac – Skyscape. I bought this sharp looking filly for €17,000 for first season trainer Henry Spiller. He trained under Godolphin, so he'll know how to ready a 2-y-o. I thought this filly was great value and she's by a brilliant sire. Henry Spiller.

UNNAMED
b.c. Mastercraftsman – Wosaita. A lovely, big, scopey colt. He won't be the earliest but he's the type to keep on improving and he has a pedigree to match his looks. Ed De Giles.

ROBIN SHARP
LOLWAH
ch.f. Pivotal – Palace Affair. Bought by one of the best in John Warren, which says it all, but she won't be early. Sir Michael Stoute.

POLLY'S SERENADE
b.f. Kyllachy – Flamenco Dancer. I'm sure she'll keep everybody on their toes at the trainer's yard but I think she'd run through a brick wall for you. Sure to win. Clive Cox.

UNNAMED
ch.c. Exceed And Excel – Indian Love Bird. This was a smashing colt with a great action who has gone to one of the best young trainers in the country. Andrew Balding.

UNNAMED
b.f. Iffraaj – Pitrizza (Machiavellian). A fantastic looking filly, she could be very classy and I hope she is lucky for one of the best couples in racing, Clare and Denis Barry. Richard Hannon.

AMANDA SKIFFINGTON
ARCHANGEL GABRIEL
b.f. Arch – Princess Kris. 200,000 Gns. A strong two year old type who is a sister/ half-sister to two Group One winners, let's hope this one can make it three for the dam. Roger Charlton.

BAY OF ST MALO
b.f. Canford Cliffs – Distant Skies. 45,000 Gns. She looked to go really well when I was at the Hannon's a couple of weeks ago, and there were a few polite words about her from them. Richard Hannon.

HAWKSMOOR (IRE)
b.f. Azamour – Bridal Dance. €80,000. This filly just glides up the gallops looking every inch an athlete and I really look forward to seeing her on the racecourse, probably mid-season. Hugo Palmer.

HIGH SHIELDS
b.c. Shamardal – Marine City. A lovely Shamardal colt, he cost 100,000 Gns. I think I stole him – in fact I know I did, as I was offered a large profit on him afterwards which his owner bravely turned down. Hopefully he

will be repaid by this great moving colt. Roger Charlton.

MAGICAL PATH
gr.f. Zebedee – Road to Reality. €20,000. A very strong filly who looks a real sprinter; she did her first piece of faster work this week and certainly impressed me. Hugo Palmer.

WALL OF FIRE
b.c. Canford Cliffs – Bright Sapphire. This horse cost 270,000 Gns. He reminded me strongly of Havana Gold; I just hope he is as good! Possibly not really early, but worth mentioning. Richard Hannon.

ZEBEDIAH
b.c. Zebedee – Kiva. He cost 140,000 Gns. He's a good looking two year old, by a sire I have a soft spot for. I hear the Hannon team are very keen on this one. Richard Hannon.

LARRY STRATTON
ELDEY
ch.f. Medicean – Royal Arruhan. Bred by Louise Parry and me, and one who slipped through the cracks at Tatts Ireland, probably because the 'judges' continue to disregard the sire. Out of a non-winner who hasn't yet bred a winner, but from a great speed family – Averti, Reesh, Pastoral Player, et al – and a little runner herself. Endo Botti, Italy.

WAY AHEAD
b.c. Kyllachy – On Her Way. I hope the name is not tempting fate. Partnership-bred by Whatton Manor Stud, Adam Driver and me, first foal of a good winning mare and a 47,000 guineas Rabbah yearling purchase. James Tate.

UNNAMED
b.c. Vale of York – Kinnego. Half-brother to two multiple winners from two previous foals, one of them the really tough filly Balladienne, which I bought as a foal. Didn't look an obvious early sort, but there is plenty of speed in the family and I think he is a sleeper. Trained in Ireland by John Levins.

UNNAMED
b.c. Footstepsinthesand – Eraadaat. First foal of a non-winner, but from a good classy

winning family and by a sire who continues to churn out winners but be underrated by the market. A neat, sharp, good-looking and the epitome of 'racy'. John Levins.

ANTHONY STROUD

SANTE (IRE)
b.f. Dream Ahead – Zeiting. This is a nice filly with a good pedigree. At the moment she is pleasing Jamie Osborne.

GOROKAI (IRE)
b.c. Kodiac – Damask. A nice moving, good looking horse who is going well at the moment. Alan McCabe.

PAUL THORMAN
'It's been a good start to the 2015 season for Trickledown Stud with the winning two-year-olds Powerallied and Tribesman'.

FRENCHMAN
b.c. La Havre – Como. We sold him at Tattersalls Book 2 and he was bought by the ever expanding 'Team Howson'. He's a very nice horse with a good way of going. He's with a good trainer, so has every chance. Charlie Hills.

REPUTATION
b.c. Royal Applause – Semaphore. As good a looker as we sold all year, if he runs half as well as he looks he'll win races. Probably a mid-season horse. John Quinn.

REGAL GAIT
b.c. Tagula – Babylonian. I'm going to single-handedly wreck a trainer's year by selecting three from Henry Candy who has three of our Trickledown Stud 2-y-o's. Sara and I both think he's as good a judge of yearling as there is out there. This colt was the best walker we sold last year and by the way he's named somebody agrees! Sometimes the fantastic walker can be slow, but we'd be gutted if this lad wasn't useful. Henry Candy.

VIBRANT CHORDS
b.c. Poet's Voice – Lovely Thought. This horse is our No.1 pick of the Henry Candy 2-y-o's. A half-brother to a good horse Jamie Osborne

trained, we thought this colt had "IT" in spades. He wasn't a typical Poet's Voice in that we felt he could be quite precocious. A wonderfully balanced horse with a solid temperament. Henry Candy.

UNNAMED
b.f. Hellvelyn – Talampaya. We sold her as a foal to a great judge and Tally Ho Stud sold her as a yearling to David Redvers. I'm told she was actually Sheikh Fahad's pick. The mare looks special, with all three of her foals winning and two of them getting black type as 2-y-o's. This was a big filly so she might need a bit of time but she's with the right outfit for patience. Henry Candy.

CHARLIE & TRACY VIGORS

COMMODITY
ch.c. Dutch Art – Royale Danehill. Tattersalls October Sale, Book 1: A lovely athletic colt who will probably be one for the second half of the season.

HIGH SHIELDS
b.c. Shamardal – Marine City. A big, strong colt who was a lovely mover and very well balanced. He'll be one for the second half of the season. We were surprised there wasn't more opposition to Amanda Skiffington in the ring when she bought him. Roger Charlton.

LORD TOPPER
b.c. Sir Percy – Fugnina. We were surprised that he didn't sell but such was our faith in him that we put him in training rather than breeze him. He could be a Chesham type and if he wins his maiden is still for sale! Charlie Hills.

ORVAR (IRE)
b.c. Dandy Man – Roskeen. Doncaster Premier Sale: A strong colt who reminded us a lot of Royal Ascot winning two year old Extortionist (also by Dandy Man) who we sold at Doncaster as well. Richard Hannon.

SHARARA
ch.c. Dutch Art – Tafawut. A muscular, precocious looking colt from a family full of top class two year olds. Brian Meehan.

UNNAMED

gr.c. Kodiac – Krasotka. Sold for 40,000 gns at Tattersalls December Sale. A strong two year old type by one of the leading sires of two year olds. David Lanigan.

Top Lots at The Tattersalls Craven Breeze Up Sales
(15–16 April 2015)

b.c. War Front – Rehear (Coronado's Quest).
850,000 Gns. Jamie McCalmont/A C Elliott (for Michael Tabor).

b.f. Exchange Rate – Ruler's Charm (Cape Town).
350,000 Gns. Oliver St Lawrence.

JACKFISH. b.c. Exceed And Excel – Torentosa (Oasis Dream).
310,000 Gns. China Horse Club/David Redvers.

SPARTE QUERCUS. b.c. Canford Cliffs – Khaizarana (Alhaarth).
300,000 Gns. Charlie Gordon-Watson.

b.c. Elusive Quality – Shady Reflection (Sultry Song).
300,000 Gns. Gerard Hourigan.

b.c. Exceed And Excel – Shepherdia (Pivotal).
290,000 Gns. Sackville/Donald.

b.c. Oasis Dream – Independence (Selkirk).
250,000 Gns. John Ferguson.

ch.c. Showcasing – Nizhoni (Mineshaft).
240,000 Gns. George Moore/Sackville/Donald.

ch.c. Stormy Atlantic – Bea Remembered (Doyen).
200,000 Gns. Sackville/Donald.

b.c. Showcasing – Night Symphonie (Cloudings).
200,000 Gns. George Moore/Sackville/Donald.

b.c. Lope D Vega – Saik (Riverman).
200,000 Gns. Jamie McCalmont.

b.c. Galileo – Theann (Rock Of Gibraltar).
200,000 Gns. Peter & Ross Doyle.

b.f. Shamardal – Two Marks (Woodman).
200,000 Gns. John Ferguson.

Trainers' Bargain Buys

It's always interesting to find out the trainers' picks from those purchases bought with a relatively modest sum. Each spring I put the following to each trainer 'Name one of your two-year-olds, bought at the yearling sales for 30,000 Guineas or less, you think will prove to be a bargain?' The horses listed below are their recommendations.

In 2014 we got 16 winners of 21 races in this section, a bit less than the previous year but still not bad going. Those with the most handsome starting prices were Belvoir Diva, Blackbriar and L'Addition (all 16-1).

Still 'Queen of the Bargain Buys' is Eve Johnson Houghton, with five winners from five selections (Orientalist, Bling King, Vestibule, Drive On and British Embassy). I know she's very keen to keep up her good record!

Other trainers to note in this section are Tom Dascombe and Mick Channon (each with four winners from five selections', followed by James Given (three winners).

AFRICAN SHOWGIRL	£25,000	George Baker
MONTAGUE WAY	16,000 Gns	Andrew Balding
SHORT WORK	26,000 Gns	Ralph Beckett
SCIARRA	£17,000	Michael Bell
HAZELY	15,000 Gns	James Bethell
ch.f. Dutch Art – Strictly	24,000 Gns	Marco Botti
SWIRRAL EDGE	£10,500	David Brown
JACK NEVISON	£10,000	Henry Candy
b.c. Lawman – Mauresmo	26,000 Gns	Peter Chapple-Hyam
PACCHES	23,000 Gns	Mick Channon
WESTBOURNE GROVE (USA)	$25,000	Robert Cowell
BANKSEA	14,000 Gns	Luca Cumani
DARK DEFENDER	£15,000	Keith Dalgleish
FOUR'S COMPANY (IRE)	€13,000	Tom Dascombe
b.c. Kodiac – Cabopino	€30,000	Ed de Giles
RISK ADJUSTED	€15,000	Ann Duffield
KASHTAN	€15,000	Harry Dunlop
AL FOUZ	€28,000	Charlie Fellowes
STRANDS OF SILK	€24,000	James Given
b.f. Vale Of York – Barbera	€16,000	Rae Guest
BARGAIN BUY	25,000 Gns	William Haggas
ARIZONA SUNRISE	10,000 Gns	Richard Hannon
TERRAPLANE	€15,000	Richard Hannon
IRISH ECLARE	20,000 Gns	Charlie Hills
HIGHWAY DREAM	10,000 Gns	William Jarvis
CARA'S MUSE	26,000Y	Eve Johnson Houghton
LADY MACAPA	£7,000	William Knight
HILLTOP RANGER	£13,000	Dan Kubler
FRANK COOL	22,000 Gns	David Lanigan
BUKLE	£22,000	Rod Millman
b.f. Poet's Voice – Dignify.	29,000 Gns	Gary Moore

THREEBAGSU	£10,000	**Stan Moore**
BAHAMIAN BOY	22,000 Gns	**Hughie Morrison**
FINE BLEND	€10,000	**Willie Muir**
SECRET TALE	€7,000	**Jamie Osborne**
br.f. Dark Angel – Embassy Pearl	20,000 Gns	**Hugo Palmer**
LADY ROCKA	7,500 Gns	**Amanda Perrett**
PINCH A KISS	7,000 Gns	**Jonathan Portman**
br.f. Captain Rio – Five Sisters	€7,200	**Noel Quinlan**
gr.f. Sir Percy – Altitude	28,000 Gns	**David Simcock**
SHOW AYA	£27,000	**Olly Stevens**
LONE ANGEL	9,000 Gns	**James Tate**
b.f. Royal Applause – Astromancer	2,000 Gns	**Mark Tompkins**
b.c. Equiano – Nouvelle Amie	16,000 Gns	**Roger Varian**
b.f. Equiano – Italian Connection	20,000 Gns	**Ed Vaughan**
ATLANTEIA	20,000 Gns	**Ed Walker**
SONG OF PARADISE	18,000 Gns	**Chris Wall**

Two-Year-Olds of 2015

CHARLIE APPLEBY
(GODOLPHIN)
As with all the horses in this, the main section of the book, the trainer's comments appear in italics under the pedigree. I've added five extra horses (without comments or star ratings) to these Godolphin two-year-olds because I feel their pedigrees and purchase prices will be of interest to the reader.

1. BLOSSOMTIME ★★★★
b.f. Shamardal – Bal De La Rose (Cadeaux Genereux). April 17. Fifth foal. €150,000Y. Arqana Deauville August. R O'Gorman. Half-sister to the minor French 3-y-o winner Askania Nova (by New Approach). The dam won 4 races at 2 and 3 yrs in France including a Group 3 event in Lyon and a listed race. She is a half-sister to 6 winners including the French 2,000 Guineas and French Derby winner Loup de Vega. The second dam, Lady Vettori (by Vettori), won the Group 3 Prix du Calvados and is a half-sister to 5 winners. *"A good-looking filly that shows a bit of class and should be out towards the end of May".*

2. BRAMBLES ★★★
ch.f. Street Cry – Peace Camp (Storm Cat). February 5. First foal. The dam, a French listed 6f winner, is a sister to one winner and a half-sister to another. The second dam, Loving Kindness (by Seattle Slew), winner of the Group 3 6f Prix de Cabourg at 2 yrs, is a half-sister to the Group 1 Prix Marcel Boussac winner Denebola, to the listed Prix Imprudence and minor US stakes winner and Grade 2/Group 2 second Glia, the US triple Grade 3 winner Snake Mountain and the dam of the 'Arc' winner Bago. *"A nice, strong filly who has a nice go about her. She shows natural ability and will be introduced in seven furlong maidens".*

3. BY THE LAW ★★★★
b.c. New Approach – Walk On Bye (Danehill Dancer). February 24. Second foal. 280,000foal. Tattersalls December. John Ferguson. The dam won the Group 3 Anglesey Stakes at 2 yrs, was third in the Group 1 6f Phoenix Stakes and is closely related to a minor winner by Danehill. The second dam, Pipalong (by Pips Pride), won 10 races including the Group 1 6f Haydock Park Sprint Cup, the Group 3 Duke Of York Stakes and the Group 3 Palace House Stakes and is a half-sister to 10 winners including the fairly useful 2-y-o 6f listed winner Out Of Africa. *"A nice, strong individual that shows some natural speed. He should be out in the early part of the season".*

4. CARRINGTON (FR) ★★★
b.c. New Approach – Winning Family (Fasliyev). May 25. Half-brother to the French 10f to 12.5f winner and Group 3 12.5f Prix de Royallieu third La Conquerante (by Hurricane Run). The dam, a French dual 2-y-o winner in France, is a half-sister to 4 winners including the US dual Grade 3 winner Ballast. The second dam, Suedoise (by Kris), is an unraced half-sister to the Group 2 12f winner Wagon Master. *"A late foal, but he's showing a lot of natural speed and he would be one to produce for the Guineas meeting".*

5. CHESS MASTER (IRE) ★★★
br.c. Shamardal – Cassandra Go (Indian Ridge). May 7. Tenth foal. 1,700,000Y. Tattersalls October Book 1. John Ferguson. Half-brother to 6 winners including the Irish 1,000 Guineas, Nassau Stakes and Sun Chariot Stakes winner Halfway To Heaven (by Pivotal), the very useful Group 3 5f and Group 3 6f winner Tickled Pink (by Invincible Spirit), the Group 3 6f Summer Stakes winner Theann (by Rock Of Gibraltar) and the fairly useful dual 5f winner Neverletme Go (by Green Desert). The dam won the Group 2 5f Kings Stand Stakes and is a full or half-sister to 8 winners including the Group 3 6f Coventry Stakes winner and sire Verglas. The second dam, Rahaam (by Secreto), a fairly useful 7f winner, is a half-sister to 8 winners. *"A good, strong bodied individual, he's showing a good level of ability to date but with his pedigree we'll wait until July before introducing him to the racecourse".*

6. G K CHESTERTON (IRE) ★★★

ch.c. Poet's Voice – Neptune's Bride (Bering). February 20. Half-brother to the fair 9f to 12f winner and UAE listed-placed Submariner (by Singspiel), to the French 6f and 9f winner Poseidon's Bride, the moderate 7f winner Pytheas (both by Seeking The Gold), the fair 6f winner Salacia (by Echo Of Light), the fair 6f winner Marshland (by Kheleyf) and the fair 10f winner Evening Affair (by Kingmambo). The dam won the Group 3 10.5f Prix Fille de l'Air and is a half-sister to 4 winners including the Group 2 1m Goffs International Stakes winner Sea Dart (by Diesis). The second dam, Wedding Of The Sea, (by Blushing Groom), a very useful filly, won the Group 3 6f Prix de Ris-Orangis. *"The Poet's Voice's look to be very strong individuals but may need a bit of time. He's a very good moving horse who shows potential".*

7. HAWKBILL (USA) ★★★★

ch.c. Kitten's Joy – Trensa (Giant's Causeway). March 6. Second foal. $350,000Y. Keeneland September. John Ferguson. The dam, a US Grade 3 placed winner, is closely related to the US triple Grade 3 winner Batique and a half-sister to 3 winners. The second dam, Serape (by Fappiano), won the US Grade 1 Ballerina Stakes. *"A very athletic individual, he's showing plenty of natural speed. He's a good mover and will be ready to run early".*

8. HIBOU ★★★★

ch.c. Street Cry – Arlette (King Of Kings). February 15. Brother to the fairly useful 2-y-o 6f and 7f winner of 3 races Autumn Lily and half-brother to 4 winners including the 2-y-o Group 3 6f Prix de Cabourg and UAE Group 3 9f winner and dual Group 1 third Alexandros, the fair 1m winner A'Juba (both by Kingmambo) and the French 2-y-o 1m winner Margravine (by King's Best). The dam, a French 8.5f (at 2 yrs) to 9.5f winner, is closely related to the Breeders Cup Turf, Coronation Cup and Grand Prix de Saint-Cloud winner In The Wings and to the Group 2 10.5f Prix Greffulhe winner Hunting Hawk. The second dam, High Hawk (by Shirley Heights), won the Group 1 Premio Roma. *"An attractive and well bodied colt who moves well. He'll be ready to introduce to the track from July onwards".*

9. LAKE HAMANA ★★★

b.f. Shamardal – Lake Toya (Darshaan). February 16. Half-sister to the minor French 1m winner Naruko (by Street Cry). The dam, a useful dual listed 10f winner, is a half-sister to several winners including the fairly useful 1m winner and Group 3 Musidora Stakes second Glen Innes and the smart Japanese winner Er Nova. The second dam, Shinko Hermes (by Sadler's Wells), is an unplaced sister to 1,000 Guineas second Strawberry Roan and a half-sister to the top-class colt Generous. *"A nice, strong filly who looks straightforward and will be ready to be introduced over 6f".*

10. LOVELL

b.c. Dubawi – Cosmodrome (Bahri). February 13. Fourth foal. 725,000Y. Tattersalls October Book 1. John Ferguson. The dam, a listed 10f winner, is a half-sister to 4 winners including listed 10f winner Splashdown and the US triple turf winner at around 1m and 9f and Grade 3 placed Tadreeb. The second dam, Space Time (by Bering) was placed over 7f at 2 yrs in France and is a half-sister to 6 minor winners.

11. MAXIMIAN (IRE) ★★★★

ch.c. Shamardal – Via Milano (Singspiel). March 30. Seventh foal. 370,000Y. Tattersalls October Book 2. John Ferguson. Half-brother to 5 winners including the Group 3 1m Prix des Lieurey and listed 1m Prix des Lilas winner Via Medici (by Medicean), the fairly useful 2-y-o 5f and 6f winner Fifth Commandment (by Holy Roman Emperor), the fairly useful Irish 6f and 7f winner of 4 races Via Ballycroy and the French 10f winner Corso Como (both by Lawman). The dam won the Group 3 1m Prix des Reservoirs at 2 yrs and is a half-sister to one winner. The second dam, Salvinaxia (by Linamix), a French listed-placed 2-y-o winner, is a half-sister to 8 winners. *"A good looking colt, he's showing natural speed and he'll be ready to run early".*

12. MORSIAN

ch.f. Dubawi – Misheer (Oasis Dream). April 3. Second foal. 750,000Y. Tattersalls October Book 1. John Ferguson. Half-sister to the 2014 2-y-o 6f winner, from two starts, Mistrusting (by Shamardal). The dam, a winner of 3 races including the Group 2 6f Cherry Hinton Stakes and second in the Group 1 Cheveley Park Stakes, is a full or half-sister to 3 winners. The second dam, All For Laura (by Cadeaux Genereux), a fairly useful 2-y-o 5f winner, is a full or half-sister to 5 winners.

13. NEW DISCOVERY ★★★
b.c. New Approach – Copperbeech (Red Ransom). April 28. The dam, a useful dual 2-y-o 1m winner, was third in the Group 1 Prix Marcel Boussac and is a half-sister to 5 winners. The second dam, Aynthia (by Zafonic), a Group 3 12f winner in Italy, is a half-sister to 5 winners including the 1m and listed placed Alamanni. *"A big, lengthy colt that covers a lot of ground. He'll be one for the back end of the season".*

14. PURE NOTE ★★★★
b.c. Dubawi – Crystal Music (Nureyev). April 1. Eighth foal. 1,600,000Y. Tattersalls October Book 1. John Ferguson. Half-brother to the useful 2-y-o dual 7f winner and listed-placed Treasury Devil (by Bernardini), to the fairly useful listed-placed 2-y-o 6f winner Crystany (by Green Desert) and the US stakes-placed winner Crystal Moment (by Distorted Humor). The dam, winner of the Group 1 Fillies' Mile, is closely related to the Group 3 12f John Porter Stakes winner Dubai Success and the Irish Derby third Tchaikovsky and a half-sister to the Group 3 winners Solar Crystal and State Crystal. The second dam, Crystal Spray (by Beldale Flutter), a minor Irish 4-y-o 14f winner, is a half-sister to 8 winners including the Group 3 Scottish Classic winner Crystal Hearted. *"A good looking son of Dubawi who has a very nice go about him. Looks to have some class and will be out in mid-season".*

15. ROARING FORTIES (IRE) ★★★
b.c. Invincible Spirit – Growling (Celtic Swing). February 8. First foal. The dam is an unraced half-sister to several winners including the dual Group 1 10f winner Pressing. The second dam, Rafif (by Riverman), was a fair 10f winner. *"A strong individual that has a nice go about him. We'll be aiming him for seven furlong maidens".*

16. SEASTROM
b.c. Oasis Dream – Seta (Pivotal). April 30. First foal. 425,000Y. Tattersalls October Book 1. John Ferguson. The dam, a very useful triple listed winner over 7f and 1m, was third in the Group 3 May Hill Stakes and is a half-sister to 7 winners including the Group 2 Prix de Pomone winner Armure and the listed winners Gravitas, Berlin Berlin and Affirmative Action. The second dam, Bombazine (by Generous), a useful 10f winner, is a half-sister to 7 winners including the Group 1 winners Barathea and Gossamer (herself dam of the Group 1 winner Ibn Khaldun) and the US Grade 3 winner Free At Last (herself dam of the US multiple Grade 2 winner Coretta).

17. SENSE OF FUN (USA) ★★★
b.f. Distorted Humor – Abhisheka (Sadler's Wells). April 21. Sister to the very smart 6f (at 2 yrs) and Group 1 1m Prix Jean Prat winner Aesop's Fables. The dam, a useful listed-placed 1m and 10f winner, is a half-sister to the Derby, King George and Arc winner Lammtarra. The second dam, Snow Bride (by Blushing Groom), was awarded the Oaks on the disqualification of Aliysa and won the Group 3 Musidora Stakes and the Group 3 Princess Royal Stakes. *"A neat individual that shows natural speed and will be ready to run early".*

18. SLEEPTALKER (USA) ★★★
b.f. Street Cry – Suez (Green Desert). April 20. Sister to the 1,000 Guineas winner Lyric Of Light and half-sister to the quite useful 2-y-o 6f winner Bitter Lake (by Halling) and the moderate 7f winner De Lesseps (by Selkirk). The dam, a very useful 2-y-o listed 6f winner, was second in the Group 1 6f Cheveley Park Stakes. The second dam, Repeat Warning (by Warning), a fair 8.3f placed 3-y-o, is a half-sister to 9 winners including the high-class winners Bella Colora (dam of the Prince Of Wales's Stakes winner Stagecraft), Colorspin (dam of the Group 1 winners Zee Zee Top, Opera House and Kayf Tara) and Cezanne. *"A full sister to Lyric Of Light, she's a neat and precocious filly and will be ready to run over 6f".*

19. UNNAMED ★★★★★
b.f. Elusive Quality – Causeway Lass (AUS) (Giant's Causeway). Half-sister to the fairly useful 2014 2-y-o 7f winner and listed placed Good Place and to the quite useful 9.5f (at 2 yrs) to 11f winner Press Room (both by Street Cry). The dam was a 2-y-o 5f winner in Australia. The second dam, Canny Lass (by Bletchingly), was a Group 1 1m winner in Australia. *"A good-looking filly who has a lot of class and will be introduced during the summer. We'd be hopeful of her being above average".*

20. UNNAMED
b.f. War Front – Icon Project (Empire Maker). March 10. Second foal. 950,000Y. Tattersalls October Book 1. John Ferguson. The dam, winner of the Grade 1 Personal Ensign Stakes and the Grade 3 New York Stakes, is a half-sister to 6 winners including the US Grade 2 winner Lasting Approval. The second dam, La Gueriere (by Lord At War), a US Grade 1 Queen Elizabeth II Challenge Cup Stakes winner, is a sister to a stakes winner and a half-sister to 11 winners including the US Grade 1 winner Al Mamoon.

21. UNNAMED ★★★
b.c. Street Cry – Meeznah (Dynaformer). March 15. First foal. 1,000,000Y. Tattersalls October Book 1. John Ferguson. The dam, winner of the Group 2 Park Hill Stakes and the Group 3 Lillie Langtry Stakes, is a half-sister to 5 winners including the smart Group 2 12f Princess Of Wales's Stakes second Shahin. The second dam, String Quartet (by Sadler's Wells), a 12.5f listed winner in France and third in the Group 3 Lancashire Oaks, is a sister to the Irish listed 10f winner Casey Tibbs and a half-sister to 4 winners. *"A big, strong colt that has a good go about him. He'll be trained by his pedigree, meaning he'll be introduced in the second half of the season".*

22. UNNAMED ★★★
b.c. Dubawi – Moonlife (Invincible Spirit). February 16. Brother to the fairly useful 2015 3-y-o 1m winner Emirates Airline. The dam, a very useful 7f (at 2 yrs) and listed 1m winner, is a half-sister to one winner out of the Italian winner of 2 races at 2 and 3 yrs Marania (by Marju). *"A well-bodied colt, he's a good mover and shows natural ability. He'll be out in second half of the season".*

23. UNNAMED ★★★★
b.br.f. More Than Ready – Silver Reunion (Harlan's Holiday). March 6. Second foal. $500,000Y. Keeneland September. John Ferguson. The dam won 5 races in the USA including the Grade 3 Endeavour Stakes and is a half-sister to 3 winners. The second dam, Silver Comic (by Silver Hawk), a US Grade 2 winner, is a half-sister to the Group/Grade 3 winners Lucayan Prince and Comic Strip. *"A nice strong filly, she's a good mover and will be ready to be introduced over 6f".*

24. UNNAMED ★★★
b.br.f. Kitten's Joy – Wild Chant (War Chant). March 23. Third foal. $350,000Y. Fasig-Tipton Saratoga August. John Ferguson. The dam, a minor 2-y-o winner in Canada, is a half-sister to 3 winners including the US Grade 1 winners Paddy O'Prado and Untapable. The second dam, Fun House (by Prized), won the US Grade 2 Buena Vista Handicap and is a half-sister to the US Grade 2 winner Early Flyer. *"A nice, strong filly who is very well balanced and a good mover. She'll be ready to run over 6f"*

25. UNNAMED
b.c. Oasis Dream – Zee Zee Top (Zafonic). February 17. Seventh foal. 625,000Y. Tattersalls October Book 1. Not sold. Half-brother to the 2014 7f placed 2-y-o Jazzy Top (by Danehill Dancer), to the Group 1 10f Pretty Polly Stakes and Group 1 10f Prix Jean Romanet winner Izzi Top (by Pivotal) and the fairly useful 1m to 11f winner of 4 races Rock N Roll Ransom (by Red Ransom). The dam won the Group 1 10f Prix de l'Opera and is a half-sister to the Group 1 winners Opera House and Kayf Tara and to the unraced dam of the Group 1 winner Necklace. The second dam, Colorspin (by High Top), won the Irish Oaks and is a half-sister to the Irish Champion Stakes winner Cezanne.

GEORGE BAKER
26. AFRICAN SHOWGIRL ★★★
ch.f. Showcasing – Georgie The Fourth (Cadeaux Genereux). March 22. Second foal.

£25,000Y. Doncaster Premier. Stephen Hillen. The dam was placed from 7f (at 2 yrs) to 12f and is a half-sister to the useful sprinter Mass Rally. The second dam, Septembers Hawk (by Machiavellian), is an unraced half-sister to several winners. (PJL Racing). *"My beautiful bride bought this horse so it's her fault if it all goes wrong! The sire had a fantastic start to his career last year and we're delighted to have this filly of his. She's showing plenty of precocity and I would expect to run her in a six furlong maiden from mid-May onwards".* **TRAINERS' BARGAIN BUY**

27. FUNNY OYSTER (IRE) ★★★
gr.f. Dark Angel – Carpet Lover (Fayruz). April 12. Seventh foal. £32,000Y. Doncaster Premier. Stephen Hillen. Half-sister to the fair 2014 5f placed 2-y-o Grazed Knees (by Majestic Missile) and to the fair 5f winner of 5 races (including at 2 yrs) Beau Mistral (by Windsor Knot). The dam ran once unplaced and is a half-sister to 4 winners including Misty Eyed (Group 3 5f Molecomb Stakes). The second dam, Bold As Love (by Lomond), is an unraced half-sister to 3 winners. (Skinner, Baker & Partners). *"We've had plenty of success with Dark Angel's, they tend to like plenty of ease in the ground and the way this filly moves suggests the same. She's done well, she's strong and well put together and should be out by the middle of May over six furlongs, but she's the type that'll develop and do well throughout the year. The Dark Angel's we've had previously have improved dramatically for their first run and go on".*

28. HOT STUFF ★★
b.c. Assertive – Even Hotter (Desert Style). March 3. Fourth foal. Brother to the moderate 5f winner of 4 races (including at 2 yrs) Spray Tan and to the moderate dual 5f winner Warm Order. The dam, a moderate 1m placed maiden, is a half-sister to 4 winners. The second dam, Level Pegging (by Common Grounds), unplaced on her only 2 starts at 2 yrs, is a sister to the listed Scarborough Stakes winner and Group 2 Kings Stand Stakes second Flanders (herself dam of the US Grade 3 winner Louvain) and a half-sister to 6 winners. (Lady Whent). *"This colt will set off in a five furlong median auction in late April. He's a speedy type".*

29. MAGNIFICENT MADIBA ★★
b.c. Mount Nelson – Mrs Penny (Planchet). February 5. First foal. 48,000Y. Tattersalls October Book 2. Stephen Hillen. The dam, a quite useful dual 5.5f winner in Australia, won over 6f here and is a half-sister to 5 minor winners in Australia. The second dam, Respective (by Noalcoholic), won 3 races in Australia and is a half-sister to 7 winners there. (PJL Racing). *"We won't be in any rush with him and I'd be surprised if he runs before August. He's a big, raw colt that covers plenty of ground but he's like a gangly teenager who needs to grow into himself in every way. So we'll be patient with him, but he's a very good-looking horse and it's no surprise he fetched such a reasonable price. Madiba was the clan name of Nelson Mandela".*

30. MAVROS ★★
br.c. Authorized – Barley Bree (Danehill Dancer). March 26. Third foal. 42,000Y. Tattersalls October Book 3. Stephen Hillen. The dam is an unplaced half-sister to 6 winners including the fairly useful 2-y-o 6f winner and Group 3 Firth Of Clyde Stakes second Mary's Daughter. The second dam, Aunty Mary (by Common Grounds), a quite useful 2-y-o 5f winner, is a half-sister to 4 winners including the multiple Group 1 winner Attraction. (George Baker). *"A lovely, strong, compact type. He won't be rushed and I imagine he'll be on the track in the mid-to-late summer over seven furlongs. He's very strong through the neck, developing all the time and I like him".*

31. PAPOU TONY ★★
b.c. Raven's Pass – Lukrecia (Exceed And Excel). March 20. Third foal. 25,000Y. Tattersalls October Book 2. Stephen Hillen. The dam, a winner at 3 yrs in Germany and Group 3 placed over 1m, is a half-sister to 2 winners. The second dam, Quecha (by Indian Ridge), placed once at 2 yrs in France, is a half-sister to one winner. (PJL and Nick & Linda Clark). *"He's quite a feisty individual, but in a good way because he does have something about him. A very willing worker, there's definitely some fire in the belly and we just have to channel it in the right direction. He'll make a 2-y-o around June time but I don't think I'll over-cook him this year. He's more of a 3-y-o type".*

32. RED TROOPER (FR) ★★★

ch.c. Shamardal – Solar Midnight (Lemon Drop Kid). January 28. First foal. 65,000Y. Tattersalls October Book 2. Stephen Hillen. The dam, a listed-placed 1m winner in France, is a half-sister to 5 winners including the French listed winner It's Midnight. The second dam, Witching Hour (by Fairy King), a minor winner at 3 yrs in France, is a half-sister to 10 winners including the triple listed winner Party Doll (dam of the dual Group 2 winner and sire Titus Livius). (PJL Racing). *"He's the apple of my eye really, even though he's just a frame of a horse at the moment. He's cantering away for now and waiting for the penny to drop, but there's nothing wrong with that because he's one for much later on and particularly for next year".*

ANDREW BALDING

33. ABLE JACK ★★

b.c. Iffraaj – Solva (Singspiel). February 21. Third foal. 120,000Y. Tattersalls October Book 1. Norris/Huntingdon. Half-brother to the modest 10f winner Solvanna (by Haafhd). The dam, a dual 10f and subsequent US stakes winner, was second in the Grade 2 Beverly Hills Handicap and is a half-sister to 6 winners. The second dam, Annapurna (by Brief Truce), a useful 2-y-o 7f winner, was listed placed over 9f and is a half-sister to 5 winners including the 2-y-o Group 3 7f Rockfel Stakes and listed 7f winner Name Of Love. (Happy Valley Racing and Breeding). *"Quite backward and just going through a slightly awkward stage at the moment, he's grown a lot since the sale but I'm sure he was a nice yearling and they usually come back to what they were. It'll be mid-summer before he does any fast work and he'll want seven furlongs to a mile this year".*

34. BINGO GEORGE (IRE) ★★★

b.c. Holy Roman Emperor – Kalleidoscope (Pivotal). February 9. First foal. The dam, a fair 2-y-o 7f winner, is a half-sister to 6 winners including the listed-placed Craft Fair. The second dam, Brush Strokes (by Cadeaux Genereux), is an unraced sister to one winner and a half-sister to 6 winners including the very useful 2-y-o dual 7f winner and Group 1 Racing Post Trophy second Mudeer. (The Smith Family). *"He's a nice horse, he's done little bits upsides, goes very well and I would have thought he'd be ready for six furlongs in* June. A good, solid, well-made horse reared by David and Trish Brown for the Smith family, they've always liked him and were keen we should train him rather than send him to the sales. So we're grateful for that because he does look nice".

35. BLUFF CRAG ★★★

b.c. Canford Cliffs – Camp Riverside (Forest Camp). February 11. Fourth foal. 30,000Y. Tattersalls October Book 2. Andrew Balding. Half-brother to the fair 2014 7.5f placed 2-y-o Willow Creek and to the quite useful triple 7f winner Admiralty (both by Iffraaj). The dam won 3 minor races in the USA at 3 and 4 yrs and is a half-sister to 5 winners including the Group 3 Somerville Tattersall Stakes winner River Proud. The second dam, Da River Hoss (by River Special), is an unraced half-sister to 5 winners including Da Hoss (Grade 1 Breeders Cup Mile, twice). (James, Michaelson, Greenwood). *"A lovely big colt, he's closely related to Tagula. He's a bigger, rangier colt than Tagula was at this age but he has a similar temperament. He'll be a six/seven furlong 2-y-o".*

36. BOTH SIDES ★★★

b.c. Lawman – Pearl Dance (Nureyev). February 10. Half-brother to the Group 3 9f Prix Chloe winner Sparkling Beam (by Nayef), to the very useful 9f winner and Group 1 Prix Marcel Boussac third Rainbow Springs, the useful 2-y-o dual 7f winner Ridge Dance (both by Selkirk) and the fairly useful dual 1m winner Born In Bombay (by Shamardal). The dam, a useful 2-y-o 6f winner and third in the Group 1 Moyglare Stud Stakes, is a half-sister to the German listed winner and Group 1 German Derby fourth Ocean Sea and the US winner and Grade 3 third Dixie Splash. The second dam, Ocean Jewel (by Alleged), is an unraced half-sister to 6 minor winners. (Mr G Strawbridge). *"He came in late but he's a good, hardy type and one to crack on with. I would have thought he'd want seven furlongs this year".*

37. BRIEF VISIT ★★

b.f. Fastnet Rock – Brevity (Street Cry). February 5. First foal. The dam, a useful 2-y-o listed 6f winner, is a half-sister to 4 winners including the quite useful 2-y-o 1m winner and subsequent US Grade 1 third Concise. The second dam, Cut Short (by Diesis), a quite useful 1m (here) and US winner, is a sister to the dual Group 2 2-y-o winner Daggers Drawn and a half-sister to 3 winners. (Mr P Freedman). *"She's only just come into the yard and she's a fine, big filly with plenty of size and scope but I haven't seen enough of her yet to form an opinion. Fastnet Rock hasn't exactly kicked goals yet, but who knows?"*

38. BROROCCO ★★★★
b.c. Shirocco – Lady Brora (Dashing Blade). March 31. Third foal. Half-brother to the high-class 2014 2-y-o Group 1 1m Racing Post Trophy and Group 2 1m Royal Lodge Stakes winner Elm Park (by Phoenix Reach). The dam, a fair 1m winner, is a half-sister to 2 winners. The second dam, Tweed Mill (by Selkirk), a quite useful 3-y-o 8.5f winner, is a half-sister to 5 winners. (Kingsclere Racing Club). *"A very nice horse and very similar to his brother Elm Park at this stage last year. He has plenty of scope and has a great big raking stride on him. It wouldn't surprise me if he was running in some good races in the autumn. He looks pretty nice at this stage and seven furlongs would be his minimum trip".*

39. BURMESE WHISPER ★★★
b.c. Approve – Annellis (Diesis). April 11. Fifth foal. €15,000Y. Tattersalls Ireland September. Andrew Balding. The dam is an unraced half-sister to 2 winners. The second dam, Japanese Whisper (by Machiavellian), a minor US 3-y-o winner, is a half-sister to 3 winners including the French Group 2 winner and Group 1 placed Maiden Tower. *"A nice, forward-going horse, he's done plenty upsides and we like him. He should be out in May".*

40. CALLIOPE ★★★★
b.f. Poet's Voice – Costa Brava (Sadler's Wells). March 26. €80,000Y. Arqana Deauville October. Anthony Stroud. Half-sister to the French 10f winner Mr Chance (by Dalakhani). The dam is an unraced sister to the listed winner and Group 1 1m Criterium International third Acropolis and a half-sister to 4 winners including the Group 2 1m Falmouth Stakes winner Tashawak, and the dual Group 2 winner Fairy Queen. The second dam, Dedicated Lady (by Pennine Walk), a

2-y-o 5f and 6f winner, is a half-sister to 5 winners. (Thurloe Thoroughbreds XXXVI). *"A lovely, quality filly, she's good-bodied has a lovely, generous eye on her. A filly with a really good outlook, she's athletic and will make a 2-y-o from the mid-season onwards".*

41. CHARMY ★★★
b.f. Yeats – Saturday Girl (Peintre Celebre). March 22. Second foal. Half-sister to the useful 2014 2-y-o 6f winner and Group 2 7f Vintage Stakes third Room Key (by Mount Nelson). The dam is an unraced half-sister to 5 winners including the 7f (at 2 yrs) and listed 10f winner Splashdown, the listed 10f winner Cosmodrome and the fairly useful stakes-placed Boogie Shoes and Tadreeb. The second dam, Space Time (by Bering), was placed over 7f at 2 yrs in France and is a half-sister to 6 minor winners in France and Australia. (Mr R Wilmot-Smith). *"I'm quite keen on Yeats – I think he's an underrated stallion. This filly is lovely, has a bit of an attitude, but she ticks a lot of boxes. She's good-bodied, a good mover, looks nice and will need a mile this year".*

42. DANCING STAR ★★★
b.f. Aqlaam – Strictly Dancing (Danehill Dancer). April 17. Second foal. Half-sister to the quite useful 2014 2-y-o 1m and 8.5f winner Dance Of Fire (by Norse Dancer). The dam, a quite useful 6f winner, is a half-sister to 3 winners here and abroad. The second dam, Lochangel (by Night Shift), a very smart winner of the Group 1 5f Nunthorpe Stakes, is a half-sister to the champion sprinter Lochsong. (J C Smith). *"As with all Jeff Smith's home-breds she's from a good family. He breeds a lot of winners and a lot of nice horses, but it's always difficult to gauge them when they come in because they're usually a bit behind the Sales horses. She's just cantering at the moment, she's good-bodied, slightly upright in front and it's early days but we like her. She's likely to turn out a bit sooner than her half-brother Dance of Fire did last year (he's pretty smart and will run in a Derby Trial)".*

43. DARK SHOT ★★★
br.c. Danehill Dancer – Dark Missile (Night Shift). February 21. Second foal. Brother to Midnight Dance (by Danehill Dancer), unplaced in two starts at 2 yrs in 2014. The

dam, a very useful 6f winner of 4 races and second in the Group 2 6f Diadem Stakes, is a full or half-sister to several winners including the fairly useful dual 1m winner Breakheart. The second dam, Exorcet (by Selkirk), a fair 3-y-o 6f winner, is a half-sister to 2 winners including the useful UAE 7f and 1m winner Rock Music. (J C Smith). *"We trained the mare who was really good and he's quite similar to her in that she was quite heavy topped and got better with racing. He's been sick this spring and we haven't done a huge amount with him but he's grand type".*

44. DREAM OF SUMMER (IRE) ★★★
b.c. Canford Cliffs – Danehill's Dream (Danehill). May 6. Sixth foal. €80,000Y. Goffs Orby. Norris/Huntingdon. Half-brother to the fairly useful 12f to 14f winner of 6 races and listed-placed Viking Storm (by Hurricane Run) and to the quite useful 11f winner Maldowney (by Dalakhani). The dam is an unraced sister to the 2-y-o winner and Group 1 Criterium de Saint-Cloud second Summerland and a half-sister to 2 minor winners. The second dam, Summerosa (by Woodman), a fair 3-y-o 8.5f winner, is a half-sister to 4 winners including the Group 1 Racing Post Trophy third Zind and to the unraced dam of the Derby winner Dr Devious. (Happy Valley Racing & Breeding). *"He's a fine big, strong horse that went through a bit of a growth spurt after the Sales but I'm sure he'll come back to himself. When he does he'll be a strong, good type for June and July".*

45. EMPEROR NAPOLEON ★★
b.c. Champs Elysees – Amarullah (Daylami). March 3. Third foal. 30,000Y. Tattersalls October Book 2. Not sold. Half-brother to the modest 2014 6f placed 2-y-o Entente (by Mawatheeq). The dam is an unraced half-sister to the fairly useful 11f and 14f winner and Group 3 2m Queen's Vase second Amerigo. The second dam, Geminiani (by King Of Kings), winner of the Group 3 7f Prestige Stakes and second in the Group 3 Musidora Stakes, is a half-sister to 4 winners including the 2-y-o Group 1 6f Phoenix Stakes and Group 2 5f Queen Mary Stakes winner Damson (herself dam of the Group 2 Flying Childers Stakes winner Requinto). *"Very scopey and a future middle-distance horse. Probably*

one for a mile at the back-end, he's a good mover and athletic".

46. FRENCH LEGEND ★★★
b.f. Pour Moi – Fast Flow (Fasliyev). April 22. First foal. The dam is an unraced half-sister to the useful 2-y-o 1m winner, Group 3 1m Prix des Reservoirs second and Group 3 12f St Simon Stakes third Cocktail Queen. The second dam, Premier Prize (by Selkirk), a useful 7f (at 2 yrs) and listed 10f winner, was third in the Group 2 Sandown Mile and is a half-sister to 7 winners including the Group 2 15f Prix Kergorlay winner Gold Medallist. (J C Smith). *"We haven't had any of the family before but she's nice, she's a good mover and has quality. The dam was unraced but they rated her. I've got a couple of Pour Moi's and I like them both".*

47. GALLEY BAY ★★★
ch.c. Bahamian Bounty – Rosabee (No Excuse Needed). March 11. Third foal. 60,000Y. Tattersalls October Book 1. Andrew Balding. The dam, a fairly useful 2-y-o 5f and 6f winner, was second in the Group 3 Princess Margaret Stakes and is a half-sister to 5 winners. The second dam, Tilbrook (by Don't Forget Me), won over 1m at 3 yrs in Ireland and is a half-sister to 8 winners including the listed winner and Group 1 Phoenix Stakes second Maledetto. (Mick and Janice Mariscotti). *"He looks every inch a 2-y-o but unfortunately he met with a setback in December. He's back now though and he's a smashing, well-made, easy-going horse. All being well he'll be out in July".*

48. GONE GIRL ★★★
b.f. Arcano – Siren's Gift (Cadeaux Genereux). February 1. Second foal. Half-sister to the fairly useful 2014 2-y-o 5f winner Merdon Castle (by Acclamation). The dam, a fairly useful triple 5f winner (including at 2 yrs) was listed-placed and is a sister to the useful 2-y-o listed 5.2f winner and Group 2 Flying Childers Stakes third Speed Cop and a half-sister to 2 winners. The second dam, Blue Siren (by Bluebird), a very useful winner of three races from 5f to 7f, was disqualified from first place in two more, notably the Group 1 5f Nunthorpe Stakes (the winner on merit) and is a half-sister to several winners including the

quite useful 9f winner Northern Habit. (Mr J C Smith). *"A solid, strong-looking filly, she had a slight setback but we've started with her again now and she's a nice type that looks reasonably racy".*

49. HUSBANDRY ★★★
b.c. Paco Boy – Humdrum (Dr Fong). February 7. First foal. The dam, a fairly useful 7f and 1m winner of 4 races (including at 2 yrs), is a half-sister to 5 winners including the useful listed 6f winner of 4 races Musical Comedy. The second dam, Spinning Top (by Alzao), a useful 10f winner, is a half-sister to numerous winners including the fairly useful 3-y-o 7f and subsequent US dual 9f winner Daytime. (The Queen). *"He would be one of our earlier types. One for late May, he's a good, strong type and reasonably precocious".*

50. IAN FLEMING ★★
b.c. Makfi – High Cross (Cape Cross). April 29. Second foal. 50,000Y. Tattersalls October Book 2. Andrew Balding. The dam, a fair 9f winner, is a half-sister to 5 winners including the Group 1 Irish Oaks winner Vintage Tipple. The second dam, Overruled (by Last Tycoon), a quite useful 1m (at 2 yrs) and 10.2f winner, is a half-sister to 6 winners including the Grade 2 American Derby winner and Italian and German Derby second Overbury. (Chelsea Thoroughbreds). *"A lovely horse, he's likely to want to start at seven furlongs in July but he's not backward".*

51. IBERICA ROAD (USA) ★★
b.br.c. Quality Road – Field Of Clover (Bluegrass Cat). February 5. First foal. €65,000Y. Goffs Orby. Andrew Balding. The dam, a minor winner at 3 yrs in Canada, is a half-sister to 4 winners including the US Grade 1 Stephen Foster Handicap winner Pool Play. The second dam, Zuri Ridge (by Cox's Ridge), a minor US 3-y-o winner, is a half-sister to 9 winners including the US dual Grade 1 winner Voodoo Dancer. (The Mucho Macho Men Partnership). *"He's gone through a massive growth spurt. Funnily enough all the ones we bought at Goffs have done their growing and changed at the same time. He was a lovely yearling and he'll be one for seven furlongs around August time".*

52. LADY PERIGNON ★★★★
b.f. Poet's Voice – Amallna (Green Desert). February 3. First foal. €185,000Y. Arqana Deauville August. S Hillen & Hugo Merry. The dam is an unraced half-sister to 5 winners including the Group 1 Nassau Stakes winner Zahrat Dubai. The second dam, Walesiana (by Star Appeal), won the German 1,000 Guineas and is a half-sister to 8 winners. (Mrs F H Hay). *"A lovely, scopey filly out of a Green Desert mare, which I like. She's got a lot of quality, she won't be early and is one for late summer, but we're hopeful for her".*

53. LE TISSIER ★★
ch.g. Sir Percy – Incarnation (Samum). April 6. Third foal. €17,000Y. Tattersalls Ireland September. Emma Balding. Half-brother to the moderate 12f winner Impertinent (by Halling). The dam, a modest 10f winner, is a half-sister to 8 winners including the Group 3 Earl Of Sefton Stakes and Group 3 Sovereign Stakes winner and multiple Group 1 placed Norse Dancer. The second dam, River Patrol (by Rousillon), a fairly useful 10.2f winner, is a half-sister to smart middle-distance stayer Dry Dock and to the dams of the Group/Grade 1 winners Mail The Desert, Good Faith and Band Gipsy. (Mrs L E Ramsden & Mr R Morecombe). *"He's from the family of Norse Dancer and we had a bit of luck for the owners with another footballer-themed horse called Van Percy. One for the back-end but he's athletic and nice".*

54. LORD ASLAN (IRE) ★★★
b.c. Thewayyouare – Lunar Lustre (Desert Prince). February 13. Ninth foal. 85,000Y. Tattersalls October Book 2. J Brummitt. Half-brother to the Italian 2-y-o winner and 6f listed-placed Light Lustre (by Rock Of Gibraltar), to the quite useful Irish 10f to 12f and hurdles winner Sharjah (by Shamardal) and the modest triple 12f and hurdles winner Whatever It Takes (by High Chaparral). The dam ran twice unplaced and is a half-sister to 9 winners including the French Group 2 winners Majorien and America (herself dam of the Melbourne Cup winner Americain). The second dam, Green Rosy (by Green Dancer), a French 10f winner and listed-placed, is a full or half-sister to 10 winners including the US Grade 3 winner Rose Bouquet. (D E

Brownlow). *"He's a nice horse, a good mover and it would be nice to have another good horse for David Brownlow again. He's got two 2-y-o's with me and I like them both. This one is a lovely horse, a good, easy mover and one to start off at seven furlongs in mid-summer. He should be up to winning races this year".*

55. LORD HUNTINGDON ★★★

b.c. Lord Of England – Marajuana (Robellino). January 12. Half-brother to the quite useful 7f and 1m winner of 4 races Tartan Trip (by Selkirk). The dam, a quite useful 2-y-o 5f winner on her debut, is a half-sister to several winners including the useful 5f to 1m winner of 8 races (from 2-6 yrs) Border Music. The second dam, Mara River (Efisio), a quite useful 6f to 1m winner, is a half-sister to several winners. (Kingsclere Racing Club). *"From one of the more precocious families we have, he's nice enough and by a German sire who is a son of a good horse we had called Dashing Blade".*

56. MAKE FAST ★★

b.f. Makfi – Raymi Coya (Van Nistelrooy). March 10. Third foal. Half-sister to the unplaced 2014 2-y-o Beauty Of The Sea (by Elusive Quality). The dam, a useful 2-y-o Group 3 7f Oh So Sharp Stakes winner, is a half-sister to 5 winners including the US 2-y-o and 4-y-o winner and stakes-placed Olympia Fields. The second dam, Something Mon (by Maria's Mon), is an unraced half-sister to 5 winners including the champion German 2-y-o and Group 2 winner Somethingdifferent. (The Queen). *"She's not very big but she looks fairly racy and forward going. Like a lot of my 2-y-o's she's still backward in her coat at the moment".*

57. MONTAGUE WAY (IRE) ★★★

b.c. Rock Of Gibraltar – Shanghai Lily (King's Best). March 12. Seventh foal. 16,000Y. Tattersalls October Book 2. Andrew Balding. Brother to the fair dual 10f winner Morocco and half-brother to the fairly useful 2-y-o 6f and 1m winner Cafe Elektric (by Pivotal). The dam, a very useful 2-y-o 6f and 7f winner, is a half-sister to 3 winners including the very useful listed-placed General Eliott. The second dam, Marlene-D (Selkirk), a minor Irish 3-y-o 9f winner, is a half-sister to 7 winners including the Queen's Vase winner Arden, the French

listed winner Kerulen and the dam of the US Grade 1 winner Kiri's Clown. (Martin and Valerie Slade). *"He goes nicely, he's reasonably forward and will probably have the speed to start at six furlongs".* **TRAINERS' BARGAIN BUY**

58. MOON OVER MOBAY ★★★

b.f. Archipenko – Slew The Moon (Kitwood). March 24. Half-sister to the quite useful 8.5f (at 2 yrs) to 2m winner of 6 races Bowdler's Magic (by Hernando), to the Irish 2-y-o 1m winner, from two starts, Luz De La Luna (by Cozzene) and the moderate 9.5f winner Always Eager (by With Approval). The dam won five Graded stakes in Argentina including a Grade 1 and is a sister to the Argentine Grade 2 winner Spice Girl and a half-sister to the Argentine triple Grade 1 winner Slew Of Reality. The second dam, Slew Of Reasons (by Seattle Slew) was unraced. (Miss K Rausing). *"It's lovely to have a horse for Kirsten Rausing again and the sire Archipenko is doing very well. A nice filly that's just been ticking away quietly, she's from a reasonably hardy family. I would have thought seven furlongs would be her starting point".*

59. MR ANDROS ★★

b.c. Phoenix Reach – Chocolada (Namid). January 27. £35,000Y. Doncaster November. Andrew Balding. Brother to the fair triple 5f winner (including at 2 yrs) Pixilated, to the fair 5f winner of 10 races from 2 to 4 yrs Roy's Legacy and the modest 1m winner Soul Of Motion. The dam was unraced. The second dam, Cocorica (by Croco Rouge), was a modest Irish 7f (at 2 yrs) and 6f winner. (Andrew Christou). *"A home bred, he's typical of the sire in looks so we'll just take our time with him, but he's nice. The half-brother won over five furlongs but he won't be doing that!"*

60. NODACHI (IRE) ★★★★

b.c. Rip Van Winkle – Jabroot (Alhaarth). April 25. Third foal. 170,000Y. Tattersalls October Book 2. Stephen Hillen. The dam, a modest 12f placed maiden, is a half-sister to 5 winners including the Group 1 10f Nassau Stakes and Group 10.4f Musidora Stakes winner Zahrat Dubai. The second dam, Walesiana (by Star Appeal), won the German 1,000 Guineas and is a half-sister to 8 winners.

(Mrs F H Hay). *"He's nice, we liked him at the sale but didn't buy him because our order book was full and then fortunately he was sent to us anyway. He goes very well and it looks like he'll make a 2-y-o from August onwards. He was quite a late foal but doesn't look it".*

61. PARIS BOUND ★★

b.c. Champs Elysees – Averami (Averti). February 13. Half-brother to the very smart Australian Group 1 10f, Sandown Group 3 1m and Epsom Group 3 8.5f winner Side Glance, to the quite useful 10f to 14.5f winner Spectator, the fair 7f (at 2 yrs) and 1m winner Advertise (all by Passing Glance), the useful listed-placed 8.5f to 14f winner Rawaki (by Phoenix Reach) and the fair 12f, 15f and hurdles winner Taglietelle (by Tagula). The dam, a moderate 7f winner, is a sister to 2 winners. The second dam, Friend For Life (by Lahib), was unplaced. (Kingsclere Racing Club). *"He's a lovely, big, long-striding horse that'll take time but he's a grand type with lots of scope".*

62. PREDETERMINED (IRE) ★★★★

b.c. Lope De Vega – Queen Bodicea (Revoque). May 14. Fifth foal. €170,000Y. Arqana Deauville August. Stephen Hillen. Half-brother to the 2-y-o Group 2 6f July Stakes winner Classic Blade (by Daggers Drawn), to the useful 5f winner of 9 races and Group 3 Prix de Saint-Georges second Captain Dunne (by Captain Rio) and the fair 6f winner Sitting Pritty (by Compton Place). The dam is an unplaced sister to the Italian listed winner Meanya and a half-sister to the fairly useful winner of 8 races at around 7f Santisima Trinidad. The second dam, Brazilia (by Forzando), a modest 6f placed 2-y-o, is a half-sister to 4 winners including the Group 2 5f Kings Stand Stakes winner Dominica. (Mrs F H Hay). *"A lovely horse, he's done bits upsides but he's a May foal and so isn't an early type. Without doubt he's got some ability and he's one for seven furlongs around August time".*

63. REHEARSE (IRE) ★★

b.c. Big Bad Bob – And Again (In The Wings). March 3. Third foal. €170,000Y. Goffs Orby. John Warren. Half-brother to the minor French 4-y-o winner of 3 races Dylanelle (by Dylan Thomas). The dam, a quite useful 10f and 12f

winner, is a half-sister to 5 winners including the Group 1 9f Prix Jean Prat winner Olden Times and the useful listed 6f winner and Group 1 Cheveley Park Stakes third Festoso. The second dam, Garah (by Ajdal), a very useful winner of 4 races over 6f, was third in the Group 32 Temple Stakes and is a half-sister to 6 winners. (Highclere Thoroughbred Racing – Disraeli). *"We had to back-off him because of a minor setback he's had but he's a grand horse that'll do better in time. We like him".*

64. ROCK OPERA ★★★★

b.f. Fastnet Rock – Opera Glass (Barathea). March 21. Half-sister to the very useful listed 10f and listed 12f winner Opera Gal (by Galileo), to the 2015 3-y-o 12f winner Opera Lad (by Teofilo) and the modest 14f winner Opera Buff (by Oratorio). The dam, a quite useful 8.5f winner, is a sister to the very smart 2-y-o Group 3 7f Solario Stakes winner and Group 1 Dewhurst Stakes third Opera Cape and a half-sister to the high-class stayer Grey Shot and the smart sprint winner of 4 races Night Shot. The second dam, Optaria (by Song), was a quite useful 2-y-o 5f winner. (J C Smith). *"She's lovely and has a bit more quality than some of the Fastnet Rock's we've had in the past. The mare is from a great family and the 3-y-o Opera Lad won the other day and we like him a lot. She'll be nice, no doubt".*

65. SHONGOLOLO ★★★

b.c. Manduro – Nipping (Night Shift). April 10. Sixth foal. €30,000Y. Baden-Baden. Richard Venn. Half-brother to the French 5f and 6.5f winner Xenophanes (by Shamardal), to the 3-y-o 5f winner on his only start Jaywalk (by Footstepsinthesand) and the minor French 3-y-o winner Constant Lover (by King's Best). The dam won the Group 3 5f Prix du Petit Couvert and is a half-sister to the Group 2 5.5f Prix Robert Papin winner Zipping and the Group 3 5f Prix du Bois winner Zelding. The second dam, Zelda (by Caerleon), a French 6.5f winner, is a half-sister to the Breeders Cup Mile and William Hill Sprint Championship winner Last Tycoon, the Group winners Astronef and The Perfect Life and the dams of the Group 1 winners Immortal Verse, Tie Black and Valentine Waltz. (Martin and Valerie Slade & Partner). *"Not very big, but bred on similar lines to the Dante Stakes winner we had called Bonfire. He's small, close-coupled, quite racy, willing and straightforward at the moment. Hopefully we'll be cracking on with him".*

66. SIGNAL HILL (IRE) ★★★
b.c. Rock Of Gibraltar – Izzy Lou (Spinning World). February 22. Second foal. €32,000Y. Goffs Orby. Kern/Lillingston. Brother to the quite useful 2-y-o dual 7f winner Juan Alonso. The dam, a modest 7f placed 2-y-o, is a half-sister to 4 winners including the US Grade 2 winner Missit. The second dam, High Spot (by Shirley Heights), is a placed half-sister to 3 winners. (Kennet Valley Thoroughbreds). *"He's done nothing but grow since the sales and is 'up behind' at the moment. I'm a big fan of the sire, this is a really nice type and Kennet Valley have been very lucky owners for us".*

67. SWASHBUCKLE ★★
b.c. Dashing Blade – Inhibition (Nayef). March 23. The dam, a fairly useful 12f winner, is a half-sister to numerous winners including the very smart Group 2 1m Oettingen-Rennen and Group 3 8.5f Diomed Stakes winner Passing Glance, the smart Group 3 7f Prix de Palais-Royal and European Free Handicap winner Hidden Meadow and the smart listed winners Scorned and Kingsclere. The second dam, Spurned (by Robellino), a fairly useful 2-y-o 7f winner, later stayed 10f. (Kingsclere Racing Club). *"A great big, long-striding type rather like his mother, he looks like the damsire Nayef. It's a family that's been good to us in the past and we'll take our time with him but he'll be alright".*

68. SUNFLOWER ★★★★
ch.f. Dutch Art – Swan Wings (Bahamian Bounty). February 24. Second foal. Half-sister to Dutch Garden (by Fastnet Rock), unplaced in one start at 2 yrs in 2014. The dam, a fairly useful 2-y-o 5f winner, is a half-sister to 7 winners. The second dam, Star Tulip (by Night Shift), a useful winner of 3 races over 6f including the listed Sandy Lane Stakes, is a half-sister to 4 minor winners. (Coln Valley Stud). *"She looked very sharp and decent but unfortunately she's had a setback. We should get her back in mid-summer and she's as fast as anything I've trained at this stage. Hopefully*

she'll be alright because she looked pretty talented with lots of speed".

69. THE GRADUATE (IRE) ★★★
gr.c. Mastercraftsman – Ballyvarra (Sadler's Wells). February 18. Third foal. 100,000Y. Tattersalls October Book 1. Andrew Balding. The dam is an unraced half-sister to 4 winners including the very useful 5f and 6f winner and Group 1 Cheveley Park Stakes second Tanami (dam of the Group 2 Rockfel Stakes winner Cairns) and the dam of the Cheveley Park Stakes winner Wannabe Grand. The second dam, Propensity (by Habitat), a fairly useful 2-y-o 5f winner, was second in the Queen Mary Stakes. (Mick & Janice Mariscotti). *"A grand, big horse, but he's going through a growth spurt now and we're backing off him for now. The sire can't do anything wrong and as he's out of a Sadler's Wells mare you wouldn't expect him to do anything until September".*

70. THIS IS FOR YOU ★★★
b.c. Paco Boy – Waypoint (Cadeaux Genereux). May 6. £10,000Y. Doncaster Premier. Andrew Balding. Half-brother to the 2-y-o Group 2 5.5f Prix Robert Papin winner Never A Doubt (by Night Shift), to the fairly useful 6f to 1m winner of 5 races Primo Way (by Primo Dominie), the useful 5f to 7f winner Jonny Mudball (by Oasis Dream) and the modest 7f winner Fabine (by Danehill Dancer). The dam, a fairly useful 6f and 7f winner, is a half-sister to 5 winners including the Group 2 6f Diadem Stakes winner and good sire Acclamation. The second dam, Princess Athena (by Ahonoora), won the Group 3 5f Queen Mary Stakes, was sprint placed in numerous Group events and is a half-sister to 4 winners. (Mr J Dwyer & Mr P Brend). *"He was cheaply bought and looks quite racy but being a May foal we wouldn't be getting after him until July time".*

71. THREE LOVES (IRE) ★★★
b.f. Duke Of Marmalade – Three Moons (Montjeu). February 9. Second foal. €62,000Y. Goffs Orby. Norris/Huntingdon. The dam, a useful 10f winner and second in the listed Pretty Polly Stakes, is a half-sister to 4 winners including the useful 2-y-o 5f winner and listed-placed Black Velvet. The second dam,

Three Owls (by Warning), a fair 1m winner, is a half-sister to 7 winners including Thames (Group 2 Prix Noailles). (Happy Valley Racing and Breeding). *"She's a nice filly and I've loved her all the way through since seeing her as a yearling. She's beautifully made, very straightforward and a good mover. One for seven furlongs to start off with".*

72. VERNE CASTLE ★★★

ch.c. Sakhee's Secret – Lochangel (Night Shift). March 21. Half-sister to the quite useful 7f winner Star Pupil (by Selkirk), to the quite useful 6f winner Strictly Dancing (by Danehill Dancer) and the fair 5f winner Celestial Dream (by Oasis Dream). The dam, a very smart winner of the Group 1 5f Nunthorpe Stakes, is a half-sister to the champion sprinter Lochsong. The second dam, Peckitts Well (by Lochnager), was a fairly useful winner of five races at 2 and 3 yrs from 5f to 6f. (Mr J C Smith). *"He looks to be the most forward of all Jeff Smith's 2-y-o's. He's well made, forward-going and would hopefully be ready to run by the end of May. Jeff always jokes that I don't find my 2-y-o's until too late in the summer and that he's going to send them in painted fluorescent so I can't miss them! This one almost looks fluorescent already because he's that sort of colour. Hopefully he'll be a nice 2-y-o for him".*

73. VISCOUNT BARFIELD ★★★★★

b.c. Raven's Pass – Madonna Dell'orto (Montjeu). March 16. First foal. 90,000Y. Tattersalls October Book 2. Andrew Balding. The dam, a fair 1m and 10f placed maiden, is a half-sister to 8 winners including the French 2,000 Guineas, Grade 1 Keeneland Turf Mile Stakes and Coventry Stakes winner Landseer and the listed 10f winner and Group 1 Prince Of Wales's Stakes third Ikhtyar. The second dam, Sabria (by Miswaki), is an unraced half-sister to 5 winners. (Mr D Brownlow). *"Taking everything we've done so far with the 2-y-o's into consideration you'd have to say that this colt is very nice indeed. He's reasonably precocious, his dam is a half-sister to the Coventry winner Landseer and he goes very well. He should be ready to run in May over six furlongs and he looks smart".*

74. WENSARA DREAM ★★

b.f. Lilbourne Lad – Emerald Fire (Pivotal). April 29. Sixth foal. £15,000Y. Doncaster Premier. Andrew Balding. Half-sister to the fair 5f and 6f winner Henry Bee (by Cadeaux Genereux) and to the modest 2-y-o dual 5f seller winner Severn Bore (by Tiger Hill). The dam, a fair dual 6f winner including at 2 yrs, is a half-sister to 7 winners including the useful 2-y-o listed 5f winner Four-Legged-Friend, the dual US Grade 3 winner Superstrike and the dam of the Group 1 winning sprinters Goodricke and Pastoral Pursuits. (Martin & Valerie Slade). *"She's not very big, looks quite precocious and yet she's still very backward in her coat. I trained the dam to win a nursery at two and she wanted soft ground whereas this filly has a quick action, so she should go on any ground".*

75. WYNFORD (IRE) ★★★

ch.g. Dylan Thomas – Wishing Chair (Giant's Causeway). April 28. Fourth foal. £6,500Y. Doncaster Premier. Emma Balding (private sale). Half-brother to the 2014 2-y-o 6f winner on his only start Use Your Filbert (by Acclamation), to the quite useful dual 7f winner Wilde Inspiration (by Dandy Man) and the fair 2-y-o dual 5f winner Done Dreaming (by Diamond Green). The dam is an unraced half-sister to 7 winners including the US stakes winner and Grade 3 placed Dawn Princess. The second dam, Fighting Countess (by Ringside), a US stakes winner of 5 races, is a half-sister to 3 stakes winners including the US dual Grade 1 winner Countess Diana. (I A Balding). *"He was well-bought I think. A nice, big, scopey horse that'll take a bit of time but we like him".*

76. UNNAMED ★★★

b.c. Champs Elysees – Belladera (Alzao). February 2. Tenth living foal. 65,000Y. Tattersalls October Book 2. David Redvers. Half-brother to 7 winners including the fairly useful 2-y-o triple 6f winner Musicora, the quite useful listed-placed 6f and 7f winner Little Scotland (both by Acclamation), the quite useful Irish 12f to 2m winner Mrs Gillow (by Danzero), the listed-placed Italian winner of 8 races from 2 to 5 yrs Sgiaff (by Spinning World) and the modest 2-y-o 5f winner

Irrational (by Kyllachy). The dam won over 6f at 2 yrs and is a half-sister to 7 winners including the listed 6f winner Silca Blanka. The second dam, Reality (by Known Fact), a Group 3 placed winner, is a half-sister to the Group 2 Champagne Stakes winner Unblest. (Qatar Racing Ltd). *"He's a little bit backward and is going to take some time but we really liked him at the sale. David Redvers bought him and sent him here which was great. I like the sire but we won't be in any hurry with this colt".*

77. UNNAMED ★★★

b.f. Holy Roman Emperor – Crystal Gaze (Rainbow Quest). March 24. Sixth foal. Half-sister to the Group 3 6f Premio Tudini winner Spirit Quartz (by Invincible Spirit), to the quite useful 5f to 1m winner of 10 races here and in France Caspian Prince (by Dylan Thomas), the fair 2015 3-y-o 5f winner Crystal Quartz (by Rock Of Gibraltar) and the minor French 2-y-o 7f winner Contrary (by Mark Of Esteem). The dam is an unraced sister to the useful dual 10f winner Desert Quest. The second dam, Jumilla (by El Gran Senor), a quite useful 2-y-o 6f winner, is a half-sister to 6 winners including Spurned (dam of the stakes winners Hidden Meadow, Kingsclere, Passing Glance and Scorned) and the German champion 2-y-o Winter Quarters. (Qatar Racing Ltd). *"She's bred to be fast and she looks fast too, but she's got a mind of her own and we'll have to get round that. She was bred by Sheikh Fahad but the family goes back to one of our own".*

78. UNNAMED ★★

b.c. Dalghar – Ela's Giant (Giant's Causeway). May 19. Fourth foal. Half-brother to the modest dual 12f winner Elegant Ophelia (by Osorio). The dam is an unraced half-sister to the fairly useful 2-y-o 1m winner and listed placed Elas Diamond (by Danehill Dancer). The second dam, Ela Athena (by Ezzoud), a winner of 3 races including the Group 3 Lancashire Oaks, was placed in 7 Group/Grade 1 events and is a half-sister to 5 winners. The sire, a half-brother to Dalakhani, won a Group 3 and a Listed event at around 7f in France. (Mr N N Botica). *"Bred by the owner, he's a late foal but has a lot of quality. The sire is standing in New Zealand now".*

79. UNNAMED ★★★★ ♠

ch.c. Exceed And Excel – Indian Love Bird (Efisio). February 7. Sixth living foal. 200,000Y. Tattersalls October Book 1. Oliver St Lawrence. Brother to the useful 7f (including at 2 yrs) and 1m winner of 4 races Correspondent and half-brother to the Group 2 6f Duke Of York Stakes and Group 3 1m Craven Stakes winner and triple Group 1 placed Delegator (by Dansili). The dam is an unraced sister to the smart Group 1 7f Prix de la Foret winner Tomba and the French Derby winner Holding Court. The second dam, Indian Love Song (by Be My Guest), a modest middle-distance placed maiden, is a full or half-sister to 4 winners. (Salem Rashid). *"A half-brother to Delegator, he goes well and some of the Exceed And Excels I've had in the past have been fairly wild but this one looks very straightforward. We're looking forward to him, he's one for six furlongs I would have thought and he's a nice horse".*

80. UNNAMED ★★★★

b.f. Dream Ahead – Jessica's Dream (Desert Style). May 2. Eleventh foal. 170,000foal. Tattersalls December. David Redvers. Half-sister to the Group 1 1m Prix Jean Prat winner Havana Gold (by Teofilo), to the fair 5f winner of 8 races (including at 2 yrs) Rocker (by Rock Of Gibraltar) and minor winners in Hong Kong (by Royal Applause) and Germany (by Montjeu). The dam, a very smart sprinter, won the Group 3 Ballyogan Stakes and the Group 3 Premio Omenoni and is a half-sister to the listed winner and dual Group 1 placed Majors Cast. The second dam, Ziffany (by Taufan), a 2-y-o 7f seller winner, is a half-sister to one winner abroad. (Qatar Racing Ltd). *"She's lovely. We've just had to back off her because her knees need a bit more time to mature but she's a filly with a great attitude. A lovely mover and a thoroughly nice filly from a very good family, she's one for seven furlongs this year I would have thought".*

81. UNNAMED ★★

b.f. Makfi – Loulou (El Prado). March 1. Second foal. 52,000Y. Tattersalls October Book 2. David Redvers. The dam, a modest 10f winner, is a half-sister to 4 winners. The second dam, Hatoof (by Irish River), a high-class filly and winner of 9 races notably the 1,000 Guineas, the Champion Stakes and the Beverly D Stakes, is a sister to the US Grade 1 winner Irish Prize and a half-sister to the French listed winners Fasateen and Insijaam. (Qatar Racing Ltd). *"She was a bit late coming in, but she's a nice mover. The Makfi's seem to need time, so I'd say we'll see her out from the mid-summer onwards".*

82. UNNAMED ★★★
b.br.c. Cape Blanco – Real Doll (Known Fact). February 3. Seventh foal. 60,000Y. Tattersalls October Book 1. Andrew Balding. Half-brother to 2 winners including the minor US winner Barbies M (by Afleet Alex). The dam, a Canadian stakes winner of 3 races at 3 and 4 yrs, is a half-sister to 2 minor winners. The second dam, Magic Spin (by Lord Avie), won 3 minor races in the USA at 3 and 4 yrs and is a half-sister to 10 winners including the multiple Group 1 winner Divine Proportions and the Prix Jacques Le Marois winner Whipper. (Mick & Janice Mariscotti). *"A fine, big, long-striding horse, he's a lovely mover and a galloping type of horse that will want seven furlongs to start with".*

83. UNNAMED ★★★
b.f. Cape Cross – Sabria (Miswaki). March 30. Fourteenth living foal. Closely related to a minor winner at 3 yrs in Japan by Green Desert and half-brother to 7 winners including the French 2,000 Guineas and Grade 1 Keeneland Turf Mile Stakes winner Landseer (by Danehill), the very smart listed 10f winner and Group 1 Prince Of Wales's Stakes third Ikhtyar (by Unfuwain), the useful Irish 10f winner Song Of Hiawatha, the fairly useful Irish 9f winner Maurice Utrillo (both by Sadler's Wells) and the quite useful 10.2f winner Sabreon (by Caerleon). The dam is an unraced half-sister to 5 winners. The second dam, Flood (by Riverman), a 6f winner in the USA, is a half-sister to the US Grade 1 winner Sabona. (Walter Swinburn). *"Owned and bred by Walter Swinburn, this is a half-sister to the dam of the nice Raven's Pass 2-y-o we have. She had a bit of a setback early on so we're giving her time, but she's a lovely filly in every other way and she'll be nice in time".*

84. UNNAMED ★★
b.f. Pour Moi – Saturn Girl (Danehill Dancer). January 20. Second foal. The dam, a fair 1m winner, is a half-sister to 8 winners including the useful listed 10f winner Livadiya. The second dam, Lilissa (by Doyoun), a French 9f and 10.5f winner, is a half-sister to 5 winners including the Group 3 12f Prix Minerve winner Linnga. (Mr M Tabor). *"A nice filly with plenty of quality, but she'll be wanting a trip later in the season I'd say".*

85. UNNAMED ★★★
gr.c. Cacique – Strawberry Morn (Travelling Victor). March 27. Tenth foal. 105,000Y. Tattersalls October Book 2. Oliver St Lawrence. Closely related to the fairly useful 2014 2-y-o dual 6f winner Wentworth Falls and to the Group 2 1m Windsor Forest Stakes and Group 3 9f Dahlia Stakes winner Strawberrydaiquiri (both by Dansili) and half-brother to the quite useful 9f and 10f winner Strawberry Lolly (by Lomitas), the fair 6f and 7f winner of 5 races Strabinios King (by King's Best) and the fair 9f winner Strawberrymystique (by Motivator). The dam, a triple Canadian stakes winner of 15 races, is a half-sister to 6 winners. The second dam, Strawberry's Charm (by Strawberry Road), a minor US 3-y-o winner, is a half-sister to 5 winners. (Salem Rashid). *"He's had a little break because his knees were immature. The sire has had fertility problems but he's done well with what he's had. I like this colt, he's nice, has a lot of scope and he's a good mover".*

86. UNNAMED ★★★
b.f. Frozen Power – Symbol Of Peace (Desert Sun). March 15. Third living foal. €42,000Y. Goffs Sportsmans. David Redvers. Half-sister to the 2-y-o Group 3 7f Acomb Stakes winner Treaty Of Paris (by Haatef) and to the fair 9.5f winner of 3 races (including at 2 yrs) All Nighter (by Bertolini). The dam, a fair 9.5f winner, is a half-sister to 5 other minor winners. The second dam, Rosy Lydgate (by Last Tycoon), is a placed half-sister to 5 winners including the US Grade 3 winner Supreme Sound. (Qatar Racing Ltd). *"She's very solid, a little bit workmanlike looking, but she's done a few bits and pieces of work and seems to have a great appetite for it. We're looking forward to her making her debut over six furlongs by the end of May".*

DAVID BARRON

87. ANGEL GRACE (IRE)

gr.f. Dark Angel – Light Sea (King's Best). March 11. Second foal. 30,000Y. Tattersalls October Book 2. Yeomanstown Stud. Half-sister to the 2014 2-y-o winner Squats (by Dandy Man). The dam is an unplaced half-sister to 7 winners including the dual Group 2 Sandown Mile winner Hurricane Alan. The second dam, Bint Al Balad (by Ahonoora), a modest 7f placed 3-y-o, is a sister to the useful Group 3 7f Nell Gwyn Stakes winner and Irish 1,000 Guineas fourth A-To-Z. (Mr C A Washbourn).

88. BARRON'S LAD ♠

ch.c. Compton Place – Dance Away (Pivotal). February 13. Seventh foal. £50,000Y. Doncaster Premier. C&C Barriers. Half-brother to the useful 2-y-o 5f and 6f winner Foghorn Leghorn, to the fair 2-y-o 6f winner Medici Dancer and (both by Medicean) and the modest 5f winner Azif (by Where Or When). The dam, a fairly useful 2-y-o 5f winner, is a half-sister to 5 winners. The second dam, Dance On (by Caerleon), a fairly useful 2-y-o dual 5f winner, was listed-placed and is a half-sister to 7 winners. (C & C Bloodstock Ltd).

89. BIGMOUTH STRIKES (IRE)

ch.c. Raven's Pass – Chiosina (Danehill Dancer). February 14. Sixth foal. 120,000Y. Tattersalls October Book 1. Harrowgate Bloodstock. Half-brother to the French listed 6f and listed 7f winner and Group 2 placed Mixed Intention, to the French 7f and 1m winner Mixed Evidence (both by Elusive City), the quite useful 2-y-o 5f and 6f winner Meritocracy and the poor 6f winner Kerfuffle (both by Kheleyf). The dam is an unraced half-sister to 4 winners including the Italian listed winner and Group 2 placed Aria Di Festa. The second dam, Alarme Belle (by Warning), a useful Irish dual 6f winner, was listed-placed and is a half-sister to 4 winners. (Mr C A Washbourn).

90. RANTAN (IRE)

b.c. Kodiac – Peace Talks (Pivotal). February 25. First foal. £65,000Y. Doncaster Premier. Mr H D Atkinson. The dam is an unraced half-sister to 3 minor winners. The second dam, Subtle Charm (by Machiavellian), is an unplaced half-sister to 7 winners including the Oaks winner Snow Bride (herself the dam of Lammtarra). (Mr H D Atkinson).

91. RHOSTAL (IRE)

b.f. Canford Cliffs – Galeaza (Galileo). March 17. Second foal. £31,000Y. Doncaster Premier. C&C Barriers. Half-sister to the quite useful 2014 2-y-o 6f winner Caius College Girl (by Royal Applause). The dam is an unraced half-sister to 4 winners including the fairly useful dual 5f winner (including at 2 yrs) Deserted Dane. The second dam, Desertion (by Danehill), a fairly useful 6f and 1m winner, is a sister to the National Stakes, Irish 2,000 Guineas and Irish Derby winner Desert King and to the Group 2 7f Champagne Stakes third Chianti and a half-sister to 5 winners. (C & C Bloodstock Ltd).

92. UNNAMED

b.c. Makfi – Present Danger (Cadeaux Genereux). January 31. First foal. £50,000Y. Doncaster Premier. David Redvers. The dam, a fair 6f (at 2 yrs) and 1m winner, is a half-sister to 5 winners including the fairly useful 2-y-o 5f winner and listed placed All For Laura (herself the dam of the Group 2 Cherry Hinton Stakes winner Misheer). The second dam, Lighthouse (by Warning), a fairly useful 3-y-o 8.3f winner, is a half-sister to 4 winners including the Group 1 Middle Park Stakes, Group 3 July Stakes and Group 3 Richmond Stakes winner First Trump. (Qatar Racing Ltd).

93. UNNAMED

b.f. Kodiac – River Bounty (Bahamian Bounty). February 17. First foal. £30,000Y. Doncaster Silver. Harrowgate Bloodstock. The dam, a modest triple 6f winner, including twice at 2 yrs, is out of the unraced Artistic Merit (by Alhaarth), herself a half-sister to 5 winners. (Twinacre Nurseries).

RALPH BECKETT

94. ABACO RIDGE ★★★

b.f. Bahamian Bounty – Echo Ridge (Oratorio). February 12. First foal. The dam, a fair 2-y-o 6f winner, is a half-sister to the fairly useful 2-y-o 6f winner and Group 2 fourth City Girl. The second dam, a smart listed 6f winner of 5 races, is a half-sister to 4 winners including the useful listed 5f winner Loch Verdi. (J C Smith). *"I always felt her mother was better than she* showed. *This filly has better knees than she had, I like her and thought she was going to be earlyish but she's just mentally immature. We'll give her a bit of time and she should be ready in mid-summer over six furlongs. I like her and it's a great family".*

95. ALYSSA ★★★

b.f. Sir Percy – Almiranta (Galileo). January 28. Second foal. Half-sister to the 2014 2-y-o Group 3 1m Prix Thomas Bryon winner Alea Iacta (by Invincible Spirit). The dam, third over 8.5f on her only start, is a half-sister to 3 winners including the Irish Group 3 10f winner Alla Speranza. The second dam, Alvarita (by Selkirk), a French listed 10.5f winner, is out of the dual Champion Stakes winner Alborada (by Alzao). (Miss K Rausing). *"A lovely, tall filly that's going to need a bit of time but it's a terrific family and I believe the dam's 3-y-o with Andre Fabre is highly thought of. She has a bit about her but she's quite leggy now and won't be ready to run until the autumn over seven furlongs and a mile".*

96. CARNTOP ★★

b.c. Dansili – Milford Sound (Barathea). February 10. Second foal. Brother to the minor French 10.5f winner Quebec. The dam, a fair French 1m winner, is a half-sister to numerous winners including the Prix de l'Arc de Triomphe and Grand Prix de Paris winner Rail Link (by Dansili), the French Group 2 12f and dual Group 3 10f winner Crosshabour and the smart French 1m and 10f performer Chelsea Manor. The second dam, Docklands (by Theatrical), a French 1m and 10f performer, is a half-sister to the smart performer at up to 9f Wharf. (The Prince Of Wales & Duchess Of Cornwall). *"A big, tall, leggy horse that'll need some time but he gets across the ground well and we'll take a look at him in the second half of the year. He'll need a mile this year".*

97. CROSSED ARROW ★★

b.f. Cape Cross – Snoqualmie Star (Galileo). February 27. First foal. The dam, a quite useful 1m and 10f winner, is a half-sister to 8 winners including the smart listed 10f winner and Group 2 Dante Stakes third Snoqualmie Boy and the very useful listed 1m (at 2 yrs) and listed 10f winner Snoqualmie Girl. The second

dam, Seattle Ribbon (by Seattle Dancer), placed over 9f and 10f at 3 yrs, is a sister to the 2-y-o Group 1 1m winner Seattle Dancer. (Mr J C Smith). *"She has a bit of quality about her and has a very good head. She's quite long-backed but is a good-moving filly and I'd say she'll come to hand from mid-to-late season. She's a good-bodied filly and I like her".*

98. CROWNING GLORY (FR) ★★

b.f. Speightstown – Forest Crown (Royal Applause). February 13. First foal. The dam, a fairly useful listed-placed 6f (at 2 yrs) and 1m winner, is a sister to the fairly useful listed-placed dual 6f winner (including at 2 yrs) Riotous Applause and a half-sister to 6 winners including the 2-y-o Group 1 1m Racing Post Trophy winner Crowded House and the French listed 11f winner and Group 3 placed On Reflection and to the dam of the US dual Grade 1 winner Ticker Tape. The second dam, Wiener Wald (Woodman), is an unplaced half-sister to 6 minor winners. (Eclipse Partnership). *"The dam didn't come to hand as a 2-y-o until quite late on. This filly is growing at the moment and is quite immature, she'll make a 2-y-o but not until the second half of the summer".*

99. DESERT HAZE ★★★★★

br.f. New Approach – Ensemble (Iron Mask). April 8. First foal. 420,000Y. Tattersalls October Book 1. B Le Metayer. The dam, a minor French 3-y-o winner, is a half-sister to 8 winners including the Group 1 7f Prix de la Foret and Group 1 6.5f Prix Maurice de Gheest winner and smart broodmare Occupandiste and the dual listed 7f winner Only Green. The second dam, Only Seule (by Lyphard), a winner over 7.5f in France at 2 yrs, is a half-sister to 9 winners including Mehthaaf (Irish 1,000 Guineas and Celebration Mile), Elnadim (July Cup and Diadem Stakes) and Khulood (Group 3 Nell Gwyn Stakes). (Sheikh Mohammed bin Khalifa Al-Thani). *"A lovely, quality, athletic filly. She's done very well since the sale and you couldn't fault her as an individual. She's a cracking filly with a good temperament and we'll have another look at her in the second half of the year. She should appear this year and make up into a really nice 3-y-o".*

100. EMERALD LOCH ★★★
ch.f. Danehill Dancer – Loch Verdi (Green Desert). April 5. Fourth foal. Half-sister to the fair 2014 6f placed 2-y-o Green Tornado (by Equiano), to the modest 2-y-o 6f winner Gift Of Music (by Cadeaux Genereux) and the moderate 2-y-o 5f winner Green Music (by Oratorio). The dam, a useful listed 5f winner of 4 races, is a half-sister to 4 winners including the smart listed 6f winner of 5 races Lochridge. The second dam, Lochsong (by Song), a champion sprinter and winner of the Prix de l'Abbaye (twice), the Kings Stand Stakes and the Nunthorpe Stakes, is a half-sister to the Nunthorpe Stakes winner Lochangel. (Mr J C Smith). *"She's quite a tall, scopey filly. Her half-brother Green Tornado was quite a 'set' horse with limited size and scope, but you couldn't say that about this one. She's a good-moving filly that'll need a bit of time, but she'll be a six furlong 2-y-o, have a couple of runs this year and then make up into a better 3-y-o".*

101. GOLDEN CHAPTER ★★
b.f. Danehill Dancer – Farfala (Linamix). January 26. Tenth foal. 200,000Y. Tattersalls October Book 1. Pan Sutong. Half-sister to 6 winners including the 2-y-o listed 10f Zetland Stakes winner and Group 2 12f Lancashire Oaks second Under The Rainbow (by Fantastic Light), the useful dual 12f winner and Group 2 Park Hill Stakes second Starfala (by Galileo) and the quite useful 2-y-o 1m winners Swingland (by Pivotal) and Speightstown (by Grand Lodge). The dam, a French listed 12f winner, is a sister to 6 winners including Alpine Rose (Group 1 Prix Jean Romanet) and Fragrant Mix (Group 1 Grand Prix de Saint-Cloud). The second dam, Fragrant Hill (by Shirley Heights), won the listed 10f Lupe Stakes. (Mr S Pan). *"A long, scopey filly from a middle-distance filly, she's likely to go for a spring break and then we'll aim for a couple of runs at the back-end. A long-term project".*

102. GOLDEN STUNNER (IRE) ★★★
ch.f. Dream Ahead – Pina Colada (Sabrehill). February 26. Eighth foal. €115,000Y. Goffs Orby. Mr Pan Sutong. Half-sister to the quite useful Irish 2-y-o 5f and subsequent US winner Mr Mojito and to the quite useful dual 1m winner Colonel Carter (both by Danehill

Dancer). The dam, a winner of 3 races here and in the USA including a minor stakes, was Grade 2 placed and is a half-sister 6 winners including Triple Threat (Group 2 Prix Eugene Adam) and to the unraced dam of Canford Cliffs. The second dam, Drei (by Lyphard), is a placed full or half-sister to 3 winners. (Mr S Pan). *"Probably a bit further forward than I initially thought. She was quite an early foal, goes about her work in a very straightforward manner and is one of those fillies you almost don't notice because she's never in trouble and just gets on with it. There's a bit of speed in the pedigree, she'll be a six furlong 2-y-o and I was a fan of Dream Ahead as a racehorse so I hope he makes it as a sire".*

103. GOLD FAITH (IRE) ★★★★
gr.c. Dark Angel – Livadream (Dalakhani). February 26. First foal. 200,000Y. Tattersalls October Book 2. Pan Sutong. The dam is an unraced half-sister to 2 minor winners. The second dam, Livadiya (by Shernazar), an Irish triple listed winner from 9f to12f, was second in the Group 1 Tattersalls Gold Cup and is a half-sister to 8 winners including the dam of the triple Group 2 winner Linngari. (Mr S Pan). *"A lovely horse, but I think there's a bit of the damsire Dalakhani about him so although he's an early foal I wouldn't be certain he's all Dark Angel. Physically I think he'll progress through the year. A very straightforward individual, he gets on with his work and he's a good mover with a low action. I would think he'd be ready to start off at six furlongs in July, but he might come earlier".*

104. HOLY ROMAN PRINCE (IRE) ★★★
b.c. Holy Roman Emperor – Princess Ellen (Tirol). April 17. Closely related to the useful listed 1m winner Prince Of Dance (by Danehill Dancer) and half-brother to 4 winners including the French and Belgian winner and 2-y-o listed 5f placed Candelabro (by Elusive Quality), the quite useful 9.5f (at 2 yrs) to 2m and hurdles winner of 28 races La Estrella (by Theatrical) and the fair 1m winner Stravella (by Stravinsky). The dam, a smart 2-y-o listed 7f Sweet Solera Stakes winner, was second in the 1,000 Guineas and the Coronation Stakes and is a half-sister to one winner out of the unraced Celt Song (by Unfuwain). (Five Horses Ltd). *"A neat colt and pretty forward, he's quite light*

framed so we may do a bit of work with him soon to see if we can press on or if he needs more time. He's got the make and shape of a 2-y-o and should see plenty of action this year".

105. MATCH MY FIRE (IRE) ★★
ch.c. Makfi – High Lite (Observatory). April 14. Fourth foal. €42,000Y. Goffs Orby. Kern/Lillingston. Half-brother to the fairly useful 7f (at 2 yrs) to 12f winner Azurite (by Azamour). The dam is an unplaced half-sister to 7 winners including the 2-y-o Group 2 Gimcrack Stakes winner Bannister. The second dam, Shall We Run (by Hotfoot), is a placed full or half-sister to 8 winners including Dead Certain (Group 1 Cheveley Park Stakes). (Kennet Valley Thoroughbreds). *"Although this colt has a speedy pedigree the Makfi 2-y-o's didn't show up last year until the season was almost over. I think he's probably of that type and I doubt us getting on with him that early. He has a good way of going but physically he looks in two halves at the moment".*

106. MISS MONEYPENNY ★★★★
b.f. Kodiac – Pearly Brooks (Efisio). April 14. Ninth foal. £42,000Y. Doncaster Premier. McCalmont Bloodstock. Half-brother to the quite useful 2014 2-y-o 5f winner Pearl's Azinger (by Zebedee), to the quite useful 2-y-o 5f winner Fine 'n Dandy (by Dandy Man), the fair dual 1m winner, including at 2 yrs, Classic Voice (by Oratorio) and a hurdles winner by High Chaparral. The dam, a fair 3-y-o 6f winner, is a sister to 4 winners including the Group 1 Phoenix Stakes winner Pips Pride and a half-sister to 4 winners. The second dam, Elkie Brooks (by Relkino), is a placed half-sister to one winner. (Chelsea Thoroughbreds – Cap Ferrat). *"She looks really forward and should be racing in April or May. I love the page, Kodiac above Efisio, and she looks to have all the toughness that her pedigree should impart. I like her, we should have a bit of sport with her over five and six furlongs and we won't be hanging around".*

107. PILLAR ★★★
b.c. Rock Of Gibraltar – Ceilidh House (Selkirk). March 5. The dam, a useful 1m (at 2 yrs) and listed 10f winner, is a sister to two quite useful 10f winners and a half-sister to 3 winners. The second dam, Villa Carlotta (by Rainbow

Quest), a smart 12f listed winner of four races, is a half-sister to 9 winners including the US dual Grade 2 winner Battle Of Hastings. (Mr J H Richmond-Watson). *"A nice colt out a dam who won as a 2-y-o late on but was much better as a 3-y-o. He looks a bit more forward than that, he's quite a strong colt and he's inherited all of the dam's robustness. He should make a seven furlong 2-y-o in the second half of the year, I like the horse and he's got a good temperament".*

108. POINT OF WOODS ★★★★
b.c. Showcasing – Romantic Myth (Mind Games). February 27. Eighth foal. 110,000Y. Tattersalls October Book 2. BBA (Ire). Half-brother to 5 winners including the fair 2-y-o dual 5f winner Heartbreak (by Iffraaj), the fair 2-y-o 6f winner Mythicism (by Oasis Dream) and the modest 7f winner of 4 races Headache (by Cape Cross). The dam, winner of the Group 3 5f Queen Mary Stakes, is a half-sister to 11 winners including another Queen Mary winner in Romantic Liason. The second dam, My First Romance (by Danehill), ran twice unplaced and is a half-sister to 6 winners. (Mr & Mrs David Aykroyd). *"He's all speed and we're just starting to crank him up now. He was quite a burly yearling but he's doing well and I'd be fairly hopeful of him appearing before the end of May. Five or six furlongs will suit him and he's a nice horse".*

109. PURE ART ★★★
b.f. Dutch Art – Pure Song (Singspiel). March 20. Fourth foal. 80,000Y. Tattersalls October Book 1. Not sold. Closely related to the fair 2014 2-y-o 9.5f winner Wolf Albarari (by Medicean) and half-sister to the smart 11f winner and Epsom Derby third Romsdal (by Halling). The dam, a fair 12f and 14f placed maiden, is a half-sister to 4 winners including the smart 7f (at 2 yrs) and Group 3 10.5f Prix Fille de l'Air winner Goncharova. The second dam, Pure Grain (by Polish Precedent), won 5 races including the Group 1 12f Irish Oaks and the Group 1 12f Yorkshire Oaks and is a half-sister to 8 winners including the dam of the Japanese Group 1 winner Fine Grain. (R Barnett). *"She's not a particularly big filly but she's strong and has plenty of Dutch Art about her. A good moving filly for the second half of the summer".*

110. SACRAMENT (IRE) ★★★★

b.f. Acclamation – Alstemeria (Danehill). February 4. Sixth foal. 75,000Y. Tattersalls October Book 1. Half-sister to the very useful 6f (at 2 yrs) and 7f winner and dual Group 3 placed Kitty Kiernan (by Pivotal) and to the modest 7f winner Fernando Torres (by Giant's Causeway). The dam, a useful Irish 6f winner and fourth in the Group 1 Irish 1,000 Guineas, is a sister to the Group 1 1m Gran Criterium winner Spartacus and to the Group 2 10f Gallinule Stakes and Hong Kong Derby winner Johan Cruyff. The second dam, Teslemi (by Ogygian), a fair 3-y-o 1m winner, is a half-sister to 5 minor winners. (Highclere Thoroughbred Racing - Disraeli). *"A strong, forward-going filly, she's just growing slightly at the moment but she'll make a 2-y-o alright, over five/six furlongs. A filly with a good outlook, she has a big, broad head on her and just gets on with life, so she should be fine".*

111. SANDAHL (IRE) ★★

b.g. Footstepsinthesand – Little Scotland (Acclamation). April 4. Second foal. €80,000Y. Goffs Orby. BBA (Ire). Half-brother to the fair 2014 6f placed 2-y-o Ertidaad (by Kodiac). The dam, a quite useful 6f and 7f winner, was listed-placed and is a half-sister to 6 winners. The second dam, Belladera (by Alzao), won over 6f at 2 yrs and is a half-sister to 7 winners including the listed Woodcote Stakes winner Silca Blanka. (Mr & Mrs David Aykroyd). *"He was a very fiery individual so we gelded him and that's made a big difference to his and our lives. He has a high head carriage, he's growing at the moment and we won't crack on with him until late April/early May".*

112. SECRET SENSE (USA) ★★★

b.f. Shamardal – Shastye (Danehill). February 14. Half-sister to the 2014 7f placed 2-y-o (on his only start) Sir Isaac Newton and to the smart listed 10f and listed 11.5f winner and Group 1 Oaks second Secret Gesture (by Galileo). The dam, a useful listed-placed 12f and 13f winner, is a half-sister to 8 winners including the Prix de l'Arc de Triomphe winner Sagamix, the Group 1 Criterium de Saint-Cloud winner Sagacity and the Group 2 winner Sage Et Jolie (dam of the Group 1 winner Sageburg). The second dam, Saganeca (by Sagace), won the Group 3 12.5f Prix de Royallieu and was second in the Group 1 Gran Premio di Milano. (Newsells Park Stud). *"A huge filly, she's twice the size of her half-sister Secret Gesture but very light on her feet and she gets along well. She'll need plenty of time but I like her a very much, as you'd expect with that pedigree. I'd be surprised if she didn't get a mile this year".*

113. SHADAD (IRE) ★★★

b.c. Zamindar – Tender Morn (Dayjur). April 29. €200,000Y. Arqana Deauville August. B Le Metayer. Brother to the 2-y-o Group 3 1m Prix d'Aumale winner and the Group 1 Prix Marcel Boussac third Zantenda and half-brother to several winners including the French 2-y-o 1m winner and Group 3 Prix d'Aumale second Single (by Singspiel) and the French 2-y-o dual 7f winner Elusif (by Elusive Quality). The dam was listed-placed over 5f at 2 yrs and is a half-sister to the listed 5.5f winner Diableneyev. (Sheikh Mohammed bin Khalifa Al Maktoum). *"Quite fiery, every Zamindar I've had have been contradictions because they've been fiery but with delicate constitutions at the same time. It's a very fast family, I think he's really nice but he needs handling with kid gloves at the moment. He'll get better as time goes on and I think he may get seven furlongs this year".*

114. SHORT WORK ★★★

ch.c. Kyllachy – Agony Aunt (Formidable). April 23. Eleventh foal. 26,000Y. Tattersalls October Book 2. A C Elliott/R Beckett. Closely related to the quite useful 6f winner Cool Tune and to the modest 5f (at 2 yrs) to 7f winner Only If I Laugh (both by Piccolo) and half-brother to 6 winners including the listed 1m winner Agony And Ecstasy, the fair 2-y-o winners Captain Revelation and Rio's Pearl (all by Captain Rio) and the fairly useful 6f winner of 7 races Doctor Hilary (by Mujahid). The dam, a quite useful 10f winner, is a half-sister to 2 winners. The second dam, Loch Clair (by Lomond), is an unplaced half-sister to 6 winners including the German Group 1 winner Wind In Her Hair (dam of the champion Japanese horse Deep Impact). (The Pickford Hill Partnership). *"His joints are quite immature and he's quite top-heavy as well, so we've had to back off him a bit. I hope he'll emulate his sister Agony And Ecstasy by getting better with age* and racing. One for auction races in the middle of the year". **TRAINERS' BARGAIN BUY**

115. SIGHTLINE ★★★★
b.f. Rock Of Gibraltar – Look So (Efisio). January 29. Half-sister to the useful 1m (at 2 yrs) and listed 10f winner and Group 3 9.5f second Regardez (by Champs Elysees) and to the fairly useful 6f (at 2 yrs) and 7f winner and listed-placed Compton (by Compton Place). The dam, a quite useful 7f and 1m winner of 4 races, is a half-sister to numerous winners including the Oaks winner Look Here. The second dam, Last Look (by Rainbow Quest), is an unraced half-sister to two minor winners. (Mr J H Richmond-Watson). "Her breeder had a sneaking suspicion that the dam would be a good broodmare and so it's proved because she's bred two stakes horses. They're both very tough horses and you couldn't break either of them with work. This filly has done very well lately, as you'd expect, because the whole family get better with time, age and work. I suspect she'll develop significantly throughout the year and is more like her half-brother Compton than Regardez. Six furlongs might be a bit sharp for her, but she'll make a 2-y-o at around seven furlongs. I expect her to improve with racing".

116. SPARRING QUEEN (USA) ★★★
b.f. War Front – Spa Break (Giant's Causeway). March 25. The dam is an unraced half-sister to numerous winners including the US Grade 2 7f winner Exchange Rate and the Group 3 7f Rose Of Lancaster Stakes winner Sabre d'Argent. The second dam, Sterling Pound (by Seeking The Gold), won five races including the Grade 3 Honey Bee Handicap. "Quite a strong, slightly raw filly at the moment, she's a bit behind in her coat and in her manner, but she's going to develop. It's a very fast family and although we won't kick on with her yet we'll take a look at her in August or September. War Front is an excellent stallion, so I'm looking forward to her".

117. THE KING'S STEED ★★
b.c. Equiano – King's Siren (King's Best). February 4. Half-brother to the quite useful 2014 2-y-o 8.5f winner Magic Dancer (by Norse Dancer). The dam, a fair 2-y-o 7f winner, is a half-sister to the useful 2-y-o listed 5.2f winner and Group 2 Flying Childers Stakes third Speed Cop and the fairly useful dual 5f winner (including at 2 yrs) Siren's Gift. The second dam, Blue Siren (by Bluebird), a very useful winner of three races from 5f to 7f, was disqualified from first place in two more, notably the Group 1 5f Nunthorpe Stakes (the winner on merit) and is a half-sister to several winners including the quite useful 9f winner Northern Habit. (Mr J C Smith). "A big, plain colt. His half-brother Magic Dancer is a big, fine, good-looking colt but this one is much plainer. He has a big, rolling action too so he'll be one for later in the year".

118. TOUMAR ★★★
ch.f. Sea The Stars – Tingling (Storm Cat). March 4. Fourth foal. 100,000Y. Tattersalls October Book 1. Not sold. Closely related to the fair 10f winner Lybica (by Galileo). The dam, a quite useful 7f and 1m placed 2-y-o in Ireland, is a half-sister to 3 winners including the Canadian Grade 3 winner Rosberg. The second dam, Bosra Sham (by Woodman), an outstanding filly and winner of three Group 1 events, is a sister to the multiple Group 1 winner Hector Protector and a half-sister to the French 2,000 Guineas winner Shanghai and the dams of the Group/Grade 1 winners Ciro and Internallyflawless. (Mr N Bizakov). "A strong, butty filly, not very big and she copes with her work quite well. She may be a bit more forward than most by Sea The Stars. A pretty straightforward filly, she'll want plenty of graft so we'll keep on top of her and see how we go".

119. UNNAMED ★★★
ch.f. Dutch Art – Agony And Ecstasy (Captain Rio). February 14. First foal. £115,000Y. Doncaster Premier. F Barberini/J Murtagh. The dam, a listed 1m winner, is a half-sister to 6 winners including the fairly useful 6f winner of 7 races Doctor Hilary. The second dam, Agony Aunt (by Formidable), a quite useful 10f winner, is a half-sister to 2 winners. (Clipper Group Holdings Ltd). "She did a little bit this morning for the first time and we trained her dam who won at two and got better at three and four. I like her, she's strong and forward-going so we'll be getting on with her. Very like her mother with a bit of Dutch Art thrown in, which can't be bad".

120. UNNAMED ★★★
b.f. Montjeu – Festoso (Diesis). February 3. Third foal. 105,000Y. Tattersalls October Book 1. Steve Parkin. The dam, a useful 1m (at 2 yrs) and listed 6f winner, was third in the Group 1 Cheveley Park Stakes and is a half-sister to 5 winners including the Group 1 9f Prix Jean Prat winner Olden Times. The second dam, Garah (by Ajdal), a very useful winner of 4 races over 6f, was second in the Group 3 5f Duke Of York Stakes and is a half-sister to 6 winners. (Clipper Group Holdings Ltd). *"The dam was a real 2-y-o and was third in the Cheveley Park, but the Montjeu's generally need plenty of TLC. We'll keep cantering away with her for now and maybe give her a spin in June/July and see how she goes on. She'll want a mile this year I should think and some juice in the ground going off the way she moves".*

121. UNNAMED ★★★
b.c. Acclamation – Greek Easter (Namid). April 5. Second living foal. 70,000Y. Tattersalls October Book 2. Robert Ng. The dam, a 7f and 1m winner in Germany and subsequently a fair 10f winner here, is a half-sister to the 2-y-o 5f and 6f winner, Group 1 Middle Park Stakes third and subsequent US Grade 3 winner Doc Holiday. The second dam, Easter Heroine (by Exactly Sharp), was placed over 7f (at 2 yrs) and 10f in Ireland and is a half-sister to 4 winners. (Mr R Ng). *"A tallish horse, he's not typical of the sire, but he's quite a good mover and covers the ground well. I'd say he wants fast ground and six furlongs and he has a good attitude".*

122. UNNAMED ★★★
b.f. Rock Of Gibraltar – Green Room (FR) (In The Wings). March 20. Fifth foal. Half-sister to L'Ingenue (by New Approach), placed fourth over 1m on her only start at 2 yrs in 2014 and to the modest 2m winner Duke's Den (by Duke Of Marmalade). The dam, a useful Italian listed 12f winner of 4 races, was placed in two other listed events here and is a half-sister to 4 winners. The second dam, Scarlet Plume (by Warning), won 2 races including the Group 3 1m Premio Dormello and is a half-sister to 4 winners out of the Oaks winner Circus Plume. (Aylesfield Farm Stud). *"I train her half-sister L'Ingenue and this one is probably not as backward. I would think she'd want seven*

furlongs or a mile around September time. A tallish filly, I like her".

123. UNNAMED ★★★★
b.f. Galileo – Landmark (Arch). March 30. Sixth foal. 420,000Y. Tattersalls October Book 1. David Redvers. Sister to the very useful 12f winner and Group 2 Ribblesdale Stakes second Field Of Miracles and to the very useful 9f, 10f and listed 12f winner Cameron Highland and half-sister to the fairly useful dual 10f winner Sour Mash (by Danehill Dancer) and the quite useful 7f winner Supposing (by Invincible Spirit). The dam, a minor 2-y-o winner in the USA, is a sister to the US dual Grade 1 winner Arravale. The second dam, Kalosca (by Kaldoun), won 3 races in France and the USA, was Grade 2 placed and is a half-sister to the Group 2 Prix Foy winner Crillon. (Sheikh Khalifa, Sheikh Suhaim & QRC). *"A gorgeous filly but quite mentally immature, she needs plenty of time. She likes to get on with it but we'll be holding on to her for a while yet".*

124. UNNAMED ★★★
b.c. Kodiac – Right After Moyne (Imperial Ballet). April 20. Sixth foal. €50,000Y. Tattersalls Ireland September. Robert Ng. Half-brother to the useful 2-y-o 5f winner and Group 3 Molecomb Stakes third Choose Wisely (by Choisir), to the quite useful 7f to 10.5f winner of 5 races Ardmay (by Strategic Prince), the fair 6f (including at 2 yrs) winner Zain Zone (by Pastoral Pursuits) and the fair 6f (at 2 yrs) and 10f winner Tamanaco (by Catcher In The Rye). The dam is an unraced half-sister to 3 winners. The second dam, Trojan River (by Riverman), won twice over 10f and 14f and is a half-sister to 6 winners including Air Marshall (Group 2 Great Voltigeur). (M R Ng). *"A big, solid, quite gross colt, he needs plenty of work and he's bigger than most you'll see by the sire. He looks pretty honest, he covers the ground well and we should be fine with him. The dam has bred a number of 2-y-o winners and this colt should make up into a 3-y-o because he's got plenty of size and scope".*

125. UNNAMED ★★
b.f. Dutch Art – Roscoff (Daylami). January 25. Fourth foal. Half-brother to the 2014 Italian 2-y-o 7.5f winner Hero Look (by Lope De Vega). The dam, a French

listed-placed 7.5f winner, is a half-sister to 2 winners. The second dam, Traou Mad (by Barathea), a French listed 2-y-o winner, was Group 3 placed four times and is a half-sister to 7 winners including the Group 2 6f Gimcrack Stakes and dual Group 3 winner Josr Algharoud and the dual Group 2 5f Prix du Gros-Chene winner Saint Marine. (Merriebelle Stables). *"A very backward filly, she's nice but she's going to need plenty of time"*.

126. UNNAMED ★★★
ch.f. Exceed And Excel – Sensational Mover (Theatrical). May 16. Seventh foal. Sister to the useful 2-y-o listed 6f winner Shamandar and half-sister to the French 2-y-o listed 7f winner Hung Parliament (by Numerous). The dam, a moderate 12f placed maiden, is out of the US Grade 2 8.5f winner Blushing Heiress (by Blushing John). (Mr P K Gardiner). *"Quite a tall filly with a very straight hind leg, but she goes OK and although I had her boxed as a filly that needs time I'm not so convinced about that now. She might come to hand a bit earlier than I thought, but her late foaling date suggests she'll be one to run towards the back-end over six furlongs"*.

MICHAEL BELL
127. ACADEMY HOUSE (IRE) ★★★
b.c. Kodiac – Joyfullness (Dixieland Band). March 4. Ninth foal. €72,000Y. Goffs Orby. A C Elliott. Half-brother to the Italian listed-placed 2-y-o winner Flying Teapot (by King Charlemagne), to the quite useful Irish 1m winner Song In My Heart (by Spartacus), the fair 7f winner of 6 races Khajaaly (by Kheleyf), the fair 2-y-o 1m winner Sir Trevor (by Refuse To Bend) and the modest 6f and 7f winner Contented (by Orpen). The dam is an unraced half-sister to 11 winners including the dam of the Group 2 Royal Lodge Stakes winner Mons. The second dam, Arewehavingfunyet (by Sham), won the Grade 1 Oak Leaf Stakes and is a half-sister to 6 winners. (W J and T O C Gredley). *"A relatively early foal by a sire that gets plenty of 2-y-o's, he's from a nice family and looks like being a 2-y-o. Just about to start fast work, he'll definitely have the ability and speed for six furlongs"*.

128. ALCANAR (USA) ★★★
ch.c. Teofilo – Badalona (Cape Cross). March 21. Half-brother to the fair 2014 2-y-o 1m winner Banditry (by Iffraaj). The dam, a quite useful 2-y-o 1m winner, is a sister to one winner and a half-sister to numerous winners including the very useful 2-y-o 6f winner and Group 1 Cheveley Park Stakes third Badminton, the useful 2-y-o 7f winner and Group 3 7f Vintage Stakes third Fox and the useful 6f and 7f winner and Group 3 Nell Gwyn Stakes second Cala. The second dam, Badawi (by Diesis), was a useful 1m and 9f winner of 4 races. (Sheikh Marwan Al Maktoum). *"A particularly good mover, he's furnished significantly since he's been with us and is one for the back-end of the season and next year. Doing everything right at the moment, he looks nice"*.

129. BIG SKY ★★
b.f. Fastnet Rock – Sheppard's Watch (Night Shift). April 19. Half-sister to the minor French 4-y-o winner Satwa Star (by King's Best) and a hurdles winner by Dansili. The dam, a very useful 6f (at 2 yrs), Group 3 7.5f Concorde Stakes and dual listed winner, is a full or half-sister to 2 winners. The second dam, Sheppard's Cross (by Soviet Star), a quite useful triple 7f winner, is a half-sister to 5 winners. (Lady Bamford). *"The mare has been disappointing but this filly moves well, she's precocious and athletic"*.

130. BLUE MOON RISING ★★★
ch.f. Dream Ahead – Wedding Gown (Dubai Destination). February 2. Third foal. 65,000Y. Tattersalls October Book 1. Not sold. The dam, placed once at 3 yrs in France, is a half-sister to 7 winners including the Japanese $3.5 million earner Gold Tiara and the Group 1 1m Queen Elizabeth II Stakes winner Poet's Voice. The second dam, Bright Tiara (by Chief's Crown), a minor 2-y-o winner in the USA, is a sister to the Grade 1 Brooklyn Handicap winner Chief Honcho and a half-sister to 10 winners. (Chris Wright). *"She's very popular in the yard and is out of a half-sister to Poet's Voice. She's precocious, moves well and is a good advertisement for the sire. Will definitely make a 2-y-o"*.

131. BOCKING END (IRE) ★★★
b.f. Paco Boy – Miss Wells (Sadler's Wells). March 1. Third foal. 30,000foal. Tattersalls

December. W J Gredley. Sister to the modest 2014 6f placed 2-y-o Cisco Boy and half-sister to the quite useful 6f winner of 4 races at 2 and 3 yrs Archie Stevens (by Pastoral Pursuits). The dam is an unraced sister to the winner and dual Group 3 placed Temple Place and a half-sister to 3 winners. The second dam, Puzzled Look (by Gulch), a stakes winner in the USA, is a half-sister to 8 winners including four US stakes winners. (W J and T C O Gredley). *"An easy-moving filly by Paco Boy, she's out of a mare by Sadler's Wells which might slow her up a bit. I see her as a nice seven furlong filly in the making. A particularly good mover".*

132. BONHOMIE ★★★

b.f. Shamardal – Bonnie Doon (Grand Lodge). April 23. Fifth foal. Half-sister to the fairly useful 8.5f (at 2 yrs) and 10f winner Border Legend (by Selkirk) and to the fair 12f winner Banks And Braes (by Red Ransom). The dam is an unraced half-sister to 6 winners including the French listed and US stakes winner Calista and the US stakes-placed winner Earthrise. The second dam, Proskona (by Mr Prospector), a high-class 3-y-o winner of the Group 3 6f Prix de Seine et Oise and the Group 2 6f Premio Umbria, is a half-sister to 10 winners including the top-class broodmare Korveya (dam of the classic winners Hector Protector, Shanghai and Bosra Sham). (The Queen). *"About to go back to the Royal Studs for a bit of spring grass, she's a very uncomplicated filly. Not over-big, she's probably one to start over seven furlongs and from August onwards".*

133. CAPE ORFORD ★★★★ ♠

ch.c. Cape Blanco – Latte (Pleasant Tap). April 20. Fifth foal. $200,000Y. Keeneland September. David Redvers. Half-brother to 4 winners abroad including the Panama stakes winner Citizen Bags (by Proud Citizen) and two minor stakes-placed winners by Langfuhr and Cowboy Cal. The dam is a US placed half-sister to 4 winners including the Grade 1 Gamely Handicap winner Mea Domina. The second dam, Madame Pandit (by Wild Again), a US Grade 3 winner, was Grade 1 placed and is a half-sister to the US Grade 3 winner Fiscally Speaking. (Qatar Racing Ltd). *"This is a nice horse and the dam's bred three 2-y-o winners. The riders really like him, he's a very*

good mover, very well-balanced and 'together'. A nice, late summer 2-y-o".

134. CARTER PACE ★★★★

b.f. Lawman – Kyniska (Choisir). March 6. Second foal. €110,000Y. Arqana Deauville August. F Barberini. The dam, a useful Irish 2-y-o 7f winner, was second in the Group 3 C L Weld Park Stakes and is a half-sister to 4 winners. The second dam, Lunadine (by Bering), is an unplaced half-sister to 3 winners including the Group 3 winner Prix Corrida winner Luna Mareza. (Clipper Logistics). *"She looks sharp, a very good mover and quite 'together'. The mare was speedy and this filly could be a six furlong 2-y-o. Lawman is a good sire of fillies in particular and the damsire Choisir ought to put a bit of boot into it. She's named after a woman who was the first lady sheriff of Kentucky".*

135. DUCHY ★★

b.f. Kyllachy – Albavilla (Spectrum). February 25. Fifth foal. 105,000Y. Tattersalls October Book 2. John Warren. Half-sister to the fairly useful 10f and subsequent UAE winner Antinori (by Fasliyev) and to the quite useful listed 1m Montrose Stakes winner Pure Excellence (by Exceed And Excel). The dam, a fair 14f winner, is a half-sister to 9 winners including the Irish listed winner Barolo. The second dam, Lydia Maria (by Dancing Brave), a moderate 1m and 10f placed maiden, is a half-sister to 7 winners. (Michael & Michelle Morris). *"She has an interesting pedigree in that she's by a sprinter and out of a mare that stayed all day. She doesn't look particularly sharp and she's quite big so we're taking our time, but she's done everything right and nothing wrong at this stage. A nice, fluent mover that seems to be taking after the dam's side".*

136. DUCK A L'ORANGE ★★★

ch.c. Duke Of Marmalade – Incheni (Nashwan). March 15. Fifth foal. 32,000Y. Tattersalls December. W J Gredley. Half-brother to the quite useful 10f winner Inchina (by Montjeu). The dam, a useful 7f (at 2 yrs) and listed 10f winner, was second in the Group 3 Nell Gwyn Stakes and is a sister to the very useful 2-y-o 7f winner and UAE Group 3 third Inchlonaig and a half-sister to 6 winners including the triple Group 3 7f winner and sire Inchinor. The second dam, Inchmurrin (by Lomond), a very useful winner of 6 races including the Group 2 Child Stakes and second in the Group 1 1m Coronation Stakes, is a half-sister to 7 winners including Welney (Mill Reef Stakes). (Mr J Barnett). *"I hope you like the name because I chose it! This colt has a cracking pedigree and he's a fine, strong colt. He gets up the hill nicely and he's one for the second half of the season. I like him".*

137. FORECASTER ★★★★
b.f. Fastnet Rock – Aurore (Fasliyev). January 31. Third foal. Half-sister to the fair 7f winner Enliven (by Dansili). The dam was placed over 6f and 7f in France at 2 yrs and is a half-sister to several winners including the triple Group 1 winner Aquarelliste and the dual US Grade 1 10f winner Artiste Royal. The second dam, Agathe (by Manila), won the Group 3 10f Prix de Psyche and is a half-sister to numerous winners including the Grade 1 Breeders Cup Classic winner Arcangues. (The Queen). *"A very precocious filly, she was a January foal and is much-liked in the yard. Good and strong, she has a very good Wildenstein pedigree. I had two Fastnet Rock's the year before last and they were very slow, but the two I have this year both look nice. This filly is very powerfully built".*

138. GENERAL HAZARD (IRE) ★★★
gr.c. Cacique – In The Soup (Alphabet Soup). March 2. Fourth foal. 32,000Y. Tattersalls October Book 3. R Frisby. Half-brother to the moderate 12f winner San Quentin (by Lawman). The dam, a minor winner of 2 races at 3 yrs in France, is a half-sister to 7 winners including two stakes winners in the USA. The second dam, Je Comprend (by Caerleon), is a placed sister to the Australian Group 2 winner Alquoz and a half-sister to two Grade 3 winners. (Mr R P B Michaelson). *"This is a good-moving horse, but he'll take a bit of time. A nice, back-end of the season type with a bit of size and scope and a good mover. I like him and the sire certainly punches above his weight. A big, strong horse for seven furlongs and a mile later in the season".*

139. GIANT SHADOW ★★★
b.c. Clodovil – Aldburgh (Bluebird). April 10.

Tenth foal. €52,000Y. Goffs Sportsmans. A.C. Elliott. Half-brother to the modest 2014 6f placed 2-y-o Aprovado (by Approve), to the quite useful 2-y-o 1m and subsequent US winner Montreaux (by Jade Robbery), the quite useful 10f and hurdles winner West Brit (by High Chaparral), the modest 10f and hurdles winner Peter Grimes (by Alhaarth) and a 3-y-o winner in Japan by Timber Country. The dam ran once unplaced and is a half-sister to 4 winners and to the dam of the high-class filly Attraction. The second dam, Eastern Shore (by Sun Prince), is a placed half-sister to 7 winners. (Michael Lowe). *"Named after my first pony! This is a very strong, robust 2-y-o type that looks like an early bird. One for us to be getting on with".*

140. GOLDEN HELLO (IRE) ★★★★
b.c. Zebedee – Your Opinion (Xaar). April 28. Second foal. 35,000Y. Tattersalls October Book 1. R Frisby. Half-brother to the unplaced 2014 2-y-o Trust Your Opinion (by Kodiac). The dam is an unraced sister to the Group 2 7f Hungerford Stakes, Group 2 7f Park Stakes and Group 2 6f Criterium de Maisons-Laffitte winner Balthazaar's Gift. The second dam, Thats Your Opinion (by Last Tycoon), a poor Irish 12f placed maiden, is a half-sister to 7 winners including the listed 1m Prix de Bagatelle winner and dual Group 3 placed Green Lady. (W J and T O C Gredley). *"Probably our sharpest colt, he does everything very easily but he's a late April foal so we're not rushing him. The riders really like him and he hasn't been off the bridle yet, so he could be quite nice. I'm bearing in mind that his second birthday isn't until late April but he's going to be a 2-y-o for sure. He looks sharp, it's a fast family and he's one for five/six furlongs".*

141. LOUD APPLAUSE ★★
b.f. Royal Applause – New Assembly (Machiavellian). March 6. Half-sister to 6 winners including the fairly useful 2014 2-y-o 6f winner and listed-placed Pack Together (by Paco Boy), the useful dual 6f winner at 2 and 3 yrs Instalment (by Cape Cross), to the quite useful 10f winner Regent's Park (by Green Desert) and the quite useful 7f winner Victoria Reel (by Danehill Dancer). The dam, a useful 9f and 10f winner, is a sister to the 7f (at 2 yrs) and Group 1 9f Dubai Duty Free Stakes

winner Right Approach and a half-sister to 6 winners. The second dam, Abbey Strand (by Shadeed), a fair 10f winner, is a half-sister to the 2-y-o Group 3 winners Grand Chelem and Splendid Moment. (The Queen). *"She's slightly unfurnished at this stage and is likely to need a bit of time. A nice, easy-moving filly but one for the autumn".*

142. MERRIMENT ★★★

ch.f. Makfi – Trianon (Nayef). March 8. Fourth foal. Half-sister to the quite useful 2014 2-y-o 6f winner Touchline (by Exceed And Excel). The dam, a fair 2-y-o 1m winner, is a half-sister to numerous winners including the smart Group 2 12f Ribblesdale Stakes and Group 2 13.3f Geoffrey Freer Stakes winner Phantom Gold (herself dam of the Oaks second Flight Of Fancy) and the useful 10f listed winner Fictitious. The second dam, Trying For Gold (Northern Baby), was a useful 12f and 12.5f winner at 3 yrs. (The Queen). *"We have the 3-y-o out of the mare, Touchline. This one is by Makfi who seems to be getting horses that take a bit of time to develop. She's a very tall filly but a particularly good mover. She's about to have a break, but we like her and the dam could end up being alright as a broodmare. One for later in the season and next year".*

143. ROSECOMB (IRE) ★★★

b.f. Rip Van Winkle – Malyana (Mtoto). March 19. Fourth foal. €50,000Y. Goffs Orby. R Frisby. Half-sister to the modest 2-y-o 7f winner Bint Malyana (by Bahamian Bounty). The dam, a quite useful 1m (at 2 yrs) to 10f winner, is a sister to the Group 2 10f Pretty Polly Stakes winner Tarfshi and half-sister to 5 winners including the champion 2-y-o filly and Group 1 6f Cheveley Park Stakes winner Embassy. The second dam, Pass The Peace (by Alzao), winner of the Cheveley Park Stakes and second in the 1,000 Guineas, is a half-sister to 3 winners. (Sir Thomas Pilkington, B T & W E A Fox). *"She's done particularly well since we bought her and she looks quite sharp. The grandam Pass The Peace was our first ever winner and she's created quite a dynasty considering there was virtually nothing on the page until she came along. This filly should come to hand pretty quickly".*

144. SCIARRA ★★★

ch.f. Monsieur Bond – Tibesti (Machiavellian). March 22. 17,000Y. Doncaster Premier. R Frisby. Sister to the modest 2014 2-y-o 6f winner Magh Meall, to the Group 1 5f Prix de l'Abbaye winner Move In Time and the moderate 7f winner Absolute Diamond and half-sister to the quite useful 5f winner of 4 races at 2 and 3 yrs Meadway (by Captain Gerrard). The dam is an unraced sister to the UAE Group 3 winner and Group 1 second Tropical Star. The second dam, Tropical (by Green Desert), a multiple Group 3 sprint winner, is a half-sister to 5 winners including the Coronation Stakes winner Shake The Yoke. (Qatar Racing Ltd). *"It's a proper pedigree and after we bought her Move In Time, her full-brother, won the Abbaye. So she certainly represents a bargain. She looks precocious, onward bound, easy-moving, enthusiastic and strong. A nice filly, she's named after the Bond girl character in the next James Bond film".*
TRAINERS' BARGAIN BUY

145. THE MAJOR ★★

b.c. Major Cadeaux – Ballerina Suprema (Sadler's Wells). April 22. Eighth foal. 4,500Y. Tattersalls October Book 4. A C Elliott. Half-brother to the modest 10f to 13f winner of 6 races Rockweiller (by Rock Of Gibraltar). The dam, a quite useful 2-y-o 8.2f winner, is a half-sister to numerous winners including the Irish 9f winner and Group 1 National Stakes second Coliseum. The second dam, Gravieres (by Saint Estephe), won the Grade 1 Santa Ana Handicap and the Grade 3 California Jockey Club Handicap and is a half-sister to 9 winners. (Lady Clara Law). *"He was a bargain I think. A nice colt out of a mare I trained that cost 300,000 and she's out of a Grade 1 winner. He's turned inside out since we bought him, so I'm happy with him".*

146. TOWERLANDS PARK (IRE) ★★★

b.c. Danehill Dancer – Strategy (Machiavellian). January 15. Sixth foal. 120,000Y. Tattersalls October Book 1. W J Gredley. Brother to the US Grade 3 winner and Grade 1 placed Justaroundmidnight (by Danehill Dancer) and half-brother to the useful Irish 2-y-o 5f winner and Group 3 6f Anglesey Stakes third Boris Grigoriev (by Excellent Air) and the fair 1m (at 2 yrs) and 10f winner Havelovewilltravel (by Holy Roman Emperor). The dam, a quite useful 10f and 11f winner, is a half-sister to 2 winners. The second dam, Island Story (by Shirley Heights), a quite useful 10f winner, is a half-sister to 6 winners. (W J Gredley). *"A fine, big, strong colt that hasn't been in the yard that long but he's got a nice pedigree, he was an early foal and he looks like being a summer 2-y-o. He looks a classy horse on Warren Hill and I see him being a seven furlong colt to start with".*

147. UNNAMED ★★★

b.f. Medicean – Agrippina (Timeless Times). February 22. Sixth foal. 70,000Y. Tattersalls October Book 1. Kern/Lillingston. Sister to the dual listed 6f winner and Group 3 third Cartimandua and half-sister to the useful 5f winner of 5 races (including at 2 yrs) Terentia (by Diktat), the fair 2-y-o 9f winner Sejanus (by Dubai Destination) and the moderate 1m winner Jay Jays Joy (by Diktat). The dam, a useful 2-y-o listed 7f winner, is a half-sister to 2 winners. The second dam, Boadicea's Chariot (by Commanche Run), an Irish 12f and hurdles winner, is a half-sister to 6 winners. (Paddy Barrett). *"We haven't pressed any buttons with her yet, but she gets up the gallop easily and looks like one for seven furlong races this year. A typical, strong 2-y-o that'll be out when the seven furlong races start".*

148. UNNAMED ★★★★

b.f. Kyllachy – Coy (Danehill). March 11. First foal. 28,000Y. Tattersalls December. M Bell Racing. Closely related to the unplaced 2014 2-y-o What Asham, to the fair 2-y-o 7f winner Resolute and the modest 4-y-o UAE 6f winner Redden (all by Pivotal). The dam won over 6f (at 2 yrs) and the listed 1m Valiant Stakes and is a sister to one winner and a half-sister to 5 winners including the very useful dual listed winner Il Warrd. The second dam, Demure (by Machiavellian), is an unraced half-sister to 9 winners including the very smart Group 2 6f Diadem Stakes winner Diffident. (Mr M V Magnier). *"She's quite sharp and will definitely be alright over six furlongs. A real little 2-y-o and a pocket rocket".*

149. UNNAMED ★★

b.f. Poet's Voice – Juniper Girl (Revoque). February 24. Third foal. 35,000Y. Tattersalls

October Book 3. Not sold. Half-sister to the fair 2014 2-y-o 10f winner Kifaaya and to the fair 10f (at 2 yrs), 13f and hurdles winner Forced Family Fun (by Refuse To Bend). The dam, a useful 7f (at 2 yrs), 12f and 2m winner, is a half-sister to the Group 2 Italian 1,000 Guineas winner Golden Nepi. The second dam, Shajara (by Kendor), is a placed half-sister to 4 winners. (Mr M B Hawtin). *"She was late being broken in and hasn't arrived yet, so I can't really comment other than she's not bred to be precocious".*

150. UNNAMED ★★★

b.c. Authorized – Local Spirit (Lion Cavern). January 22. Sixth foal. Brother to the quite useful 7f (at 2 yrs) to 12f winner of 6 races Al Saham and half-brother to the quite useful 2014 2-y-o 7f winner Classic Collection (by Cape Cross) and the quite useful 6f winner Active Spirit (by Pivotal). The dam, a useful 10f winner, was second in the Group 2 12f Lancashire Oaks and is a sister to the Irish 1,000 Guineas, Coronation Stakes and Nassau Stakes winner Crimplene and a half-sister to 7 winners including the smart Group 3 12.3f Chester Vase winner Dutch Gold. The second dam, Crimson Conquest (by Diesis), a quite useful 2-y-o 6f winner, is a half-sister to the US stakes winner Sword Blade. (Sheikh Marwan Al Maktoum). *"Just ticking over at the moment but his sire gets stacks of winners and he looks another in the making. That won't be until the second half of the season over seven furlongs plus".*

151. UNNAMED ★★★

b.c. Sir Percy – My First Romance (Danehill). February 11. Fifteenth foal. 55,000Y. Tattersalls October Book 2. A C Elliott/M Bell. Half-brother to 12 winners including the Group 3 5f Queen Mary Stakes winners Romantic Myth (by Mind Games) and Romantic Liason (by Primo Dominie), the 2-y-o 5f winner Power Packed (by Puissance), the 1m and 9f winner Chapter Seven (by Excellent Art), the 2-y-o 6f winner Alkhafif (by Royal Applause), the dual 5f winner Zargus (by Zamindar) – all four fairly useful, and the quite useful 2-y-o winners Wedaad (by Fantastic Light) and Fantacise (by Pivotal). The dam is an unplaced half-sister to 6 winners. The second dam, Front Line Romance (by Caerleon), was a Group 3 placed 1m 2-y-o winner. (Secular Stagnation). *"The mare has an incredible record for producing winners and this colt looks quite precocious. He may be one for the Chesham Stakes at Royal Ascot. He's sound and ready to move into work".*

JAMES BETHELL

152. AIRTON ★★
b.c. Champs Elysees – Fly In Style (Hernando). March 23. Ninth foal. 30,000Y. Tattersalls October Book 2. J Bethell. Half-brother to the fairly useful 6f and 7f winner and listed placed Percy Jackson (by Sir Percy), to the fair 2-y-o 6f winner Khaleeji, the fair 6f winner Shotgun Start (both by Kyllachy), the modest 9f and 10f winner Sternian (by Where Or When) and the moderate 2-y-o 6f seller and subsequent Spanish winner Distant Flash (by Mujahid). The dam is an unraced half-sister to 2 minor winners abroad. The second dam, Fly Don't Run (by Lear Fan), is a placed sister to the Group 2 Premio Ellington winner Run Don't Fly and a half-sister to 5 winners. (Clarendon Thoroughbred Racing). *"A nice colt, but he's quite leggy and definitely more of a 3-y-o type than for this year. We'll hopefully get him out in September over seven furlongs or a mile. He's quite weak but has actually just started to improve and he's a very good mover".*

153. BIT OF A COUP (FR) ★★★
b.c. Henrythenavigator – Watchful (Galileo). January 29. Second foal. €26,000Y. Arqana Deauville October. C de Moubray. The dam, a quite useful 11f and 12f winner, is a half-sister to 5 winners including the Group 3 placed Rabi and Kawagino. The second dam, Sharakawa (by Darshaan), is an unraced half-sister to 4 winners including the Group 3 placed Mempari and to the unraced dams of the US Grade 2 winner Sans Adieu and the Group 1 placed sprinter Hamish McGonagall. (Mr Buckingham). *"A very nice colt but backward at the moment, he's quite classy and he may be one for a mile this season in mid to late summer. Should be a better 3-y-o".*

154. CHIRINGUITA (USA) ★★★
gr.f. Hard Spun – Silver Games (Verglas). April 6. First foal. The dam, a quite useful 7f (at 2 yrs) and 1m winner, is a half-sister to the Group 1 1m Falmouth Stakes and Group 2 6f Lowther Stakes winner Nahoodh. The second dam, Mise (by Indian Ridge), is an unraced half-sister to 6 winners including the Group 3 Prix du Hedouville winner Not Just Swing. (Chris Wright). *"She's lovely, a very nice filly that should be one for July or August. She's grown quite a lot since we've had her, she's quite rangy but very nice. She's a little bit narrow at the moment but she'll fill out, she moves very well and is probably a six/seven furlong 2-y-o".*

155. FAST AND FURIOUS (IRE) ★★★
b.c. Rock Of Gibraltar – Ocean Talent (Aptitude). January 30. Second foal. 25,000Y. Tattersalls October Book 2. J Bethell. Half-brother to Kelloura (by Mastercraftsman), unplaced over 7f on her only start at 2 yrs in 2014. The dam is an unraced half-sister to 7 winners including the useful listed-placed 6f (at 2 yrs) and 7f winner Imroz and the useful 3-y-o listed 1m winner Insinuate (dam of the Group 3 winner Stronghold). The second dam, All At Sea (by Riverman), a high-class winner of 5 races from 1m to 10.4f including the Group 1 Prix du Moulin, is a half-sister to 8 winners including the dual Group 3 Free Handicap winner Over the Ocean. (Mr Buckingham). *"A very nice horse, I thought he'd be early than he is, but he still could be out in May over six furlongs. He's very well put together, he's not that big and I don't think he'll grow a lot, so he'll definitely make a 2-y-o".*

156. HAZELY ★★★
b.f. Cape Cross – Sentimental Value (Diesis). May 1. Seventh foal. 15,000Y. Tattersalls October Book 2. J Bethell. Half-sister to the fairly useful 9.5f (at 2 yrs) and 12f winner Personal Opinion (by New Approach), to the quite useful 9f and 10f winner Oriental Cat (by Tiger Hill), the quite useful dual 10f winner Barwell Bridge (by Red Ransom) and the fair 9f, 10f and hurdles winner Memorabilia (by Dansili). The dam, a winner of 2 stakes events in the USA and Grade 3 placed, is a half-sister to 6 winners in Japan. The second dam, Stately Star (by Deputy Minister), a stakes winner of 6 races in the USA, is a half-sister to 9 winners. (Clarendon Thoroughbred Racing). *"She's very nice and I'm hoping she'll be out around July or August over seven furlongs. She's very well put together and has a really good temperament".*
TRAINERS' BARGAIN BUY

157. LADY CANFORD (IRE) ★★★
b.f. Canford Cliffs – Soul Mountain (Rock Of Gibraltar). March 8. Fifth foal. 42,000Y. Tattersalls October Book 2. J Bethell. Half-sister to the quite useful Irish 2-y-o 1m winner and 3-y-o Italian Group 3 10f second French Quebec (by Excellent Art), to the minor French 10f winner Secret Shine (by Raven's Pass) and the modest 1m winner Caliso Bay (by High Chaparral). The dam, a quite useful 10.5f and 11f winner, is a sister to the French winner and listed 10.5f placed Londonintherain and a half-sister to 3 winners including the US Grade 2 winner Girl Warrior. The second dam, Qhazeenah (by Marju), a useful 6.5f (at 2 yrs) to 7f winner, is a half-sister to 9 winners including the smart Group 2 14.6f Park Hill Stakes winner Ranin. (Clarendon Thoroughbred Racing). *"She's just gone through a growing period but previously I thought she might come early. Even so she may still be out in late May and she's quite well put together".*

158. RICH PURSUITS ★★★
ch.c. Pastoral Pursuits – Salvia (Pivotal). April 9. Fourth foal. 38,000Y. Tattersalls October Book 3. J Bethell. Closely related to the fair triple 6f winner Spiraea (by Bahamian Bounty) and half-brother to the modest 12f winner Highsalvia Cosmos (by High Chaparral) and the moderate 2-y-o 1m winner Salvationist (by Invincible Spirit). The dam ran once unplaced and is a half-sister to 7 winners including the very useful 6f (at 2 yrs) and 9f winner Zabaglione. The second dam, Satin Bell (by Midyan), a useful 7f winner, is a half-sister to 4 winners including the useful listed 6f winner Star Tulip. (R T Vickers). *"He's quite big and will probably make a 2-y-o by season. A very nice colt, I'll probably start him over six furlongs although the pedigree suggests he'll get further than that. I'll try and aim him for the Book 3 Sales race".*

159. RONALDJAMESSACH ★★★
ch.c. Lord Shanakill – Boschendal (Zamindar). April 17. Second foal. 19,000Y. Tattersalls December. J Bethell. The dam is an unplaced half-sister to 4 winners including the smart winner of four Group 3 races from 7f to10f and Group 1 placed Mac Love. The second dam, My Lass (by Elmaamul), won over 12f

at 3 yrs, was third in the listed 10f Trigo Stakes and is a half-sister to 4 minor winners. (Clarendon Thoroughbred Racing). *"He's probably as forward as any of my 2-y-o's. A six furlong type 2-y-o, he's nice and I would hope he'd be out in May".*

160. WESTWARD HO (IRE) ★★
b.c. Fastnet Rock – Thought Is Free (Cadeaux Genereux). April 12. Fourth foal. 35,000Y. Tattersalls October Book 2. J Bethell. Half-brother to the fairly useful dual 1m winner and listed 10.5f third Merry Me (by Invincible Spirit). The dam, a fairly useful 6f listed-placed 2-y-o, is a half-sister to 6 winners including the Group 3 third Day Of Conquest and the dam of the Group 1 winner Hearts Of Fire. The second dam, Dayville (by Dayjur), a quite useful triple 6f winner, is a half-sister to 4 winners including the Grade 1 Yellow Ribbon Handicap winner Spanish Fern. (Mr G N van Cutsem). *"He's a nice colt, but very backward like a lot of these Fastnet Rock's seem to be. I would think he'll want seven furlongs to start with in August/September. Well put together, I think he's still got a bit of growing to do. A straightforward 2-y-o".*

SAEED BIN SUROOR
(GODOLPHIN)
I must say a big 'Thank You' to Saeed's Assistant Trainer, Tony Howarth, for going through many of the most promising of Saeed's Godolphin two-year-olds with me on my visit to their yard in the spring.

161. AZHAR ★★★★
b.f. Exceed And Excel – Nitya (Indian Ridge). January 23. Third foal. 210,000foal. Tattersalls December. John Ferguson. Half-sister to the quite useful dual 1m winner Pleasure Bent and the fair 10f winner Heho (both by Dansili). The dam is an unraced sister to the Grade 1 Breeders Cup Mile winner Domedriver and a half-sister to 5 winners including the French Group 3 winner Tau Ceti and the dam of the Group 2 winner Freedonia. The second dam, Napoli (by Baillamont), a winner of 3 listed races in France and Group 3 placed, is a sister to the French Group 3 winner D'Arros. *"A nice, sweet filly who is showing some precocity at present. Medium-sized, there's plenty on her – she carries a fair amount of condition. A good*

mover, she shows a bit of speed, has a great attitude and will probably go into faster work soon. Could be an early season type".

162. BRAVE HERO ★★★★
ch.c. Poet's Voice – Classical Dancer (Dr Fong). March 29. Seventh foal. 75,000Y. Tattersalls October Book 1. John Ferguson. Half-brother to the fair 2014 6f placed 2-y-o Pressure (by Equiano), to the quite useful 7f, 1m (both at 2 yrs) and 12f winner Zaaqya and the fair 9f winner Topanga Canyon (both by Nayef). The dam, a fairly useful 8.3f winner, was listed-placed twice and is a half-sister to 6 winners including the Group 1 Premio Roma winner Imperial Dancer. The second dam, Gorgeous Dancer (by Nordico), an Irish 3-y-o 1m winner and third in the listed Irish Oaks Trial, is a half-sister to 3 winners. *"Hasn't been with us long but he's a lovely, big, strong colt with a very nice action. He can be a bit playful but once we step up his work I'm sure he'll knuckle down to it. A nice horse".*

163. BRAVE TIMES ★★★★
b.f. Exceed And Excel – Marie De Medici (Medicean). March 12. Second foal. Half-sister to the 2014 2-y-o Group 3 7f Oh Sharp Stakes and 2015 UAE Group 3 9.5f winner Local Time (by Invincible Spirit). The dam, a useful 7f (at 2 yrs) and listed 10f winner, was second in the Group 3 1m Prix des Reservoirs and is a half-sister to 2 winners. The second dam, Mare Nostrum (by Caerleon), won the Group 3 Prix Vanteaux and was placed in the Prix Vermeille and Prix Saint-Alary and is a half-sister to 7 winners including the US Grade 1 winner Aube Indienne. *"A strong-topped, straightforward filly who actually hasn't done much work yet. She moves considerably well and has a beautiful topline. Not one to rush and has plenty of scope. Probably a seven furlong/mile filly".*

164. CAPE OF THE EAST (IRE) ★★★★
b.f. Iffraaj – Cala (Desert Prince). February 2. Sixth foal. Half-sister to the fairly useful 7f, 9f (both at 2 yrs) and 12.5f winner Shrewd (by Street Sense) and to the fair 7f winner Top Draw (by Elusive Quality). The dam, a useful 6f and 7f winner and second in the Group 3 Nell Gwyn Stakes, is a half-sister to 9 winners including the very useful 2-y-o 6f

winner and Group 1 Cheveley Park Stakes third Badminton, the useful 2-y-o 7f winner and Group 3 7f Vintage Stakes third Fox and the useful 7f winner Rafferty. The second dam, Badawi (by Diesis), was a useful 1m and 9f winner of 4 races. *"A beautiful looking filly who is an extremely good mover, she hasn't done much at present but seems to have a little bit of class about her. A seven furlong/mile two-year-old".*

165. CHANGE THE GAME (USA) ★★★
ch.c. Distorted Humor – Joanie's Catch (First Tour). February 23. First foal. $550,000Y. Fasig-Tipton Saratoga August. John Ferguson. The dam, a US winner of 4 races at 2 and 3 yrs and placed in six Graded stakes, is a half-sister to one winner. The second dam, Caught Speeding (by Saint Ballado), a minor US winner at 2 and 3 yrs, is a half-sister to 5 other minor winners. *"A lovely, big, strong individual, he's probably one for the middle-to-back end of the season. He has a bit of a knee action so probably wouldn't want summer ground and will not be rushed".*

166. CLEAR LEADER (USA) ★★★★
b.c. Hard Spun – Laureldean Gale (Grand Slam). May 6. Second foal. The dam, a very smart 2-y-o 6f winner and second in the Group 3 7f Prix du Calvados, is a half-sister to numerous winners including the Group 3 Musidora Stakes Secret History and the US stakes winner Costume Designer. The second dam, Ravnina (by Nureyev), is an unraced half-sister to 2 stakes-placed winners. *"A good-looking colt that's doing everything right. He's not one to be rushed and although he does show us bits of speed he hasn't done much at present. He'll be one for the middle part of the season".*

167. CLEAR WATER (IRE) ★★★
b.f. Hard Spun – Storm Lily (Storm Cat). February 11. Half-sister to the 2014 US 2-y-o 6.5f winner First Down (by Street Sense), to the useful dual 6f (at 2 yrs) and UAE 7f winner and dual Group 3 second Gold City (by Pivotal) and the quite useful 5f winner of 5 races Storm Moon (by Invincible Spirit). The dam is an unplaced half-sister to the useful 2-y-o dual 6f winner and Group 3 placed Crimson Sun. The second dam, Crimplene (by

Lion Cavern), won the Irish 1,000 Guineas, the Coronation Stakes and the Nassau Stakes and is a half-sister to numerous winners including the smart Group 3 12.3f Chester Vase winner Dutch Gold. *"A rather hot individual who probably wouldn't take a lot of work. She's very racy in her training, shows a good degree of precocity and hopefully will be running sometime in May/June. Certainly one of the more forward-going types – she just wants to please and could be running in May".*

168. CONFIDENT KID ★★★★

b.c. Dubawi – Longing To Dance (Danehill Dancer). April 2. Fourth foal. 500,000Y. Tattersalls October Book 1. John Ferguson. Half-brother to the quite useful 2014 6f and 7f placed 2-y-o Foreign Diplomat (by Oasis Dream) and to the very useful Group 3 10f Prix de Psyche winner Be My Gal (by Galileo). The dam, second in the listed 6f Flame Of Tara Stakes, is a half-sister to 5 winners including the champion Swedish 2-y-o 5f to 1m winner King Quantas and to the unplaced dam of the dual Group 1 winner and sire Dutch Art. The second dam, Palacegate Episode (by Drumalis), a sprint winner of a Group 3 in Italy and numerous listed events here and abroad, is a full or half-sister to 5 winners. *"A good-looking son of Dubawi, he shows a fair level of ability already albeit in his slower paces. We wouldn't be in any rush with him but he has size and scope on his side".*

169. DIFFERENT JOURNEY ★★★

b.c. Poet's Voice – Vintage Gardenia (Selkirk). March 20. First foal. 82,000foal. Tattersalls December. John Ferguson. The dam, a minor French winner at 3 yrs, is a sister to the smart Group 3 10f Winter Hill Stakes and subsequent US Grade 2 1m winner Tam Lin and a half-sister to 5 winners. The dam won over 7f at 2 yrs and was placed in both the French and Irish 1,000 Guineas. *"A good, strong-topped colt who will need plenty of time. He is a very laid-back type, has a very big stride and is a good walker. Not one to rush, the back-end of the season will be very much in mind for this horse".*

170. DUBAI FASHION (IRE) ★★★★

b.f. Dubawi – Oriental Fashion (Marju). March 3. Half-sister to 7 winners including

the very useful 2-y-o 6f and 7f winner Oriental Warrior, the useful 1m winner of 4 races (including at 2 yrs) and Group 3 Irish 2,000 Guineas third Famous Warrior (both by Alhaarth), the very useful 7f and UAE 1m winner and Group 2 second Green Coast, the fairly useful 7f and 1m winner Desert Chief (both by Green Desert) and the fairly useful 2-y-o 6f winner Bulbul (by Shamardal). The dam won the Group 2 1m Premio Ribot and is a half-sister to 3 winners including the US Grade 2 winner Makderah. The second dam, Wijdan (by Riverman), a useful 1m and 10.4f winner, is a sister to the listed 1m winner Sarayir and a half-sister to Nashwan, Nayef and Unfuwain. *"An attractive filly with lots of scope, a good action and a good temperament to go with it. She'll go into faster work in early April and looks a nice sort. Very straightforward, she's very nice I think".*

171. ENJOY LIFE (IRE) ★★★★

b.f. Acclamation – Jeu De Plume (Montjeu). January 28. First living foal. €180,000Y. Arqana Deauville August. R O'Gorman. The dam is a placed half-sister to 6 winners including the Group 3 winner Hearthstead Maison and the listed winners Rave Reviews and Fermion. The second dam, Pieds De Plume (by Seattle Slew), second once over 1m at 3 yrs in France, is closely related to the French listed and US stakes winner Slew The Slewor and a half-sister to the Group 1 Prix Lupin winner and sire Groom Dancer. *"Showing lots of speed, she's a rather nice filly who is precocious but has plenty of scope to go with it. She's already showing us a fair level of ability and with luck will be one of the early season runners".*

172. FIRST VICTORY ★★★

b.c. Dubawi – Ocean Silk (Dynaformer). April 7. Half-brother to the quite useful 12f winner Just Like Silk (by Elusive Quality) and to a hurdles winner by Manduro. The dam, a winner of 4 races including the listed Lupe Stakes, was second in the Group 1 Yorkshire Oaks and is a half-sister to 2 winners including the useful 10f winner Seven Magicians. The second dam, Mambo Jambo (by Kingmambo), a minor winner at 3 yrs in France, is a sister to the multiple Group 1 winner Divine Proportions and a half-sister to the dual Group 1 winner Whipper. *"Not very tall, so we'll have to see how we get on with him, but he's straightforward and in full training".*

173. GREAT ORDER (USA) ★★★

b.br.c. Street Cry – Michita (Dynaformer). February 16. Brother to the quite useful 1m and 9.5f winner Thatchmaster and half-brother to the minor US 1m winner Gavroche (by Distorted Humor). The dam, winner of the Group 2 12f Ribblesdale Stakes and the listed 10f Height Of Fashion Stakes winner, was third in the Yorkshire Oaks and the Prix Vermeille (both Group 1) and is a sister to one winner and a half-sister to the US 6f to 1m winner and Grade 3 placed Thunder Mission. The second dam, Thunder Kitten (by Storm Cat), a US 6.5f to 8.5f winner (including a Grade 3), is a half-sister to the Japanese Group 1 1m winner Nobo True. *"A very nice-looking colt but very big, he stands over a lot of ground and would be one of our bigger two-year-olds although in his training he doesn't show it. Not one to be rushed, he's one for the middle-to-end of the season".*

174. HUGE FUTURE ★★★★

b.c. Shamardal – Time Honoured (Sadler's Wells). March 25. Seventh living foal. €260,000Y. Goffs Orby. John Ferguson. Half-brother to the quite useful 12f winner Infinitum (by Dalakhani), to the fair 10f to 12f winner of 3 races Bona Fortuna (by Mark Of Esteem) and a hurdles winner by Daylami. The dam, a quite useful 2-y-o 1m winner, is a sister to the Group 3 12f Princess Royal Stakes winner Time Allowed and a half-sister to the Group 3 12f Jockey Club Stakes winner Zinaad and the dams of five Group winners. The second dam, Time Charter (by Saritamer), won the Oaks, the King George VI and Queen Elizabeth Diamond Stakes, the Champion Stakes and the Coronation Cup. *"A really nice type for the middle part of the season, he is very laid-back and has a great temperament. One not to be rushed but already showing signs of strong progression. He has plenty of size and scope and a nice way of going".*

175. JUFN ★★★★

b.c. Nayef – Deyaar (Storm Cat). February 2. Half-brother to the fair 2-y-o 6f winner Khobaraa (by Invincible Spirit). The dam is an unraced sister to the US Grade 3 winner Habaya and Grade 3 laced winner Hatheer. The second dam, Golden Apples (by Loon), won the Del Mar Oaks, the Yellow Ribbon Stakes and the Beverly D Stakes (all Grade 1) and is a half-sister to 6 winners including Alexander Three D (Group 3 Park Hill Stakes). *"A good, strong-topped colt who is showing plenty of speed but may just be lacking mental strength at present. Hopefully he's one to go forward with and could be making his debut around June time. Despite being by Nayef he's showing lots of speed and he's built like a sprinter. Not over-big, but strong and very wide, he covers a lot of ground and he'll probably start off at six furlongs".*

176. LOOKS GREAT ★★★★

b.f. New Approach – Danehill Dreamer (Danehill). March 17. Fifth foal. 200,000Y. Tattersalls October Book 1. John Ferguson. Sister to the fairly useful 2014 2-y-o 6f winner Sulaalaat and half-sister to the quite useful 2-y-o 1m winner Madeed and the Qatar winner Khudoua (both by Nayef). The dam is an unraced half-sister to 8 winners including Compton Admiral (Group 1 10f Coral Eclipse Stakes), Summoner (Group 1 1m Queen Elizabeth II Stakes) and the dam of the multiple Group 1 winner The Fugue. The second dam, Sumoto (by Mtoto), a useful 6f (at 2 yrs) and 7f winner, is a half-sister to 5 winners including the dam of the Group/Graded stakes winners Adagio and Arvada. *"A lovely filly with a great temperament, she shows plenty of precocity but just needs to fill out a little. A very nice type, she'll probably start at six furlongs before stepping up to seven".*

177. MOST CELEBRATED (IRE) ★★★★★

b.c. New Approach – Pietra Santa (Acclamation). March 18. Second foal. €170,000Y. Arqana Deauville August. R O'Gorman. The dam, a listed winner of 5 races from 2 to 4 yrs in France, is a half-sister to 2 winners. The second dam, Margie Queen (by Sternkoenig), won twice in Germany at 3 and 4 yrs and is a half-sister to 8 winners. *"A lovely, rangy colt who has a very good action and a great temperament to go with it. Could be a July runner with a bit of luck. He has plenty of size and scope, good bone and he looks like an athlete. A very nice type".*

178. MOVE UP ★★★★
b.c. Dubawi – Rosinka (Soviet Star). May 14. Fourth foal. Half-brother to the fair 12f winner Moshe (by Dansili). The dam, a useful 2-y-o 6f winner, subsequently won a US Grade 3 event over 11f and was Grade 1 placed twice. She is a half-sister to 6 winners including the US Grade 1 12f and triple Grade 2 winner King's Drama and the US Grade 1 placed Self Feeder. The second dam, Last Drama (by Last Tycoon), won and was listed placed twice over 10f in France and is a sister to the listed winner and smart broodmare Tycoon's Drama. *"A nice, sharp individual with a good action and a good topline. He carries plenty of condition but he shows lots of speed and looks quite strong. He could be racing in May/June".*

179. NAJM KABIR (IRE) ★★★★★
b.c. Dubawi – Comic (Be My Chief). February 23. Tenth foal. 1,400,000Y. Tattersalls October Book 1. John Ferguson. Half-brother to 6 winners including the US dual Grade 1 winner Laughing (by Dansili), to Viva Pataca (by Marju), a listed winner of 5 races here at 2 yrs from 7f to 9f prior to winning the Grade 1 Queen Elizabeth II Cup in Hong Kong (twice) and £5.9 million and the quite useful 10f to 14f and hurdles winner Comedy Act (by Motivator). The dam, a quite useful 10f and 11.5f winner, is a half-sister to 4 winners including the 2-y-o Group 3 Solario Stakes and multiple US Grade 2 winner Brave Act. The second dam, Circus Act (by Shirley Heights), is an unraced sister to the listed winner Lady Shipley and a half-sister to the listed winner Ellie Ardensky. *"A lovely individual who seems to have a lot of class. A great walker with a really nice action and a good temperament. A medium-sized colt with very good bone, he's very good-looking and we'll be hoping for nice things for him".*

180. PEACEFUL JOURNEY ★★★★
ch.f. Exceed And Excel – Dove (Sadler's Wells). January 28. Third foal. Half-brother to the fair 2014 8.5f placed 2-y-o International Name (by Iffraaj). The dam, a quite useful 10f winner, is a half-sister to 4 winners including the very smart Group 3 10f Winter Hill Stakes and

Group 3 7f Champagne Lanson Vintage Stakes winner Naheef. The second dam, Golden Digger (by Mr Prospector), was placed fourth 3 times from 6f (at 2 yrs) to 1m and is a sister to the dam of the Irish Oaks winner Lailani and a half-sister to the high-class Group 2 10f Prince Of Wales's Stakes winner Faithful Son and the very smart Coventry Stakes and Prix Quincey winner Always Fair. *"A good-looking individual with plenty of scope and a nice action. He does everything very easily but I wouldn't think he'd be too early. Just needs a bit of time. A nice horse".*

181. PERFECTLY FAIR ★★★★
b.f. Invincible Spirit – She Storm (Rainbow Quest). March 22. Third foal. 150,000foal. Tattersalls December. John Ferguson. The dam is an unraced half-sister to 7 winners including two listed winners in Italy and a minor US stakes winner. The second dam, She Bat (by Batshoof), won the Group 3 Premio Bagutta and is a half-sister to 5 winners. *"A nice, straightforward filly who shows plenty of speed. Just lacking a bit of mental strength at present in that she gets a bit 'hot' in between exercise, but she should be racing in the first half of the season".*

182. STEADY PACE ★★★★
b.c. Dark Angel – Cool Kitten (One Cool Cat). April 6. First foal. 80,000foal. Tattersalls December. John Ferguson. Half-brother to the quite useful 2014 2-y-o dual 1m winner Prince of Paris (by Champs Elysees). The dam, a moderate 7f and 1m winner, is a half-sister to 8 winners including the smart 2-y-o Group 2 1m Royal Lodge Stakes winner Atlantis Prince. The second dam, Zoom Lens (by Caerleon), placed once over 7f at 2 yrs, is a half-sister to 4 winners. *"A medium-sized, precocious type, he's a nice, strong-topped colt who is just about to go into faster work. All being well he should be an early season runner, probably starting off at five furlongs".*

183. STRONG CHALLENGE ★★★★
ch.c. Exceed And Excel – Miss Brief (Brief Truce). April 20. Seventh foal. 200,000Y. Tattersalls December. John Ferguson. Brother to the smart 2-y-o dual 6f winner and dual Group 2 placed Crown Prosecutor and half-brother to 3 winners including the useful

2014 2-y-o 6f winner and Group 3 Horris Hill Stakes second Fox Trotter (by Bushranger) and the useful 2-y-o listed 5f winner of 5 races Riskit fora Biskit (by Kodiac). The dam, a fair 5f placed maiden, is a half-sister to 6 winners including the 2-y-o Group 3 Sirenia Stakes winner and Group 1 placed Dhanyata. The second dam, Preponderance (by Cyrano de Bergerac), a quite useful 2-y-o dual 5f winner, is a half-sister to 6 winners. *"A nice, precocious type who is showing a lot of speed, but possibly when we step him up in work he may well be on the weak side because he is quite leggy and scopey. Nonetheless he'll go into fast work to see if he's going to be an early runner. All being well he may even be our first two-year-old runner, so he'll be aimed at the Newmarket Guineas meeting".*

184. VERY HONEST ★★★★
b.f. Poet's Voice – Cercle D'Amour (Storm Cat). February 5. Half-sister to the fair 11f winner Dorfman (by Halling). The dam is an unraced sister to the listed Irish 1,000 Guineas Trial winner Royal Tigress and to the 2-y-o winner and Group 3 5.5f Prix d'Arenburg third Thunderous Mood and a half-sister to the Group 3 Norfolk Stakes winner Warm Heart and the 2-y-o listed 6f winner Miguel Cervantes,. The second dam, Warm Mood (by Alydar), won 4 races at up to 9f in the USA and is a half-sister to a stakes winner in Japan. *"A lovely, strong-topped individual who covers a lot of ground in her canters. We'll step her up to faster work soon and she could be an early season runner. She looks quite strong, there doesn't seem to be any weakness about her and she's more mature than most at the moment with a nice way about her".*

185. VERY TALENTED (IRE) ★★★★
b.c. Invincible Spirit – Crystal House (Golden Voyager). February 1. Half-brother to a Grade 3 1m placed winner in Argentina by Smarty Jones and to a minor winner in the USA by Rahy. The dam, a champion 3-y-o filly in Peru, won two Grade 1 stakes and is a sister to the Chilean Grade 1 winner Crystal Clear and a half-sister to 10 winners. The second dam, Cristalline (by Northair), a champion 3-y-o filly in Chile, won the Grade 1 Premio Las Oaks. *"A handsome, strong individual who will not be early but is showing plenty of ability and has a great attitude to training at present. He*

has plenty of size and scope about him, but he could be a July/August type two-year-old. He just grabs the ground, has a big action and just looks a nice horse".

186. WINNING STORY ★★★★
b.c. New Approach – Tanzania (USA) (Darshaan). April 3. Half-brother to the dual listed 9f winner and Group 2 Dante Stakes third True Story (by Manduro) and to the fairly useful 8.5f (at 2 yrs) and dual 10f winner Serengeti (by Singspiel). The dam is an unraced half-sister to 3 winners including the very useful listed 10f Predominate Stakes winner Roscius. The second dam, Rosefinch (by Blushing Groom), a smart winner of the Group 1 10f Prix Saint-Alary, is a half-sister to the Grade 2 Long Island Handicap winner Shaima out of the Fillies' Triple Crown winner Oh So Sharp. *"A lovely, big, strong colt doing everything right at the moment. He covers a lot of ground in his canter exercises and looks to be a nice type for July onwards. Looks a bit lengthier than his half-brother True Story and probably has more scope".*

187. YATTWEE (USA) ★★★
b.br.c. Hard Spun – Alzerra (Pivotal). March 18. Half-brother to the listed 7f (at 2 yrs) and listed 1m winner and Group 2 May Hill Stakes second Majeyda (by Street Cry). The dam won 3 races over 5f and 6f at 2 yrs including the Group 3 Cornwallis Stakes and is a full or half-sister to 4 winners. The second dam, Belle Argentine (by Fijar Tango), a listed winner in France and third in the French 1,000 Guineas, is a half-sister to one winner. *"He had a little setback early on, but now he's ready to step up. A small, strong-topped colt who is showing natural speed, he should be in faster work by the end of April".*

188. UNNAMED ★★★
b.c. Shamardal – Express Way (ARG) (Ahmad). February 20. Brother to the fair 10f and 12f winner Arabian Beauty and half-brother to the Group 1 7f Prix Jean-Luc Lagardere and Italian dual Group 1 winner Rio De La Plata, the quite useful 2-y-o 7f winner Ihsas (both by Rahy), the Argentine Grade 1 winner El Expresivo (by Candy Stripes) and the fairly useful 1m winner Expressly (by Street Cry). The dam, placed in Argentina, is a half-sister to 2 minor winners

out of the unraced Escaline (by Hawk). *"He won't be early but he's a nice individual. He has a really nice action and does everything easily but he's quite rangy and scopey, so he won't be rushed. One to make his debut towards the back-end of the season I would think".*

JIM BOLGER

189. AM CAILIN ORGA (IRE)
ch.f. Galileo – Finsceal Beo (Mr Greeley). March 7. Fourth foal. Closely related to the 2014 2-y-o Group 2 1m Beresford Stakes winner Ol' Man River (by Montjeu) and to the fair 2-y-o 10f winner Too The Stars (by Sea The Stars). The dam, winner of the Prix Marcel Boussac, 1,000 Guineas and Irish 1,000 Guineas, is a half-sister to the German Group 2 1m winner Frozen Power and the fairly useful winners and listed-placed Musical Bar and Zabeel Park. The second dam, Musical Treat (by Royal Academy), a useful 3-y-o 7f winner and listed-placed twice, subsequently won four races at 4 yrs in Canada and the USA and is a half-sister to 6 winners. (Mr M D Ryan).

190. BENIGNUS
ch.c. Galileo – Saoire (Pivotal). April 26. Seventh foal. Brother to the fairly useful 12f winner Sundara and half-brother to the useful 1m (at 2 yrs) and listed 7f winner Requisition, the Swedish 2-y-o winner Polar Desert (both by Invincible Spirit) and the fair 2-y-o 6f winner Pink Diva (by Giant's Causeway). The dam, winner of the Irish 1,000 Guineas and third in the Group 1 Moyglare Stud Stakes, is a half-sister to 6 winners. The second dam, Polish Descent (by Danehill), is an unraced half-sister to 4 winners. (Mrs J S Bolger).

191. CLEAR CUT ♠
b.c. Acclamation – Claiomh Solais (Galileo). March 1. First foal. €300,000Y. Goffs Orby. BBA (Ire). The dam, a very useful Irish 1m winner and dual Group 3 placed, is a sister to the smart 2-y-o dual Group 3 6f winner and 1,000 Guineas second Cuis Ghaire, to the Group 3 9f winner Scintillula and the Irish 2-y-o 7f winner and Group 1 Coronation Stakes second Gile Na Greine. The second dam, Scribonia (by Danehill), is an unraced half-sister to 6 winners including the 2-y-o listed 6f winner and dual Group 1 placed Luminata. (Mrs J S Bolger).

192. HERALD THE DAWN (IRE)
b.c. New Approach – Hymn Of The Dawn (Phone Trick). May 20. Eighth foal. Brother to the Group 1 National Stakes, Dewhurst Stakes, 2,000 Guineas and St James's Palace Stakes winner Dawn Approach and half-brother to the fair 5f (at 2 yrs) to 7f winner Comadoir (by Medicis). The dam, placed fourth once at 2 yrs, is a half-sister to 3 winners including the Grade 1 third Galantas. The second dam, Colonial Debut (by Pleasant Colony), was placed in the USA and is a half-sister to 6 winners. (Mrs J S Bolger).

193. KING OF SAXONY (IRE)
b.c. Pivotal – Turmalin (Dalakhani). April 11. Second foal. 150,000Y. Tattersalls October Book 1. John Ferguson. The dam is an unraced half-sister to 3 winners including the German Group 2 winner Emerald Commander. The second dam, Brigitta (by Sadler's Wells), won over 1m and 10f at 3 yrs in France and is a sister to the 2-y-o Group 1 1m Racing Post Trophy winner Commander Collins, closely related to the Grade 1 Breeders Cup Sprint winner Lit de Justice and the 2,000 Guineas, Derby and Irish Derby placed Colonel Collins and a half-sister to the Group 2 Royal Lodge Stakes winner City Leader. (Godolphin).

194. LANDLOCKED
b.c. Street Cry – Land Of Dreams (Cadeaux Genereux). January 27. Half-brother to 4 winners including the multiple Group 1 winning sprinter Dream Ahead (by Diktat) and the listed 10f and listed 11f winner Into The Dark (by Rainbow Quest). The dam won the Group 2 5f Flying Childers Stakes and the Group 3 5f King George V Stakes and is a half-sister to 6 winners. The second dam, Sahara Star (by Green Desert), winner of the Group 3 5f Molecomb Stakes, was third in the Lowther Stakes and is a half-sister to 6 winners including Yalaietanee (Group 3 7f Greenham Stakes). (Godolphin).

195. PARTY FOR EVER (IRE)
b.f. Iffraaj – Miss Party Line (Phone Trick). May 2. Seventh foal. 210,000Y. Tattersalls October Book 1. BBA (Ire). Half-sister to the French 2-y-o listed 6f winner Corsario (by Zafonic), the very useful 7f (at 2 yrs) and 6f winner of 4 races Bentong (by Anabaa), the

useful 5f and 6f winner and listed-placed Line Of Reason (by Kheleyf), the quite useful 2-y-o 7f winner Noafal (by Bahamian Bounty) and the fair 5f and 6f winner Sister Clement (by Oasis Dream). The dam won once at 3 yrs and is a sister to the US Grade 2 winner All Chatter. The second dam, La Mimosa (by Bold Forbes), a stakes winner of 5 races in the USA, is a half-sister to the US Grade 1 winner Caline. (Mrs June Judd).

196. QUEEN OF SICILY (USA)

b.f. Cape Cross – Jealous Again (Trippi). April 27. The dam the Group 2 5f Queen Mary Stakes winner and is a full or half-sister to several winners. The second dam, Chi Sa (by Bold Ruckus), won twice at around a mile in Canada. (Godolphin).

197. SPLIT DECISION (IRE)

b.f. Teofilo – Night Visit (Sinndar). April 1. Sixth foal. €950,000Y. Goffs Orby. John McCormick. Sister to the Irish Derby winner Trading Leather and to the fairly useful 11f and 12f winner Wexford Town and half-sister to the fair 7f winner Gleadhradh (by Chevalier). The dam is an unraced half-sister to 3 minor winners. The second dam, Moonlight Sail (by Irish River), a French 2-y-o 7f winner, is a sister to the Champion Stakes, 1,000 Guineas and Prix de l'Opera winner Hatoof and to the US Grade 1 1m winner Irish Prize and a half-sister to the dual 10f listed winner Insijaam and the 12f listed winner Fasateen. (Mrs J S Bolger).

198. TIPSTAFF

b.c. Street Cry – Firth of Lorne (Danehill). March 4. Brother to the listed 1m and UAE Group 3 10f winner Falls Of Lora and half-brother to the fairly useful 2014 2-y-o dual 7f winner Latharnach (by Iffraaj), the French 1m (at 2 yrs) and German listed 7f winner Etive, the useful 1m winner Loch Linnhe (both by Elusive Quality) and the fair dual 1m winner (including at 2 yrs) Bint Almatar (by Kingmambo). The dam, a French 2-y-o listed 1m winner and second in the French 1,000 Guineas, was Grade 2 placed in the USA is a half-sister to 5 winners. The second dam, Kerrera (by Diesis), won the Group 3 Cherry Hinton Stakes and second in the 1,000 Guineas. (Godolphin).

199. UNNAMED

b.f. Dansili – Tyranny (Machiavellian). May 20. Eighth foal. 700,000Y. Tattersalls October Book 1. Solis/Litt. Sister to the 2-y-o Group 1 6f Phoenix Stakes winner Zoffany and half-sister to the 2-y-o Group 3 6f Anglesey Stakes winner Wilshire Boulevard (by Holy Roman Emperor), the fairly useful 7f to 10.5f winner That's Plenty (by Dr Fong) and the quite useful 6f winner Queen Of Mean (by Pivotal). The dam, a fairly useful dual 7f winner, is a half-sister to 5 winners including the listed 1m and US Grade 2 winner Spotlight. The second dam, Dust Dancer (by Suave Dancer), won the Group 3 Prix de la Nonette. (Solis/Litt Bloodstock).

MARCO BOTTI

200. ALJAZZI ★★★★

b.f. Shamardal – Nouriya (Danehill Dancer). January 31. First foal. The dam, a very useful dual listed 10f winner, is a half-sister to the fairly useful 2-y-o 7f winner and triple listed 10f placed Lady Nouf. The second dam, Majestic Sakeena (by King's Best), is an unraced half-sister to the German listed sprint winner Shy Lady (dam of the St James's Palace Stakes winner Zafeen) and to the French listed winner Sweet Story. (Saleh Al Homaizi & Imad Al Sagar). *"A very scopey filly, she's a lovely mover but I won't be in a rush to train her because she needs plenty of time. She looks more of a 3-y-o than a 2-y-o, so whatever she does this year will be a bonus. She could definitely be a talented filly though".*

201. ANTIOCO (IRE) ★★★★

b.c. Motivator – Haraplata (Platini). March 8. Ninth foal. £39,000Y. Tattersalls December. A Panetta. Half-brother to the German winner at 2 and 5 yrs and Group 3 third Hashbrown (by Big Shuffle), to the French 12f and 15f winner Hungarian Dance (by Sinndar) and the placed dam of the Group 3 Prix des Chenes winner Evasive's First. The dam, a listed-placed winner at 3 and 4 yrs in Germany, is a half-sister to 4 winners including the Irish listed winner Jane Austen. The second dam, Harasava (by Darshaan), is an unraced half-sister to 5 winners. *"He goes really well, especially for a horse that on pedigree should be a 3-y-o rather than a 2-y-o. He's very forward and shows plenty of ability. Being by Motivator we'll wait for when the seven furlong races start".*

202. APPROCAILLIS ★★★

ch.c. New Approach – Capercaillie (Elusive Quality). April 27. First foal. The dam, a fairly useful dual 5f winner at 2 yrs, was listed-placed and is a half-sister to 5 winners. The second dam, Silent Eskimo (by Eskimo), won a Grade 2 and three Grade 3 stakes in the USA and is a half-sister to 5 winners. *"Physically he's still a bit weak but he's going nicely and hasn't done anything fast yet. We'll take our time with him and hope to see him out in September".*

203. COUP DE MAIN (IRE) ★★★★

b.f. Oasis Dream – Termagant (Powerscourt). March 3. First foal. 350,000foal. Tattersalls December. RBS. The dam, winner of the Group 1 7f Moyglare Stud Stakes, is a half-sister to 4 winners including the fairly useful 1m (at 2 yrs) to 10f winner of 7 races and listed-placed Splinter Cell. The second dam, Rock Salt (by Selkirk), placed twice at 3 yrs in France, is a sister to the Group 2 10f Prix Eugene Adam and Group 3 9f Prix de Guiche winner Kirkwall and a half-sister to 4 winners. *"An expensive filly at the sales, she's nice and compact, looks a 2-y-o but isn't that precocious. So she's just doing routine canters at the moment, no fast work, but all I can say is that she's straightforward, has a lovely attitude and we like her".*

204. DIVINE JOY ★★

b.f. Rip Van Winkle – Joyeaux (Mark Of Esteem). March 3. First foal. 28,000Y. Tattersalls October Book 2. Marco Botti. The dam, a modest 5f and 6f winner of 6 races, is a half-sister to 5 winners including the Group 1 Premio Lydia Tesio winner Aoife Alainn and the Italian listed winner and Group 2 Italian 2,000 Guineas third Adorable Fong. The second dam, Divine Secret (by Hernando), is an unraced half-sister to 6 minor winners here and abroad. (Mr W A Tinkler). *"A nice individual. We like her and she has a good temperament, but like a number of our 2-y-o's she's likely to want seven furlongs to begin with so we're going carefully with her at the moment. She's athletic and light on her feet".*

205. DREAM LORD (IRE) ★★★

ch.c. Dream Ahead – Silent Secret (Dubai Destination). February 10. Third foal. 60,000Y. Tattersalls October Book 2. Mark Crossman. Half-brother to the modest Irish 2-y-o 5f winner Gwen Lady Byron (by Dandy Man). The dam, a fair 2-y-o 5f winner, is a half-sister to 4 winners including the smart Irish Group 3 7f and Group 3 1m winner Cheyenne Star and to the dam of the triple Group 1 winner Gordon Lord Byron. The second dam, Charita (by Lycius), a listed 1m winner in Ireland, is a half-sister to 4 winners including the Italian Group 2 winner Stanott. (K A Dasmal). *"He's grown a lot since the sales and he's going to end up quite a big size. His sire wasn't an early type and I can see this colt starting in July. A straightforward colt".*

206. FEEL THIS MOMENT (IRE) ★★★

b.c. Tamayuz – Rugged Up (Marju). March 14. Third foal. £26,000Y. Doncaster Premier. Jamie Lloyd/Marco Botti. Half-brother to the modest 2015 6f placed 3-y-o Red Tycoon (by Acclamation). The dam is an unraced half-sister to the Japanese Group 3 winner Meiner Eternel and to the very useful Irish 2-y-o listed 5f winner Warsaw. The second dam, For Evva Silca (by Piccolo), placed once at 2 yrs, is a half-sister to 9 winners including the 2-y-o Group 1 6f Prix Morny winner Silca's Sister and the dual Group 2 winner Golden Silca. (Mrs L Botti). *"He's done so well since we bought him and has come to hand much quicker than we expected. We've already stepped him up to fast work, he's doing well and showing ability, so he's a horse we like and he should be relatively early".*

207. JASSUR ★★★

b.c. Canford Cliffs – Child Bride (Coronado's Quest). February 6. Eighth foal. £140,000Y. Doncaster Premier. Tony Nerses. Half-brother to the US Grade 2 12f and 14f winner Juniper Pass (by Lemon Drop Kid), to two minor winners in the USA by Out Of Place and Holy Bull and a minor winner in Argentina by Theatrical. The dam is an unraced half-sister to 6 winners including the dam of the US Grade 2 winner Postponed and to the dam of the Group 1 Racing Post Trophy winner Crowded House. The second dam, Chapel Of

Dreams (by Northern Dancer), won 7 races in the USA including two Grade 2 events and is a half-sister to 5 winners including the Grade 1 winner and top-class sire Storm Cat. (Saleh Al Homaizi & Imad Al Sagar). *"A nice, very compact individual that looks a 2-y-o, he's quite forward in his work and he's showing some speed. We'll probably press on with him and I should think he'll be racing around June time. He shows ability".*

208. MAJESTIQUE ★★
br.f. High Chaparral – Germane (Distant Relative). April 14. Fourteenth foal. €49,000Y. Tattersalls Ireland September. Brian Grassick Bloodstock. Sister to the Italian listed winner and US Grade 2 second Lucky Chappy (by High Chaparral) and half-sister to 5 winners including the useful 1m and 8.3f winner and triple listed placed Granted and the quite useful 7.5f and 1m winner Robema (both by Cadeaux Genereux). The dam, a useful winner of the Group 3 7f Rockfel Stakes and placed in two listed events, is a half-sister to 9 winners including the very useful German listed 10f winner Fabriano. The second dam, Fraulein Tobin (by J O Tobin), a fair 1m winner, is a half-sister to the very smart 10f performer Running Stag. *"She's not the biggest but she looks very athletic, has a very light action and I like her. But both her pedigree and her physique suggest she needs time and she won't be in fast work any time soon. A filly with a lovely attitude and she goes nicely for what she's been doing at this stage".*

209. MAY ROSE (IRE) ★★★★
b.f. Lawman – Rose De France (Diktat). March 24. Fourth foal. €520,000Y. Goffs Orby. Tony Nerses. Closely related to the smart 2-y-o 6f winner and Group 1 7f Dewhurst Stakes second Cable Bay and to the fair 5f winner Tanghan (both by Invincible Spirit) and half-sister to the 2014 2-y-o 5f and 7f winner Sea Wolf (by Amadeus Wolf). The dam, placed four times at 3 yrs in France, is a half-sister to 4 winners including the Group 3 winner and French 2,000 Guineas third Bowman and the dam of the Group 1 winners Kirklees and Mastery. The second dam, Cherokee Rose (by Dancing Brave), won the Group 1 Haydock Park Sprint Cup and the Group 1 Prix Maurice de Gheest and is a half-sister to 4 winners.

(Saleh Al Homaizi & Imad Al Sagar). *"She came in quite late but she's a smart filly and a great mover. I can see why she was expensive because she's got plenty of class. Being by Lawman she won't be early but she's very correct and strong, so she could be anything".*

210. MISTY LORD (IRE) ★★★
b.c. Lilbourne Lad – Misty Night (Galileo). February 20. First foal. £54,000Y. Doncaster Premier. Jamie Lloyd/Marco Botti. The dam is an unraced half-sister to 2 winners including the useful 7f and 1m winner and listed-placed Greyfriarschorista. The second dam, Misty Heights (by Fasliyev), an Irish listed 9f winner, was Group 3 placed twice and is a half-sister to 10 winners including the Group 3 winner Madeira Mist, herself the dam of Joshua Tree (winner of the Grade 1 Canadian International three times). (Fabfive). *"He's a bit long-backed and he's out of a Galileo mare, so I don't think he'll be a sprinter. He's growing a lot and changing shape all the time, I like him and he's a nice mover. One for July onwards, he could be an interesting horse later in the season".*

211. MR KHALID ★★★★
b.c. Pour Moi – Island Dreams (Giant's Causeway). January 9. Second foal. 135,000Y. Tattersalls October Book 1. Jamie Lloyd/Marco Botti. Half-brother to the quite useful 2014 2-y-o 1m winner Who'sthedude (by Duke Of Marmalade). The dam, placed fourth over 10f on her only start, is a half-sister to 3 winners including the Group 2 Betfred Mile winner and Group 1 Champion Stakes second Rob Roy. The second dam, Camanoe (by Gone West), ran unplaced twice and is a half-sister to 8 winners including the US Grade 1 winner Super Staff. (Saleh Al Homaizi & Imad Al Sagar). *"I think he's got plenty of ability and plenty of class. He goes well, his temperament is fine and we're very pleased with him. He could make his debut around June time and I see him being suited by a mile later on. Possibly a classic prospect for next year".*

212. ONESIE (IRE) ★★★
br.c. Dandy Man – Easee On (Hawk Wing). April 20. First foal. £40,000Y. Doncaster Premier. Jamie Lloyd/Marco Botti. The dam is an unraced half-sister to 5 winners including a listed winner in Italy. The second dam, Fairy

Lore (by Fairy King), won once at 3 yrs and is a half-sister to 4 winners. (Mr W A Tinkler). *"He goes nicely, he looks a 2-y-o and is responding well to fast work. One of our early types, he has a great temperament and so he ticks all the boxes".*

213. PACOMMAND ★★★★
b.c. Paco Boy – Indian Story (Indian Ridge). April 28. Second foal. €43,000Y. Goffs Orby. Jamie Lloyd. The dam ran once unplaced and is a half-sister to 5 winners including the Italian listed winner of 7 races Group 2 Italian 1,000 Guineas second Love Roi. The second dam, Law Tudor (by Law Society), a minor winner at 3 yrs in Italy, is a half-sister to 5 winners. (G Manfredini). *"A nice type, I don't think he was too expensive but maybe that's because he's not a good walker. But on the canter he's a beautiful mover and we like him a lot. We're taking our time with him, but he could be an exciting 2-y-o later on".*

214. PIACERE (IRE) ★★★
b.f. New Approach – Aneedah (Invincible Spirit). February 10. First foal. 220,000Y. Tattersalls October Book 1. Not sold. The dam, a fairly useful 2-y-o 1m winner, was listed-placed and is a half-sister to 2 winners including the 2-y-o Group 3 7f C L Weld Park Stakes winner My Titania. The second dam, Fairy Of The Night (by Danehill), an Irish 7f listed and 9.5f winner, is a sister to one winner and a half-sister to 2 winners including the US Grade 3 12f and Irish listed 11f winner Dress Rehearsal. (The Great Partnership). *"I don't know why she wasn't sold because she's very correct and very strong. She'll need a bit of time but she does everything easily and she's showing plenty of ability. One for the mid-summer".*

215. RECONSIDER ★★★
ch.c. Approve – Singora Lady (Intikhab). March 25. €20,000Y. Goffs Sportsmans. Jamie Lloyd/Marco Botti. Half-brother to the Italian dual listed 1m winner Lucky Serena (by Bertolini). The dam, a modest 7f (at 2 yrs) to 10f winner, is a half-sister to 4 winners. The second dam, Unicamp (by Royal Academy), a quite useful 2-y-o 6f winner, is a half-sister to 5 winners including the useful dual 2-y-o 7f and subsequent UAE winner Dulcet Spear. *"A*

cheap purchase but a nice individual, he goes well and is straightforward. He shows some speed so we'll keep him going and aim for the six furlong races. We're still looking for an owner for him".

216. RIAL (IRE) ★★★
b.f. Dark Angel – Coin Box (Dubai Destination). January 31. First foal. €33,000Y. Tattersalls Ireland September. Marco Botti. The dam is an unplaced half-sister to one minor winner. The second dam, Small Change (by Danzig), a fairly useful 2-y-o 7f winner, is a sister to the smart Group 1 6f Middle Park Stakes winner Zieten and to the Group 1 6f Cheveley Park Stakes winner Blue Duster and closely related to numerous winners including the French listed 1m winner Slow Jazz. *"When we bought her she was on the small side but she's grown and done well physically. She's coming to hand quickly and definitely showing speed, so I'm very pleased with her. I can see her being on the track in May".*

217. SURBETT (IRE) ★★★
b.c. Rock Of Gibraltar – Causeway Queen (Giant's Causeway). February 5. Second foal. €85,000Y. Goffs Orby. Jamie Lloyd/Marco Botti. Half-brother to Azamaara (by Azamour), unplaced in one start at 2 yrs in 2015. The dam is an unraced half-sister to 2 winners including the Group 3 Dee Stakes winner and Epsom Derby third Astrology. The second dam, Ask For The Moon (by Dr Fong), won 5 races including the Group 1 10f Prix Saint-Alary and is a half-sister to one winner. (Scuderia Rencati SRL). *"Quite forward both mentally and physically, he looks a 2-y-o and we've stepped him up in fast work. He's responded well, showing definite ability and shows some speed".*

218. UNNAMED ★★★
b.f. Exceed And Excel – Alamouna (Indian Ridge). March 3. Fifth foal. 52,000Y. Tattersalls October Book 1. Jamie Lloyd/Marco Botti. Half-sister to the French 1m and 9f winner Almoradi (by Barathea) and the minor French 11f winner Almadan (by Azamour). The dam, a quite useful 10f winner, is a half-sister to 8 winners including the useful 7f (at 2 yrs) and listed 1m winner Alasha (herself the dam of two stakes winners). The second dam, Alasana

(by Darshaan), won twice in France over 1m and 9f and is a half-sister to 8 winners including the French dual Group 2 winner Altayan. (Sheikh M B K Al Maktoum). *"Quite a smart filly, she's doing everything easily, has a good temperament and we're stepping up her work now. She's quite a big filly so I'm not putting her under too much pressure at the moment".*

219. UNNAMED ★★★

ch.c. Rip Van Winkle – Apache Dream (Indian Ridge). May 7. Fifth foal. 85,000Y. Tattersalls October Book 2. Jamie Lloyd/Marco Botti. Half-brother to the quite useful Irish 2-y-o 1m winner and Group 3 Mooresbridge Stakes third Hall Of Mirrors (by Duke Of Marmalade). The dam, a fair 2-y-o 6f winner, is a half-sister to 4 winners including the Group-placed Middlemarch and Lady High Havens. The second dam, Blanche Dubois (by Nashwan), is an unraced half-sister to 10 winners including Indian Haven (Irish 2,000 Guineas), Count Dubois (Group 1 Gran Criterium). *"A nice colt, he was weak at the sales but is doing well physically now. He's very tall and not ready for fast work yet but he has a good pedigree, Indian Ridge is a good broodmare sire and he could be a nice horse for the future".*

220. UNNAMED ★★★

ch.c. Zoffany – Attalea (Monsun). February 15. First foal. £18,000foal. Tattersalls December. Not sold. The dam is an unraced sister to the German listed winner Andorn and a half-sister to 3 winners. The second dam, Anthyllis (by Lycius), a 2-y-o winner in Germany and listed-placed in Italy, is a half-sister to 7 winners including the Group 1 German Derby winner Adlerflug and the German Group 2 winner Arrigo. (Coolmore). *"He's a beautiful horse with a great temperament, he's quite big so he'll take a bit of time but he could end up a stakes horse later in the year".*

221. UNNAMED ★★★★★ ♠

b.c. Champs Elysees – Dahama (Green Desert). March 2. Third foal. 320,000Y. Tattersalls October Book 1. John Warren. Half-brother to the 2014 2-y-o Group 2 7f Rockfel Stakes and listed 7f winner Al Thakhira (by Dubawi). The dam is an unplaced half-sister to 8 winners including the French 7f listed winner Bezrin.

The second dam, Darling Flame (by Capote), a useful 6f (at 2 yrs) and 7f winner, is a half-sister to 7 winners including the very smart Japanese Group 1 winning miler Heart Lake. (Al Shaqab Racing). *"A different type to his half-sister Al Thakhira. She's quite small but this colt has plenty of scope. He's a very nice mover, mentally he's quite forward and he's showing plenty of ability. One of my top picks".*

222. UNNAMED ★★★

br.f. Poet's Voice – Hear My Cry (Giant's Causeway). April 9. Second foal. €47,000Y. Tattersalls Ireland September. Jamie Lloyd/Marco Botti. Half-sister to the minor 2014 Italian 2-y-o winner Magia Nera (by Bellamy Road). The dam was unplaced in the USA on her only start and is a half-sister to 8 winners including the US Grade 2 winner Blingo and the listed winner Hold To Ransom (herself dam of the Australian dual Group 3 winner Retrieve) and to the dam of the UAE Grade 1 winner Prince Bishop. The second dam, Wassifa (by Sure Blade), a fairly useful 11f winner here, subsequently won 3 minor races in the USA and was stakes-placed. (Sheikh M B K Al Maktoum). *"A very good-looking filly and she may well have cost more at a different sale because the Poet's Voice yearlings were popular. We like her but because she's quite big I'm in no hurry to step her up into fast work. I can see her starting her career in June/July over seven furlongs or a mile".*

223. UNNAMED ★★★

ch.f. Dutch Art – Strictly (USA) (Fusaichi Pegasus). March 9. First foal. 24,000Y. Tattersalls December. Jamie Lloyd/Marco Botti. The dam, a dual 3-y-o winner in the USA, is a half-sister to 4 minor winners. The second dam, Dancing (by Spectrum), won the Group 2 Santa Ynez Stakes in the USA and is a half-sister to 4 winners. (Sheikh M B K Al Maktoum). *"A racy type, she should be early enough and she's already doing fast work. She goes nicely but she can be a little bit hot, which probably comes from Fusaichi Pegasus. However, we're very pleased with her and I thought she was a relatively cheap buy".* **TRAINERS' BARGAIN BUY.**

224. UNNAMED ★★

b.f. Oasis Dream – Ulfah (Danzig). March

21. Half-sister to the quite useful 7f and 1m winner Narmin (by Pivotal). The dam, an Irish dual listed 6f winner, is a sister to the Group 2 6f Diadem Stakes winner Haatef, to the listed winner and Group 1 Moyglare Stud Stakes second Shimah and the listed 6f (at 2 yrs) and Group 3 7f Athasi Stakes winner Waleyef. The second dam, Sayedat Alhadh (by Mr Prospector), a US 7f winner, is a sister to the US Grade 2 7f winner Kayrawan and a half-sister to the useful winners Amaniy, Elsaamri and Mathkurh. (Sheikh M. B. K Al Maktoum). *"Still in pre-training, she's a backward type but she moves nicely".*

JIM BOYLE

225. BLACK BESS ★★

b.f. Dick Turpin – Spring Clean (Danehill). January 21. Half-sister to the quite useful 6f and 7f winner of 4 races Duster (by Pastoral Pursuits), to the fair 2-y-o dual 5f winner Amis Reunis (by Bahamian Bounty), the fair 5f and 6f winner of 4 races Clearing and the fair dual 6f winner Hoover (both by Sleeping Indian). The dam, a quite useful 2-y-o 6f winner, is a half-sister to 2 winners in France. The second dam, Spring Haven (by Lear Fan), is a placed half-sister to 7 winners including the German Group 3 winner Tahreeb. *"She's a half-sister to a few that we've trained including the 4-y-o we have now, Clearing, so we know the family well. She's a very tall, big filly and she's going to take a bit of time but she has a bit of quality about her. I like her, she's quite athletic, has a lot of substance but still has a bit of filling out to do. The earliest we'll see her out will be mid-season".*

226. BOURNE SYMPHONY ★★

b.f. Lilbourne Lad – Song To The Moon (Oratorio). March 31. First foal. €10,000Y. Tattersalls Ireland September. The dam, a fair 1m to 10f winner of 5 races, is a half-sister to 3 winners including the Hong Kong Group 2 winner Charles The Great. The second dam, Jojeema (by Barathea), is an unraced half-sister to 5 winners including the high-class Group 2 12f Jockey Club Stakes and Group 3 12f Cumberland Lodge Stakes winner Riyadian. (Epsom Ups & Downs Partnership). *"Not over-big but she's a real sharp sort with a superb attitude and she'll be ready to rock n roll really soon. One for five furlong maidens in the coming weeks, she's the sharpest of my 2-y-o's, she's got a bit of speed about her and she really sticks her neck out. So I'm looking forward to getting her out and having some fun with her".*

227. EBBISHAM (IRE) ★★★★

b.c. Holy Roman Emperor – Balting Lass (Orpen). March 9. Fifth foal. €65,000Y. Goffs Orby. Peter & Ross Doyle. Half-brother to the French dual 1m winner Grande Amore (by Refuse To Bend). The dam is an unraced half-sister to 7 winners including the French listed winner and US Grade 2 placed Wedding Ring and the dam of the Group 3 Dee Stakes winner Gypsy King. The second dam, Fleur d'Oranger (by Northfields), a listed 12f winner in France and placed in three Group 3 events, is a half-sister to 9 winners including the German Group 3 winner and French Oaks third Premier Amour. (In Recovery Partnership). *"A very nice colt that's doing nice canters and he's definitely got a bit of quality about him. Big and strong, he'll be out in late May/early June and I really like him. I would think he'd be one to start off at six furlongs".*

228. MASTER OF HEAVEN ★★

b.c. Makfi – Maid In Heaven (Clodovil). January 22. First foal. 40,000Y. Tattersalls October Book 2. David Redvers. The dam, a fairly useful dual 7f winner, was listed-placed and is a half-sister to 5 winners. The second dam, Serious Delight (by Lomond), is an unraced half-sister to 8 winners. (Maid In Heaven Partnership). *"A bull of a horse, with plenty of bone and plenty of substance, he has a nice attitude but he won't be sharp. I can see him starting off in six furlong maidens and progressing to seven".*

229. NORTHMAN (IRE) ★★

b.c. Frozen Power – Chifney Rush (Grand Lodge). April 10. €15,000Y. Goffs Sportsmans. Peter & Ross Doyle. Half-brother to the 12f and hurdles winner Seamour (by Azamour) and to the moderate 5f winner Prince Of Prophets (by Intikhab). The dam, placed fourth once over 10f from two starts, is a half-sister to 4 winners including the listed-placed Reine De Neige. The second dam, Don't Rush (by Alleged), a fairly useful dual 12f winner, is a half-sister to the US Grade 1 winners Seaside Attraction (dam of the US Grade 1 winners Cape Town and Golden Attraction) and Gorgeous, to the champion Canadian 3-y-o Key to the Moon and the placed dam of Fantastic Light. (Harrier Racing 3). *"A horse we like, he's very straightforward and although he doesn't look early he's doing fast work and I'd expect him to run quite soon. I'll wait for the six furlong maidens for him, he's a good-looking and very willing horse".*

CLIVE BRITTAIN

230. UNNAMED
b.c. Dream Ahead – Anadolu (Statue Of Liberty). February 20. First foal. 40,000Y. Tattersalls October Book 2. Rabbah Bloodstock. The dam, a fairly useful 2-y-o listed 5f winner, is a half-sister to 7 winners. The second dam, Afto (by Relaunch), won the Grade 2 Railbird Stakes in the USA and is a half-sister to 7 winners. (Saeed Manana).

231. UNNAMED
b.f. Poet's Voice – Bezant (Zamindar). April 16. Seventh foal. 50,000Y. Tattersalls October Book 2. Rabbah Bloodstock. Half-sister to Deposer (by Kheleyf), a 2-y-o 6f and subsequent Hong Kong winner and placed in the Group 3 Jersey Stakes, the Group 3 Diomed Stakes and a US Grade 1 event. The dam, placed once at 3 yrs over 1m, is a half-sister to 3 winners including the Group 2 Beresford Stakes third Sant Jordi. The second dam, Foresta Verde (by Green Forest), is a placed half-sister to 8 winners including the smart broodmare Tanouma. (Sheikh J D Al Maktoum).

232. UNNAMED
ch.c. Poet's Voice – Calakanga (Dalakhani). March 19. Third foal. 35,000Y. Tattersalls October Book 2. Not sold. The dam, a quite useful 12f winner, is a half-sister to 10 winners including the very smart Group 1 1m Racing Post Trophy and Group 2 10.4f Dante Stakes winner Dilshaan and the listed winner and Group 1 second Darrfonah. The second dam, Avila (by Ajdal), a fair 7f placed maiden, is a half-sister to the smart middle-distance colts Alleging, Monastery and Nomrood. (Saeed Manana).

233. UNNAMED ♠
b.c. Manduro – Krynica (Danzig). April 8. Fourth living foal. 24,000Y. Tattersalls October

Book 3. Rabbah Bloodstock. Half-brother to the fair dual 1m winner Songburst (by Singspiel). The dam, a quite useful 2-y-o 5f winner, is a half-sister to 5 winners including the Group 3 9f Earl Of Sefton Stakes winner and multiple Group 1 second Phoenix Tower. The second dam, Bionic (by Zafonic), a very useful 2-y-o 7f winner, is a half-sister to the Group 3 7f Prestige Stakes winner Sense Of Joy and the multiple Group 3 middle-distance winner and French Derby fourth Day Flight.

234. UNNAMED
ch.c. Kyllachy – Rhal (Rahy). February 7. First foal. 27,000Y. Tattersalls October Book 2. Rabbah Bloodstock. The dam, a fair 5f and 6f winner, is a half-sister to one winner in Japan. The second dam, Queen Of Stars (by Green Desert), is an unraced half-sister to the Group 3 1m Premio Dormello winner and Group 1 Italian Oaks third Lady Catherine. (Saeed Manana).

235. UNNAMED
ch.c. Iffraaj – Soxy Doxy (Hawk Wing). February 6. Third foal. 25,000Y. Tattersalls October Book 2. Rabbah Bloodstock. Half-brother to the modest 8.5f and 10f winner Mister Mayday (by Kheleyf) and to a winner in Singapore by Verglas. The dam, a moderate 12f placed maiden, is a half-sister to 5 winners including the listed King Charles II Stakes and subsequent US Grade 3 winner and Grade 1 placed Millennium Dragon. The second dam, Feather Bride (by Groom Dancer), won once at 3 yrs in France and is a half-sister to 5 winners. (Saeed Manana).

236. UNNAMED
ch.c. Arcano – Star Approval (Hawk Wing). April 19. Fourth foal. 50,000Y. Tattersalls October Book 2. Rabbah Bloodstock. Half-brother to the quite useful dual 5f winner at 2 and 3 yrs Katchy Lady (by Kyllachy). The dam is an unraced half-sister to 3 winners including the Group 1 7f Moyglare Stud Stakes winner and Coronation Stakes third Mail The Desert. The second dam, Mail Boat (by Formidable), is an unraced half-sister to 4 winners including the Group 3 Chester Vase winner and St Leger third Dry Dock and the dam of the dual Group 3 winner and multiple Group 1 placed Norse Dancer. (Sheikh J D Al Maktoum).

DAVID BROWN

237. ARIZE (IRE) ★★★
b.f. Approve – Raise (Seattle Slew). March 31. Eighth living foal. 12,000Y. Tattersalls October Book 3. Peter Onslow. Half-sister to the modest 2014 2-y-o 6f winner, on her only start, X Raise (by Speightstown) and to two minor winners in the USA by Arch and Horse Chestnut. The dam, a minor US winner at 4 yrs, is a half-sister to 7 winners including the Irish Group 2 Railway Stakes winner Lizard Island and to the dam of the US Grade 1 winner Corinthian. The second dam, Add (by Spectacular Bid), a stakes placed winner of 4 races at 3 and 4 yrs, is a half-sister to 8 winners including the Group 1 Grand Criterium winner Jade Robbery. (Peter Onslow). *"She's had one run but was totally green on that occasion. She's certainly going to win races and she's a big, strong filly, probably a bit weak at the moment, but we gave her a run for experience. A long term filly, she'll be a six/seven furlong 2-y-o".*

238. BIT OF A LAD (IRE) ★★★
b.c. Lilbourne Lad – Sacred Love (Barathea). January 5. Eighth foal. 16,000Y. Tattersalls December. D H Brown. Half-brother to the 2-y-o 7f winner Secret Love (by Dalakhani), to the 6f to 7.5f winner of 9 races Illustrious Prince and the 7f winner Mastoora (both by Acclamation) – all quite useful and the modest Irish 12f winner Heart In The Air (by Cape Cross). The dam, placed fourth once over 1m, is a half-sister to 5 winners. The second dam, Abstraction (by Rainbow Quest), is an unraced sister to the Group 2 Prix du Conseil de Paris winner De Quest and to the listed winner Source Of Light and a half-sister to the US triple Grade 1 winner Wandesta. (Mr D H Brown). *"He's a lovely colt and I can see him being a very nice 2-y-o, he's not come in his coat yet but what bits he has done have been pleasing. He should be out by the end of May".*

239. FISHERMAN'S FRIEND ★★★
b.c. Equiano – Tiana (Diktat). April 2. Fifth foal. 22,000Y. Tattersalls October Book 3. David Brown. Half-brother to the fairly useful 2014 2-y-o 6f winner Salt Island (by Exceed And Excel), to the fair 5f (at 2 yrs) and 6f winner Royal Warrior (by Royal Applause) and a winner abroad by Bahamian Bounty. The dam, a fairly useful 2-y-o 6f winner, was listed-placed over 7f and is a half-sister to 6 winners including the useful 2-y-o Group 3 Molecomb Stakes second Mary Read. The second dam, Hill Welcome (by Most Welcome), was placed twice at 2 yrs and is a half-sister to 5 winners including the Group 1 6f Middle Park Stakes winner Stalker. (Mrs F Denniff). *"I think he's going to be a very nice colt. He'll start off at six furlongs and he does everything right. He does have ability".*

240. GUILTLESS (USA) ★★★★
b.f. Bernardini – Getaway Girl (Silver Deputy). May 5. $100,000Y. Keeneland September. David Redvers. Half-sister to the Canadian Grade 3 9f winner Northern Causeway (by Giant's Causeway). The dam won 3 minor races in the USA and is a half-sister to 5 winners including the multiple US Grade 1 winner Ghostzapper and the US Grade 1 Hopeful Stakes winner City Zip. The second dam, Baby Zip (by Relaunch), a stakes winner of 4 races in the USA, is a half-sister to 4 winners. (Qatar Racing Ltd). *"She's a lovely filly and it won't be too long before she's out. She'll start at five furlongs but she'll progress to six and possibly seven".*

241. HOME AGAIN ★★★
b.c. Bahamian Bounty – Celestial Welcome (Most Welcome). March 25. Ninth foal. £34,000Y. Doncaster Premier. John Fretwell. Brother to the quite useful 6f (including at 2 yrs) and 7f winner of 5 races Shesastar and half-brother to 4 winners including the quite useful 2-y-o dual 7f winner and listed-placed Startori (by Vettori), the fair 2-y-o 7f winner Celestial Tryst (by Tobougg) and the fair 1m and 9.5f winner Gabrial's Wawa (by Dubai Destination). The dam, a useful 7f to 12f winner of 8 races, is a full or half-sister to 5 winners including the Group 2 King Edward VII Stakes second Snowstorm. The second dam, Choral Sundown (by Night Shift), a quite useful winner of 4 races at up to 12f, is a half-sister to 5 winners. (J C Fretwell). *"A nice colt, he'll be a sprinter and is probably a mid-season type 2-y-o".*

242. MIDNIGHT MACCHIATO (IRE) ★★
b.c. Dark Angel – Lathaat (Dubai Destination). April 12. Second foal. 19,000Y. Tattersalls

December. D H Brown. The dam, a fair dual 7f placed maiden, is a half-sister to 2 winners. The second dam, Khulood (by Storm Cat), a useful listed 7f (at 2 yrs) and Group 3 7f Nell Gwyn Stakes winner, is a half-sister to 9 winners including the Irish 1,000 Guineas winner Mehthaaf and the July Cup winner Elnadim. (D A West). *"One for the middle of the season but he's coming forward like a nice horse. He's one for seven furlongs and a mile".*

243. PALPITATION ★★★
b.c. Fast Company – Sensation (Soviet Star). May 10. Twelfth foal. 20,000Y. Tattersalls December. D H Brown. Half-brother to 6 winners including the smart dual Group 3 middle-distance winner of 8 races Systematic (by Rainbow Quest), the fairly useful 10f to 2m 2f winner Scatter Dice (by Manduro) and the quite useful 2-y-o 7f winner Sunday Smile (by Sunday Silence). The dam won the Group 2 1m Falmouth Stakes and is a half-sister to 5 winners including the US Grade 2 placed Outlasting (dam of the Grade 2 winner Fortitude). The second dam, Outstandingly (by Exclusive Native), a champion US 2-y-o filly, won the Grade 1 Breeders Cup Juvenile Fillies and the Grade 1 Hollywood Starlet Stakes and is a half-sister to 7 winners. (D A West). *"He's a May foal but he might have had a run before his birthday. He's showing me quite a bit and he'll be quite sharp too. A five/six furlong 2-y-o".*

244. ST GEORGES CROSS ★★★
b.c. Showcasing – Garter Star (Mark Of Esteem). April 8. Third foal. 42,000Y. Tattersalls October Book 3. J C Fretwell. Half-brother to the moderate 2014 7f placed 2-y-o Star Pursuits (by Pastoral Pursuits). The dam ran twice unplaced and is a half-sister to 4 winners including the listed winner Queen's Grace. The second dam, Palace Affair (by Pursuit Of Love), a smart winner of 5 listed races from 5f to 7f, is a sister to one winner and a half-sister to 10 winners including the Group 1 6f July Cup winner and sire Sakhee's Secret. (J C Fretwell). *"He looks like he's going to be a sprinter but he's still backward and I don't think we'll see him out before mid-season".*

245. SWIRRAL EDGE ★★★★
b.f. Hellvelyn – Pizzarra (Shamardal). February 15. First foal. £10,500Y. Doncaster Silver. D H Brown. The dam, a moderate 5f and 6f placed maiden, is a half-sister to numerous winners including the 2-y-o Group 2 5f Flying Childers Stakes and Group 3 5f Molecomb Stakes winner Wunders Dream, the very useful Irish Group 3 Ridgewood Pearl Stakes winner Grecian Dancer and the fairly useful 6f winners Nocturne and Go Between (by Daggers Drawn). The second dam, Musianica (by Statoblest), a modest 5f and 5.3f winner at 3 yrs, is a half-sister to 5 winners including the high-class Hong Kong horses Mensa and Firebolt. (Mr D H Brown). *"A very nice filly indeed. Well put-together, she'll be running soon and looks the part. It's a fast family and she's inherited that speed. Swirral Edge is the name of a walk to Helvellyn in the Lake District".* **TRAINERS' BARGAIN BUY**

246. TAKE CHARGE ★★★
b.c. Showcasing – Be Decisive (Diesis). April 2. Tenth living foal. £41,000Y. Doncaster Premier. John Fretwell. Half-brother to the quite useful 2-y-o 5f winner To The Point (by Refuse To Bend) and to the quite useful Irish 2-y-o 6f and subsequent German winner Be Fantastic (by Fantastic Light). The dam, a fair 1m winner, is a half-sister to 7 winners including the listed 7f winner Miss Ivanhoe. The second dam, Robellino Miss (by Robellino), won 7 races at up to 9f in the USA, was stakes-placed and is a half-sister to the listed winners Grangeville and Palana. (J C Fretwell). *"He's going to be a 2-y-o for later on, he'll be alright but he needs seven furlongs".*

247. TICKING AWAY ★★★
gr.c. Monsieur Bond – Pendulum (Pursuit Of Love). February 15. Eighth foal. 38,000Y. Tattersalls December. J C Fretwell. Half-brother to the quite useful 2-y-o 5f winner Every Second , to the moderate 6f winner Abraham Monro (both by Kyllachy), the quite useful 5f and 6f winner of 8 races Medici Time (by Medicean), the quite useful 5f to 7.5f winner of 8 races My Son Max (by Avonbridge) and the fair 1m winner Pendulum Star (by Observatory). The dam, a quite useful 7f winner, is a half-sister to 6 winners. The second dam, Brilliant Timing (by The Minstrel), is a placed half-sister to the US Grade 1 winners Timely Writer and Timely Assertion. (J

C Fretwell). *"He's a big, strong horse, probably one for five and six furlongs. We're just at a crossroads with him at the moment, wondering whether to push on with him or wait a bit. A very nice horse".*

248. TIKTHEBOX (IRE) ★★★

b.c. Approve – Nicene (Pulpit). April 22. Sixth foal. 12,500Y. Tattersalls December. D H Brown. Half-brother to the unplaced 2014 2-y-o Katniss (by Champs Elysees) and to the modest 10.5f winner Shisha Threesixty (by High Chaparral). The dam, placed once at 2 yrs in the USA, is a half-sister to 4 winners including the 2-y-o listed Washington Singer Stakes winner and Group 3 second Prizeman. The second dam, Shuttle (by Conquistador Cielo), a minor US 3-y-o winner, is a sister to the US Grade 2 winner Dotsero and a half-sister to 4 winners. (Mr D H Brown). *"He'll be a touch above average I'd say and he'll be racing in April. He's got speed, so I'll start him over five furlongs, but he may be better over six".*

249. TIME AGAIN ★★

b.f. Kyllachy – Record Time (Clantime). March 12. Half-sister to the smart dual Group 3 5f winner Moorhouse Lad (both by Bertolini), to the useful 5f (including at 2 yrs) and 6f winner of 5 races Off The Record (by Desert Style) and the modest 2-y-o 5f winner Pro Tempore (by Fraam). The dam, a fair 5f winner at 3 and 4 yrs, is a sister to the listed winning sprinter Lago Di Varano and a half-sister to 3 winners. The second dam, On The Record (by Record Token), a fair dual sprint winner at 2 and 4 yrs, is a half-sister to 3 winners. (Peter Onslow). *"She'll take a bit of time, because that's what the family does. One for later on, she'll be a sprinter but she won't make a 2-y-o until the back-end of the season".*

250. TRIBESMAN ★★★★

ch.c. Equiano – Millsini (Rossini). February 18. Fourth foal. £35,000Y. Doncaster Premier. John Fretwell. The dam is an unplaced half-sister to 6 winners including the French Group 3 5f winner Mirza and the useful listed 6f placed Millybaa. The second dam, Millyant (by Primo Dominie), winner of the Group 2 5f Prix du Gros-Chene, is a half-sister to 5 winners including the Group 2 5f Flying Childers winner and very useful sire Prince Sabo and to

the Irish listed winner Bold Jessie (herself dam of the Gimcrack Stakes winner Abou Zouz). (J C Fretwell). *"Well, you've seen him run haven't you?! He won his first start and I think he's well up to Coventry Stakes standard, so we're excited about him. We'll give him a run in a Conditions event next, he's well put together, not over-big but well balanced and he ticks all the boxes for a smart early 2-y-o".*

251. WAR QUEEN ★★★★ ♠

b.f. Acclamation – New Deal (Rainbow Quest). April 8. Sixth foal. €67,000Y. Tattersalls Ireland September. David Redvers. Sister to the useful 6f (at 2 yrs) and 12f winner Alrasm, to the fairly useful 2-y-o 5f winner New Pearl and the quite useful 7.5f (at 2 yrs) and 10.5f winner New Street. The dam, a minor 3-y-o 1m winner in France, is a half-sister to 6 winners including the Group 2 Lowther Stakes third Dunloskin. The second dam, Dalinda (by Nureyev), a winner at 4 yrs in France, is a half-sister to 4 winners. (Qatar Racing Ltd). *"Yes, she looks like one that'll be out early, she's promising and shows a bit of class. A five/six furlong 2-y-o".*

252. UNNAMED ★★★★

b.f. Smart Strike – More Hennessy (Hennessy). March 21. Third foal. $350,000Y. Keeneland September. David Redvers. Half-sister to the 2014 2-y-o listed 5f Windsor Castle Stakes winner and Group 1 Prix Morny second Hootenanny (by Quality Road) and to a minor US winner by Not For Love. The dam, unplaced in one start, is a half-sister to 6 winners including the US Grade 1 Prioress Stakes winner Cat Moves. The second dam, Dance Move (by Capote), is an unraced half-sister to 5 winners out of the US Grade 1 winner Dance Teacher. (Qatar Racing Ltd). *"A half-sister to a fast horse in Hootenanny, she looks like a classy filly but probably won't start until six furlongs sometime in May. She's ticking all the right boxes and doing everything right".*

253. UNNAMED ★★

b.f. Compton Place – Never Lose (Diktat). April 5. Third foal. £32,000Y. Doncaster Premier. David Redvers. Half-sister to the fair 2-y-o 7f winner Miss Lillie (by Exceed And Excel). The dam, a fairly useful 6f and 7f winner, was third in the listed Cecil Frail Stakes and is a half-sister to 3 winners including the fairly useful 6f winner of 4 races (including at 2 yrs) and listed-placed Morache Music. The second dam, Enchanted Princess (by Royal Applause), a fair 3-y-o 8.3f winner, is a half-sister to 5 winners including the dam of the Group 3 winner and dual Group 1 placed High Standing. (Qatar Racing Ltd). *"A late-season 2-y-o, probably for seven furlongs, but she's a nice filly".*

HENRY CANDY

254. BOUNCE ★★★★

b.f. Bahamian Bounty – Black Belt Shopper (Desert Prince). April 2. Ninth foal. 32,000Y. Tattersalls October Book 2. R Frisby. Closely related to the modest 6f winner Exit Strategy (by Cadeaux Genereux) and half-sister to 4 winners including the quite useful 2-y-o 7f winner Cheque Book (by Araafa), the Japanese winner of 8 races from 3 to 7 yrs Leo Parade, the fair 12f winner Black Label (both by Medicean) and the modest 6f winner Sushi (by Kyllachy). The dam, a quite useful 2-y-o 6f winner, was listed-placed and is a half-sister to one winner. The second dam, Koumiss (by Unfuwain), a French maiden that stayed 10f, is a half-sister to 8 winners including the listed Queen's Vase winner Arden. (Landmark Racing Ltd). *"She's very muscular and hasn't done a lot yet but she'll be starting work soon and I think she'll come to hand pretty quickly. She looks a proper sprinter and should be racing in May".*

255. DENHAM SOUND ★★★

ch.f. Champs Elysees – Presbyterian Nun (Daylami). February 7. The dam, a fairly useful 2-y-o 7f winner, was listed-placed and is a half-sister to 5 winners including the Group 3 7f Minstrel Stakes winner Jedburgh. The second dam, Conspiracy (by Rudimentary), a useful 2-y-o listed 5f winner, is a half-sister to 7 winners including the Group 2 10f Sun Chariot Stakes winner Ristna and the dual listed winner Gayane. (Earl Cadogan). *"She's a big, strong filly for the late summer or autumn and I like the way she goes".*

256. FREE PASSAGE ★★★

ch.c. Medicean – Free Offer (Generous). March 1. Half-brother to the smart listed 1m winner Cape Peron (by Beat Hollow)

and to the fair 8.5f winner Faure Island (by Myboycharlie). The dam was a quite useful 7f (at 2 yrs) and dual 10f winner. The second dam, Proserpine (by Robellino), a fairly useful 2-y-o 1m winner, is a half-sister to the 1m and 10f winner and subsequent US Grade 1 14f placed Chelsea Barracks. (Earl Cadogan). *"I think he'll be a nice horse, but I think he'll take a bit of time. That's what the family do and Medicean wouldn't make it any more precocious. Probably one for seven furlongs to start with and he should make up into a nice horse".*

257. JACK NEVISON ★★★

b.c. Dick Turpin – Creative Mind (Danehill Dancer). April 27. Fourth foal. £10,000Y. Doncaster Silver. Henry Candy. Half-brother to the French 2-y-o 6f winner Hidden Talent (by Kyllachy). The dam, a quite useful 7f winner including at 2 yrs, was third in the Group 3 Chartwell Stakes and is a half-sister to 6 minor winners. The second dam, Inventive (by Sheikh Albadou), a quite useful 2-y-o dual 5f winner, is a half-sister to 3 minor winners in France. (Henry Candy and Partners). *"He looks very sharp and a very muscular horse. You'd be looking at around June time for him and he looks a proper sprinter. Apparently it was 'Swift Jack Nevison' that did the famous ride from London to York and not Dick Turpin. We thought it was a bit too bold to keep 'Swift' in the name, so we dropped it!"* **TRAINERS' BARGAIN BUY**

258. LIMONATA (IRE) ★★★

b.f. Bushranger – Come April (Singspiel). January 28. Second living foal. 90,000Y. Tattersalls October Book 2. H Candy. Half-sister to the very smart 2014 2-y-o dual listed 6f winner Limato (by Tagula). The dam, a fair 10f winner, is a half-sister to 3 minor winners. The second dam, So Admirable (by Suave Dancer), is an unraced sister to the Group 1 10f Coral Eclipse Stakes winner Compton Admiral and a half-sister to 7 winners including the Group 1 1m Queen Elizabeth II Stakes winner Summoner and the dam of the multiple Group 1 winner The Fugue. (P G Jacobs). *"She goes nicely and looks very strong. I would hope she'd be running around June time over six furlongs".*

259. MEDICIMAN ★★★★

b.c. Medicean – Quintrell (Royal Applause). April 7. Sixth foal. 25,000Y. Tattersalls October Book 2. H Candy. Half-brother to the fair dual 1m winner Snooky (by Exceed And Excel), to the fair dual 7f winner Tiger Jim (by Tiger Hill) and the fair 2-y-o 7f winner Cornish Path (by Champs Elysees). The dam, a fair dual 7f winner at 3 yrs, is a half-sister to 8 minor winners. The second dam, Peryllis (by Warning), a modest 6f (at 2 yrs) to 10.2f placed maiden, is a half-sister to 6 winners including the very useful sprinter Cragside. (One Too Many, N Agra, M Silver). *"He's quite big, but he looks quite mature and he moves well. He's done a couple of bits of work and he seems to go alright, but with that pedigree and size you wouldn't want to run him before June at the earliest. One to start at six furlongs I'd say and he looks a nice horse".*

260. NICARRA ★★★

b.f. Kodiac – Nassma (Sadler's Wells). February 16. Thirteenth foal. Half-sister to 8 winners including the Group 3 7.5f and dual listed winner Lady Wingshot (by Lawman), the 2-y-o listed 5f Dragon Stakes winner and Group 2 5f Flying Childers Stakes second Bahama Mama (by Invincible Spirit), the useful 2-y-o 6f and 7f and subsequent UAE winner Calchas (by Warning) and the quite useful 9f winners Traprain (by Mark Of Esteem) and Dansker (by Darshaan). The dam, a listed middle-distance winner of 2 races, is a half-sister to 5 minor winners. The second dam, Pretoria (by Habitat), a useful 7f (at 2 yrs) and listed 10f winner (in Italy), is a half-sister to 4 winners including Ivanka (Group 1 Fillies' Mile). (Mrs Patricia Burns). *"Out of a Sadler's Wells mare, she's growing and developing quite a lot at the moment. So I should think she'd need a spring break, but she's a lovely moving filly, covers a lot of ground and looks the part".*

261. PAST MASTER ★★★★

b.c. Mastercraftsman – Millestan (Invincible Spirit). April 26. Third foal. 40,000Y. Tattersalls October Book 2. Not sold. Half-brother to the moderate 6f winner Seraphima (by Fusaichi Pegasus). The dam, a quite useful 2-y-o 8.3f and subsequent US winner, is a half-sister to 5 winners including the useful French 9.5f (at 2 yrs) to 15f winner and listed-placed

Grey Mystique. The second dam, Atnab (by Riverman), a modest 12f winner, is a half-sister to 6 winners including the listed winner Dansili Dancer. (Mr D B Clark, Mr A R Bentall, Mr H Candy). *"He's one that will take a bit of time but I suspect we'll get him out in late summer. He's a strong, classy looking colt that moves well and he's out of a decent Invincible Spirit mare, so I should think he'll be a nice type for six and seven furlongs".*

262. REGAL GAIT (IRE) ★★★ ♠

b.c. Tagula – Babylonian (Shamardal). May 2. Second foal. £45,000Y. Doncaster Silver. Henry Candy. Half-brother to the fair 2-y-o 5f and 6f winner Pull The Plug (by Sleeping Indian). The dam, placed twice over 6f at 2 yrs, is a half-sister to 4 winners including the 1m (at 2 yrs) and listed 10f winner and Group 1 Criterium de Saint-Cloud third Empire Day. The second dam, Evil Empire (by Acatenango), a Group 3 12f winner in Germany, is a sister to the German triple listed winner El Tango and a half-sister to 9 winners including the German listed winner El Tiger. (P G Jacobs). *"A late foal, he's immature at the moment but he's a lovely mover and a horse that we like. I couldn't see him running before July or August and looking at him you'd think he may be a seven furlong type rather than an out-and-out sprinter".*

263. ROSIE ROYCE ★★★★

b.f. Acclamation – Rebecca Rolfe (Pivotal). February 5. First foal. The dam, a French listed 5f winner and Group 3 5f second, is a half-sister to 2 winners. The second dam, Matoaka (by A P Indy), a fairly useful 7f winner, is a half-sister to 2 winners including the 2-y-o listed 1m winner and 3-y-o Group 3 placed Battle Chant. (Hunscote Stud). *"She seems quite strong and straightforward and I should think she'd be capable of running in June. One to watch out for I should think".*

264. SHOWING OFF (IRE) ★★★

ch.c. Notnowcato – Walk On Water (Exceed And Excel). January 25. First foal. The dam, a fairly useful 2-y-o dual 6f winner, is a half-sister to the 2-y-o 6f winner (on her only start) Pussycat Dream. The second dam, The Cat's Whiskers (Tale Of The Cat), a winner over 7f and 1m in New Zealand, is a half-sister to 6 winners including the Australian Group

3 winner and Group 1 placed Tully Dane. (Dowager Duchess Of Bedford). *"He looks quite forward for a Notnowcato and he's out of a good Exceed And Excel mare too. I could see him running in mid-summer and he's a good-moving, strong sort of horse that I like".*

265. VIBRANT CHORDS ★★★ ♠
b.c. Poet's Voice – Lovely Thought (Dubai Destination). April 11. Third foal. £75,000Y. Doncaster Premier. Henry Candy. Half-brother to the useful 5f winner of 5 races High On Life (by Invincible Spirit). The dam, a quite useful 7f (at 2 yrs) and dual 6f, was listed-placed and is a half-sister to the 6f (at 2 yrs), Group 2 7f Challenge Stakes and Group 3 7f Jersey Stakes winner Just James and to the listed winner and Group 3 placed Blue Jack. The second dam, Fairy Flight (by Fairy King), a 2-y-o 6f winner in Ireland, is a sister to one winner and a half-sister to the French listed 10.5f winner Titled Ascent and the Irish listed winning sprinter Northern Tide. (P G Jacobs). *"A small, neat horse, he's very much like Poet's Voice's sire Dubawi. Very muscular and a good mover, he's going to take a bit of time and is one for the second half of the year. We like him".*

266. UNNAMED ★★★
b.f. Kyllachy – Floating (Oasis Dream). March 2. Third foal. £20,000Y. Doncaster Premier. Henry Candy. Half-sister to the modest dual 1m winner Like A Prayer (by Compton Place). The dam is an unplaced half-sister to 6 winners. The second dam, Bonne Etoile (by Diesis), a fairly useful winner of 3 races at 3 yrs including a listed event over 10f, is a half-sister to 5 winners. (Potensis Bloodstock). *"She's very muscular and knows what to do with herself. I can see her running in June time, she's not very big, but strong and a nice mover".*

267. UNNAMED ★★★
ch.f. Dandy Man – High Chart (Robellino). April 22. Fourth foal. £21,000Y. Doncaster Premier. Henry Candy. The dam, a modest 5f (at 2 yrs) to 1m winner, is a half-sister to 3 winners. The second dam, Bright Spells (by Salse), won once at 2 yrs and was listed-placed. (Potensis Bloodstock). *"A very, very muscular, nice-moving filly, she just needs to grow up a little bit in front. We like her a lot and she'll be an out-and-out sprinter I think".*

268. UNNAMED ★★★★ ♠♠
b.f. Hellvelyn – Talampaya (Elusive Quality). February 4. Fourth foal. 50,000Y. Tattersalls October Book 2. David Redvers. Half-sister to the useful 2014 2-y-o 6f winner and Group 3 6f Princess Margaret Stakes second Pastoral Girl, to the fairly useful 2-y-o triple 5f winner and listed-placed Lilbourne Lass (both by Pastoral Pursuits) and the fair 5f winner Flirtinaskirt (by Avonbridge). The dam is an unraced half-sister to 5 minor winners here and in the USA. The second dam, Argentina (by Storm Cat), a minor US 2-y-o winner, is a full or half-sister to 7 winners. (Qatar Racing Ltd). *"A very big, very strong filly, she's done a couple of bits of work and if she wasn't so big she'd almost be running now. We'll give her a bit more time and bring her out in May or June. Should be one to follow".*

LADY JANE CECIL
269. ALMEDA
b.f. Champs Elysees – Bionic (Zafonic). April 22. Half-sister to the high-class Group 3 9f Earl Of Sefton Stakes winner and multiple Group 1 second Phoenix Tower (by Chester House), to the quite useful 2-y-o 7f winner Winter Bloom (by Aptitude) and the quite useful 2-y-o 5f winner Krynica (by Danzig). The dam, a very useful 2-y-o 7f winner, is a half-sister to the Group 3 7f Prestige Stakes winner Sense Of Joy (by Dansili) and the multiple Group 3 middle-distance winner and French Derby fourth Day Flight. The second dam, Bonash (by Rainbow Quest), a very useful filly, won 4 races in France from 1m to 12f including the Prix d'Aumale, the Prix Vanteaux and the Prix de Malleret and is a full or half-sister to 4 winners. (Khalid Abdulla).

270. CAJOLED (FR)
b.f. High Chaparral – Dolphina (Kingmambo). February 15. Second foal. The dam, a fair 10f winner, is a half-sister to one winner. The second dam, Sea Of Showers (by Seattle Slew), won once over 1m and was third in the Group 2 1m Prix de Sandringham and is a half-sister to the triple US Grade 1 winner (over 7f and 1m) Aldebaran and the Canadian Grade 1 Atto Mile winner Good Journey. (Niarchos Family).

271. FORMATIVE
b.c. Champs Elysees – Chasing Stars

(Observatory). March 27. Third foal. The dam, a French listed 1m winner of 4 races, is a half-sister to the useful 1m and 11f winner and Group 3 Chester Vase third Risk Taker. The second dam, Post Modern (by Nureyev), is an unraced sister to the Oaks and the Fillies Mile winner Reams of Verse and a half-sister to 10 winners including Elmaamul (Coral Eclipse Stakes and Phoenix Champion Stakes) and the Group winners Manifest, Modernise and Modern Day and the dam of the high-class middle-distance filly Midday. (Khalid Abdulla).

272. HIGHLY PRIZED
b.c. Manduro – Razzle (USA) (Danzig). April 1. Sixth foal. Half-brother to the quite useful 7f and 1m winner Defendant (by Medicean). The dam is an unraced half-sister to Danehill, the US Grade 2 9f winner Eagle Eyed, the very smart Group 3 Criterion Stakes winner Shibboleth, the US Grade 3 winner Harpia and the listed 7f winner Euphonic. The second dam, Razyana (by His Majesty), was placed over 7f at 2 yrs and 10f at 3 yrs. (Khalid Abdulla).

273. IMPERIAL STATE
b.c. Holy Roman Emperor – Seldemosa (Selkirk). April 26. Fifth foal. £40,000Y. Doncaster Premier. A.C.E/Scott. Half-brother to the quite useful 6f (at 2 yrs) and 10f winner Lucky Henry (by Lucky Story) and to the fair 6f to 1m winner Lady Bayside (by Ishiguru). The dam, a modest 8.5f winner, is a half-sister to 4 winners including the very useful 7f winner of 4 races here and in the UAE Sirocco Breeze. The second dam, Baldemosa (by Lead On Time), won over 1m in France at 3 yrs and is a half-sister to 4 winners including the Group 1 5.5f Prix Robert Papin winner Balbonella (herself dam of the top-class sprinter Anabaa and the French 1,000 Guineas winner Always Loyal). (The Harnage Partnership).

274. ROYAL BEEKEEPER
ch.c. Champs Elysees – Lasso (Indian Ridge). May 5. Fifth foal. 58,000Y. Tattersalls October Book 2. A C Elliott/G Scott. Half-sister to the quite useful 2-y-o 7f winner Goldoni (by Dylan Thomas) and to the fairly useful 7f (at 2 yrs) and 1m winner Gunner Lindley (by Medicean). The dam, a modest 7f winner, is a half-sister to 5 winners. The second dam, Rosse (by Kris), a

useful dual 7f winner, was listed-placed and is a half-sister to 9 winners including the Group 1 1m Coronation Stakes winner Rebecca Sharp and the smart Group 3 11.5f Lingfield Derby Trial winner Mystic Knight. (Wellington Group Syndicate).

275. SHADEN (IRE)
b.f. Kodiac – Lady Avenger (Namid). February 19. Second foal. 40,000Y. Tattersalls October Book 2. Tony Nerses. Half-sister to the winner I'll Be Your Clown (by Aqlaam). The dam, a fairly useful 2-y-o 5f winner, was second in the listed National Stakes. The second dam, Shioda (by Bahri), is an unplaced half-sister to 8 winners.(Saleh Al Homaizi & Imad Al Sagar).

276. WAVELESS
b.f. Three Valleys – Wemyss Bay (Sadler's Wells). February 18. Third foal. The dam is an unraced sister to the 1m (at 2 yrs) and Group 1 10f Grand Prix de Paris winner Beat Hollow and a half-sister to 3 winners including the US Grade 3 winner Yaralino. The second dam, Wemyss Bight (by Dancing Brave), a very smart filly, won 5 races including the Group 1 12f Irish Oaks and the Group 2 12f Prix de Malleret. (Khalid Abdulla).

277. ZEEBEE
gr.f. Zebedee – Etta Place (Hawk Wing). April 6. First foal. The dam is an unplaced half-sister to 4 winners including the listed placed Ti Adora. The second dam, Wavy Up (by Brustolon), won once at 3 yrs in France and is a half-sister to 5 winners including the US Grade 2 and French Group 3 winner Wavy Up. (Biddestone Racing Partnership).

MICK CHANNON
278. ACTS OF FOLLY (SPA) ★★★★
ch.f. King's Best – Jezebel (Owington). March 18. Eighth foal. 20,000Y. Tattersalls December. Nawara Stud. Sister to the fair French 9f winner Crown Prince and half-sister to the 2014 French 2-y-o 7f winner Isis, the fairly useful triple 6f winner Pearl Ice (both by Iffraaj) and a winner in Italy by Royal Applause. The dam, a useful Italian 2-y-o listed 6f winner, was third in the Group 3 6f Prix de Seine-et-Oise. The second dam, Just Ice (by Polar Falcon), a fairly useful winner over 5f and 6f here and in France including

a listed event, is a half-sister to 11 winners including the listed winners Always On A Sunday and Palmetto Express. (Prince A A Faisal). *"She's very nice. I haven't done a lot with her yet but she looks to have a very good temperament for a King's Best. I'd certainly mark her down as one to keep your eyes open for. I like her a lot – she's very nice and I'd guess seven furlongs would be her starting point".*

279. ANGELIC GUEST (IRE) ★★★★

b.f. Dark Angel – Kelsey Rose (Most Welcome). March 6. Ninth foal. 155,000Y. Tattersalls October Book 1. Gill Richardson. Sister to the useful 6f (at 2 yrs) to 1m winner and Group 1 Lockinge Stakes second Sovereign Debt and half-sister to the very useful 6f (at 2 yrs) and Group 3 Fred Darling Stakes winner Puff (by Camacho), the quite useful 2-y-o dual 7f winner Marked Card (by Kheleyf), and the fair 2-y-o 6f winner Golden Rosie (by Exceed And Excel). The dam, a fairly useful listed-placed 2-y-o 5f winner of 3 races, is a half-sister to 3 winners. The second dam, Duxyana (by Cyrano de Bergerac), is an unraced half-sister to 8 winners. (John Guest Racing Ltd). *"She's very nice but not one of your early Dark Angel's. A lovely big filly with a lot of size and scope, I think she'll be ready come Goodwood time in late July".*

280. ASHJAN ★★

b.c. Medicean – Violet (Mukaddamah). March 18. Twelfth foal. £58,000Y. Doncaster Premier. Gill Richardson. Half-brother to 5 winners including the dual 6f and subsequent US Grade 2 winner and Grade 1 second Starlarks (by Mujahid), the quite useful 1m to 9.3f winner of 5 races Boo (by Namaqualand) and the modest 7f and 1m winner Kannon (by Kyllachy). The dam, a fair 6f and 8.5f winner, is a full or half-sister to 8 winners including the 10.4f John Smiths Handicap and triple Hong Kong stakes winner and Group 2 third Sobriety. The second dam, Scanno's Choice (by Pennine Walk), a middle-distance placed maiden, is a half-sister to the US Grade 2 winner Dilmoun. (Jaber Abdullah). *"He's going to be a six/seven furlongs colt but you'd expect that from his pedigree. He's fine and I'm happy with him but we haven't got stuck into our two-year-olds yet. They've done away with a lot of the early 2-y-o races unfortunately, so there's not a lot to aim for during April".*

281. BETSY COED ★★★

b.f. Raven's Pass – Lucky Norwegian (Almutawakel). April 21. Sixth foal. €95,000Y. Goffs Orby. Gill Richardson. Half-sister to the quite useful 2-y-o dual 7f winner Astonishment (by Desert Style) and the fair 6f and 7f winner Charter (by Elusive City). The dam won one race in Norway at 3 yrs and is a half-sister to 3 other minor winners and to the dams of Elusive Wave (Group 1 French 2,000 Guineas) and Langs Lash (Group 2 Queen Mary Stakes). The second dam, Echoes (by Niniski), won the Group 3 Prix Corrida and is a half-sister to 5 winners. (Nick and Olga Dhandsa & John and Zoe Webster). *"She's a nice filly, very good-looking and just needs some sunshine like a lot of them at this time of the year. She's got a bit of size and scope so we'll be looking at six/seven furlongs for her in mid-season".*

282. BLACKLISTER ★★★

br.c. Lawman – Lebenstanz (Singspiel). April 1. Sixth foal. 22,000Y. Tattersalls October Book 2. Gill Richardson. Half-brother to the moderate 10f winner My Renaissance (by Medicean) and to the minor Italian 1m (at 2 yrs) and 7.5f winner Sapperton (by Key Of Luck). The dam, a minor winner in France, is a half-sister to 5 winners including the dual Group 3 winner Boreas. The second dam, Reamur (by Top Ville), is a placed half-sister to 5 winners. *"He's not supposed to be an early colt but he goes very well and he's a nice colt. He's a 2-y-o for sure and you could possibly run him over five furlongs by the way he looks and how he's developing, but he's defnitely more of a six/seven furlong 2-y-o".*

283. BRESLIN ★★★

ch.c. Atlantic Sport – Aries (Big Shuffle). March 9. £3,000Y. Ascot December. Not sold. Half-brother to the quite useful 6f (including at 2 yrs) and 5f winner of 3 races Jinky (by Noverre), to the quite useful 2-y-o 6f winner Planet Red (by Bahamian Bounty) and the modest 1m (at 2 yrs), 10f and hurdles winner McVicar (by Tobougg). The dam, a fair 2-y-o 7f winner, is a full or half-sister to 6 winners in Germany. The second dam, Auenlust (by Surumu), won 3 races over 1m in Germany and is a full or half-sister to 11 winners. (Living Legend Racing Partnrship). *"He's a half-brother to a few winners we've had and is named after the owner of all of them who passed away last year. He's not going to be really early but I like him, he's a nice colt and he'll certainly have the speed for six furlongs. These Atlantic Sport 2-y-o's of mine are good".*

284. CIZOUS ★★★★
b.f. Sixties Icon – Rose Cheval (Johannesburg). March 17. Third foal. Sister to the fair 2-y-o dual 5f winner Scargill and half-sister to the modest 2014 5f and 6f placed 2-y-o El Che (by Winker Watson). The dam, a fair 7f (at 2 yrs) to 9f placed maiden, is a half-sister to 2 winners in North America. The second dam, La Samanna (by Trempolino), won 2 minor races at 3 and 4 yrs in the USA and is a half-sister to 5 winners. (Norman Court Stud). *"Very nice, she ought to be a 2-y-o to watch out for. She's well put together, solid and good-bodied. Looks a 2-y-o type".*

285. COOPERESS ★★★
b.f. Sixties Icon – Vilnius (Imperial Dancer). March 27. Second foal. Half-sister to the quite useful 2014 2-y-o 5f and 6f winner Honest Bob'S (by Winker Watson). The dam, a modest 5f (including at 2 yrs) and 6f winner of 5 races, is a half-sister to the fairly useful 2-y-o dual 5f winner Lyric Ace. The second dam, Aces Dancing (by Big Shuffle), a quite useful 2-y-o 5f winner, is a sister to the German Group 2 winner Auenklang and to the German listed winner Auenweise and a half-sister to 6 winners. (Norman Court Stud). *"A filly with a bit of size to her, I'll wait for the six furlong races because she's a bit unfurnished, but she's nice and I could see her winning in May or June".*

286. CUPPATEE ★★★
b.f. Canford Cliffs – Fanditha (Danehill Dancer). March 21. First foal. The dam, a quite useful 7f (at 2 yrs) to 10f winner of 4 races, was listed-placed and is a half-sister to the useful 2-y-o 7f winner and Group 3 second Lord High Admiral. The second dam, Splendid (by Mujtahid), was placed once over 6f at 2 yrs and is a half-sister to the listed 12f winner

Peking Opera. (Mrs T Burns). *"A little Canford Cliffs filly out of a mare I trained, she was fairly late coming in but she's a good, strong 2-y-o".*

287. CUSTOM ★★★★
b.f. Lilbourne Lad – Margaux Magique (Xaar). February 20. Second foal. 13,000Y. Tattersalls October Book 2. Gill Richardson. Half-sister to the fair 2014 7f placed 2-y-o Hawkin (by Big Bad Bob). The dam, a minor winner at 4 yrs in Germany, is a half-sister to 4 winners including the Group 2 German 2,000 Guineas winner Royal Power. The second dam, Magic Touch (by Fairy King), is an unraced half-sister to 5 winners including the German 2,000 Guineas winner Sharp Prod. (Insignia). *"She goes well and could run at five furlongs but would certainly be a six furlong 2-y-o. You need to put her in your list".*

288. EPSOM ICON ★★★
b.f. Sixties Icon – Hairspray (Bahamian Bounty). March 22. Second foal. 9,500Y. Tattersalls December. Not sold. Half-sister to the unplaced 2015 2-y-o First Class Mail (by Winker Watson). The dam, a fairly useful 6f winner of 4 races (including at 2 yrs), is a sister to one winner and a half-sister to 4 winners including the quite useful 6f (at 2 yrs) and 1m winner Watneya. The second dam, Quickstyx (by Night Shift), a fair 1m winner, is a half-sister to 5 winners including the smart 12f listed winner and US dual Grade 1 placed Red Fort and the useful 12f listed winner Red Carnation. (Epsom Stars Racing). *"She's tall and will probably be better when the six/seven furlong races come along, but she shows a bit of speed and we're happy with her. The dam was a six furlong type and this filly will definitely get further".*

289. ETTIE HART (IRE) ★★
b.f. Bushranger – Miss Megs (Croco Rouge). February 11. €8,000Y. Tattersalls Ireland September. Gill Richardson. Half-sister to the quite useful 2-y-o 6f winner Chips O'Toole (by Fasliyev), to the fair 6f to 1m winner of 5 races Presumido (by Iffraaj) and to a winner in Norway by Danetime. The dam, a fair 9f and 11f winner in Ireland, is a half-sister to 3 winners including the listed winner Santa Isobel. The second dam, Atlantic Record (by Slip Anchor), is an unraced full or half-sister to

4 winners. (Lord Ilsley Racing). *"She was fine and then pulled a hamstring which has held us up a bit, but give these horses a month and they turn themselves inside out. She'll be one for the second half of the season".*

290. FERNTINA ★★★
b.f. Sixties Icon – The Screamer (Insan). April 8. Sister to the quite useful 2014 2-y-o 6f winner Juventas and to a hurdles winner by Imperial Dancer. The dam, a 12f winner on the flat, won 5 races over jumps. The second dam, Augusta Victoria (by Callernish), is an unraced half-sister to 5 winners. (Norman Court Stud). *"Very nice, she's had the odd little setback but she's very good-looking. To look at her she's one to die for and she would be a 2-y-o, but I haven't had a clear run with her yet".*

291. FIUNTACH (IRE) ★★★
b.f. Sixties Icon – Fiumicino (Danehill Dancer). February 18. The dam, a fairly useful 2-y-o 1m winner, was listed-placed and is a half-sister to the German 2-y-o 7f winner Bagutta Sun. The second dam, Valhalla (by Sadler's Wells), ran twice unplaced and is a half-sister to the winners and Group 3 placed Sugar Ray and Gaspar Van Wittel. (Norman Court Stud). *"A lovely filly but one for seven furlongs. She goes alright now, which makes me think she'll be fine when she fills out later on".*

292. GANDVIK (IRE) ★★★
b.c. Baltic King – Regal Lustre (Averti). March 30. Fifth foal. €4,000Y. Tattersalls Ireland September. Gill Richardson. Half-brother to the Swedish winner at 2 and 3 yrs Catch A Grenade (by Kodiac). The dam, a modest dual 5f placed 2-y-o, is a half-sister to 4 winners including the fairly useful listed-placed and subsequent US stakes winner Royal Rebuke. The second dam, Noble Lustre (by Lyphard's Wish), was a modest 4-y-o 6f winner. (Lord Ilsley Racing). *"Quite a nice colt that goes well, he's had a touch of sore shins but he's a 2-y-o alright".*

293. HARLEQUEEN ★★★
b.f. Canford Cliffs – Aurelia (Rainbow Quest). March 26. Seventh foal. 32,000Y. Tattersalls October Book 1. Gill Richardson. Half-sister to Wardell (by Rip Van Winkle), unplaced in one start at 2 yrs in 2014, to the quite useful 7f (at 2 yrs) and 12f winner Aurorian (by Fantastic Light) and the fair 7f to 10f winner of 4 races Six Silver Lane (by Aussie Rules). The dam, a fair 2-y-o 10f winner, is a half-sister to 8 winners including the dam of the Grade 1 Northern Dancer Turf Stakes winner Forte Dei Marmi. The second dam, Fern (by Shirley Heights), a fairly useful 12f winner and listed 10f Lupe Stakes third, is a half-sister to 6 winners including the Group 1 Fillies Mile winner and Oaks second Shamshir. (Harlequin Direct). *"A nice filly with a bit of size, she's a rangy type. We've just got started with her".*

294. HARLEQUIN ROCK ★★★★
b.c. Rock Of Gibraltar – Berry Baby (Rainbow Quest). February 25. Fourth foal. 35,000Y. Tattersalls October Book 2. Gill Richardson. Half-brother to the fair 12f winner Mabdhool (by Mount Nelson) and to the modest 1m winner The Codger (by Observatory). The dam, a modest 14f winner, is a half-sister to the very useful 2-y-o dual 7f winner and multiple Group 3 placed Measuring Time. The second dam, Inchberry (by Barathea), was placed 7 times including when second in a listed event over 1m at 2 yrs and fourth in the Oaks and is a half-sister to 5 winners including the very useful 12f listed winner Inchiri. (Harlequin Direct). *"A smashing colt, we're just a bit behind at present so he's not on the early list. He's built like a bull".*

295. HARLEQUIN TWIST ★★★
b.f. Acclamation – Triton Dance (Hector Protector). January 25. Fifth living foal. 80,000Y. Tattersalls October Book 2. Gill Richardson. Half-sister to the fair 2-y-o 7f winner Miblish (by Teofilo) and to the useful Irish dual 7f winner and Group 3 Tetrarch Stakes third Count John (by Intikhab). The dam, an Irish 2-y-o 5f winner, is a half-sister to 4 winners including the 2-y-o Group 2 6f Cherry Hinton Stakes winner Jewel In The Sand and the German 3-y-o listed 6f winner Davignon. The second dam, Dancing Drop (by Green Desert), a useful dual 6f winner, was listed-placed 5 times and is a half-sister to 9 winners. (Harlequin Direct). *"She had a little bit of a setback so she hasn't done much yet but she's a nice filly, not an early type, but she'll be fine".*

296. HARRISON ★★★
b.c. Sixties Icon – Excellent Day (Invincible Spirit). February 23. Second foal. Half-brother to the unplaced 2014 2-y-o May One (by Winker Watson). The dam, a fair 5f (at 2 yrs) and 7f winner, is a half-sister to 2 winners including Dalkey Girl, a quite useful 2-y-o 5f winner here and listed placed over 12f at 4 yrs in Scandinavia. The second dam, Tosca (by Be My Guest), is an unraced half-sister to 8 minor winners here and abroad. *"He's going to need six/seven furlongs and he shows bags of ability. I like him, he's got a bit of size about him and he should get a trip eventually but the dam won over five furlongs, so I don't know. A nice colt though".*

297. JAADU (FR) ★★★★
b.c. Holy Roman Emperor – Reine Violette (Fly To The Stars). May 9. Third foal. €90,000Y. Goffs Orby. Gill Richardson. The dam is an unraced half-sister to 5 minor winners. The second dam, Princesse Mimi (by American Prince), a minor dual 3-y-o winner in France, is a sister to the French Group 3 winner Prince Ruffian and a half-sister to 2 winners. *"A big, strong horse, one with a bit of size about him and he's certainly one to put in the book. He's a real nice horse and whether it's five or six furlongs the trip wouldn't matter to him".*

298. JERSEY BREEZE ★★★★
gr.f. Dark Angel – Sixfields Flyer (Desert Style). January 20. Fourth foal. €105,000Y. Goffs Orby. Gill Richardson. Sister to the quite useful 2-y-o 6f and 7f winner Malachim Mist and half-sister to the fair 6f winner Rich Forever and the Singapore winner Flambard House (both by Camacho). The dam, a moderate 1m placed maiden, is a half-sister to 6 winners including Rich Ground (Group 3 July Stakes). The second dam, Gratclo (by Belfort), a modest winner of 5 races from 2 to 4 yrs, is a half-sister to 3 winners. (Mrs S G Bunney). *"Yes, she's smashing – she's got to be in the book. We haven't really done much speed work but what bits we've done she shows plenty. Everything is nice about her".*

299. KASSIA ★★★★
b.f. Acclamation – Speedy Sonata (Stravinsky). April 27. Fifth foal. €400,000Y. Goffs Orby. Gill Richardson. Half-sister to the very useful 2-y-o 6f winner and Group 2 Mill Reef Stakes second Rufford (by Invincible Spirit) and to the fairly useful 2-y-o 6f winner Yesnabay (by Grand Slam). The dam won 6 races from 2 to 4 yrs in the USA and was stakes-placed and is a half-sister to 6 winners. The second dam, Sandshell (by Silver Hawk), is a placed sister to the Prix de Diane winner Lady In Silver and a half-sister to 8 winners. (Jon & Julia Aisbitt). *"An absolute cracker – she could be anything. She was expensive but I don't think the money was wasted. She could win over five furlongs but six would be perfect for her".*

300. LUNAR SON ★★★★
gr.c. Medicean – Moon Empress (Rainbow Quest). March 20. Fourth foal. 50,000Y. Tattersalls October Book 3. Gill Richardson. Half-brother to the useful 2014 2-y-o 1m winner and Group 3 Autumn Stakes second Restorer (by Mastercraftsman). The dam, a fair dual 12f winner, is out of the French listed-placed winner Diamoona (by Last Tycoon), herself a half-sister to 8 winners including the French Group winners Diamond Mix, Diamond Dance and Diasilixa. *"He's a smasher, goes really well and shows plenty of dash. He looks sharp but we'll probably wait for six furlongs with him. One to look out for".*

301. MINDBENDER ★★★
b.c. Acclamation – Magic Eye (Nayef). February 28. First foal. 60,000Y. Tattersalls October Book 1. Not sold. The dam, a German multiple listed 1m winner, is a half-sister to 7 winners including the useful 6f to 1m winner and listed-placed Dabbers Ridge. The second dam, Much Commended (by Most Welcome), a useful 2-y-o 7f winner, was second in the Group 2 Italian 1,000 Guineas and is a sister to the Grade 2 San Marcos Handicap and Dee Stakes winner Prize Giving and a half-sister to 5 winners and to the placed dam of the dual US Grade 1 winner Alpride. (Chris Wright and Emily Asprey). *"A nice, big colt, he needs a bit of time to furnish".*

302. MALAIKA ★★★
b.f. Sixties Icon – Evanesce (Lujain). May 4. Sister to the fair 2-y-o dual 7f winner Yorkshire Icon and to the fair 2-y-o 5f winner Amahoro and half-sister to the modest 2-y-o dual 5f seller winner Selinda (by Piccolo) and the fair

6f winner (including at 2 yrs) to 2m and jumps winner Alfraamsay (by Fraam). The dam, a fair 2-y-o 6f winner, is a half-sister to 4 winners. The second dam, Search Party (Rainbow Quest), a fair 8.3f and 10f placed maiden, is a half-sister to 5 winners including the 6f (at 2 yrs) and US Grade 1 10f winner Bequest. (Gill & Dave Hedley). *"Not an early 2-y-o but she's from a family that all seem to win and she'll be the same. Probably a seven furlong type for the second half of the season".*

303. MOTDAW ★★
b.f. Motivator – Dawnus (Night Shift). April 28. Eighth foal. 30,000Y. Tattersalls October Book 2. G Howson. Sister to the quite useful dual 10f winner Initiator and half-sister to the very useful Irish 2-y-o listed 6f and subsequent US 1m winner Longhunter and the quite useful 2-y-o 6f and 7f winner Beedee (by Beat Hollow). The dam, a useful listed 10f winner, is a half-sister to 4 winners. The second dam, the French 1m winner Dame's Violet (by Groom Dancer), is a full or half-sister to 6 winners including the Group 2 Princess Of Wales's Stakes winner Wagon Master. (Derek & Jean Clee). *"She's a backward filly and not very big, but she's done well. Quite a nice filly for the second half of the season".*

304. OCTOBER STORM ★★
b.c. Shirocco – Cyber Star (King's Best). January 25. First foal. 85,000Y. Tattersalls October Book 1. Gill Richardson. The dam is an unplaced half-sister to the Oaks and Irish Oaks second Shirocco Star. The second dam, Spectral Star (by Unfuwain), a fair 11.8f winner, is a half-sister to 7 winners including the Group 3 7f Tetrarch Stakes winner and Irish 2,000 Guineas second France. (Jon & Julia Aisbitt). *"One for later on, he was expensive but Shirocco's don't usually make 2-y-o's and this colt is from a staying family".*

305. OPAL TIARA (IRE) ★★★
b.f. Thousand Words – Zarafa (Fraam). March 18. First foal. 1,800Y. Ascot December. Not sold. The dam is an unraced half-sister to 5 winners. The second dam, Search Party (Rainbow Quest), a fair 8.3f and 10f placed maiden, is a half-sister to 5 winners including the 6f (at 2 yrs) and US Grade 1 10f winner

Bequest. (Gill & Dave Hedley). *"This filly goes well and she'll be a real fun 2-y-o we can get on with".*

306. PACCHES ★★★★
b.br.f. Clodovil – Ringarooma (Erhaab). April 7. Fifth foal. 23,000Y. Tattersalls October Book 3. Gill Richardson. Half-brother to the 2014 Italian 2-y-o winner Starting Grid (by Fast Company) and to a minor 4-y-o winner abroad by Kyllachy. The dam, a moderate 4-y-o 10f winner, is a half-sister to 2 winners and to the dams of the Group 2 winners Wi Dud and Tariq. The second dam, Tatouma (by The Minstrel), a quite useful 2-y-o 5f and 6f winner, is a half-sister to 4 winners. (The Wentworth Amigos). *"They'll have a lot of fun with this filly. She'll win, shows plenty of speed and is exactly what you want. The partnership came here and picked her out by themselves, so I'm delighted for them".* **TRAINERS' BARGAIN BUY**

307. ROCKCLIFFE ★★★
b.c. Notnowcato – Hope Island (Titus Livius). March 8. Fifth foal. €30,000Y. Tattersalls Ireland September. Gill Richardson. Half-brother to the quite useful triple 6f winner Rocksilla (by Rock Of Gibraltar). The dam, a modest 1m winner at 3 yrs, is a half-sister to 4 winners including the smart Group 3 6f Greenlands Stakes winner of 6 races Moon Unit. The second dam, Chapka (by Green Desert), is a placed half-sister to 7 winners including the top-class middle-distance colt Old Vic. *"I like him, he'll need six furlongs at least but he's a nice sort and he seems to be improving as time goes on".*

308. SHINE LIKEADIAMOND ★★★★
ch.f. Atlantic Sport – Solmorin (Fraam). Half-sister to the modest 6f (at 2 yrs) and 5f winner Majestic Rose (by Imperial Dancer), to the fairly useful dual 5f winner (including at 2 yrs) Lucky Leigh, the modest 6f (including at 2 yrs) and 5f winner of 4 races Saxonette (both by Piccolo) and the modest dual 1m winner (including at 2 yrs) Alfredtheordinary (by Hunting Lion). The dam is an unplaced half-sister to 2 winners. The second dam, Reclusive (by Sunley Builds), was unraced. *"She does exactly as her name suggests. All the family*

*win, this filly goes really well and looks like a
2-y-o but she's got a bit of size about her too.
An absolute smasher".*

309. SIRI ★★★

br.f. Atlantic Sport – Search Party (Rainbow
Quest). March 20. Half-sister to the 5f and 6f
winner of 8 races, including at 2 yrs, Bateleur
(by Fraam), to the 2-y-o 6f winner Evanesce
(by Lujain), the dual 1m winner at 2 and 3 yrs
Shimba Hills (by Sixties Icon), the 10f to 2m
and hurdles winner Foster's Road (by Imperial
Dancer) – all fair winners, and a 2-y-o winner
in the Czech Republic by Sixties Icon. The
dam, a fair 8.3f and 10f placed maiden, is a
half-sister to 4 winners including the 2-y-o
6f and subsequent US Grade 1 10f winner
Bequest. The second dam, Quest (by The
Minstrel), a winner of 3 races from 9f to 10f, is
a sister to Treizieme (Group 1 Grand Criterium)
and a half-sister to Eastern Mystic (Group 2
Yorkshire Cup). (Gill & Dave Hedley). *"The sire
only covered six mares and all six foals are in
training here. This one isn't going to be racing
until the back-end of the season, but she's nice".*

310. SOPHISTICA ★★★

b.f. Thousand Words – Texas Queen
(Shamardal). March 22. First foal. €56,000Y.
Tattersalls Ireland September. Gill Richardson.
The dam, a fair dual 5f winner, is a half-sister
to 3 minor winners. The second dam, Min Asl
Wafi (by Octagonal), a fair 7f placed 3-y-o, is
a half-sister to 7 winners including the high-
class Group 1 1m St James's Palace Stakes and
Group 2 6f Mill Reef Stakes winner Zafeen, the
2-y-o Group 3 7f Prix du Calvados winner Ya
Hajar and the listed 7f winner Atlantic Sport.
(Nick and Olga Dhandsa & John and Zoe
Webster). *"She's a nice filly, she goes well but
won't be real early. One for six furlongs".*

311. SPECIAL QUEEN ★★★

gr.f. Clodovil – Special Lady (Kaldoun). March
3. Tenth foal. 20,000Y. Tattersalls October
Book 3. Gill Richardson. Half-sister to the
dual Group 2 Prix Daniel Wildenstein winner
Special Kaldoun (by Alzao), to the Canadian
3-y-o winner and French listed-placed
Privalova (by Pivotal) and the fairly useful 10f
and 14f winner of 5 races Duke Of Clarence
(by Verglas). The dam was placed at 2 yrs in
France and is a half-sister to 5 minor winners.
The second dam, Macedoine (by King Of
Macedon), won once in France and is a half-
sister to the US Grade 1 Gamely Handicap
winner La Koumia. (Jaber Abdullah). *"She just
needs that little bit of time but shows a bit of
dash. Six furlongs should suit her".*

312. STAR BLAZE ★★★★

b.c. Shamardal – Gallic Star (Galileo). January
28. First foal. The dam, a useful 2-y-o 6f and
listed 1m winner, was third in the Group 2 12f
Ribblesdale Stakes and is a half-sister to one
winner. The second dam, Oman Sea (by Rahy),
a quite useful 2-y-o 6f winner, is a sister to the
Group 3 Criterion Stakes winner Racer Forever.
(Jon & Julia Aisbitt). *"An absolutely smashing
horse and almost the pick of the crop, he's
a lovely colt that appears to have a great
temperament and he could be anything. He
does everything right, he's by the right stallion
and out of a very good Galileo mare who we
also trained. I think we'll be starting him off at
six furlongs".*

313. THAT'LL HAPPEN ★★★

b.c. Atlantic Sport – Musiara (Hunting Lion).
February 20. The dam, a moderate dual 5f
placed 2-y-o, is a half-sister to 5 winners. The
second dam, Search Party (Rainbow Quest),
a fair 8.3f and 10f placed maiden, is a half-
sister to 5 winners including the 6f (at 2 yrs)
and subsequent Grade 1 10f Santa Barbara
Handicap winner Bequest. *"He's sharp and
he goes well. I'm not sure he's one for five
furlongs, but certainly six".*

314. TIGERWOLF (IRE) ★★★★

br.c. Dream Ahead – Singing Field (Singspiel).
April 26. Third living foal. 120,000Y. Tattersalls
October Book 1. Gill Richardson. The dam
is an unraced sister to the French listed 12f
winner and US dual Grade 1 placed Fast And
Furious and a half-sister to 9 winners including
the US Grade 2 winner Herboriste. The second
dam, Helvellyn (by Gone West), a quite useful
2-y-o 8.3f winner, is a half-sister to 6 winners.
(George Materna & Roger Badley). *"He's
certainly one to consider. He's smashing and
goes really well. He could win over five, six,
seven – or whatever. A nice colt, he's got to be
in the book".*

315. UNLIT (IRE) ★★★
b.f. Approve – Riymaisa (Traditionally). March 12. Fourth foal. £20,000Y. Doncaster Premier. Gill Richardson. Half-sister to a 2-y-o winner in Sweden by Majestic Missile. The dam, placed at 3 yrs in France, is a half-sister to 5 winners including the listed 10f Pretty Polly Stakes winner Riyalma. The second dam, Riyafa (by Kahyasi), was a listed 12f winner at Ascot. (Insignia). *"She goes really well. The Insignia syndicate look to have two really nice 2-y-o's with me. This filly is sharp and the sire got plenty of winners last year".*

316. WITHOUT DOUBT ★★★
gr.f. Clodovil – Justice System (Criminal Type). April 21. Twelfth foal. €32,000Y. Goffs Orby. Gill Richardson. Sister to the fairly useful 7f and 1m (here) and Australian triple Group 2 middle-distance winner Moriarty and half-sister to 3 winners including the quite useful 1m and subsequent US winner Leave To Appeal (by Victory Note) and the modest 2-y-o 5f and 6f winner Just A Carat (by Distinctly North). The dam is an unplaced half-sister to 10 winners including Lear Spear (Group 2 Prince of Wales's Stakes). The second dam, Golden Gorse (by His Majesty), won 5 minor races in the USA and is a half-sister to 10 winners including Lotus Pool (listed Irish 2,000 Guineas Trial and US dual Grade 3). (Jaber Abdullah). *"She's a nice filly and a half-sister to a very good horse in Moriarty. She's OK and doing everything right".*

317. UNNAMED ★★★
b.c. Sakhee's Secret – Blakeshall Rose (Tobougg). May 3. Sixth foal. Half-brother to the quite useful listed-placed 5f and 6f winner of 4 races at 2 and 3 yrs Effie B (by Sixties Icon) and the modest 2-y-o dual 6f winner Miss Muga (by Imperial Dancer). The dam, a modest 6f placed maiden, is a half-sister to 2 winners. The second dam, Giggleswick Girl (by Full Extent), was a modest 6f (at 2 yrs) and 5f winner of 4 races. *"A homebred that came in a bit late, so he's a bit behind, but he's a nice colt and I think he'll be a 2-y-o. Nice and strong, you wouldn't think he was a May foal".*

318. UNNAMED ★★★
b.c. Air Chief Marshal – Bonne Mere (Stepneyev). March 13. Fifth foal. 16,000Y.

Tattersalls October Book 2. Gill Richardson. Half-brother to the very useful listed winner of 5 races at 2 and 3 yrs, including a listed event, Mister Hughie and to the fair 6f winner Big Tex (by Captain Rio). The dam, a listed-placed winner of 5 races, is a half-sister to 2 minor winners in France. The second dam, Gardine (by Fast Topaze), a listed-placed winner of 5 races, is a half-sister to 3 winners. (Jaber Abdullah). *"A bloody lovely horse he is. He could be anything, he hasn't missed a day and the sire has had a lot of winners in France. Probably more of a back-end type 2-y-o".*

319. UNNAMED ★★★
b.f. Bahamian Bounty – Clodilla (Clodovil). February 6. First foal. The dam, a minor Italian 3-y-o winner, is a sister to one winner and a half-sister to 3 winners including the fairly useful 2-y-o 7f winner and listed-placed One More Road and the fairly useful 5f winner of 4 races and Group 3 Molecomb Stakes third Archers Road. The second dam, Somoushe (by Black Minnaloushe), is an unraced half-sister to 9 winners including the 1m 2-y-o and subsequent German Group 1 10f winner Ransom O'War. *"She was showing all the right signs of being early and then had a bit of a setback. She's back cantering now though and if I can get on with her I will do, because she's a real sharp little sort".*

320. UNNAMED ★★
b.f. Sixties Icon – Fading Away (Fraam). April 27. Sister to the fair 2-y-o 6f and 7f winner of 3 races Porteous and to the fair 2-y-o 6f winner Fadeintoinfinity and half-sister to the moderate 2014 7f placed 2-y-o Invisible Eye (by Winker Watson), the modest 10f and hurdles winner Brilliant Barca (by Imperial Dancer) and the modest 2-y-o 7f winner Alphacino (by Hunting Lion). The dam is an unraced sister to the useful 5f (at 2 yrs) to 1m winner Dayglow Dancer out of the unraced Fading (by Pharly). (Peter Taplin). *"She's nice, probably one for mid-season and there are loads of winners in the family".*

321. UNNAMED ★★★
gr.c. Lawman – Indian Dumaani (Indian Ridge). May 2. Second foal. 20,000Y. Tattersalls October Book 2. Gill Richardson. The dam won 4 minor races at 2 and 3 yrs in Italy and

is a half-sister to 2 winners. The second dam, Mubadalah (by Dumaani), a modest 7f fourth placed 2-y-o, is a half-sister to 8 winners including the Group 1 Queen Elizabeth Stakes II winner Maroof. *"I have two very nice Lawman 2-y-o's. He was a May foal and he'll be a seven furlong type but he shows enough now to say he'll be alright".*

322. UNNAMED ★★★★
b.c. Intense Focus – Royal Esteem (Mark Of Esteem). March 19. Fourth foal. £48,000Y. Doncaster Premier. Gill Richardson. Half-brother to the fair triple 1m winner Hostile Fire (by Iffraaj) and to a 2-y-o winner in Russia by Ramonti. The dam, a dual winner at 3 yrs in the USA, is a half-sister to one winner abroad. The second dam, Inchacooley (by Rhoman Rule), an Irish and US listed winner of 6 races at 3 to 8 yrs, is a half-sister to one winner. (Malih Al Basti). *"He's a smashing horse. I don't think we'll see him until May or June, but physically he was always real nice and he's made up into a really lovely individual now. A strong colt, I haven't done enough with him to say when exactly he'll be ready, but it'll certainly be in the first half of the season".*

323. UNNAMED ★★★
b.f. Sixties Icon – Summer Cry (Street Cry). April 17. Fourth foal. 800foal. Tattersalls December. Norman Court Stud. The dam is an unraced half-sister to 2 minor winners in the USA. The second dam, Midsummer Sun (by Coronado's Quest), a minor US 3-y-o winner, is a half-sister to 2 winners. (Norman Court Stud). *"She's a scopey type and one for much later on, but she goes very well".*

324. UNNAMED ★★★
b.f. Sixties Icon – Sweet Pilgrim (Talkin' Man). February 23. Second foal. 1,000foal. Tattersalls December. Norman Court Stud. Sister to Run By Faith, placed fourth once over 7f from two starts at 2 yrs in 2014. The dam, a modest 6f winner, is a half-sister to 4 winners. The second dam, Faraway Moon (by Distant Relative), is a placed half-sister to 5 minor winners. (Norman Court Stud). *"She was cheap but she goes well and shows a bit of speed. Not a big filly, but she looks like making a 2-y-o a bit earlier than some by the sire".*

325. UNNAMED ★★★
b.c. Zamindar – Valoria (Hernando). April 23. Third foal. 14,000Y. Tattersalls December. Gill Richardson. Half-brother to the 2014 8.5f placed 2-y-o Vanishing (by Sir Percy). The dam is an unraced half-sister to 3 winners including the smart listed 10f winner and Group 1 Oaks third Volume and the useful dual 1m winner (including at 2 yrs) Validus (by Zamindar). The second dam, Victoire Finale (by Peintre Celebre), a useful French 1m winner, is a half-sister to numerous winners including the French Group 2 winner Vertical Speed out of the Group 1 Prix du Cadran winner Victoire Bleue. *"A nice horse he is, but he was quite late coming in and is one of the most backward ones we've got. I'm very pleased with him and he's a good-looking colt but he wouldn't be an early 2-y-o".*

PETER CHAPPLE-HYAM

326. AHRAAM ★★
b.c. Roderic O'Connor – Simla Sunset (One Cool Cat). April 24. First foal. 23,000Y. Tattersalls October Book 2. A Elliott. The dam, a quite useful 7f and 1m winner of 4 races at 3 to 5 yrs, is a half-sister to 4 winners including the useful 1m to 11f winner of 12 races Emerald Wilderness and the fairly useful dual 5f (at 2 yrs) and 6f winner and listed-placed Ooh Aah Camara. The second dam, Simla Bibi (by Indian Ridge), placed over 1m at 2 yrs, is a half-sister to 10 winners including the German Group 1 winner Lady Jane Digby and the triple Group 3 winner Gateman. (Mr A R Elliott). *"He'll want plenty of time but he moves nicely and I see him as being one for seven furlongs in July or August. He's a straightforward colt".*

327. BEAST MODE (IRE) ★★★★
b.c. Cape Cross – Faithful One (Dubawi). April 7. €130,000Y. Arqana Deauville October. David Redvers. The dam, a quite useful listed-placed 7f and 1m winner, is half-sister to one winner. The second dam, Have Faith (by Machiavellian), a quite useful 2-y-o 7f winner, is a sister to the useful UAE winner of 7 races and Group 3 third Opportunist and a half-sister to the Group 1 Nassau Stakes winner Favourable Terms and the French listed winner Modern History. (Qatar Racing Ltd). *"He does everything perfectly, not the biggest horse in*

the world but he's a sharpish colt for a Cape Cross and a good mover. He should be out in mid-season, he'll be a seven furlong horse and I do like him".

328. EMARATI BIN DUBAI ★★★
b.c. Royal Applause – Umseyat (Arch). February 11. First foal. €20,000Y. Tattersalls Ireland September. Allan Bloodlines. The dam, a quite useful 2-y-o 1m winner, is a half-sister to 3 winners the smart listed 11f winner and Group 2 12f Princess Of Wales's Stakes second Alwaary. The second dam, Tabrir (by Unfuwain), is an unraced sister to 2 winners including the 1,000 Guineas and Group 2 7f Rockfel Stakes winner Lahan and a half-sister to 2 winners. (Khalifa Ahmad Al Shaikh Association). *"He's quite sharp and the plan will be to run him over six furlongs in May and then see how we go. I don't mind him at all".*

329. FREDDIE FREELOADER ★★★
b.c. Zoffany – Spinning Wings (Spinning World). March 2. First foal. £22,000Y. Doncaster Premier. Global Equine. The dam, a quite useful 12f to 2m winner of 4 races, is a half-sister to a hurdles winner. The second dam, Wings To Soar (by Woodman), is a placed half-sister to 4 minor winners. (Paul Hancock). *"He's quite a small colt but I've done a bit with him already and he doesn't go too bad. He'll win races, without being a superstar, and I don't mind him at all. I'll try him at five furlongs but he'll probably be better at six".*

330. GEMMULAL ★★★
b.f. Acclamation – Elvira Delight (Desert Style). February 9. First foal. 55,000Y. Tattersalls October Book 1. Not sold. The dam, a modest 1m winner, is a half-sister to 4 winners including the dual Group 1 King's Stand Stakes winner and sire Equiano and the useful listed 7f winner Evita Peron. The second dam, Entente Cordiale (by Ela-Mana-Mou), placed third once over 12f from 3 starts, is a half-sister to 4 winners. (Saleh Al Homaizi & Imad Al Sagar). *"She's coming on really nice and is quite a big, strong filly. She's pulled herself together and I can't knock her whatsoever. She hits the ground a bit hard so she may want a bit of cut in the ground. One for six furlongs around June time, all being well. She's got plenty of pace and she's not bad at all".*

331. GINGER JOE ★★★ ♠
ch.c. Medicean – Susi Wong (Selkirk). March 21. Ninth foal. £32,000Y. Doncaster Premier. Blandford Bloodstock. Half-brother to 6 winners including the Group 3 St Simon Stakes and Group 3 13f Ormonde Stakes winner Buccellati (by Soviet Star), the Italian listed 2-y-o winner and Group 3 6f Premio Primi Passi second Golden Stud (by In The Wings) and the Scandinavian listed winner La Petite Chinoise (by Dr Fong). The dam, a listed-placed 3-y-o winner in Germany, is a half-sister to 4 winners. The second dam, Stay That Way (by Be My Guest), is an unraced full or half-sister to 8 winners including the Coronation Stakes winner Chalon (dam of the dual Group 1 winner Creator). (Burnham Plastering). *"He's been doing some faster work just lately and he goes well but he shows he's a six furlong horse rather than five. A typical Medicean, he's very laid back, doesn't give you any clues but every now and then he'll go well.*

332. LOHALVAR (FR) ★★
ch.c. Le Havre – Loup The Loup (Loup Solitaire). March 29. €75,000Y. Arqana Deauville October. Stephen Hillen. Half-brother to the French 2-y-o 5f winner and Group 2 5.5f Prix Robert Papin second Louve Rouge (by Gold Away), to the minor French 2m winner Poliloup (by Poliglote) and the French dual 9.5f winner Loenrique (by Enrique). (Mrs Fitri Hay). *"He's done nothing wrong, he'll take a bit of time but I don't mind him at all. Hopefully he's one for July/August, but he will want a trip".*

333. MARSHAL DAN TROOP (IRE) ★★
b.c. Lawman – Corrozal (Cape Cross). March 3. Fourth foal. 35,000Y. Tattersalls October Book 2. P Chapple-Hyam. The dam, a minor German 3-y-o winner, is a half-sister to 3 winners. The second dam, Casanga (by Rainbow Quest), a German Group 3 11f winner, is a half-sister to 11 winners. (Paul Hancock). *"He's just gone a bit weak and backward, but there are no problems with him whatsoever and he's another one for the second half of the season".*

334. MZYOON (IRE) ★★★
b.f. Galileo – High Society (Key Of Luck). April 11. Eighth foal. €240,000Y. Goffs Orby.

Stephen Hillen. Half-sister to the Group 1 Golden Jubilee Stakes and Group 1 6f Haydock Sprint Cup winner Society Rock (by Rock Of Gibraltar), to the fair 14f winner Byron Blue (by Dylan Thomas), the minor German 2-y-o 6f winner Johannesburg Cat (by Johannesburg) and a winner in Greece by One Cool Cat. The dam, an Irish 2-y-o listed 6f and subsequent US stakes winner, was Grade 2 placed and is a half-sister to 4 winners. The second dam, Ela's Gold (by Ela-Mana-Mou), a moderate 6f placed maiden, is a full or half-sister to 6 winners. (Hussain Alabbas Lootah). *"She'll need plenty of time – probably one for around August/September time. She's very nice and a very good specimen – you can't fault her".*

335. PARAFIN YOUNG ★★★★

ch.c. Cape Blanco – Hasty (Invincible Spirit). March 11. First foal. The dam, a fairly useful 7f and subsequent US winner, was third in the Group 3 Oh So Sharp Stakes and is a sister to 2 minor winners and a half-sister to 2 more. The second dam, Saramacca (by Kahyasi), a 12f winner at 4 yrs, is a half-sister to 6 winners. (Mrs Fitri Hay). *"I like him, he's not the biggest horse in the world and he's just got a touch of a sore shin at the moment which is holding us up. He's well put together, the mare was quite quick and initially I thought he'd be one of my first 2-y-o's out. I like him a lot and if I've got one for the Chesham at Royal Ascot it might be him".*

336. PERICLES (IRE) ★★★

ch.c. Danehill Dancer – Althea Rose (Green Desert). April 14. Third foal. 90,000Y. Tattersalls October Book 1. Hugo Merry. Brother to the fair 2014 6f fourth placed 2-y-o Lord North. The dam ran once unplaced and is a half-sister to 9 winners including the top-class National Stakes, Irish 2,000 Guineas and Irish Derby winner Desert King and the Group 3 Mooresbridge Stakes winner Cairdeas. The second dam, Sabaah (by Nureyev), a modest 8.2f placed maiden, is a full or half-sister to 8 winners including the Group 1 1m Queen Elizabeth II Stakes winner Maroof and to the placed dam of the Canadian Grade 2 winner Callwood Dancer. (Mrs Fitri Hay). *"I thought he was quite sharp so I did a bit with him just to have a look but he's gone a bit weak at the*

moment and he needs a bit of time. A good specimen of a horse and a good mover, we'll probably start him off at six furlongs, maybe in July if we're lucky".

337. PLEASURE DOME ★★★

b.f. Makfi – Nouvelle Lune (Fantastic Light). April 28. Fourth foal. 45,000Y. Tattersalls October Book 1. Not sold. Closely related to the fair 6f and 7f winner Glassy Posse (by Dubawi) and half-sister to the quite useful 7f to 9f winner of 8 races Maverik (by Iceman) and the fair 8.5f winner Valley Of Destiny (by Three Valleys). The dam is an unraced half-sister to 6 winners including Audacieuse (Group 3 Prix de Flore winner and dam of the St Leger winner Kingston Hill) and Waiter's Dream (Group 3 Acomb Stakes). The second dam, Sarah Georgina (by Persian Bold), a quite useful 2-y-o 6f winner, is a half-sister to 11 winners including the French 1,000 Guineas winner Danseuse du Soir (dam of the Group 1 Gran Criterium winner Scintillo). *"She's a big filly but floats along the ground. I like her a lot and she's the nicest Makfi I've had. So she could be alright over seven furlongs around about August. Bear in mind that Makfi's all seem to want some cut in the ground".*

338. RESONATOR ★★★

b.c. Compton Place – Saddlers Bend (Refuse To Bend). April 8. Second foal. £26,000Y. Doncaster Premier. Blandford Bloodstock. The dam, a fair winner 6f to 9f winner of 7 races, is a half-sister to 6 winners. The second dam, Sudden Interest (by Highest Honor), a minor dual 3-y-o winner in France, is a half-sister to 4 winners including Sudden Love (Grade 1 E P Taylor Stakes). *"He's just starting to do a bit of work now and he's coming on well. Probably no superstar, but I would have thought he'd be out at the end of May over six furlongs. His conformation is spot on and he'll win races without setting the world alight".*

339. SABRE SQUADRON (IRE) ★★★★

b.c. Lope De Vega – Caravan Of Dreams (Anabaa). March 2. Third foal. 75,000Y. Tattersalls December. Sackville/Donald. Half-brother to the fairly useful 12.5f and 14f winner Weather Watch (by Hurricane Run). The dam, a fair 2-y-o 1m placed maiden, is a half-sister to the dual Group 3 winner and multiple Group 2 placed Royal And Regal and to the listed winner and Group 2 Dante Stakes second Celtic Silence. The second dam, Smart 'n Noble (by Smarten), won the Group 2 Barbara Fritchie Handicap in the USA and is a half-sister to 7 winners. (Mrs Fitri Hay). *"The sire can do nothing wrong and this colt is probably my favourite 2-y-o but he's backward and won't be out until August. He goes really well, he has plenty of pace and six or seven furlongs will suit. He's a good specimen, very correct and good bodied".*

340. SAUTTER ★★★
b.c. Kyllachy – Regency Rose (Danehill). May 3. Fifth foal. 220,000Y. Tattersalls October Book 2. Tony Nerses. Half-brother to the useful 2-y-o Group 3 6.3f Anglesey Stakes winner Regional Counsel, to the fair 1m winner Regal Salute (both by Medicean) and the fair dual 5f winner Eternitys Gate (by Dutch Art). The dam is an unraced sister to the Group 1 6f Cheveley Park Stakes winner Regal Rose and to the Japanese 10f stakes winner Generalist and a half-sister to 8 winners. The second dam, Ruthless Rose (by Conquistador Cielo), ran twice unplaced and is a half-sister to 9 winners including the high-class miler Shaadi. (Saleh Al Homaizi & Imad Al Sagar). *"He cost plenty of money and I've got his half-brother Eternitys Gate here but they're totally different horses. Eternity's Gate is small but this is a big colt that's just gone through a growing phase and he's gone weak, but he does go along well and there are no problems with him whatsoever. Six furlongs around July time will suit him".*

341. SAYEDAATI SAADATI (IRE) ★★★
b.c. Montjeu – Guessing (Kingmambo). February 7. First foal. The dam ran unplaced twice and is a half-sister to numerous winners including the 2-y-o Group 1 7f Prix Jean Luc Lagardere winner Horatio Nelson, the UAE Group 2 winner and Group 1 Eclipse Stakes third Viscount Nelson, the Group 2 7f Rockfel Stakes winner Kitty Matchem and the dual Group 1 placed Red Rock Canyon. The second dam, Imagine (by Sadler's Wells), won the Irish 1,000 Guineas and the Epsom Oaks and is a half-sister to Generous, winner of the Derby, the Irish Derby and the King George VI. (Ahmad Abdulla Al Shaikh & Co). *"There's nothing wrong with him at all, he's from a*

pretty good family and he goes well – in fact he goes too well for a Montjeu at this time of the year so I'm taking him steady. Being a first foal he's just a bit on the small side and he's one for the second half of the season".

342. TIMES LEGACY ★★★
b.c. Cape Cross – Simply Times (Dodge). March 28. Tenth foal. 48,000Y. Tattersalls October Book 1. Not sold. Half-brother to the 2014 7f placed 2-y-o Time Flies (by Exceed And Excel) and to 7 winners including the Group 2 7f Hungerford Stakes and Group 3 6f winner Welsh Emperor (by Emperor Jones), the listed 5f winner of 4 races Majestic Times (by Bluebird), the useful 6f and 7f winner and Group 3 third Brave Prospector (by Oasis Dream) and the fairly useful 5f (at 2 yrs) to 7f winner Forever Times (by So Factual). The dam is an unplaced half-sister to 5 winners. The second dam, Nesian's Burn (by Big Burn), a winner and stakes-placed in the USA, is a half-sister to 9 winners. (Mr A Belshaw). *"I think I've had nearly all of the dam's foals and this one is sharper than most of them. They're all sprinters but they all took a bit of time. He's not the biggest horse in the world but I don't mind him at all and I reckon he'll be out around June time over six furlongs. A good-looking horse, you can't fault him whatsoever".*

343. UNNAMED ★★★★
b.c. Lawman – Mauresmo (Marju). March 25. Second foal. 26,000Y. Tattersalls October Book 2. Troy Steve. The dam is an unraced sister to the winner of 6 races and Group 2 Diadem Stakes second Munjiz and a half-sister to 3 winners. The second dam, Absaar (by Alleged), a fair 11f winner, is a half-sister to 10 winners including Group/Grade 1 winners Annoconnor and At Talaq. (Paul Hancock). *"This is a very big horse but he goes really well and I like him a lot. He'll be better as a 3-y-o than at two, but he could be fairly useful at the back-end I think. He'll want a mile, so no doubt he'll end up in that mile maiden at Doncaster in September I like to target. Hopefully I can get him out before then".* **TRAINERS' BARGAIN BUY**

344. UNNAMED ★★★★
b.c. Lawman – Millay (Polish Precedent). March 31. Eighth foal. €140,000Y. Goffs Orby. David Redvers. Half-brother to the useful 2-y-

o listed 1m winner Chief Barker (by Azamour), to the fairly useful 2-y-o 6f winner Salford Art (by Sir Percy), the moderate 2m winner M'Lady Rousseau (by Selkirk) and a winner in Switzerland by Red Ransom. The dam, a minor winner at 3 yrs in France, is a half-sister to 6 winners including the listed winner Millstreet. The second dam, Mill Path (by Mill Reef), ran once unplaced and is a half-sister to 4 winners including the Irish Oaks winner Give Thanks. (Qatar Racing Ltd). *"He goes along really well. A typical Lawman in that he has a bit of an attitude, but he does nothing wrong at all and he's sharper than my other two Lawman 2-y-o's. He should be out around July time I would have thought over six or seven furlongs. He's got a bit of speed and I like him".*

345. UNNAMED ★★★

b.c. Equiano – Owdbetts (High Estate). March 18. £22,000Y. Doncaster Premier. Blandford Bloodstock. Half-brother to the smart Group 3 5.2f and 6f Wokingham Handicap winner Ratio (by Pivotal), to the fairly useful 5f to 10f of 11 races winner Rochdale (by Bertolini), the fairly useful 6f (including at 2 yrs) and 7f winner Heywood (by Tobougg), the quite useful triple 7f winner Sam Nombulist (by Sleeping Indian) and the fair 2-y-o 6f winners Existentialist (by Exceed And Excel) and Alice Blackthorn (by Forzando). The dam, a fair 7f to 10.2f winner of 4 races, is a half-sister to 3 minor winners. The second dam, Nora Yo Ya (by Ahonoora), ran once unplaced at 2 yrs and is a half-sister to 3 winners. *"He was quite sharp but then he changed a lot and went weak. But recently he's done a couple of bits of faster work and he does go along really nice. I see him as one for July time and he could be pretty useful".*

ROGER CHARLTON

346. ARCHANGEL GABRIEL ★★★★ ♠

b.br.f. Arch – Princess Kris (Kris). January 17. Twelfth foal. 200,000Y. Tattersalls October Book 1. Amanda Skiffington. Sister to the US Grade 1 11f winner Prince Arch and to the minor US winner of 4 races Arty Crafty and half-sister to the 2-y-o Group 1 National Stakes winner Kingsfort (by War Chant) and a minor winner in the USA by Boundary. The

dam, a quite useful 1m winner, is half-sister to 8 winners including Intimate Guest (Group 3 May Hill Stakes) and the dam of the US Grade 1 winner Luas Line. The second dam, As You Desire Me (by Kalamoun), a dual French listed winner over 7.5f and 1m, is a half-sister to the King Edward VII Stakes winner Classic Example. (Chris Humber & Steven Smith). *"A neat, well-built, strong filly that looks fairly forward. She shows speed and looks like making a 2-y-o by the middle of the season, despite this being a middle-distance family".*

347. BANHAM ★★★★

gr.c. Exchange Rate – Palisade (Gone West). May 4. Half-brother to the 2014 6f placed 2-y-o Scooner, to the US Grade 3 7f and Grade 3 1m winner and Grade 1 second Jibboom, the quite useful 7f (at 2 yrs) and 1m winner Hidden Treasure (all by Mizzen Mast), the useful 7f and 1m winner (including at 2 yrs) Self Evident (by Known Fact) and the quite useful 12f winner Action Front (by Aptitude). The dam, a quite useful 2-y-o 7f winner, is a half-sister to the useful 1m winners Boatman (at 2 yrs) and Emplane. The second dam, Peplum (by Nijinsky), a useful winner of the listed Cheshire Oaks, is a half-sister to the 1,000 Guineas winner Al Bahathri. (Khalid Abdulla). *"A nice, attractive colt, although he's a late foal he should be racing from July onwards and he looks promising at this stage. The sire tends to be an influence for speed, so I expect this colt to be a six/seven furlong 2-y-o".*

348. BATTLEMENT ★★★★

gr.f. Dansili – Scuffle (Daylami). March 13. Closely related to the 2014 2-y-o 7f winner, on her only start, Suffused (by Champs Elysees) and half-sister to the quite useful 5.5f and 6f winner Sleep Walk (by Oasis Dream). The dam, a useful triple 1m winner, was listed-placed and is a half-sister to the high-class Group 1 9f Dubai Duty Free and triple Group 3 winner Cityscape and to the very smart Group 2 5f Temple Stakes and multiple Group 1 placed Bated Breath. The second dam, Tantina (by Distant View), a smart winner of 4 races including two listed events over 7f, was Group 3 placed and is a half-sister to 2 winners. (Khalid Abdulla). *"A very well-made, strong, big filly. She hasn't done any work yet but she looks promising and will be a 2-y-o by the middle of the year. You would imagine she'd end up being a miler".*

349. BITTER ORANGE ★★★

ch.f. Dutch Art – Pearl Mountain (Pearl Of Love). February 9. First foal. £27,000Y. Doncaster Premier. Sackville/Donald. The dam, placed over 2m, is a half-sister to 7 winners including the Irish Group 3 Boland Stakes winner Social Harmony and the dam of the Group 1 Tattersalls Gold Cup winner Casual Conquest. The second dam, Latest Chapter (by Ahonoora), is an unraced half-sister to the Grade 1 Belmont Stakes winner Go And Go. (De La Warr Racing). *"A small, neat, sharp filly that's had a bit of a setback. I was hoping she might be reasonably early, but she won't be. It's a mixed pedigree because there's speed on one side and stamina on the other".*

350. BLUE BUTTERFLY ★★★

b.f. Kyllachy – Raysiza (Alzao). May 11. Eleventh foal. Sister to the fairly useful 2-y-o 6f winner and Group 3 Firth Of Clyde Stakes third Highland Daughter and half-sister to 5 winners including the Italian triple listed winner Ryan (by Generous), the fair 7f winners Tikka Masala (by One Cool Cat) and Claim (by Acclamation) and the Italian 2-y-o sprint winner Casina Valadier (by Fath). The dam, a listed 1m winner in Italy, is a half-sister to 5 winners and to the dam of Kinnaird (Prix de l'Opera). The second dam, Raysiya (by Cure The Blues), an Irish 10f and 12f winner, is a half-sister to 5 winners. (A & S Brudenell). *"It's a nice family and she's a good-moving, athletic filly with a bit of scope to her – more than most Kyllachy's I guess. I would have thought she'd be a 2-y-o for July/August".*

351. CHESTER STREET ★★★★ ♠

b.c. Invincible Spirit – Expressive (Falbrav). April 22. Third foal. 70,000Y. Tattersalls October Book 1. Charlie Gordon-Watson. Half-brother to the fair 2-y-o 6f winner Expect (by Invincible Spirit). The dam, a fair 9f winner, is a half-sister to 5 winners including the Group 1 1m Matron Stakes winner Echelon (dam of the Falmouth Stakes winner Integral) and the dual Group 2 1m winner Chic. The second dam, Exclusive (by Polar Falcon), winner of the Group 1 1m Coronation Stakes, is a half-sister to 9 winners including the 2,000 Guineas winner and Derby fourth Entrepreneur and the Epsom Oaks second Dance a Dream. (Sultan Ahmad Shah). *"An attractive horse from a good female family of Cheveley Park Stud's. I think that for an Invincible Spirit he was quite well-bought. He's done well and has a good temperament for one by that sire, I like him, but he was quite a late foal and he won't be early".*

352. CLODIANNA ★★★

gr.f. Clodovil – Indiannie Moon (Fraam). April 24. Fifth foal. 25,000Y. Tattersalls December. Amanda Skiffington. Sister to a winner in the Czech Republic and half-sister to the fair 2014 2-y-o 7f winner Fingal's Cave (by Fast Company) and the fairly useful listed 1m winner Audacia (by Sixties Icon). The dam ran once unplaced and is a sister to the winner and listed-placed Indiannie Star and a half-sister to 4 winners including the German 2-y-o Group 2 6f winner Ajigolo and the useful 5f (including at 2 yrs) and 6f winner of 5 races and Group 3 Cornwallis Stakes third Kickboxer (by Clodovil). The second dam, Ajig Dancer (by Niniski), a quite useful 7f winner of 4 races, is a half-sister to 2 winners. (Paul Inglett & Partners). *"She's had a slight setback this week but she's neat and bred for speed. Clodovil has a good strike rate with his 2-y-o's, but when she runs I don't know. She should be a five furlong filly though".*

353. EGLANTYNE DREAM (FR) ★★★★

b.f. Oasis Dream – Bright Morning (USA) (Storm Cat). April 14. Third foal. Half-sister to Skye Morning (by Invincible Spirit), unplaced over 1m on her debut at 3 yrs in 2015. The dam is an unraced half-sister to 8 winners including Observatory (Group 1 Queen Elizabeth II Stakes, Prix d'Ispahan, etc) and the dual Group 1 winner High Praise. The second dam, Stellaria (by Roberto), won from 5f to 8.5f including the listed 6f Rose Bowl Stakes and is a half-sister to 8 winners. (Paul Hearson). *"Likely to be one of our first 2-y-o runners. She's not very big, very athletic and bred to be speedy. Quite nippy at the moment, she'll be a 2-y-o in April or May".*

354. EXECUTOR ★★★

b.c. Cacique – Star Cluster (Observatory).
March 1. Sixth foal. Half-brother to the fair
12f winner Asterism (by Motivator) and to
the moderate 5.5f winner Encapsulated (by
Zamindar). The dam, a useful 7f (at 2 yrs) and
listed 1m winner, is a half-sister to numerous
winners including the smart 6f (at 2 yrs) to
8.5f winner Didina, the smart French 10f
winner Espionage and the very useful dual 10f
winner Explode. The second dam, Didicoy (by
Danzig), a useful winner of 3 races over 6f, is
closely related to the Group 3 1m Prix Quincey
winner Masterclass and a half-sister to the
champion 2-y-o Xaar. (Khalid Abdulla). *"It's a
very good family and you'd have to argue that
so far the dam has been disappointing. I've got
three 2-y-o's by Cacique but I've never had any
before and this colt looks quite nice, he's quite
forward and sensible. A seven furlong type for
July or August".*

355. HIGH SHIELDS ★★★ ♠♠

b.c. Shamardal – Marine City (Carnegie). May
11. Eighth foal. 100,000Y. Tattersalls October
Book 1. Amanda Skiffington. Brother to
the quite useful 1m winner Feared In Flight
and half-brother to 3 winners including the
modest 2m winner Dubai Diva (by Dubai
Destination) and the moderate 12f, 14f and
hurdles winner Light The City (by Fantastic
Light). The dam, a fair 12f winner, is a half-
sister to 5 winners including the Group 1 12f
Prix de l'Arc de Triomphe and dual German
Group 1 winner Marienbard. The second
dam, Marienbad (by Darshaan), a French 1m
winner at both 2 and 3 yrs, is a half-sister to
6 winners. (M Pescod). *"He's a nice horse and
was well-bought I think because Shamardal's
yearling average shot up last year. He was also
a Darley cast-off which is always encouraging
because they usually do quite well. There's a lot
of stamina in his pedigree and he's a May foal,
very big, attractive, strong and very 'together'.
He's unlikely to be out before the autumn".*

356. HORRAH ★★★

b.c. Royal Applause – Aegean Shadow
(Sakhee). February 23. Second foal. 26,000Y.
Tattersalls October Book 2. Not sold. The dam,
a fair 6f and 7f winner of 3 races at 3 and 4
yrs, is a half-sister to 5 winners including the
useful 2-y-o listed 6f winner of 3 races and

Group 2 7f Vintage Stakes third Corporal
Maddox. The second dam, Noble View (by
Distant View), placed fourth over 5f and 6f
at 2 yrs, is a half-sister to 5 winners including
the French 1,000 Guineas winner Houseproud.
(Mrs Thomson-Jones). *"A strong colt, he's
related to others by Royal Applause that have
done well such as Corporal Maddox and he
didn't cost a lot. I think he'll be reasonably
early".*

357. INTERMITTENT ★★★

b.f. Cacique – Innocent Air (Galileo). May 2.
Half-sister to the fairly useful 12f and 14f
winner Fledged (by Dansili) and to the quite
useful 7f winner Angelic Air (by Oasis Dream).
The dam won two listed events over 7f and
10f at 2 and 3 yrs and is a half-sister to 6
winners including the French listed and US
stakes winner and US Grade 1 placed Skipping
and the dual Group 3 placed Minority. The
second dam, Minskip (by The Minstrel), won
once at 2 yrs and is a sister to the US Grade 2
winner Savinio and a half-sister to the Italian
dual Group 1 winner St Hilarion and the
dam of the dual Group 1 winner Muhtarram.
(Khalid Abdulla). *"An attractive filly, she moves
well, won't be particularly early but I like her".*

358. IRREVOCABLE (IRE) ★★★

b.f. Big Bad Bob – Out Of Time (Anabaa).
March 18. Fourth foal. 35,000Y. Tattersalls
October Book 2. Amanda Skiffington. Half-
sister to the Irish 2-y-o 7f winner and Group
3 1,000 Guineas Trial second What Style and
to the minor French 7f winner Via Lattea (by
Teofilo). The dam is an unraced half-sister
to 4 winners including the Group 2 placed
Drill Sergeant and Nobilis. The second dam,
Dolydille (by Dolphin Street), won 7 races
including two listed events from 9f to 12f
and is a half-sister to 9 winners including the
listed 1m winner and high-class broodmare
La Meilleure. (The Pyoneers). *"Everything by
the sire tends to look the same. They're not
very robust, they're very dark in colour and
light-framed but he's a successful stallion. This
filly looks OK but she's one for the autumn I
should think".*

359. KUANTAN ★★

b.c. Acclamation – Gay Mirage (Highest
Honor). March 21. First foal. 140,000Y.

Tattersalls October Book 2. Beckhampton Stables. The dam, a modest 12f placed maiden, is a half-sister to the fairly useful 11f and 14f winner and Group 3 2m Queen's Vase second Amerigo. The second dam, Geminiani (by King Of Kings), winner of the Group 3 7f Prestige Stakes and second in the Group 3 Musidora Stakes, is a half-sister to 4 winners including the 2-y-o Group 1 6f Phoenix Stakes and Group 2 5f Queen Mary Stakes winner Damson (herself dam of the Group 3 Molecomb Stakes winner Requinto). (Sultan Ahmad Shah). *"Like most Acclamations he's a good-natured, solid horse. The dam was disappointing on the racecourse and there's plenty of stamina in the family. This colt doesn't look like a sharp, early 2-y-o and is more like a stayer, but he does have a nice temperament".*

360. NOBLEWOMAN ★★★
b.f. Showcasing – Rare Virtue (Empire Maker). March 20. Half-sister to the quite useful 8.5f winner Seldom Seen (by Observatory). The dam was unplaced on her only start. The second dam, Heat Haze (by Green Desert), winner of the Grade 1 Matriarch Stakes and the Grade 1 Beverly D Stakes, is closely related to the Coronation Stakes, Prix Jacques Le Marois and Breeders Cup Filly & Mare Turf winner Banks Hill, to the Grade 1 winners Intercontinental, Cacique and Champs Elysees and the Group 2 winner and high-class sire Dansili. (Khalid Abdulla). *"I haven't had any by the sire Showcasing but he did very well with his first runners last year. This filly is a very big, powerful, sprinting type of filly. She hasn't been here long and I don't know much about her, but she's a big filly and I can only imagine she'll need a bit of time".*

361. PACIFIC SALT (IRE) ★★★★
gr.c. Zebedee – Villa Nova (Petardia). January 23. Eleventh foal. 210,000Y. Tattersalls October Book 1. Harriet Jellett & Anglia Bloodstock. Half-brother to 7 winners including the fairly useful 5f (at 2 yrs) to 9f winner and listed-placed Prince Of Denmark, the modest 7f winner Alexander Family (both by Danetime), the fairly useful triple 10f and subsequent Hong Kong winner Six Of Diamonds (by Redback) and the US 2-y-o winner and stakes-placed Forbidden Paradise (by Chineur). The dam is an unplaced half-sister to 6 winners including the Group 3 winner and Group 1 Dewhurst Stakes third Impressionist. The second dam, Yashville (by Top Ville), is an unraced half-sister to 8 winners. (Mr J S Kelly). *"A nice horse, he looks quite 'together', he's very attractive and a good mover. He's grown plenty since the sales and although I could run him any time I won't rush him. One for the middle of the summer, he seems to go quite nicely".*

362. PALING ★★★
b.c. Zamindar – Solar Pursuit (Galileo). February 21. First foal. The dam is an unraced half-sister to 8 winners including Meteor Storm (Grade 1 10f Manhattan Handicap), Polish Summer (Group 2 12.5f Grand Prix de Deauville), the listed 10f winner Morning Eclipse and the French Group 3 2m winner Host Nation. The second dam, Hunt The Sun (by Rainbow Quest), is an unraced sister to the high-class Rothmans International, Prix Royal-Oak and Prix Kergorlay winner Raintrap and to the very smart Criterium de Saint-Cloud and Prix du Conseil de Paris winner Sunshack. (Khalid Abdulla). *"He hasn't been here very long so it's hard to assess him yet. He's big, strong, attractive and a good moving horse for the second half of the year".*

363. PROJECTION ★★★
b.c. Acclamation – Spotlight (Dr Fong). February 24. Seventh foal. £90,000Y. Doncaster Premier. John & Jake Warren. Half-sister to three placed horses. The dam, a listed 1m and subsequent US Grade 2 Lake Placid Handicap winner, is a full or half-sister to 4 winners including the dam of the Group 1 Phoenix Stakes winner Zoffany. The second dam, Dust Dancer (by Suave Dancer), won 4 races including the Group 3 10f Prix de la Nonette and is a half-sister to 6 winners including the Group 3 7.3f Fred Darling Stakes winner Bulaxie (herself dam of the Group 2 winner Claxon). (The Royal Ascot Racing Club). *"He's more forward the other Acclamation colt we have, looks like a 2-y-o and is starting to move into a bit of work, but the mare has been very disappointing. I'm happy with him and he's doing well".*

364. PURE FANTASY ★★
b.f. Fastnet Rock – Fictitious (Machiavellian).

March 30. Closely related to 3 winners including the useful 6f, 7f (both at 2 yrs) and 1m winner and listed-placed Quadrille and the fairly useful 2-y-o 6f and 7f winner Free Verse (both by Danehill Dancer) and half-sister to the quite useful dual 1m winner Hunting Tower (by Sadler's Wells) and the fair triple 6f winner Cardinal (by Pivotal). The dam, a useful listed 10f winner, is a sister to the Group 2 12f Ribblesdale Stakes and Group 2 13.3f Geoffrey Freer Stakes winner Phantom Gold (dam of the Oaks second Flight Of Fancy). The second dam, Trying For Gold (by Northern Baby), was a useful 12f and 12.5f winner. (The Queen). *"She's an attractive filly and a good mover, but the sire hasn't bred early types in Europe. So I see this filly as being one to run in the second half of the year".*

365. PURE VANITY ★★★ ♠

b.f. New Approach – Miss Pinkerton (Danehill). February 1. Sister to the winner Vanity Rules and half-sister to 4 winners including the quite useful dual 10f winner This Is The Day (by Footstepsinthesand), the modest 1m to 12f winner of 16 races General Tufto (by Fantastic Light) and the modest 1m to 10f winner Smart Step (by Montjeu). The dam, a useful 6f (at 2 yrs) and listed 1m winner, is a half-sister to 5 winners including the smart 7f (at 2 yrs) and 10f winner Grand Central. The second dam, Rebecca Sharp (by Machiavellian), won the Group 1 1m Coronation Stakes and is a half-sister to 8 winners. (A E Oppenheimer). *"She's not here yet but she's quite nice. In pre-training at the moment, she should be here sometime during April I would think".*

366. QUICK MARCH ★★★

b.f. Lawman – Strut (Danehill Dancer). March 31. Fifth foal. Half-brother to the quite useful 2014 2-y-o 6f winner Skate (by Verglas), to the Group 3 6f Bengough Stakes and triple listed 6f winner Mince (by Medicean) and the quite useful dual 6f winner Stomp (by Nayef). The dam, a 2-y-o listed 5.2f winner, was Group 3 placed twice and is a half-sister to 4 winners including the US Grade 3 6.5f third Vaunt. The second dam, Boast (by Most Welcome), a useful 5f and 6f winner, is a half-sister to 6 winners. (Lady Rothschild). *"A well-named filly, she's got a bit to live up to being a half-sister to Mince but I guess Lawman fillies are possibly*

more attractive than the colts. *Not very big, but strong and bred to be a 2-y-o so I'm hopeful".*

367. SALAD DAYS ★★★

b.f. Pivotal – Scarlet Runner (Night Shift). January 26. The dam, a very useful Group 3 Princess Margaret Stakes (at 2 yrs) and Group 3 7f Nell Gwyn Stakes winner, is a half-sister to 2 winners. The second dam, Sweet Pea (by Persian Bold), a quite useful 1m winner of 4 races, is a half-sister to numerous winners including the listed 6f winner Star Tulip. (N Jones). *"I like her, she's a full sister to a disappointing filly called Scarlet Plum but looks more forward than that filly. She won't be early, but the dam was a good six furlong filly and you'd hope this filly will have the speed for six as well".*

368. SCAMPER ★★★

b.f. Oasis Dream – Wince (Selkirk). March 7. Sister to the fair 7f to 9f winner Dream Win and to the fair 1m winner Dream Wild and half-sister to the Group 1 Yorkshire Oaks winner Quiff, the useful 10f winner and Group 3 Chester Vase second Arabian Gulf and the useful 12f winner and Group 3 placed Total Command (all by Sadler's Wells). The dam won the 1,000 Guineas and is a sister to one winner and a half-sister to 3 winners including the very smart middle-distance winner Ulundi. The second dam, Flit (by Lyphard), a fair 10f winner, is a half-sister to the US Grade 1 winner Contredance and the stakes winners Old Alliance, Shotiche and Skimble (dam of the dual US Grade 1 winner Skimming). (Khalid Abdulla). *"She seems to be more like Oasis Dream than the rest of the family and on looks you'd say she'd be a six/seven furlong 2-y-o. It's a great family and she could be anything, but she had a setback early on and we don't know what we've got yet".*

369. SOLWAY FIRTH ★★★

b.f. Cacique – Rule Of Nature (Oasis Dream). February 10. Second foal. Half-sister to the 2015 3-y-o 1m debut winner Townsville (by Zamindar). The dam, a quite useful 2-y-o 6f winner, is a sister to the French listed 12f winner Preferential. The second dam, Jolie Etoile (by Diesis), is an unplaced half-sister to 3 winners including the Group 1 Prix de la Foret winner Etoile Montante and the dam of the French Group 3 winner Glaswegian. (Khalid Abdulla). *"She hasn't been here very long but she's attractive, seems to move well and the dam was a 2-y-o winner. She could be anything, but I guess she'll be a 2-y-o in the second half of the year".*

370. UNNAMED ★★★

ch.f. Strategic Prince – Asian Lady (Kyllachy). May 20. Sister to the modest 2014 5f and 6f placed 2-y-o Oriental Splendour. The dam, a modest 5f and 6f placed 3-y-o, is a half-sister to 6 winners including the very useful 6f (at 2 yrs) and 7f listed winner Levera. The second dam, Prancing (by Prince Sabo), a useful listed-placed 2-y-o 5f winner, stayed 1m and is a full or half-sister to 4 winners including the Group 1 6f Middle Park Stakes winner First Trump. (Sultan Ahmad Shah). *"She came in quite late but looks as if she ought to be a 2-y-o. She's small and she's a sister to a horse that probably ought to have won as a 2-y-o, Oriental Splendour. She's a bit behind the others but looks as if she ought to be pressed into action soon. I think she's OK and should be a 2-y-o, so we'll press forward".*

371. UNNAMED ★★★

b.f. Dansili – Clowance (Montjeu). April 15. Second foal. The dam, winner of the Group 3 12f St Simon Stakes and a 10f listed event, was placed in the Group 1 Irish St Leger and the Group 1 Coronation Cup and is a half-sister to 3 winners out of the German Group 2 11f winner Freni (by Sternkoenig). (Seasons Holidays). *"A nice filly. She's big, rangy, attractive and shows plenty of promise for a big filly. It's hard to tell with those types but she's one for the back-end of the year I guess. I wouldn't swap her".*

372. UNNAMED ★★

ch.c. Champs Elysees – Cross Your Fingers (Woodman). April 19. Fourth foal. 36,000Y. Tattersalls December. Amanda Skiffington. Brother to the fair 11f winner Gallic Destiny and half-brother to the moderate 7f to 9.5f winner Archina (by Arch). The dam is an unraced sister to the Group 1 Cheveley Park Stakes winner Gay Gallanta (herself dam of the Group 2 winner and sire Byron) and a half-sister to 11 winners. The second dam, Gallanta (by Nureyev), a 5.5f to 1m winner and second

in the Group 1 Prix Morny, is a half-sister to 6 winners including the Group 1 winner Gay Mecene. (Kessly Equine). *"A good-moving horse, all being well he'll be ready for the autumn over a mile".*

PAUL COLE

373. ARCHIMEDES (IRE)

b.c. Invincible Spirit – Waveband (Exceed And Excel). March 27. Second foal. €240,000Y. Goffs Orby. Hugo Merry. The dam, a fairly useful listed 6f winner of 4 races, is a sister to the smart 2-y-o dual Group 3 5f winner Bungle Inthejungle and a half-sister to 7 winners including the useful 2-y-o dual 5f winner and Group 2 5f King George Stakes second Group Therapy. The second dam, Licence To Thrill (by Wolfhound), a quite useful dual 5f winner, is a half-sister to 4 winners. (Mrs F H Hay).

374. BARON BOLT

br.c. Kheleyf – Scarlet Royal (Red Ransom). March 6. Third foal. 48,000Y. Tattersalls October Book 2. P Cole. Half-brother to the fairly useful 2-y-o 6f winner and Group 3 6f Firth Of Clyde Stakes third Momalorka (by Dutch Art). The dam is an unplaced half-sister to several winners. The dam is an unraced half-sister to 8 winners including the high-class Group 1 1m Queen Elizabeth II Stakes winner Where Or When and the smart 10f and 12f winner and Group 1 St Leger fourth All The Way. (Asprey, Wright, Meyrick, PJL Racing).

375. CAITIE (IRE)

b.f. Canford Cliffs – The Shrew (Dansili). March 3. First foal. 40,000Y. Tattersalls October Book 2. Oliver Cole. The dam, a fairly useful 7.5f and 1m winner, was listed-placed twice over 1m and is a half-sister to one winner. The second dam, Whazzat (by Daylami), a useful 2-y-o listed 7f Chesham Stakes winner, is a half-sister to 5 winners including the useful 7f (at 2 yrs), listed 1m and Italian Group 3 1m winner Whazzis. (Mr H Robinson).

376. CLIFFHANGER

b.f. Canford Cliffs – Copy-Cat (Lion Cavern). February 11. Eighth living foal. 78,000Y. Tattersalls October Book 1. Oliver Cole. Half-sister to the Group 2 John Of Gaunt Stakes winner and dual Group 3 placed Pastoral Player (by Pastoral Pursuits), to the smart listed 1m winner and Group 2 placed Chil The Kite (by Notnowcato) and the fairly useful 2-y-o winners Copywriter (by Efisio), Chataway (by Mujahid), Laudatory (by Royal Applause) and Gilt Linked (by Compton Place). The dam is an unplaced half-sister to the Group 3 5f King George Stakes winner Averti. The second dam, Imperial Jade (by Lochnager), a useful sprint winner of 4 races and second in the Group 2 Lowther Stakes, is a sister to the triple sprint Group winner Reesh. (Mr F Stella).

377. HOUSE OF COMMONS (IRE)
b.c. Sea The Stars – Reality (Slickly). March 23. First foal. 150,000Y. Tattersalls October Book 2. Hugo Merry. The dam, a French 6.5f (at 2 yrs) and listed 1m winner, is a half-sister to one winner. The second dam, Rose Des Charmes (by Cozzene), is an unraced half-sister to the US Grade 2 winner Blue Moon. (Mrs F H Hay).

378. INDRAPURA (IRE)
ch.c. Cape Blanco – A Mind Of Her Own (Danehill Dancer). March 30. Second foal. £43,000Y. Doncaster Premier. Ollie Cole. The dam, third in the Group 3 6f Coolmore Stud Sprint Stakes, is a half-sister to 2 winners including the dual Group 2 placed Birdman. The second dam, Gilded Vanity (by Indian Ridge), a minor Irish 5f winner, is a sister to 2 winners including the smart 1m winner and Irish 2,000 Guineas second Fa-Eq and a half-sister to 4 winners including the smart listed 7.3f and 1m winner Corinium and the useful dual 5f winner (including at 2 yrs) Ellway Star.

379. JAZZ CAT (IRE)
ch.f. Tamayuz – Chelsea Rose (Desert King). April 10. Sixth foal. €350,000Y. Goffs Orby. Stephen Hillen. Sister to the smart Group 3 6f Prix de Ris-Orangis and listed 1m winner Thawaany and half-sister to the fairly useful listed 1m second Hamlool (by Red Ransom) and the quite useful 5f and 6f winner of 5 races Pale Orchid (by Invincible Spirit). The dam won the Group 1 7f Moyglare Stud Stakes and three listed events, was Group 1 placed twice and is a half-sister to the Irish listed 1m winner and US Grade 2 placed European. The second dam, Cinnamon Rose (by Trempolino), an Irish 10f winner, is a half-sister to the Group 2 winner River Warden

and the US Grade 3 winner Sweettuc. (Mrs F H Hay).

380. PILOT HILL (IRE)
b.f. Intikhab – Song Of Passion (Orpen). March 29. Third foal. 48,000Y. Tattersalls October Book 3. Oliver Cole. Sister to the useful 2014 7f to 10f winner of 4 races Crafty Choice and to the quite useful 2-y-o 6f winner The Clan Macdonald. The dam, a useful 6f to 7.6f winner of 5 races at 2 to 4 yrs, is a half-sister to 6 winners including the Group 2 Sandown Mile and Group 3 Craven Stakes winner Hurricane Alan and the fairly useful 2-y-o 8.6f winner and listed-placed winner of 6 races Aaim To Prosper. The second dam, Bint Al Balad (by Ahonoora), a modest 7f placed 3-y-o, is a sister to the useful Group 3 7f Nell Gwyn Stakes winner A-To-Z. (Prince Faisal Salman).

381. RECENT ACQUISITION (IRE)
b.c. Approve – Dear Catch (Bluebird). April 16. Tenth foal. 45,000Y. Tattersalls October Book 2. Oliver Cole. Brother to the fair 2014 2-y-o 5f winner Free Entry and half-brother to 5 winners including the fairly useful 5f and 6f winner of 5 races and Group 3 second Golden Destiny (by Captain Rio) and the quite useful 6f and 7f winner Bluegrass Blues (by Dark Angel). The dam, a 9f winner in Ireland, is a sister to the Group 3 5f Ballyogan Stakes winner and Group 1 Haydock Park Sprint Cup third Catch The Blues and a half-sister to 5 winners. The second dam, Dear Lorraine (by Nonoalco), a French 10f winner, is a half-sister to 4 winners. (Mr R Green).

382. SWEET DRAGON FLY
b.f. Oasis Dream – Sweet Cecily (Kodiac). February 5. First foal. 140,000Y. Tattersalls October Book 1. Stephen Hillen. The dam won the 2-y-o listed 6f Bosra Sham Stakes. The second dam, Yaqootah (by Gone West), a fair 5f winner at 3 yrs, is a half-sister to 6 winners including the useful 2-y-o 6f winner and listed-placed Elshabiba and the minor US stakes winner Jah. (Mrs F H Hay).

383. TERENTUM LAD (IRE)
b.c. Lilbourne Lad – Montefino (Shamardal). April 26. Second foal. 58,000Y. Tattersalls December. Oliver Cole. Half-brother to the

useful 2014 2-y-o 5f and 6f winner of 3 races and Group 3 6f Firth Of Clyde Stakes second Parsley (by Zebedee). The dam is an unraced half-sister to 2 minor winners. The second dam, Monturani (by Indian Ridge), winner of the Group 2 10f Blandford Stakes and two listed events over 1m and 10f, is a half-sister to 7 winners including the listed 6f and listed 7f winner Monnavanna. (Mr T A Rahman).

ROBERT COWELL

384. ABU AL HAWA ★★

ch.c. Le Havre – Sainte Colombe (Danehill Dancer). February 13. The dam is an unplaced sister to the very smart 2-y-o Group 2 7f Champagne Stakes winner and French 2,000 Guineas and French Derby third Westphalia and a half-sister to 5 winners including the US Grade 3 El Camino Real Derby winner and Grade 2 placed Cliquot. The second dam, Pharapache (by Lyphard), won over 10f in France and is closely related to the French Group 3 winner Antheus and a half-sister to the French Group 3 winner Alexandrie (dam of the Group 1 10f Criterium de Saint-Cloud winner Poliglote) and to the placed dam of the Group 1 Prix Ganay winner Indian Danehill. (Jaber Abdullah). *"He wouldn't be the biggest in the world but he actually moves quite well and he looks a game horse. He'll probably need a bit of time, but if he doesn't grow much we'll crack on with him".*

385. FINGERTIPS ★★

b.f. Royal Applause – Hanging On (Spinning World). April 15. Third foal. Half-sister to 2 minor winners in Germany (by Barathea) and Qatar (by Leporello). The dam, a fairly useful 2-y-o 7f winner, is a half-sister to 9 winners including the Irish listed winner Barolo. The second dam, Lydia Maria (by Dancing Brave), a moderate 1m and 10f placed maiden, is a half-sister to 7 winners. (Fingertips Partnership). *"Although she's a Royal Applause she needs a bit of time. Her knees are still a bit immature so we can't move on with her just yet".*

386. JUMEIRAH STAR (USA) ★★★

b.br.f. Street Boss – Cosmic Wing (Halo). March 18. Twelfth foal. Half-sister to 7 winners including the useful 6f (at 2 yrs) and 5f winner and UAE Group 3 third Speed Hawk (by Henny Hughes). The dam, a US stakes-placed winner

at 2 and 3 yrs, is a half-sister to the US stakes winner and Grade 3 placed Charley Tango and to the dam of the US Grade 2 winner Tizaqueena. The second dam, Ziggy's Act (by Danzig), won the Grade 3 Pucker Up Stakes in the USA. (K A Dasmal). *"She's a similar size and a similar sort to her half-brother Speed Hawk who is continuing to do well. She'll be a 2-y-o by the middle of the season, she's cantering at the moment and hasn't done any fast work yet, but when she is ready she'll be a sprinter for sure".*

387. KING COLE (USA) ★★★★

ch.c. Scat Daddy – Volver (Danehill Dancer). February 28. Second foal. $115,000Y. Keeneland September. Robert Cowell. The dam, a 1m and 9.5f winner of 3 races at 3 and 4 yrs in France, is a half-sister to 4 winners including the French listed-placed winner Katerini. The second dam, Chanteleau (by A P Indy), won over 10.5f in France and is a half-sister to 3 winners. (K A Dasmal). *"I really like this horse. He's quite rangy but having said that he covers the ground really well. He looks more than capable and once we start working him I think he'll show us he's got an engine. A likeable individual, I think we'll be stepping up his work very soon".*

388. ROCKING RUDOLPH ★★★

b.f. Discreetly Mine – Empire Spring (Empire Maker). January 22. First foal. $40,000Y. Keeneland September. Robert Cowell. The dam, a minor winner of 3 races at 3 and 4 yrs in the USA and Canada, is a half-sister to 3 minor winners. The second dam, Our Rite Of Spring (by Stravinsky), a stakes winner of 3 races at 3 yrs in the USA, is a half-sister to 4 winners including the Grade 1 King's Bishop Stakes winner and sire Hard Spun. (Glen Johnson). *"A strongly made filly, she's not dissimilar to her another of our 2-y-o's Jumeirah Star. She has a good attitude, she's very fast-looking and powerful. Because she's so big we won't be rushing her and she's one for the middle to back-end for sure".*

389. ROSE ZAFONIC ★★★

b.f. Poet's Voice – With Distinction (Zafonic). March 29. Eighth foal. 32,000Y. Tattersalls October Book 1. Rabbah Bloodstock. Half-sister to the useful 2-y-o listed 7f winner

Talking Hands (by Mujahid), to the fair 7f (at 2 yrs) and 1m winner Herbert Crescent (by Averti) and the modest 2-y-o 5f winner Palladius (by Sakhee's Secret). The dam, placed once over 12f, is a half-sister to 4 minor winners. The second dam, Air Of Distinction (by Distinctly North), won 3 races including the Group 3 Anglesey Stakes and is a full or half-sister to 9 winners. (Jaber Abdullah). *"She's in full work and is quite speedily-bred. I quite like her and she looks an early type. Looks set for an early seasonal debut".*

390. SHE'S MY PRINCESS (IRE) ★★★★
b.f. Kodiac – Aguilas Perla (Indian Ridge). March 15. Seventh foal. 100,000Y. Tattersalls October Book 1. Robert Cowell. Half-sister to 5 winners including the fairly useful Irish listed-placed 2-y-o 5f and 7f winner Spirit Of Pearl (by Invincible Spirit), the fair 6f (at 2 yrs) to 1m winner Annes Rocket (by Fasliyev), the fair 2-y-o 6f winner Al Mahmeyah (by Teofilo) and the modest Irish dual 6f winner Hazelwood Ridge (by Mozart). The dam is an unraced sister to the Irish listed 7f winner Cool Clarity and a half-sister to the listed winners Artistic Blue and Queen Of Palms. The second dam, Tapolite (by Tap On Wood), a listed 7f winner, is a sister to Sedulous (2-y-o Group 3 1m Killavullen Stakes). (Malih Al Basti). *"She was quite expensive but looks money well spent judging by what I see on the gallops. She's got a huge back-end on her, she's fast and typical of the sire – good looking with an attractive head. She could be as early as I want her to be. I just need to let the hand brake off once before she runs".*

391. WESTBOURNE GROVE ★★★
b.c. Munnings – Catch Me Later (Posse). March 25. First foal. $25,000Y. Keeneland September. R Cowell. The dam, a minor US 2-y-o winner, is a half-sister to 7 winners, three of them stakes-placed in the USA. The second dam, Douce Douce (by Bold Ruckus), won 8 minor in the USA from 3 to 6 yrs and is a half-sister to 8 winners. (K Quinn, C Benham, I Saunders). *"He looks like money well-spent because he's really good-looking , he's already done some work and it looks like he'll be a runner". **TRAINERS' BARGAIN BUY***

392. UNNAMED ★★★
b.c. Royal Applause – Acicula (Night Shift). April 28. Eleventh foal. 30,000Y. Tattersalls October Book 3. Rabbah Bloodstock. Half-brother to the smart Group 3 6f Sirenia Stakes winner of 6 races Elnawin, to the quite useful dual 5f winner at 2 and 3 yrs Normal Equilibrium, the quite useful 5f to 1m winner of 10 races Elna Bright (all by Elnadim), the 2-y-o 5f and 6f seller winner Raphoola (by Raphane) and the moderate 7f and 1m winner Alucica (by Celtic Swing). The dam, a useful 2-y-o 5f and 6f winner, is a half-sister to 5 winners. The second dam, Crystal City (by Kris), a minor 10f winner at 3 yrs in France, is a half-sister to 2 winners. (Mr M Al Shafar). *"He's not particularly big but he's stocky, he's fast and he knows his job. One of my earliest 2-y-o's".*

393. UNNAMED ★★
b.f. Aqlaam – Areyaam (Elusive Quality). May 12. Half-sister to the useful 2-y-o 7f and listed 1m winner Go Angellica, to the fair 7f winner Arabian Music (both by Kheleyf) and the quite useful 2-y-o dual 6f winner My Lucky Liz (by Exceed And Excel). The dam, a fair maiden, was placed three times over 1m and is a half-sister to 2 winners. The second dam, Yanaseeni (by Trempolino), is an unplaced sister to the German-trained middle-distance dual Group 1 winner Germany (by Trempolino) and to 4 minor winners in the USA. (Mr Ahmed Jaber). *"She's attractive, quite tall and leggy, but she was a late foal and just needs a bit of time and possibly seven furlongs".*

394. UNNAMED ★★★
b.c. Lilbourne Lad – Blondie's Esteem (Mark Of Esteem). March 16. Second foal. 40,000Y. Tattersalls October Book 2. Rabbah Bloodstock. The dam is an unplaced half-sister to 4 winners including the useful Irish 5f (at 2 yrs) and listed 6f winner and multiple Group 3 placed Croisultan. The second dam, Zoudie (by Ezzoud), a fair 10f winner, is a half-sister to 7 winners including the dual Group 3 winner Redback. (Mr A Al Mansoori). *"A good-looking horse, physically he's a nice specimen and he's just starting to do a bit of work. I like him, he seems to have a lot of decent attributes, he moves well and has a good attitude. One for six furlongs I'd say".*

395. UNNAMED ★★★
b.c. Blame – Fiscal Policy (Wildcat Heir).
February 28. First foal. $67,000Y. Keeneland
September. Robert Cowell. The dam, a US
stakes-placed dual 2-y-o winner, is a half-sister
to 2 winners. The second dam, Betty's Courage
(by Montbrook), is an unraced half-sister to 6
winners. (Malih Al Basti). *"A real good-looking
horse, slightly 'up behind' at the moment so
he'll need a bit of time but he's got a very good
attitude. He's a good-looking, sturdy 2-y-o type
and I'd say he'd be fast but we haven't done
any fast work with him yet".*

396. UNNAMED ★★★★
ch.f. Notnowcato – Instructress (Diktat). First
foal. The dam, a fair dual 5f winner at 2 and
3 yrs, is a half-sister to 5 winners including
the quite useful 2-y-o dual 5f winner and
listed-placed Smooch. The second dam, Two
Step (by Mujtahid), a modest 5f and 7f winner
at 4 and 5 yrs, is a half-sister to 3 winners.
(Bottisham Heath Stud). *"The first foal out
of a mare I trained – she won as a 2-y-o at
Windsor. This is a pretty attractive filly, she's
come a long way in a short space of time and
is just about to start fast work. I think she'll be
quick and I'm quite excited about the mare
because I think she'll be a good one. I wish this
filly was by a more productive sire, but I think
she'll be alright and she's one to follow".*

397. UNNAMED ★★★
b.c. Holy Roman Emperor – Love Thirty
(Mister Baileys). February 5. Sixth foal.
€90,000Y. Goffs Orby. R Cowell. Closely
related to the moderate 2014 7.5f placed
2-y-o Chefchaouen (by Dylan Thomas) and
half-brother to the fair 7f winner (on her
only start) Royal Temptress (by Strategic
Prince) and the moderate 6f winner Game
All (by Acclamation). The dam, a fairly
useful 2-y-o 6f winner, is a half-sister to
one winner. The second dam, Polished Up
(by Polish Precedent), a modest 10f placed
3-y-o, is a half-sister to 9 winners including
the champion sprinter and high-class sire
Cadeaux Genereux and the dam of the listed
winning sprinters Ya Malak and Dominio. (Mr
A Al Banwan). *"A very good-looking colt, he's
already done some work and we're giving him
some time off because he's got sore shins. He's
very sturdy, looks fast and is well developed. I'd
say he'll be a fairly early type and I've got a lot
of time for him".*

398. UNNAMED ★★★
ch.c. Halling – Masaya (Dansili). February 23.
First foal. 50,000Y. Tattersalls October Book 2.
Rabbah Bloodstock. The dam, a useful listed-
placed 2-y-o 5f and 7f winner, is a half-sister
to 3 minor winners. The second dam, Anbella
(by Common Grounds), a French 2-y-o listed
7f winner, is a half-sister to 8 winners including
the Group 1 Criterium de Saint-Cloud winner
Spadoun and the Group 1 Prix de l'Opera
winner Satwa Queen. (Mr A Al Mansoori).
*"Although he's not a particularly tall horse, for
a Halling he shows a lot of speed and looks
more like a speedster than one by the sire
would generally look. He'll be a mid-season
2-y-o and will have the speed for six furlongs".*

399. UNNAMED ★★★
b.f. Danehill Dancer – Shaanara (Darshaan).
March 18. Eighth foal. €85,000Y. Goffs Orby.
R Cowell. Sister to the smart 1m and 9f winner
and Group 3 10f Royal Whip Stakes third
Fortify and half-sister to the quite useful 12f
to 2m 2f winner of 5 races Never Can Tell (by
Montjeu), the modest 10f winner Fantastic
Lass (by Fantastic Light) and a hurdles winner
by Lomitas. The dam, a quite useful 2-y-o 7f
winner, is a half-sister to 3 winners including
the smart Group 3 7f Gladness Stakes winner
Cool Edge. The second dam, Mochara (by
Last Fandango), placed once over 5f at 2 yrs
in Ireland, is a half-sister to 4 winners. (Mr A
Al Banwan). *"A good, strong looking filly. Being
by Danehill Dancer I thought she'd need a bit
of time but actually she's going quite nicely
already. She's almost ready for a piece of work
now and if all goes well she could be out in
June".*

400. UNNAMED ★★
b.f. Elnadim – Startori (Vettori). February 9.
Fourth living foal. 22,000Y. Tattersalls October
Book 3. Rabbah Bloodstock. Half-sister to the
modest 2014 2-y-o dual 6f winner White Vin
Jan (by Hellvelyn), to the fair 2-y-o listed-
placed 5f and 6f winner Liber and the fair
2-y-o dual 5f winner Guru Girl (by Ishiguru).
The dam, a quite useful 2-y-o dual 7f winner,
was listed-placed and is a half-sister to 5
winners. The second dam, Celestial Welcome

(by Most Welcome), a useful 7f to 12f winner of 8 races, is a full or half-sister to 5 winners including the smart Group 2 12f King Edward VII Stakes second Snowstorm. (Mr M Al Shafar). *"She's done nothing but grow and now she's probably too tall to get her going early, so we'll give her a bit of time to fill her frame because she's looking quite leggy now. A back-end type 2-y-o".*

SIMON CRISFORD

401. FIRST SELECTION (SPA) ★★★
b.c. Diktat – Villa Sonata (Mozart). February 10. £42,0002-y-o. Ascot Breeze Ups. S Crisford. Half-brother to 3 minor winners abroad by Silent Times, Keltos and Green Tune. The dam, a quite useful 10f winner, is a half-sister to numerous winners including the useful 1m (at 2 yrs) and listed 10f winner Ceilidh House. The second dam, Villa Carlotta (by Rainbow Quest), a smart 12f listed winner of four races, is a half-sister to the fairly useful 10f winner Seeyaaj. *"He's a nice colt and I'd like to get him out sooner rather than later, but he looks like he'll stay further than five furlongs eventually. He's going nicely and he'll be one of our first 2-y-o runners. This is my first season as a trainer and I've chosen this selection of two-year-olds in the expectation that most of them will be amongst the first wave of runners from the yard. I'm very pleased with my squad of 2-y-o's, most of them are later developing types for mid-summer onwards and I'm taking my time with them".*

402. HIGHWAY ROBBER ★★★
b.c. Dick Turpin – Lawyers Choice (Namid). April 6. Third foal. 15,000Y. Tattersalls October Book 3. Not sold. Half-brother to the quite useful 6f (at 2 yrs) and 7f winner Dutch Art Dealer (by Dutch Art). The dam, a fair 7f and 1m winner, is a half-sister to 4 winners including the Italian listed winner Far Hope (herself dam of the Italian dual Group 1 winner Voila Ici). The second dam, Finger Of Light (by Green Desert), a fairly useful 2-y-o 6f winner, is a half-sister to 6 winners including the listed winners Lady Shipley and Ellie Ardensky and to the dams of the Australian Grade 1 winner Serenade Rose and the multiple US Grade 2 winner Brave Act. *"We're looking towards running him over five furlongs towards the end of April. He looks like an early,* sharp sort and he's doing everything right. He looks like he's got enough toe for five furlongs, he's working nicely and I'm very pleased with the way he's developed over the winter".*

403. KINDLY ★★★
b.f. Kyllachy – Touching (Kheleyf). February 7. Second foal. 75,000Y. Tattersalls October Book 2. Simon Crisford. Half-sister to the fair 2014 2-y-o Prince Of Time (by Bahamian Bounty), placed fourth over 6f and 7.5f. The dam, a fairly useful 2-y-o 6f winner, was listed-placed and is a half-sister to 3 winners. The second dam, Feminine Touch (by Sadler's Wells), is an unraced half-sister to 3 winners. *"She's a little bit behind schedule and won't be out until mid-summer. A nice filly, she's been growing a bit recently and hasn't done anything more than cantering, but she'll definitely make a 2-y-o and I very much hope she'll go on next year".*

404. LUCKY LOT ★★★★ ♠
b.f. Exceed And Excel – Sweetie Time (Invincible Spirit). February 4. First foal. €165,000Y. Arqana Deauville August. Anthony Stroud. The dam, a fairly useful 2-y-o 6f winner, was listed placed twice over 7f. The second dam, Blessing (by Dubai Millennium), is an unraced half-sister to 7 winners. *"She should be racing by mid-summer, she's got a lot of quality about her. We haven't been in a rush with her because she's not over-big and she's just grown a bit recently but she's a very nice filly and I like her a lot".*

405. PENNY POET (IRE) ★★★
b.f. Intikhab – Mneme (Ocean Of Wisdom). March 18. Second foal. 70,000Y. Tattersalls October Book 2. Rabbah Bloodstock. The dam is an unplaced half-sister to 5 winners including the French listed winner and Group 1 Prix Ganay third Sensible. The second dam, Raisonnable (by Common Grounds), a listed 1m winner, was placed in three Group 3 1m events and is a half-sister to 7 winners including the US Grade 1 Yellow Ribbon Invitational winner Aube Indienne. *"She's potentially in my most forward group, does everything easily and looks nice. You should give her a mention in the book".*

406. PRIDE OF ANGELS ★★★
gr.f. Dark Angel – Openness (Grand Lodge).

February 1. Fifth foal. 65,000Y. Tattersalls October Book 2. Simon Crisford. Half-sister to the fair 5f (at 2 yrs) to 8.5f winner Almanack (by Haatef) and to a winner in the Czech Republic by Motivator. The dam is an unraced half-sister to 7 winners including the Group 1 1m Coronation Stakes winner Balisada (herself the dam of a listed winner). The second dam, Balisada (by Lomond), a modest 1m winner, is a sister to the Child Stakes winner Inchmurrin (herself dam of the very smart and tough colt Inchinor) and a half-sister to 7 winners including the Mill Reef Stakes winner Welney. *"A nice, active filly, she was just held up for a short time because of a small splint, but she's back in training now. She'll be a nice, sharp, five/six furlong 2-y-o".*

407. TAFTEESH (IRE) ★★★
b.c. Kodiac – Mudalalah (Singspiel). April 12. Second foal. €120,000Y. Goffs Orby. Shadwell Estate Co. The dam, a quite useful 1m to 10f placed maiden, is a half-sister to 6 winners including the Group 3 Ballysax Stakes winner Moiqen and the Group 2 Beresford Stakes second Rekaab. The second dam, Za Aamah (by Mr Prospector), is an unraced sister to the listed Pretty Polly Stakes winner Siyadah and a half-sister to the dual listed winner and Fillies Mile third Esloob. *"He's done a few bits of fast work and he looks like a nice 2-y-o to follow for the season. He's doing everything right, we'll start him off at six furlongs and he's bred to stay further than that".*

408. WAFI STAR (IRE) ★★★
b.c. Showcasing – Ophelia's Song (Halling). March 8. Second foal. €80,000Y. Goffs Orby. S Crisford (private sale). The dam is an unraced half-sister to 8 winners including the useful listed 10f Pretty Polly Stakes winner Musetta and to the placed dam of the Group 2 July Stakes winner Alhebayeb. The second dam, Monaiya (by Shareef Dancer), a French 7.5f and 1m winner, is a full or half-sister to 9 winners including the Canadian Grade 2 winner Vanderlin. *"He's on the same programme as another one of our 2-y-o's, Tafteesh. A nice colt for the six furlong races, he's progressing and doing everything right".*

409. WASSEEM (IRE) ★★★
ch.c. Approve – Vintage Escape (Cyrano

De Bergerac). March 18. Twelfth foal. 28,000Y. Tattersalls October Book 2. Rabbah Bloodstock. Half-brother to the French listed 5f winner Lisselan Diva, to the useful 1m (at 2 yrs) and listed 8.5f winner Vinthea (both by Barathea), the fair Irish 10f winners Protestant (by Papal Bull) and High Vintage (by High Chaparral) and the fair 2-y-o 5f winner Extra Power (by Acclamation). The dam was placed 6 times in Ireland at up to 9f and is a half-sister to one winner. The second dam, Overstay (by Be My Guest), is an unraced half-sister to 10 winners including the Melbourne Cup and Irish St Leger winner Vintage Crop. *"He looks a 2-y-o type, he's shaping up well, going forward and we're looking forward to getting him going. We like him".*

410. ZANJABEEL ★★★ ♠
b.c. Aussie Rules – Grain Only (Machiavellian). March 31. Sixth foal. 210,000Y. Tattersalls October Book 2. Shadwell Estate Co. Half-brother to the modest 2014 7.5f 2-y-o winner Multi Grain (by Sir Percy), to the Australian Group 3 12f winner of 7 races Caravan Rolls On, the quite useful 2-y-o 1m winner Gabrial's Star (both by Hernando) and the quite useful 2-y-o 7f winner Noble Metal (by With Approval). The dam is an unraced half-sister to 4 minor winners. The second dam, All Grain (by Polish Precedent), a useful 12.6f winner and third in the Group 3 Lancashire Oaks, is a sister to the Irish Oaks and Yorkshire Oaks winner Pure Grain and a half-sister to 7 winners. (Hamdan Al Maktoum). *"A lovely colt with a good attitude, he covers the ground well and will come to hand from the summer onwards. He should appreciate starting off over seven furlongs on good ground".*

411. UNNAMED ★★★
b.c. Acclamation – Winged Harriet (Hawk Wing). March 10. Third foal. €70,000Y. Goffs Orby. John Ferguson. Half-brother to the fair 2-y-o 7f winner Archibald Thorburn (by Duke Of Marmalade). The dam, a quite useful 6f winner at 3 yrs, is a half-sister to 8 winners including the smart Group 3 7f Minstrel Stakes winner and Group 1 6f Phoenix Stakes second Air Chief Marshal, the listed winners and Group 3 placed Misu Bond and Slip Dance and the Group 1 Irish 2,000 Guineas second Foxtrot Romeo. The second dam, Hawala (by

Warning), a useful 8.3f winner, is a half-sister to 4 winners including Afaf (Group 3 Prix Fille de l'Air). *"He looks like a 2-y-o and he's going very nicely now. He won't be that early but he has a real 2-y-o stamp about him. We'll start him off at six furlongs and he looks a nice type to continue throughout the season".*

LUCA CUMANI

412. ANGELA NORTH ★★

b.f. Canford Cliffs – Vallota (Polish Precedent). April 29. Eighth foal. Half-sister to the Group 3 5f and listed 5f winner Ialysios (by So Factual) and the quite useful 1m winner (on his only start) Wistar (by Dubawi). The dam is an unraced half-sister to 5 winners including the useful 6f (at 2 yrs) and 7f listed winner Epagris. The second dam, Trikymia (by Final Straw), was placed third over 5f at 2 yrs on her only outing and is a half-sister to 9 winners including the Irish Derby winner Tyrnavos, the champion 2-y-o Tromos, the Coronation Stakes winner Tolmi and the Middle Park Stakes winner Tachypous. (Mr M Marinopoulos). *"A nice enough girl, she's a bit on the small side and needs to grow and furnish. The family don't really produce 2-y-o's but being by Canford Cliffs this one could catch up and be alright from the summer onwards. It's a fast family so she could well be a sprinter, but she's just immature at present".*

413. BANKSEA ★★★

b.c. Lawman – Stars In Your Eyes (Galileo). March 12. First foal. 14,000Y. Tattersalls December. Charlie Gordon-Watson. The dam, a fair 12f winner, is a half-sister to 5 winners including the listed 1m winner New Mexican and the Group 2 Dante Stakes third Co-ordinated Cut. The second dam, Apache Star (by Arazi), a fairly useful 7f (at 2 yrs) to 9f winner, was listed placed twice at up to 11.4f and is a half-sister to 6 winners including the US stakes winner and Grade 3 placed Duke Of Green. (Mr L Marinopoulos). *"He was a very cheap horse and I don't know why. There's nothing wrong with him – in fact he's quite likeable. He'll make a 2-y-o by mid-summer, he's grown, strengthened and is going the right way".* **TRAINERS' BARGAIN BUY**

414. BEAUTIFUL MORNING ★★★

b.f. Galileo – Date With Destiny (George Washington). March 15. First foal. 650,000Y. Tattersalls October Book 1. McCalmont Bloodstock. The dam, a fairly useful 2-y-o 7f winner and third in the listed Oaks Trial, is a half-sister to 6 winners including the Group 3 10.5f Prix Penelope winner Ombre Legere and the US Grade 1 9f second Flawly (herself the dam of three stakes winners). The second dam, Flawlessly (by Rainbow Quest), is a placed full or half-sister to 9 winners including the French listed winners and Group-placed Video Rock and Lady Day. (Mr J S Kelly). *"A lovely filly, she's big, strong and really good-looking but more of a 3-y-o type. She'll make a 2-y-o at some point from mid-season onwards and could be anything. Her damsire being George Washington makes her a bit special".*

415. BLIND FAITH (IRE) ★★★

ch.f. Zoffany – Guajira (Mtoto). April 27. Fifth foal. 60,000Y. Tattersalls October Book 2. Charlie Gordon-Watson. Half-brother to the very useful dual 5f (at 2 yrs) and listed Doncaster Mile winner and Group 1 Sussex Stakes third Gabrial (by Dark Angel), to the fair 9f and 12f winner Innocent Touch (by Intense Focus) and a minor winner in France by Beat Hollow. The dam, a minor French 11f winner of 3 races, is a half-sister to 9 winners including Jaunatxo and Iron Deputy (both US Grade 2 winners) and the dam of the German Group 2 winner Shamalgan. The second dam, Femme de Fer (by Iron Duke), won twice in France and is a half-sister to 3 winners. (Mr C Wright & Mr W Asprey). *"A nice filly, she's very tall and very big. You probably wouldn't think she'd be a 2-y-o but she finds everything very easy. So I wouldn't be surprised if she won races as a 2-y-o".*

416. CRYPTIC (IRE) ★★★

br.c. Lord Shanakill – Privet (Cape Cross). April 28. Third foal. 65,000Y. Tattersalls October Book 2. John Warren. Half-brother to the fair 2014 7f placed 2-y-o Just A Penny (by Kodiac) and to the minor French 7f winner Bilge Kagan (by Whipper). The dam, a fair 6f placed 2-y-o, is a sister to the useful German 2-y-o Group 2 winner Mokabra and a half-sister to 6 winners. The second dam, Pacific Grove (by Persian Bold), a fairly useful 2-y-o listed-placed winner of 3 races from 7f to 1m, is a half-sister to 5 winners including the listed winners Mauri Moon and Kimbridge Knight. (Mrs A Silver). *"A precocious colt, he's strong enough to make a 2-y-o from the early summer onwards over six/seven furlongs".*

417. DAILY NEWS ★★★

b.c. Street Cry – Zeeba (Barathea). March 11. Half-brother to the very smart Group 3 Huxley Stakes winner of 6 races at around 10f Danadana and to the fairly useful 10f to 14f winner of 6 races Semeen (both by Dubawi). The dam, a fair 12f winner, is a sister to the useful listed 14f winner Lost Soldier Three and a half-sister to 5 winners including the useful 10.5f and 12f winner Altaweelah. The second dam, Donya (Mill Reef), was placed once over 10f from 2 outings and is a half-sister to the Rothmans International winner French Glory and the useful Irish winner at up to 12f Golden Isle. (Sheikh Mohammed Obaid Al Maktoum). *"He'll take a bit of time and the half-brothers weren't particularly forward, but he's well-developed so I can see him being out in September. Whether he'll win this year it's too early to say, but there's no reason why not".*

418. DIAMOND GEYSER ★★★

b.c. Champs Elysees – Triomphale (Nureyev). May 2. Ninth living foal. 55,000Y. Tattersalls October Book 2. Charlie Gordon-Watson. Half-brother to 7 winners including the very useful 6f listed winner of 4 races (including at 2 yrs) One Putra (by Indian Ridge), the fairly useful 7f (at 2 yrs) and 3-y-o listed 7f winner Teophilip (by Teofilo), the quite useful 2-y-o 5f winner Maggie Lou (by Red Ransom) and the quite useful 10f winner Rondelet (by Bering). The dam, a French 2-y-o 6f winner, is a half-sister to 4 winners including the US Grade 3 winner Tresoriere. The second dam, Time Deposit (by Halo), is an unraced half-sister to 4 winners including the Group 2 Richmond Stakes winner Gallant Special. (Mr L Marinopoulos). *"He's a bit small and a fairly late foal so he needs to develop, but he's nice. He's a horse that catches your eye and does things easily, but isn't one we'll see racing before the second half of the season".*

419. EL VIP (IRE) ★★★

b.c. Pivotal – Elle Danzig (Roi Danzig). April 10. Twelfth foal. 250,000Y. Tattersalls October Book 1. Charlie Gordon-Watson. Half-brother to 9 winners including the German triple Group 3 winner Elle Shadow (by Shamardal), the German and Italian listed winners El Comodin (by Monsun) and Elle Gala (by Galileo) and the fairly useful 10f winner and listed-placed Lyric Street (by Hurricane Run). The dam won the Group 1 Premio Roma (twice) and the Group 1 10f Grosser Preis Bayerisches Zuchtrennen and is a half-sister to 10 winners. The second dam, Elegie (by Teotepec), won 3 races in Germany and is a half-sister to 8 winners including the Group 1 Preis von Europa winner Ebano. (Al Shaqab Racing UK Ltd). *"A nice horse, he's one for the summer onwards but Pivotal wouldn't exactly be a 2-y-o sire. A likeable colt".*

420. GADWA ★★★★

b.f. Oasis Dream – Lady Of Everest (Montjeu). March 10. Third foal. 500,000Y. Tattersalls October Book 1. Tony Nerses. Half-sister to the fairly useful 2014 listed-placed 2-y-o 1m winner Lady Of Dubai (by Dubawi) and to the quite useful 12f winner Got To Dream (by Duke Of Marmalade). The dam is an unraced half-sister to the Irish listed winner and Group 1 Irish Oaks second Roses For The Lady. The second dam, Head In The Clouds (by Rainbow Quest), won the Group 3 12f Princess Royal Stakes and is a sister to the high-class St Leger, Chester Vase and Jockey Club Stakes winner Millenary and a half-sister to the very smart 1m (at 2 yrs) and 10f winner and Derby third Let The Lion Roar. (Saleh Al Homaizi & Imad Al Sagar). *"She's just as nice as her sister Lady Of Dubai was at this stage. She's likeable, goes well and I suspect she'll be out even earlier than Lady of Dubai – possibly in June or July".*

421. HAGGLE ★★★

ch.f. Pivotal – Barter (Daylami). March 29. Third foal. Half-sister to the fair 10f winner Petticoat Lane (by High Chaparral). The dam is an unplaced half-sister to 11 winners including the very useful listed 12f winner and good broodmare Puce and the dam of the Group 1 winners Alexandrova and Magical Romance. The second dam, Souk (by Ahonoora), a fairly useful 7f winner, was listed placed over 1m and is a half-sister to 3 winners. (Fittocks Stud). *"Funnily enough, despite her breeding she seems to be fairly forward. She goes well, she's not big and she's well put together, so she could be one for June/July from six furlongs upwards".*

422. KILIM ★★★
b.f. Dansili – Kibara (Sadler's Wells). May 5. Seventh foal. Closely related to the fairly useful 1m (at 2 yrs) to 12f winner of 3 races Kikonga (by Danehill Dancer) and half-sister to the quite useful 10f and 12f winner Kinshasa (by Pivotal) and the quite useful 11f and 12f winner of 3 races Kiwayu (by Medicean). The dam, a fair 11f winner, is a sister to 5 winners including the St Leger and Great Voltigeur Stakes winner Milan and half-sister to 3 winners. The second dam, Kithanga (by Darshaan), was a smart winner of 3 races including the Group 3 12f St Simon Stakes and the listed 12f Galtres Stakes. (Fittocks Stud). *"She's a May foal and it's a middle-distance family, but having said that she's going well and finds everything really easy. I'm not going to push her but she's likeable and the target is the summer onwards".*

423. KISS ★★
b.f. Sir Percy – Kintyre (Selkirk). March 2. First foal. The dam is an unraced half-sister to 3 winners including the fairly useful 1m (at 2 yrs) to 12f winner of 3 races Kikonga. The second dam, Kibara (by Sadler's Wells), a fair 11f winner, is a sister to 5 winners including the St Leger and Great Voltigeur Stakes winner Milan and half-sister to 3 winners including the Group 2 Great Voltigeur Stakes third Go For Gold. (Fittocks Stud Ltd). *"A backward filly, but she should run in the autumn".*

424. MATERIALISTIC ★★★★
b.f. Oasis Dream – Pongee (Barathea). May 6. Sixth foal. 550,000Y. Tattersalls October Book 1. Not sold. Half-sister to 4 winners including the listed 10f winner Pinzolo (by Monsun), the quite useful listed-placed 2-y-o 1m winner Poplin (by Medicean) and the fair 10f winner Paisley (by Pivotal). The dam, a Group 2 12f Lancashire Oaks winner, is closely related to the listed 12f and listed 14f winner Lion Sands and to the listed-placed 11f winner Pukka and a half-sister to 5 winners. The second dam, Puce (by Darshaan), a listed 12f winner, is a half-sister to 10 winners including the dam of the dual Oaks winner Alexandrova and the Cheveley Park Stakes winner Magical

Romance. (Fittocks Stud). *"She's very nice, seems quite forward and is well put together. A June/July filly, she's strong and likeable".*

425. MISSION MARS ★★★★
b.c. Kyllachy – Ashraakat (Danzig). April 22. Twelfth foal. 65,000Y. Tattersalls October Book 2. John Warren. Half-brother to the fair 2014 triple 5f placed 2-y-o Rock Follies (by Rock Of Gibraltar) and to 4 winners including the quite useful 6f to 10f winner of 12 races El Dececy (by Seeking The Gold), the quite useful 7f winner Ahdaaf (by Bahri) and the quite useful 7f (at 2 yrs) to 12f winner Hezaam (Red Ransom). The dam, a very useful 6f and 7f listed winner, is a sister to 2 winners including the July Cup winner Elnadim, closely related to the Irish 1,000 Guineas winner Mehthaaf and a half-sister to 6 winners. The second dam, Elle Seule (by Exclusive Native), won the Group 2 1m Prix d'Astarte and is a half-sister to three Group/Grade 1 winners and to the dam of Dubai Millennium. (Mr L Marinopoulos). *"He's nice, fairly forward and he could be running over six furlongs in mid-summer. Well developed and well put together".*

426. MY FAVOURITE THING ★★
b.f. Oasis Dream – The Sound Of Music (Galileo). March 21. Half-sister to the UAE listed 10f and listed 11f placed Seema (by Dubawi). The dam is an unraced half-sister to 6 winners including the St Leger and Coronation Cup winner Scorpion, the US Grade 2 and Grade 3 winner Memories and the listed winners Danish Rhapsody and Garuda. The second dam, Ardmelody (by Law Society), is an unraced half-sister to 8 winners. (Sheikh Mohammed Obaid Al Maktoum). *"She's not a typical Oasis Dream and it looks like she needs time and a bit of furnishing. It's hard to categorize her but I'd say there seems to be more Galileo in her than Oasis Dream".*

427. NADA ★★
b.f. Teofilo – Zomaradah (Deploy). March 20. Half-sister to 6 winners including the National Stakes (at 2 yrs), Irish 2,000 Guineas and Prix Jacques le Marois winner and sire Dubawi (by Dubai Millennium), the Group 2 12f Lancashire Oaks winner Emirates Queen (by Street Cry), the listed 10f winner Princess Nada (by Barathea) and the fairly useful listed-placed

1m winner Dubai Queen (by Kingmambo). The dam won the Group 1 Italian Oaks, the Group 2 Royal Whip Stakes and the Group 2 Premio Lydia Tesio. The second dam, Jawaher (by Dancing Brave), placed over 1m and 9f, is a half-sister to the Derby winner High-Rise. (Sheikh Mohammed Obaid Al Maktoum). *"She's a bit 'on the leg' at the moment and I don't see her being much of a 2-y-o until the autumn, but she's a good-looking filly just like all of them out of Zomaradah".*

428. PACHARANA ★★
b.f. Oasis Dream – Cascata (Montjeu). February 22. The dam, a fair 2-y-o 1m winner, is a sister to the high-class multiple Group 1 winning middle-distance colt St Nicholas Abbey and a half-sister to 2 winners including the US dual Grade 2 winner and Grade 1 placed Grammarian. The second dam, Leaping Water (by Sure Blade), is an unraced half-sister to the high-class St James's Palace Stakes and Prix Jean Prat winner Starborough, the Criterium de Saint-Cloud and Criterium International winner Ballingarry, the Racing Post Trophy winner Aristotle and the Prix de Royaumont winner Spanish Falls. (Stuart Stuckey). *"She's not very precocious because she looks more of a Montjeu than Oasis Dream, but she could run this year over seven furlongs or a mile. It's a staying family".*

429. POINT OF VIEW (IRE) ★★★
b.c. New Approach – Artisti (Cape Cross). April 12. Fourth foal. 400,000Y. Tattersalls October Book 1. John Warren. Half-brother to the German Group 3 10f winner Magic Artist (by Iffraaj) and to a winner in Austria by Nayef. The dam is an unraced half-sister to 5 winners including the Group 1 winner Gran Criterium winner Kirklees and the Group 1 St Leger and Hong Kong Vase winner Mastery and to the dam of the Group 1 Eclipse Stakes winner Mukhadram. The second dam, Moyesii (by Diesis), won once at 3 yrs in France and is a half-sister to 3 winners including the Group 3 Prix de Fontainebleau winner Bowman. (Sheikh Mohammed Obaid Al Maktoum). *"He's done very well physically and has the makings of a nice horse over seven furlongs and a mile later on. Probably more of a 3-y-o type, but he should win this year".*

430. ROYAL MAHOGANY ★★★★
b.c. Kodiac – Chiba (Timber Country). April 22. Third foal. 47,000Y. Tattersalls December. Charlie Gordon-Watson. The dam is an unraced half-sister to 4 winners including the Group 2 Prix de Sandringham winner and French 1,000 Guineas second Maiden Tower and the French listed winner Tokyo Rose. The second dam, Sawara (by Danzig), is an unraced half-sister to 8 winners including the French Group 2 and Group 3 winner Affidavit. (Sheikh Mohammed Obaid Al Maktoum). *"He should be a 2-y-o because he's well-grown, forward and quite strong. He should be out in May or June although it's too early to say how good he might be".*

431. SILK SUIT (FR) ★★★
b.c. Rip Van Winkle – Silk Gallery (Kingmambo). March 14. Second foal. 65,000Y. Tattersalls October Book 2. Charlie Gordon-Watson. Half-brother to a minor 2-y-o winner abroad by Mastercraftsman. The dam, a moderate 4-y-o 5f winner, is a half-sister to 7 winners including the Australian Grade 2 winner Fantastic Love. The second dam, Moon Flower (by Sadler's Wells), a winner over 1m (at 2 yrs) and 10f in Ireland, is a sister to the listed winners Side Of Paradise (dam of the dual Group 1 winner Immortal Verse) and Flowerdrum and a half-sister to 8 winners including the triple Grade 1 winner Last Tycoon, the Group 2 Premio Melton winner Astronef and the dam of the Group 1 winners Valentine Waltz, Tie Black and Sense Of Style. (Buxted Partnership). *"He's fine and should win a race or two this year hopefully, starting in the summer over seven furlongs".*

432. SUBOTAL (IRE) ★★★★★
ch.c. Pivotal – Suba (USA) (Seeking The Gold). April 3. Third foal. Brother to Pivotique, unplaced on her only start at 2 yrs in 2014. The dam, a quite useful 8.5f winner, is a half-sister to the high-class National Stakes (at 2 yrs), Irish 2,000 Guineas and Prix Jacques le Marois winner and sire Dubawi, to the listed 10f winner Princess Nada and the listed-placed winners Emirates Queen and Dubai Queen. The second dam, Zomaradah (by Deploy), won the Group 1 Italian Oaks, the Group 2 Royal Whip Stakes and the Group 2 Premio Lydia Tesio and is a half-sister to several winners.

(Sheikh Mohammed Obaid Al Maktoum). *"A nice colt – we like him. He's shown a bit more at this stage than your average Pivotal and he may even be a six furlong horse to begin with. Certainly one of my picks".*

433. SUN LOVER ★★★★
b.c. Oasis Dream – Come Touch The Sun (Fusaichi Pegasus). April 16. Second foal. 360,000Y. Tattersalls October Book 1. John Warren. The dam, a minor US 3-y-o winner, is a half-sister to the Group 1 Moyglare Stud Stakes, Prix Marcel Boussac (both at 2 yrs), Irish 1,000 Guineas and Pretty Polly Stakes winner Misty For Me and to the useful 7f (at 2 yrs) and listed 9f winner and dual Group 3 placed Twirl. The second dam, Butterfly Cove (by Storm Cat), is an unraced sister to the Group 3 Irish 1,000 Guineas Trial winner Kamarinskaya and a half-sister to 5 winners including the champion 2-y-o colt Fasliyev. (Sheikh Mohammed Obaid Al Maktoum). *"A lovely looking horse, he's very athletic, more compact and stronger than his 3-y-o half-brother Archery Peak and is by a more precocious stallion. So hopefully this colt will be both earlier and better! He could start at six, but more likely seven furlongs".*

434. TIPTREE ★★
b.f. Duke Of Marmalade – Taking Liberties (Royal Academy). April 12. Twelfth foal. €80,000Y. Goffs Orby. John Warren. Closely related to 4 winners including the listed 1m winner of 7 races here and in Hong Kong Troubadour, the fair 2-y-o 6f winner Danapali (both by Danehill) and the fair 2-y-o 7f winner Fistful Of Dollars (by Holy Roman Emperor) and half-brother to 5 winners including the French 2-y-o winner and 5f listed-placed Agapimou (by Spectrum). The dam ran once unplaced and is a sister to the 2-y-o Group 3 1m Futurity Stakes winner Equal Rights and a half-sister to 6 winners. The second dam, Lady Liberty (by Noble Bijou), a Group 1 12f winner in Australia, is a half-sister to 4 winners. (Mr M Morris). *"A nice, big filly, she's grown a lot and it would be nice to get her out in the autumn. Much more of a 3-y-o, she was named after the marmalade of course!"*

435. UAE PRINCE (IRE) ★★
b.c. Sea The Stars – By Request (Giant's Causeway). April 22. Second foal. 650,000Y. Tattersalls October Book 1. Charlie Gordon-Watson. The dam is an unplaced half-sister to 3 winners including the Group 2 Irish Derby Trial winner, Irish Derby second and St Leger second Midas Touch. The second dam, Approach (by Darshaan), a 7.5f (at 2 yrs) and listed 10f winner, was second in a US Grade 2 9.5f event and in the Group 3 May Hill Stakes and is a sister to the very useful 2-y-o 8.5f winner Intrigued and a half-sister to 7 winners including the French 2,000 Guineas and US Grade 1 winner Aussie Rules. (Sheikh Mohammed Obaid Al Maktoum). *"A lovely-looking horse, but not a 2-y-o. We may see him out at the back-end of the season".*

436. ZABEEL PRINCE(IRE) ★★★
ch.c. Lope De Vega – Princess Serena (Unbridled's Song). March 7. Sixth foal. 325,000Y. Tattersalls December. Charlie Gordon-Watson. Closely related to the Australian dual Group 2 winner Puissance de Lune and to the quite useful 7f winner Majesty (both by Shamardal) and half-brother to the quite useful 2-y-o 7f winner Serena's Storm (by Statue Of Liberty and herself dam of the dual Group 1 winner Rizeena), the fairly useful dual 7f winner Invincible Fresh (by Footstepsinthesand) and the fair 7f winner of 4 races (including at 2 yrs) Serene Oasis (by Oratorio). The dam, a minor 4-y-o winner, is a half-sister to the US Grade 2 winner Doubles Partner. The second dam, Serena's Sister (Rahy), is an unplaced sister to the outstanding US winner of eleven Grade 1 events Serena's Song (dam of the Coronation Stakes winner Sophisticat). (Sheikh Mohammed Obaid Al Maktoum). *"A nice, scopey horse for the summer onwards. I can't tell you what trip he'll want but he's not a sprinter. A lovely looking horse, as his price tag suggests".*

437. UNNAMED ★★★
b.c. Rock Of Gibraltar – Amaya (Kingmambo). March 6. First foal. 90,000Y. Tattersalls October Book 2. Charlie Gordon-Watson. The dam is an unraced half-sister to 3 winners here and abroad. The second dam, Saree (by Barathea), a fairly useful 2-y-o 7f winner, subsequently won once in the USA, was Grade 3 placed in Canada and is a sister to the 2-y-o Group

1 6f Cheveley Park Stakes winner Magical Romance and a half-sister to the Oaks, Irish Oaks And Yorkshire Oaks winner Alexandrova. (Mr Nagy El Azar). *"A nice, good-looking horse, he's scopey and lengthy. More of a seven furlong/mile 2-y-o rather than a sprinter".*

438. UNNAMED ★★★

b.f. Galileo – Danedrop (Danehill). March 15. Half-sister to the multiple Group 1 winner (including the Prix de l'Arc de Triomphe) Danedream (by Lomitas), to the modest 6f (at 2 yrs) to 12f winner of 5 races Valdan (by Val Royal) and the French listed-placed Debutante (by Gold Away). The dam is an unraced half-sister to 6 winners. The second dam, Rose Bonbon (by High Top), a winner over 13f in France, is a half-sister to the French Group 1 winners Le Nain Jaune, Indian Rose and Vert Amande and to the dam of Groom Dancer. (Coolmore). *"A very nice filly, she's not big and backward but as she's a sister to an Arc winner it's difficult to be sure about her trip this year. I'd say she could be a July/August 2-y-o".*

439. UNNAMED ★★★

ch.f. Rock Of Gibraltar – Rivara (Red Ransom). April 30. First foal. 425,000Y. Tattersalls October Book 1. John Ferguson. The dam is an unraced half-sister to 8 winners including the Group 2 Prix de Pomone winner Armure and the listed winners Affirmative Action, Berlin Berlin, Gravitas and Seta. The second dam, Bombazine (by Generous), a useful 10f winner, is a half-sister to 7 winners including the Group 1 winners Barathea and Gossamer (herself dam of the Group 1 winner Ibn Khaldun) and the US Grade 3 winner Free At Last (herself dam of the US multiple Grade 2 winner Coretta). (Miss S J E Leigh). *"A nice, forward-going filly, she's not bred to be a sprinter and is more of a seven furlong type, but she shows enough to suggest she could start off at six furlongs in the summer".*

440. UNNAMED ★★★★ ♠

ch.c. New Approach – Wadaat (Diktat). March 1. Third foal. 150,000Y. Tattersalls October Book 1. John Warren. The dam, a useful 1m winner and second in the Group 2 Italian Oaks, is a half-sister to 5 winners including the Italian Group 3 placed Mrs Snow. The second dam, Shining Vale (by Twilight Agenda), is an unraced half-sister to the German and Italian Group 2 winner Walzerkoenigin (herself dam of the Group 1 German Derby winner Wiener Walzer). (Al Shaqab Racing UK Ltd). *"He goes well and for a New Approach he shows more speed and precocity than most of them. A nice horse, he could even be a six furlong horse to begin with in June or July. Very likeable".*

KEITH DALGLEISH

441. AUSSIE EXPRESS ★★

gr.g. Aussie Rules – Bolshaya (Cadeaux Genereux). April . Twelfth foal. £5,000Y. Doncaster Premier. Bobby O'Ryan/Keith Dalgleish. Half-brother to the fair 2-y-o dual 6f winner Karuga (by Kyllachy), to the fair 2-y-o 5f winner Inagh River (by Fasliyev), the Irish 2-y-o 7f and subsequent Hong Kong winner Carnegie Hall (by Danehill) and a minor winner in Greece by Pivotal. The dam, a fair triple 6f winner, is a half-sister to 8 winners including the very smart King's Stand Stakes and Temple Stakes winner Bolshoi and the useful sprinters Mariinsky, Great Chaddington and Tod. The second dam, Mainly Dry (by The Brianstan), is an unraced half-sister to 4 winners. (Equus Syndicate). *"He's been a bit slower to come to come to hand than I expected, but he should be racing in May over five or six furlongs".*

442. CHARMED COMPANY (IRE) ★★★

b.f. Fast Company – Lucky Leigh (Piccolo). January 14. Second foal. £55,000Y. Doncaster Silver. Tom Malone/Keith Dalgleish. Half-sister to the 2014 French 2-y-o 5.5f and 6.5f winner Something Lucky (by Clodovil). The dam, a fairly useful dual 5f winner (including at 2 yrs), was fourth in the Group 2 Queen Mary Stakes and is a full or half-sister to three modest 2-y-o winners. The second dam, Solmorin (by Fraam), is an unplaced half-sister to 2 minor winners. (Straightline Construction Ltd). *"A nice filly, she's strong and from a fast family. She'll be out in late April/early May".*

443. DARK DEFENDER ★★★

b.c. Pastoral Pursuits – Oh So Saucy (Imperial Ballet). January 26. First foal. £15,000Y. Doncaster Premier. Tom Malone/Keith Dalgleish. The dam, a fair 7f and 1m winner of 5 races, is a half-sister to 2 minor winners.

The second dam, Almasi by Petorius), a fair 7f winner of 8 races, is a half-sister to 2 winners. (Prestige Thoroughbred Racing). *"I like him, he's a nice size, goes well and should be out in early May over five furlongs. He'll get six by the end of the year I'd say".* **TRAINERS BARGAIN BUY**

444. FARKLE MINKUS ★★★
b.g. Kheleyf – Majestic Diva (Royal Applause). January 18. Brother to the useful 5f to 7f winner of 4 races from 2 to 6 yrs Stonefield Flyer. The dam is an unraced half-sister to several winners including the fairly useful 2-y-o listed-placed 6f winner Prince Of Elegance. The second dam, Elegant Lady (by Selkirk), was a quite useful 6f winner. (Mr G R Leckie). *"He was quite highly strung so he's been gelded and naturally he's taken a bit of time to get over it. So we're a little bit behind with him but he should be racing by the end of June. We trained his brother Stonefield Flyer but this horse is slightly bigger than he was at this stage. He's quite scopey and a good-looking horse".*

445. FOREVER A LADY (IRE) ★★★
b.f. Dark Angel – Unicamp (Royal Academy). February 23. Tenth foal. £27,000Y. Doncaster Premier. Tom Malone/Keith Dalgleish. Half-sister to 4 winners including the quite useful Irish 2-y-o 7f, 1m and hurdles winner Kempes, the quite useful 7f and 1m winner of 13 races (including at 2 yrs) Smarty Socks (by Elnadim) and the modest 7f (at 2 yrs) to 10f winner Singora Lady (by Intikhab). The dam, a quite useful 2-y-o 6f winner, is a half-sister to 5 winners including the useful dual 2-y-o 7f and subsequent UAE winner Dulcet Spear. The second dam, Honeyspike (by Chief's Crown), placed over 1m, is a half-sister to 6 winners including the Irish listed 10f winner and US Grade 1 second Casey Tibbs. (Straightline Construction Ltd). *"A small, strong, 2-y-o type, she's very laid-back in her work and I think there's more there than she's giving us at the minute. I'm not sure when she'll be out, but I guess she'll be racing in June and she'll be a sprinting type".*

446. HOLLYWOOD KEN (IRE) ★★★
b.c. Arcano – Third Dimension (Suave Dancer). March 20. Eighth foal. €70,000Y. Goffs Orby.

Tom Malone. Half-brother to 6 winners including the 14f winner and Group 2 Beresford Stakes second Orgilgo Bay (by Lawman), the quite useful winner of 4 races at around 2m Theola (by Kalanisi), to the Italian winner of 6 races and listed placed My Pension (by Kendor) and the minor French winner of 6 races from 2 to 4 yrs Marie Octobre (by Daylami). The dam, a minor French 3-y-o winner, is a half-sister to 7 winners. The second dam, Fly Me (by Luthier), won the Group 3 10.5f Prix Corrida and the Group 3 10.5f Prix de Flore and is a half-sister to the Group 1 Grand Prix de Paris winner Galiani. (Straightline Construction Ltd). *"A lovely horse, he's big, strong and has a great attitude. He's a quick learner – everything just clicks with him. Looking at his pedigree you could think he'd need more time, but if he continues taking his work like this then I'll be happy to run him around May time".*

447. LIVELLA FELLA (IRE) ★★★
b.f. Strategic Prince – Ardent Lady (Alhaarth). March 16. Seventh living foal. £12,000Y. Doncaster Silver. Bobby O'Ryan/Keith Dalgleish. Half-sister to the fairly useful Irish 1m winner and listed placed Gatamalata (by Spartacus), to the Italian winner and 7.5f listed placed Denusa (by Aussie Rules), the fair 2-y-o 6f and 8.5f winner Daniella de Bruijn (by Orpen) and the fair 2-y-o 5f winner First Choice (by Choisir). The dam, a fair 9.5f winner, is a half-sister to 6 winners. The second dam, Arvika (by Baillamont), a minor French 3-y-o winner, is a half-sister to 5 winners. (Middleham Park Racing XXIII). *"She's working OK, seems to have plenty of speed and she's likely to be racing in May".*

448. MR GRUMPY ★★
b.c. Sir Percy – Panna (Polish Precedent). April 4. Tenth foal. £26,000Y. Doncaster Premier. Tom Malone/Keith Dalgleish. Half-brother to the quite useful 10f and hurdles winner Hot Diamond (by Desert Prince), to the fair 12f winners Kunegunda (by Pivotal) and Wulfrida (by King's Best) and the modest 9f winner Red Lily (by Red Ransom). The dam, a useful 10f winner, is a half-sister to 7 winners including Pentire (King George VI and Queen Elizabeth Diamond Stakes, Irish Champion Stakes etc). The second dam, Gull

Nook (by Mill Reef), a smart winner over 10.5f at 3 yrs and second in the Group 2 12f Ribblesdale Stakes, is a half-sister to the Group 3 winners Banket and Mr Pintips. (Straightline Construction Ltd). *"He's a back-end type going off what I've seen so far. It's a middle distance pedigree anyway and not surprisingly the penny hasn't dropped yet, so I'll let him come in his own time".*

449. NORTH SPIRIT (IRE) ★★★★
b.c. Zebedee – Zara's Girl (Tillerman). March 23. First foal. €45,000Y. Tattersalls Ireland September. Bobby O'Ryan/Keith Dalgleish. The dam is an unplaced half-sister to 10 winners including the smart listed 7f winner of 8 races and multiple Group 3 placed Dohasa. The second dam, Zara's Birthday (by Waajib), placed from 7f (at 2 yrs) to 2m, is a half-sister to 4 winners. *"He's likely to be one of our first 2-y-o runners. He has loads of speed, he'll start off at five furlongs and I think he may want top of the ground".*

450. SATTELAC ★★★
b.f. Kodiac – Sattelight (Fraam). February 24. Sixth foal. £23,000Y. Doncaster Premier. Bobby O'Ryan/Keith Dalgleish. Half-sister to the Swedish 2-y-o winner Little Miss Take (by Royal Applause) and to the minor Italian 3-y-o winner Bounty Sat (by Bahamian Bounty). The dam, placed once in a bumper race, is a sister to the listed-placed winner Indiannie Star and a half-sister to 4 winners including the 2-y-o Group 2 6f winner in Germany Ajigolo and the multiple sprinter winner and Group 3 placed Kickboxer. The second dam, Ajig Dancer (by Niniski), a quite useful 7f winner of 4 races, is a half-sister to 2 winners. *"I like her, she's got a great attitude and she's done everything we've asked of her. She's a lovely size and has a nice big stride on her. In her work she's very straightforward – it's there if you want it but if not she's happy to just slot in".*

451. UNNAMED ★★★
b.f. Elnadim – Bijan (Mukaddamah). April 2. Eighth foal. £10,000Y. Doncaster Silver. Tom Malone/Keith Dalgleish. Half-sister to the fair 6f winner of 5 races (including at 2 yrs) Gung Ho Jack (by Moss Vale), to the modest 6f (at 2 yrs) and 5f winner Ramblin Bob (by Piccolo), the moderate 5f winner Cliffords Reprieve (by

Kheleyf) and a winner abroad by Sleeping Indian. The dam, a modest 5f (at 2 yrs) and 6f winner, is a half-sister to 6 winners including the Group 3 Ballyogan Stakes winner Yomalo. The second dam, Alkariyh (by Alydar), a fairly useful 2-y-o 6f winner, is a half-sister to 5 winners. *"A speedy filly, we'll start her off at five furlongs, she's strong enough and straightforward".*

452. UNNAMED ★★
b.f. Zebedee – Derval (One Cool Cat). January 16. Second foal. £25,000Y. Doncaster Premier. Tom Malone/Keith Dalgleish. The dam is an unplaced half-sister to 5 winners including the French listed winner Arikaria and the Hong Kong stakes winner Sacred Nuts. The second dam, Sagrada (by Primo Dominie), a minor German 3-y-o winner, is a full or half-sister to 10 winners including two listed winners in Germany. *"A strong filly with plenty of bone, she was showing us plenty early on but we backed off her a bit. So she's only just starting back now and I haven't done enough with her to be able to say much more".*

453. UNNAMED ★★★★
b.f. Dark Angel – Jemima's Art (Fantastic Light). February 14. Third foal. €43,000Y. Goffs Sportsmans. Bobby O'Ryan/Keith Dalgleish. Sister to the quite useful 2014 2-y-o 1m winner Shalimah. The dam, a moderate 10f winner, is a half-sister to 11 winners including the US dual Grade 2 10f winner Battle Of Hastings and the smart listed 12f winner Villa Carlotta. The second dam, Subya (by Night Shift), was a very useful winner of 5 races from 5f (at 2 yrs) to 10f including the Lupe Stakes, the Masaka Stakes and the Star Stakes (all listed events). *"I like her, a good-looking, athletic filly, she's been working well, has a good attitude and should be out in midsummer. Her full brother won last year as a 2-y-o but only at the back-end over a mile. So it seems the dam is a stamina influence".*

454. UNNAMED ★★★
b.f. Roderic O'Connor – Maundays Bay (Invincible Spirit). April 10. First foal. €45,000Y. Goffs Sportsmans. Bobby O'Ryan/Keith Dalgleish. The dam, a fair Irish 2-y-o 7f winner, is a half-sister to 2 winners. The second dam, Mystic Mile (by Sadler's Wells), a fairly useful

10f and 11.6f winner, was listed-placed and is a half-sister to 3 minor winners. (Weldspec Glasgow Ltd). *"She's small, shows a lot of speed and she'll be one of a number of fillies I have that'll be making their debuts in May or June. From what I've seen so far I'll be starting her at five furlongs".*

455. UNNAMED ★★

ch.f. Compton Place – Pink Delight (Rock Of Gibraltar). February 14. First foal. £14,000Y. Doncaster Premier. Tom Malone/Keith Dalgleish. The dam ran twice unplaced and is a half-sister to 2 winners including the Group 2 Prix Robert Papin winner Irish Field. The second dam, Turkana Girl (by Hernando), is a placed half-sister to 5 winners including Leo (Group 2 Royal Lodge Stakes). *"A workmanlike filly, she gets on with things and she's another in that batch of 2-y-o's that should be making their debuts around May time. Like a lot of first foals she's not over-big but she's tough and gets on with the job. She's still for sale if anyone is looking for a nice filly".*

456. UNNAMED ★★

b.c. Jeremy – Step With Style (Gulch). May 2. Eighth foal. €70,000Y. Goffs Sportsmans. Bobby O'Ryan/Keith Dalgleish. Half-brother to the useful 6f (at 2 yrs) and 9f winner and dual Group 3 placed Firey Red (by Pivotal), to the quite useful Irish 12f winner Comedic Art (by Dansili), the minor Irish 2-y-o 1m winner Sansibar (by Linamix) and the modest Irish 1m winner Shy Smile (by Peintre Celebre). The dam, a quite useful 1m winner, is a half-sister to 4 winners including the Group 3 placed Absolute Glee. The second dam, Looking Brill (by Sadler's Wells), won over 12f in Ireland and is a half-sister to 10 winners. (Weldspec Glasgow Ltd). *"A big, strong type with great bone, he's very backward and doesn't really know what's expected of him yet. I won't force him and he'll tell me when he's ready".*

TOM DASCOMBE
457. ARCANADA (IRE) ★★

ch.c. Arcano – Bond Deal (Pivotal). March 5. Fourth foal. £42,000Y. Doncaster Premier. Sackville/Donald. The dam, a winner of 6 races in Italy and the USA including a minor stakes, was third in the Group 3 1m Premio Carlo Chiesa and is a half-sister to 3 winners

including the fairly useful triple 6f winner and listed-placed Dawn Eclipse. The second dam, Prima (by Primo Dominie), a fair 5f and 6f placed 2-y-o, is a half-sister to 4 minor winners. *"A lovely colt, probably the most laid-back 2-y-o I've ever seen, he's a pleasure to deal with. He's got a white face and four white socks and is very 'up behind' at the moment. I'm surprised at how forward he is and how much he can do at this early stage, so he may get a run in mid-May even if it's just for experience. He needs further than five furlongs and he copes well".*

458. BIG AMIGO (IRE) ★★★★

b.c. Bahamian Bounty – Goldamour (Fasliyev). March 4. Second foal. €65,000Y. Goffs Orby. Sackville/Donald. The dam, placed at 3 yrs in France, is a half-sister to 3 winners. The second dam, Glamadour (by Sanglamore), a winner over 11.5f in France, is a half-sister to 10 winners including the outstanding multiple Group 1 winner Goldikova and the Group 1 Prix Vermeille winner Galikova. (L A Bellman). *"A big colt and a lovely animal, we've gone steady with him but he finds it all easy. A good-moving horse, he's had no setbacks and I should think he'd be out over six furlongs in the middle of May. If he proves good enough we'll go to Ascot. He's been cantering alongside horses that have been here for six weeks longer than him and has already caught up to them".*

459. BULGE BRACKET ★★★

b.c. Great Journey (JPN) – Baldovina (Tale Of The Cat). February 17. Fourth foal. Half-brother to the Group 2 5f Queen Mary Stakes winner Ceiling Kitty (by Red Clubs) and to the fair 2-y-o triple 5f winner Van Go Go (by Dutch Art). The dam is a placed half-sister to the Japanese dual Group 3 winner One Carat. The second dam, Baldwina (by Pistolet Bleu), won the Group 3 Prix Penelope and is a half-sister to 5 winners. The sire was smart at around a mile in Japan. (Chasemore Farm). *"A half-brother to a nice filly we had called Ceiling Kitty. He's a different model to her but he seems to be quite forward, he's going well and I'd be hopeful he'd be good enough to win a maiden".*

460. CALDER PRINCE (IRE) ★★★

br.c. Dark Angel – Flame Of Ireland (Fasliyev).

May 22. Third foal. €30,000Y. Tattersalls Ireland September. Sackville/Donald. Half-brother to a winner in Greece by Marju. The dam, a fair Irish 2-y-o 6f winner, is a half-sister to 9 winners. The second dam, Grenouillere (by Alysheba), is a placed half-sister to 4 winners including Oczy Czarnie (Group 1 Prix de la Salamandre) and Glaieul (Group 1 Criterium de Saint-Cloud). (Calderprint Ltd). *"He was a very late foal and as a result he was quite a small yearling, which meant we bought him for a bit less than I expected. He's by a sire that I really like in Dark Angel and he's grown an awful lot. We won't be in a rush with him and if he doesn't run before June there's no panic".*

461. CANCAN KATY ★★

b.f. Canford Cliffs – Katy Nowaitee (Komaite). March 1. Seventh living foal. 50,000Y. Tattersalls October Book 2. Blandford Bloodstock. Half-brother to the US Grade 3 9f and listed winner Tottie (by Fantastic Light), to the fairly useful 8.5f and 10.5f winner and Group 3 Chester Vase second Mister Impatience and the quite useful 10f, 11f and jumps winner Harry Tricker (both by Hernando). The dam, a useful listed 10f winner of 5 races, is a half-sister to 3 winners. The second dam, Cold Blow (by Posse), a modest 7f placed 2-y-o, is a half-sister to 3 minor winners. (Chasemore Farm). *"Bought by Andrew Black at the sales, the dam was a good filly and winner of the Cambridgeshire. This filly was a real madam when she came in, we had to re-break her, then pony her around the place for weeks and she just got better and better. She's a sweet filly now. The pedigree suggests she'll want seven furlongs as a 2-y-o so we'll go slowly with her, but she's improving all the time. That's the most important thing".*

462. CAPONOVA (IRE) ★★

b.c. Bushranger – Satin Cape (Cape Cross). April 11. Fifth foal. £18,000Y. Doncaster Silver. Sackville/Donald. Half-brother to the fairly useful 6f to 8.5f winner of 6 races Capo Rosso (by Red Clubs), to the quite useful Irish 2-y-o 5f winner Jolly Snake, the fair 2-y-o 5f winner Molamento and the moderate Irish 7f winner Elusive Gent (all by Elusive City). The dam, placed once over 5f at 2 yrs from 2 starts, is a half-sister to 6 winners abroad. The second dam, Marylou Whitney (by Fappiano),

was placed in the USA and is a half-sister to 3 winners. (Deva Racing Partnership). *"A half-brother to Capo Rosso who has done us proud over the years, he's owned by the same Partnership. Both Capo Rosso and this one go everywhere with their tongues hanging out of their mouths, so that trait must come from the mare! Capo Rosso improved with age and I think this lad will probably be similar, he's going to want six and probably seven furlongs, but he's a nice horse".*

463. CHESHAM ROSE (IRE) ★★★

ch.f. Mastercraftsman – Rose's Destination (Dubai Destination). April 24. Fourth foal. €22,000Y. Tattersalls Ireland September. Sackville/Donald. Closely related to the Italian winner at 2 and 3 yrs Choisir Roses (by Choisir). The dam is an unraced half-sister to 6 winners including the dual listed winner and Group 1 7f National Stakes second Golden Arrow. The second dam, Cheal Rose (by Dr Devious), was placed 8 times at up to 1m in Ireland and is a half-sister to 6 winners including the US Grade 3 winner Buffalo Berry (herself dam of the US Grade 3 winner and Grade 1 placed Chattahoochee War). (Chesham Rose Partnership). *"A lovely filly, she was quite small when we bought her but she's been doing more than I expected. She's had a touch of sore shins so we've backed off her a bit, but she's grown into a nice filly. One would assume that she'd want seven furlongs".*

464. CRESCENT QUEEN ★★

ch.f. Nayef – Lilac Moon (Dr Fong). February 19. First foal. The dam, a modest 1m to 12f winner of 4 races, is a half-sister to 4 other minor winners. The second dam, Luna De Miel (by Shareef Dancer), placed five times in Germany, is a full or half-sister to 4 winners including the dam of the Group 1 Prix de l'Opera winner Lady Marian. (Chasemore Farm & Owen Promotions). *"By Nayef, a sire you wouldn't normally associate with precocity, and out of a mare that we trained. She's a little bit small so we'll give her a bit more time to grow and it would be nice to get her to win for the mare".*

465. DUTCH GALLERY ★★★

b.c. Dutch Art – Luluti (Kheleyf). February 28. Second foal. 65,000Y. Tattersalls October Book 2. D Ffrench Davis. The dam ran once unplaced and is a half-sister to 5 winners including the Group 3 Princess Margaret Stakes third Excellerator. The second dam, Amsicora (by Cadeaux Genereux), is an unraced half-sister to 3 minor winners. (Saleh Al Homaizi & Imad Al Sagar). *"A colt that was bred by his owners and bought back at the sales, he looks very much like a 2-y-o. He's a lovely, big horse and being by Dutch Art you would hope he'd be speedy. I guess he'll be out around June time".*

466. FALCON ANNIE (IRE) ★★★
b.f. Kodiac – Frosted (Dr Fong). March 16. Third foal. €70,000Y. Goffs Orby. Sackville/ Donald. The dam ran unplaced twice and is a sister to the triple listed winner and Group 2 6f Gimcrack Stakes second Andronikos and a half-sister to 3 winners. The second dam, Arctic Air (by Polar Falcon), a quite useful 2-y-o 7f winner, is a sister to the useful listed 7f winner Arctic Char and a half-sister to 6 winners including the Group 2 winners Barrow Creek and Last Resort and the dam of the Group 2 winner Trans Island. (S Burns, M Smyth, D Studholme). *"A lovely filly, very sharp and racy and just how you'd hope a Kodiac would be. She looks like she's ready to run, so she'll hopefully make her debut sometime in April. A strong, early type, but with a bit of size to her so hopefully she'll continue".*

467. FIRE DIAMOND ★★★
b.c. Firebreak – Diapason (Mull Of Kintyre). March 4. First foal. £2,600Y. Ascot November. Not sold. The dam, a fair 6f and 7f winner of 3 races at 3 and 4 yrs, is a half-sister to the useful 2-y-o winner and Group 2 Richmond Stakes third Mullaad. The second dam, Suaad (by Fools Holme), was a fair 2-y-o 7f winner. (Mr John Brown). *"A home-bred of the Browns, he's out of a mare I trained and he looks just like her. That's not a bad thing because she won three races. We're pleased with him, he's pretty straightforward and we're pushing ahead. He's pretty laid-back, knows his job quite well and he'll be out in May".*

468. FIRESNAKE ★★★
b.c. Dandy Man – La Bataille (Out Of Place). April 3. Seventh foal. £70,000Y. Doncaster Premier. Sackville/Donald. Half-brother to the modest 2014 dual 6f placed 2-y-o

Battleranger (by Bushranger), to the fair 7f (at 2 yrs) and 8.5f winner Aint Got A Scooby (by Red Clubs) and a minor German 3-y-o winner by Kodiac. The dam, placed at 2 yrs in the USA, is a half-sister to 4 winners including the useful 2-y-o 6f winner and Group 3 Sweet Solera Stakes second Don't Forget Faith. The second dam, Contredance (by Danzig), won the Grade 1 Washington Lassie Stakes in the USA and is a full or half-sister to 8 winners including the US Grade 2 winner and smart broodmare Skimble. (Pritchard & Woodward). *"A lovely horse, he's sure to want six furlongs but he's ready to run now so he'll start over five furlongs in mid-April".*

469. FOUR'S COMPANY (IRE) ★★★
b.f. Fast Company – Mrs Beeton (Dansili). January 24. Second foal. €13,000Y. Tattersalls Ireland September. Sackville/Donald. The dam, a fair 1m winner, is a half-sister to the very smart multiple Group 3 10f winner Stotsfold. The second dam, Eliza Acton (by Shirley Heights), a fair 2-y-o 1m winner, is a half-sister to 4 winners including listed 10f Winter Derby and subsequent US Grade 3 winner Supreme Sound and to the unraced Why So Silent (dam of the Group 3 winner Leporello and the listed winners Calypso Grant and Poppy Carew). (Morris, O'Halloran, Satchell, Willcock). *"A nice filly. I like these Fast Company's – I'm surprised by them because they've got a bit of speed but they stay as well. She looks the type to be out early but she'll get six furlongs and maybe seven. She was a cheap filly I thought".*
TRAINERS' BARGAIN BUY

470. FRESH ARUGULA (IRE) ★★★★
b.c. Fast Company – Temecula (High Chaparral). February 4. First foal. 55,000Y. Tattersalls October Book 2. Sackville/Donald. The dam, a fair 10f and 10.5f winner, is a half-sister to one winner. The second dam, Gujarat (by Distant View), is an unraced half-sister to 5 winners. *"He looks a proper 2-y-o and his owner has had some luck with us with horses like Walkingonthemoon and Hung Parliament. This one could be the best he's had, because he's a lovely horse. He's got the speed for five furlongs but will probably want further, he's tall, muscular and has a great attitude. A straightforward 2-y-o, he'll be running in April I should think".*

471. GAMBIT ★★

b.c. New Approach – Sospel (Kendor). January 22. Thirteenth foal. 120,000Y. Tattersalls October Book 1. Sackville/Donald. Half-brother to 10 winners including the Group 3 6f Premio Tudini winner Charming Woman (by Invincible Spirit), the Italian listed winner Men's Magazine (by Dr Devious) and the Italian listed-placed winner Vanity Woman (by Nayef). The dam, a minor German 2-y-o winner, is a half-sister to 4 other minor winners. The second dam, Scene Galante (by Sicyos), won 3 minor races at 4 yrs in France and is a half-sister to 6 winners including the German dual Group 3 winner Ladoni. (L A Bellman & Caroline Ingram). *"The biggest horse I've ever bought, he weighs 550kgs, so although he was an early foal and he looks ready, he's not. His size tells you he'll need time, we'll just go steady with him and if we get a run or two out of him before the end of the season I'll be delighted. He's a lovely colt, looks sure to want a bit of a trip and is hopefully one that'll develop into a nice 3-y-o".*

472. GAMESTERS BOY ★★

b.c. Firebreak – Gamesters Lady (Almushtarak). April 4. Second foal. Brother to the moderate Gamesters Lad, placed fourth once over 6f at 2 yrs in 2014. The dam, a modest 6f (at 2 yrs) to 12f and hurdles winner, is a half-sister to a winner over jumps. The second dam, Tycoon Tina (by Tina's Pet), was a moderate 1m to 12f winner. (Bryn Vyrnwy Caravan Park Ltd). *"He's one for six/seven furlongs but we'll get him out early enough to see what he can do. Hopefully we can get him to win a little race".*

473. GOLDEN GLIMMER (IRE) ★★★

b.f. Danehill Dancer – Gilded Vanity (Indian Ridge). March 14. Eighth foal. 320,000Y. Tattersalls October Book 1. Peter & Ross Doyle. Sister to the useful 2-y-o dual 6f winner and Group 2 Superlative Stakes second Birdman and to the Irish 2-y-o Group 3 6f placed A Mind Of Her Own, closely related to the fair 2-y-o 5f winner Roman Seal (by Holy Roman Emperor) and half-sister to the fair 6f winner of 4 races Desert Icon (by Desert Style). The dam won over 5f in Ireland and is a sister to the Irish 2,000 Guineas second Fa-Eq and a half-sister to 5 winners including the listed winner Corinium. The second dam, Searching Star (by Rainbow Quest), was a modest 6f to 11.3f placed half-sister to 8 winners. (Chasemore Farm). *"She's a half-sister to a filly we had called Roman Seal who we really liked but unfortunately she broke her pelvis. It's Danehill Dancer's last crop so I hope she's good because it would be nice for the owner to have a Danehill Dancer broodmare. Hopefully she'll win a race or two but it's difficult to assess her trip because she came in very late and she's been backward in her coat. She's coming now and looking better all the time, but she won't work until May".*

474. HAPPY TIDINGS ★★★★

b.f. Exceed And Excel – Helena Molony (Sadler's Wells). April 12. Fifth foal. €105,000Y. Arqana Deauville August. Private sale. Half-sister to the quite useful 10f winner Dance Of Heroes (by Danehill Dancer), to the fair 10f winner Red Hand (by Mr Greeley) and the fair 9.5f winner Heavenly Sound (by Street Cry). The dam won once over 10f at 3 yrs and was listed-placed in Ireland and is a sister to the Derby, Irish Derby and Breeders Cup Turf winner High Chaparral and the Group 2 Dante Stakes winner Black Bear Island. The second dam, Kasora (by Darshaan), is an unraced full or half-sister to 8 winners. (Newsells Park Stud & Manor House Stables). *"A lovely horse that was led out of the ring unsold at Arqana. I couldn't believe she didn't sell because I loved her. We managed to do a deal with her owners, Newsells Park. She's elegant, tall and everything you'd want in a filly. I don't know what sort of a trip she'll want because the dam's side suggests stamina but her sire certainly doesn't. At the moment she's doing everything right and she's a lovely filly".*

475. ICE DREAM (IRE) ★★

b.f. Frozen Power – Mikes Baby (Key Of Luck). March 30. Sixth foal. €28,000Y. Tattersalls Ireland September. Sackville/Donald. Half-sister to the US winner and stakes-placed Ace Of Aces (by Antonius Pius) and to the minor Italian winner of 8 races from 2 to 6 yrs Su Contadori (by Indian Haven). The dam, a modest 4-y-o 6f winner, is a half-sister to 5 winners including the listed placed Palace Royale. The second dam, Trojan Tale (by Critique), is an unplaced half-sister to 4 winners. (Mr D J Lowe). *"Frozen Power is a first season sire so we don't know what to expect from him yet. This filly was my favourite yearling at the time I bought her, she's lovely to look at and just has a bit of a temperament so we've just got to nurse her in the right way. We'll feel our way with her and I'd like to think she'll be a six furlong 2-y-o".*

476. IDEAL RECRUIT (IRE) ★★
br.c. Lord Shanakill – Gemma's Pearl (Marju). March 16. First foal. €22,000Y. Tattersalls Ireland September. Sackville/Donald. The dam, placed once at 3 yrs in Italy, is a half-sister to the very useful listed-placed winner Yes Mr President. The second dam, Royals Special (by Caerleon), is an unplaced half-sister to 5 winners including Ezzoud, winner of the Eclipse Stakes and the Juddmonte International Stakes (twice) and Distant Relative, winner of the Sussex Stakes and the Prix du Moulin. (Mr R Jones). *"This horse was very forward but he's just had a bit of a setback in the last few days which will probably hold us up for a few weeks. He's quite tall but I still think he'll be out in May, he's sharp enough and he probably wants six furlongs".*

477. LA CELEBS VILLE (IRE) ★★★
b.f. Sea The Stars – Bryanstown (Galileo). February 1. First foal. 70,000Y. Tattersalls October Book 2. Sackville/Donald. The dam, placed fourth over 9f at 4 yrs on her only start, is a half-sister to 4 minor winners. The second dam, Stiletta (by Dancing Brave), is an unraced sister to the Epsom and Irish Derby winner Commander In Chief and a half-sister to the champion 2-y-o and miler Warning, the US Grade 1 winner Yashmak, the Irish Derby second Deploy and the Great Voltigeur Stakes winner Dushyantor. (Newport Rangers). *"I liked her at the sales and her dam is a half-sister to the dam of a horse we have called Double Discount who is rated 95. She's slightly small so you'd like to see her grow, but she's by a great racehorse and sire, so on pedigree she has every chance of being useful. We won't be in a rush with her, but she has a fantastic pedigree".*

478. LEMBIT AND BUTLER (IRE) ★★★
b.c. Lilbourne Lad – Fathoming (Gulch). April 7. Fourth foal. £58,000Y. Doncaster Premier. Sackville/Donald. Closely related to the fairly useful 2-y-o 6f winner and listed-

placed Mister Marc and to the fair 2-y-o 7f winner Zeshov (both by Acclamation). The dam ran once unplaced and is a half-sister to 3 minor winners. The second dam, Ocean Ridge (by Storm Bird), winner of the Group 2 6f Prix Robert Papin and second in the Group 1 1m Coronation Stakes, is a half-sister to 6 winners including the Group 2 Gimcrack Stakes second Fokine. (The Amarone Partnership). *"A nice, big colt, he's just a little bit lazy, which doesn't matter because I'm sure he'll come good in his own time. I've given him one piece of work just to try and wake him up a bit and he's going the right way. He's a bit backward thinking so he's not one you'd expect to win first time out".*

479. MICKEY (IRE) ★★
b.c. Zoffany – Enchantment (Compton Place). April 15. Fourth foal. £18,000Y. Doncaster Premier. Manor House Stables. Half-brother to the moderate 6f winner Heroic Endeavour (by Ishiguru) and to the moderate 5f winner Dream Sika (by Elnadim). The dam, a useful 5f and 6f winner of 5 races, is a half-sister to 5 winners. The second dam, Tharwa (by Last Tycoon), a modest 5.2f and 6f winner, is a half-sister to 8 winners including the French listed winner Blushing All Over and good broodmare Come On Rosi (the dam of 4 stakes winners). (Mrs Janet Lowe). *"I liked him when I saw him at Doncaster Sales. He's a good-looking colt and yet he didn't cost much for a colt from Doncaster. I think Zoffany has every chance of being a successful sire. This colt has grown so much it's unbelievable, I like him a lot but he pleases you one week and then disappoints you the next, so I just need him to put two pieces of good work together".*

480. MONSIEUR GLORY ★★
ch.c. Monsieur Bond – Chushka (Pivotal). April 15. Second foal. £40,000Y. Doncaster Premier. Sackville/Donald. Half-brother to Emblaze (by Showcasing), placed fourth on all three of his starts at 2 yrs in 2014. The dam, a fair 6f winner, is a half-sister to 4 winners including the 2-y-o Group 2 6f July Stakes winner Captain Hurricane. The second dam, Ravine (by Indian Ridge), a quite useful 3-y-o 6f and 7f winner, is a half-sister to 4 winners including the Lowther Stakes and Falmouth Stakes winner Niche. (Ms A A Yap & Mr F

Ma). *"He's a huge horse and has the neck of a stallion. He's been doing some cantering, but some swimming as well to try and get some weight off him. I quite like the sire, but this colt is one that's going to take time".*

481. OUR ELTON (USA) ★★★

ch.c. Speightstown – Warsaw Ballet (El Prado). February 22. Second foal. €80,000Y. Goffs Orby. Sackville/Donald. The dam, a German 3-y-o listed-placed winner, is a half-sister to one winner in the USA. The second dam, Whiletheiron'shot (by Smart Strike), a US stakes-placed winner of 4 races at 3 and 4 yrs, is a half-sister to 8 winners including two US stakes winners. (D Studholme, M Smyth & S Burns). *"He seems to go through stages where he does a bit of work but then goes backward. I thought he was going to be quite early but he seems to have lengthened and there's plenty of him now. His owners aren't in any rush and we'll let him tell us when he's ready. He'll be out before mid-season".*

482. REFLEKTOR (IRE) ★★★

ch.c. Bahamian Bounty – Baby Bunting (Wolfhound). April 10. Tenth foal. £45,000Y. Doncaster Premier. Sackville/Donald. Half-brother to the fairly useful 5f winner of 4 races (including a listed event at 2 yrs) Bahamian Babe, to the fairly useful 5f and 6f winner of 8 races (including at 2 yrs) Victorian Bounty, the fair 6f winner Ventura Cove (all by Bahamian Bounty) and the fair triple 6f winner including at 2 yrs Nova Champ (by Intikhab). The dam, a modest sprint-placed maiden, is a half-sister to 7 winners including the dual Group winners Atraf and Son Pardo. The second dam, Flitteriss Park (by Beldale Flutter), a modest 1m winner, is a half-sister to 5 winners. (Mr D J Lowe). *"He's not over-big but he's surprised me because although he was looking lazy he didn't half shift when we gave him a gallop. He's a very laid-back horse that doesn't really know what he's doing yet, but we took him for a canter at Nottingham racecourse yesterday and he was good. There's a bit of speed there and I can imagine him making his debut at Bath in a class 5 maiden and then if he's good enough he'll go to Chester".*

483. ROMAN TIMES (IRE) ★★★

b.f. Holy Roman Emperor – Timeless Dream (Oasis Dream). March 28. Third foal. Half-sister to the 2015 1m placed 3-y-o Happy Dreams (by Fastnet Rock). The dam, a modest 6f winner, is half-sister to 7 winners including Welsh Emperor (Group 2 7f Hungerford Stakes) and the listed 5f winner Majestic Times. The second dam, Simply Times (by Dodge), ran twice unplaced at 2 yrs and is a half-sister to 5 winners. *"Chester racecourse rang us up to say they'd like a horse in training with us. This filly came from Goldford Stud which is just up the road from us, but we were told her sire was Henrythenavigator. When we found out the mistake we were very pleased because we much prefer Holy Roman Emperor! She didn't arrive until February and by the middle of April she was galloping. She's got a bit of speed and we'll set her off at five furlongs before moving up to six. I'm really pleased with her".*

484. SHARP JACK ★★★

ch.c. Pivotal – Sharp Terms (Kris). March 20. Eighth foal. 50,000Y. Tattersalls October Book 1. Sackville/Donald. Half-brother to the 2-y-o Group 2 6f Lowther Stakes and Group 2 Queen Mary Stakes winner Best Terms (by Exceed And Excel), to the Group 3 placed Italian winner Sunsemperchi (by Montjeu), the quite useful 10f and hurdles winner Helvelius (by Polish Precedent) and the fair 9f winner Miss Chicane (by Refuse To Bend). The dam is an unraced half-sister to 9 winners including the Group 2 winners First Charter and Anton Chekhov. The second dam, By Charter (by Shirley Heights), a 2-y-o winner and second in the listed Cheshire Oaks, is a sister to the smart Group 2 winner Zinaad. (P Bamford, L A Bellman, C McKee). *"I was delighted when Jack Berry came to one of our owner's days in October. This colt was his favourite of our yearlings, so that's a good endorsement and hence we gave the colt the name Sharp Jack! Although he's a half-brother to a champion 2-y-o filly in Best Terms, his sire Pivotal isn't the most precocious 2-y-o sire there is, but he can gallop alright and I think he'll want six furlongs. We'll try to find a maiden for him in the middle of May with one eye on Royal Ascot if he proves good enough. He looks like a 2-y-o, he's muscular, strong and well put together, but being by Pivotal suggests we should give him a bit more time".*

485. SIMPLY ME ★★★★
b.f. New Approach – Ego (Green Desert).
March 27. Eighth living foal. 90,000Y.
Tattersalls October Book 1. Sackville/Donald.
Half-sister to 7 winners including the modest
2014 2-y-o 7f winner Frosty Times (by Silver
Frost), the useful 7f (at 2 yrs) and 1m winner
and listed-placed Chef, the fair 7f winner
I'm Sensational (both by Selkirk), the quite
useful 2-y-o 7f winner and listed-placed Self
Centred (by Medicean) and the fair dual 7f
winner (including at 2 yrs) Cut And Thrust
(by Haafhd). The dam, a very useful 2-y-o
dual 6f winner, was listed-placed twice and
is a half-sister to 3 winners. The second dam,
Myself (by Nashwan), a smart winner of the
Group 3 7f Nell Gwyn Stakes, is a half-sister
to 12 winners including the Bluebook (Group
3 Princess Margaret Stakes). (L A Bellman).
*"Well named, being out of Ego, she's a beautiful
looking horse. I gave her a bit of time because
her pedigree suggested it, but we've started
doing a bit with her and she's coping really
well. She's very feminine, quite narrow and
reasonably tall, if she continues to cope with
her work she'll be racing in May. I can see her
wanting at least seven furlongs later on".*

486. SPEY SECRET (IRE) ★★★
br.c. Kyllachy – Chiarezza (Fantastic Light).
March 18. Second foal. £75,000Y. Doncaster
Premier. Sackville/Donald. Half-brother to a
minor winner in Australia by Bernardini. The
dam, a minor 2-y-o winner in Australia, is a
half-sister to 2 winners including the US stakes
winner Silvestris. The second dam, the quite
useful 7f winner Kafhanee (by Seeking The
Gold), is a half-brother to 6 winners including
the Group 3 1m Prix d'Aumale winner
Birthstone and the useful 9f to 14f winner and
Group 3 12f St Simon Stakes third Songcraft.
(Spey Whisky). *"A lovely, big horse, I just hope
he's not too big for the early part of the season.
We'll take our time with him and if he was
good enough the owners may send him out to
Hong Kong because their business is based out
there. We'll try and get him to Royal Ascot if
we can, that's what the owners would like. He's
a big, strong horse that moves well but he may
just want a bit more time".*

487. SPIRIT OF THE VALE (IRE) ★★
b.f. Royal Applause – Nesmeh (More Than

Ready). March 13. Second foal. 25,000Y.
Tattersalls October Book 3. Sackville/Donald.
Half-sister to Roman De Brut (by Rock Of
Gibraltar), a modest 8.5f fourth at 2 yrs in
2014. The dam is an unraced sister to the
minor US stakes winner Ready Racer and a
half-sister to the US listed winner Speedway.
The second dam, Freefourracing (by French
Deputy), won the 2-y-o Group 3 Prestige
Stakes and is a half-sister to 4 winners.
(Messrs' DB, L and MW Salmon). *"You can't
miss her because she's got four white socks
and a big white face. She's got a fair attitude,
she looks like a Royal Applause and I guess
she'll want six furlongs and maybe seven. She's
a reasonable size and you wouldn't say she's
without a chance of making a 2-y-o".*

488. SWANSWAY ★★★
ch.c. Showcasing – Spring Stroll (Skywalker).
March 16. Fifth foal. €55,000Y. Arqana
Deauville August V2. Sackville/Donald.
Half-brother to the French listed-placed 10f
winner Dinner's Out (by War Front). The dam
was placed in the USA and is a half-sister to
4 minor winners. The second dam, Annora
Springs (by Kris S) won 2 minor races and is a
half-sister to 8 winners including Alice Springs
(three US Grade 2 wins). (M Smyth, S Burns,
D Studholme & T Flaherty). *"I don't think I've
ever known a 2-y-o to change so much. We
bought him in August and was a light looking
horse. So we were taking a bit of a chance on
him because we had to hope he'd develop,
but my God he has done. He's huge now, has
a great shape to him, beautiful arches, neck
and quarters and looks like a real racehorse.
The sire did incredibly well in his first season
last year, this horse looks like he'll want further
than five furlongs but that's fine. I should think
if you sent him to the Breeze Ups now he'd
make a lot of money. He'd be about as good-
looking a 2-y-o as we've got".*

489. TOP OF THE ROCKS (FR) ★★
b.c. Rock Of Gibraltar – Runaway Top
(Rainbow Quest). February 12. Third foal.
£38,000Y. Doncaster Premier. Sackville/Donald.
The dam, placed over 12f in France, is a half-
sister to 2 winners including the French Group
3 placed Kakofonic. The second dam, Brooklyn
Gleam (by Caerleon), won at 3 yrs and is a
half-sister to 11 winners including the Arc

winner Solemia and the Group 2 Prix Greffulhe winner Prospect Wells. (The Mad March Hares). *"The first colt we bought at Doncaster last year, the stallion's not that hot so he was reasonably good value. He's a really good-looking horse, good natured, copes well and we have to give him a bit of work because he gets a bit fresh. He's going to want seven furlongs and a mile I should think".*

490. WORKING FROM HOME ★★★
b.f. Rip Van Winkle – Work Shy (Striking Ambition). February 26. First foal. The dam won over 5f at 3 yrs on her only start and is a half-sister to one winner. The second dam, Angel's Camp (by Honour And Glory), was a moderate Irish 1m winner, is a half-sister to 3 winners. (Chasemore Farm & Owen Promotions). *"I bought and trained the mare who unfortunately had knee problems and she only ran once, but she won. She was quite useful and if we could have run her more she'd have won more. This filly looks just like her, she's had a little setback which is irritating because previous to that I was surprised how forward she was. You wouldn't expect a very precocious 2-y-o by this sire and the dam didn't run until late on as a 2-y-o. I like her, she's big and very strong looking and you'd think she'd win over five or six furlongs in the second half of the season".*

491. UNNAMED ★★★★
b.c. Iffraaj – Clever Day (Action This Day). April 13. Second foal. €60,000Y. Goffs Orby. Sackville/Donald. The dam is an unraced half-sister to 5 winners including the US stakes winner and Grade 3 placed Mavoreen. The second dam, Bloomin Genius (by Beau Genius), is an unplaced half-sister to 2 stakes winners in the USA. *"Every year some of the best 2-y-o's we have are the ones we can't sell, like last year when we couldn't sell Angelic Lord who is now rated 108 and was fifth at Royal Ascot. This colt is beautiful and yet he's still for sale. He's going to be a decent animal and if necessary Manor House Stables will own him. He'll want at least six furlongs".*

492. UNNAMED ★★★
b.c. Kyllachy – Dubai Bounty (Dubai Destination). March 5. First foal. £52,000Y. Doncaster Premier. Sackville/Donald. The

dam, a fair 8.5f (at 2 yrs) to 12.5f winner, is a half-sister to one winner. The second dam, Mary Read (by Bahamian Bounty), a useful 2-y-o dual 5f winner, was second in the Group 3 Molecomb Stakes and is a half-sister to 6 winners. *"One of the few we haven't yet sold, I think most Kyllachy's want six furlongs and this colt could well be the same, but he shows plenty of speed and precocity. He has a great attitude and he can shift, so he'll be a proper 2-y-o.*

493. UNNAMED ★★★ ♠
ch.c. Exceed And Excel – Hill Welcome (Most Welcome). April 27. Eleventh foal. £85,000Y. Doncaster Premier. Sackville/Donald. Brother to the fairly useful dual 5f winner (including at 2 yrs) Exceedance and half-brother to 6 winners including the useful 2-y-o dual 5f winner and Group 3 Molecomb Stakes second Mary Read (by Bahamian Bounty), the useful listed-placed 2-y-o 6f winner Tiana (by Diktat) and the quite useful 6f (at 2 yrs) and 7f winner Dubai Hills (by Dubai Destination). The dam, placed twice at 2 yrs, is a half-sister to 5 winners including the Group 1 6f Middle Park Stakes winner Stalker. The second dam, Tarvie (by Swing Easy), was a useful sprint winner of 3 races. *"He looks an out-and-out speedy 2-y-o. He's professional and ready to go but because we haven't sold him we won't be trying to get him out in April. The dam has bred a few 2-y-o winners and I can't see any reason why this one won't be another. Everything about him is nice, he's a proper racy 2-y-o".*

494. UNNAMED ★★★
b.c. Captain Rio – Inourthoughts (Desert Style). March 3. Third foal. €48,000Y. Tattersalls Ireland September. Sackville/Donald. Half-brother to the fair 2-y-o dual 6f winner Focusofourthoughts (by Intense Focus). The dam, a quite useful Irish 2-y-o 5f winner, is a half-sister to 3 winners including Green Door (2-y-o Group 2 Flying Childers Stakes). The second dam, Inourhearts (by Pips Pride), a useful listed 5f winner of 4 races, is a half-sister to 2 winners. (M Khan X2). *"He cost 48 Grand which is an awful lot for a Captain Rio, but Murt Khan rang me up straight away and said he'd like to have him. He said that a Captain Rio costing so much must be bloody*

beautiful! He's a gorgeous horse and a cracking individual, we'll take our time because I don't think the sire's stock want more than five furlongs, generally speaking. They tend to go well at Southwell and when there's some ease in the ground. I really like him".

495. UNNAMED ★★

b.c. Bushranger – Munaawashat (Marju). March 11. Fourth foal. 9,500foal. Tattersalls December. Not sold. Brother to the modest Haarib, placed fourth over 6f and 7f at 2 yrs in 2014. The dam, a fair 6f (at 2 yrs) to 8.5f winner of 5 races, is a half-sister to the Group 3 10f Mooresbridge Stakes winner Windsor Palace, the Irish listed winner Anna Karenina and the useful dual 7f winner and Group 3 Queen Mary Stakes second Al Ihsas. The second dam, Simaat (by Mr Prospector), a fair 1m winner, is a half-sister to 2 winners. (Mr John A Duffy). *"This colt is available for lease and he has a reasonable pedigree under the second dam. Every Bushranger we've had has won a race and this colt is very straightforward and well-mannered. He'll want six or seven furlongs and probably a bit of cut in the ground".*

496. UNNAMED ★★

b.f. Zamindar – Veiled Beauty (Royal Academy). February 10. Half-sister to the smart Group 3 7f John Of Gaunt Stakes and listed 6f Cammidge Trophy winner The Cheka (by Xaar), to the useful 9f and 10f winner and listed-placed Wall Of Sound (by Singspiel), the fair 2-y-o 7f winner Azlaa (by Dubawi) and the fair 1m winner Vettorenjoy (by Vettori). The dam is an unplaced half-sister to 6 winners including the French listed winner Arabride. The second dam, Model Bride (by Blushing Groom), is an unraced half-sister to 6 winners including the dam of Zafonic and Zamindar. (Chasemore Farm). *"Not yet in training, apparently she's very big and just not ready to be trained yet. Her half-sister Wall Of Sound didn't even enter training as a 2-y-o, but hopefully this filly will do".*

ED DE GILES

497. CAY LOCATION (IRE) ★★★

b.c. Bahamian Bounty – Desert Location (Dubai Destination). March 2. First foal. £16,000Y. Doncaster Premier. Sackville/Donald.

The dam, a modest 8.5f fourth placed 2-y-o, is a half-sister to 3 winners including the dual listed winner Free Agent. The second dam, Film Script (by Unfuwain), a useful listed 10f and listed 12f winner, is a half-sister to 5 winners including the Group 3 winner Barney McGrew and the listed National Park. (Clarke, King and Lewis). *"He's a nice big horse with a good attitude and he's doing everything we ask. I think he'll be out earlyish, starting off at six furlongs, he has a great stride on him and I should imagine he'll be an out-and-out galloper".*

498. JINKO'S APPROVAL (IRE) ★★★★

ch.c. Approve – Felin Gruvy (Tagula). March 28. Fifth foal. €25,000Y. Tattersalls Ireland September. Sackville/Donald. Half-brother to the fair 5.5f (at 2 yrs) and 12f winner Uncle Roger (by Camacho). The dam, placed once over 6f at 2 yrs, is a half-sister to 5 winners. The second dam, Felin Special (by Lyphard's Special), an Irish 2-y-o 6.5f winner, is a half-sister to 5 winners. (Clarissa Castagli). *"I love this horse, he's one of the most precocious of our 2-y-o's and he has plenty of speed. He has a great attitude and is one of my favourites".*

499. OPERATIVE ★★★

ch.c. Pastoral Pursuits – Gilt Linked (Compton Place). April 2. Fifth foal. £44,000Y. Doncaster Premier. Sackville/Donald. Half-brother to the fairly useful triple 7f winner at 2 and 3 yrs Lincoln (by Clodovil). The dam, a quite useful 2-y-o 5f winner, is a half-sister to 5 winners including the Group 3 John Of Gaunt Stakes winner and dual Group 2 placed (including at 2 yrs) Pastoral Player. The second dam, Copy-Cat (by Lion Cavern), is an unplaced half-sister to 7 winners including the very useful Group 3 5f King George Stakes winner Averti. (Gwyn & Samantha Powell). *"He's big and rangy so he won't be early but I'd like to see him out in June. He's got plenty of toe, so I imagine we'll start him over six furlongs and I love him to bits".*

500. ZLATAN (IRE) ★★

b.c. Dark Angel – Guard Hill (Rahy). April 18. Second foal. Doncaster Premier. Sackville/Donald. Half-brother to the poor 6f seller winner River Dreamer (by Intense Focus). The dam, an Irish 2-y-o 6f winner from two starts, is a half-sister to 4 winners. The second dam, Dream Bay (by Mr Prospector), is an unraced half-sister to 7 winners including Nadia (Group 1 Prix Saint-Alary). (Gwyn Powell and Richard Meakes). *"He's taking a bit of time to come to hand but with a bit of luck he will do by July. I like him but I haven't put a gun to his head yet".*

501. UNNAMED ★★★
b.c. Kodiac – Awwal Malika (Kingmambo). April 30. Fifth foal. 55,000Y. Tattersalls October Book 2. Sackville/Donald. Closely related to the fair 7f and 1m winner of 5 races Desert Colours (by Exceed And Excel) and half-brother to 2 winners including the modest dual 6f winner Bosham (by Sadler's Wells). The dam, a fair 3-y-o 6f winner, is a half-sister to 2 winners in Japan. The second dam, First Night (by Sadler's Wells), a useful listed-placed 1m winner, subsequently won a minor event at 4 yrs in the USA. She is closely related to the Oaks and Irish Derby winner Balanchine and to the Group winners Romanov and Red Slippers (herself dam of the Group 1 Prix de Diane winner West Wind). (Simon Treacher). *"He's taking time to come to hand but he's a great mover and a strong colt. He was quite a late foal and probably won't be out until August, but he's quite strong. A very nice horse".*

502. UNNAMED ★★★★
b.f. Holy Roman Emperor – Be Amazing (Refuse To Bend). February 7. First foal. 52,000Y. Tattersalls October Book 2. Sackville/ Donald. The dam, a modest maiden, was 7f placed at 2 and 3 yrs and is a half-sister to 3 winners including the triple listed winner and Group 2 placed Asset. The second dam, Snow Peak (by Arazi), a 1m winner in France, is a half-sister to 6 winners. (Bernard & Sarah Taylor and John Manser). *"A lovely little horse, she's compact and has a great attitude. Likely to be my first or second runner, she's all there and has a great big backside on her".*

503. UNNAMED ★★★
b.c. Kodiac – Cabopino (Captain Rio). April 28. Third foal. €30,000Y. Tattersalls Ireland September. Sackville/Donald. Half-brother to the moderate 7f winner Cahal (by

Bushranger). The dam is a placed half-sister to 6 winners including the Group placed Miss Trish, Crystal View and Pride And Joy. The second dam, Fey Rouge (by Fayruz), is an unplaced half-sister to 9 winners. *"Not over-big but very strong and with a good attitude, he's got plenty of toe and I'd imagine we'd start him over six furlongs. He's still for sale".* **TRAINERS' BARGAIN BUY**

504. UNNAMED ★★★
b.c. Iffraaj – Engraving (Sadler's Wells). April 8. Fifth foal. 70,000Y. Tattersalls October Book 2. Sackville/Donald. Half-brother to the Italian listed 1m (at 2 yrs) and listed 10f winner Virtual Game (by Kheleyf) and to the fair 2-y-o 6f winner Ladykin (by Holy Roman Emperor). The dam is an unraced half-sister to 2 winners including the multiple French listed winner and Group 2 second Kocab. The second dam, Space Quest (by Rainbow Quest), won the listed Prix Joubert and is a half-sister to 7 winners including the French Group winner Dance Routine (dam of the Group 1 Grand Prix de Paris winner Flintshire). (Simon Treacher). *"I think we'll run him from late summer onwards this year because he's taking everything we're doing with him, but he's going to be a very nice 3-y-o. He's going very well and I'm very pleased with what I see".*

505. UNNAMED ★★
b.f. Shamardal – Gower Song (Singspiel). April 7. Fourth foal. 80,000Y. Tattersalls October Book 2. Sackville/Donald. Half-sister to the 2014 7f placed 2-y-o (from two starts) Melodious (by Cape Cross). The dam, a very useful listed 10f winner here and subsequently a Group 3 12f winner in Dubai, is a half-sister to 7 winners including the Group 2 placed Prince Of Denial and the dam of the listed winner and Oaks second Something Exciting. The second dam, Gleaming Water (by Kalaglow), a quite useful 2-y-o 6f winner, is a sister to the Group 3 Solario Stakes winner Shining Water (dam of the Group 1 Grand Criterium winner Tenby) and a half-sister to 8 winners. (Simon Treacher & Ali Mortazavi). *"Her looks are to die for, but she's quite big and we'll definitely be taking our time with her. I don't think she'll be out before late summer and I can see her wanting seven furlongs or more this year.*

506. UNNAMED ★★★

b.c. Kodiac – Mark One (Mark Of Esteem). April 17. Fifth foal. 62,000Y. Tattersalls October Book 2. Sackville/Donald. Half-brother to the useful 6f (at 2 yrs) and 7f winner and listed-placed Factory Time (by Baltic King) and to the fair 6f (at 2 yrs) to 2m and hurdles winner Ambrose Princess (by Chevalier). The dam, a quite useful 10f and 12f winner, is a half-sister to 2 winners. The second dam, One Wild Oat (by Shareef Dancer), won once at 3 yrs in France and is a half-sister to 12 winners including Arctic Owl (Group 1 Irish St Leger) and Marooned (Group 1 Sydney Cup) and the very smart broodmare Much Too Risky (the dam of four stakes winners). (Simon Treacher & Clarissa Castagli). *"He's had a few weeks off but he's back now and he'll be racing in mid-summer. He's pleased us with everything he's done and he'll be a sprint type 2-y-o".*

507. UNNAMED ★★★ ♠

b.c. Mastercraftsman – Wosaita (Generous). January 21. Thirteenth foal. 50,000Y. Tattersalls October Book 1. Sackville/Donald. Half-brother to 6 winners including the useful 7f (at 2 yrs), listed 1m and Italian Group 3 1m winner Whazzis (by Desert Prince), the useful 2-y-o listed 7f Chesham Stakes winner Whazzat (by Daylami), the quite useful 2-y-o 8.6f winner Whatizzit (by Galileo) and the quite useful 2-y-o 7f and 1m winner Special Envoy (by Barathea). The dam, a fair 12.3f placed maiden, is a half-sister to 10 winners including the Group 1 10.5f Prix de Diane winner Rafha (the dam of Invincible Spirit). The second dam, Eljazzi (by Artaius), a fairly useful 2-y-o 7f winner, is a half-sister to 8 winners including the high-class miler Pitcairn. *"A horse with a lovely pedigree, he's big but by no means weak and he's an early foal so I can imagine him being out in July. We'll probably see the best of him next year, but he moves well and ticks every box. One to do well over 7f this year and be even better next year".*

ANN DUFFIELD

508. ARCTIC ROYAL (IRE) ★★★

ch.f. Frozen Power – Bronze Queen (Invincible Spirit). February 27. Third foal. €28,000Y. Tattersalls Ireland September. Ann Duffield. Half-sister to the useful listed-placed 5f winner Abstraction (by Majestic Missile) and to the fair 5f and 6f winner The Dandy Yank (by Dandy Man). The dam is an unplaced half-sister to one winner. The second dam, Sheba (by Lycius), won twice at 2 yrs in France and is a half-sister to 4 winners including the Group 3 Prix Vanteaux winner and US Grade 1 third Campsie Fells. (Mr J Dance). *"A nice filly, she's compact, quite precocious and bred to be quick. A good-looking filly, she goes well and we like her".*

509. DANZEB ★★★

b.c. Zebedee – Daneville (Danetime). April 14. Sixth foal. 25,000Y. Tattersalls October Book 2. Ann Duffield. Half-brother to the fair 5f (at 2 yrs) and 6f winner of 4 races Dancheur (by Chineur), to the fair 1m and hurdles winner Jubail (by Redback) and two minor 3-y-o winners in Italy by Tillerman. The dam is an unraced half-sister to 4 winners. The second dam, Loveville (by Assert), is an unplaced half-sister to 9 winners. *"A good looking colt, he's straightforward and we're just stepping up his work now. A sprint type 2-y-o for the mid-summer onwards".*

510. HILARY J ★★★

b.f. Mount Nelson – The Terrier (Foxhound). February 12. Fifth foal. £40,000Y. Doncaster Premier. Ann Duffield. Half-sister to the useful triple 2-y-o 5f and Group 3 Flying Five winner Dutch Masterpiece (by Dutch Art), to the quite useful dual 6f winner Dinneratmidnight (by Kyllachy), the fair 5f and 6f winner Miss Bunter (by Bahamian Bounty) and the modest 6f and 7f winner Beachwood Bay (by Tobougg). The dam, a fair 2-y-o 5f winner, is a half-sister to 4 minor winners. The second dam, Branston Gem (by So Factual), placed over 5f at 2 yrs, is a half-sister to 3 winners including the dual listed winner Falcon Hill. (E & R Stott). *"A quality filly for mid-summer onwards, she's from a very nice family and the mare was quick. Quite a big, imposing filly, she's attractive and racy with lots of bone. I like her very much".*

511. LADY NAHEMA ★★★

b.f. Zoffany – Jamary (Grand Reward). March 26. Second foal. £30,000Y. Doncaster Premier. Not sold. Half-sister to Takafol (by Fast Company), placed fourth once over 5f at 2 yrs in 2014. The dam ran once unplaced and is a half-sister to 7 winners including the US listed winners Dawaytogold and Cherry Moon (herself dam of the triple Group 1 winner Cherry Mix). The second dam, Datsdawayitis (by Known Fact), a minor US winner of 3 races at 4 yrs, is a half-sister to 8 winners. (Mr David Barker & Mr Douglas McMahon). *"A quality filly, I like her but she's quite big and a little bit backward still. She wants a bit of time and won't run until mid-to-late summer".*

512. MR STRAVINSKY (IRE) ★★★

b.c. Zebedee – Galvano (Galileo). March 29. First foal. £28,000Y. Doncaster Premier. Ann Duffield. The dam is an unraced half-sister to 2 minor winners. The second dam, Vanishing River (by Southern Halo), is an unplaced half-sister to 6 winners including the Group 2 winners Vetheuil and Verveine (dam of the Group 1 winners Volga and Vallee Enchantee). (Mrs Ann Starke and Mr John Dance). *"He's very nice and I'd be surprised if he didn't win. A very strong and well-built horse that looks like a sprinter, despite being out of a Galileo mare".*

513. MY AMIGO ★★★

gr.c. Stimulation – Blue Crest (Verglas). February 1. First foal. £38,000Y. Doncaster Premier. Ann Duffield. The dam, a minor dual winner at 3 yrs in France, is a half-sister to 4 winners. The second dam, Ideale Dancing (by Shining Steel), a minor winner at 2 and 3 yrs in France, is a half-sister to 3 winners. (Mr J Dance). *"He's a nice horse, we like him. He's tall, very attractive and he'll make a 2-y-o from mid-summer onwards. The type to make up into a fine 3-y-o as well".*

514. NINETTA ★★

b.f. New Approach – Pine Chip (Nureyev). February 17. Eleventh foal. 60,000Y. Tattersalls October Book 1. Horse France. Half-sister to 5 winners including the French triple listed 12f winner Pouvoir Absolu (by Sadler's Wells) and the French 9f and 10f winner and listed 12f placed Perfect Murder (by Desert King). The dam is a placed sister to the Prix de l'Arc de Triomphe, French Derby and Grand Prix de Paris winner Peintre Celebre and a half-sister to the French Group winners Peinture Rare and Pointilliste. The second dam, Peinture Bleue (by Alydar), a US Grade 2 12f and French listed 10f winner, is a half-sister to the

US Grade 3 winner Provins and the French Group 3 winner Parme. (Mrs J F Bianco). *"She's the best bred horse here because her dam is a full sister to an Arc winner. She's a lovely filly but we're taking our time with her and haven't asked her any questions yet. She's a backward filly but she looks the part and is very well-balanced. One for the back end of the season and especially for next year".*

515. RISK ADJUSTED (IRE) ★★★

b.c. Bushranger – Silk Fan (Unfuwain). May 8. €15,000Y. Tattersalls Ireland September. Ann Duffield. Half-brother to the useful 5f (at 2 yrs) and 6f winner and Group 3 third Haikbidiac (by Kodiac), to the quite useful 5f and 6f winner of 5 races (including at 2 yrs) Fanrouge (by Red Clubs), the quite useful 12f and hurdles winner Eagle Rock (by High Chaparral) and the fair 12f winner Widezain (by Chineur). The dam, a fairly useful triple 7f winner (including at 2 yrs), is a half-sister to 5 winners. The second dam, Alikhlas (by Lahib), a fair 3-y-o 1m winner, is a half-sister to 4 winners including the listed winner and Group 2 Lancashire Oaks second Sahool and the dam of the multiple Group winner Maraahel. (Mr J Dance). *"He's bred to get seven furlongs but he'll start his career in April over five. We like him, he's quite a big, imposing colt and his family is full of winners".* **TRAINERS' BARGAIN BUY**

516. SILHUETTE (IRE) ★★

b.f. Canford Cliffs – Lisfannon (Bahamian Bounty). March 24. Fifth foal. £18,000Y. Doncaster Premier. Ann Duffield. Half-sister to the Irish 2-y-o 6f winner Mironica (by Excellent Art) and to the quite useful 2-y-o 5f winner Dress Up (by Noverre). The dam, placed fourth three times from 5f to 6.5f, is half-sister to 4 winners including the listed 5f winner of 5 races Dazed And Amazed. The second dam, Amazed (by Clantime), a modest 5f placed 3-y-o, is a sister to the Group 3 Prix du Petit Couvert winner Bishops Court and a half-sister to 5 winners including the listed winning sprinter Astonished. (Mr J Dance). *"A very nice filly but she's leggy and she'll want time. Everyone seems to be saying that about their Canford Cliffs 2-y-o's. I wouldn't say she'd want a trip because she's bred to be quick, but she just isn't precocious".*

517. SILVER STREAK (IRE) ★★★
gr.c. Dark Angel – Happy Talk (Hamas).
April 16. Eighth foal. €45,000Y. Tattersalls
Ireland September. Ann Duffield. Brother to
the fair 2-y-o 6f winner Evoke and half-
brother to the fairly useful 2-y-o 5f winner
Nagham (by Camacho), the fair 2-y-o dual 5f
winner Frisky Talk (by Fasliyev), the modest
5f and 6f winner Foreign Rhythm (by Distant
Music) and the fair 7f to 12.5f and hurdles
winner Mica Mika (by Needwood Blade).
The dam, an Irish 10f and hurdles winner, is
a half-sister to 8 winners including the US
Grade 3 winner Storm Dream. The second
dam, Mamara Reef (by Salse), a modest 14f
and hurdles winner, is a half-sister to the listed
winner and smart broodmare Nibbs Point.
(Punchbowl Racing). *"A very nice colt, we hope
to get him out around June time. He covers
a lot of ground, he's athletic and has a great
stride on him".*

518. SOUTHERN SEAS ★★
ch.f. Archipenko – Sourire (Domedriver).
April 17. Fourth foal. The dam, a dual 2-y-o
7f winner, later won a listed event over 1m
in Sweden and is a half-sister to 5 winners
including the 2-y-o Group 3 1m Prix des
Reservoirs winner Songerie, the German
listed winner and Group 1 Italian Oaks third
Souvenance and the French listed winner and
Group 3 placed Soft Morning. The second
dam, Summer Night (by Nashwan), a fairly
useful 3-y-o 6f winner, is a half-sister to 7
winners including the Group 3 Prix d'Arenburg
winner Starlit Sands. (Miss K Rausing). *"This
filly looks like she's going to need time, but
she's a good mover and looks tough. Mentally
she needs to run sooner rather than later,
because we need to give her something to
think about. Otherwise on pedigree you'd
be forgiven for thinking she'd be one for late
summer onwards".*

519. WHISPERING SOUL (IRE) ★★★
b.f. Majestic Missile – Belle Of The Blues (Blues
Traveller). March 11. €45,000Y. Tattersalls
Ireland September. Ann Duffield. Half-sister
to 8 winners including the 2014 2-y-o 6f
winner Fruity (by Camacho), the 6.5f (at 2 yrs)
to 1m winner Talitha Kum (by Chineur), the
8.5f to 10f winner Yojojo (by Windsor Knot)
and the 8.5f (at 2 yrs) to 14f winner Dunhoy

(by Goodricke) – all quite useful. The dam
ran twice unplaced and is a half-sister to 5
winners including Croft Pool (Group 2 Temple
Stakes). The second dam, Blackpool Belle (by
The Brianstan), won 3 races at 2 and 3 yrs. (Mr
John Dance & Mr John Gatenby). *"A lovely filly
for the mid-summer onwards. We're taking out
time with her, she's a well-balanced, attractive,
medium sized filly that stands over a bit of
ground. Very nice".*

520. TEEPEE TIME ★★★★
b.f. Compton Place – Deora De (Night Shift).
January 16. Second foal. £30,000Y. Doncaster
Premier. David Redvers. The dam ran once
unplaced and is a sister to the fairly useful 2-y-
o 5f winner and subsequent US stakes winner
Deal Breaker and a half-sister to the Group
2 6f Richmond Stakes winner Prolific (by
Compton Place). The second dam, Photo Flash
(by Bahamian Bounty), a fair 1m winner, is a
half-sister to 8 winners including the Group
2 Royal Lodge Stakes winner Atlantis Prince.
(Qatar Racing Ltd). *"A very nice filly, she looks
capable and she's very athletic and forward
going. A powerful filly, she's built like a colt and
I'd like to get her out before the end of May".*

ED DUNLOP
521. AHDAATH (IRE)
b.f. Kodiac – Sonny Sunshine (Royal Applause).
March 25. Second foal. £120,000Y. Doncaster
Premier. Shadwell Estate Co. Half-sister to
Rasha (by Zebedee), unplaced in two starts
at 2 yrs in 2014. The dam is an unraced
half-sister to 3 winners including the multiple
Group 1 winning sprinter Sole Power. The
second dam, Demerger (by Distant View), is an
unraced half-sister to 5 winners. (Hamdan Al
Maktoum).

522. AMAZING RED
b.c. Teofilo – Artisia (Peintre Celebre). April
25. Seventh living foal. 220,000foal. Tattersalls
December. Charlie Gordon-Watson. Half-
brother to the Group 1 Hong Kong Vase and
Group 2 Yorkshire Cup winner of 7 races and
triple Melbourne Cup second Red Cadeaux
(by Cadeaux Genereux), to the modest 11f
and 14f winner Artisan (by Medicean) and a
winner in Norway by Fantastic Light. The dam
was placed over 1m and is a half-sister to 8
winners including the Hong Kong Group 1

winner Rave and the dual Group 3 5f winner
Almaty. The second dam, Almaaseh (by
Dancing Brave), placed once over 6f at 3 yrs,
is a half-sister to 7 winners including the 2,000
Guineas and Champion Stakes winner Haafhd.
(Mr R Arculli).

523. COGENT
b.c. Paco Boy – Logic (Slip Anchor). January
7. Eleventh foal. Brother to the fair 2-y-o 6f
winner Illogical and half-brother to 8 winners
including the 2-y-o 7f winner Crowley's
Law (by Dubawi), the 1m and 10f winner
Everybody Knows (by King's Best), the 1m to
14f winner Rationale (by Singspiel) and the
6f (at 2 yrs) to 9f winner of 7 races Logsdail
(by Polish Precedent) – all quite useful. The
dam, a useful 1m placed 2-y-o, is a half-sister
to 4 winners including the listed Oaks Trial
winner and Group 2 Park Hill Stakes third Port
Helene. The second dam, Docklands (by On
Your Mark), a listed-placed winner of 3 races,
is a half-sister to 11 winners including the
1,000 Guineas winner Night Off. (W J & T C O
Gredley).

524. GABRIELLA
b.f. Paco Boy – Bounty Box (Bahamian Bounty).
February 3. First foal. 31,000Y. Tattersalls
October Book 3. A Bengough. The dam, a
useful dual listed 6f winner of 6 races from 2
to 5 yrs, is a sister to the French 2-y-o winner
and listed-placed Bahamian Box and a half-
sister to 3 winners. The second dam, Bible Box
(by Bin Ajwaad), was a quite useful 7f to 9f
winner of 3 races from 3 to 5 yrs. (The Belfour
Partnership).

525. GIRL WITH A PEARL
ch.f. Dutch Art – Pointed Arch (Rock Of
Gibraltar). March 31. Fourth foal. 120,000Y.
Tattersalls October Book 1. Kern/Lillingston.
Half-sister to the fairly useful 8.5f (at 2 yrs) to
12f winner Farquhar (by Archipenko) and to
the quite useful 2-y-o dual 6f winner Dream
Maker (by Bahamian Bounty). The dam, a
modest 12f winner, is closely related to the
listed 12f winner Chartres and a half-sister to
7 winners including the listed 10f and listed
14f winner Pugin and the dam of the 2-y-o
Group 2 Railway Stakes winner Lilbourne Lad.
The second dam, Gothic Dream (by Nashwan),

won over 7f in Ireland at 2 yrs, was third in
the Irish Oaks and is a half-sister to 3 winners.
(Racing Fillies).

526. GLORYETTE
b.f. Raven's Pass – Cara Fantasy (Sadler's Wells).
April 27. Seventh foal. Half-sister to 7 winners
including the useful 2014 2-y-o listed 1m
winner Prince Gagarin (by Dubawi), the very
smart 2-y-o Group 3 7f Acomb Stakes and
Group 3 1m Craven Stakes winner and Group
1 Racing Post Trophy second (by Elusive
Quality), the smart 1m (at 2 yrs), Group 3 10f
Strensall Stakes and listed 9f winner Palavicini
(by Giant's Causeway) and the quite useful
8.5f (at 2 yrs) and 12f winner Oasis Fantasy (by
Oasis Dream). The dam, a quite useful dual 12f
winner, is a half-sister to the Group 2 Topkapi
Trophy winner Lucky Guest. (The Belfour
Partnership).

527. HAJEER
b.f. Cape Cross – Mejala (Red Ransom).
January 22. Second foal. Half-sister to
Thanaaya (by Haatef), unplaced in one start
at 2 yrs in 2014. The dam, a fair 10f winner, is
a half-sister to the smart dual 7f winner and
Group 3 placed Muwaary, the very useful 2-y-
o listed 7f Star Stakes winner and Group 3 7f
Prestige Stakes second Mudaaraah, the useful
listed 6f winner Ethaara and the useful 2-y-o
listed 7f winner Sudoor. The second dam,
Wissal (Woodman), is an unraced sister to the
2-y-o Group 2 7f Laurent Perrier Champagne
Stakes Bahhare and a half-sister to the St
James's Palace Stakes and Queen Elizabeth II
Stakes winner Bahri. (Hamdan Al Maktoum).

528. KAFOO
b.c. Dansili – Nidhaal (Observatory). April 18.
Sixth foal. Half-brother to the useful 2-y-o
5f winner and dual Group 2 placed Burwaaz
(by Exceed And Excel), to the quite useful 6f
(at 2 yrs) and 5f winner of 4 races Sharaarah
and the quite useful 2-y-o 5f and 6f winner
Sadafiya (both by Oasis Dream). The dam, a
very useful 2-y-o listed 6f winner and second
in the Group 3 6f Princess Margaret Stakes,
is a half-sister to 2 winners. The second dam,
Jeed (by Mujtahid), a quite useful 2-y-o 6f
winner, is a half-sister to 2 winners. (Hamdan
Al Maktoum).

529. MUJAMALA ♠
b.f. Exceed And Excel – Habaayib (Royal Applause). March 6. Second foal. The dam, a useful 2-y-o Group 3 6f Albany Stakes winner, was second in the Group 2 Cherry Hinton Stakes and is a sister to a winner. The second dam, Silver Kestrel (by Silver Hawk), a minor winner of 2 races at 3 and 4 yrs in the USA, is a half-sister to 5 winners. (Hamdan Al Maktoum).

530. QEYAADAH (IRE)
b.c. Acclamation – Effervesce (Galileo). February 28. First foal. 160,000Y. Tattersalls October Book 2. Shadwell Estate Co. The dam, a fair 10f winner, is a half-sister to 4 winners including the dual Group 3 6f Greenlands Stakes and UAE Group 3 6f winner of 11 races (including at 2 yrs) Hitchens. The second dam, Royal Fizz (by Royal Academy), won once over 6.5f at 2 yrs in France and is a half-sister to 7 winners here and abroad including the £1.4m Hong Kong earner Floral Pegasus. (Hamdan Al Maktoum).

531. QUEENSBURY ODYSSEY
ch.c. Poet's Voice – Russian Spirit (Falbrav). April 21. First foal. 70,000Y. Tattersalls October Book 2. W J Gredley. The dam, a fairly useful listed 6f winner of 3 races, is a half-sister to 2 winners. The second dam, Russian Rhapsody (by Cosmonaut), a fairly useful 7f and 1m winner, is a half-sister to 3 winners. (W J & T C O Gredley).

532. RAASMAAL
b.c. Poet's Voice – Luminda (Danehill). April 4. Eighth foal. 160,000Y. Tattersalls October Book 2. Shadwell Estate Co. Half-brother to the listed 1m and subsequent US Grade 2 winner Rhythm Of Light (by Beat Hollow), to the French 1m listed-placed 2-y-o winner Lazy Afternoon (by Hawk Wing), the quite useful 6f (at 2 yrs) to 9f winner Lunar Deity (by Medicean) and the quite useful triple 7f winner She's In The Money (by High Chaparral). The dam won 2 races in France at 2 and 4 yrs and is a half-sister to 3 winners including the US Grade 2 winner Little Treasure. The second dam, Luminosity (by Sillery), won once at 2 yrs in France and is a half-sister to 4 minor winners. (Hamdan Al Maktoum).

533. ROCKERY (IRE)
b.f. Fastnet Rock – Rain Flower (Indian Ridge). January 26. Tenth foal. 350,000Y. Tattersalls October Book 1. BBA (Ire). Closely related to the Group 1 Oaks and Group 1 German Oaks winner Dancing Rain, to the fair 7f (at 2 yrs) and 1m winner Captain Dancer (both by Danehill Dancer), the 2-y-o listed 5f winner Sumora (dam of the Group 1 Moyglare Stud Stakes winner Maybe) and the useful Irish 2-y-o 7f winner Fleeting Shadow (both by Danehill) and half-sister to one winner. The dam is an unraced three-parts sister to the Epsom Derby, Irish Champion Stakes and Dewhurst Stakes winner Dr Devious and a half-sister to 5 winners including the Group 3 winners Royal Court and Archway. The second dam, Rose Of Jericho (by Alleged), is an unraced half-sister to 5 winners. (Sir Peter Vela & Hon Mrs Peter Stanley).

534. SHARAAKAH (IRE)
b.f. Roderic O'Connor – Lanark Belle (Selkirk). February 24. Fifth foal. €22,000Y. Goffs Orby. F Barberini/Ed Dunlop. Half-sister to the fair 2014 dual 6f placed 2-y-o Aledaid (by Acclamation), to the fairly useful 2-y-o 7f and subsequent multiple US winner Diamond Geezah (by Diamond Green) and the 6f (at 2 yrs) and 9f winner and Italian listed-placed Quissisana (by Antonius Pius). The dam is an unplaced half-sister to 6 winners including the listed Winter Derby winner Adiemus. The second dam, Anodyne (by Dominion), a useful 6f winner, is a sister to the very useful US Grade 3 winner Domynsky and a half-sister to 9 winners. (M Jaber).

535. SNOW PIXIE (USA)
b.f. Flower Alley – Woodland Dream (Charnwood Forest). May 5. Half-sister to the outstanding filly and six-time Group 1 winner Snow Fairy (by Intikhab). The dam, a quite useful 7f winner, is a half-sister to numerous winners including the 2-y-o Autumn Stakes and German 3 winner and useful sire Big Bad Bob. The second dam, Fantasy Girl (by Marju), is an unplaced half-sister to 4 winners very useful listed 11.5f winner of 6 races Persian Lightning. (Windflower Overseas Holdings Inc).

HARRY DUNLOP

536. D'NIRO (IRE) ★★★
br.c. Big Bad Bob – Causeway Charm (Giant's Causeway). March 5. Fourth foal. €75,000Y. Goffs Orby. Badgers Bloodstock. Half-brother to the 2014 6f fourth-placed 2-y-o Seeking Approval (by Approve) and to the fairly useful 2-y-o 6f and 7f winner and Group 3 Musidora Stakes second Lily Rules (by Aussie Rules). The dam is an unplaced half-sister to 6 winners including the German dual listed winner Chan Chan. The second dam, Candy Charm (by Capote), is an unraced half-sister to 7 winners. (Weston Brook Farm, Bromfield & Whitaker). *"A nice, big horse that hasn't been with us long. I very much like what I see but I think we'll have to wait a while with him. I suspect he'll want a mile".*

537. GREAT COMPANY (IRE) ★★★
b.c. Fast Company – Sunlit Silence (Green Desert). March 5. Fifth foal. £60,000Y. Doncaster Premier. Mark Crossman. Brother to the fair 2014 2-y-o 5f and 6f winner Low Cut Affair. The dam is an unplaced half-sister to 2 winners. The second dam, Magical Cliché (by Affirmed), was placed in the listed Irish 1,000 Guineas Trial and is a sister to 4 stakes winners including the Irish 1,000 Guineas winner Trusted Partner (herself dam of the US Grade 1 winner Dress To Thrill). (Khalifa Dasmal). *"He's a bonny little horse, we thought he'd be sharp and early but now he's looking more like a mid-season type. He looks a nice horse and we like him".*

538. INCREDIBLE THUNDER ★★★
b.c. Kheleyf – Glitz (Hawk Wing). March 8. Third foal. £9,500Y. Doncaster Premier. Half-brother to the fair 2014 2-y-o 5.5f winner Amber Crystal and to the modest 7f (at 2 yrs) and 1m winner Dark Crystal (both by Multiplex). The dam, a moderate 12f placed maiden, is a half-sister to 3 winners. The second dam, Lunar Lustre (Desert Prince), ran twice unplaced and is a half-sister to 9 winners including the Group 2 Prix du Conseil du Paris winner Majorien and the Group 2 Prix de Malleret winner America. (Windsor House Stables Partnership). *"We like him, he was quite weak as a yearling but physically he's done very well. Hopefully he'll give us a bit of sport and be a nice little horse to follow*

throughout the year. My son William named him after a Superhero!"

539. KASHTAN ★★★
ch.f. Sakhee's Secret – Gitane (Grand Lodge). April 1. Ninth foal. €15,000Y. Tattersalls Ireland September. Anthony Stroud/Harry Dunlop. Sister to the fairly useful 6f and 7f winner Pool House and half-sister to the French winner of 3 races and 1m listed-placed Mega Back (by Zamindar) and a winner in Austria by Shirocco. The dam, a minor French 11f winner, is a half-sister to 9 winners. The second dam, Grenouillere (by Alysheba), is a placed half-sister to 4 winners including the Group 1 Prix de la Salamandre winner Oczy Czarnie. (Gehring, Whitaker & Partners). *"We like this filly, she's done some work and I think she'll be one to start off in May over six furlongs. She's a strong filly that will improve with time because she still has some developing to do".*
TRAINERS' BARGAIN BUY

540. MR MARBIN (IRE) ★★★
b.c. Raven's Pass – Ultra Finesse (Rahy). March 25. Fourteenth foal. 26,000Y. Tattersalls October Book2. Crimbourne Stud. Half-brother to 6 winners including the useful 2-y-o 6f winner and listed placed Proceed With Care (by Danehill), the useful 6f and 7f winner and listed-placed Dramatic Quest (by Zafonic) and quite useful 2-y-o 1m winner Defence Of Duress (by Motivator) and the fair 7f (at 2 yrs) and 1m winner Debonnaire (by Anabaa). The dam, a useful French 8.5f and 10f winner, was second in the Group 2 12f Prix de Malleret and is a half-sister to 6 winners including the Arc winner Suave Dancer. The second dam, Suavite (by Alleged), a winner of four races and second in the Grade 3 7f Comely Stakes, is a half-sister to 4 winners. (Crimbourne Stud). *"He's a half-brother to the dam of Roz who was a good filly we had and also the recent Australian Group 1 winner Hartnell. He's a bonny little horse that should be doing his stuff over six and seven furlongs I would say".*

541. POULICHE ★★
ch.f. Monsieur Bond – Tarneem (Zilzal). May 14. Fourteenth foal. €6,000Y. Tattersalls Ireland September. Anthony Stroud. Half-sister to 8 winners including the smart 7f (at 2 yrs) and Group 3 9f Darley Stakes winner and

SEEK THEM HERE!

Elusive Pimpernel

- Consistent miler with quality juveniles in training with Ger Lyons, Jessica Harrington, Richard Hannon....etc

- From the Family of Big Bad Bob

- Won (Gr.3) Acomb Stakes, (Gr.3) Craven Stakes, (Gr.1) 2nd Racing Post Trophy

- Timeform rated 117 'big strong colt: smart performer'

- Great success at the sales, €50,000, £36,000, £26,000 etc

- 2015 fee: €1,000

sires, top of the pile is Irish National Stud resident **Elusive Pimpernel** whose progeny fetched an average price last year of £12,018 – almost 16 times his stud fee of €1,000. Cristina Patino's Craven Stakes winner, who covered superstar Snow Fairy last year, began his career at Islanmore Stud in 2012 but, like fellow resident and former Patino colour-bearer Big Bad Bob, relocated to the Irish National Stud shortly after. As a result the son of Elusive Quality can be expected to be represented by larger crops in coming years, but from just 16 **yearlings to sell last year the statistic is an eyecatching one**

Katherine Fidler,
Racing Post, 5-2-2015

IRISH NATIONAL STUD
www.irishnationalstud.ie

John Osborne, Gary Swift, Sinead Hyland or Helen Boyce
Tel: +353 (0)45 521251 Gary +353 (0)86 6031979

Group 1 Coronation Cup third Enforcer, the quite useful 2-y-o dual 5f winner Lord Of The Inn, the modest 1m winner Uncle Brit (all by Efisio), the quite useful triple 5f winner Zalzilah (by Kheleyf) and the fair dual 10f winner and subsequent US listed-placed Canaveral (by Cape Cross). The dam, a quite useful 1m winner, is a half-sister to 4 minor winners. The second dam, Willowy Mood (by Will Win), won two Grade 3 events in the USA and is a half-sister to 9 winners. (Hot To Trot Racing Club). *"A filly that hasn't been here that long and she's a late foal. I think we'll start her off at six furlongs in June or July".*

542. THREE BROTHERS (FR) ★★★
b.br.c. Slickly – Vivartic (Verglas). March 28. Third foal. €27,000Y. Arqana Deauville October. Anthony Stroud. Brother to the minor French winner Algar. The dam won 6 minor races in France at 3 and 5 yrs and is a half-sister to 9 minor winners. The second dam, Arctic Bride (by Arctic Tern), a minor winner at 3 yrs, is a half-sister to 4 winners. (Nicholas Pascall). *"A French bred colt, we like him and we'll campaign him over there to some extent to take advantage of the French premiums. He probably wants seven furlongs hopefully he's one we can look forward to".*

543. TORQUAY ★★
b.f. Aqlaam – Torcross (Vettori). April 19. Sixth living foal. Half-sister to the fair 10f, 12f and hurdles winner Bagber (by Diktat) and to the modest 2-y-o dual 8.5f winner Rural Affair (by Pastoral Pursuits). The dam, a useful 2-y-o 7f winner, is a half-sister to the very useful 6f (at 2 yrs), Group 3 7.5f Concorde Stakes and dual listed winner Sheppard's Watch. The second dam, Sheppard's Cross (by Soviet Star), a quite useful 7f winner of 3 races, is a half-sister to 5 winners including the Irish listed sprint winner Clean Cut. (Mr R J McCreery). *"I've had a couple out of the family and I'd say she's going to need time and won't be doing a great deal this season. She'll have a break shortly and come back in later for some action in the autumn".*

544. UNNAMED ★★
br.c. Dutch Art – Passing Stranger (Dixie Union). March 15. First foal. The dam, a fair 6f winner, is a half-sister to one winner. The second dam, Square Pants (King Of Kings), a minor US 4-y-o winner, is a half-sister to 4 winners including the Group 2 Cherry Hinton Stakes and Group 3 Albany Stakes winner Sander Camillo. (Mrs Susan Roy). *"He's out for a spring break at the moment but when we had him he looked quite backward despite being by Dutch Art. He's one for later in the season".*

TIM EASTERBY
545. EXCESSABLE ♠
ch.c. Sakhee's Secret – Kummel Excess (Exceed And Excel). January 26. First foal. £6,000Y. Doncaster Premier. Tim Easterby. The dam, a modest 5f (at 2 yrs) and 6f winner, is a half-sister to 4 minor winners here and abroad. The second dam, Ipanema Beach (by Lion Cavern), a modest 1m and 8.5f winner, is a half-sister to 3 winners.

546. FLYING PURSUIT
ch.c. Firebreak – Choisette (Choisir). April 6. Fourth foal. 21,000Y. Doncaster Premier. Tim Easterby. Half-brother to the fair 2014 2-y-o 6f winner Straightothepoint (by Kyllachy). The dam, a modest triple 5f winner (including at 2 yrs), is a half-sister to 2 winners. The second dam, Final Pursuit (by Pursuit Of Love), a fairly useful 2-y-o 5.7f winner, is a half-sister to 10 winners including the very useful dual 6f winner and Group 3 Coventry Stakes second Sir Nicholas (subsequently very successful in Hong Kong), the smart sprint winner and Ayr Gold Cup second Double Action and the very useful 2-y-o listed 6f Sirenia Stakes winner Lipstick. (Ontoawinner, M Hulin & Partner).

547. FLYING ROYAL
b.f. Dutch Art – Royal Punch (Royal Applause). March 21. Sixth foal. 60,000Y. Tattersalls December. J Walsh. Half-sister to the listed 6f Rockingham Stakes winner and Group 2 Lowther Stakes third Royal Rascal (by Lucky Story), to the quite useful 2-y-o 5f winner Cocktail Charlie (by Danbird) and the modest dual 6f winner Another Royal (by Byron). The dam ran once unplaced and is a half-sister to 4 winners including the US Grade 3 winner Tigah. The second dam, Macina (by Platini), a winner in Germany and Group 3 third, is a half-sister to 4 winners.

548. POPPYPICCOLINA
b.f. Piccolo – Popocatepetl (Nashwan).
April 7. Seventh foal. Half-sister to the fairly
useful 7f (at 2 yrs) and 1m winner Mariachi
Man (by Haafhd), to the quite useful 7f (at 2
yrs) and 1m winner Guacamole (by Inchinor),
the modest 5f and 6f winner Miss Firefly, the
moderate 1m winner Poppy Golightly (both
by Compton Place) and the Italian winner of
11 races King London (by Beat Hollow). The
dam, a modest 12f and 14f placed maiden,
is a half-sister to 5 winners. The second dam,
Dimakya (by Dayjur), a fair 7.5f winner in
France, is a half-sister to 8 winners including
the listed winners Loyalize and Remuria. (J
Gompertz).

549. ROCK ON (IRE)
ch.c. Rock Of Gibraltar – Spectacular Show
(Spectrum). March 27. Fourth foal. £42,000Y.
Doncaster Premier. Stephen Hillen. Half-
brother to the useful listed 6f winner Valbchek
and to the minor French winner Premier
Acclaim (both by Acclamation). The dam, a
quite useful 2-y-o 5f winner, is a half-sister
to 3 winners including the Group 3 7f Sweet
Solera Stakes winner and Group 1 Fillies'
Mile third English Ballet. The second dam,
Stage Presence (by Selkirk), a quite useful
3-y-o 7f and 1m winner, is a half-sister to 6
winners including the 6f (at 2 yrs) and Group
3 7f Ballycorus Stakes winner Rum Charger
(herself dam of the US triple Grade 1 winner
Winchester). (Mrs J E Pallister).

550. SILVER SANDS (IRE)
ch.c. Zebedee – Eloquent Rose (Elnadim).
March 29. Fourth foal. £30,000Y. Doncaster
Premier. Tim Easterby. Half-brother to the
useful 6f and 7f winner of 7 races and
listed-placed Dutch Rose (by Dutch Art). The
dam, a quite useful 2-y-o dual 5f winner, is
a half-sister to 4 winners. The second dam,
Quintellina (by Robellino), was a quite useful
2-y-o 7f winner. (C H Stevens).

551. UNNAMED
b.c. Frozen Power – Liscoa (Foxhound). March
20. Fifth foal. 25,000Y. Tattersalls October
Book 2. Tim Easterby. Half-brother to the fairly
useful 2014 2-y-o 5.5f and 6f winner Dougal
(by Zebedee), to the fair 5f (at 2 yrs) and 1m
winner Megamunch (by Camacho), the Italian

dual 2-y-o winner Last Child (by Night Shift)
and the fair Irish 5f winner Red Army Blues (by
Soviet Star). The dam, a fair Irish 1m and 10f
winner, is a half-sister to 4 winners including
the useful Irish listed 6f winner Spencers
Wood. The second dam, Ascoli (by Skyliner),
an Irish, 10f, 12f and hurdles winner, is a half-
sister to 3 winners.

DAVID ELSWORTH
552. AUSTRALIAN QUEEN ★★★
b.f. Fastnet Rock – Barshiba (Barathea).
May 7. Half-sister to the 2015 2-y-o Group
2 6f Duchess Of Cambridge Stakes winner
Arabian Queen (by Dubawi). The dam, a dual
Group 2 Lancashire Oaks winner of 7 races, is
a half-sister to several winners including the
useful 2-y-o listed 1m winner Doctor Dash
and the fairly useful 1m (at 2 yrs) and 10f
winner Dashing Star. The second dam, Dashiba
(by Dashing Blade), a useful 9f and 10f winner,
is a half-sister to several winners including the
fairly useful 10f and 12f winner Smart Blade.
(J C Smith). *"She's a big filly and just like both
her sire and dam she's got a big head, so she
wasn't bred to be a beauty queen, but she
could still be a 2-y-o in the second half of the
season. Fastnet Rock has yet to prove himself
here after having loads of Group 1 winners in
Australia, so that's a bit worrying. She's done
nothing wrong yet and does what she has to
do".*

553. DASHING APPROACH ★★★★★
ch.f. New Approach – Dashiba (Dashing
Blade). February 15. Half-sister to the dual
Group 2 Lancashire Oaks winner of 7 races
Barshiba (by Barathea), to the useful 2-y-o
listed 1m winner Doctor Dash, the fair 2-y-o
1m winner Dashing Doc (both by Dr Fong),
the fairly useful 1m (at 2 yrs) and 12f winner
Dashing Star (by Teofilo) and the modest dual
10f winner Westhaven (by Alhaarth). The dam,
a useful 9f and 10f winner, is a half-sister to
several winners including the fairly useful 10f
and 12f winner Smart Blade. The second dam,
Alsiba (by Northfields), a modest winner of
one race at 4 yrs, was a staying half-sister to
several winners and to the dam of the Irish
St Leger winner Oscar Schindler. (J C Smith).
*"She'll be our star 2-y-o this year I think. A
very nice filly that reeks class, she's athletic
and racy. I like her a lot and although she's not*

necessarily bred to be an early 2-y-o I think she might be".

554. DAYLIGHT ROBBERY ★★

br.c. Dick Turpin – Imperialistic (Imperial Ballet). Half-brother to the smart Group 2 German 1,000 Guineas winner Electrelane (by Dubawi), to the fairly useful listed-placed 2-y-o 5f and subsequent US winner Imperialistic Diva (by Haafhd) and the fair dual 1m winner Quite Sparky (by Lucky Story). The dam, a fairly useful 6f (at 2 yrs) to 1m winner of 5 races, was listed-placed and is a half-sister to 3 winners. The second dam, Shefoog (by Kefaah), a fairly useful dual 7f winner (including at 2 yrs), is a half-sister to 3 winners. (The National Stud & David Elsworth). *"A horse that could run in mid-summer, he looks very nice but he only came in late so I don't know much about him".*

555. JUSTICE ANGEL (IRE) ★★★★

gr.f. Dark Angel – Malaica (Roi Grande). April 22. Half-sister to the fairly useful 2014 2-y-o 7f winner Success Days (by Jeremy). The dam, a French 2-y-o 5f and 6f winner, was second in the Group 3 Prix Miesque and is a half-sister to 3 winners. The second dam, Carmel (by Highest Honor), is an unraced half-sister to 7 winners including the Group 1 Prix Ganay winner Execute and the Group 3 winners Tot Ou Tard and Ing Ing. (Mr R Ng). *"A lovely, very quick filly, she'll be a nice 2-y-o and is one to watch out for".*

556. JUSTICE BOLD (IRE) ★★

gr.c. Zebedee – Chantilly Beauty (Josr Algarhoud). May 16. Third foal. The dam, an Italian 2-y-o 6f listed winner, was second in the Group 2 Premio Regina Elena and in the Group 3 7f Chartwell Fillies' Stakes and is a half-sister to 3 winners in France. The second dam, Lysabelle (by Lesotho), a listed-placed winner of 5 races in France, is a half-sister to 7 winners. (Mr R Ng). *"A big, strong horse that just needs to develop more, so he needs more time and is one for the second half of the season".*

557. JUSTICE FOCUSED ★★

b.c. Intense Focus – Moon Shine (Groom Dancer). April 28. Eighth foal. Half-brother to the unplaced 2014 2-y-o Lucy (by Tomorrow's

Cat). The dam is an unraced half-sister to 3 winners. The second dam, Marsoumeh (by Green Dancer), won 6 races in France including over jumps. (Mr R Ng). *"A strong colt, we bred him and I think he'll be nice, so although he doesn't have much of a page I think you ought to give him a mention".*

558. JUSTICE LADY (IRE) ★★★

br.f. Dream Ahead – Celestial Dream (Oasis Dream). April 8. Third foal. 55,000Y. Tattersalls October Book 2. Suzanne Roberts. Half-sister to the fair 2014 1m fourth placed 2-y-o The Last Marju (by Marju) and to the fair 1m winner Hesbaan (by Acclamation). The dam, a fair 5f winner, is a half-sister to 3 winners here and abroad and to the unraced dam of the Group 2 winner Norse King. The second dam, Lochangel (by Night Shift), a very smart winner of the Group 1 5f Nunthorpe Stakes, is a half-sister to the champion sprinter Lochsong. (Mr R Ng). *"A filly with a speedy pedigree, she's very nice, looks precocious and goes nicely. I expect her to be winning by June".*

559. JUSTICE LASS (IRE) ★★★★

b.f. Canford Cliffs – Dibiya (Caerleon). February 11. Half-sister to the useful 2-y-o 7f winner and dual listed-placed Dibayani (by Shamardal), to the fairly useful Irish 7f winning 2-y-o's Dirar (by King's Best) and Dilinata (by Spinning World), the quite useful Irish 9f winner Diylawa (by Mastercraftsman) and the quite useful Irish 12f winner Dibella (by Observatory). The dam, a fairly useful 12f and 14f winner, was listed-placed. The second dam, Dabtiya (by Shirley Heights), won the listed Ballyroan Stakes. (Mr R Ng). *"A very nice 2-y-o. I like her a lot and she'll be early".*

560. JUSTICE LUCKY (USA) ★★★

b.c. Scat Daddy – Lucky Be Me (Peaks And Valleys). April 9. First foal. €60,000Y. Goffs Orby. Robert Ng. The dam, a stakes winner of 3 races in Canada, is a half-sister to 6 winners. The second dam, Timely Search (by Regal Search), a US stakes-placed winner, is a half-sister to 3 winners. (Mr R Ng). *"You ought to put this one in, he's a very nice horse, but he won't be early".*

561. JUSTICE PLEASING ★★★

b.c. Kodiac – Spangle (Galileo). April 15. Third

foal. 60,000Y. Tattersalls October Book 2.
Suzanne Roberts. Half-brother to a winner
in Germany by Dutch Art. The dam ran once
unplaced. The second dam, Yakutia (by Polish
Precedent), is an unraced sister to the dual
Group 2 winner Predappio and a half-sister to
3 winners. (Mr R Ng). *"He's not got much of a
pedigree but he's a good mover and a bonny,
nice-topped little horse. The jury is out as to
how early he'll be, especially as he's the first
Kodiac I've had".*

562. JUSTICE ROCK ★★★★
b.c. Acclamation – Fashion Rocks (Rock
Of Gibraltar). April 14. Third foal. 75,000Y.
Tattersalls October Book 3. Suzanne Roberts.
The dam, a useful 2-y-o listed 6f winner, is
a half-sister to 4 winners. The second dam,
La Gandilie (by Highest Honor), a dual 2-y-o
winner in France including a listed event, was
third in the Group 3 Prix Chloe and is a half-
sister to 4 winners including the Italian listed
winner Totostar and to the placed dams of the
French Group 3 winners Linda Regina and Star
Of Akkar. (Mr R Ng). *"A lovely horse, he's one
to keep an eye on this year because I think he'll
be one of our better colts".*

563. SEA OF FLAMES ★★★
ch.c. Aqlaam – Hidden Fire (Alhaarth). March
30. The dam, a fair 7f and 1m winner, is a half-
sister to 2 winners including the useful 2-y-o
1m winner, Group 3 1m Prix des Reservoirs
second and Group 3 12f St Simon Stakes third
Cocktail Queen. The second dam, Premier
Prize (by Selkirk), a useful 7f (at 2 yrs) and
listed 10f winner, was third in the Group 2
Sandown Mile and is a half-sister to 7 winners
including the Group 2 15f Prix Kergorlay
winner Gold Medallist. (J C Smith). *"I trained
the dam who sadly died recently. This is a
good, strong colt that looks like he'll win as a
2-y-o but he won't be that early. One for July
onwards".*

564. THE NEW MASTER ★★★★
br.c. New Approach – Maziona (Dansili). April
26. Third foal. 60,000Y. Tattersalls December.
Suzanne Roberts. The dam, a quite useful Irish
2-y-o 7f winner, is a half-sister to 5 winners
including the very smart Group 3 Gordon
Stakes winner and Group 1 St Leger second
The Geezer. The second dam, Polygueza (by

Be My Guest), a minor 3-y-o 7f winner in
Ireland, is a half-sister to 4 winners including
the Irish listed winner Lepoushka. (J C Smith).
*"He's a very nice horse, I like him a lot and
took an interest in him at the sales because I
trained the dam's half-brother The Geezer. So I
bought him and then sold him to The Geezer's
owner Jeff Smith. He has an air of superiority
about him and he does everything very easily.
I wouldn't be dismissive about his 2-y-o career
but I think he's more of a mile/ten furlong
horse. Having said that, it won't stop him
winning over six or seven furlongs as a 2-y-o".*

565. UNNAMED (IRE) ★★★
b.f. Dream Ahead – Dorothy Dene (Red
Ransom). March 24. 25,000Y. Tattersalls
October Book 2. Suzanne Roberts. Half-sister
to the quite useful 2014 2-y-o 6f winner
Navigate (by Iffraaj). The dam is an unraced
half-sister to 3 winners including the Group
1 Middle Park Stakes winner Primo Valentino
and the Group 2 6f Cherry Hinton Stakes
winner and Group 1 6f Phoenix Stakes third
Dora Carrington. The second dam, Dorothea
Brooke (by Dancing Brave), won over 9f and
is a half-sister to 6 winners. (GB Partnership).
*"She's still growing so she'll take a bit of time,
but I think she'll make a six furlong 2-y-o".*

JAMES EUSTACE
566. APACHE MYTH ★★
ch.f. Sakhee's Secret – Indian Angel (Indian
Ridge). March 15. Third foal. Half-sister to
the 2014 1m placed 2-y-o, from 2 starts,
Chief Spirit (by Norse Dancer). The dam is an
unraced half-sister to 3 winners. The second
dam, Lochangel (by Night Shift), a very smart
winner of the Group 1 5f Nunthorpe Stakes,
is a half-sister to the champion sprinter
Lochsong. (J C Smith). *"She's big, like her half-
brother Chief Spirit, but I like her already and
I like to think she has a touch of class. One for
second half of the season over seven furlongs,
she gets up Warren Hill easily enough despite
her size".*

567. GLITTERING ★★
ch.f. Firebreak – Razzle (Green Desert). March
10. £6,000Y. Doncaster Silver. J Eustace.
Half-sister to the fairly useful dual 7f winner
Infiraad and to the fair 8.5f and 9f winner of 3
races Double Cee (both by Haafhd). The dam,

a modest 10f placed 3-y-o, is a sister to the very smart triple Group 3 6f and 7f winner and sire Desert Style and a half-sister to 2 winners. The second dam, Organza (by High Top), a useful 3-y-o 10f winner, is a full or half-sister to 7 winners including the Group 1 Prix de la Foret winner Brocade (herself dam of the Group 1 winners Barathea and Gossamer). (Sherin Lloyd & Friends). *"She was cheap but actually it's not a bad family at all and if she won a race she'd be worth breeding from. I like the Firebreaks because he was a tough, durable horse and both my 2-y-o fillies by that stallion seem to have unusually good temperaments. This is a filly with a good-action, I wouldn't do anything too soon with her but she's not a slow, backward filly".* **TRAINERS' BARGAIN BUY**

568. LONG ISLAND ★★★

b.f. Firebreak – Fakhuur (Dansili). March 11. First foal. The dam, a fair 1m winner, is a half-sister to one winner on the flat and two winners over hurdles. The second dam, Halska (Unfuwain), is an unraced half-sister to 7 winners including the top-class French and Irish Derby winner Old Vic, the Group 3 Prix Foy winner Splash of Colour and the listed winners Bobinski and Green Lucia. (R J McCreery). *"Of my two Firebreak's this is the more precocious. She's strengthened up well, I like her, she's not very tall but she is very strong. She could be a 2-y-o and she has a great attitude".*

569. NEXT TRAIN'S GONE ★★

b.g. Rail Link – Coh Sho No (Old Vic). March 16. Half-brother to the quite useful 2015 10f winner Wind Place and Sho, to the moderate 2m and hurdles winner Iron Butterfly (both by Shirocco), the fair 11f and dual 12f winner Iron Condor (by Tobougg) and the fair 14f to 2m and hurdles winner At The Money (by Robellino). The dam was a modest 15.4f and hurdles winner. The second dam, Castle Peak (by Darshaan), a fairly useful 12f winner, is a half-sister to the Prix du Cadran winner Sought Out and to the listed winners Queen Helen and Greektown (herself dam of the Geoffrey Freer Stakes winner Multicolored) and the dam of the Great Voltigeur Stakes winner Bonny Scot. (H D Nass). *"He's a very good mover and for a horse that, on pedigree,*

shouldn't be able to canter up Warren Hill yet, he's a very good-moving horse too. He'll probably want a mile this year and middle-distances as a 3-y-o".

570. NORSE CUSTOM ★★

b.f. Norse Dancer – Accustomed (Motivator). February 10. First foal. The dam, modest 7.5f placed 2-y-o, is a half-sister to one winner. The second dam, Duty Paid (by Barathea), a useful 2-y-o listed 6f winner, is a sister to the useful 1m winner and listed-placed Lady Miletrian and a half-sister to 3 winners. (J C Smith). *"If there is such a thing as a typical Norse Dancer this is it, because she's a big, impressive-looking filly. She'll want time, but in the second half of the season she could be OK".*

571. PENNERLEY ★★

b.f. Aqlaam – Penelewey (Groom Dancer). February 10. Seventh foal. Half-sister to the 2014 6f placed 2-y-o, from 2 starts, Pencil (by Excellent Art), to the useful 1m (at 2 yrs) and 10f winner Jedediah (by Hernando) and the modest 7f and 9f winner Marksbury (by Mark Of Esteem). The dam, a useful 6f and 7f winner of 3 races, is a half-sister to 7 winners here and abroad. The second dam, Peryllys (by Warning), is a placed half-sister to 6 winners. (Major M G Wyatt). *"She's the nicest looking filly out of the mare, she's done nothing wrong and the way she's going she'll be a mid-season 2-y-o. There are just a few signs that she might be more forward than you'd expect".*

572. POCKET ★★

b.f. Paco Boy – Take The Plunge (Benny The Dip). February 14. Third foal. 5,000Y. Tattersalls October Book 3. J Eustace. Half-sister to a minor winner in Denmark by Royal Applause. The dam is an unplaced half-sister to 8 winners. The second dam, Pearly River (by Elegant Air), a fair 7f (at 2 yrs) and 12f winner, is a half-sister to 5 winners. (P F Charter). *"A cheap filly, but she has a bit of speed and an attitude a bit like her father in that she wants to be a racehorse. So I think she'll be pretty tough on the racecourse. She needs to grow into herself and level off a bit more, but I can see her being alright as a 2-y-o. She's built like a sprinter and looks quick enough to start off at six furlongs".*

573. SHADOW SPIRIT ★★
b.f. Makfi – Highland Shot (Selkirk). April 5. Half-sister to the smart German Group 2 1m, Group 3 9f Darley Stakes and listed 1m Pomfret Stakes winner of 6 races Highland Knight (by Night Shift), to the fair dual 1m winner Great Shot (by Marju) and a hurdles winner by Dr Fong. The dam, a fairly useful 7f to 9f winner, is a half-sister to 8 winners including the very smart 2-y-o Group 3 7f Solario Stakes winner and Group 1 Dewhurst Stakes third Opera Cape, the high-class stayer Grey Shot and the smart sprint winner of 4 races Night Shot. The second dam, Optaria (by Song), a quite useful 2-y-o 5f winner, is out of the unplaced Electo (by Julio Mariner). (J C Smith). *"It's a staying family and the sire's stock seem to need time too, but this filly isn't big. She isn't doing anything wrong at all and she should make a 2-y-o by mid-season".*

574. THE NAME IS JAMES ★★
br.c. Equiano – Miss Bond (Danehill Dancer). February 14. First foal. The dam is an unraced half-sister to 2 winners including the fairly useful dual 6f winner at 2 and 3 yrs and listed Carnarvon Stakes second City Girl. The second dam, Lochridge (by Indian Ridge), a smart listed 6f winner of 5 races, is a half-sister to 3 winners including the useful listed 5f winner Loch Verdi. (J C Smith). *"He's not very tall so although on looks you might think he'd make a 2-y-o, actually he's got some growing and levelling out to do and he came into the yard late. We won't see much of him before the latter part of the season".*

575. UNNAMED ★★
ch.f. Champs Elysees – Rainbow Queen (Spectrum). February 17. Seventh foal. 10,000Y. Tattersalls October Book 2. Not sold. Half-sister to the quite useful dual 7f winner Sir Isaac (by Key Of Luck) and the quite useful 10f and 12f of 3 races winner Quixote (by Singspiel). The dam won 4 races from 6f to 1m at 3 and 4 yrs in Belgium and France and is a half-sister to 4 winners including the Group 3 Prix Miesque winner Stella Blue (herself dam of the triple listed winner Sirius Prospect). The second dam, Libanoor (by Highest Honor), won 4 races at 3 yrs in France and is a sister to the French triple Group 3 winner Take Risks and to 3 listed-placed winners. (Mr & Mrs R Scott). *"There's a lot of stamina in the pedigree and she's a bit of a character without being nasty. She's well grown, has lots of bone and is very strong even at this early stage, but she is bred to want a trip. One for the back-end over a mile I would say".*

RICHARD FAHEY

576. ABU KHADRA (IRE)
ch.c. Dubawi – Flashy Wings (Zafonic). May 2. Fourth foal. Half-brother to the 2014 2-y-o 7f winner, on his only start, Flashy Memories (by Dubawi) and to the fairly useful Irish 7f winner Flashy Approach (by New Approach). The dam, a winner of 4 races including the Group 2 6f Lowther Stakes and Group 2 5f Queen Mary Stakes, was Group 1 placed three times and is a half-sister to 5 winners. The second dam, Lovealoch (by (by Lomond), a very useful 7f (at 2 yrs) and 9f winner here and placed in the Group 2 Falmouth Stakes and the Group 2 Premio Lydia Tesio, subsequently won once in the USA and is a half-sister to 7 winners. (Jaber Abdullah).

577. ANOTHER TOUCH
b.c. Arcano – Alsalwa (Nayef). March 25. Second foal. €80,000Y. Goffs Sportsmans. Robin O'Ryan. Half-brother to Mufrad (by New Approach), placed fourth over 7f from two starts at 2 yrs in 2014. The dam, a quite useful Irish dual 1m winner, is a half-sister to 5 winners including the listed-placed Liberating. The second dam, Ros The Boss (by Danehill), a quite useful 7f and 1m winner, is a half-sister to 9 winners including the Irish 2-y-o listed 9f winner and Group 1 second Yehudi.

578. APPLETON
ch.c. Showcasing – Valentina Guest (Be My Guest). April 8. Fifth foal. 73,000Y. Tattersalls October Book 2. Highfield Farm Ltd. Half-brother to Beardwood (by Dutch Art), a promising second over 6f on his only start at 2 yrs in 2014. The dam, a fairly useful 7f (at 2 yrs) and 10f winner of 4 races, was listed-placed twice and is a half-sister to 5 winners. The second dam, Karamiyna (by Shernazar), a French listed 10.8f winner, is a sister to the Group 1 10.5f Prix Ganay, Group 2 10f Nassau Stakes, Group 2 10f Sun Chariot Stakes and

Group 1 10f German winner Kartajana and a half-sister to the Australian Group 1 winner Karasi.

579. ASTLEY HALL

ch.c. Dutch Art – Haigh Hall (Kyllachy). February 15. Second foal. Half-brother to Robin Park (by Invincible Spirit), a modest 5f and 6f placed 2-y-o on all three of her starts in 2014. The dam, a quite useful 2-y-o 5f winner, is a half-sister to 5 winners including the very useful 7f (at 2 yrs) and listed 1m winner and Group 3 Dahlia Stakes third Don't Dili Dali, the useful 7f and 1m winner and listed-placed Balducci and the fairly useful 1m winner and listed-placed Ada River. The second dam, Miss Meltemi (by Miswaki Tern), a 7f and 1m 2-y-o winner in Italy, was third in the Group 1 Italian Oaks and is a half-sister to 2 winners. The second dam, Blu Meltemi (by Star Shareef), won 5 races at 2 and 3 yrs in Italy and was second in the Italian Oaks. Despite being green this colt won on his debut at Redcar on the 13th April.

580. AWOHAAM (IRE)

b.f. Iffraaj – Horatia (Machiavellian). April 25. Tenth foal. 75,000Y. Tattersalls October Book 2. Rabbah Bloodstock. Half-sister to the Group 3 12f Pinnacle Stakes winner Moment In Time (by Tiger Hill), to the fairly useful listed-placed 7f (at 2 yrs) and 1m winner Fontley (by Sadler's Wells), the quite useful 7f and 1m winner Muzdaher (by Danzig) and the fair 9f winner Some Site (by Nayef). The dam, a 10f winner here, subsequently won a Grade 3 in the USA and is a half-sister to 7 winners including the triple Group 2 winner Opinion Poll. The second dam, Ahead (by Shirley Heights), a Group 3 placed 12f winner, is a half-sister to the top-class miler Markofdistinction. (Jaber Abdullah).

581. BINT KODIAC (IRE)

b.f. Kodiac – Magnificent Bell (Octagonal). March 12. Sixth foal. €70,000Y. Goffs Orby. Rabbah Bloodstock. Half-sister to the fairly useful 10f to 2m and hurdles winner Inventor (by Alzao), to the quite useful 5f (at 2 yrs) to 10f winner Las Verglas Star (by Verglas), the moderate 6f winner Crystalized (by Rock Of Gibraltar) and a winner in Russia (by Celtic

Swing). The dam is an unraced half-sister to 6 winners including the listed 10f winner Esyoueffcee (by Alzao). The second dam, Familiar (by Diesis), a fairly useful 1m winner, is a half-sister to 8 winners including the high-class Prix du Moulin winner and Epsom Oaks second All At Sea and the smart French dual Group 3 winner Over The Ocean.

582. BIRCHWOOD (IRE)

b.c. Dark Angel – Layla Jamil (Exceed And Excel). January 21. First foal. 77,000Y. Tattersalls October Book 2. Highfield Farm. The dam, a fair dual 7f winner at 2 and 3 yrs, is a half-sister to 2 winners. The second dam, Guana Bay (by Cadeaux Genereux), is an unraced sister to one winner and a half-sister to 5 winners including the Group 2 winners Prince Sabo and Millyant, and the listed winner Bold Jessie (dam of the Group 2 Gimcrack Stakes winner Abou Zouz).

583. BLACK MAGIC

gr.c. Poet's Voice – Centifolia (Kendor). March 9. Sixth foal. €45,000Y. Goffs Orby. R F Racing. Half-brother to the French dual 1m winner Heronchelles (by New Approach), to the fair 6f (including at 2 yrs) and 5f winner of 4 races Dissent (by Dansili) and the modest 5f and 6f winner of 6 races Colourbearer (by Pivotal). The dam won 4 races at 2 yrs in France including the Group 2 Criterium de Maisons-Laffitte and is a half-sister to 2 winners. The second dam, Djayapura (by Fabulous Dancer), won once at 3 yrs in France and is a half-sister to 4 winners.

584. CURTAIN CALL

b.f. Acclamation – Apace (Oasis Dream). March 8. First foal. The dam, a quite useful 7f (at 2 yrs) and 5f winner, is a sister to the useful listed 5f winner and Group 3 third Sugar Free and a half-sister to the useful 1m (at 2 yrs) and 9f winner High Twelve (by Montjeu). The second dam, Much Faster (Fasliyev), a winner of 4 races including the Group 2 6f Prix Robert Papin and second in the Group 1 Prix Morny, is a half-sister to 4 winners.

585. DANCING YEARS ♠

ch.f. Iffraaj – Daganya (Danehill Dancer). March 29. Seventh foal. €175,000Y. Goffs Orby.

Cheveley Park Stud. Half-sister to the 1m to 11f winner of 7 races Akasaka (by King's Best), to the dual 12f winner Cape Of Good Grace (by Cape Cross), the 5f and 6f winner Kernoff (by Excellent Art) – all fairly useful, and the modest dual 6f winner Chasca (by Namid). The dam won 2 races including a listed 6f event in Ireland and was second in the Group 2 5f Flying Five. She is a sister to the listed 5f winner Snaefell and a half-sister to 4 winners. The second dam, Sovereign Grace (by Standaan), won over 5f in Ireland and is a half-sister 9 winners.

586. DEANSGATE (IRE)
b.c. Dandy Man – Romarca (Raise A Grand). March 24. Third foal. £62,000Y. Doncaster Premier. Highfield Farm. The dam, a minor Irish 12f winner, is a half-sister to one winner. The second dam, Billy Buzz (by Fayruz), was a minor 7f and 9f winner.

587. DREAMING OF STELLA (IRE)
ch.f. Giant's Causeway – Sweeter Still (Rock Of Gibraltar). February 1. First foal. 100,000foal. Keeneland November. Steve Rudolf. The dam, winner of the Grade 3 Senorita Stakes in the USA, is a sister to one winner and a half-sister to numerous winners including the 2-y-o Group 1 1m Racing Post Trophy winner Kingsbarns and the Group 3 Irish 1,000 Guineas Trial winner Belle Artiste. The second dam, Beltisaal (by Belmez), placed 5 times at 3 yrs in France, is a half-sister to 5 winners including the listed winner and Group 2 placed Kafhar.

588. EDISIA
b.f. Holy Roman Emperor – Penchant (Kyllachy). February 7. Half-sister to the Group 1 6.5f Prix Maurice de Gheest and Group 2 7f Lennox Stakes winner Garswood (by Dutch Art). The dam is an unraced half-sister to 5 winners including the Group 3 7f Nell Gwyn Stakes winner and dual Group 1 placed Infallible. The second dam, Irresistible (by Cadeaux Genereux), a fairly useful 5f (at 2 yrs) and listed 6f winner, was Group 3 placed and is a half-sister to 2 winners.

589. EVANGELICAL
b.f. Dutch Art – Pious (Bishop Of Cashel). April 11. Tenth foal. Sister to the fair 2-y-o

5f winner My Boy Bill and half-sister to the smart 2-y-o Group 2 Mill Reef Stakes winner Supplicant, to the smart 7f and listed 1m winner of 5 races Penitent (both by Kyllachy) and to four winners by Pivotal including the fairly useful 2-y-o 7f winner Blithe. the quite useful 5f winner of 10 races Solemn. The dam, a fair dual 6f winner (including at 2 yrs), is a half-sister to 5 winners. The second dam, La Cabrilla (by Carwhite), a fairly useful 2-y-o 5f and 6f winner and third in the Group 3 Princess Margaret Stakes, is a half-sister to the Group 1 Nunthorpe Stakes winner Ya Malak. (Cheveley Park Stud).

590. FIRST TO POST (IRE)
b.c. Acclamation – Aoife Alainn (Dr Fong). February 22. First foal. 50,000Y. Tattersalls October Book 1. Rabbah Bloodstock. The dam, a winner of 5 races including the Group 1 Premio Lydia Tesio, is a half-sister to 5 winners including the Italian listed winner and Group 2 Italian 2,000 Guineas third Adorabile Fong. The second dam, Divine Secret (by Hernando), is an unraced half-sister to 7 minor winners here and abroad.

591. FISHERGATE
b.c. Pastoral Pursuits – Miss Meggy (Pivotal). May 5. Fifth foal. Half-brother to the quite useful 2015 dual 5f placed 3-y-o Crawford Avenue (by Equiano), to the quite useful 2-y-o 5f winner Eccleston (by Acclamation) and the quite useful 2-y-o 7f and 1m winner of 3 races and subsequent US 3-y-o Grade 3 1m winner Charlie Em (by Kheleyf). The dam won a listed 5f event at 2 yrs and a class 4 handicap over 7f at 4 yrs. The second dam, Selkirk Rose (by Pips Pride), a fair 5f (at 2 yrs) and 6f winner, is a half-sister to 5 minor winners. (Highfield Farm).

592. GALLIPOLI (IRE)
b.c. Compton Place – Altadena Lady (Imperial Ballet). May 9. Second foal. 30,000Y. Tattersalls October Book 2. Robin O'Ryan. The dam is an unraced half-sister to 4 winners including the useful listed 5f winner of 6 races Our Little Secret (herself dam of the dual listed winner Pearl Secret). The second dam, Sports Post Lady (by M Double M), a fair 5f winner of 4 races, is a half-sister to 5 winners including the useful sprinter Palacegate Episode (a winner of

11 races here and abroad including a Group 3 race in Italy and numerous listed events).

593. GARCIA
b.c. Paco Boy – Birdie (Alhaarth). February 17. Seventh foal. 50,000Y. Tattersalls October Book 2. John Warren. Half-brother to the fairly useful 2014 2-y-o 7f winner and Group 3 Acomb Stakes third Il Paparazzi (by Royal Applause) and to the French 12f winner Salvation (by Montjeu). The dam, a 1m and listed 11.5f winner, is a half-sister to 7 winners including the French middle-distance winner of 10 races (including four listed events) Faru and the listed winner Fickle (herself dam of the Group 3 winner Tarfah). The second dam, Fade (by Persepolis), is an unraced half-sister to Tom Seymour, a winner of five Group 3 events in Italy.

594. GIN IN THE INN
b.c. Alfred Nobel – Nose One's Way (Revoque). March 28. Fifth foal. €35,000Y. Tattersalls Ireland September. O'Ryan/Fahey. Half-brother to the 2014 2-y-o 5f winner Grandad's World (by Kodiac), to the Irish 4-y-o 1m winner Kavaco (by Choisir) and to a minor winner in Italy by Oratorio. The dam, a winner over hurdles, is a half-sister to 5 winners including the 2-y-o Group 3 Sirenia Stakes winner and Group 1 Cheveley Park Stakes second Dhanyata. The second dam, Preponderance (by Cyrano de Bergerac), a quite useful 2-y-o dual 5f winner, is a half-sister to 6 winners. This colt won well on his debut in a 6 runner maiden at Leicester on the 10th April.

595. HILLDALE
b.f. Exceed And Excel – Miss Meltemi (Miswaki Tern). March 21. Tenth foal. 67,000Y. Tattersalls October Book 2. Highfield Farm. Closely related to the very useful 7f (at 2 yrs) and listed 1m winner and Group 3 Dahlia Stakes third Don't Dili Dali, to the useful listed-placed 7f to 8.5f winner Balducci and the fairly useful listed-placed 1m winner Ada River (all by Dansili) and half-sister to 3 winners including the quite useful 2-y-o 5f winner Haigh Hall (by Kyllachy) and the quite useful 12f winner Zafarana (by Tiger Hill). The dam, a 2-y-o winner in Italy and third in the Group 1 Italian Oaks, is a half-sister to 2 winners. The second dam, Blu Meltemi (by Star Shareef), a winner

of 5 races at 2 and 3 yrs in Italy and second in the Italian Oaks, is a half-sister to 3 winners.

596. HYLAND HEATHER
b.f. Lilbourne Lad – Maidservant (Seeking The Gold). March 6. First foal. €85,000Y. Goffs Orby. Robin O'Ryan. The dam is an unraced half-sister to 4 winners including the French Group 3 second Woven Lace. The second dam, Do The Honours (by Highest Honor), won the Group 3 Prix de Meautry and is a half-sister to 8 winners including Seba (listed Chesham Stakes).

597. KEPT UNDER WRAPS
gr.f. Clodovil – Chatifa (Titus Livius). April 13. Ninth foal. 40,000Y. Tattersalls October Book 2. Amanda Skiffington. Half-sister to the unplaced 2014 2-y-o Jellwa (by Iffraaj), to the French 10f winner Akaaleel (by Teofilo), a hurdles winner by Key Of Luck and the unraced dam of the Italian Group 3 winner Salford Secret. The dam, a quite useful 1m winner, is a half-sister to 6 winners including the Group 1 winners Homecoming Queen (1,000 Guineas), Queen's Logic (Cheveley Park Stakes) and the top-class Dylan Thomas. The second dam, Lagrion (by Diesis), placed 5 times in Ireland, stayed 12f and is a full or half-sister to 3 winners.

598. KIRI SUNRISE (IRE)
b.f. Iffraaj – Lucky Flirt (Gulch). March 15. Fifth foal. €110,000Y. Goffs Orby. R F Racing. Half-sister to the quite useful dual 6f winner Dreese (by Dandy Man), to the fair Irish 2-y-o 1m and Hong Kong winner Lucked Out (by Ramonti) and the minor winner of 6 races abroad Lucky Peter (by Marju). The dam, unplaced in the USA at 2 yrs, is a half-sister to 9 winners including a stakes winner. The second dam, Bashful Charmer (by Capote), a minor US 2-y-o stakes winner, is a half-sister to 5 winners in the USA.

599. LATHOM
b.c. Compton Place – Wigan Lane (Kheleyf). April 19. Second foal. £39,000Y. Doncaster Premier. Highfield Farm. The dam, a fair 2-y-o 6f winner, is a half-sister to 2 winners including the useful 5f and 6f winner of 4 races from 2 to 6 yrs Hoh Hoh Hoh. The second dam, Nesting (by Thatching), is an unplaced full or

half-sister to 3 winners and to the dams of the Group 2 winners Tariq and Wi Dud.

600. LEE LANE

b.f. Compton Place – Canukeepasecret (Mind Games). February 3. First foal. £58,000Y. Doncaster Premier. Highfield Farm. The dam is an unraced half-sister to 3 winners including the listed winner and Group 1 King's Stand Stakes third Pearl Secret. The second dam, Our Little Secret (by Rossini), a useful listed 5f winner of 6 races, is a half-sister to 3 winners.

601. LINE SPORT (IRE)

ch.c. Exceed And Excel – Majestic Dubawi (Dubawi). February 3. First foal. The dam was a useful 2-y-o Group 3 6f Firth Of Clyde Stakes winner. The second dam, Tidal Chorus (by Singspiel), ran twice unplaced and is a half-sister to 6 winners including the French listed winner South Rock. (Jaber Abdullah).

602. LYDIATE (IRE)

b.f. Acclamation – Maid To Order (Zafonic). March 19. Eighth foal. £50,000Y. Doncaster Premier. Highfield Farm. Sister to the quite useful 2-y-o 5f winner Storm Trooper and to the fair 7f (at 2 yrs) and 1m winner Jibaal and half-sister to the modest 2-y-o 5f winner Rightcar Ellie (by Namid) and 2 minor winners abroad by Authorized and Barathea. The dam, a modest Irish 1m winner, is a half-sister to 10 winners including the Group 1 Phoenix Stakes third Catch A Glimpse (herself the dam of a US Grade 3 winner). The second dam, Spring To Light (by Blushing Groom), a 6f and 7f winner and second in the Group 3 C L Weld Park Stakes, is a half-sister to 7 winners.

603. NICE NAME (IRE)

b.c. Royal Applause – Grand Zafeen (Zafeen) February 26. Second foal. Half-brother to Grand Beauty (by Kheleyf), placed second over 5f and 6f on both her starts at 2 yrs in 2014. The dam, a fair 5f (at 2 yrs) and 6f winner of 4 races, is a half-sister to one winner. The second dam, Majestic Desert (by Fraam), a smart winner of the Group 3 Fred Darling Stakes and the Group 3 Oak Tree Stakes, was second in the Group 1 Cheveley Park Stakes. (Jaber Abdullah).

604. OROTAVEO (IRE)

b.f. Frozen Power – Gala Style (Elnadim). April 27. Eighth foal. 60,000Y. Tattersalls October Book 1. Not sold. Half-sister to the very useful dual listed 7f winner and dual Group 3 placed Majestic Myles, to the 2-y-o winner Majestic Moon (both by Majestic Missile), the smart 2-y-o 6f winner, Group 2 Coventry Stakes second and Group 2 Gimcrack Stakes third Parbold (by Dandy Man) and the quite useful 7f winner Oonagh (by Arakan). The dam is an unraced half-sister to 2 minor winners. The second dam, Style N' Elegance (by Alysheba), is a placed half-sister to 11 winners including the Group 2 winner Easy To Copy (herself the dam of 3 stakes winners) and the Irish 1,000 Guineas winner Trusted Partner (dam of the high-class filly Dress To Thrill).

605. PADDY POWER (IRE)

ch.c. Pivotal – Rag Top (Barathea). April 7. Sixth living foal. 80,000Y. Tattersalls October Book 2. Not sold. Half-brother to the fair 2-y-o 6f winner Brick Tops (by Danehill Dancer), to the modest 2-y-o 6f winner Ragsta (by Key Of Luck) and a winner in Spain by Zamindar. The dam, a useful 2-y-o Group 3 7f C L Weld Park Stakes and listed 6f Swordlestown Stud Sprint Stakes winner, is a half-sister to 8 winners including the listed-placed Red Top and the dam of the 2-y-o listed winner Elhamri. The second dam, Petite Epaulette (by Night Shift), a fair 5f winner at 2 yrs, is a half-sister to 3 winners.

606. POWERALLIED

b.c. Camacho – Kaplinsky (Fath). April 30. Second foal. £16,000Y. Doncaster Silver. Robin O'Ryan. The dam, a modest dual 7f winner, is a half-sister to a winner. The second dam, Cossack Princess (by Lomond), was placed fourth once over 10f in Ireland. This colt won on his debut at Musselburgh on the 5th April, some way off his second birthday.

607. RIBCHESTER (IRE)

b.c. Iffraaj – Mujarah (Marju). March 24. First foal. €105,000Y. Goffs Orby. Highfield Farm. The dam is an unplaced half-sister to 4 winners including the Group 3 14f Curragh Cup winner Tactic. The second dam, Tanaghum (by Darshaan), a useful listed-placed 10f winner, is a half-sister to 8 winners including the smart Group 2 10f Premio Lydia Tesio winner Najah.

608. ROSE MARMARA
ch.f. Exceed And Excel – Show Rainbow (Haafhd). March 10. First foal. The dam, a fairly useful 6f (at 2 yrs) and listed 6f winner, is a half-sister to one winner. The second dam, Rainbow Sky (by Rainbow Quest), was a fair 10.5f winner. (Jaber Abdullah).

609. SANAADH
ch.c Exceed And Excel – Queen's Logic (Grand Lodge). April 28. Half-brother to 6 winners including the Group 2 6f Lowther Stakes, Group 3 6f Princess Margaret Stakes (both at 2 yrs) and Group 2 6f Diadem Stakes winner Lady Of The Desert (by Rahy), the fairly useful dual 10f winner Prince Of Stars (by Sea The Stars),the quite useful 2-y-o 1m and subsequent UAE 6f winner Go On Be A Tiger (by Machiavellian) and the quite useful Irish 11f winner Abu Nayef (by Nayef). The dam, a champion 2-y-o filly and winner of the Group 1 6f Cheveley Park Stakes and the Group 2 6f Lowther Stakes, is a half-sister to the top-class multiple Group 1 winner Dylan Thomas. The second dam, Lagrion (by Diesis), was placed 5 times in Ireland and stayed 12f and is a full or half-sister to 3 winners. (Jaber Abdullah).

610. SUNNUA (IRE)
b.f. Dark Angel – Island Sunset (Trans Island). March 31. Second foal. €48,000Y. Tattersalls Ireland September. A O'Ryan/Middleham Park. The dam, a fairly useful 7f (at 2 yrs) to 10f winner of 5 races, is a half-sister to 5 winners. The second dam, Islandagore (by Indian Ridge), a 3-y-o 7f winner in Ireland, was second in a listed event over 9f on her only other start and is a half-sister to the 2-y-o listed 6f winner Lady Of Kildare.

611. YA JAMMEEL
b.c. Dubawi – Silver Touch (Dansili). April 30. Fourth foal. Half-brother to the quite useful 10f winner Sayed Youmzain (by Dalakhani). The dam won the Group 3 7f Criterion Stakes and was third in the Group 1 Maurice de Gheest and is a half-sister to 2 winners. The second dam, Sanpala (by Sanglamore), is an unplaced half-sister to 10 winners including

four stakes winners and the dam of the US multiple Grade 1 winner Ventura. (Jaber Abdullah).

612. YOUNG JOHN (IRE)
b.c. Acclamation – Carpet Lady (Night Shift). April 20. Tenth foal. 130,000Y. Tattersalls October Book 2. Not sold. Brother to the useful 2-y-o listed 5f winner of 4 races and Group 3 Cornwallis Stakes third Cake and to the fair 2-y-o 7f winner Heskin and half-brother to 5 winners including the quite useful 5f and 6f winner of 7 races Tagula Night, the quite useful 7f and 1m winner Suited And Booted (both by Tagula) and the modest 2-y-o 6f winner Wachiwi (by Namid). The dam, a fair dual 6f placed 2-y-o, is a half-sister to 5 winners including the Hong Kong stakes winner Classic Fountain. The second dam, Lucky Fountain (by Lafontaine), is an unraced sister to the Group 2 Geoffrey Freer Stakes winner Shambo.

613. ZAHRAT NARJIS
b.f. Exceed And Excel – Nijoom Dubai (Noverre). March 24. Third foal. The dam, winner of the 2-y-o Group 3 Albany Stakes, is a half-sister to 2 winners including the Group 3 Albany Stakes winner and Group 1 Fillies' Mile second Samitar. The second dam, Aileen's Gift (by Rainbow Quest), is an unraced half-sister to 3 winners including the fairly useful listed-placed Roker Park and the dam of the Group 2 Gimcrack Stakes winner Shameel.

614. ZAINA RIZEENA
ch.f. Shamardal – Sweet Lilly (Tobougg). March 9. Third foal. Half-sister to the fair 1m winner Lilly Junior (by Cape Cross). The dam, a smart listed 1m and listed 1m winner of 6 races and second in the Group 3 Musidora Stakes, is a half-sister to the useful 9f and 10f winner of 7 races Ofaraby. The second dam, Maristax (by Reprimand), a fair 2-y-o 7f winner, is closely related to the useful 2-y-o listed 5f winner Four-Legged-Friend and a half-sister to 6 winners including the dual US Grade 3 winner Superstrike and the dam of the Group 1 winning sprinters Goodricke and Pastoral Pursuits. (Jaber Abdullah).

615. UNNAMED
ch.c. Showcasing – Malelane (Prince Sabo).

April 9. Fourth living foal. 90,000Y. Tattersalls October Book 2. Robin O'Ryan. Half-sister to the quite useful 5f winner of 5 races (including at 2 yrs) Secret Missile (by Sakhee's Secret), to the modest 5f and 6f winner Compton Prince (by Compton Place) and the moderate 5f to 7f winner of 6 races Novalist (by Avonbridge). The dam, a poor 5f placed maiden, is a half-sister to 6 winners including the Group 3 Prix du Petit Couvert winner Bishops Court and the listed winning sprinter Astonished. The second dam, Indigo (by Primo Dominie), a quite useful 2-y-o 5f winner, is a half-sister to 5 winners.

CHARLIE FELLOWES

616. AL DALLAH ★★
b.f. Footstepsinthesand – Fillthegobletagain (Byron). March 12. First foal. €26,000Y. Tattersalls Ireland September. Charlie Gordon Watson. The dam is an unraced half-sister to 6 winners including the Italian and Hong Kong stakes winner Romancero. The second dam, Batilde (by Victory Piper), was placed in Italy and is a half-sister to 7 minor winners. (Mr Sehail bin Khalifa Al Kuwari). *"She's quite sharp, not over-big but very athletic with a lovely, long stride. One day you see her zipping up the hill and you think she might be early, but then when you see her in the box she doesn't look like an early 2-y-o. She does everything easily, I'm hoping to get her out in June because she thrives on her exercise".*

617. AL FOUZ ★★★
b.c. Footstepsinthesand – Zawariq (Marju). February 15. Fourth foal. €28,000Y. Tattersalls Ireland September. Charlie Gordon-Watson. Brother to the hurdles winner Rockabilly Riot. The dam is an unplaced half-sister to 6 winners including the fairly useful triple 7f winner (including at 2 yrs) Silk Fan. The second dam, Alikhlas (by Lahib), a fair 3-y-o 1m winner, is a half-sister to 4 winners including the listed winner and Group 2 Lancashire Oaks second Sahool and to the dam of the dual Group 2 winner Maraahel. (Mr Sehail bin Khalifa Al Kuwari). *"A really nice horse and one for the second half of the season, he's very attractive and a beautiful mover. He's scopey and covers a lot of ground but I'd be hoping to get him out in August or September".*
TRAINERS' BARGAIN BUY

618. AL MAFTOON ★★
b.c. Lilbourne Lad – Mooching Along (Mujahid). April 6. Fifth foal. €28,000Y. Tattersalls Ireland September. Charlie Gordon-Watson. Half-brother to the quite useful 2014 Irish 2-y-o 5f winner and listed-placed Primo Uomo, to the quite useful dual 6f winner Strategic Force (both by Strategic Prince) and the quite useful 7f (at 2 yrs) and 6f winner Great Spirit (by Tagula). The dam is an unraced half-sister to one winner. The second dam, Inching (by Inchinor), was placed 9 times over 5f and 6f from 2 to 4 yrs and is a half-sister to 7 winners including the triple Group 3 winning sprinter Majestic Missile. (Mr Sehail bin Khalifa Al Kuwari). *"Very immature and one for the end of the season. He had a minor problem which meant he had to have some time off but I think he'll be all the better for it. He's filled out, strengthen up and done really well. A nice, scopey horse for the end of the season".*

619. ENDLESS ACRES ★★
b.c. Champs Elysees – Eternity Ring (Alzao). May 5. Seventh foal. 35,000Y. Tattersalls October Book 2. Charlie Gordon-Watson. Half-brother to the unplaced 2014 2-y-o Bounty Bah (by Bahamian Bounty) and to the quite useful dual 6f winner Sedenoo (by Cape Cross). The dam is an unraced half-sister to 7 winners including the Group 3 winners Baron Ferdinand and Love Everlasting. The second dam, In Perpetuity (by Great Nephew), a fairly useful 10f winner, is a half-sister to 6 winners including the Derby winner and high-class sire Shirley Heights and to the placed Bempton (herself dam of the Group winners Gull Nook, Mr Pintips and Banket). (Saffron House Stables Partnership). *"A beautiful mover but he's a May foal and a Champs Elysees, so he won't be doing anything very early. Still weak, he'll be one for the mid-to-end of the year. He's a good size and I'd be disappointed if I didn't get him out this year. A nice horse and a lovely mover".*

620. RIP IT UP ★★★★
b.c. Rip Van Winkle – Monaazalah (Green Desert). March 31. Fourth foal. €65,000Y. Goffs Orby. Grove Stud. Half-brother to Classical Rose (by Amadeus Rose), unplaced in one start at 2 yrs in 2014. The dam, a quite useful 2-y-o 6f winner, is a half-sister to 2 winners. The second dam, Karamah (by Unfuwain),

a fair 6f placed 2-y-o, is a half-sister to 6 winners. (Terry Jennings). *"As good-looking as you could want in a horse. A great, big, strong, scopey individual with a touch of class. If only one of my 2-y-o's are going to be any good this is it. He was broken quite late so we haven't had him as long as the rest but he's joined in no problem and he's doing plenty. He'll not be early and is probably one for September time over seven furlongs and a mile. I'm very pleased with him".*

621. SALVO ★★★

b.f. Acclamation – Passe Passe (Lear Fan). March 6. Twelfth foal. Closely related to the quite useful winner of 5 races (including over 5f at 2 yrs) Ryedale Ovation (by Royal Applause) and half-sister to 5 winners including the fair 2014 2-y-o 7f winner Pasticcio (by New Approach), the fairly useful 10.2f and 12f winner and Australian Grade 2 placed Magic Instinct (by Entrepreneur) and the fairly useful 7f (at 2 yrs) and 10f winner Cabinet (by Grand Lodge). The dam, a fair 7f to 12f placed maiden, is a half-sister to the Irish listed winner and French Group 2 placed Windermere. The second dam, Madame L'Enjoleur (by L'Enjoleur), a US 2-y-o stakes winner and Grade 1 placed twice, is a half-sister to the Grade 1 winner Labeeb. (Mr A Oppenheimer). *"A nice little filly, she's plenty forward enough to be racing in the first half of the season. A lovely mover with a great attitude, I'm very happy with her and she's coming along nicely".*

622. TRODERO ★★★

b.f. Mastercraftsman – Jules (Danehill). March 30. Eighth foal. 10,000Y. Tattersalls October Book 3. Charlie Gordon-Watson. Half-sister to the useful 6f and 7f winner of 7 races from 2 to 5 yrs Golden Desert (by Desert Prince), to the quite useful dual 7f winner (including at 2 yrs) Romantic Wish (by Hawk Wing), the quite useful dual 1m winner Stosur (by Mount Nelson), the modest 1m to 14f winner of 8 races The Blue Dog (by High Chaparral) and a winner in Hungary by Fasliyev. The dam, a fair 3-y-o 7f winner, is a half-sister to 10 winners including the dam of the Australian Group 1 winner Prowl. The second dam, Before Dawn (by Raise A Cup), a champion US 2-y-o filly, won two Grade

1 events and is a half-sister to 6 winners. (Newpinewood Stables). *"All things considered I think I bought her quite cheaply, she's a good-looking filly and one for the mid-to-latter part of the season over seven furlongs. A nice attitude and a good mover, I'm very pleased with her and I think it could be ten grand well-spent".*

623. VROOM ★★★★ ♠

ch.c. Poet's Voice – Shivaree (Rahy). April 22. Sixth foal. 45,000Y. Tattersalls October Book 3. Charlie Gordon-Watson. Half- sister to the fairly useful 2-y-o 5f winner and listed-placed Tomintoul Singer (by Johannesburg), to the fair 2-y-o listed 5f winner Geesala (by Barathea) and a 2-y-o winner in Sweden by Amadeus Wolf. The dam, a fair 2-y-o 6f winner, is a half-sister to 2 winners. The second dam, Shmoose (by Caerleon), a useful 2-y-o 6f winner and third in the Group 3 6f Prix de Seine-et-Oise, is a half-sister to 6 winners and to the good broodmare June Moon. (Emma Capon and Simon Marsh). *"A very sharp little horse. He's done two pieces of work already, he'll be out very early and I'm really pleased with the way he's going. A flashy chestnut with a white face and four white socks, he's got a beautiful action so he wouldn't want soft ground. We'll aim him at a maiden sometime in April or possibly the Conditions race at Newmarket".*

624. UNNAMED ★★

b.c. Desert Party – Ras Shaikh (Sheikh Albadou). February 28. Half-brother to the Group 3 7f Criterion Stakes winner Racer Forever, to the quite useful dual 10f winner Wrood (by Invasor), the quite useful 2-y-o 6f winner Oman Sea (both by Rahy) and the fair 10f and 12f winner Caribbean Pearl (by Silver Hawk). The dam, a useful 2-y-o 6f winner, was second in three listed events at 3 yrs and is a half-sister to several winners. The second dam, Aneesati (by Kris), a quite useful 1m winner, is a half-sister to several winners including the Prix de la Salamandre second Bin Nashwan. (M Obaida). *"A gorgeous horse and a powerful individual, I've gone easy on him because he had a little niggle in front but all being well he'll be fine towards the latter part of the season. He looks like a sprinter but I'm hoping he'll stay seven furlongs or a mile later on".*

625. UNNAMED ★★★
b.c. Shirocco – Storming Sioux (Storming Home). March 28. Third foal. The dam, a fair 1m placed maiden including at 2 yrs, is a half-sister to numerous winners including the smart Group 3 7f Solario Stakes (at 2 yrs) and Group 1 Prix Jean Prat winner Best Of The Bests and the smart 6f (at 2 yrs) and 9f winner and Group 2 Dante Stakes third Dunhill Star. The second dam, Sueboog (by Darshaan), a very useful winner of the Group 3 7.3f Fred Darling Stakes, was third in the Musidora Stakes and the Nassau Stakes and is a half-sister to 6 winners. (M Obaida). *"He's a nice, scopey individual but hopefully he's not fooling me into thinking he's one of the more forward of my 2-y-o's, because that's what he appears to be, despite his pedigree. A good size, a nice mover with very good conformation, he has an engine and I'm very pleased with him. To date he looks like one for the first half of the season and I really like him".*

JAMES GIVEN
626. CHARAMBA ★★
b.f. Sir Percy – Rahcak (Generous). April 8. Seventh foal. Half-brother to the fair 7f and 7.5f winner Fenella Fudge (by Rock Hard Ten) and to a jumps winner by Sunday Silence. The dam is a placed half-sister to 3 winners including the top-class colt Mark of Esteem, winner of the 2,000 Guineas, the Queen Elizabeth II Stakes and the Tripleprint Celebration Mile. The second dam, Homage (by Ajdal), was unraced and is closely related to the very smart Group 1 9.2f Prix Jean Prat winner Local Talent and a half-sister to the Group 2 6f Mill Reef Stakes winner Local Suitor. (Peter Onslow & James Given). *"We bought the mare at Keeneland and the interesting point about this filly's pedigree is that she's closely related to Mark Of Esteem who is both her grandsire and a half-brother to her dam. She's a bit backward, which is what you'd expect given that the dam is by Generous and that Sir Percy doesn't get that many precocious sorts. She's a decent shape and size, so we'll hopefully bring her out over seven furlongs later in the season. She's no shrinking violet – she's got a decent back-end on her".*

627. COOL IT ★★
ch.f. Medicean – Pantile (Pivotal). May 2.

Second foal. £5,000Y. Doncaster Premier. Cool Silk /Anthony Stroud. The dam is an unraced half-sister to 5 minor winners. The second dam, Tahirah (by Green Desert), a useful 3-y-o 7f and 1m winner, was listed-placed twice and is a sister to one winner and a half-sister to 5 winners. (The Cool Silk Partnership). *"Not a big filly, she was a late foal so we've not done much with her yet, especially as the pedigree isn't that precocious. She'll take a bit of time, but she wasn't expensive by any means".*

628. COOL SILK BOY ★★★★
b.c. Big Bad Bob – Kheleyf's Silver (Kheleyf). March 18. Third foal. 50,000Y. Tattersalls October Book 2. Anthony Stroud. Half-brother to the 2014 champion 2-y-o filly and Group 1 Cheveley Park Stakes winner Tiggy Wiggy (by Kodiac) and to the fair 6f winner Iftaar (by Bushranger). The dam, a fairly useful 2-y-o 5f winner, is a half-sister to 4 winners including the very useful Group 3 6f Norfolk Stakes winner of 6 races Masta Plasta. The second dam, Silver Arrow (by Shadeed), was placed once at 2 yrs and is a half-sister to 4 winners. (The Cool Silk Partnership). *"Considering she's a half-sister to a champion 2-y-o filly I think he was relatively cheap. Maybe people were put off because they thought Richard Hannon would be keen to buy him, which he wasn't as it turned out. I think that was fortunate for us because this is a strong, good-sized horse, pretty precocious but with scope as well. We really like him, he's done a few sharp bits of work and he'll be running in May. From what we've seen so far we're more than happy with him and we'd love to think he could be a Norfolk Stakes 2-y-o".*

629. COOL SILK GIRL ★★★★
br.f. Motivator – Captain's Paradise (Rock Of Gibraltar). May 12. Second foal. 160,000Y. Tattersalls October Book 1. Cool Silk/Anthony Stroud. The dam, unplaced in two starts at 2 yrs, is a half-sister to 6 winners including the Singapore Gold Cup and Gran Premio del Jockey Club winner Kutub, the Irish 2-y-o listed 9f winner On The Nile and the Irish listed 1m winner In The Limelight. The second dam, Minnie Habit (Habitat), an Irish 4-y-o 9f winner, is closely related to the 5f Curragh Stakes and 6f Railway Stakes winner Bermuda Classic (herself dam of the Coronation Stakes

winner Shake The Yoke and the Phoenix Sprint Stakes winner Tropical) and a half-sister to 6 winners. (The Cool Silk Partnership). *"A late foal, she was quite expensive, she's very laid-back and has taken everything in her stride. Nothing bothers her, she's a lovely shape and size and has a lovely nature. We haven't taken the handbrake of yet because it's all about being patient with her, but she's as nice a filly as we've had, with middle-distance potential, for a long time. I really like her and I'm hoping to have her out from late summer onwards".*

630. FEELIN DICKY ★★
b.c. Dick Turpin – Feelin Foxy (Foxhound). April 23. First foal. The dam, a quite useful 5f and 6f winner of 9 races over 5f and 6f and from 2 to 7 yrs, is a half-sister to 6 winners including the useful 2-y-o dual 6f winner and listed-placed Josh and the quite useful 2-y-o winners Valley Of Fire, Russian Reel and Yes Two. The second dam, Charlie Girl (by Puissance), a 2-y-o 5f winner, is a half-sister to 4 winners. (The Cool Silk Partnership). *"The dam was a tough sprinting racemare and I trained her for a good part of her career, so I know her well. This colt didn't go through the sales ring so his prep came much later and he's a bit behind the others. Hopefully he's one for mid-season and he certainly has a 2-y-o look about him. His name should amuse plenty of people!"*

631. GIRLS IN A BENTLEY ★★★
b.f. Acclamation – Laurelei (Oratorio). February 9. First foal. £60,000Y. Doncaster Premier. Cool Silk/Anthony Stroud. The dam, a minor winner in France at 3 yrs, is a half-sister to 5 winners including the multiple Group 1 winner (including the Irish Derby) Cape Blanco and the US dual Grade 2 winner Mr O'Brien. The second dam, Laurel Delight (by Presidium), a useful winner of 4 races over 5f, is a half-sister to 5 winners including the high-class sprinter Paris House. (The Cool Silk Partnership). *"She's given us a good feel, zips along nicely and despite not being totally bred for speed I don't she's far away from running, probably by the end of May. She has a chunky, squat, 2-y-o physique".*

632. ITSINTHESTARS ★★
b.f. Zoffany – Gemini Gold (King's Best). March

5. Fifth foal. £32,000Y. Doncaster Premier. BBA (Ire). Half-sister to the fair 2014 5.5f and 6f placed 2-y-o Lady Gemini (by Myboycharlie), to the fair 6f (at 2 yrs) and 1m winner Disclosure (by Indesatchel) and a hurdles winner by Danehill Dancer. The dam, a fairly useful Irish 7f winner, was third in the Group 3 Park Express Stakes and is a half-sister to 6 winners. The second dam, Wakria (by Sadler's Wells), won 3 races including the listed 1m Prix de Saint-Cyr and is a half-sister to 3 minor winners. (Bearstone Stud Ltd). *"A home-bred from Bearstone Stud, she's nicely put together and a good, strong type. We haven't had her as long as most of the 2-y-o's and we haven't done a lot with her. She has a willing attitude but I'm not sure she'll be that early. She'll make a 2-y-o by mid-season I should think".*

633. SEARCH FOR ED ★★
b.c. Monsieur Bond – Spontaneity (Holy Roman Emperor). February 19. First foal. £55,000Y. Doncaster Premier. Cool Silk/Anthony Stroud. The dam, a modest 5f placed maiden, is a half-sister to 5 winners including the dual listed winner and Group 2 Flying Childers Stakes second and smart broodmare Swiss Lake. The second dam, Blue Iris (by Petong), a useful winner of 5 races over 5f and 6f including the Weatherbys Super Sprint and the Redcar Two-Year-Old Trophy, was listed-placed three times and is a half-sister to 10 winners. (The Cool Silk Partnership). *"He hasn't come to hand as quickly as I expected. He doesn't do anything without a great deal of zip yet, although looks a 2-y-o type, so I think we need to progress with him slowly. He's inbred 2x3 to Danehill and I do think he'll be a speedy type when the penny drops".*

634. SIGN OF THE KODIAC (IRE) ★★★
b.c. Kodiac – Summer Magic (Desert Sun). May 13. Fourth foal. £50,000Y. Doncaster Premier. Cool Silk/Anthony Stroud. Brother to the fairly useful 7f (at 2 yrs) and 1m winner Vector Force. The dam, a quite useful 6f to 1m winner of 6 races, is a half-sister to a hurdles winner and to the dam of the Irish Group 3 winner Ansgar. The second dam, Cimeterre (by Arazi), is a placed half-sister to 4 winners including the dam of the dual Group 3 winning sprinter Captain Gerrard. (The Cool Silk Partnership). *"A very nice horse, he's big*

but his foaling date means he's the youngest of our 2-y-o's. Nevertheless he has done some fast work because he was ready for it and he went very nicely indeed. His full brother Vector Force won as a 2-y-o and is currently rated 93, this colt is certainly showing ability and I would hope to have him out shortly after his birthday, so before the end of May. He has a very willing attitude and he'll probably start at six furlongs before progressing to seven".

635. SILK BOW ★★

b.f. Elusive City – Ishraaqat (Singspiel). March 12. Second foal. £31,000Y. Doncaster Premier. Anthony Stroud. The dam, a fair 1m winner, is a half-sister to 9 winners including the useful triple 6f (including at 2 yrs) and subsequent UAE listed 5f winner Taqseem. The second dam, Elshamms (by Zafonic), a fairly useful 2-y-o 7f winner and third in the Group 3 Prestige Stakes, is a half-sister to 10 winners. (The Cool Silk Partnership). *"She ran in the Brocklesby where she broke well but then ran with the choke out and just did too much. She shows a lot of speed but as the season goes along she'll probably go six furlongs by mid-summer and maybe even seven later on".*

636. SIR DUDLEY (IRE) ★★★

b.c. Arcano – Rosy Dudley (Grand Lodge). February 10. Sixth foal. £52,000Y. Doncaster Premier. Cool Silk/Anthony Stroud. Half-brother to the fairly useful 6f (at 2 yrs) to 1m winner of 5 races Apostle (by Dark Angel), to the quite useful 2-y-o 5f and 7f winner Grand Honour (by Verglas), the quite useful 1m winner Shafrah (by Acclamation) and a winner in Qatar by Refuse To Bend. The dam, a fair Irish 8.5f winner at 3 yrs, is a half-sister to 6 winners including the Group 2 Criterium des Ans winner Deadly Dudley and the listed winner Miss Nosey Parker. The second dam, Renzola (by Dragonara Palace), is an unraced half-sister to the dam of the Group 1 and Grade 1 winner Millkom. (The Cool Silk Partnership). *"He was fifth in the Brocklesby where he wasn't as fit as we thought he could have been. The jockey reported it was hard to pull him up afterwards, which is nice for a 2-y-o. He's a great walking horse, has a good attitude and is nice and strong. He'll be running again in mid-April and I wouldn't be surprised to see him going six furlongs and possibly*

seven by the end of the year. He should be winning before too long". Sir Dudley won a maiden at Nottingham on April 18th.

637. STONE QUERCUS (IRE) ★★

b.c. Rock Of Gibraltar – Redglow (Fasliyev). March 23. Second foal. €60,000Y. Arqana Deauville October. Anthony Stroud. The dam is an unraced half-sister to 5 winners including the smart Irish dual Group 3 7f winner Redstone Dancer and the useful dual 6f (at 2 yrs) and listed 7f winner Red Liason. The second dam, Red Affair (by Generous), an Irish listed 10f winner, is a half-sister to 6 winners including the smart 7.6f to 10f winner Brilliant Red. (The Cool Silk Partnership). *"He was quite backward when he arrived from the sales, but he's been catching up all the time and he's a biggish horse now. He's done well and he's cantering away nicely, but he's very much one for the last third of the season because he's going to take a bit of coming together".*

638. STRANDS OF SILK (IRE) ★★★

b.f. Kodiac – Saldenaera (Areion). March 19. First foal. £24,000Y. Doncaster Premier. Cool Silk/Anthony Stroud. The dam, a minor 3-y-o winner in Germany, is a sister to the German listed winner Saldenart and a half-sister to 5 winners. The second dam, Saldengeste (by Be My Guest), a minor dual 3-y-o winner in Germany, is a half-sister to 9 winners. (The Cool Silk Partnership). *"She's quite a 'buzzy' filly but we gave her a few bits of work a few weeks ago where she showed some ability, but we've had to teach her to settle. She's had a little break and she's working again now in a much more settled fashion. I'd hope to have her out by the end of May".* **TRAINERS' BARGAIN BUY**

JOHN GOSDEN
639. AMANAAT (IRE) ★★★

b.c. Exceed And Excel – Pietra Dura (Cadeaux Genereux). February 21. Ninth foal. 280,000Y. Tattersalls October Book 1. Shadwell Estate Co. Half-brother to the quite useful 7f and 1m and subsequent US Grade 3 10f winner Turning Top (by Pivotal), to the quite useful 2-y-o 6f winner Curly Wee (by Excellent Art) and the 9f winner (on his only start) Hollander (by Fasliyev). The dam, a listed-placed 2-y-o 7f winner, is a half-sister to 4 winners. The second dam, Bianca Nera (by Salse), won the Group 1 7f Moyglare Stud Stakes and the Group 2 6f Lowther Stakes and is a half-sister to 4 winners including the Moyglare Stud Stakes second Hotelgenie Dot Com (herself dam of the dual Group 1 winner Simply Perfect). *"A well-balanced, good-moving colt, I imagine he'll be out in May or June over a stiff six furlongs. I like the stallion".*

640. AUNTINET ★★★
b.f. Invincible Spirit – Cozy Maria (Cozzene). March 7. Eighth foal. Sister to the 2-y-o Group 2 5f Flying Childers Stakes and Group 3 5f Molecomb Stakes winner of 6 races Zebedee and closely related to the fair 7f winner Pategonia (by Oasis Dream). The dam, a useful 10f winner, was listed-placed twice and is a half-sister to 7 winners. The second dam, Mariamme (by Verbatim), won twice at 3 yrs in the USA and is a half-sister to 7 winners including the Grade 1 Breeders Cup Turf winner Miss Alleged. *"A sweet filly, she's a good mover but just going through a growing stage now, which isn't a bad thing because she looked as if she was going to be somewhat petite. I see her being out around July time. Given the fact that she's related to Zebedee I think she'll be a sprinter".*

641. BLUEBEARD ★★★
b.c. Dansili – Arabesque (Zafonic). February 28. Eleventh foal. Closely related to the very smart listed 6f winner Camacho (by Danehill) and half-brother to numerous winners including the Group 2 6f Gimcrack Stakes winner Showcasing, the useful 2014 2-y-o 6f winner Tendu and the fairly useful triple 6f winner (including at 2 yrs) and listed-placed Bouvardia (both by Oasis Dream). The dam, a useful listed 6f winner, is a sister to 2 winners including the useful 5f and 6f winner Threat and a half-sister to 5 winners including the Group 2 1m Prix de Sandringham winner Modern Look. The second dam, Prophecy (by Warning), a useful winner of the Group 1 6f Cheveley Park Stakes, was second in the Group 3 7f Nell Gwyn Stakes. (Khalid Abdulla). *"A very attractive horse and a good mover, he's quite a 'jack the lad' around the place and lets you know he's there the whole time. A lovely moving colt".*

642. CACHAO ★★★
br.c. New Approach – Mambo Halo (Southern Halo). March 14. Sixth foal. 120,000Y. Tattersalls October Book 1. Rabbah Bloodstock. Half-brother to the fair 2014 2-y-o 5f winner Mambo Paradise (by Makfi), to the very useful 2-y-o listed 6f winner Earl Of Leitrim (by Johannesburg) and the fair 10.5f and 12.5f winner Mambo Rhythm (by Authorized). The dam, a 2-y-o winner in Argentina, is a half-sister to two winners including the listed Lupe Stakes winner and Group 1 Yorkshire Oaks second Ocean Silk. The second dam, Mambo Jambo (by Kingmambo), a minor 3-y-o winner in France, is a sister to 3 winners including the multiple Group 1 winners Divine Proportions and Whipper and a half-sister to 7 winners. *"A strong type, he didn't cost that much for a New Approach and he'll make a 2-y-o by July time".*

643. CARTAGO ★★★
b.c. Dansili – Kilo Alpha (King's Best). March 7. Second foal. Half-brother to the 2014 French 2-y-o 1m winner and Group 3 1m Prix Thomas Bryon second Alpha Bravo (by Oasis Dream). The dam, a French listed 1m winner, is a sister to the very smart triple listed 10f winner Runaway. The second dam, Anasazi (Sadler's Wells), was placed over 9f and 10f in France and is a half-sister to the outstanding colt Dancing Brave and the Prix Vermeille and Prix de Diane winner Jolypha. *"A good moving, athletic and very lively colt. There's a lot of spirit about him and his riders have to sit tight".*

644. CASTLE HARBOUR ★★★
b.c. Kyllachy – Gypsy Carnival (Trade Fair). February 14. First foal. 200,000Y. Tattersalls October Book 1. John Warren. The dam, a fair 1m winner, is a half-sister to 3 winners including the very smart listed 1m winner of 7 races and Group 2 third Mabait. The second dam, Czarna Rosa (by Polish Precedent), is an unraced half-sister to 9 winners including the dam of the Group 2 Queen Mary Stakes winner Elletelle. *"A strong colt, he's a good mover with a good attitude and I'd like to see him out around June time over six furlongs. Like a lot of Kyllachy's he'll probably like a bit of cut in the ground".*

645. CITY OF IDEAS ★★★
b.c. Dansili – Gertrude Bell (Sinndar). March 8. First foal. The dam, a Group 2 12f Lancashire Oaks winner, is a half-sister to 2 winners including the useful listed 10f winner Dick Doughtywylie. The second dam, Sugar Mill (by Polar Falcon), a French 10f winner, was listed-placed twice. *"He's a nice type of colt, medium-sized and looks like a mid-season type 2-y-o. A strong colt and a good mover"*.

646. DHAROOS (IRE) ★★★ ♠
ch.c. New Approach – Cailiocht (Elusive Quality). April 12. Second foal. The dam is an unraced half-sister to the 2-y-o Group 1 7f Moyglare Stud Stakes winner and 1,000 Guineas third Maybe. The second dam, Sumora (by Danehill), a 2-y-o listed 5f St Hugh's Stakes winner, is a sister to the useful Irish 7f winner Fleeting Shadow and a half-sister to the Oaks and German Oaks winner Dancing Rain. *"A big, rangy colt, he's going to be very much one for the mile maidens around September. He's got a great attitude and a good, relaxed mind on him"*.

647. EPSOM DAY (IRE) ★★★
b.c. Teofilo – Dubai Flower (Manduro). March 21. First foal. The dam is an unplaced half-sister to numerous winners including the smart Group 3 7f Solario Stakes (at 2 yrs) and Group 1 Prix Jean Prat winner Best Of The Bests and the smart 6f (at 2 yrs) and 9f winner and Group 2 Dante Stakes third Dunhill Star. The second dam, Sueboog (by Darshaan), a very useful winner of the Group 3 7.3f Fred Darling Stakes, was third in the Musidora Stakes and the Nassau Stakes and is a half-sister to 6 winners. *"A nice colt, he's attractive and a good mover. His knees are a bit immature but he's a grand type and I'd hope to have him out around July or August"*.

648. EXIST ★★★ ♠♠
b.f. Exceed And Excel – Harryana (Efisio). February 5. Tenth foal. 180,000Y. Tattersalls October Book 2. Cheveley Park Stud. Half-sister to 6 winners including the fair 2014 2-y-o 5f winner Showstoppa (by Showcasing), the 2-y-o Group 2 6f Mill Reef Stakes winner Temple Meads (by Avonbridge), the useful 2-y-o 6f winner and Group 3 Firth of Clyde Stakes second Sneak Preview (by Monsieur

Bond), the quite useful 2-y-o 5f winner O'Gorman (by Sleeping Indian) and the fair 2-y-o 5f winner Hot Secret (by Sakhee's Secret). The dam, a fair 2-y-o dual 5f winner, is out of the quite useful 3-y-o 5f winner Allyanna (by Thatching), herself a half-sister to 8 winners. *"She's quite a character and was a lot of fun to break in! I'd like to see her out around June time if possible. A five/six furlong 2-y-o"*.

649. EYESHINE ★★★★
b.f. Dubawi – Casual Look (Red Ransom). February 27. $1,450,000Y. Keeneland September. Flaxman Stables. Half-sister to the fairly useful 1m to 10f winner of 4 races Mushreq (by Distorted Humor), to the minor US dual 1m winner Casual Trick (by Bernardini) and the minor US winner Hidden Glance (by Kingmambo). The dam, an Epsom Oaks winner, was second in the Group 1 Fillies' Mile and is a sister to the listed Prix de Liancourt winner and Grade 1 Yellow Ribbon Stakes third Shabby Chic and a half-sister to 5 winners including the US winner and Grade 2 placed American Style. The second dam, Style Setter (by Manila), a stakes-placed winner of 3 races in the USA, is a half-sister to 2 winners. *"A good-looking, strong filly and I can see a lot of the mother coming through as well. She'll be happiest coming through in September/ October time because she's a big girl and I don't think she'll appreciate me trying to go for her any sooner. A fine looking filly"*.

650. FLYWEIGHT ★★★
b.f. Teofilo – Morinqua (Cadeaux Genereux). March 18. Second foal. 200,000Y. Tattersalls October Book 1. John Ferguson. Half-sister to the 2014 2-y-o Cornwallville (by Makfi), a winner of 5 races from 6f to 1m including a listed event. The dam, a useful listed 5f winner of 5 races at 2 to 4 yrs, is a half-sister to the useful 5f (at 2 yrs) and listed 6f winner and triple Group 3 placed Topkamp. The second dam, Victoria Regia (by Lomond), a stakes winner of 3 races from 6f to 1m here and in the USA, is a half-sister to 9 winners including the listed winners Fight To The Last and Seattle Victory. John couldn't enlighten me about this filly because he only got her a week after I'd spoken to him. I'm particularly interested in her because my Partnership

had the mare in training with James Given as a 3-y-o and she was very fast but barely got five furlongs. I managed to glean some information from her pre-training yard and apparently she's done well, goes nicely and looks like a 2-y-o. ST.

651. FOUNDATION (IRE) ★★★★ ♠

ch.c. Zoffany – Roystonea (Polish Precedent). February 24. Seventh foal. €190,000Y. Goffs Orby. John Warren. Half-brother to the fairly useful 2014 2-y-o 7f winner Misterioso (by Iffraaj), to the fairly useful 7f (at 2 yrs) to 8.5f winner Vastonea (by Verglas), the quite useful Irish 2-y-o 7f winner Take A Chance (by Hawk Wing) and a minor 2-y-o winner abroad by Xaar. The dam, a listed-placed winner of 2 races over 7f and 1m in France, is a half-sister to 4 winners including the French listed winners Bermuda Grass and Bermuda Rye. The second dam, Alleluia Tree (by Royal Academy), a French 2-y-o winner, is a half-sister to 7 winners and to the unraced dam of the triple Group 1 winner Scorpion. *"A grand colt, he's filled his frame out well, he has a good action and he catches the eye. I see him as being happiest over seven furlongs or a mile this year".*

652. GENERALSHIP ★★★★

b.c. New Approach – Ahla Wasahl (Dubai Destination). March 8. Second foal. 600,000Y. Tattersalls October Book 1. John Ferguson. The dam, a useful 6f (at 2 yrs) and listed 1m winner, was third in the Group 2 Cherry Hinton Stakes and is a half-sister to 4 winners including the dam of the Group 1 Italian Oaks winner Menhoubah. The second dam, In Full Cry (by Seattle Slew), a winner at 2 and 3 yrs in the USA, was second in the Grade 2 6f Adirondack Stakes and is a half-sister to 6 winners including the top-class miler Posse. *"A nice, medium-sized, strong colt with a good manner about him. He should be a mid-season 2-y-o and there's speed on the dam's side".*

653. GRADIENT ★★★

b.c. Oasis Dream – Very Good News (Empire Maker). January 15. First foal. The dam is an unraced half-sister to the Grade 1 Matriarch Stakes and Grade 1 Beverly D Stakes winner Heat Haze, to the Coronation Stakes, Prix Jacques Le Marois and Breeders Cup Filly &

Mare Turf winner Banks Hill, the US Grade 1 winners Intercontinental, Champs Elysees and Cacique, and the Group 2 1m winner and top-class sire Dansili. The second dam, Hasili (by Kahyasi), won over 5f at 2 yrs and stayed a mile. *"He was an early foal and I've done some half-speed work with him. I'll leave him alone for now and pick him up again in the middle of May. He goes OK, no more than that at the moment".*

654. INVESTITURE ★★★★

b.f. Invincible Spirit – Highest (Dynaformer). January 28. First foal. The dam, a fairly useful listed-placed 12f winner, is a half-sister to 5 winners including the French listed 12f and US Grade 2 12f Long Island Handicap winner Olaya and the smart listed-placed 7f (at 2 yrs) to 10f winner Wasan. The second dam, Solaia (by Miswaki), winner of the listed Cheshire Oaks and second in the Group 3 12f Lancashire Oaks, is a half-sister to 3 winners. *"A nice type of filly, we had the mother here who was a big, rangy mare. This is a well-balanced, good type and I could see her first appearance being at the July course in late July/August over seven furlongs".*

655. JOHN MILTON (IRE) ★★★

b.c. Poet's Voice – Kelly Nicole (Rainbow Quest). February 25. Sixth foal. 200,000Y. Tattersalls October Book 1. John Ferguson. Half-brother to the very smart Group 2 Summer Mile and listed 7f winner and Group 2 Celebration Mile second Aljamaaheer (by Dubawi) and to the fairly useful dual 7f (at 2 yrs) and 1m winner and Group 3 Dee Stakes third Tinkertown (by Verglas). The dam, a fair 1m to 10f winner of 3 races, is a half-sister to 8 winners including the Group 1 placed Robin Hood. The second dam, Banquise (by Last Tycoon), a French 2m winner, is a half-sister to 8 winners including the French Group 2 winners Modhish and Russian Snows and the good broodmare Truly Special. *"He's a scopey colt and still growing, but he's got plenty of scope and is a nice type for the second half of the season".*

656. KARAAMA ★★★★

b.c. Oasis Dream – Eshaadeh (Storm Cat). February 10. Closely related to the very useful 2-y-o Group 2 5f Queen Mary Stakes winner and Group 1 6f Cheveley Park Stakes third Maqaasid (by Green Desert). The dam, unplaced in 2 starts, is a half-sister to 7 winners including the 1,000 Guineas and Coronation Stakes winner Ghanaati and the Group 3 12f Cumberland Lodge Stakes winner Mawatheeq. The second dam, Sarayir (by Mr Prospector), a listed 1m winner, is closely related to the top-class Champion Stakes winner Nayef and a half-sister to the 2,000 Guineas, Eclipse, Derby and King George winner Nashwan. (Hamdan Al Maktoum). *"A nice colt, he's a little bit immature at the moment and I wouldn't want to push him forward. I could see him being more of an August type 2-y-o, obviously we know the family well and I think this colt will be speedy. He's blocky and strong".*

657. KAKASHAN (IRE) ★★★★
b.f. Kodiac – Barracade (Barathea). April 22. Fourth foal. 250,000Y. Tattersalls October Book 2. Hugo Lascelles. Half-sister to the fairly useful 2-y-o dual 6f winner and Group 2 Rockfel Stakes second Blockade (by Kheleyf) and to the fair dual 7f winner Black Rider (by Elnadim). The dam, a modest 10f placed 3-y-o in Ireland, is a half-sister to the US stakes winner and triple Group 2 placed Spider Power. The second dam, America Calling (by Quiet American), a fair 6f winner at 3 yrs, is a half-sister to 8 winners. *"An attractive, good-shaped filly and a good mover with a good attitude. I planned to go early with her but she just has a touch of immaturity. I'd like to move along with her as soon as she's ready to go but I'll wait for her to tell me".*

658. KHALEESY (IRE) ★★★
b.f. Galileo – Fleeting Spirit (Invincible Spirit). February 22. First foal. The dam won the Group 1 6f July Cup, the Group 2 5f Flying Childers Stakes (at 2 yrs) and the Group 2 5f Temple Stakes and is a half-sister to 2 winners including the fairly useful Irish 6f to 1m winner of 7 races and listed-placed Alone He Stands (by Flying Spur). The second dam, Millennium Tale (Distant Relative), is an unraced half-sister to 5 winners. *"A neat filly and very much a first foal, she's racy and might be out by mid-season".*

659. KHOR AL UDAID ★★★★
b.c. Invincible Spirit – Brusca (Grindstone). February 26. Ninth foal. 680,000Y. Tattersalls October Book 1. John Warren. Half-sister to 7 winners including the Group 3 Prix La Force winner and French Derby third Baraan (by Dalakhani), the French listed-placed Brampour (by Daylami) and Bruxcalina (by Linamix). The dam won 3 minor races at 3 and 4 yrs in the USA and is a half-sister to 6 winners including the US dual Grade 3 winner and Grade 1 placed Somali Lemonade. The second dam, Chic Corine (by Nureyev), is an unraced half-sister to 6 winners including the US Grade 2 winners Waldoboro and Tara Roma. *"A quality horse with a bit of scope. He's a lovely mover and has a very good mind on him. Definitely not your early type, he's one for the middle of the season onwards over seven furlongs and a mile. Naturally athletic".*

660. LA MORTOLA ★★★
b.f. Dubawi – Claba Di San Jore (Barathea). April 13. Ninth foal. Half-sister to 6 winners including the Italian Group 1 10f winner Crackerjack King (by Shamardal), the Italian Group 1 12f winners Jakkalberry (by Storming Home) and Awelmarduk (by Almutawakel), the Italian listed 10f and listed 12f winner and Group 2 Prix Niel third Kidnapping (by Intikhab). The dam, a minor Italian 3-y-o winner, is a half-sister to 9 winners. The second dam, Claw (by Law Society), a listed-placed Italian winner of 7 races, is a half-sister to 5 winners. *"A sweet filly with a nice temperament, she enjoys her canters and is a seven furlong type 2-y-o from July onwards. She's named after some famous gardens near San Remo".*

661. LEE BAY ★★★
b.c. Cacique – Bantu (Cape Cross). April 30. Second foal. 100,000Y. Tattersalls October Book 3. Blandford Bloodstock. Half-brother to the fairly useful 2014 2-y-o 8.5f winner Banzari (by Motivator). The dam, a fair 10f placed maiden, is a half-sister to the Grade 2 La Prevoyante Handicap winner Arvada and to the Group 3 7f Craven Stakes winner Adagio. The second dam, Lalindi (by Cadeaux Genereux), a fair middle-distance winner of 7 races, is a half-sister to 5 winners including the

useful 2-y-o winner Sumoto (herself dam of the Group 1 winners Summoner and Compton Admiral). *"A nice colt with a good mind on him, he's strengthening and doing well all the time. I see him very much as a horse for around September time".*

662. LINGUISTIC (IRE) ★★★★
b.c. Lope De Vega – Dazzle Dancer (Montjeu). January 16. Second foal. 650,000Y. Tattersalls October Book 1. John Ferguson. The dam, a fair Irish 4-y-o 12f winner, is a half-sister to 3 winners including the fairly useful triple listed-placed Lunduv. The second dam, Another Dancer (by Groom Dancer), won the Group 2 Prix de Malleret and is a half-sister to 6 winners. *"A nice sort of horse with a good attitude, he's a good mover and a grand sort of colt. We'll wait for seven furlongs with him".*

663. LIZZIE SIDDAL ★★★
b.f. Dansili – Selinka (Selkirk). February 17. Third living foal. 150,000Y. Tattersalls October Book 1. Blandford Bloodstock. Half-sister to the fair 6f (at 2 yrs) and 7f winner Pivotal Movement (by Pivotal) and to a minor winner abroad by Green Desert. The dam, a useful listed 6f (at 2 yrs) and listed 7f winner, is a half-sister to 2 winners. The second dam, Lady Links (by Bahamian Bounty), a dual listed 6f winner (including at 2 yrs), is a half-sister to 5 winners. *"A very attractive filly, she moves nicely, catches the eye and does everything easily. She's not going to be asked any questions early on, we'll wait for the seven furlong maidens at the July course. She's named after the artist Rossetti's model".*

664. MAGIC MIRROR ★★★
b.f. Dutch Art – Balatoma (Mr Greeley). February 10. First foal. 35,000Y. Tattersalls October Book 1. Rabbah Bloodstock. The dam, a modest 10f winner, is a half-sister to 6 winners including the Irish 2-y-o and subsequent Hong Kong winner and Group 3 Tetrarch Stakes second Creekview. The second dam, Honfleur (by Sadler's Wells), a useful French listed 13.5f winner, is a sister to the Prix de l'Arc de Triomphe winner Carnegie, closely related to the Group 2 Prix Guillaume d'Ornano winner Antisaar and a half-sister to the Group 3 St Simon Stakes winner Lake Erie. *"A strong, big-barrelled filly, she's doing*

her canters and there's a bit of stamina on her dam's side but I can see her running over six furlongs. Let's hope so. She wasn't very expensive for a Book 1 yearling".*

665. MAS A TIERRA ★★★★
ch.c. Footstepsinthesand – Celestial Girl (Dubai Destination). February 18. First foal. 70,000Y. Tattersalls October Book 1. Blandford Bloodstock. The dam, a fair 10f winner of 5 races, is a half-sister to 4 winners including the Italian 1m to 10f winner of 14 races from 3 to 6 yrs Strepadent. The second dam, Brightest Star (by Unfuwain), was placed over 10f and 11f is a half-sister to the Oaks winner Lady Carla. *"A grand colt, he moves well, has a good attitude and a good action. I'm very happy with him and he should be racing by the second half of May".*

666. MIDDLEMAN ★★★★★
b.c. Oasis Dream – Sense Of Pride (Sadler's Wells). February 10. The dam, a fair 10.5f winner, is a sister to the multiple Group 3 middle-distance winner and French Derby fourth Day Flight and a half-sister to the very useful 2-y-o 7f winner Bionic, the Group 3 7f Prestige Stakes winner Sense Of Joy and the useful 2-y-o dual 7f winner Ashdan. The second dam, Bonash (by Rainbow Quest), a very useful filly, won 4 races in France from 1m to 12f including the Prix d'Aumale, the Prix Vanteaux and the Prix de Malleret and is a full or half-sister to 4 winners. *"I trained the mother and this is a grand horse that's already doing a little bit of work. He's doing everything fine, I'm happy with him and he's a really likeable colt with a good attitude. Look out for him."*

667. NATHRA (IRE) ★★★★
b.f. Iffraaj – Rada (Danehill). March 25. Fifth foal. 270,000Y. Tattersalls October Book 2. John Warren. Half-sister to the fairly useful 2-y-o 6f and 7f winner Tickle Time (by Kheleyf) and to the quite useful 7f (at 2 yrs) to 9f winner of 6 races Angelic Upstart (by Singspiel). The dam is an unplaced half-sister to 9 winners including the high-class Group 1 6f July Cup winner Owington. The second dam, Old Domesday Book (by High Top), a fairly useful 10.4f winner, was listed placed. *"A nice filly, well-balanced and strong with a good*

action. She has a good mind on her and is the type of filly that could be running from mid-May onwards over six furlongs".

668. NEOCLASSICAL ★★★★
ch.c. Dubawi – Teeky (Daylami). February 23. Third foal. Half-brother to the fairly useful 2014 2-y-o 1m winner Timba and to the quite useful dual 6f winner Secret Hint (both by Oasis Dream). The dam, a quite useful 12f winner, is a half-sister to numerous winners including the Group 2 7f Challenge Stakes winner Sleeping Indian, the Group 2 12f Grand Prix de Chantilly winner Aiken and the listed 1m winner Nationalism. The second dam, Las Flores (by Sadler's Wells), a useful 10f winner, was second in the Lingfield Oaks Trial and third in the Italian Oaks and is a full or half-sister to numerous winners. *"A solid colt by a proper stallion, his mother was a good staying type. A very likeable horse".*

669. AL EGDA ★★★
b.f. Poet's Voice – Perfect Spirit (Invincible Spirit). February 3. Fourth living foal. 700,000Y. Tattersalls October Book 1. Al Shaqab. Closely related to the Group 3 7f Chartwell Stakes and listed 6f Pavilion Stakes winner Perfect Tribute (by Dubawi) and half-sister to the fair 10f winner Perfect Delight (by Dubai Destination). The dam is an unraced half-sister to 4 winners including the triple listed winner Swift Tango and the Group 3 Chester Vase third First Row. The second dam, Ballet Society (by Sadler's Wells), ran once unplaced and is a sister to the listed winner Synergetic and a half-sister to Group 3 winner and 2,000 Guineas second Enrique. *"A nice filly, she's grown quite a bit through the winter and won't be an early 2-y-o at all. I think the sire's 2-y-o's are looking more like second half of the season types and for next year. She has a lovely frame, goes fine and is a likeable filly for later on".*

670. PERSUASIVE (IRE) ★★★
gr.f. Dark Angel – Choose Me (Choisir). March 16. Second foal. €180,000Y. Goffs Orby. Cheveley Park Stud. Half-sister to the quite useful 2014 2-y-o Amazour (by Azamour), placed three times over 6f. The dam, a very useful 6f (at 2 yrs) to 10f winner of 4 races including a listed 7f event in Ireland, was third in the Group 2 Blandford Stakes and is a half-

sister to 4 winners. The second dam, Hecuba (by Hector Protector), a fairly useful 10f winner, is a half-sister to 7 winners including the German Group 2 winner Bad Bertrich Again and the Group 3 Scottish Classic winner Prolix. *"She ran a temperature around Christmas time but she's doing really well now and I'd hope to have her out around mid-season. A nice 2-y-o type and a neat filly".*

671. PREDILECTION (USA) ★★★★
b.c. First Defence – Summer Shower (Sadler's Wells). January 30. Fifth foal. Half-brother to the smart 7f (at 2 yrs) and Group 3 10f Prix du Prince d'Orange winner Starboard (by Zamindar). The dam, a French listed-placed dual 12f winner, is a sister to the very smart 1m (at 2 yrs) and Group 2 12f Princess of Wales's Stakes winner Doctor Fremantle. The second dam, Summer Breeze (Rainbow Quest), won over 1m at 2 yrs, was third in the Group 3 1m Prix des Reservoirs and is sister to the high-class Rothmans International and Prix Royal-Oak winner Raintrap and to the very smart Criterium de Saint-Cloud and Prix du Conseil de Paris winner Sunshack. (Khalid Abdulla). *"He's an early 2-y-o type you should put in the book. He's doing well and should be worth keeping an eye on during the first half of the season".*

672. PREQUEL (IRE) ★★★
b.f. Dark Angel – Miss Indigo (Indian Ridge). April 9. Ninth foal. 360,000Y. Tattersalls October Book 1. Charlie Gordon-Watson. Sister to the fairly useful 2014 2-y-o 7f winner Azmaam and to the useful 2-y-o Group 3 6f July Stakes winner Alhebayeb and half-sister to the useful listed 5f winner and Group 3 third Humidor (by Camacho) and four modest sprint winners by Camacho, Distant Music (2) and Desert Style. The dam is a placed half-sister to 8 winners including the useful listed 10f Pretty Polly Stakes winner Musetta. The second dam, Monaiya (by Shareef Dancer), a French 7.5f and 1m winner, is a full or half-sister to 9 winners including the Canadian Grade 2 winner Vanderlin. *"A nice filly, she's a good mover and has a good attitude – she's a very expressive filly when she's out. Very likeable, she's grown a lot and is naturally still a bit weak for a young horse but no more than you'd expect".*

673. PRINCELY SUM (USA) ★★★

b.f. Lemon Drop Kid – Honoria (Sadler's Wells). January 24. Third foal. $400,000Y. Keeneland September. Blandford Bloodstock. Half-sister to the minor US stakes winner Maximova (by Danehill Dancer). The dam was an Irish listed 12f winner. The second dam, Tedarshana (by Darshaan), won 3 races in France and the USA, was third in the Grade 2 La Prevoyante Handicap and is a half-sister to 6 winners including the US stakes winner and Grade 2 placed The Key Rainbow. *"A grand sort, I like her and she's an attractive filly with a good action. Her pedigree suggests she won't be ready until the autumn, but she's a lovely type of filly and very much one to look forward to next year".*

674. REMARKABLE ★★★

b.c. Pivotal – Irresistible (Cadeaux Genereux). March 25. Brother to the very smart 7f (at 2 yrs) and Group 3 7f Nell Gwyn Stakes winner and Coronation Stakes and Falmouth Stakes second Infallible, to the useful dual 6f winner Watchable, the quite useful dual 7f winner at 2 and 3 yrs Thrill and the fair 7f (at 2 yrs) and 6f winner of 4 races New Decade and closely related to the fairly useful 7f and 1m winner Chilled (by Iceman). The dam, a fairly useful 5f (at 2 yrs) and listed 6f winner, is a half-sister to 2 winners. The second dam, Polish Romance (by Danzig), a minor 7f winner in the USA, is a sister to the US stakes winner Polish Love and a half-sister to 5 minor winners. *"We know the family well. She's nice and good bodied but needs time, so she'll be one to start off in September over seven furlongs".*

675. SHALAA (IRE) ★★★★ ♠♠

b.c. Invincible Spirit – Ghurra (War Chant). February 23. Fifth foal. 170,000Y. Tattersalls October Book 1. Charlie Gordon-Watson. Half-brother to the quite useful 1m (at 2 yrs), 10f and hurdles winner Pearl Castle (by Montjeu). The dam, a quite useful 2-y-o 6f winner, subsequently won in the USA and was Grade 3 placed. She is a sister to the winner and US Grade 2 third Zizfaf and a half-sister to 7 winners including the smart 2-y-o Group 1 6f Middle Park Stakes winner Hayil and the US Grade 2 second Tamhid. The second dam, Futuh (by Diesis), a fairly useful 2-y-o 6f winner, is a half-sister to 7 winners including

the Canadian stakes winner Rose Park (dam of the dual US Grade 1 winner Wild Rush). *"A grand colt, he's a good mover with a good attitude. He's done a bit of work already, goes nicely and is the type I'd like to have out before the end of April".*

676. SOUTHERN STARS ★★★★

b.f. Smart Strike – Stacelita (Monsun). February 9. First foal. The dam, a winner of six Group 1 events from 9.5f to 12f in France and the USA, is a half-sister to several minor winners. The second dam, Soignee (by Dashing Blade), a German listed winner and second in the Group 3 Prix des Reservoirs, is a half-sister to 5 winners including the German Group 2 winner Simoun. *"A very athletic filly with a good stride on her, she's the first foal of a good racemare. She looks quite a lot like her mother and has taken after her rather more than Smart Strike. She does everything very easily and you could be tempted to go earlier with her than you should. I think she's one to wait for the seven furlong maidens".*

677. SOVEREIGN PARADE (IRE) ★★★★★

b.f. Galileo – Dialafara (Anabaa). February 8. Second foal. 480,000Y. Tattersalls October Book 1. John Warren. Sister to the 2014 2-y-o 7f winner and Group 3 Acomb Stakes fourth Jamaica. The dam, a minor winner at 3 yrs in France, is a half-sister to 5 winners including the 2-y-o 7f winner and Group 3 9f Prix de Conde second Diaghan. The second dam, Diamilina (by Akarad), won the Group 2 Prix de Malleret and the Group 3 Prix de la Nonette and is a sister to Diamonixa (Group 3 Prix Cleopatre) and a half-sister to 7 winners including the Group 3 winner and triple Group 1 placed Diamond Green. *"A very nice filly, she's a good mover, athletic and leggy but covers the ground easily. One for seven furlongs at the July course, if all goes well. Quality".*

678. STANLEY ★★★

ch.c. Sea The Stars – Deirdre (Dubawi). January 29. Second foal. The dam, a fairly useful 2-y-o 1m winner, was listed-placed and is a half-sister to the very smart Group 1 Irish St Leger, Group 2 Lonsdale Cup and Group 2 Prix Foy winner Duncan and the smart Group 2 Doncaster Cup winner Samuel. The second dam, Dolores (by Danehill), a listed 1m winner and second in the Group 2 1m Sun Chariot Stakes, is a half-sister to one winner. *"A grand colt, he'll take some time because he's got a lot of scope about him, like a lot by the sire. A likeable colt, I see him very much as a September/October 2-y-o".*

679. SYMBOLIC ★★★★
b.c. Shamardal – Resort (Oasis Dream). February 2. Third foal. Half-brother to the fair 6f winner Supersta (by Pivotal). The dam, a fairly useful 7f and 1m winner, is a half-sister to 8 winners including the smart 2-y-o Group 2 6f Mill Reef Stakes and Group 2 Lennox Stakes winner Byron. The second dam, Gay Gallanta (by Woodman), a very smart winner of the Group 1 6f Cheveley Park Stakes and the Group 3 5f Queen Mary Stakes, was second in the Group 2 1m Falmouth Stakes and is a half-sister to 11 winners including the smart Group 2 10f Gallinule Stakes winner Sportsworld. *"A strong colt, he's very good-bodied and powerful. He moves well and I'd like to see him out by the end of May over six furlongs".*

680. TAQAAREED ★★★
ch.f. Sea The Stars – Ezima (Sadler's Wells). February 3. Sister to the 1m (at 2 yrs), Group 1 12f Epsom Oaks and Group 1 12f King George VI winner Taghrooda. The dam, a smart 1m, listed 10f and listed 12f winner, is a full or half-sister to 3 winners including the listed placed Ezalli. The second dam, Ezilla (by Darshaan), is an unraced sister to the top-class broodmare Ebaziya, a triple listed winner from winner from 7f (at 2 yrs) to 12f in Ireland (herself dam of the Group 1 winners Edabiya, Ebadiyla and Enzeli) and a half-sister to 7 winners. *"A strong filly, she stands over a good bit of ground and has quite a feisty temperament. She enjoys her exercise but she's not one you would argue with. One to bring out in September time over a mile".*

681. TAQDEER (IRE) ★★★★
ch.c. Fast Company – Brigantia (Pivotal). January 29. First foal. £140,000Y. Doncaster Premier. Shadwell Estate Co. The dam is an unraced half-sister to 5 winners including the French 12f and German 11f winner and Group 3 placed Britannic. The second dam,

Anka Britannia (by Irish River), placed at 3 yrs in France, is a half-sister to 4 winners including the US Grade 1 10f winner Deputy Commander. *"An attractive horse, his knees are just starting to close and mature. He's a lovely type of horse and a great mover but he doesn't look a speed horse. He looks very much like one to race over seven furlongs".*

682. TASHWEEQ (IRE) ★★★
b.c. Big Bad Bob – Dance Hall Girl (Dansili). January 10. Second foal. £150,000Y. Doncaster Premier. Shadwell Estate Co. Half-brother to the fairly useful 2014 Irish 2-y-o 5f winner Kasbah (by Acclamation). The dam, a quite useful Irish 7f winner, is a half-sister to 3 winners including the listed winner Solar Deity. The second dam, Dawn Raid (by Docksider), a quite useful Irish 3-y-o 7f winner, is a half-sister to 8 winners including the French and Irish 2,000 Guineas and Richmond Stakes winner Bachir. *"A strong boy, he's looking like an autumn 2-y-o but having said that if I could get him out in August over seven furlongs I'd be happy. A good-bodied horse".*

683. WAJEEZ (IRE) ★★★
ch.c. Lope De Vega – Chanter (Lomitas). February 13. Fifth foal. 190,000Y. Tattersalls October Book 2. Shadwell Estate Co. Half-brother to the quite useful 2-y-o 7f winner Edge (by Acclamation) and to the quite useful 10f winner Music Man (by Oratorio). The dam is an unraced half-sister to 8 winners including King George VI and Queen Elizabeth Diamond Stakes winner Belmez and the dam of the Grade 1 Arlington Million winner Debussy. The second dam, Grace Note (by Top Ville), a fairly useful 10f winner and second in the Group 3 12f Lingfield Oaks Trial, is a half-sister to 7 winners including the dam of the Prix de Diane winner Lypharita. *"A nice type of horse, he's neat, a good mover and has a good mind on him. We'll set off with him in the middle of the season over seven furlongs".*

684. WANNABE FRIENDS ★★★
ch.c. Dubawi – Wannabe Posh (Grand Lodge). February 15. Fifth foal. Brother to the smart Group 3 1m winner Wannabe Yours and half-brother to the fairly useful 10f and 12f winner Wannabe Loved (by Pivotal) and the fair 14f winner Wannabe Your Man (by Halling). The

dam won four races including the listed 12f Galtres Stakes, was second in the Group 3 14f Lillie Langtry Stakes and is a half-sister to the Group 1 6f Cheveley Park Stakes winner Wannabe Grand. The second dam, Wannabe (Shirley Heights), a quite useful 1m and 10f winner, is a half-sister to the Group 1 Cheveley Park Stakes second Tanami (dam of the Group 2 Rockfel Stakes winner Cairns). *"This is a neat colt with a quick action. He's does his canters fine, has a good mind on him, doesn't quite have the scope of his brother but there's plenty of time for him to grow. He may be out around June time, but I'll let the horse tell me".*

685. WHITE HOT (IRE) ★★★

b.f. Galileo – Gwynn (Darshaan). February 27. Eighth foal. 1,250,000Y. Tattersalls October Book 1. James Delahooke. Sister to the 1m (at 2 yrs) and listed 10f winner Kissed and closely related to the Group 1 Epsom Derby winner Pour Moi (by Montjeu), to the Group 3 1m Prix des Reservoirs and Group 3 10.5f Prix Penelope winner and Group 1 placed Gagnoa and the fairly useful French 2-y-o 1m winner Rendezvous (both by Sadler's Wells). The dam is an unraced half-sister to 2 minor winners. The second dam, Victoress (by Conquistador Cielo), won over 11f and is a half-sister to 7 winners including the dual Group 1 winner Awaasif (dam of the Oaks winner Snow Bride). *"A lovely filly, she's attractive and a good mover. Very much a Galileo – Darshaan type, which means we'll wait for September/October for her. A nice filly for the future".*

686. UNNAMED ★★★

b.f. Zebedee – Baileys Cream (Mister Baileys). April 7. Ninth foal. 82,000Y. Tattersalls October Book 1. Blandford Bloodstock. Closely related to the 2-y-o listed 6f winner and Group 3 second Baileys Cacao (by Invincible Spirit) and half-sister to the moderate 7f winner Aqua Vitae (by Camacho) and three minor winners in Italy, France and Switzerland by Imperial Ballet, Captain Rio and Camacho. The dam, a fair 2-y-o 7f winner, is a full or half-sister to 5 winners including the listed Chesham Stakes winner Fair Cop. The second dam, Exclusive Life (by Exclusive Native), won once in the USA and is a half-sister to 8 winners including the US Grade 2 winner Special Warmth. *"She's a nice type, does everything fine and she's a*

good, strong filly with plenty of substance. One for June time and she'll be a five/six furlong 2-y-o".

687. UNNAMED ★★★ ♠

b.c. Rip Van Winkle – Chehalis Sunset (Danehill Dancer). March 21. Fourth foal. 260,000Y. Tattersalls October Book 2. Blandford Bloodstock. Half-brother to the unplaced 2014 2-y-o Why No Rein (by Tagula) and to the fair 2-y-o 7f winner Gown (by Excellent Art). The dam is an unraced half-sister to 6 winners including the US Grade 2 9f Honeymoon Handicap winner and Grade 1 placed Country Garden. The second dam, Totham (by Shernazar), a quite useful 12f winner, is a half-sister to 6 winners. *"An athletic colt with a very good attitude. He just needs to strengthen and I'll give him the chance to do so. I won't try and wing him early and I could see him being out around July time, over seven furlongs".*

688. UNNAMED ★★★★

b.c. War Front – City Sister (Carson City). February 3. $750,000foal. Keeneland November. Aisling Duignan. Half-brother to the US 2-y-o Grade 2 9f Demoiselle Stakes winner Dixie City and to the US stakes-placed winner Union City (both by Dixie Union). The dam, a winner of 3 races and Grade 3 placed, is a half-sister to 2 winners including the US Grade 3 winner Fast Decision. The second dam, Demi Soeur (by Storm Bird), is an unraced half-sister to the champion US 2-y-o colt Dehere. *"A very powerful colt, he could pass as a 3-y-o right now he's such a big, strong horse. He moves well and I'm not in any hurry with him. I see him being one to bring out around August time".*

689. UNNAMED ★★★ ♠

b.c. Fastnet Rock – Crystal Maze (Gone West). February 19. Fourth foal. 80,000Y. Tattersalls October Book 1. Blandford Bloodstock. Half-brother to the French 1m (at 2 yrs) and Group 2 10f Prix Greffulhe winner Ocovango (by Monsun). The dam is an unraced half-sister to 3 winners including the fairly useful 2-y-o winners and listed-placed Treasury Devil and Crystany. The second dam, Crystal Music (by Nureyev), won the Group 1 Fillies' Mile at 2 yrs and is closely related to the Group 3 12f John Porter Stakes winner Dubai Success and the smart 7f (at 2 yrs) and 10f winner Tchaikovsky and a half-sister to the Group 3 winners Solar Crystal and State Crystal. *"He's doing fine, I know the family very well and he's a strong boy like a lot by the sire. He seems to have a good mind on him too, some of them by the sire seem to be a bit wayward but he's not. A very likeable colt, but he's very much an autumn horse".*

690. UNNAMED ★★★
b.c. Pour Moi – Glen Rosie (Mujtahid). January 30. Eighth foal. €85,000Y. Arqana Deauville August. Charlie Liverton. Closely related to the useful 2-y-o listed 7f winner Kings Quay, to the fairly useful 10f winner of 3 races Milne Garden (both by Montjeu) and the modest 10f winner Calculated Risk (by Motivator) and half-brother to the quite useful listed placed 10f and 11f winner Fastback (by Singspiel). The dam, a 2-y-o 5.2f winner and second in the Group 3 Fred Darling Stakes, is a half-sister to 5 winners including the Irish Group 3 10f and triple US stakes winner Artema. The second dam, Silver Echo (by Caerleon), is an unraced sister to the listed 6f winner Dawn Success and a half-sister to the Gladness Stakes winner Prince Echo. *"He's a nice type out of a Mujtahid mare and there's a lot of Mujtahid about him. He's strong, he's not going to be big but Pour Moi's won't be, and he's a nice little horse to be a mid-season 2-y-o".*

691. UNNAMED ★★★
br.f. Dark Angel – Jasmine Flower (Kyllachy). January 25. Second foal. 130,000Y. Tattersalls October Book 2. Blandford Bloodstock. The dam is an unraced sister to the listed-placed winner Nasri and a half-sister to 3 winners including the Group 2 third Ellmau. The second dam, Triple Sharp (by Selkirk), a quite useful 10f and hurdles winner, is a half-sister to 6 winners including the Group 2 Prix Eugene Adam winner Triple Threat and to the unraced dam of the top-class miler Canford Cliffs. *"A strong filly, she's coming along fine but she has a big ribcage on her and she'll take a bit of getting fit. If possible I'd like to have her out in late May or June".*

692. UNNAMED ★★★
ch.c. Dutch Art – Kelowna (Pivotal). February

26. Second foal. 340,000Y. Tattersalls October Book 2. Al Mirqab Racing. Half-brother to the promising 2014 2-y-o 8.5f winner Nebulla (by Iffraaj). The dam, a quite useful 1m winner here, was subsequently a stakes-placed winner in North America. The second dam, Kootenay (by Selkirk), a very useful winner of three listed races over 1m and 9f and third in the Group 2 Falmouth Stakes, is a half-sister to 5 winners including the Group 1 Irish St Leger winner Sans Frontieres. *"A nice, grand colt with plenty of scope, he's a good looking horse and a good mover. He's a big boy for a Dutch Art, so we wouldn't want to hurry him. He's one for the seven furlong maidens around August time".*

693. UNNAMED ★★★★
ch.f. Intikhab – Luanas Pearl (Bahri). March 17. Third foal. 27,000Y. Tattersalls October Book 2. J Shack. Half-sister to the fair 11.5f winner Cosette (by Champs Elysees). The dam is an unraced half-sister to 7 winners including the Chester Vase, September Stakes and Winter Derby winner (all Group 3 events) Hattan and the Group 3 Jockey Club Cup winner Tastahil. The second dam, Luana (by Shaadi), a useful triple 6f winner (including at 2 yrs), was listed-placed and is a half-sister to 5 winners including the high-class middle-distance horses and Group 1 winners Warrsan and Luso and the Group winners Cloud Castle and Needle Gun, and to the dams of the Group 3 winners Blue Monday, Nideeb, Queen's Best and Laaheb. *"She's a well-made filly with a nice action and I think she was well-bought. She'll make a June/July 2-y-o and she's doing well".*

694. UNNAMED ★★★
b.f. Galileo – Miarixa (Linamix). January 18. Sixth foal. Half-sister to the 1,000 Guineas, Irish Oaks and Yorkshire Oaks winner Blue Bunting (by Dynaformer) and to the modest 2m and hurdles winner Descaro (by Dr Fong). The dam is an unraced sister to the French winner and Group 3 placed Mister Kick and a half-sister to 3 winners including the French listed winner Marque Royale (herself the dam of two listed winners). The second dam, Mrs Arkada (by Akarad), a listed winner and third in the Group 1 Prix Saint-Alary, is a half-sister to the Group 3 winners Mister Sicy, Manninamix and Mister Riv. *"A big, rangy, elegant filly with a lot of Linamix there. She's*

light framed and light on her feet. One for the mile maidens in the autumn".

695. UNNAMED ★★★ ♠♠

b.c. Shamardal – Multicolour Wave (Rainbow Wave). April 10. Tenth foal. 550,000Y. Tattersalls October Book 1. Peter & Ross Doyle. Half-brother to 6 winners including the Group 1 French 1,000 Guineas winner Elusive Wave (by Elusive City), the Irish 2-y-o 7f winner and listed-placed Million Waves (by Mull Of Kintyre) and the quite useful 2-y-o 7f winners Million Spirits (by Invincible Spirit) and Wealdmore Wave (by Oratorio). The dam is a placed half-sister to 4 winners and to the unraced dam of the Group 2 Queen Mary Stakes winner Langs Lash. The second dam, Echoes (by Niniski), won the Group 3 Prix Corrida, was Group 2 placed and is a half-sister to 5 winners. *"He'll need plenty of time. A lovely type for the back-end and then as a 3-y-o".*

696. UNNAMED ★★★★

ch.c. Shamardal – Nightime (Galileo). March 7. Fifth foal. 400,000Y. Tattersalls October Book 1. John Warren. Half-brother to the fairly useful Irish 10f winner and listed-placed Sleeping Beauty (by Oasis Dream) and to the modest 8.5f winner New Year's Night (by Raven's Pass). The dam won 2 races at 3 yrs including the Irish 1,000 Guineas and is a half-sister to 7 winners. The second dam, Caumshinaun (by Indian Ridge), won 5 races from 6f to 1m in Ireland at 3 and 4 yrs including a listed event and is a half-sister to one winner. *"This is a quality colt, he's a good mover with a bit of class about him. That doesn't mean he'll be winging it for Royal Ascot – that wouldn't be his game. I see him as a seven furlong or mile horse this year".*

697. UNNAMED ★★

b.c. Poet's Voice – Past The Post (Danzig). March 18. Seventh foal. 475,000Y. Tattersalls October Book 1. Al Shaqab. Closely related to the French listed 1m winner and Group 2 Premio Ribot second Dancing Sands (by Dubai) and half-brother to 3 winners including the 2-y-o 7f winner Post And Rail (by Silver Hawk) and the fair 1m winner For Posterity (by Shamardal). The dam, a winner in the USA, is a sister to 4 winners including the

Group 2 1m Lockinge Stakes winner Emperor Jones and the Group 1 Middle Park Stakes third Majlood and a half-sister to 5 winners including Bakharoff (Group 1 1m William Hill Futurity Stakes). The second dam, Qui Royalty (by Native Royalty), a winner of 5 races at up to 1m in the USA, was Grade 3 placed and is a half-sister to 8 winners. *"He's a big, rangy boy with plenty of scope about him. It's all going to happen for him as a 3-y-o, but you'd want to race him at the back-end of his 2-y-o career for experience".*

698. UNNAMED ★★★

b.f. Sea The Stars – Pursuit Of Life (Pursuit Of Love). April 28. Seventh foal. 320,000Y. Tattersalls October Book 1. Al Mirqab Racing. Closely related to a minor winner in Italy by Cape Cross and half-sister to the Group 3 Italian 1,000 Guineas winner Stay Alive (by Iffraaj), the Italian Group 3 winner and Group 1 Gran Premio de Milano third Gimmy (by Lomitas) and a minor winner in Italy by Diktat. The dam, a winner of 4 races in Italy at 2 and 3 yrs and listed-placed three times, is a half-sister to 5 winners including the French dual Group 3 winner Di Moi Oui. The second dam, Biosphere (by Pharly), a listed-placed winner in Italy, is a sister to the triple listed winner Scribano. *"A sweet filly that moves well, she's medium-sized and carries herself well. I'll take my time and bring her out in the second half of the year".*

699. UNNAMED ★★★

b.f. Dansili – Real Sense (Galileo). January 29. First foal. $325,000Y. Keeneland September. John Ferguson. The dam, placed at 3 yrs in France, is closely related to Saddex, a winner of two Group 1 12f races in Italy and Germany. The dam is an unplaced half-sister to the multiple US Grade 1 winner Denon, to the listed 6f winner and Group 1 6f Cheveley Park Stakes second Imperfect Circle (dam of the top-class miler Spinning World) and the Moyglare Stud Stakes, Coronation Stakes, Child Stakes and Cherry Hinton Stakes winner Chimes of Freedom (dam of the multiple US Grade 1 winner Aldebaran). *"A nice type of filly, she has a bit of class about her, moves well and has a very good temperament. One for September/October".*

700. UNNAMED ★★★
b.f. Galileo – Shadow Song (Pennekamp).
January 18. Sixth foal. Sister to the 2-y-o
Group 3 7f Silver Flash Stakes winner, multiple
Group 1 placed and subsequent US Grade
1 9f winner Together and to the fairly useful
2-y-o 7f and 1m winner Terrific and closely
related to the fairly useful 7f (at 2 yrs) and 12f
winner Kingdom and to the 2-y-o Group 1 1m
Criterium International winner and Irish Derby
third Jan Vermeer (both by Montjeu). The dam
won once at 3 yrs in France and is a half-
sister to the Group 3 May Hill Stakes winner
Midnight Air (herself dam of the Group 3 and
subsequent US Grade 2 winner Midnight Line)
and to the placed dam of the Group 1 Prix de
l'Abbaye winner Imperial Beauty. The second
dam, Evening Air (by J O Tobin), is an unraced
half-sister to 5 winners. *"Despite being an early
foal she's going to need some time. She has
scope and there's no rush with her, so I see her
as a filly for September time".*

701. UNNAMED ★★★
b.f. Zoffany – Sioduil (Oasis Dream). March 3.
Third foal. 260,000Y. Tattersalls October Book
2. Blandford Bloodstock. Half-brother to the
useful 2014 2-y-o listed 5f winner and Group
2 Norfolk Stakes second Mind Of Madness
(by Azamour). The dam, a fairly useful Irish 5f
winner, is a half-sister to 3 winners here and
abroad. The second dam, Indian Belle (by
Indian Ridge), a fairly useful Irish 10f winner,
is a half-sister to 3 winners. *"She's a nice,
attractive filly but she's grown a lot and now
needs to strengthen back".*

702. UNNAMED ★★★★
ch.c. Raven's Pass – Turkana Girl (Hernando).
April 7. Fifth living foal. €70,000Y. Goffs Orby.
John Ferguson. Half-brother to the 2-y-o
Group 2 Prix Robert Papin winner Irish Field
(by Dubawi) and the French 3-y-o 6f and
1m winner Thats Notall Folks (by Kheleyf).
The dam, placed once over 7f, is a half-sister
to 5 winners including the Group 2 Royal
Lodge Stakes winner Leo and the dual Italian
listed winner Balkenhol. The second dam,
Miss Penton (by Primo Dominie), was placed
3 times at up to 7f and is a half-sister to 8
winners including the very useful listed 6f
Sirenia Stakes winner Art of War. *"He's done a

little bit of early work, he's a neat colt and he
goes well. A racy, early type".*

703. UNNAMED ★★★ ♠
gr.c. Oasis Dream – Warling (Montjeu).
February 4. First foal. 550,000Y. Tattersalls
October Book 1. Charlie Gordon-Watson.
The dam, a fairly useful 11f winner, is closely
related to the French 2-y-o 10f winner of 3
races and Group 3 Prix Exbury second War
Is War and a half-sister to 3 winners. The
second dam, Walkamia (by Linamix), won the
Group 3 10.5f Prix Fille de l'Air and is a sister
to 2 winners including the Group 2 11f Prix
Noailles winner Walk On Mix and a half-sister
to 8 winners. *"Although he's by Oasis Dream
his second dam is by Linamix and he looks a
lot more like the female side. A rangy, lovely-
moving, grey colt, he's going to be all about
seven furlongs and a mile later this year".*

RAE GUEST

704. A LOVE STORY ★★
gr.f. Archipenko – Albacocca (With Approval).
January 29. First foal. €17,000Y. Goffs
Sportsmans. Not sold. The dam, a moderate
11.5f winner, is a half-sister to 3 winners. The
second dam, Ballymac Girl (by Niniski), a
modest winner of 5 races in Ireland at up to
15f, is a half-sister to the Nassau Stakes winner
Last Second (dam of the French 2,000 Guineas
winner Aussie Rules), the Group 3 Doncaster
Cup winner Alleluia (dam of the Prix Royal-
Oak winner Allegretto) and the Moyglare Stud
Stakes third Alouette (dam of the Champion
Stakes winner Alborada and the multiple
German Group 1 winner Albanova) and to the
placed dam of the Group 1 winners Yesterday
and Quarter Moon. (Miss K Rausing). *"We've
had two by the sire and they've both won, but
I think most of them need a trip. This is a nice
filly from a great family, but more of a 3-y-o
type than a 2-y-o really".*

705. EARLY SUNSET (IRE) ★★★
gr.f. Dark Angel – Dear Gracie (In The Wings).
March 15. Second foal. 16,000Y. Tattersalls
October Book 3. Rae Guest. Half-sister
to the fair 10f winner Sweet Cherry (by
Mastercraftsman). The dam, a quite useful
10f winner, is a sister to the Irish 2-y-o listed
6f winner and Group 2 placed He's A Decoy
and a half-sister to 6 winners including the

high-class 6f Stewards Cup winner and smart sire Danetime. The second dam, Allegheny River (by Lear Fan), won once over 7f at 3 yrs in Ireland and is a half-sister to one winner. (Barry Stewart and Sakal, Davies & Jennings). *"She's done well since she came in, has matured a lot and I could see her being out by late summer. I think she'll start off at six furlongs but I can see her wanting seven because she's out of an In The Wings mare. Not a big filly, but a nice size".*

706. LASTMANLASTROUND ★★★

b.c. Azamour – Lastroseofsummer (Haafhd). March 2. First foal. £40,000Y. Doncaster Premier. Rae Guest. The dam, a fair 13f to 2m and hurdles winner, is a half-sister to 6 winners including the smart 7f (at 2 yrs) to 2m winner and Group 2 placed Romantic Affair. The second dam, Broken Romance (by Ela-Mana-Mou), is an unraced half-sister to 6 winners including the Grade 1 9f Hollywood Derby winner Foscarini and the Group-placed Cobblers Cove and Guns Of Navarone. (The Boot Sarratt Racing Syndicate). *"We trained the dam who was a stayer but this colt seems quite sharp, he's not very big and may well be a mid-season type 2-y-o. He doing really well and despite being by Azamour he looks like being earlier than you'd think. I'm pleased with him and he'll be sharp enough for six furlongs".*

707. MAYBERAIN (IRE) ★★★★

b.f. Acclamation – Luckbealadytonight (Mr Greeley). January 22. First foal. €72,000foal. Goffs November. Rathbarry Stud. The dam, a moderate 6f placed maiden at 2 and 3 yrs, is a half-sister to the 2-y-o Group 1 7f Moyglare Stud Stakes winner and 1,000 Guineas third Maybe. The second dam, Sumora (by Danehill), a 2-y-o listed 5f St Hugh's Stakes winner, is a sister to the useful Irish 7f winner Fleeting Shadow and a half-sister to the Oaks and German Oaks winner Dancing Rain. (Thomas Radley). *"She's got a great pedigree and for a first foal she's a big filly. She'll want a mile as time goes on, I think Mr Greeley is doing well as a broodmare sire and I could see her running over seven furlongs or a mile from August onwards. A lovely filly, she moves well and there are no problems with her. All being well she'll be up to Group class".*

708. UNNAMED ★★★

ch.f. Tamayuz – Allegrissimo (Redback). April 2. Second foal. 17,000Y. Tattersalls October Book 2. Rae Guest. The dam, a minor French 2-y-o winner, is a half-sister to 2 winners including the Group 3 second Silver Grey. The second dam, Operissimo (by Singspiel), is an unraced sister to the 2-y-o Group 3 1m Prix Thomas Bryon winner Songlark and a half-sister to 5 winners including the Dubai Group 3 winner Blatant and the dam of the multiple Group 1 winner Sky Lantern. (C J Murfitt). *"I like the sire because we've had two others by Tamayuz and they've both won plenty of races. This filly has everything going for her at the minute, she looks a 2-y-o and should be one of our earlier runners. Not very big, but a nice, solid 2-y-o type I could see being suited by six furlongs".*

709. UNNAMED ★★★

b.f. Vale Of York – Barbera (GER) (Night Shift). February 26. Seventh foal. €16,000Y. Goffs Sportsmans. Robbie Mills/Rae Guest. Sister to the modest 2014 2-y-o 5f winner Millar Rose and half-sister to the quite useful 5f winner of 3 races at 2 and 3 yrs Berberana (by Acclamation) and 2 winners abroad by Rakti and Strategic Prince. The dam, a minor German 3-y-o winner, is a half-sister to 7 winners. The second dam, Briscola (by General Assembly), won 3 races at 3 yrs in Germany and is a half-sister to 4 winners. (Guy Carstairs and Sakal, Davies & Jennings). *"All the family have been winners and I love Night Shift as a broodmare sire because we've had some good luck with horses bred that way. This filly has grown a lot since the sales, she's done well and looks the part".* ***TRAINERS' BARGAIN BUY***

710. UNNAMED ★★★

b.f. Lilbourne Lad – Christmas Tart (Danetime). March 22. Fifth foal. Half-sister to the modest 2014 dual 5f placed 2-y-o Tarando (by Equiano), to the useful 2-y-o listed 5f winner and Group 2 Queen Mary Stakes second Hoyam (by Royal Applause) and the moderate 6f winner Make Up (by Kyllachy). The dam, a fair 2-y-o 5f winner, is a half-sister to 8 winners including the smart Group 3 6f Prix de Meautry winner Andreyev. The second dam, Missish (by Mummy's Pet), is an unraced full or half-sister to 4 minor winners here and abroad including the dam of the Group 3 winners Asian Heights and St Expedit. (The Storm Again Syndicate). *"One that came in late from the stud because she was quite small, but she has plenty of 'go' about her. She looks like she'll be a five furlong 2-y-o but she's still playing catch up with the others".*

711. UNNAMED ★★★
b.f. Elusive City – Distant Dreamer (Rahy). January 19. Third foal. The dam is an unplaced half-sister to 6 winners. The second dam, Khazayin (Bahri), was placed twice over 10f and is a sister to the Arc winner Sakhee and a half-sister to numerous winners. (Claydon Bloodstock). *"A very strong looking filly by a sire that gets loads of winners, particularly in France, she looks like being a 2-y-o".*

712. UNNAMED ★★
ch.c. Duke Of Marmalade – Guilia (Galileo). March 16. Fifth foal. Half-sister to the promising 2014 2-y-o 7f winner, on her only start, Goodyearforroses (by Azamour), to the quite useful 9.5f winner and listed-placed God's Speed (by Oratorio) and to the modest 10f and 12f winner Guiletta (by Dalakhani). The dam, a useful 2-y-o 7f winner, was listed-placed over 10f and 13f and is a half-sister to 2 winners. The second dam, Lesgor (by Irish River), won over 10f in France, was third in the Group 3 10f Prix de Psyche and is a half-sister to 3 winners. (The Hornets). *"I trained the dam who was fifth in the Oaks. So far she's bred three winners from four foals and we've trained them all. Being by Duke Of Marmalade this colt is backward now and is one to start off in late summer. He looks a nice type for his 3-y-o career".*

713. UNNAMED ★★★★
b.f. Kyllachy – Noble Desert (Green Desert). February 25. Sister to the fair 5f (including at 2 yrs) and 6f winner of 6 races Mr Optimistic and half-sister to the fair 6f (including at 2 yrs) and 7f winner The Human League (by Tobougg), the fair 6f winner Star Of Rohm (by Exceed And Excel) and the modest 2-y-o 1m winner Noble Dictator (by Diktat). The dam is an unplaced half-sister to 9 winners. The second dam, Sporades (by Vaguely Noble), won the Group 3 10.5f Prix de Flore and is a half-sister to 9 winners including Mill Native

(Grade 1 10f Arlington Million) and the Group 3 winners French Stress and American Stress. (C J Murfitt). *"A home-bred filly out of a mare that's bred four winners from five runners. Looking at the way she's going and the fact that she's be Kyllachy she looks like making a nice 2-y-o but we'll not rush her. A good-looking filly, I'm very pleased with her at the moment and we'd like to think she'll be stakes-class".*

714. UNNAMED ★★★
b.f. Kyllachy – Wise Melody (Zamindar). February 5. Second foal. Half-sister to the 2014 French 2-y-o 6f winner Sallal (by Exceed And Excel). The dam, a quite useful dual 6f winner, is a half-sister to 5 winners including the useful 2-y-o 5f winner and Group 3 Prix d'Arenburg third Racina. The second dam, Swellegant (by Midyan), won once at 2 yrs and is a half-sister to 5 winners including the Group 2 winners Prince Sabo and Millyant. (Redgate Bloodstock). *"She's only been in the yard a month but it's a family I know very well. Typical of the family, this filly is a sprinter type, being muscular and well-built. But we're still getting to know her really".*

WILLIAM HAGGAS
715. AL HAWRAA ★★★
b.f. Iffraaj – Kashoof (Green Desert). January 8. Fourth foal. Closely related to Ehtifaal (by Teofilo), placed fourth once over 7f from two starts at 2 yrs in 2013. The dam, a quite useful 2-y-o 5f winner, is a half-sister to one winner. The second dam, Khulood (by Storm Cat), a useful listed 7f (at 2 yrs) and Group 3 7f Nell Gwyn Stakes winner, is a half-sister to numerous winners including the Irish 1,000 Guineas winner Mehthaaf and the July Cup winner Elnadim. (Hamdan Al Maktoum). *"A tall, leggy, good-moving filly. She's really nice but will take a bit of time – I can't work out how much yet because despite her speedy pedigree she's as tall as this room".*

716. ALPINE DREAM ★★★★
b.f. Dream Ahead – Infamous Angel (Exceed And Excel). February 12. Third foal. 40,000foal. Tattersalls December. BBA (Ire). Half-sister to the unplaced 2014 2-y-o Pretty Famous (by Invincible Spirit). The dam won two races at 2 yrs including the Group 2 6f Lowther Stakes.

The second dam, Evangeline (by Sadler's Wells), is an unraced half-sister to 4 winners. "She's a nice filly and I like my Dream Ahead 2-y-o colt as well. The dam won the Lowther and this filly will be a 2-y-o alright".

717. AUXILIARY ★★★ ♠
b.g. Fast Company – Lady Xara (Xaar). February 1. Fourth foal. £70,000Y. Doncaster Premier. John & Jake Warren. Half-brother to the quite useful 6f winner Lady Horatia (by Mount Nelson). The dam is an unraced half-sister to 5 winners including the Group 3 Meld Stakes winner Khalafiya (herself dam of the dual Group 2 winner Predappio). The second dam, Khalisiyn (by Shakapour), a fairly useful 7f and 1m winner at 3 yrs, is a half-sister to 5 winners including the US Grade 2 Dixie Handicap and listed Scottish Derby winner Kadial and the Group 2 placed Kalim. (Highclere Thoroughbred Racing, Walpole). *"Definitely a 2-y-o, he's strong and well-made. He should be racing in May but I don't quite know how good he'll be. I don't think he's a really good one but he's tough and not bad at all".*

718. BAAHY (IRE) ★★★
br.c. Arcano – Amjaad (Dansili). February 13. The dam is an unraced half-sister to the Group 1 National Stakes winner Power and the Group 2 12f Ribblesdale Stakes winner Thakafaat. The second dam, Frappe (by Inchinor), a fairly useful 2-y-o 6f winner, is a half-sister to 3 winners including the 2,000 Guineas winner Footstepsinthesand. (Hamdan Al Maktoum). *"The Arcano's haven't been that early even though he was a 2-y-o himself and this one looks like being a mid-season 2-y-o. The dam was expensive but never ran. She was small and neat but not very precocious, so I'm wary of that. This colt is alright though".*

719. BARGAIN BUY ★★★
ch.f. Tamayuz – Peace Summit (Cape Cross). March 19. Third foal. 25,000Y. Tattersalls October Book 2. Rabbah Bloodstock. The dam is an unraced half-sister to 5 winners including the useful 2-y-o 7f winner Grosvenor Square and to the unraced dam of the Group 1 winner King's Apostle. The second dam, Embassy (by Cadeaux Genereux), a champion 2-y-o filly and winner of the Cheveley Park

Stakes, is a half-sister to 6 winners including the Group 2 Pretty Polly Stakes winner Tarfshi. (Sheikh Rashid Dalmook Al Maktoum). *"A big filly but a nice mover, she's got something about her. She won't be that early, but I like her".* Take a look at my Introduction to read the story about how she was given this name! **TRAINERS' BARGAIN BUY**

720. BESHARAH (IRE) ★★★★
b.f. Kodiac – Dixieland Kiss (Dixie Union). February 18. First foal. 85,000Y. Tattersalls October Book 2. Rabbah Bloodstock. The dam is an unraced half-sister to 3 winners including the US stakes winner and triple Grade 3 placed Kiss Mine. The second dam, Kiss The Devil (by Kris S), a US Grade 3 winner of 6 races from 3 to 5 yrs, is a half-sister to 4 winners. (Sheikh Rashid Dalmook Al Maktoum). *"She's very sharp. This filly and Emerald Bay are the two to look out for early doors. I've worked some 2-y-o fillies a few times and these two have risen to the top. She's nice and this will be her year".*

721. CURRICULUM ★★★★
b.c. New Approach – Superstar Leo (College Chapel). March 19. Half-brother to 6 winners including the very smart Group 3 5f Molecomb Stakes and Group 3 5f King George Stakes winner Enticing (by Pivotal), to the useful 3-y-o 7f and listed 1m winner and Group 3 7f Jersey Stakes second Sentaril, the fair 7f winner Cloud Line (both by Danehill Dancer) and the quite useful dual 5f winner (including at 2 yrs) Speed Song (by Fasliyev). The dam won 5 races including the Group 2 5f Flying Childers Stakes and the Weatherbys Super Sprint and is a full or half-sister to numerous winners. The second dam, Council Rock (by General Assembly), a fair 9f and 10f placed 3-y-o, is a half-sister to 6 winners including Glatisant, winner of the Group 3 Prestige Stakes and dam of the 2,000 Guineas winner Footstepsinthesand. (Lael Stable). *"A lovely horse, he's big but we're going to train him now to see what he's made of. I see him as a possible Chesham Stakes horse because he's strong, well-made and doesn't look immature at all. So he's got a chance and has real quality".*

722. DAWN HORIZONS ★★★★
ch.f. New Approach – Hidden Hope (Daylami).

March 5. Half-sister to the useful 1m (at 2 yrs), 10f and listed 12f winner Our Obsession (by Shamardal), to the fairly useful dual 1m winner Westwiththenight (by Cape Cross) and the modest 11f winner Fine Style (by Pivotal). The dam, a useful listed 11.4f Cheshire Oaks winner, is a half-sister to 9 winners including Rebecca Sharp (Group 1 1m Coronation Stakes) and the Group 3 Lingfield Derby Trial winner Mystic Knight. The second dam, Nuryana (by Nureyev), a useful winner of the listed 1m Grand Metropolitan Stakes, is a half-sister to 5 winners. (Mr A E Oppenheimer). *"She's lovely – one with a bit of quality. She's having a break at the moment, but she could be useful just as her half-sister the Galtres Stakes winner Our Obsession was. New Approach is quite a hard stallion to assess, but I guess this filly will be best at around mile this year".*

723. DREAM OF TARA (IRE) ★★★

b.f. Invincible Spirit – Spirit Of Tara (Sadler's Wells). April 4. Tenth foal. Half-sister to the high-class Group 2 1m and Group 3 1m and 9f winner Echo Of Light (by Dubai Millennium), to the smart dual 12f listed winner Akarem, the Irish listed-placed 1m and 9f winner Multazem (both by Kingmambo), the useful 1m winner and Group 1 Coronation Stakes third Irish History (by Dubawi) and the useful listed-placed 10f winner Flame Of Gibraltar (by Rock Of Gibraltar). The dam, a 12f winner and second in the Group 2 Blandford Stakes, is a sister to Salsabil (1,000 Guineas, Oaks, Irish Derby and Prix Vermeille) and a half-sister to the Group 1 St James's Palace Stakes winner Marju. The second dam, Flame Of Tara (by Artaius), won the Coronation Stakes. (Miss Pat O'Kelly). *"She's fine, not a sharp one but she has a lot of quality. One for the back-end of the season, she has a nice temperament, a nice outlook and is an elegant filly. She's very genuine and the owner tells me she was the nicest yearling she had last year".*

724. EASY CODE ★★★★

b.c. Bahamian Bounty – Skirrid (Halling). February 14. Second foal. 80,000Y. Tattersalls October Book 1. Rabbah Bloodstock. The dam is an unraced half-sister to 5 winners including the smart 10f and 12f and subsequent US Grade 2 8.5f and dual Grade 3 winner Spice

Route. The second dam, Zanzibar (by In The Wings), winner of the Group 1 11f Italian Oaks, is a half-sister to 2 winners. (Sheikh Juma Dalmook Al Maktoum). *"I like him a lot, he's not early but he moves well and should be racing in July. I've got a few Bahamian Bounty's that I like but I don't know if that's good or bad!"*

725. ELECTRA VOICE ★★★★

b.f. Poet's Voice – Electra Star (Shamardal). February 2. First foal. The dam, a fairly useful triple 1m winner, is a half-sister to numerous winners including to the useful 2-y-o 5f and 7f winner Asia Winds and the useful 2-y-o dual 6f winner Fancy Lady. The second dam, Ascot Cyclone (by Rahy), a fairly useful 5.7f (at 2 yrs) and 7f winner, is a full or half-sister to 13 winners including the Group 1 7f Prix de la Salamandre second Bin Nashwan and the US Grade 2 winner Magellan. (Salem Obaida). *"I like her, she's by a first season sire and out of a dam we trained who was quite useful and had a bit of a temperament. This one is feisty, she'll be alright and a July type 2-y-o. Not bad for a first foal, she's quite small but quite a nice 2-y-o. We've got two by Poet's Voice and I like them both".*

726. EMERALD BAY ★★★★ ♠

b.f. Kyllachy – Bahia Emerald (Bahamian Bounty). February 5. First foal. The dam, a modest dual 6f winner, is a sister to one winner and a half-sister to 6 winners including the listed 6f winner and Group 3 Princess Margaret Stakes second Vital Statistics. The second dam, Emerald Peace (by Green Desert), a useful listed 5f winner of 4 races and second in the Group 2 5f Flying Childers Stakes, is a half-sister to 5 winners. (Cheveley Park Stud). *"A sharp filly, she wants fast ground which is unlike most by the sire and she'll be out in April or May. Very keen to please, she's not very big but strong and definitely quick".*

727. ENTSAR (IRE) ★★★★

b.f. Fastnet Rock – Starfish (Galileo). March 5. Fifth foal. 260,000Y. Tattersalls October Book 1. John Warren. Half-sister to the 2-y-o Group 1 6f Phoenix Stakes winner and Group 1 1m Matron Stakes winner La Collina, to the fair 1m (at 2 yrs) to 12f winner Kuantan One (both by Strategic Prince) and the quite useful 7f (at

2 yrs) and 9f winner Next Edition (by Antonius Pius). The dam is an unraced half-sister to 3 winners including the Group 3 placed Icon Dream. The second dam, Silver Skates (by Slip Anchor), is a placed half-sister to 8 winners including the Group 2 Derrinstown Derby Trial winner Fracas. (Al Shaqab Racing). *"Oh yes, I like her! She's grown a lot and is a half-sister to a 2-y-o Group 1 winner. We were underbidder for her at Tattersalls and fortunately she was sent to us by Al Shaqab. Hopefully she'll be a late summer 2-y-o and she's a very nice filly".*

728. FASHIONATA (IRE) ★★★
ch.f. Fast Company – Red Red Rose (Piccolo). March 6. Second foal. €26,000Y. Goffs Sportsmans. Jill Lamb. Half-sister to the quite useful 2014 2-y-o 5f winner Pillar Box (by Sakhee's Secret). The dam is an unraced half-sister to 6 winners including Temple Meads (2-y-o Group 2 Mill Reef Stakes) and the useful 2-y-o 6f winner and Group 3 Firth of Clyde Stakes second Sneak Preview. The second dam, Harryana (by Efisio), was a fair 2-y-o dual 5f winner. (The Super Sprinters). *"This filly has a bit more scope than her half-sister Pillar Box, a filly we trained. She's got a bit of a splint at the moment but I see her as one for the Supersprint at Newbury. That's what she was bought for".*

729. FOL O'YASMINE ★★★★
b.f. Dubawi – Sewards Folly (Rudimentary). March 5. Half-sister to the Group 2 6f Diadem Stakes winner and Group 1 6f Middle Park Stakes second Sayif (by Kheleyf), to the useful Group 3 5f Cornwallis Stakes winner and Group 2 Flying Childers Stakes second Hunter Street (by Compton Place) and a hurdles winner by Tobougg. The dam was placed at 2 yrs and is a half-sister to 6 minor winners. The second dam, Anchorage (by Slip Anchor), won twice at 3 yrs and is a half-sister to 6 winners including the Group 3 Ormonde Stakes winner Brunico. (Saleh Al Homaizi & Imad Al Sagar). *"Not a great mover and not a great walker, but she's quite small, strong and very typical of the sire. She'll be a 2-y-o alright".*

730. HIJRAN ★★★★
ch.f. Mastercraftsman – Sunny Slope (Mujtahid). April 11. Eighth foal. 60,000Y. Tattersalls October Book 2. Tony Nerses. Half-

sister to the Irish 2-y-o 7f and subsequent US Grade 2 winner Indigo River (by Kodiac), to the quite useful 7f, 1m (including at 2 yrs) and 11f winner of 6 races Lake Pontchartrain (by Invincible Spirit), the modest 6f (at 2 yrs) and 1m winner of 7 races Royal Holiday (by Captain Rio) and the quite useful 2-y-o 5.5f winner Excitement (by Xaar). The dam, a modest 1m and 9f winner, is a half-sister to 2 minor winners. The second dam, Scottish Eyes (by Green Dancer), is an unraced half-sister to 4 winners. (Saleh Al Homaizi & Imad Al Sagar). *"I like her a lot. Light on her feet, she's doing very well and is a nice filly".*

731. I CAN'T STOP ★★★
gr.f. Kyllachy – Vellena (Lucky Story). March 26. Fourth foal. 50,000Y. Tattersalls October Book 2. Rabbah Bloodstock. Half-sister to the modest dual 6f winner Koharu (by Ishiguru). The dam is an unraced half-sister to 9 winners including the Group 2 Coventry Stakes winner Hellvelyn. The second dam, Cumbrian Melody (by Petong), a quite useful 2-y-o 5f and 6f winner, is a half-sister to 5 winners. (Sheikh Rashid Dalmook Al Maktoum). *"I quite like her. She's nice, willing, enthusiastic and should be a summer 2-y-o".*

732. IN THE CITY ★★★ ♠
ch.c. Exceed And Excel – Soft Morning (Pivotal). April 3. Fourth foal. 100,000Y. Tattersalls October Book 1. Highflyer Bloodstock. Half-brother to the French 2-y-o 6f winner So In Love (by Smart Strike) and to the 2-y-o 7f winner Savanna La Mar (by Curlin) – both listed-placed. The dam, a useful listed 9.5f winner of 3 races, is a half-sister to 8 winners including the 2-y-o Group 3 1m Prix des Reservoirs winner Songerie and the fairly useful 2-y-o 7.2f winner and Group 3 1m Prix des Reservoirs third Souvenance. The second dam, Summer Night (by Nashwan), a fairly useful 3-y-o 6f winner, is a half-sister to 7 winners including Starlit Sands (Group 3 Prix d'Arenburg). (Simon Munir & Isaac Suede). *"I like him. He's a sweet horse and he's keen to please. One for seven furlongs this year I'd say".*

733. LAPILLI ★★★★★
b.c. Bahamian Bounty – Blue Lyric (Refuse To Bend). February 2. Second foal. 70,000Y. Tattersalls October Book 2. Shadwell Estate Co.

Half-brother to the moderate 2014 5f placed 2-y-o Fine Judgement (by Compton Place). The dam was a fair 2-y-o dual 7f winner. The second dam, Powder Blue (by Daylami), placed twice over 7f (both her starts), is a half-sister to 3 minor winners including the dam of the Group 3 winners Fantasia and Pink Symphony. (Sheikh Ahmed Al Maktoum). *"If you had a poll in the yard about which 2-y-o would make it to Royal Ascot they'd all point to this colt. He's a natural, he's strong and he'll run early too. A well-made horse that wants fast ground, he's a really fluent mover. A nice horse, I think he'll start at the Guineas meeting. I don't tend to train them to win first time out and I think he'll run at least twice before Ascot".*

734. LIKE NO OTHER ★★★
b.c. Approve – Blue Beacon (Fantastic Light). February 26. Fourth foal. 70,000Y. Tattersalls October Book 2. Jill Lamb. Half-brother to the fair 2014 2-y-o 7f winner Light Fantastic (by Acclamation) and to the modest 11f and 12f winner of 3 races Asian Wing (by Hawk Wing). The dam, a modest 7f and 9f placed maiden, is a half-sister to 3 winners including the dam of the Group 3 winners Pink Symphony and Fantasia. The second dam, Blue Duster (by Danzig), won the Group 1 6f Cheveley Park Stakes and is a sister to the smart Group 1 6f Middle Park Stakes winner Zieten and a half-sister to 9 winners. (Mr L Sheridan). *"Yes, I like him, he's done very well. I thought he'd be really early, but now I think he'll be a June/July 2-y-o. He's grown up a lot but I'm not sure how good the stallion is yet. I think he needs a good one this year".*

735. MANSHOOD (IRE) ★★★★
b.c. Iffraaj – Thawrah (Green Desert). February 27. Fifth living foal. 380,000Y. Tattersalls October Book 1. Shadwell Estate Co. Half-brother to the Group 3 6f Hackwood Stakes winner Heeraat (by Dark Angel), to the useful 2-y-o listed 5f winner and Group 3 5f Molecomb Stakes third Ambiance (by Camacho) and a minor winner in Germany by Chineur. The dam is an unraced half-sister to 6 winners including Malhub (Group 1 Golden Jubilee Stakes) and the US Grade 3 winner Dhaamer. The second dam, Arjuzah (by Ahonoora), winner of the listed 7f Sceptre Stakes and third in the Group 2 7f Challenge

Stakes, is a half-sister to 2 winners. (Hamdan Al Maktoum). *"I like him, his half-brother Heeraat did quite well for us and he's so like him in his mannerisms and his nature. I'm not sure how precocious he'll be, especially as Heeraat got stronger after his 2-y-o career, but he'll be a lovely horse in time".*

736. MELABI (IRE) ★★★★ ♠♠
b.c. Oasis Dream – Briolette (Sadler's Wells). March 19. Sixth foal. 250,000Y. Tattersalls October Book 1. Charlie Gordon-Watson. Half-brother to the fairly useful Irish 2-y-o 1m winner Thomasgainsborough (by Dansili) and to the quite useful 6f to 8.5f winner of 5 races Point North (by Danehill Dancer). The dam won the listed 10f Trigo Stakes, was second in the Group 3 12f Princess Royal Stakes and is a sister to the Irish listed winner Peach Out Of Reach and a half-sister to 6 winners including the multiple Grade 1 winner Pilsudski and the champion Japanese filly Fine Motion. The second dam, Cocotte (by Troy), a very useful 10.2f winner, was second in the Group 3 Prix de Psyche. (Al Shaqab Racing). *"He's a very nice horse, he's strong and should be a 2-y-o. Six/seven furlongs should suit him this year".*

737. MUSAANADA ★★★
b.f. Sea The Stars – Gaze (Galileo). March 7. Fourth foal. 235,000foal. Tattersalls December. Shadwell Estate Co. Half-sister to the useful 2-y-o 1m and subsequent Australian listed 9f winner Greatwood (by Manduro), to the fair 6f and 7f winner Ganimede (by Oasis Dream) and the modest 12f and 14f winner Bridgehampton (by Lando). The dam, placed over 10f and 12f here, won twice in Germany and is a half-sister to the Irish Derby, Coronation Cup and Tattersalls Gold Cup winner Fame And Glory and the listed-placed Guaranda (dam of the Group 3 winner Gravitation). The second dam, Gryada (by Shirley Heights), a fairly useful 2-y-o 7f and 8.3f winner, was third in the Group 3 1m Premio Dormello and is a full or half-sister to 4 winners and to the unraced dam of the German dual Group 1 winner Gonbarda. (Hamdan Al Maktoum). *"A lovely filly but she needs time and will be a mile and a half filly next year. She has a lovely way about her and is a very nice, attractive filly. She's also inbred 2x3 to the fantastic broodmare Urban Sea".*

738. MUTAYYAM ★★★
ch.c. Aqlaam – Sant Elena (Efisio). April 21.
Fourth foal. 200,000foal. Tattersalls December.
Shadwell Estate Co. Half-brother to the 2-y-o
Group 1 Prix Morny and Group 1 Middle Park
Stakes winner of 5 races Reckless Abandon
(by Exchange Rate), to the fair 7f winner Free
Rein (by Dansili) and the modest triple 8.5f
winner Jumbo Prado (by El Prado). The dam,
a quite useful dual 6f winner (including at 2
yrs), was then listed-placed in Canada and is a
half-sister to the US Grade 1 9f and 10f winner
Ticker Tape. The second dam, Argent Du Bois
(by Silver Hawk), placed five times at 2 and 3
yrs in France, stayed 1m and is a half-sister to
7 winners including the Group 1 Racing Post
Trophy winner Crowded House. (Hamdan Al
Maktoum). *"This colt has changed a lot and
we've had some luck with Sheikh Hamdan
horses that were bought as foals – including
Aqlaam and Mukhadram. When he arrived
I didn't like him very much, but he's really
developed and he'll just go on improving.
One for the back-end of the season".*

739. MUZDAWAJ ★★★★★
b.c. Dansili – Shabiba (Seeking The Gold).
April 16. Fourth foal. Half-brother to Sharqeyi
(by Shamardal), placed second over 7f on
both her starts at 2 yrs in 2014, to the useful
6f (at 2 yrs) and dual listed 7f winner Ertijaal
(by Oasis Dream) and the useful 2-y-o 6f
winner and listed-placed Odooj (by Pivotal).
The dam, a useful 6f (at 2 yrs) and listed 1m
winner, was third in the Group 3 7f Oak Tree
Stakes and is a half-sister to the useful 2-y-o
6f winner and Group 3 placed Darajaat. The
second dam, Misterah (by Alhaarth), a very
useful listed 6f (at 2 yrs) and Group 3 7f Nell
Gwyn Stakes winner, is sister to one winner
and a half-sister to the useful 2-y-o 6f winner
Muqtarb. (Hamdan Al Maktoum). *"A lovely
colt and one of my favourites. We've trained
everything out of the dam and this is the nicest.
Ertijaal was beautiful but temperamental. This
colt is beautiful too and he's doing really well.
One for September time".*

740. NIETZSCHE ★★★★
ch.c. Poet's Voice – Ganga (Generous). April
10. Thirteenth foal. 65,000Y. Tattersalls
October Book 2. John Warren. Half-brother to
8 winners in France including the French listed

12f winner of 4 races Light Impact. The dam, a
quite useful 1m and 10f winner, is a half-sister
to 7 winners. The second dam, Congress Lady
(by General Assembly), a winner in France and
Group 3 second in Ireland, is a half-sister to 9
winners. (Michael Morris). *"A nice horse and
he'll be a 2-y-o too. We'll start him off over six
furlongs in May and he could develop into an Ascot
horse. I like him, he's tall and quite leggy but
he's got speed and covers some ground".*

741. NOKHADA (IRE) ★★★★
b.c. Lilbourne Lad – Silverdreammachine
(Marju). March 20. Third foal. 70,000Y.
Tattersalls October Book 2. Shadwell Estate
Co. Half-brother to the French 2014 2-y-o
winner Aimee (by Alfred Nobel). The dam is
an unplaced half-sister to 7 winners including
the German Group 2 winner Stormont. The
second dam, Legal Steps (by Law Society),
won once at 3 yrs and is a half-sister to 6
winners including the South African Group 1
winner Super Sheila. (Hamdan Al Maktoum).
*"A lazy little beggar but I think he can go and
he's a good-looking model. Definitely a 2-y-o,
he's a nice colt that'll want quick ground".*

742. OLYMPIC RUNNER ★★★
ch.f. Exceed And Excel – Lochridge (Indian
Ridge). February 4. Half-sister to the fairly
useful 2-y-o 6f winner City Girl (by Elusive
City) and to the fair 2-y-o 6f winner Echo
Ridge (by Oratorio). The dam, a smart listed 6f
winner of 5 races, is a half-sister to 3 winners
including the useful listed 5f winner Loch
Verdi. The second dam, Lochsong (by Song),
a champion sprinter and winner of the Prix
de l'Abbaye (twice), the Kings Stand Stakes
and the Nunthorpe Stakes, is a half-sister to
the Nunthorpe Stakes winner Lochangel. (J C
Smith). *"A very racy filly, she's quite leggy but
I think she'll be a 2-y-o and hopefully she'll
be better than either of the dam's previous
two winners, because she's by a better sire in
Exceed And Excel".*

743. ORNATE ★★★★
b.c. Bahamian Bounty – Adorn (Kyllachy).
April 16. Half-brother to the useful 2014 2-y-o
dual 5f winner Fendale (by Exceed And Excel)
and to the 2-y-o Group 2 Richmond Stakes
winner Saayerr (by Acclamation). The dam,
a useful 2-y-o 6f winner, is closely related to

the US 5f (minor stakes) to 8.5f winner Red
Diadem and a half-sister to 4 winners. The
second dam, Red Tiara (by Mr Prospector), a
moderate 7.6f fourth-placed maiden, is closely
related to the Japanese sprint stakes winner
Meiner Love and a half-sister to 4 winners.
(Cheveley Park Stud). *"He's alright this colt and
the mare has done really well with her first
two foals. He's maybe not quite as precocious
as Saayerr was, but he's strong and he'll be a
summer 2-y-o. These Bahamian Bounty's want
to get on with it".*

744. OUT AND ABOUT (IRE) ★★★★
b.c. Fastnet Rock – Starship (Galileo). March
25. Sixth foal. Closely related to the smart 7f,
1m (both at 2 yrs) and Group 3 10f Gallinule
Stakes winner Packing Tycoon (by Danehill
Dancer), to the quite useful 7f (at 2 yrs) and
1m winner Bilimbi, the quite useful dual 10f
winner Martian (both by Duke Of Marmalade)
and the fairly useful 2-y-o 7f and 1m winner
Pickled Pelican (by Dylan Thomas). The dam,
a fair 7f (at 2 yrs) to 8.3f winner, is a half-sister
to numerous winners including Superstar
Leo (Group 2 5f Flying Childers Stakes).
The second dam, Council Rock (by General
Assembly), a fair 9f and 10f placed 3-y-o, is
a half-sister to 6 winners including Glatisant
(Group 3 Prestige Stakes). (The Starship
Partnership). *"A very nice horse and very
similar to Bilimbi who has gone to Hong Kong.
I think he's got a real good look to him, he's
well-made but his pedigree tells you he'll take
a bit of time. I can see him doing well".*

745. QORTAAJ ★★★
b.g. Kyllachy – Cardrona (Selkirk).
January 28. First foal. 130,000Y. Tattersalls
October Book 2. Shadwell Estate Co. The dam
is an unplaced sister to the useful listed 6f
(at 2 yrs) and listed 7f winner Selinka and a
half-sister to 2 winners. The second dam, Lady
Links (by Bahamian Bounty), a dual listed 6f
winner (including at 2 yrs), is a half-sister to 5
winners. *"A nice, strong horse, a bit heavy but
a nice mover. He had a very high testicle so
we cut him. One for six/seven furlongs in the
second half of the season".*

746. RAHYAH ★★★★
b.f. Acclamation – Kahlua Kiss (Mister Baileys).
March 26. Fourth foal. 75,000Y. Tattersalls

October Book 1. John Warren. Half-sister
to the smart 6f (at 2 yrs) and dual listed
10f winner of 5 races Windhoek (by Cape
Cross) and to the quite useful 12f winner
Spiritoftheunion (by Authorized). The dam,
a fairly useful 7f (at 2 yrs) and 10f winner of
4 races, was listed-placed twice and is a half-
sister to the 2-y-o winner and dual Group 3
placed Mister Genepi. The second dam, Ring
Queen (by Fairy King), is an unraced half-sister
to 10 winners including the US dual Grade 1
winner Special Ring. (Ahmed Al Naboodah).
*"Definitely a 2-y-o type, she wants fast ground
and there's just something about her. One to
start off in May".*

747. RAUCOUS ★★★★ ♠
b.c. Dream Ahead – Shyrl (Acclamation).
March 23. Second living foal. 100,000Y.
Tattersalls October Book 2. John Warren. The
dam, a useful 2-y-o 5f winner, was second
in the Group 2 5f Queen Mary Stakes and is
a half-sister to 4 winners. The second dam,
Finicia (by Miswaki), was placed four times
at 2 yrs in France. (Highclere Thoroughbred
Racing, Melbourne). *"I like him, the dam was
second in the Queen Mary, he's a nice horse
with a good temperament and he should
do well. He should be a 2-y-o and he come
together quite early".*

748. RECORDER ★★★★
ch.c. Galileo – Memory (Danehill Dancer).
January 28. First foal. The dam won the Group
2 6f Cherry Hinton Stakes and is a sister to
one winner and a half-sister to 4 winners
including the 2-y-o Group 3 Tyros Stakes
winner Remember Alexander. The second
dam, Nausicaa (by Diesis), won 3 races at 2
and 3 yrs in France and the USA over 7f and
1m, was third in the Grade 3 Miesque Stakes
and is a half-sister to 3 winners. (The Queen).
*"It's widely believed that Galileo does his best
when matched with speed and I hope this colt
goes on to help prove the point. We don't have
many Galileo's and this is a nice colt out of a
mare that was very good but temperamental.
This colt is strong, well-made and doesn't
look like a Galileo, but if we can get him to
Royal Ascot I would think the Chesham would
suit. It's so exciting to see how the Queen's
pedigrees have improved dramatically over the
last few years".*

749. SAINTED ★★★

ch.f. Dutch Art – Blithe (Pivotal).
March 8. Third foal. Sister to the useful triple 6f winner Telmeyd. The dam, a fairly useful 2-y-o 7f winner, is a half-sister to 5 winners including the Group 2 1m winner Penitent. The second dam, Pious (by Bishop Of Cashel), a fair dual 6f winner (including at 2 yrs), is a half-sister to 5 winners. (Cheveley Park Stud). *"The dam was really useful but unfortunately she fractured a sesamoid at the end of her 2-y-o career, which prevented her from being a stakes filly. This is a lovely filly, although nothing at all like her half-brother Telmeyd. She'll come together in the summer and I suspect she'll be an August/September 2-y-o".*

750. SPECIAL SEASON ★★★★

ch.c. Lope De Vega – Keep Dancing (Distant Music). February 12. First foal. 95,000Y. Tattersalls October Book 2. Rabbah Bloodstock. The dam, a modest 6f winner, is a half-sister to 5 winners including the 2-y-o Group 2 July Stakes winner Alhebayeb and the listed 5f winner Humidor. The second dam, Miss Indigo (by Indian Ridge), is a placed half-sister to 8 winners including the useful listed 10f Pretty Polly Stakes winner Musetta. (Sheikh Rashid Dalmook Al Maktoum). *"I like him, but of course everyone likes the Lope De Vega's now because he's done so well. This colt got a sore shin so we backed off him and he'll be back in a month. I think he'll be a six/seven furlong 2-y-o and he's a fine, big horse".*

751. SYMPOSIUM ★★★

ch.f. Exceed And Excel – Soodad (King's Best). February 27. Second foal. 70,000Y. Tattersalls October Book 2. John Warren. The dam is an unplaced half-sister to the French listed winner Qurtaas. The second dam, Qurrah (by Zafonic), was placed twice at 3 yrs in France and is a half-sister to 5 winners including the 1,000 Guineas winner Virginia Waters. (The Royal Ascot Racing Club). *"She's done very well, she's quite strong and from a good family. A July type 2-y-o".*

752. TASLEET ★★★★

b.c. Showcasing – Bird Key (Cadeaux Generoux). March 19. Sixth foal. £52,000Y. Doncaster Premier. Shadwell Estate Co. Half-brother to the modest 2-y-o 7f seller winner Face The Future (by Green Desert) and to the fairly useful dual 7f winner Makaamen (by Selkirk). The dam ran once unplaced and is a half-sister to 7 winners including the very smart 2-y-o Group 2 7f Champagne Stakes winner Etlaala. The second dam, Portelet (by Night Shift), a fairly useful 5f winner of 4 races, is a half-sister to 4 winners. (Hamdan Al Maktoum). *"Yes, he's a runner and he'll be a 2-y-o. A cheeky beggar, he's lazy but he'll be out in May. Sheikh Hamdan likes us to buy some sharper ones to compliment his more backward home-breds and we bought Nokhada and this one. They're both precocious and their best year will be this one".*

753. WRAPPED ★★★★

ch.f. Iffraaj – Muffled (Mizaaya). March 20. Ninth foal. 110,000Y. Tattersalls October Book 2. Cheveley Park Stud. Sister to the quite useful 2-y-o dual 5f winner Rafeeej and half-sister to 5 winners including the fairly useful 2-y-o 5f winner and listed-placed Excello (by Exceed And Excel), the fair 1m winner Defiant Spirit (by Compton Place), the French 2-y-o 7f winner Hushed (by Cape Cross) and the modest 2-y-o 6f winner Chandrayaan (by Bertolini). The dam, a modest 7f winner, is a half-sister to 3 other minor winners. The second dam, Sound It (by Believe It), is a placed half-sister to the Group 1 winners Pas de Reponse and Green Tune. (Cheveley Park Stud). *"Yes, I like her. She was quite expensive but she's big and powerful and I think we'll be getting on with her. I'd be surprised if she's a five furlong 2-y-o but she could be six".*

754. UNNAMED ★★ ♠

b.f. Galileo – Baraka (Danehill). February 10. Seventh foal. €300,000Y. Arqana Deauville August. Anthony Stroud. Sister to the 12f winner Min Alemarat and to the 10f and 12f winner Beyond Conceit – both fairly useful. The dam, a listed 11f winner, is a sister to the Japanese stakes winner Fine Motion and a half-sister to 6 winners including the multiple Group 1 winner Pilsudski and the Irish 2-y-o Group 3 1m winner Glowing Ardour. The second dam, Cocotte (by Troy), a very useful 10.2f winner, was second in the Group 3 Prix de Psyche and is a half-sister to the listed winner Gay Captain. (Mr B Kantor & Mr M Jooste). *"A backward filly but she's done really well and she's lovely, but the dam's been to Galileo plenty of times and only bred one winner. One for the back-end of the season and if she's any good she'll be an Oaks filly next year".*

755. UNNAMED ★★★ ♠

b.f. Invincible Spirit – Bratislava (Dr Fong). April 23. Sixth foal. €300,000Y. Goffs Orby. Steve Parkin. Half-sister to the 2014 6f placed 2-y-o Slovak (by Iffraaj), to the useful triple listed 6f winner (including at 2 yrs) Katla (by Majestic Missile), the fair Irish 1m winner Derulo (by Arakan) and a minor winner in the USA by Diamond Green. The dam is an unplaced half-sister to 8 winners including the Group 1 7f Prix Jean-Luc Lagardere winner Wootton Bassett. The second dam, Balladonia (by Primo Dominie), a useful 9f winner, was listed-placed twice over 10f and is a half-sister to 5 winners. (Clipper Logistics). *"A nice filly that cost a lot of money and was bought by the owners of our Cheveley Park Stakes winner Rosdhu Queen who was by the same sire. She'll be out in June/July time, she's strong and will be a 2-y-o".*

756. UNNAMED ★★★

b.f. Fastnet Rock – Butterfly Blue (Sadler's Wells). May 6. Seventh foal. Closely related to the useful triple 1m winner (including at 2 yrs) and listed-placed King George River and to the fairly useful 9f winner and Group 3 Irish 1,000 Guineas Trial third Sapphire Pendant (both by Danehill Dancer) and half-sister to the Canadian listed-placed winner Lacadena (by Fasliyev). The dam, a quite useful Irish 9f winner, is a sister to the winner and Group 1 Fillies' Mile second Maryinski (dam of the Group 1 winners Thewayyouare and Peeping Fawn) and a half-sister to the Group/Grade 2 winners Better Than Honour, Turnberry Isle and Smolensk. The second dam, Blush With Pride (by Blushing Groom), a dual US Grade 1 winner, is a half-sister to the dams of the top-class 2-y-o's Xaar, El Gran Senor and Try My Best. (Sir Peter Vela, D Nagle, J Magnier). *"A gorgeous filly with a lovely temperament, she's very classy-looking but she goes at the back of the string at the moment because she needs time. She'll stay well as a 2-y-o and be better next year".*

757. UNNAMED ★★★★

ch.c. Champs Elysees – Dalvina (Grand Lodge). March 24. First foal. 110,000Y. Tattersalls October Book 1. Not sold. The dam, a smart 7f (at 2 yrs), listed 10f and subsequent US Grade 3 12f winner, is a half-sister to 2 winners including the very useful 7f (at 2 yrs) and listed 10f winner Soft Centre. The second dam, Foodbroker Fancy (by Halling), a smart 6f (at 2 yrs) and dual listed 10f winner, is a half-sister to 4 winners including the useful listed 2-y-o 6f winner Femme Fatale. (St Albans Bloodstock). *"He's the first foal out of a mare that was useful – she was the Oaks favourite at one time, but she's been very difficult to breed from and sadly for the breeder this one is a colt rather than a filly. He's a strong colt and the nicest I've had for the owner – and I've had a few. He's the type to make his debut in August and he's a nice horse".*

758. UNNAMED ★★★ ♠

b.f. Dream Ahead – Flanders (Common Grounds). April 16. Eleventh foal. 400,000Y. Tattersalls October Book 1. Kern/Lillingston. Half-sister to 10 winners including the Group 1 Haydock Park Sprint winner G Force (by Tamayuz), the US Grade 3 Miesque Stakes winner Louvain (by Sinndar and herself dam of the dual Group 1 winner Flotilla), the useful listed 10f winner Laajooj (by Azamour), the fairly useful Irish 10f winner Lagoon (by Montjeu) and the quite useful 5f (including at 2 yrs) and 6f winner and Group 3 third Desert Poppy (by Oasis Dream). The dam, winner of the listed Scarbrough Stakes and second in the Group 2 Kings Stand Stakes, is a half-sister to 8 winners. The second dam, Family at War (by Explodent), was a fair 2-y-o 5f winner. (Lordship Stud). *"She's nice, an expensive yearling from a good family, but she just needs time. She will be fast but she won't be precocious".*

759. UNNAMED ★★★★

ch.f. Champs Elysees – Fleche d'Or (Dubai Destination). March 31. Third foal. €150,000Y. Goffs Orby. Steve Parkin. Sister to the listed 10f winner Eastern Belle and half-sister to the 2014 2-y-o 8.5f winner Golden Horn (by Cape Cross). The dam is an unraced half-sister to 10 winners including the Group 1 1m Coronation Stakes winner Rebecca Sharp, the

Group 3 11.5f Lingfield Derby Trial winner Mystic Knight and the listed 11.4f Cheshire Oaks winner Hidden Hope. The second dam, Nuryana (by Nureyev), a useful winner of the listed 1m Grand Metropolitan Stakes, is a half-sister to 5 winners. (Clipper Logistics). *"She's lovely. A full sister to a stakes winner and the 3-y-o half-brother Golden Horn is supposed to be really good. This filly has a lot of white about her but she's a beautiful mover. I'm sure she'll be nice and I like her a lot".*

760. UNNAMED ★★★

ch.f. Exceed And Excel – Landela (Alhaarth). April 22. Seventh foal. €165,000Y. Goffs Orby. Rabbah Bloodstock. Half-sister to the French 2-y-o 7f winner and listed-placed Impendor (by Holy Roman Emperor), to the quite useful 2-y-o 1m and subsequent US winner Get A Grip (by Royal Applause) and the quite useful 1m and 9f winner Trumpington Street (by Noverre). The dam, placed fourth on both her starts over 7f and 1m at 4 yrs, is a half-sister to 6 winners including Zambezi Sun (Group 1 Grand Prix de Paris) and the French Group 2 winner Kalabar. The second dam, Imbabala (by Zafonic), won at 3 yrs in France and is a half-sister to 6 winners including the French Group 3 winner Short Pause. (Sheikh Juma Dalmook Al Maktoum). *"I'm not sure what to make of her. She was a lovely yearling but when she came in after being broken she wasn't half as nice. She's just coming back now and she'll make a 2-y-o later on. She's one of those that might thrive quite quickly".*

761. UNNAMED ★★★

b.f. Acclamation – Map Of Heaven (Pivotal). January 19. First foal. The dam, a fair 7f winner, is a sister to the very smart Group 3 5f Molecomb Stakes and Group 3 5f King George Stakes winner Enticing and a half-sister to several winners including the useful listed 1m winner and Group 3 7f Jersey Stakes second Sentaril. The second dam, Superstar Leo (by College Chapel), a very smart 2-y-o, won 5 races including the Group 2 5f Flying Childers Stakes and the Weatherbys Super Sprint and is a full or half-sister to numerous winners. (Lael Stable). *"She should be a 2-y-o, she's a little back of the knee but quite strong and the first foal out of a Pivotal mare who was only fair but good-looking. A January foal*

and a granddaughter of Superstar Leo, she should be a mid-summer 2-y-o so we'll be kicking on with her soon".

762. UNNAMED ★★★★

ch.f. Exceed And Excel – Miss Honorine (Highest Honor). April 15. Seventh foal. 85,000Y. Tattersalls October Book 2. John Warren. Half-sister to the unplaced 2014 2-y-o Onorina (by Arcano), to the fairly useful 2-y-o 6f winner Master Chef (by Oasis Dream) and the quite useful 7f (including at 2 yrs) and 1m winner Admire The View (by Dubawi). The dam, a winner of three listed events from 1m to 10f, was Group 3 placed twice and is a half-sister to 8 winners including the Canadian Grade 2 winner Mekong Melody. The second dam, Nini Princesse (by Niniski), won 6 races from 2 to 4 yrs in France and is a sister to the US Grade 1 winner Louis Cyphre and a half-sister to the French Group 2 winner Psychobabble. (Abdulla Al Khalifa). *"I like her, she's a very well-made 2-y-o, strong and with something about her. She'll be racing around June time and she'll be OK".*

763. UNNAMED ★★★

b.c. Iffraaj – Quaich (Danehill). February 20. Fourth living foal. 110,000Y. Tattersalls October Book 2. Shadwell Estate Co. Brother to the fairly useful 2-y-o 7f winner Diala and half-brother to the quite useful 2-y-o 1m winner Matula (by Halling). The dam, a fair 7f winner, is a half-sister to the German 3-y-o winner and Group 3 1m second Lukretia. The second dam, Quecha (by Indian Ridge), placed once over 6f at 2 yrs in France, is a half-sister to one winner. (Sheikh Ahmed Al Maktoum). *"I thought her half-sister Diala was going to be very good but she didn't train on. This colt isn't very precocious but he's quite a well-made horse and should be out in August".*

764. UNNAMED ★★★

b.f. Oasis Dream – Quan Yin (Sadler's Wells). April 3. Fourth foal. 100,000Y. Tattersalls October Book 2. Rabbah Bloodstock. Half-sister to Broughtonian (by Invincible Spirit), last on his only outing at 2 yrs in 2014 and to the quite useful Irish 12f winner Ode To Psyche (by Dansili). The dam is an unraced half-sister to 3 winners including Moon Driver (Group 3 Prix d'Arenburg). The second dam,

East Of The Moon (by Private Account), won the French 1,000 Guineas, the Prix de Diane and the Prix Jacques le Marois and is a half-sister to the top class miler and sire Kingmambo and to the smart Miesque's Son. (Sheikh Juma Dalmook Al Maktoum). *"A very sharp, racy-looking 2-y-o. She'll be a June 2-y-o because she's strong and ready-made".*

765. UNNAMED ★★★
b.f. Iffraaj – Sahara Sky (Danehill). March 11. Fourth foal. €35,000Y. Goffs February. Goodwill Bloodstock. Half-sister to the 2014 2-y-o Group 1 6f Phoenix Stakes winner Dick Whittington (by Rip Van Winkle), to the fairly useful 2-y-o 5f winner Sign From Heaven (by Raven's Pass) and the fair dual 6f winner Lisiere (by Excellent Art). The dam is an unraced half-sister to 9 winners including the Group 1 6f July Cup winner Owington. The second dam, Old Domesday Book (by High Top), a fairly useful 10.4f winner, was third in the listed 10f Sir Charles Clore Memorial Stakes. (Mr Paul Makin). *"A half-sister to a 2-y-o Group 1 winner in Dick Whittington, she's a strong filly and looks a 2-y-o but isn't the greatest mover I've ever trained. I think she might be changing so we've turned her out for a bit. I see her very much as a 2-y-o".*

MICHAEL HALFORD
766. AFZAL (FR) ★★★★
ch.c. Iffraaj – Adelfia (Sinndar). May 12. Sixth foal. Half-brother to the quite useful 2-y-o 1m winner Adelana (by Manduro) and to the fairly useful 1m (at 2 yrs) and 9f winner Adilapour (by Azamour). The dam, a quite useful 12f winner, is a half-sister to several winners including the smart dual Group 3 winner Adilabad. The second dam, Adaiyka (by Doyoun), was a smart winner of the Group 3 9f Prix Chloe. (H H Aga Khan). *"A well-balanced colt with a good action and a good attitude, he'll probably want seven furlongs. He's a late foal and he's one for a bit later on but he goes well".*

767. ANAMBA ★★★★
b.f. Shamardal – Anamato (Redoute's Choice). April 19. Second foal. The dam was a Group 1 10f winner at 4 yrs in Australia and was Group 1 placed a further three times, including over 10f in the USA. (Godolphin Management). *"A*

lovely, big, tall filly with a beautiful action, it'll be the second half of the year before we see her out. She'll be a seven furlong type and she's a lovely, long-striding filly".*

768. AL QAHWA (IRE) ★★★★
b.c. Fast Company – Cappuccino (Mujadil). March 16. Sixth foal. €130,000Y. Goffs Orby. John Ferguson. Half-brother to the fair 5f to 7f winner of 5 races from 2 to 5 yrs Barista, to a minor winner in Greece (both by Titus Livius) and the fair 2-y-o 5f winner Vodka Time (by Indian Haven). The dam is an unraced half-sister to 10 winners including the Group 3 Arc Trial winner Compton Bolter and the dam of the Group 3 winners Bezelle and Iftiraas. The second dam, Milk And Honey (by So Blessed), a useful sprint winner at 2 yrs, is a half-sister to 9 winners including the Prix Foy winner Beeshi and the dams of the Cheveley Park Stakes winner Seazun and the Prix Dollar winner Insatiable. (Godolphin Management). *"A nice horse and one of our more forward 2-y-o's, he has a lovely temperament and he shows a nice bit of pace. He could be out in late May or early June".*

769. ESHAAN (IRE) ★★
ch.c. Tamayuz – Ebalista (Selkirk). May 6. Half-brother to the French Group 2 12.5f Prix de Royallieu winner Ebiyza (by Rock Of Gibraltar) and to the useful listed-placed 10f winner Ebeyina (by Oasis Dream). The dam, a quite useful 12f winner, is a half-sister to 7 winners including the useful 1m winner and Group 1 National Stakes third Eyshal. The second dam, Ebadiyla (by Sadler's Wells), won the Group 1 Irish Oaks and the Group 1 Prix Royal-Oak and is a half-sister to the smart Group 1 7f Moyglare Stud Stakes winner Edabiya and the high-class Ascot Gold Cup winner Enzeli. (H H Aga Khan). *"A straightforward colt, he's just doing swinging canters at the moment but he does everything well. He's one for the second half of the season".*

770. GIFT WRAP (IRE) ★★★
b.f. Raven's Pass – Intapeace (Intikhab). March 1. First foal. €40,000Y. Goffs November. John Ferguson. The dam, fairly useful listed-placed Irish 6f (at 2 yrs) and 7f winner, is a sister to the smart Group 3 winning sprinter and 2-y-o Group 2 placed Hoh Mike and a half-sister

to 6 winners. The second dam, Magical Peace (by Magical Wonder), a quite useful Irish 6f winner, is a half-sister to one winner. (Godolphin Management). *"She looks like a real 2-y-o, she's good and strong and has been pleasing us in her work. She'll be running by mid-season and looks like a filly to start over six furlongs before moving up to seven".*

771. HAZAMAR (IRE) ★★★★
gr.c. Manduro – Hazarafa (Daylami). March 10. Second foal. The dam, a useful listed 12f winner, is a half-sister to the 2-y-o Group 3 7f Silver Flash Stakes winner Harasiya, to the useful dual 10f winner and Group 3 second Haziyna and the useful listed 12f winner Hazarafa. The second dam, Hazariya (by Xaar), winner of the Group 3 7f Athasi Stakes and a listed event over 7f, is a half-sister to the Group 3 Blue Wind Stakes winner Hazarista and a half-sister to numerous minor winners. (H H Aga Khan). *"He's quite a big, tall colt and a beautiful individual. He's well-balanced and one for seven furlongs or a mile at the back-end. He's well grown and levelled off and we like him a lot, although he isn't doing much yet".*

772. HOUSEMAID (IRE) ★★
b.f. Invincible Spirit – Lady Catherine (Bering). February 18. Half-sister to the quite useful 5f (at 2 yrs) to 7f winner Lady Frances (by Exceed And Excel), to the quite useful UAE 6f and 7f winner Lord Tiger (by Tiger Hill) and the German 10f winner Signora (by Indian Ridge). The dam won the Group 3 1m Premio Dormello and a listed 1m event in France (both at 2 yrs). The second dam, Queen Catherine (by Machiavellian), a useful French 2-y-o and 3-y-o 1m winner, is a half-sister to the useful 2-y-o 7f winner and Group 3 1m May Hill Stakes third Gretel. (Godolphin Management). *"She's grown a lot lately, but she goes well and had a great attitude. We'll have to take our time with her for now".*

773. INDRAHAR (IRE) ★★★
b.f. Raven's Pass – Viz (Darshaan). March 26. 140,000foal. Tattersalls December. John Ferguson. Half-sister to the Group 2 Park Stakes and Group 3 Athasi Stakes winner Viztoria (by Oratorio). The dam, a useful Italian listed 12f winner, is a half-sister to

numerous winners including the smart 1m (at 2 yrs) to 10f winner and Group 3 placed Forbearing. The second dam, For Example (by Northern Baby), an Irish 10f placed maiden, is a half-sister to 5 winners and to the dams of the Group/Grade 1 winners Awe Inspiring, Culture Vulture, Polish Precedent and Zilzal. (Godolphin Management). *"She's a nice, straightforward filly that goes well. For what she's doing we like her, but it'll be mid-season before she starts".*

774. KALASADI (IRE) ★★★
ch.c. Exceed And Excel – Kalidaha (Cadeaux Genereux). May 10. The dam, a useful 7f (at 2 yrs) and 1m winner, was third in the Group 3 Brownstown Stakes and is a half-sister to 3 winners including the useful listed UAE 1m winner Burano. The second dam, Kalimanta (by Lake Coniston), ran twice unplaced and is a half-sister to 6 winners including the top-class Champion Stakes and Breeders Cup Turf winner Kalanisi and the high-class 1m listed winner and Group 1 St James's Palace Stakes second Kalaman. (HH Aga Khan). *"A little bit backward, but he's a lovely moving colt. He covers a lot of ground but he's not very big and being a May foal we'll give him a chance to develop. We like him and whatever we've asked him to do he's done well".*

775. LOGISTICS (FR) ★★
gr.c. Iffraaj – Raisonable (El Prado). January 28. Fourth foal. €160,000Y. Arqana Deauville August. R O'Gorman. Half-brother to the quite useful 2014 2-y-o 1m winner Tom Hark (by Makfi) and to the minor French winner Revolte (by Green Tune). The dam, placed once at 2 yrs, is a half-sister to 8 winners including Legerete (Group 2 Prix de Malleret). The second dam, Sea Hill (by Seattle Slew), a minor winner at 3 yrs in France, is a half-sister to 7 winners including Groom Dancer (Group 1 Prix Lupin). (Godolphin Management). *"He grew a lot after Christmas and he's just doing half-speeds now. A nice, straightforward colt with a good action, he's one for the second half of the year over seven furlongs".*

776. MISS PHILLYJINKS (IRE) ★★★
b.f. Zoffany – Smoken Rosa (Smoke Glacken). February 2. Fourth foal. €12,500Y. Tattersalls Ireland September. M Halford. Half-sister to

the modest triple 1m winner Bosstime and to the fair 7f winner Refusetolisten (both by Clodovil). The dam, placed 3 times in the USA, is a half-sister to 4 winners including Snowdrops (three Graded stakes wins). The second dam, Roses In The Snow (by Be My Guest), a useful 1m winner and listed-placed here, subsequently won in the USA and is a half-sister to 6 winners. *"She goes really well and she's a beautiful mover. She'd catch your eye on your gallops, thriving at the moment and pleasing us.*

777. PIRQUET (IRE) ★★★
b.f. Sea The Stars – Pleasantry (Johannesburg). February 16. First foal. 200,000Y. Tattersalls October Book 1. John Ferguson. The dam is an unraced half-sister to the top-class miler and multiple Group 1 winner Kingman and to the Group 3 Tercentenary Stakes winner Remote. The second dam, Zenda (by Zamindar), won the French 1,000 Guineas, was second in the Coronation Stakes and the Grade 1 Queen Elizabeth II Challenge Cup at Keeneland and is a half-sister to the Middle Park Stakes, July Cup and Nunthorpe Stakes winner Oasis Dream. (Godolphin Management). *"A lovely filly with a beautiful temperament and a good action, she's not over-big but covers plenty of ground. We like her, she's going to take a bit of time, but it's a magnificent pedigree and she's a quality filly with a super temperament".* Pirquet is named after two Austrian brothers. Guido was a pioneer of Astronautics and has a crater on the moon named after him. Clemens developed the concept of allergies. Both clever lads! ST.

778. PROTOCOL (IRE) ★★★
b.c. Kodiac – Deportment (Barathea). April 10. Second foal. 160,000Y. Tattersalls October Book 2. John Ferguson. Brother to the fair 2014 2-y-o 5f winner Commodore. The dam, a fair 10f winner, is a half-sister to 5 winners including the 2-y-o Group 3 1m May Hill Stakes winner and triple Group 1 placed Summitville and the useful Irish 7f to 10f winner of 6 races Worldly Wise. The second dam, Tina Heights (by Shirley Heights), a quite useful 10f winner of her only start, is a half-sister to 3 winners. (Godolphin Management). *"He's grown an awful lot so we've not done much with him yet. You'd like him though, he*

has a lovely temperament and is a good-moving horse for the second half of the year".*

779. REDDOT DANCER (IRE) ★★★★
b.c. Danehill Dancer – Roselyn (Efisio). March 2. Ninth foal. €62,000Y. Goffs Orby. BBA (Ire). Half-brother to 6 winners including the useful 6f and UAE dual 1m winner and Group 3 placed Colmar Kid (by Choisir), to the useful 2-y-o 5f and 6f winner West Leake Diman (by Namid), the fair 2-y-o 6f winner Squires Gate and the fair 1m to 10f winner of 5 races Kimono My House (by Dr Fong). The dam, placed fourth 3 times at 2 yrs over 6f and 7f, is a sister to the triple listed winner Riberac and a half-sister to 5 winners. The second dam, Ciboure (by Norwick), a fair 6f (at 2 yrs) and 1m winner of 3 races, is a half-sister to 4 winners. (George Tay). *"A beautiful, big horse, he does everything easily and has a good action. He's got a good attitude and he'll make a 2-y-o in the second half of the year".*

780. REDDOT ROMAN (IRE) ★★★
br.c. Holy Roman Emperor – Zoumie (Mark Of Esteem). March 28. Second foal. €50,000Y. Goffs Orby. BBA (Ire). The dam is an unraced half-sister to 4 winners including the listed 6f winner and multiple Group 3 placed Croisultan. The second dam, Zoudie (by Ezzoud), a fair 10f winner, is a half-sister to 7 winners including the dual Group 3 winner Redback. (George Tay). *"He's a horse that's just starting to come to hand. He's doing everything well, he's a good-moving horse and we'll probably start him off at six furlongs in mid-season".*

781. SPIRIT GLANCE ★★★★
b.f. Invincible Spirit – Gonfilia (Big Shuffle). March 22. Half-sister to the fairly useful 2-y-o dual 6f winner and Group 3 7f Sirenia Stakes third Signs Of The Sand (by Cape Cross) and to the fair dual 10f winner Greek War (by Monsun). The dam won 7 races including the Group 3 8.5f Princess Elizabeth Stakes and four listed events and is a full or half-sister to 6 winners including the German dual Group 1 12f winner Gonbarda. The second dam, Gonfalon (by Slip Anchor), is a half-sister to several winners. *"A sharp type of filly, she's done everything well so far and should be one of our first fillies to run. She's very*

straightforward, does everything nicely and is one to start at six furlongs".

782. STILL LIFE ★★★
ch.c. Dutch Art – Helen Glaz (Giant's Causeway). March 4. First foal. 250,000Y. Tattersalls October Book 1. John Ferguson. The dam, placed once at 3 yrs in France, is a half-sister to 2 minor winners. The second dam, Helinska (by Pennekamp), a minor winner of 2 races in France at 4 yrs, is a half-sister to 7 winners including Shamardal. (Godolphin Management). *"A beautiful looking horse with a very good temperament, he's very lazy in his work but the penny will drop one of these days and then he'll come to hand quickly. We like him and he's done everything we've asked of him. He's a fine, big horse but very mature, with plenty of strength and presence about him".*

783. TONKINESE ★★★★
b.c. Authorized – Honky Tonk Sally (Dansili). April 4. Fourth foal. 180,000Y. Tattersalls October Book 1. John Ferguson. Half-brother to the modest 2012 2-y-o 7f winner Ragtime Dancer (by Medicean) and to the fairly useful 2-y-o triple 5f winner and listed-placed Umneyati (by Iffraaj). The dam, a quite useful 2-y-o 7f winner, is a half-sister to 7 winners including the Group 3 1m Prix Saint-Roman winner Eco Friendly. The second dam, Flower Girl (by Pharly), a winner of 5 races including the Group 3 6f Goldene Peitsche and the listed 6f Sandy Lane Stakes, is a sister to the listed 9.4f winner Farmost and a half-sister to 3 winners. (Godolphin Management). *"He's another nice horse we like a lot. He shows plenty of pace considering his pedigree and he'll want seven furlongs to start with".*

784. VITELLO ★★★
b.f. Raven's Pass – Vitoria (Exceed And Excel). March 11. Second foal. The dam, a fairly useful 7f (at 2 yrs) and 6f winner of 3 races, is a half-sister to several winners including the listed 10f Prix de la Seine winner Ghyraan and the very useful 7f and 1m winner Plum Pudding. The second dam, Karayb (by Last Tycoon), a fairly useful 6f (at 2 yrs) and 7f winner, was listed placed and is a half-sister to 2 minor winners abroad. (Godolphin Management). *"A lovely, well-made, good-moving filly. She could*

be running before the end of May over six furlongs and she goes well".

785.UNNAMED ★★
b.f. Pivotal – Fine Threads (Barathea). March 18. First foal. 120,000Y. Tattersalls October Book 2. John Ferguson. The dam, a quite useful 7f (at 2 yrs) and 10f winner, is a sister to the 2-y-o 7f and subsequent US Grade 2 Sunset Handicap winner Always First and a half-sister to 4 winners including the fairly useful listed-placed Orientalist Art. The second dam, Pink Cristal (by Dilum), a smart 3-y-o listed 1m winner, is a half-sister to 8 winners including the German Group 2 and Group 3 Scottish Classic winner Crystal Hearted and Crystal Spray (dam of the Group winners Crystal Music, State Crystal, Dubai Success and Solar Crystal). (Godolphin Management). *"She's a big, good-moving filly for the second half of the year. Everything we've asked of her she's done well".*

786. UNNAMED ★★★★
b.c. Acclamation – Hanakiyya (Danehill Dancer). January 28. The dam, a fair 1m winner, is a half-sister to 5 winners including the Irish Group 3 7.5f Concorde Stakes winner Hamairi and the Irish 5f (at 2 yrs) and 3-y-o listed 6f winner Hanabad. The second dam, Handaza (by Be My Guest), a 1m winner at 3 yrs in Ireland, is out of Hazaradjat (by Darshaan), herself a half-sister to the Middle Park Stakes winner Hittite Glory. (H H Aga Khan). *"A well-forward colt for an Aga Khan horse. He's a good moving sort and should be one of the first 2-y-o colts we run. He's strong and takes his work really well".*

787. UNNAMED ★★★
b.f. Teofilo – Paimpolaise (Priolo). March 20. March 20. Half-sister to the 2014 Irish 2-y-o 1m winner Shannon Soul, to the smart Group 2 7f Hungerford Stakes and Group 3 7f Solario Stakes winner Shakespearean (both by Shamardal) and the modest 6f and 9f winner Hamis Al Bin (by Acclamation). The dam, placed twice at 3 yrs in France, is a half-sister to 7 winners including the Group 3 Prix de Saint-Georges winner Pont-Aven (herself dam of the Group 2 winners Josr Algarhoud and Sainte Marine). The second dam, Basilea (by Frere Basile), is a placed half-sister to 7

winners including the Group winners Bold Apparel and Conte Grimaldi. (Mr Michael Enright). *"A lovely filly and a beautiful mover with a very good temperament. She'll take a bit of time and she's one for seven furlongs in the second half of the year".*

788. UNNAMED ★★★

b.f. Oasis Dream – Pearl Banks (Pivotal). April 17. Second foal. €325,000Y. Goffs Orby. Not sold. The dam, a winner of 5 races in France and Germany including a German Group 3 event, is a half-sister to 5 winners including the French listed winner Pearls Of Passion. The second dam, Pearly Shells (by Efisio), a winner of the Group 1 Prix Vermeille and the Group 2 Prix de Malleret, is a half-sister to 4 winners including the US Grade 1 Hollywood Turf Handicap and Group 3 Beresford Stakes winner Frenchpark. (Mr Michael Enright). *"She's a filly that's grown a lot recently, she has a great action and she'll come into her own in the second half of the year. A lovely filly".*

789. UNNAMED ★★★

b.f. Dansili – Song (Sadler's Wells). January 24. Third foal. €300,000foal. Goffs November. Cregg Castle Stud. The dam is an unraced sister to the Irish 1,000 Guineas winner Yesterday, to the Group 1 7f Moyglare Stud Stakes winner and Irish 1,000 Guineas, Oaks and Irish Oaks placed Quarter Moon and the Oaks and Irish Oaks third All My Loving. The second dam, Jude (by Darshaan), a moderate 10f placed maiden, is a sister to the listed 14f winner and Irish Oaks third Arrikala and to the useful Irish 12f listed winner Alouette (dam of the Champion Stakes winner Alborada and the German triple Group 1 winner Albanova) and a half-sister to the Group 2 10f Nassau Stakes and Sun Chariot Stakes winner Last Second (dam of the Irish 2,000 Guineas winner Aussie Rules). (Mr Michael Enright). *"We like her, she has a very good temperament and is very straightforward. Well-balanced and with a good action, she's a little bit weak at the moment and is one for the second half of the year over seven furlongs".*

RICHARD HANNON

My visit to Richard's yard was another enjoyable and fulfilling one. The trainer shared his thoughts about his two-year-olds with me, as did his Assistant Trainers Tony Gorman and Steve Knight.

790. ABO SIDRAH (IRE) ★★★

b.c. Dream Ahead – Blissful Beat (Beat Hollow). February 28. Second foal. €250,000Y. Arqana Deauville August. Peter & Ross Doyle. Half-brother to the useful 2014 2-y-o 6f winner and Group 3 6f Sirenia Stakes third Home Of The Brave (by Starspangledbanner). The dam is an unraced half-sister to 8 winners including the Group 3 9f Prix de Conde winner Rashbag and the Group 3 7f Criterion Stakes winner Suggestive. The second dam, Pleasuring (by Good Times), is a sprint placed half-sister to 5 winners including Rose Of Montreaux (Group 3 1,000 Guineas Trial) and the Group 3 Princess Elizabeth Stakes winner Bay Street (herself the dam of 5 stakes winners). (Al Shaqab Racing). *"He's a nice horse but he'll take a bit of time. He's a great colour and we haven't had any problems with him yet. He's grand".*

791. AGUEROOO (IRE) ★★★★

b.c. Monsieur Bond – Vision Of Peace (Invincible Spirit). February 13. First foal. 70,000Y. Tattersalls October Book 2. Peter & Ross Doyle. The dam is an unraced half-sister to the Group 3 Premio Tudini winner Victory Laurel. The second dam, Special Cause (by Fasliyev), won once over 7f at 3 yrs in France and is a half-sister to 6 winners including the dam of Zafeen (Group 1 St James's Palace Stakes). (Middleham Park Racing LXXXVI). *"One of the nicer two-year-olds we've got, a really good type, you'd like everything about him, he's really strong but we're in no hurry with him just yet so he may be one for seven furlongs. We like him a lot".*

792. ALBE BACK ★★★★

gr.c. Archipenko – Alba Stella (Nashwan). April 9. Seventh foal. 30,000Y. Tattersalls October Book 2. Peter & Ross Doyle. Closely related to the 10f to 12f winner of 6 races at 3 and 4 yrs Aleatricis (by Kingmambo) and half-brother to 4 winners including the 14f and 2m winner All My Heart (by Sadler's Wells) and the 12f winner All That Rules (by Galileo) – all three quite useful. The dam, a fairly useful dual 12f winner, is a half-sister to the dual

Champion Stakes winner Alborada and the triple German Group 1 winner Albanova. The second dam, Alouette (by Darshaan), a useful listed 12f winner, is a sister to the listed winner Arrikala and a half-sister to the dams of the Group 1 winners Quarter Moon, Yesterday, Aussie Rules and Allegretto. (Mr W P Drew). *"He needs a bit of time and has a bit of daylight underneath him, but he's a nice, classy sort of horse who might make a mid to late-summer 2-y-o, with a bit of scope. One to put in your notebook – and the owner is lucky as well".*

793. AL KHATEYA ★★★★
b.f. Acclamation – Grenadia (Thunder Gulch). February 13. Third foal. €350,000Y. Arqana Deauville August. Peter & Ross Doyle. The dam, a French listed-placed winner, was Grade 3 placed in the USA and is a half-sister to 8 winners including the Group 3 La Coupe and Group 3 Prix Gontaut-Biron winner Slew The Red and the dam of the South African Group 1 winner Mahbooba. The second dam, Great Lady Slew (by Seattle Slew), a minor US 4-y-o winner, is a half-sister to 4 winners. *"A beautiful filly, she's a little bit small and neat but she's very racy and has a nice pedigree. She ought to be an early sort".*

794. AL MARKHIYA (IRE) ★★★★
b.f. Arcano – Danetime Out (Danetime). March 1. Sixth foal. Peter & Ross Doyle. Half-sister to the 2014 2-y-o Group 2 7f Superlative Stakes and Group 2 7f Champagne Stakes winner Estidhkaar (by Dark Angel), to the 2-y-o Group 1 7f National Stakes and Group 2 7f Vintage Stakes winner Toormore (by Arakan) and the quite useful 5.5f (at 2 yrs) and 7f winner Try The Chance (by Majestic Missile). The dam is an unraced half-sister to 7 winners including the Group 3 second Easaar. The second dam, Matila (by Persian Bold), a fairly useful 3-y-o 6f winner, is a half-sister to 6 winners. (Al Shaqab Racing). *"A half-sister to two very good horses of ours, she's a real nice filly. You can't help but like her, she's a great mover and is one for the second half of the season over seven furlongs. A really nice filly she is".*

795. ALTARSHEED (IRE) ★★★★
b.c. Lilbourne Lad – Lilakiya (Dr Fong). February 23. Fifth foal. 100,000Y. Tattersalls

October Book 2. Peter & Ross Doyle. Half-sister to the quite useful 2014 2-y-o 7f winner Run The Red Light (by Alfred Nobel), to the very useful 2-y-o 6f and subsequent 10f winner Karam Albaari (by King's Best) and the fair 7f winner Minstrels Gallery (by Refuse To Bend). The dam, a modest 12f winner, is a half-sister to 4 winners including the dual 7f (at 2 yrs) and subsequent German and Italian Group 1 winner Linngari. The second dam, Lidakiya (by Kahyasi), a useful 10f and 12f winner, is a half-sister to 8 winners including the triple listed winner Livadiya. (Hamdan Al Maktoum). *"A lovely, tidy horse, he'll be really nice for the six/seven furlong races. I like him a lot".*

796. AMPLE ★★★
b.c. Arakan – Ambonnay (Ashkalani). March 30. £8,000Y. Doncaster Premier. Peter & Ross Doyle. Half-brother to four placed horses. The dam, a fairly useful 2-y-o 6f winner, is a half-sister to 5 winners including the dual Group 1 winner and sire Dick Turpin. The second dam, Babycham Sparkle (by So Blessed), a quite useful 5f and 6f winner, is a half-sister to 6 winners. (Mrs J Wood). *"We've had a lot of luck with the sire. This colt was cheap and he's no world beater but he is a real good fun horse. He'll win a couple of races alright".* Ample won at Chelmsford on his debut on the 9th April.

797. ANCIENT TRADE (USA) ★★★
b.f. Speightstown – Nafisah (Lahib). May 3. $485,000Y. Keeneland September. Al Shahania Stud. Half-brother to the useful UAE Group 3 1m winner of 5 races Snaafy (by Kingmambo), to the Irish 11.5f and hurdles winner Waaheb (by Elusive Quality) and a minor winner in the USA by Distorted Humor. The dam, a very useful 7f (at 2 yrs), 9f and listed 10f winner, was second in the Group 2 Ribblesdale Stakes and is a half-sister to 8 winners including the Irish 12f listed and hurdles winner Mutakarrim. The second dam, Alyakkh (by Sadler's Wells), a fair 3-y-o 1m winner, is a full or half-sister to 7 winners including the Champion Stakes and 2,000 Guineas winner Haafhd. (Sheikh Khalifa Al Thani). *"A lovely, big horse and a really good mover, he's not done any work yet but he's one that should be out in the middle of the summer over six/seven furlongs".*

798. ANOTHER SANCERRE ★★★
ch.c. Makfi – Mpumalanga (Observatory). February 27. Third foal. 23,000Y. Tattersalls October Book 2. Not sold. Half-brother to the fair 2-y-o 7f winner Tea In Transvaal (by Teofilo). The dam, a 2-y-o winner in France and third in the Group 3 Prix du Calvados, is a half-sister to 4 winners. The second dam, Dimakya (by Dayjur), a fair 7.5f winner in France and placed from 6f (in England) to 10f, is a half-sister to 8 winners including the listed winners Loyalize and Remuria. (David Brown and Andy Lloyd). *"He's sharp and ready to roll now. There's not a lot of him but he could win a couple of races early on".*

799. ANWAR (IRE) ★★★★
gr.f. Dark Angel – Salt Rose (Sleeping Indian). March 26. First foal. 78,000Y. Tattersalls October Book 2. Peter & Ross Doyle. The dam is an unraced half-sister to 8 winners including the Group 3 Prix de Flore winner In Clover (herself dam of the Group 1 winner We Are) and the French listed winners Bayourida and Bellona. The second dam, Bellarida (by Bellypha), won the Group 3 Prix de Royaumont and is a half-sister to 2 winners. (Sheikh J D Al Maktoum). *"She's a lovely filly that jumped into a good one on her debut. She'll improve an awful lot for that, especially as we haven't done a lot with her. She'll be winning soon".*

800. ARIZONA SUNRISE ★★★
b.c. Sakhee's Secret – Phoenix Rising (Dr Fong). March 3. Third foal. 10,000Y. Tattersalls October Book 3. Amanda Skiffington. The dam is an unraced half-sister to 9 winners including the very useful 2-y-o 5f and 6f winner and Cornwallis Stakes second Deadly Nightshade. The second dam, Dead Certain (by Absalom), a very smart winner of the Group 1 6f Cheveley Park Stakes and the Group 2 6.5f Prix Maurice de Gheest, is a half-sister to 7 winners and to the placed dam of the Group 2 Gimcrack Stakes winner Bannister. (Westward Bloodstock). *"He's a really nice colt, ready to run and better than his purchase price would suggest. He could be good enough to win at one of the nicer tracks".* **TRAINERS' BARGAIN BUY**

801. ATLANTIC SUN ★★★
b.c. Roderic O'Connor – Robema (Cadeaux Genereux). February 15. Fourth foal. £52,000Y. Doncaster Premier. Peter & Ross Doyle. The dam, a quite useful 7m and 1m winner, is a sister to the listed-placed winner Granted (the dam of two listed winners) and the US Grade 1 placed winner Lucky Chappy. The second dam, Germane (by Distant Relative), a useful winner of the Group 3 7f Rockfel Stakes and placed in two listed events, is a half-sister to 9 winners including the very useful German dual listed Fabriano. (Middleham Park Racing XLV). *"I liked him a lot and thought he'd be quite early, but he's just gone backwards a bit and he needs time. But he really is nice".*

802. BAG OF DIAMONDS ★★★
b.c. Lilbourne Lad – Milnagavie (Tobougg). March 8. First foal. 30,000Y. Tattersalls October Book 2. Peter & Ross Doyle. The dam, a quite useful 11f and 12f winner, is a half-sister to 5 winners. The second dam, a useful 10.2f winner and third in the Group 2 12.5f Prix de Royallieu, is a half-sister to 8 winners including the dual listed winner Sadlers Wings. (Stables of the Burning Man). *"The biggest Lilbourne Lad we've got, he moves very well and he'll be a nice 2-y-o over seven furlongs".*

803. BAY OF ST MALO (IRE) ★★★★ ♠
b.f. Canford Cliffs – Distant Skies (Tiger Hill). January 9. First foal. 45,000Y. Tattersalls October Book 2. Amanda Skiffington. The dam is an unraced half-sister to 3 winners including the Group1 Middle Park Stakes winner Primo Valentino and the Group 2 Cherry Hinton Stakes winner Dora Carrington. The second dam, Dorothea Brooke (by Dancing Brave), won over 9f and is a half-sister to 7 winners. (Coriolan Partnership). *"I love her to bits – she's a really nice filly and a great mover. The owners will have a lot of fun with her and she looks good enough to win over five furlongs but she may be better over six".*

804. BLACKOUT ★★★★
b.c. Dream Ahead – Belle Masquee (Oratorio). January 17. First foal. €85,000Y. Arqana Deauville August. Peter & Ross Doyle. The dam, a French 10f and 11f winner in France, is a half-sister to 5 winners. The second dam, Secret Wells (by Sadler's Wells), a minor

French 3-y-o winner, is a half-sister to 7 winners including the US Grade 1 winner Atticus. (Martin Hughes & Michael Kerr-Dineen). *"A really nice horse, he's big and strong and we put a crossed noseband on him. We'll give him all the time he needs but he's a really nice individual".*

805. BOURNEMOUTH BELLE ★★★★
b.f. Canford Cliffs – Ellbeedee (Dalakhani). March 14. First foal. 30,000Y. Tattersalls October Book 2. Peter & Ross Doyle. The dam, a fair 10f winner, is a half-sister to 6 winners including the French 2-y-o 1m winner and subsequent US Grade 2 San Clemente Handicap and Grade 2 San Gorgonio Handicap winner Uncharted Haven. The second dam, Tochar Ban (by Assert), a quite useful 10f winner, is a half-sister to 6 winners including the listed Italian winner Isticanna (herself dam of the Group 2 Royal Whip Stakes winner Chancellor). *"She's not the prettiest but she's one of the best movers I've seen. A five/six furlong filly, she's a cracker and she'll definitely win. When they see her in the parade ring people won't back her, but she's some mover".*

806. BOYCIE ★★
b.c. Paco Boy – Eve (Rainbow Quest). March 16. Eighth living foal. 12,000Y. Tattersalls October Book 3. K Ivory. Half-brother to 5 winners including the useful 7f, 11f and 12f winner Charm School (by Dubai Destination), the fairly useful listed-placed 1m winner Admission (by Azamour), the fairly useful 1m and 10f winner Dubai Twilight (by Alhaarth) and the fair 1m and 10f winner Cape Explorer (by Cape Cross). The dam, a quite useful winner of 3 races over 1m, is a half-sister to 7 winners including the listed winners Birdie, Fickle and Faru. The second dam, Fade (by Persepolis), is an unraced half-sister to the multiple Group 3 winner Tom Seymour. (Ken Ivory). *"He's ready to run now. He's sharp and he ought to win a little race".*

807. BREAK FREE ★★★
b.f. Oasis Dream – Penny's Gift (Tobougg). January 22. Second foal. Half-sister to the fair 2014 2-y-o dual 5f winner Dittander (by Exceed And Excel). The dam, a 2-y-o listed 6f and Group 2 1m German 1,000 Guineas

winner, is a sister to one winner and a half-sister to 3 winners. The second dam, Happy Lady (by Cadeaux Genereux), a fair 1m placed maiden, is a half-sister to 4 winners including the smart middle-distance stayer and Group 2 Yorkshire Cup second Rainbow Ways. (Rockcliffe Stud).

808. CACICA ★★★★
b.f. Cacique – Moonlight Mystery (Pivotal). May 3. First foal. 160,000Y. Tattersalls October Book 2. Charlie Gordon-Watson. The dam, a modest 7f winner, is a half-sister to 4 other minor winners. The second dam, Mauri Moon (by Green Desert), won 4 races including the listed Oak Tree Stakes and is a half-sister to 5 winners including the Singapore Derby winner Kimbridge Knight. (Lady Bamford). *"A beautiful filly, she had a bit of an attitude early on but that's improved the more we've done with her. She'll make a mid to late-summer 2-y-o, I really like her and she's got a bit of class. Ought to make a nice filly".*

809. CHARLOTTE ROYALE (IRE) ★★★★ ♠
gr.f. Zoffany – Lady Gray (High Chaparral). January 21. First foal. Goffs Sportsmans. Sackville/Donald. The dam is an unraced half-sister to the 2-y-o Group 3 7f Prestige Stakes winner Sesmen. The second dam, Poetry In Motion (by Ballad Rock), a modest 5f winner at 4 yrs, is a half-sister to 5 winners including the German Group 3 winner and US Grade 3 placed Neshad. (De La Warr Racing). *"She's done well since she came in, she's put on weight and I see her as a six furlong type. She's quite professional".*

810. CIARA'S BEAUTY ★★★
b.f. Aqlaam – Tanasie (Cadeaux Genereux). February 14. Twelfth foal. £10,000Y. Doncaster Premier. Peter & Ross Doyle. Half-sister the fairly useful 2-y-o listed 10f Zetland Stakes second and 3-y-o 9f winner Fiddlers Wood (by Spectrum), to the quite useful 5f and 6f winner of 6 races Doric Lady (by Kyllachy), the UAE 4-y-o winner Jamhoori (by Tiger Hill) and the German winner of 7 races Drax (by Mark Of Esteem). The dam, a French 3-y-o winner, is a full or half-sister to 3 winners including the Group 3 Meld Stakes winner of 7 races Latino Magic. The second dam, Tansy (by Shareef Dancer), a fair 2-y-o 6f winner,

is closely related to the top-class middle-distance colt Most Welcome and the useful middle-distance winner Top Guest and a half-sister to 5 winners. (Emma Ambrose & R Hannon). *"She's done very well since she came in, put on a lot of weight and she'll be aimed at the auction races. She's shown that she's quite sharp, she's ready to roll, wasn't expensive but she'll definitely win".*

811. DANEHILL KODIAC (IRE) ★★★
b.c. Kodiac – Meadow (Green Desert). April 6. Seventh foal. £30,000Y. Doncaster Premier. Sackville/Donald. Half-brother to the fair 2014 Irish 7f placed 2-y-o Mzuri (by Tagula), to the fair 2-y-o 5f and subsequent US winner Scantily Clad, the Italian winner of 5 races Dye Fore (both by Acclamation) and the fair 2-y-o dual 6f winner Reliant Robin (by Moss Vale). The dam, a modest 4-y-o 7f winner in Ireland, is a sister to one winner and a half-sister to 7 winners including the listed Sceptre Stakes winner Medley. The second dam, Marl (by Lycius), a fairly useful 2-y-o 5.2f winner, is a half-sister to 4 winners including the 2-y-o listed 5f National Stakes winner Rowaasi. (Jaber Abdullah). *"I thought he'd be one of our first runners, I like him and he's a great mover, but all of a sudden he's grown. He's just shot up and is very weak looking now. Looking at him he'll not be racing until late May".*

812. DHEBAN (IRE) ★★★★ ♠
gr.c. Exceed And Excel – Comeback Queen (Nayef). February 7. Third foal. 240,000Y. Tattersalls October Book 1. John Warren. Half-brother to the fairly useful Irish 8.5f winner Nonchalant (by Oasis Dream). The dam, a fairly useful 2-y-o 1m winner, was second in the listed Masaka Stakes and is a half-sister to 6 winners including the US Grade 2 and Grade 3 winner Worldly and the listed US 2-y-o Breeders Cup Juvenile Turf winner Donativum. The second dam, Miss Universe (by Warning), a useful 2-y-o 6f winner and third in the Group 3 Solario Stakes, is a half-sister to 5 winners. (Al Shaqab Racing). *"A lovely, very good-moving horse, he's quite forward and should be out fairly early on. He knows his job".*

813. DYLLAN ★★★
b.c. Zebedee – Luvmedo (One Cool Cat). April 2. Second foal. 13,000foal. Goffs November.

Woodstock. Half-brother to the Italian 2-y-o 6f winner and dual listed-placed Pivotal Rio (by Captain Rio). The dam, unplaced in two starts, is a half-sister to 3 winners including the smart 2009 6f Goffs Million Sprint winner Lucky General. The second dam, Dress Code (by Barathea), a quite useful 2-y-o 5f winner, is a sister to the useful 2-y-o Group 3 7f C L Weld Park Stakes winner Rag Top and a half-sister to 6 winners. (Mrs J Wood). *"We trained the mare and she was nuts! This is a strong type and one for six furlongs".*

814. ELTEZAM (IRE) ★★★ ♠
b.c. Kodiac – Tymora (Giant's Causeway). January 18. First foal. 280,000Y. Tattersalls October Book 1. Peter & Ross Doyle. The dam is an unplaced half-sister to 3 minor winners. The second dam, Shiva (by Hector Protector), a high-class winner of the Group 2 10.5f Tattersalls Gold Cup and the Group 3 10f Brigadier Gerard Stakes, is a sister to the high-class Group 2 12f Prix Jean de Chaudenay and Group 3 12f Prix Foy winner Limnos and a half-sister to the Group 1 Oaks winner Light Shift. (Al Shaqab Racing). *"A big colt, a really good sort and a good mover, we won't be in any hurry with him".*

815. FASHAAK (IRE) ★★★★ ♠
b.c. Starspangledbanner – Szabo (Anabaa). January 31. Eighth foal. 260,000Y. Tattersalls October Book 1. Peter & Ross Doyle. Half-brother to 5 winners including the fair 12f, 14f and hurdles winner Teak (by Barathea), to the modest 2-y-o 6f winner Sensational Love (by Cadeaux Genereux) and the Italian 10f winner Fuente Apache (by Hawk Wing). The dam, a fairly useful 7f placed 2-y-o, is a half-sister to the listed winners Edinburgh Knight and Nightbird. The second dam, Pippas Song (by Reference Point), a fair 12f winner, is a half-sister to 8 winners including the Prestige Stakes winner Glatisant (dam of the 2,000 Guineas winner Footstepsinthesand) and the dam of the champion 2-y-o filly Superstar Leo. (Al Shaqab Racing). *"He's a beauty and should be a lot earlier than the other we have by the same sire. He's on the small side and a good mover".*

816. FORGOTTEN WISH (IRE) ★★★
b.f. Lilbourne Lad – Khatela (Shernazar).

March 24. Eleventh living foal. €75,000Y. Goffs Orby. Peter & Ross Doyle. Half-sister to 7 winners including the 2-y-o 7.2f and listed 1m Heron Stakes winner and Group 3 9f Prix de Conde second Massive, the quite useful 2m and hurdles winner Busted Tycoon (both by Marju), the French 12f listed-placed Irish Kind (by Cape Cross), the modest 15f winner Khayar (by Refuse To Bend) and the modest 2-y-o 9f winner Khandala (by Soviet Star). The dam won over 1m and 9f in Ireland and is a half-sister to 4 minor winners. The second dam, Khatima (by Relko), won at 3 yrs and is a half-sister to the French triple listed winner Kaldoun. (Middleham Park Racing). *"A lovely filly for six furlongs in the middle of the season. Goes very well".*

817. GECKO ★★★★
b.c. Zoffany – Chameleon (Green Desert). March 29. Eighth living foal. £120,000Y. Doncaster Premier. Amanda Skiffington. Half-brother to the fairly useful 6f (at 2 yrs) to 14.7f winner of 8 races and listed-placed Merchant Of Dubai (by Dubai Destination), to the fair 6f winner Youhavecontrol (by Hawk Wing) and a hurdles winner by Hawk Wing. The dam, a fair 4-y-o 7f winner, is a sister to the Group 1 6f July Cup winner Owington and a half-sister to 7 winners. The second dam, Old Domesday Book (by High Top), a fairly useful 10.4f winner, was listed-placed over 10f. (Westward Bloodstock). *"He's just started fast work and did surprisingly well considering he's a bit fat at the moment. We like him, he could be an early type and with luck a Norfolk Stakes type".*

818. GITTAN ★★★ ♠
b.c. Kodiac – Apple Dumpling (Haafhd). March 19. First foal. 55,000Y. Tattersalls October Book 2. Tony Nerses. The dam, placed fourth once over 7f, is a half-sister to 7 winners including the listed winner Antediluvian. The second dam, Divina Mia (by Dowsing), a modest 2-y-o 6f winner, stayed 11f and is a half-sister to the dam of the Australian Grade 1 winner Markham. *"Not very big, but he should make a 2-y-o and although he's yet to come in his coat he should make an early type".*

819. GREAT PAGE (IRE) ★★★★★ ♠
b.f. Roderic O'Connor – Areeda (Refuse To Bend). January 16. Second foal. €27,000Y.

Tattersalls Ireland September. Peter & Ross Doyle. The dam, a fair 3-y-o 7f winner, is a half-sister to 8 winners including the fairly useful triple 5f winner and listed-placed Jack Spratt. The second dam, Raindancing (by Tirol), a fairly useful 2-y-o 6f winner, was third in the Group 3 6f Princess Margaret Stakes and is a sister to the smart 7f (at 2 yrs) to 10f winner and Group 1 National Stakes third Mountain Song and a half-sister to 7 winners including the Group 2 Cherry Hinton Stakes winner Please Sing. (Middleham Park Racing LXXVIII). *"I like her a lot and she could be another Tiggy Wiggy. She's built like a colt and she really does go well. All speed, she may well have won before your book is out".*

820. GREENFYRE (IRE) ★★★
b.f. Kodiac – Miss Chaumiere (Selkirk). March 15. First foal. 72,000Y. Tattersalls October Book 3. Peter & Ross Doyle. The dam, a moderate dual 1m placed maiden, is a half-sister to 4 winners including the very useful 1m winner and Australian Group 2 placed Moyenne Corniche. The second dam, Miss Corniche (by Hernando), a 7f (at 2 yrs) and listed 10f winner, is a full or half-sister to 10 winners including the listed 1m winner Miss Riviera Golf. (Mrs J K Powell). *"She goes really well and seems quite sharp, but she's hanging on to her coat and won't be ready for a few weeks".*

821. GUTAIFAN (IRE) ★★★★
gr.c. Dark Angel – Alikhlas (Lahib). April 7. €75,000foal. Goffs November. Pater & Ross Doyle. Half-brother to 6 winners including the fairly useful triple 7f winner (including at 2 yrs) Silk Fan (by Unfuwain), the 1m winner Blasket Spirit (by King's Best) and the 7f winner Anne Tudor (by Anabaa) and the Irish 2-y-o 7f and 1m winner and listed-placed Cest Notre Gris (by Verglas) – all 3 quite useful. The dam, a fair 1m winner, is a half-sister to the listed winner and Group 2 second Sahool and the dam of the dual Group 2 winner Maraahel. The second dam, Mathaayl (by Shadeed), a quite useful 6f and 10f winner, is a half-sister to the Group 3 winner Muhbubh. (Al Shaqab Racing). *"A beautiful horse, very strong and perhaps a bit heavy but he doesn't move like a heavy horse. We really like him, he hasn't done any fast work yet but he'll make a racehorse".*

822. HERMANN ★★★

b.c. Authorized – Alamanni (Elusive Quality). April 8. Fourth foal. 110,000Y. Tattersalls October Book 2. Peter & Ross Doyle. The dam, a winner over 6f and 1m in Italy and second in the Group 3 7f Premio Chiusura, is a half-sister to 6 winners including the Italian Group 3 winner Aynthia. The second dam, Altamura (by El Gran Senor), a dual listed winner, is a half-sister to three stakes winners. (Michael Kerr-Dineen & Martin Hughes). *"A very nice horse. He carries his head a bit high sometimes but that will come down as he matures and grows up. He was a horse bought for a 3-y-o career and I think that's exactly what he'll be, but he might well run as a 2-y-o. If he does I imagine he'll run pretty well because he's got some ability".*

823. HUMPHREY BOGART (IRE) ★★★ ♠

b.c. Tagula – Hazarama (Kahyasi). April 4. Eleventh foal. £33,000Y. Doncaster Premier. Peter & Ross Doyle. Brother to the quite useful 6f (at 2 yrs), 10f and hurdles winner Domino Dancer and half-brother to the fair 10f winner Devote Myself (by Kodiac) and the moderate dual 1m winner Isitcozimcool (by Shinko Forest). The dam won over 13f and is a half-sister to 6 winners including the Group 3 winners Hazariya and Hazarista. The second dam, Hazaradjat (by Darshaan), won twice at 2 and 3 yrs and is a full or half-sister to 10 winners including the Flying Childers and Middle Park Stakes winner Hittite Glory. (Chelsea Thoroughbreds – Saint Tropez). *"A smashing horse that moves very well, he's not dissimilar in looks to Canford Cliffs (also a son of Tagula). A grand horse for the mid-season onwards".*

824. ILLUMINATE (IRE) ★★★

b.f. Zoffany – Queen Of Stars (Green Desert). February 13. Sixth foal. £95,000Y. Doncaster Premier. Peter & Ross Doyle. Half-sister to the fair 5f and 6f winner Rhal (by Rahy) and to a winner in Japan by Singspiel. The dam is an unraced half-sister to the Group 3 1m Premio Dormello winner and Group 1 Italian Oaks third Lady Catherine. The second dam, Queen Catherine (by Machiavellian), a useful French 2-y-o and 3-y-o 1m winner, is a half-sister to 5 winners. (Denford Stud). *" A lovely filly, with a very pretty head, she's only cantered up the*

grass up to now but she could be anything. Probably a six furlong filly".*

825. INLAND SEA (USA) ★★★★

b.c. Scat Daddy – Cat's Eye Witness (Elusive Quality). February 23. Brother to No Nay Never, winner of the 2-y-o Group 1 6f Prix Morny and the Group 2 5f Norfolk Stakes. The dam won over 5.5f at 2 yrs in the USA and is a half-sister to 8 winners in the USA including the Grade 3 winner Cat's Career. The second dam, Comical Cat by Exceller), won 4 races in the USA from 6f to 1m and was Grade 3 placed. (Sheikh Khalifa Al Thani). *"This is a smashing horse. A strong colt that ought to be sharp, he'll hopefully turn into a Royal Ascot 2-y-o".*

826. IN THE RED (IRE) ★★★★

b.c. Elusive Pimpernel – Roses From Ridey (Petorius). March 1. Eleventh foal. £36,000Y. Doncaster Premier. Peter & Ross Doyle. Half-brother to the useful 2-y-o Group 2 6f July Stakes second Armigerent, subsequently a winner abroad, (by In The Wings), to the fair 2-y-o 7f winner Sultans Way (by Indian Ridge) and a winner abroad by Invincible Spirit. The dam is an unplaced half-sister to 6 winners including the German and Italian Group 1 winner Kutub and two listed winners in Ireland. The second dam, Minnie Habit (by Habitat), an Irish 4-y-o 9f winner, is closely related to the dual Group 3 sprint winner Bermuda Classic (dam of the Group 1 winners Shake The Yoke and Tropical). *"A big horse and a strong type for six/seven furlongs. He's nice and we like him a lot".*

827. JAYJINSKI (IRE) ★★★★

gr.c. Zebedee – Prime Time Girl (Primo Dominie). April 10. Eighth foal. 80,000Y. Tattersalls October Book 3. Peter & Ross Doyle. Half-brother to the Italian listed-placed winner of 4 races Tacma (by Baltic King), to the modest Irish 5f to 7.7f winner of 4 races Doorock (by Redback), the moderate 7f winner Cannon Bolt (by Chineur) and the minor Italian winner of 7 races Reprime (by Revoque). The dam ran twice unplaced and is a half-sister to 4 winners including Poker Face (Group 2 Flying Childers Stakes). The second dam, Timely Raise (by Raise A Man), a minor winner of 6 races from 2 to 4 yrs in the USA, is a half-sister to 8 winners. (Amanda Turner, Martin Clarke, Jim Jeffries). *"A smashing horse, he's big for a Zebedee. He hasn't worked yet but he could be anything over any trip".*

828. JET SETTING (IRE) ★★★
b.f. Fast Company – Mean Lae (Johannesburg). February 16. Second foal. €7,000foal. Goffs November. Woodstock. The dam, a fair Irish 7f winner, is a half-sister to one winner. The second dam, Plume Rouge (by Pivotal), a useful 2-y-o 6f and 3-y-o listed 7.5f winner in Ireland, is a half-sister to one winner in Italy. (Mrs J Wood). *"She goes well and ought to make an early 2-y-o. She's quite forward in her coat and will have had a run before your book is out".*

829. KESSELRING ★★★
ch.c. New Approach – Anna Oleanda (Old Vic). April 22. Ninth living foal. 90,000Y. Tattersalls October Book 1. Not sold. Half-brother to 5 winners including the smart 2-y-o Group 3 7f Horris Hill Stakes winner Piping Rock (by Dubawi), the Group 3 Prix d'Astarte winner and Group 2 Oaks d'Italia second Middle Club (by Fantastic Light), the French dual 10.5f winner and Group 3 Prix de Royaumont third Anna Mona (by Monsun) and the German listed-placed Anna Royal (by Royal Dragon). The dam won twice at 3 yrs in Germany and is a sister to the German Group 3 winner Anno Luce and a half-sister to the dams of the Group winners Annus Mirabilis, Anna of Saxony, Annaba and Pozarica. The second dam, Anna Paola (by Prince Ippi), won the Group 2 German Oaks. (R J McCreery). *"A lovely horse, we like him a lot and we had his half-brother Piping Rock here. He's a very good mover and does everything easily but he's one for back-end of the season".*

830. KING OF ROOKS ★★★★
b.c. Acclamation – Slap Shot (Lycius). March 14. Seventh foal. 67,000Y. Tattersalls October Book 2. Peter & Ross Doyle. Half-brother to the fair 2014 7f placed 2-y-o Crack Shot (by Lope De Vega) and to 4 winners including the Italian Group 3 7f winner Sandslash (by Holy Roman Emperor), the quite useful 2-y-o 7f and subsequent German winner and 1m listed-placed Samara Valley (by Dalakhani) and the minor dual Italian winner

at 4 and 5 yrs Fighting Talk (by Shamardal). The dam won 6 races in Italy including the Group 3 Gran Premio Citta di Napoli and was second in the Group 1 5f Prix de l'Abbaye and is a half-sister to 2 winners in Turkey. The second dam, Katanning (by Green Desert), is a placed half-sister to 4 winners abroad. (Jared, Palmer-Brown, R Hannon Snr). *"A nice horse, he's good-looking, well put together and a solid type. He's forward-going as well, so he's one that's on your side. I like him a lot and he could be a Royal Ascot 2-y-o".*

831. LEXINGTON LAW (IRE) ★★★★
b.c. Lawman – Tus Nua (Galileo). February 25. Second foal. 45,000Y. Tattersalls October Book 2. Peter & Ross Doyle. The dam, a winner of two bumper races, is a half-sister to 4 winners. The second dam, Sierva (by Darshaan), was placed at 2 yrs in Germany and is a half-sister to 8 winners. (Middleham Park Racing). *"A lovely horse, he's a standout to look at, hasn't done any work yet but is as nice a Lawman as we've had. A smashing horse, he's likely to want seven furlongs in the second half of the season".*

832. LIGHT INFANTRY (IRE) ★★★
ch.c. Fast Company – Convidada (Trans Island). March 7. First foal. €50,000Y. Goffs Orby. Peter & Ross Doyle. The dam won 3 races at 3 yrs in Spain and is a half-sister to 9 winners in Germany. The second dam, Provacatrice (by Irish River), won at 3 yrs in France and is a half-sister to 7 winners including Gracioso (Group 1 Prix Lupin). (Michael Pescod & Justin Dowley). *"A very nice horse, we had to give him a bit of time off but he'd been showing plenty and we'll have no problem picking him up in the middle of the season".*

833. LOG OUT ISLAND (IRE) ★★★★
b.c. Dark Angel – White Daffodil (Footstepsinthesand). February 18. Second foal. £95,000Y. Doncaster Premier. Peter & Ross Doyle. Brother to the unraced 2014 2-y-o Bushephalus. The dam, a modest 5f (at 2 yrs) and 6f winner, is a half-sister to 5 winners including the dual listed 6f winner (including at 2 yrs) Lady Links (herself dam of the dual listed winner Selinka). The second dam, Sparky's Song (by Electric), a moderate 10.2f and 12f winner, is a half-sister to the

very smart Group 1 6.5f winner Bold Edge and to the listed winner and Group 3 5f Temple Stakes second Brave Edge. (Jared Sullivan & Chris Giles). *"A grand horse with a really likeable attitude and he goes well. He'll be racing in May or early June and might even be a Royal Ascot type. He's got an engine and is one to get excited about".*

834. MANAAFIDH (IRE) ★★★★★
b.c. Zebedee – Starring (Ashkalani). February 19. Eighth foal. €330,000Y. Goffs Orby. Peter & Ross Doyle. Half-brother to the 2-y-o listed 1m winner Letsgoroundagain (by Redback), to the quite useful 7f to 9f winner of 11 races Spinning (by Pivotal), the quite useful 7f to 12f and hurdles winner Goodwood Starlight (by Mtoto), the fair 1m winners Syros (by Kheleyf) and L'Astre De Choisir (by Choisir) and the fair 2-y-o 5f winner Daisy Moses (by Mull Of Kintyre). The dam, placed once at 3 yrs in France, is a half-sister to 5 winners the very smart dual listed 5f winner Watching. The second dam, Sweeping (by Indian King), a useful 2-y-o 6f winner, is a half-sister to 10 winners. (Hamdan Al Maktoum). *"A gorgeous colt with a bit of grey in his tail which is very lucky in this yard. An outstanding looking horse, he appears to go well and to move very well, but he hasn't worked yet. A very nice colt and one to give five stars to".*

835. MANSOOB ★★★
ch.c. Paco Boy – Descriptive (Desert King). May 2. Sixth foal. 280,000Y. Tattersalls October Book 1. Shadwell Estate Co. Half-brother to the useful 2-y-o 6f winner and Group 2 7f Rockfel Stakes third Valonia (by Three Valleys) and to a 2-y-o winner in Norway by Xaar. The dam, a quite useful 2-y-o 6f winner, is a half-sister to 5 winners. The second dam, Ridiya (by Last Tycoon), an Irish 1m and 9f winner, was listed placed over 6f and is a half-sister to 6 winners. (Hamdan Al Maktoum). *"A leggier, bigger type than most of the Paco Boys, he'll be a six/seven furlong 2-y-o".*

836. MARENKO ★★★★
b.f. Exceed And Excel – Safina (Pivotal). March 7. Second foal. Half-sister to the quite useful 2014 2-y-o 6f winner Vesnina (by Sea The Stars). The dam, a fairly useful 7f winner, was listed-placed over 1m and

is a half-sister to one winner. The second dam, Russian Rhythm (by Kingmambo), won the 1,000 Guineas, Coronation Stakes, Nassau Stakes and Lockinge Stakes and is a half-sister to several winners including the 2-y-o Group 2 1m Royal Lodge Stakes winner Perfectperformance. (Cheveley Park Stud). *"A lovely, big, classy filly, she's a good mover and a good looker. One for the middle to back-end of the season".*

837. MAYFAIR MAGIC ★★★
b.f. Dick Turpin – B Berry Brandy (Event Of The Year). April 14. Fifth foal. Half-sister to Holland Park (by More Than Ready), placed third over 7f on his only start at 2 yrs in 2014, to the quite useful 2-y-o dual 7f winner Cricklewood Green (by Bob And John) and two minor winners in the USA by Forest Wildcat and Point Given. The dam is an unplaced half-sister to 3 winners including the triple Group 2 winner and Group 1 placed Strong Suit. The second dam, Helwa (by Silver Hawk), is an unraced sister to the 2-y-o listed 1m winner Silver Colours and a half-sister to 4 winners including the Japanese Grade 2 winner God Of Chance. *"She was tricky to begin with, but we persevered with her and now she's turned herself inside out. Everything must have been happening too quickly for her. I like her a lot, she could be anything but she might want seven furlongs".*

838. MERMAID ★★★
b.c. Kodiac – Ma Vie En Rose (Red Ransom). April 9. Third foal. £8,000Y. Doncaster Premier. Peter &Ross Doyle. Half-brother to the moderate 2014 5f placed 2-y-o Boann (by Vale Of York). The dam, a moderate dual 6f placed 3-y-o, is a half-sister to four winners. The second dam, Stop Out (by Rudimentary), a fairly useful listed-placed 2-y-o 5f winner, is a half-sister to several winners including the multiple Group winner from 6f to 1m Firebreak. (Mrs J Wood). *"A nice filly and an early type, she just needs to come in her coat a bit but she'll be a five/six furlong 2-y-o".*

839. NEW FOREST ★★★
b.c. Iffraaj – Through The Forest (Forestry). February 2. Second foal. 120,000Y. Tattersalls October Book 2. Peter & Ross Doyle. Half-brother to the modest 2-y-o 5f winner

Bountiful Girl (by Bahamian Bounty). The dam, a moderate 11f winner, is a half-sister to 2 winners including the minor US stakes winner Dattts Our Girl. The second dam, Lakefront (by Deputy Minister), is an unraced half-sister to 5 winners including the US listed winner Sluice (herself dam of the US Grade 1 winner Mushka). (S Suhail). *"A good sort for the latter part of the season"*.

840. NISSER ★★★★
b.c. Dream Ahead – Poppy Seed (Bold Edge). February 28. First foal. £130,000Y. Doncaster Premier. Tony Nerses. The dam won 3 races over 6f at 3 and 4 yrs and was listed-placed and is a half-sister to 4 winners. The second dam, Opopmil (by Pips Pride), was placed twice at 2 yrs and is a sister to the Group 1 6f Haydock Park Sprint Cup winner Pipalong and a half-sister to 12 winners including the 2-y-o 6f listed winner Out Of Africa. (Saleh Al Homaizi & Imad Al Sagar). *"He goes very well and hopefully he's one we'll be taking to Royal Ascot because we like him a lot. A beautiful horse, he was a standout at the sales and I like him a lot".*

841. OH THIS IS US (IRE) ★★★★ ♠
b.c. Acclamation – Shamwari Lodge (Hawk Wing). March 12. Second foal. €110,000Y. Goffs Orby. Peter & Ross Doyle. The dam, a very useful 6f (including at 2 yrs) and Irish Group 3 1m winner of 6 races, is a half-sister to 3 winners including the listed Tetrarch Stakes winner Imperial Rome. The second dam, Ripalong (by Revoque), is an unplaced half-sister to 13 winners including the Group 1 6f Haydock Park Sprint Cup and Group 3 5f Palace House Stakes winner Pipalong. (Team Wallop). *"Out of a mare we trained who was very good, this colt sometimes just holds his head a bit high, but he goes well. A typical Acclamation , he pleases and does everything on the bridle".*

842. ORVAR (IRE) ★★★ ♠
b.c. Dandy Man – Roskeen (Grand Lodge). March 5. Sixth foal. £60,000Y. Doncaster Premier. Tony Nerses. Half-brother to the modest 7f winners Great Crested (by Clodovil) and Zahr Alyasmeen (by Iffraaj). The dam is an unraced half-sister to 5 winners including the dam of the Group 2 Gimcrack Stakes winner

Shaweel and to the unraced dam of the dual Group 1 winner Samitar and the Group 3 Albany Stakes winner Nijoom Dubai. The second dam, Joyful (by Green Desert), a fair 7f winner at 3 yrs, is a half-sister to 7 winners including Golden Opinion (Group 1 1m Coronation Stakes). (Saleh Al Homaizi & Imad Al Sagar). *"An early type, he hasn't done any fast work yet but he's been finding everything pretty easy".*

843. OUT OF THE DARK (IRE) ★★★
b.f. Kyllachy – Assumption (Beckett). February 20. Fourth foal. 72,000Y. Tattersalls October Book 1. Peter & Ross Doyle. Half-sister to the German 3-y-o 7f and 1m winner Elaysa and to the moderate 7f winner Quan (both by Shamardal). The dam, a 7f seller winner at 3 yrs, is a half-sister to 3 winners including the Group 1 Golden Jubilee Stakes and Group 1 Nunthorpe Stakes winner Kingsgate Native. The second dam, Native Force (by Indian Ridge), a quite useful 1m winner, is a half-sister to 2 winners. (Mrs Boocock, Mrs Doyle, Mr Barry). *"A really nice Kyllachy filly for when the six furlong races start".*

844. PALENVILLE (IRE) ★★★
ch.f. Rip Van Winkle – Faithful Duchess (Bachelor Duke). April 21. Second foal. €22,000foal. Goffs November. Woodstock. The dam, a moderate 5f and 6f placed maiden, is a half-sister to 7 winners including the very smart 2-y-o Group 2 7f Champagne Stakes winner Etlaala. The second dam, Portelet (by Night Shift), a fairly useful 5f winner of 4 races, is a half-sister to 4 winners. (Mrs J Wood). *"A nice filly, she hasn't come in her coat yet and we'll take our time with her".*

845. PAPA LUIGI (IRE) ★★★
b.c. Zoffany – Namaadhej (Swain). April 18. First foal. €85,000Y. Goffs Orby. Peter & Ross Doyle. The dam, placed at 3 yrs in France, is a half-sister to the 2-y-o Group 3 1m Prix Thomas Bryon winner Makaan and the French listed 12f winner and Group 3 third Almail. The second dam, Khassah (by Green Desert), a very useful 2-y-o 6f and 1m winner, was second in the Group 1 Fillies' Mile and is a half-sister to 6 winners. (Middleham Park Racing XLVIII). *"One for the middle of the*

season, but he's a lovely colt and a great mover. The Zoffany's could be alright I think".

846. PARIS PROTOCOL ★★★★
b.c. Champs Elysees – Island Vista (Montjeu). March 14. Second foal. 55,000Y. Tattersalls October Book 2. Peter & Ross Doyle. The dam, a quite useful 10f winner, is a half-sister to 7 winners including the Group 1 Racing Post Trophy second Mudeer. The second dam, Colorvista (by Shirley Heights), is an unraced half-sister to 9 winners including Colorspin (Irish Oaks winner and dam of the Group 1 winners Zee Zee Top, Opera House and Kayf Tara), Bella Colora (Prix de l'Opera winner and dam of the very smart colt Stagecraft) and the Irish Champion Stakes winner Cezanne. (Macdonald, Wright, Creed, Jiggins, Miller). *"His pedigree suggests he wants time but he's showing a lot now. Ideally he'd want six and then seven furlongs".*

847. PERFORMER ★★★
b.f. New Approach – Annalina (Cozzene). March 23. Fifth foal. Half-sister to the fairly useful 2014 2-y-o 6f winner Dr No (by Aussie Rules), to the quite useful 12f winners Hepworth (by Singspiel) and Sagamore (by Azamour), the quite useful 10f and 11.5f winner Portrait (by Peintre Celebre) and the Japanese Group 3 placed Kyoei Basara (by Aussie Rules). The dam is an unraced half-sister to 4 winners including the US Grade 2 Long Island Handicap winner Olaya. The second dam, Solaia (by Miswaki), won the listed Cheshire Oaks and was second in the Group 3 Lancashire Oaks and is a half-sister to 3 winners. (Denford Stud). *"A good type and a very strong filly with plenty of bone, she's one for the middle to back end of the season".*

848. POLDARK ★★
b.c. Rip Van Winkle – Maybe I Will (Hawk Wing). April 10. Third foal. 11,000Y. Doncaster Premier. Peter & Ross Doyle. The dam, a fair 7f (at 2 yrs) to 10f winner of 4 races, is a half-sister to the Group 1 1m Matron Stakes and Group 2 7f Lennox Stakes winner Chachamaidee and to the Group 3 7f Oak Tree Stakes winner J Wonder. The second dam, Canterbury Lace (by Danehill), is an unraced sister to the Group 3 Gallinule Stakes winner and Irish Derby second Alexander Of Hales

and to the Irish 2-y-o 1m winner and Group 1 1m Criterium International second Chevalier and a half-sister to the 1,000 Guineas winner Virginia Waters. (Mrs J Wood). *"He goes OK but he's small and needs to grow. His pedigree would suggest seven furlongs this year".*

849. PREMIER CURRENCY (IRE) ★★★★ ♠
b.c. Elusive Pimpernel – Zeena (Unfuwain). March 30. Second foal. £26,000Y. Doncaster Premier. Peter & Ross Doyle. The dam, a modest 10f placed maiden, is a half-sister to 4 winners including the Hong Kong Group 1 10f and UAE Group 1 9f winner Presvis. The second dam, Forest Fire (by Never So Bold), a quite useful 1m to 12f winner of 4 races, is a half-sister to 4 minor winners here and abroad. (Mr W P Drew). *"We like both our Elusive Pimpernels, although their attitude might be a problem. They're both grand horses though and if you looked at them you'd buy them. I think this colt is even better than the other one".*

850. PRESS GANG ★★★
b.c. Mount Nelson – Rutba (Act One). February 5. Second foal. £60,000Y. Doncaster Premier. Amanda Skiffington. The dam, a modest 14f to 17f winner, is a half-sister to 4 winners including the dual listed winner Alfie Flits. The second dam, Elhilmeya (by Unfuwain), a listed-placed 11f winner, is a half-sister to 4 winners. (Michael Pescod). *"He's well put together, real sharp and one for five/six furlongs. One of the early types".*

851. RECEDING WAVES ★★★
b.c. Dick Turpin – Welanga (Dansili). April 12. Fourth foal. 22,000Y. Tattersalls October Book 3. Charlie Gordon-Watson. Half-brother to the fair 2-y-o 5f winner Chasing Dreams (by Pastoral Pursuits). The dam is an unraced half-sister to 8 winners including the listed 1m and subsequent US Grade 3 8.5f winner Out Of Reach and the 2-y-o 6f winner and Group 3 Cherry Hinton Stakes third Well Warned (herself the dam of three listed winners) and a half-sister to 4 winners. The second dam, Well Beyond (by Don't Forget Me), a 2-y-o 5f and 3-y-o listed 1m October Stakes winner, is a half-sister to 3 winners. (Michael Cohen & Michael Daffney). *"A grand little horse, he's tough, not over-big*

and we'll get him out later on. A little warrior, he's a sound sort of horse we can run plenty of times and he may not be a star but I like his attitude. I've got a share in him myself and he's a likeable horse".

852. RING OF TRUTH ★★★★
b.f. Royal Applause – Spinning Top (Alzao). April 27. Sister to the useful listed 6f winner of 4 races Musical Comedy and half-sister to 5 winners including the quite useful 2014 2-y-o 5.5f winner Kinematic (by Kyllachy), the fairly useful 7f and 1m winner of 4 races (including at 2 yrs) Humdrum (by Dr Fong) and the fairly useful 7f (at 2 yrs) to 12f winner of 7 races Full Toss (by Nayef). The dam, a useful 10f winner, is a half-sister to numerous winners including the fairly useful 3-y-o 7f and subsequent US dual 9f winner Daytime. The second dam, Zenith (by Shirley Heights), was a fairly useful 2-y-o 8.5f winner. (The Queen). *"She shows loads of speed, everyone who rides her likes her and although it's early days you could be forgiven for thinking she's a possible Queen Mary filly".* She looked a certain future winner when second on her debut in a 2-y-o five furlong Newbury maiden on the 17th April.

853. RISING SUNSHINE ★★★
b.c. Dark Angel – Little Audio (Shamardal). March 26. First foal. €240,000Y. Goffs Orby. Peter & Ross Doyle. The dam is an unraced half-sister to 3 winners including the smart 2-y-o dual listed winner Big Audio. The second dam, Tarbela (by Grand Lodge), a moderate 7f placed 2-y-o in Ireland, is a half-sister to 3 winners and to the dams of the Group 1 winners Arcano and Gilt Edge Girl. (Middleham Park Racing LXXXVIII). *"A nice, sharp, 2-y-o type. He ought to go well, we haven't done much with him yet but we'll get going with him when the weather picks up".*

854. SCOTTISH COMMAND ★★★
b.c. Kyllachy – Angel Song (Dansili). February 28. Second foal. 50,000Y. Tattersalls October Book 2. Highflyer/Shefford Bloodstock. The dam, a fair 6f winner, is a half-sister to 7 winners including the useful Group 3 5f Prix de Saint-Georges and triple sprint listed winner Mood Music. The second dam, Something Blue (by Petong), is an unplaced sister to one winner and a half-

sister to 5 winners including the dam of the smart sprinters Astonished and Bishops Court. (Henry Ponsonby). *"A lovely horse, he'll hopefully be ready when the six furlong races start. There may well be shares still available in him and you could do worse"*

855. SEE YOU WHEN (IRE) ★★★
b.c. Acclamation – Lighthouse (Warning). February 27. Ninth foal. 70,000Y. Tattersalls October Book 2. Peter & Ross Doyle. Half-sister to 6 winners including the very useful 7f and 1m winner Kehaar, the fairly useful 2-y-o 5f winner and listed placed All For Laura (herself dam of the Group 2 Cherry Hinton Stakes winner Misheer), the fair 6f (at 2 yrs) and 1m winner Present Danger (all by Cadeaux Genereux) and the quite useful 10f to 12f winner Point Of Light (by Pivotal). The dam, a fairly useful 8.3f winner, is a half-sister to the Group 1 Middle Park Stakes, Group 3 July Stakes and Group 3 Richmond Stakes winner First Trump. The second dam, Valika (by Valiyar), was placed from 1m to 12f and is a half-sister to the high-class sprinter Mr Brooks. (J Palmer-Brown, Jared, R Hannon). *"A good-moving horse, not particularly big for an Acclamation, but he's a horse we quite like".*

856. SHAWAAHID (IRE) ★★★
b.c. Elnadim – Vexacious (Shamardal). April 20. First foal. 100,000Y. Tattersalls October Book 2. Peter & Ross Doyle. The dam is an unraced half-sister to the very useful Irish Group 2 9f and Group 3 9.5f winner Mango Diva. The second dam, Mango Mischief (by Desert King), a Group 3 10f Daffodil Stakes winner of 5 races, is a half-sister to 4 winners including the useful 2-y-o 6f and 7f and subsequent US Grade 3 winner Eurolink Raindance. (Hamdan Al Maktoum). *"A lovely, big strong horse and one for the middle of the season, he'll be a six/seven furlong 2-y-o".*

857. SKEAPING ★★★
b.c. Excellent Art – Gale Green (Galileo). January 25. First foal. 24,000Y. Tattersalls October Book 3. Howson/Houldsworth Bloodstock. The dam, a fair 10f winner, is a half-sister to 7 winners including the dam of the French 2-y-o Group 2 winner Smooth Operator. The second dam, Anna Of Brunswick (by Rainbow Quest), a fair 3-y-o 10f winner,

is a half-sister to 5 winners including the German Group 3 winner Anno Luce to the dams of the Group winners Annus Mirabilis, Anna of Saxony, Annaba, Piping Rock and Pozarica. (Pall Mall Partners). *"I love him, he's done a couple of bits of work and done well, but I'd say he'd need six furlongs starting off. A smashing horse with a big white face".*

858. SNAN (IRE) ★★★
b.c. High Chaparral – Slow Sand (Dixieland Band). March 28. Fourth foal. Half-brother to the very useful 2-y-o 6f winner and listed second Dorothy B (by Fastnet Rock) and to the quite useful 10f winner Northern Star (by Montjeu). The dam ran twice unplaced and is a half-sister to 5 winners including the French listed winner and Group 2 second Slow Pace. The second dam, Slow Down (by Seattle Slew), a winner in France and a listed winner in the USA, is a half-sister to 7 winners including the US dual Grade 3 winner Olmodavor. (Al Shaqab Racing). *"I like him a lot. He didn't look the best when he came in but he's turned the corner and started to do well. I think he's a nice horse".*

859. SPATCHCOCK ★★★★
b.c. Dutch Art – Lady Hen (Efisio). April 26. Fifth foal. 78,000Y. Tattersalls October Book 2. Peter & Ross Doyle. Brother to Arthenus, unplaced in one start at 2 yrs in 2014 and half-brother to 2 minor winners in Qatar and the USA by Singspiel. The dam, a modest 8.5f winner, is a half-sister to 3 winners including the Group 3 10.5f Prix Fille de l'Air winner Antioquia. The second dam, Royale Rose (by Bering), a fair 1m winner at 3 yrs, is a half-sister to 2 winners including the French listed winner Rouen. (M Hughes. D Anderson, R Morecombe). *"A Dutch Art colt, I really like him, he's a small, racy, neat horse and we'll get going early with him. He's a horse that should certainly make a 2-y-o".*

860. SPIRITED GIRL (IRE) ★★★★
b.f. Invincible Spirit – Albarouche (Sadler's Wells). February 1. Third foal. 100,000Y. Tattersalls October Book 1. Not sold. The dam, a quite useful 10f winner, is a sister to the listed winner and Derby second Dragon Dancer and a half-sister to 3 winners. The second dam, Alakananda (by Hernando), a

fairly useful dual middle-distance winner, is a sister to one winner and a half-sister to 7 winners including the dual Champion Stakes winner Alborada and the triple German Group 1 winner Albanova. (Mrs B S Facchino). *"A nice, big filly, she moves well. A mid-season type 2-y-o with a touch of class and a lot of scope".*

861. SPONGY ★★★★
b.c. Zoffany – Eminence Gift (Cadeaux Genereux). February 10. Fourth foal. £35,000Y. Doncaster Premier. Peter & Ross Doyle. The dam, a moderate dual 10f winner is a sister to the listed-placed 1m and 8.3f winner and smart broodmare Granted and a half-sister to 4 winners including the Italian listed winner Lucky Chappy. The second dam, Germane (by Distant Relative), a useful winner of the Group 3 7f Rockfel Stakes and placed in two listed events, is a half-sister to 9 winners including the very useful German 10f winner Fabriano. (Middleham Park Racing). *"I like this colt, he goes well and he's very nice, but he's getting bored with what he's doing and getting cheeky. So we could do with getting him out soon to give him something else to think about. Could be a Royal Ascot type".*

862. STEEL OF MADRID (IRE) ★★★★ ♠
b.c. Lope De Vega – Bibury (Royal Applause). April 6. Second foal. 120,000Y. Tattersalls October Book 2. Peter & Ross Doyle. The dam, a fair 7f winner, is a half-sister to the Group 1 Ascot Gold Cup winner Rite Of Passage. The second dam, Dahlia's Krissy (by Kris S), a listed-placed winner of 5 races in the USA, is a half-sister to 5 winners. (Michael Pescod). *"He hasn't come in his coat yet but he's a really good goer. Really nice, I like him a lot. One for seven furlongs this year".*

863. STROKE OF MIDNIGHT (IRE) ★★★ ♠
br.f. Dark Angel – Timbre (Dubai Destination). January 29. First foal. €45,000Y. Tattersalls Ireland September. Kern/Lillingston. The dam is an unraced half-sister to 5 winners including the 2-y-o listed Chesham Stakes winner Champlain. The second dam, Calando (by Storm Cat), won the Group 3 1m May Hill Stakes, was second in the Group 1 Fillies Mile and third in the French 1,000 Guineas and is a half-sister to 3 winners. (Kennet Valley Thoroughbreds). *"A nice filly, she was a little bit*

weak when she came in but she's really done well and she's switched on. She's not come in her coat yet, but she's one we quite like".

864. SUNSET DREAM (IRE) ★★★★ ♠
b.f. Acclamation – Oasis Sunset (Oasis Dream). April 10. Third foal. 130,000Y. Tattersalls October Book 2. Peter & Ross Doyle. The dam, a fair 7f winner at 2 yrs, is a half-sister to 5 winners including the 2-y-o Group 1 6f Cheveley Park Stakes winner Seazun. The second dam, Sunset Cafe (by Red Sunset), a minor Irish 12f winner, is a sister to the Group 3 Prix Foy winner Beeshi and a half-sister to 8 winners including the John Smiths Magnet Cup winner Chaumiere. "A very pretty filly and a good-moving 2-y-o with a bit of class. Not necessarily an early type, but smart".

865. TABARRAK (IRE) ★★★★ ♠
b.c. Acclamation – Bahati (Intikhab). January 22. First foal. £180,000Y. Doncaster Premier. Peter & Ross Doyle. The dam, a quite useful 2-y-o 6f winner, is a half-sister to 8 winners including the Irish 7f (at 2 yrs) to 10f and subsequent Hong Kong stakes winner Solid Approach, the useful Irish 7f winner and listed-placed Dangle and the useful 5f to 7f winner of 6 races Zero Money. The second dam, Dawn Chorus (by Mukaddamah), is an unraced half-sister to 7 winners. (Hamdan Al Maktoum). "He's one of the best looking 2-y-o's we've got. Hopefully he's as good as he looks and he'll turn into a classy 2-y-o".

866. TAQWAA (IRE) ★★★★ ♠
ch.c. Iffraaj – Hallowed Park (Barathea). March 19. Third living foal. 140,000Y. Tattersalls October Book 2. Peter & Ross Doyle. Half-brother to the quite useful 9f and 10f winner Stetchworth (by New Approach) and to the fair 7f winner (including at 2 yrs) and 6f winner Shamrocked (by Rock Of Gibraltar). The dam is an unraced half-sister to 5 winners including the Derby second Walk In The Park and the listed winner Soon. The second dam, Classic Park (by Robellino), won 3 races including the Irish 1,000 Guineas and is a half-sister to 10 winners including the US Grade 2 winner Rumpipumpy. (Hamdan Al Maktoum). "A lovely, big, tall horse, he's a nice sort for the middle of the season onwards".

867. TARAABUT (IRE) ★★★★
b.c. Lilbourne Lad – Cuilaphuca (Danetime). March 31. Fourth foal. £130,000Y. Doncaster Premier. Peter & Ross Doyle. Half-brother to the quite useful 1m winner Cameo Tiara (by High Chaparral) and to the moderate 1m winner Brady's Hill (by Alhaarth). The dam, a fairly useful Irish 6f and 7f winner, was listed-placed and is a half-sister to 6 winners including the listed winner and useful broodmare Soreze. The second dam, Run Bonnie (by Runnett), won over 6f in Ireland at 3 yrs and is a half-sister to 4 winners. (Hamdan Al Maktoum). "A smashing horse, he's fine, big and strong. He has a very mature head on him, he was a standout individual at the sales and these Lilbourne Lad's appear to go very well. He won't let the side down".

868. TASKEEN (IRE) ★★★
b.c. Lilbourne Lad – Lola Rosa (Peintre Celebre). February 21. Second living foal. 140,000Y. Tattersalls October Book 2. Peter & Ross Doyle. The dam is an unraced half-sister to 2 minor winners abroad. The second dam, Snow Polina (by Trempolino), won 10 races including the Grade 1 Beverly D Stakes and is a half-sister to 2 winners. (Hamdan Al Maktoum). "A lovely, big horse, a good mover and a nice sort".

869. TELEGRAM ★★★
b.c. Dream Ahead – Miss Chaussini (Rossini). February 24. Fifth foal. 42,000Y. Tattersalls December. Peter & Ross Doyle. Half-brother to the fairly useful dual 7f (at 2 yrs) to 10f winner Strictly Silver (by Dalakhani), to the fairly useful 2-y-o 5f winner Muir Lodge (by Exceed And Excel), the fair 7f (at 2 yrs) to 10f winner Coincidentally (by Acclamation) and the fair 6f winner Chaussini (by Dubawi). The dam, a fair Irish 3-y-o 7f winner, is a half-sister to 9 winners. The second dam, Chaussons Roses (by Lyphard), is an unraced half-sister to the French dual Group 3 winner Tenue De Soiree and a half-sister to the triple Group 1 winner Baiser Vole and the dual Group 2 winner Squill. (Mr M S Al Shahi). "He's quite forward for a Dream Ahead. We like him and he hasn't done much work yet, but he's sure to make a 2-y-o".

870. TERRAPLANE (IRE) ★★★

b.f. Bushranger – Sheer Glamour (Peintre Celebre). March 13. Tenth foal. €15,000Y. Goffs Orby. Peter & Ross Doyle. Half-sister to the quite useful 10f winner Dame Lucy (by Refuse To Bend). The dam was placed over 12.5f in Ireland and is a half-sister to 4 winners including the listed 6f winner Coney Kitty. The second dam, Auntie Maureen (by Roi Danzig), a fair Irish 9f and 10f winner, is a half-sister to 3 minor winners. (Justin Dowley & Michael Pescod). *"A lovely filly by a sire who isn't particularly fashionable, but she was lovely when we bought her and she's done nothing wrong. She'll be a nice, early type of 2-y-o and she gets in the auction races off a low weight. By any other sire she'd have made 50 Grand".* ***TRAINERS' BARGAIN BUY***

871. TOLEDO ★★★★

b.c. Exceed And Excel – Alovera (King's Best). March 21. Fifth foal. Half-brother to the quite useful 2014 2-y-o 6f winner Typhoon Season, to the fair 1m winner Erodium (both by Kyllachy), the quite useful 2-y-o 6f winner Corncockle (by Invincible Spirit) and the fair 2-y-o 5f winner Balm (by Oasis Dream). The dam, a fairly useful 2-y-o 6f winner, is a sister to the smart 6f (at 2 yrs) and listed 8.3f winner Army Of Angels and a half-sister to numerous winners including the useful 2-y-o 6f winner and Group 2 Lowther Stakes second Seraphina. The second dam, Angelic Sounds (by The Noble Player), a minor 2-y-o 5f winner, is a half-sister to 7 winners including the Group 1 Prix de la Foret winner Mount Abu. (Rockcliffe Stud). *"He goes well. A nice, tidy 2-y-o, he'll be one of the earlier ones. A good-moving colt".*

872. TORMENT ★★★★ ♠

bl/gr.c. Dark Angel – Selkirk Sky (Selkirk). March 9. Fifth foal. 160,000Y. Tattersalls October Book 1. John Warren. Half-brother to the fair 2014 2-y-o 5f winner Flicka's Boy (by Paco Boy) and to the Scandinavian winner Mr Fong (by Dr Fong). The dam, a moderate 7f winner, is a half-sister to 3 winners including the triple listed winner and Group 2 6f Gimcrack Stakes second Andronikos. The second dam, Arctic Air (by Polar Falcon), a quite useful 2-y-o 7f winner, is a sister to the useful listed 7f winner Arctic Char and a half-sister to 6 winners including the Group 2 winners Barrow Creek and Last Resort and the dam of the Group 2 winner Trans Island. (Highclere Thoroughbred Racing, Palmerston). *"A smashing horse, a little bit heavy but he doesn't move like that and he's been a dream so far. The sort of horse we can't wait to do some work with".*

873. TORCH ★★★

b.c. Paco Boy – Singed (Zamindar). March 27. Ninth foal. 55,000Y. Tattersalls October Book 2. John Warren. Half-brother to the useful 2-y-o dual 1m and subsequent Hong Kong stakes winner and Group 2 1m Royal Lodge Stakes third On Our Way (by Oasis Dream) and to the quite useful 10f and 11f winner On Her Way (by Medicean). The dam won once at around 1m in France and is a half-sister to the French listed winner and Group 3 placed Inhabitant. The second dam, Infringe (by Warning), won once at 3 yrs in France and is a half-sister to 7 winners including the Group 3 winners Ecologist, Green Reef and Infrasonic. (Highclere Thoroughbred Racing). *"One of the taller Paco Boy 2-y-o's, he's a nice type and a good mover but one for the second half of the season".*

874. VENTURA FALCON (IRE) ★★★

b.f. Excellent Art – Danish Gem (Danehill). March 14. Ninth foal. €115,000Y. Goffs Orby. Peter & Ross Doyle. Half-sister to the very useful triple listed 6f winner Artistic Jewel (by Excellent Art), to the fairly useful 5f and 6f (at 2 yrs) and listed 1m winner Ponty Rossa (by Distant Music), the fair dual 6f winner Jimmy The Poacher (by Verglas), the modest dual 9f winner Midnight Strider (by Golan) and a winner in Greece by Marju. The dam, a 1m winner at 3 yrs in France, is a half-sister to 6 winners. The second dam, Gemaasheh (by Habitat), is an unraced half-sister to 5 winners. (Middleham Park Racing Ll). *"I like her quite a bit, but she's a big filly and definitely needs a bit of time. Probably one for six or seven furlongs, we won't be in a hurry with her but she's nice".*

875. WALL OF FIRE ★★★ ♠

b.c. Canford Cliffs – Bright Sapphire (Galileo). January 19. First foal. 270,000Y. Tattersalls October Book 1. Amanda Skiffington. The dam ran twice unplaced and is a half-sister to 2 minor winners. The second dam, Jewel In The Sand (by Bluebird), a winner of 4 races including the Group 2 6f Cherry Hinton Stakes and the listed Albany Stakes, is a half-sister to 4 winners including the German 3-y-o listed 6f winner Davignon. (Westward Bloodstock). *"A nice horse, he hasn't done any work yet but he ought to make a classy mid-season type 2-y-o, starting at six furlongs. He looks sharp but I don't think he is and he'll benefit with a bit of time".*

876. WAR WHISPER (IRE) ★★★★
b.c. Royal Applause – Featherweight (Fantastic Light). February 19. Second foal. €115,000Y. Goffs Orby. Peter & Ross Doyle. The dam, a quite useful dual 10f winner, is a half-sister to 7 winners including the fairly useful 1m (listed) and 9f winner of 4 races at 4 yrs Wagtail. The second dam, Dancing Feather (by Suave Dancer), a fair 4-y-o 1m winner, is a half-sister to 8 winners including the Group 3 Prix Cleopatre winner Spring Oak and the 10f Lupe Stakes winner Fragrant Hill (herself dam of the French Group 1 winners Alpine Rose and Fragrant Mix). (Mr M Daniels). *"A nice big colt, he goes well, we like him and he could be a Royal Ascot 2-y-o".*

877. WEDGE (IRE) ★★★★
ch.c. Zebedee – Jalmira (Danehill Dancer). April 28. First foal. 62,000Y. Tattersalls October Book 2. Peter & Ross Doyle. The dam, a very useful winner of 9 races from 1m to 9.5f including three listed events, is a half-sister to one winner. The second dam, Jadini (by Darshaan), is an unraced half-sister to 3 minor winners. (R Morecombe, D Anderson, M Hughes). *"He's working well, not very big and should be an early type. Hopefully he'll turn into a Royal Ascot sort".*

878. WHITECLIFF PARK ★★★★
b.c. Canford Cliffs – Venetian Rhapsody (Galileo). March 20. Third foal. 62,000Y. Tattersalls October Book 2. Peter & Ross Doyle. The dam, a minor winner at 3 yrs in France, is a half-sister to 3 minor winners in France and the Czech Republic. The second dam, Paldouna (by Kaldoun), a winner and listed-placed three times in France, is a half-sister to 8 winners. (Mr H R Heffer). *"One of the nicest*

Canford Cliffs we have. He was a standout at the sales and is physically a very nice horse, quite tall, well-built and a solid type. He's continued like that as we've trained him, he's a great mover and a real, lovely 2-y-o for six/seven furlongs".*

879. WILEY POST ★★★
b.c. Kyllachy – Orange Pip (Bold Edge). April 7. Third foal. Half-brother to the modest 2014 dual 5f placed 2-y-o Pacngo (by Paco Boy). The dam, a fair dual 6f winner, is a full or half-sister to 4 winners including the triple 6f winner and listed-placed Poppy Seed. The second dam, Opopmil (by Pips Pride), was placed twice at 2 yrs and is a sister to the Group 1 6f Haydock Park Sprint Cup winner Pipalong and a half-sister to 10 winners including the 2-y-o 6f listed winner Out Of Africa. (Lady Whent). *"He's a nice, tough, hardy little horse. He's no world beater but he'll definitely win a little race in the right place. Quite nice".*

880. WINDSWEPT ★★★★
b.c. Pivotal – Westerly Air (Gone West). April 1. Fourth foal. Half-brother to the fair 7f winner (on her only start at 2 yrs) Floodlit (by Fantastic Light). The dam, a fair 9.3f winner, is a half-sister to 4 winners including the Grade 2 Long Island Handicap, the Group 3 May Hill Stakes and Group 3 Prestige Stakes winner Midnight Line. The second dam, Midnight Air (by Green Dancer), won the Group 3 1m May Hill Stakes at 2 yrs and is a half-sister to 5 minor winners and to the dam of the Group 1 5f Prix de l'Abbaye winner Imperial Beauty. (Cheveley Park Stud). *"A lovely big filly with a bit of class. She'll take a bit of time but she has a good attitude and is a nice filly".*

881. ZEBADIAH (IRE) ★★★★ ♠
b.c. Zebedee – Kiva (Indian Ridge). May 9. Tenth foal. £140,000Y. Doncaster Premier. Amanda Skiffington. Half-brother to 6 winners including the quite useful dual 5f winner (including at 2 yrs) Annie Beach (by Redback), the fair 6f (at 2 yrs) and 5f winner of 9 races Cruise Tothelimit (by Le Vie Dei Colori), the fair 2-y-o 7f winner Cornish Rose (by Kheleyf), the modest 6f winner Red Gift (by Chineur) and the minor Italian 2-y-o winner Andouille (by Moss Vale). The dam is an unraced half-

sister to 5 winners. The second dam, Hagwah (by Dancing Brave), a multiple listed winner from 1m to 12f, is a half-sister to the 2-y-o listed 1m and subsequent US Grade 1 winner Sarafan. (Westward Bloodstock). *"A smashing horse, he was a very nice-looking yearling, he's not over-big but he looks a runner. He's sharp and ready to run now, but we'll hang on to him until the nicer races come".*

882. UNNAMED ★★★
b.c. Sea The Stars – Alshahbaa (Alhaarth). February 1. First foal. 240,000Y. Tattersalls October Book 1. Peter & Ross Doyle. The dam, a useful Irish 2-y-o 6f winner, was third in the Group 3 7f Silver Flash Stakes and is a half-sister to 4 winners including the useful 2-y-o 6f winner and Group 3 7f Killavullan Stakes third Aaraas. The second dam, Adaala (by Sahm), an Irish 7f (at 2 yrs) and listed 9f winner, is a half-sister to 2 winners. (Al Shaqab Racing). *"A good-looking filly and a really good mover, but she'll take a lot of time. One for the back-end of the season".*

883. UNNAMED ★★★★
b.f. Holy Roman Emperor – Folle Blanche (Elusive Quality). February 22. First foal. €80,000Y. Goffs Orby. Peter & Ross Doyle. The dam, placed twice at 2 and 3 yrs in France, is a half-sister to 4 winners. The second dam, Always Loyal (by Zilzal), won 3 races including the French 1,000 Guineas and the Group 3 1m Prix de la Grotte and is a half-sister to the top-class sprinter Anabaa, the Group 3 Prix d'Arenburg winner Key Of Luck and the listed winner Country Belle (dam of the Group 2 Gimcrack Stakes winner Country Reel). (Mrs F H Hay). *"A nice filly, she's sharp and goes well. She should make an early 2-y-o we think because she's pretty switched on and knows her job".*

884. UNNAMED ★★★
gr.c. Fastnet Rock – Hotelgenie Dot Com (Selkirk). April 2. Eleventh foal. 100,000Y. Tattersalls October Book 2. Howson/ Holdsworth Bloodstock. Closely related to the Group 1 Fillies' Mile and Group 1 Falmouth Stakes winner Simply Perfect (by Danehill) and half-brother to the fair 10f winner Loch Ma Naire (by Galileo) and the minor Irish 12f winner Allied Answer (by Danehill Dancer).

The dam, a 2-y-o 7f winner, was second in the Group 1 Moyglare Stud Stakes, third in the Group 1 Fillies Mile and is a half-sister to the Moyglare Stud Stakes winner Bianca Nera. The second dam, Birch Creek (by Carwhite), was third in the Group 3 1m Premio Royal Mares and is a half-sister to 7 winners including the Group 3 winning sprinter Great Deeds. (Derek & Jean Clee). *"He's shown us more than all the Fastnet Rock's we've ever had. I like him a lot, he shows plenty, wants to go forward and it won't be long before he's running".*

885. UNNAMED ★★★★
ch.c. Paco Boy – Lilli Marlane (Sri Pekan). March 29. Seventh foal. 65,000Y. Tattersalls October Book 2. Rabbah Bloodstock. Half-brother to the fair 6f (at 2 yrs) and 7f winner Pearl Rebel (by Cockney Rebel) and the moderate 7f winner Philmack Dot Com (by Traditionally). The dam, a fair and 1m and 10f winner, is a half-sister to 5 winners including the US Grade 2 Del Mar Derby winner Medici Code. The second dam, Fivefive (by Fairy King), a modest 5f (at 2 yrs) and 1m winner, is a half-sister to 4 winners. (S Manana). *"A real nice, big colt and he shows plenty too. I can see him wanting six furlongs and he could be a Royal Ascot 2-y-o".*

886. UNNAMED ★★★
b.f. Iffraaj – Love Intrigue (Marju). January 27. Second foal. 55,000Y. Tattersalls October Book 1. Rabbah Bloodstock. Half-sister to the moderate Irish 10.5f winner Eloge (by Elnadim). The dam, an Italian 2-y-o listed 6f and 3-y-o Group 3 5f winner, is a half-sister to 3 winners including the Italian listed winner Cool Contest. The second dam, Love Contest (by Love The Groom), a listed-placed winner of 3 races at 2 yrs in Italy, is a half-sister to 4 winners. (S H Altayer). *"She should be ready to run early. A good, correct filly, she'll be starting fast work in early April".*

887. UNNAMED ★★★
br.f. Poet's Voice – Lucky Token (Key Of Luck). April 19. Fourth foal. 115,000Y. Tattersalls October Book 2. Sackville/Donald. Half-sister to a winner in Honk Kong at 4 yrs by Exceed And Excel. The dam, a fair 9f winner, is a half-sister to 9 winners including the multiple Group 1 winner Sky Lantern, the 2-y-o Group

3 6f Round Tower Stakes winner Arctic and the Group 3 2m Queens Vase winner Shanty Star. The second dam, Shawanni (by Shareef Dancer), a useful 2-y-o 7f winner, is a half-sister to the UAE Group 3 winner Blatant and the Group 3 Prix Thomas Bryon winner Songlark. (Malih L Al Basti). *"A lovely filly and related to Sky Lantern, she has a bit of attitude like she has. I like her a lot".*

888. UNNAMED ★★★
b.c. Dick Turpin – Mookhlesa (Marju). March 6. Fourth foal. 70,000Y. Tattersalls October Book 2. Peter & Ross Doyle. Half-brother to the unplaced 2014 2-y-o Wiggle (by Dutch Art) and to the modest 5f winner Traditionelle (by Indesatchel). The dam, a quite useful 2-y-o 5f winner, is a half-sister to one winner. The second dam, Ikhlas (by Lahib), is an unraced sister to the 2-y-o Group 3 Horris Hill Stakes winner La-Faah and a half-sister to 6 winners. (Al Shaqab Racing). *"He's very like the sire. A nice, big horse and very strong, looking at him you might think he's a bit too big to make a 2-y-o but he seems to be very well-balanced, so I see no problems with that. He's a nice horse".*

889. UNNAMED ★★★ ♠
b.f. Iffraaj – Pitrizza (Machiavellian). February 28. Tenth foal. 300,000Y. Tattersalls October Book 1. Half-sister to 6 winners including the useful Irish 2-y-o 6f winner and Group 3 Tyros Stakes third Vilasol, the 2-y-o listed 7.5f winner Snow Watch (both by Verglas), the quite useful 1m to 12f winner of 12 races The Lock Master (by Key Of Luck) and the fair 6f and 7f winner of 4 races Perfect Treasure (by Night Shift). The dam won once over 12f in France and is a half-sister to 4 other minor winners. The second dam, Unopposed (by Sadler's Wells), is an unraced half-sister to 11 winners including the dam of the dual Group 2 winner and sire Titus Livius. (Denis Barry). *"A classy looking filly, she was expensive and she moves well. One for the back end of the season, but there's a lot to like about her".*

890. UNNAMED ★★★
b.f. Zoffany – Promise Of Love (Royal Applause). March 9. Third foal. £100,000Y. Doncaster Premier. Peter & Ross Doyle. Half-sister to the modest dual 5f winner Where

The Boys Are (by Dylan Thomas). The dam, a fair 5f and 6f placed maiden, is a half-sister to 3 winners including the 2-y-o Group 2 6f Criterium de Maisons-Laffitte winner and sire Captain Rio. The second dam, Beloved Visitor (by Miswaki), won twice over 6f in Ireland at 2 yrs, was listed-placed and is a half-sister to 6 winners. (Jared Sullivan & Chris Giles). *"She came in looking very lean but she's starting to do well and I'm really pleased with her".*

891. UNNAMED ★★★
b.f. Kodiac – Red Remanso (Redback). April 27. Second foal. €48,000Y. Tattersalls Ireland September. Peter & Ross Doyle. The dam ran twice unplaced and is a half-sister to 5 winners including the listed 1m Heron Stakes winner and Group 1 1m Criterium International third Redolent. The second dam, Esterlina (by Highest Honor), won over 1m at 3 yrs in Ireland and is a half-sister to 3 minor winners in France. (Mr M. A. Al Mannai). *"A five furlong 2-y-o type, he could be out early".*

892. UNNAMED ★★★
b.f. Dark Angel – Rose Of Battle (Averti). March 9. Fifth foal. 50,000Y. Tattersalls October Book 2. Rabbah Bloodstock. Half-brother to the moderate 2012 2-y-o 6f winner Windsor Rose (by Windsor Knot) and to the modest 2-y-o 6f winner Pendle Lady (by Chineur). The dam, a quite useful Irish 2-y-o 5f winner, is a half-sister to 4 winners including the Group 2 second Orpen Grey. The second dam, Sky Red (by Night Shift), a fair 5f winner of 3 races, is a sister to the French listed winner Shoalhaven and to the listed-placed winner Night Haven. (S Manana). *"She's a nice filly who looked small at first, but in the last three weeks she's grown, put on weight and done really well. I like her a lot but she'll want a bit of time".*

893. UNNAMED ★★★★
b.c. Exceed And Excel – Ruse (Diktat). March 14. Fourth foal. 230,000Y. Tattersalls October Book 1. Peter & Ross Doyle. Half-brother to the French 2-y-o winner and German 1m listed-placed Rowan Brae (by Haafhd) and to the modest 1m winner Confusing (by Return To Bend). The dam is a placed half-sister to 9 winners including the very useful Group 3 7f Jersey Stakes winner Ardkinglass and the dam of the listed winners Succession and Succinct.

The second dam, Reuval (by Sharpen Up), a useful winner of 2 races over 1m at 3 yrs, is a half-sister to 6 winners and to the dams of the Group 2 winners Ozone Friendly, Reprimand and Wiorno. (Al Shaqab Racing). *"A big, tall horse that goes well, he's a really nice type".*

JESSIE HARRINGTON

894. BRAVER THE BULL (IRE) ★★
b.g. Big Bad Bob – Danzelline (Danzero). March 16. Sixth foal. €28,000Y. Goffs Orby. Rabbah Bloodstock. Half-brother to the quite useful 5f (including at 2 yrs) and 6f winner of 7 races Head Space (by Invincible Spirit), to the fair Irish 2-y-o 6f winner Diva Dolce (by Domedriver) and the fair 9f winner Chevalgris (by Verglas). The dam, a fair Irish 1m and 10f winner, is a half-sister to 6 winners including the Group 1 Tattersalls Gold Cup winner Rebelline (dam of the Group 3 winner Recharge) and the Group 2 Blandford Stakes winner Quws. The second dam, Fleeting Rainbow (by Rainbow Quest), a modest 10f placed 3-y-o, is a half-sister to 3 winners. (Anamoine Ltd). *"A well-grown gelding, he won't make an early 2-y-o but he should be racing by June/July over seven furlongs".*

895. EAGER TO PLEASE (IRE) ★★★
b.f. Elusive Pimpernel – Toy Show (Danehill). March 16. 10,000foal. Goffs November. BBA (Ire). Half-brother to the fairly useful 2014 2-y-o 5f winner Cleveland Street (by Windsor Knot), to the quite useful 1m to 10f winner of 5 races Wing Play (by Hawk Wing), the fair 1m (at 2 yrs) to 2m and hurdles winner Knight's Parade (by Dark Angel) and the minor Italian winner Capo Malfatano (by Hurricane Run). The dam, a quite useful triple 10f winner (including at 2 yrs), is a half-sister to 3 winners. The second dam, March Hare (by Groom Dancer), a modest middle-distance placed maiden, is a half-sister to 7 winners including the smart 1m and 10f listed winner Inglenook. *"She looks like she could be fairly early but I have a good few of these Elusive Pimpernel's and they're all big. This one is the sharpest of them though and she's nice, so hopefully I'll get her out in May".*

896. FINAL FRONTIER (IRE) ★★★★
b.c. Dream Ahead – Polly Perkins (Pivotal). March 31. Fifth foal. €37,000Y. Goffs

Sportsmans. BBA (Ire). Half-brother to the useful 2014 2-y-o 7f winner and Group 3 7f C L & M F Weld Park Stakes second Lola Beaux (by Equiano) and to the fair triple 7f winner Marmarus (by Duke Of Marmalade). The dam, a useful 2-y-o dual listed 5f winner, is a half-sister to 2 winners. The second dam, Prospering (by Prince Sabo), a moderate 7f winner at 3 yrs, is a half-sister to 6 winners. (Vimal Khosla & Mrs P K Cooper). *"A half-brother to a filly I had last year called Lola Beaux, he's nice and although I thought he'd be backward, he isn't. He seems to be coming on well, should be running in May or June and he'll be a six/seven furlong 2-y-o".*

897. HAMLEY (FR) ★★★
b.f. Fastnet Rock – Mary Arnold (Hernando). March 19. Third foal. Half-sister to the fair 2-y-o 7f winner Stateos (by Acclamation). The dam ran once unplaced and is a half-sister to 5 winners including the Group 1 Criterium de Saint-Cloud winner Linda's Lad. The second dam, Colza (by Alleged), a quite useful 2-y-o 1m winner, is a half-sister to 10 winners including the Group 3 6f July Stakes winner Wharf and the top-class broodmare Docklands (dam of the Arc winner Rail Link). (Niarchos Family). *"She's one for July time I think and for a Fastnet Rock she's good-looking and not too big. At the moment I like her and she's done everything we want her to do, but I'm a bit mindful that Fastnet Rock's tend to look early and then end up taking longer".*

898. LOVEISALLAROUND ★★★★
gr.f. Zebedee – Shauna's Princess (Soviet Star). April 26. Fourth foal. €43,000Y. Tattersalls Ireland September. BBA (Ire). Half-sister to a minor 2-y-o winner abroad by Oratorio. The dam, a winner, is a sister to the useful 7f to 11f winner and US Grade 3 placed Ihtiraz and a half-sister to 8 winners including the Group 3 Prix Berteux winner Samsaam and the listed winner Al Ihtithar. The second dam, Azyaa (by Kris), a useful 7.5f winner, is a half-sister to 5 winners. (Mr J Carthy, Mr M O'Neill, Mr M Buckley & Partners). *"She's nice and she'll be running as soon as the ground dries up. A sharp, five furlong filly and she's done everything well".*

899. MISSGUIDED (IRE) ★★

b.f. Rip Van Winkle – Foolish Ambition (Danehill Dancer). March 15. Second foal. €22,000Y. Goffs Orby. BBA (Ire). Sister to the unplaced 2014 2-y-o Bakht A Rawan. The dam, a fairly useful listed-placed 2-y-o 6f winner, is a sister to the fairly useful 6f winner and 2-y-o Group 3 6f second True Verdict. The second dam, Foolish Act (by Sadler's Wells), is an unraced full or half-sister to 6 winners including Circle Of Gold (Group 3 Prestige Stakes) and the listed winner Crystal Crossing (dam of the St Leger winner Rule Of Law). *"A nice filly, she's big and strong but it's hard to know when she'll come to hand".*

900. MS BRINKLEYS (IRE) ★★★

b.f. Arcano – Follow My Lead (Night Shift). February 17. Sixth foal. €38,000Y. Goffs Orby. BBA (Ire). Half-sister to 5 winners including the useful 2014 2-y-o 6f winner Sixty (by Iffraaj), the smart Group 3 1m Prix Messidor and listed Doncaster Mile winner of 8 races Graphic (by Excellent Art), the quite useful Irish 9f winner Crystal Morning (by Cape Cross) and the fair 7f and 1m winner Soaring Spirits (by Tamayuz). The dam, a fair 8.3f winner, is a half-sister to 7 winners including Halicarnassus (Group 2 Superlative Stakes and Group 2 Bosphorus Cup). The second dam, Launch Time (by Relaunch), is a US placed half-sister to the US Grade 2 winner Palace March and Grade 1 placed Executive Pride. (Commonstown Racing Stables). *"She's done a bit of work, she's done well and I'm happy with her. She looks like she's going to be early. I trained her half-sister Crystal Morning, it's a great family and everything but all of the mare has won. A compact filly, she's a strong 2-y-o type and hopefully one that'll be running in late May or early June".*

901. MULLIGATAWNY (IRE) ★★★★

b.c. Lope De Vega – Wild Whim (Whipper). February 20. Second foal. 135,000Y. Tattersalls October Book 1. BBA (Ire). The dam is an unraced half-sister to 4 winners including the Group 2 Railway Stakes third Il Pirata. The second dam, Wild Bluebell (by Bluebird), won the Group 3 Concorde Stakes and is a half-sister to 7 winners including Priory Belle (Group 1 7f Moyglare Stud Stakes) and Eva's Request (Group 1 Premio Lydia Tesio).

(Millhouse LLC). *"A very good-moving horse, he's lovely and I'd be hopeful of him running in May.*

902. PROUD MARIA (IRE) ★★★

ch.f. Medicean – Foot Of Pride (Footstepsinthesand). February 6. First foal. The dam, unplaced in two starts, is a half-sister to 5 winners including the smart Irish Group 3 7f and Group 3 1m winner Cheyenne Star and to the unraced dam of Gordon Lord Byron (Group 1 Haydock Sprint Cup and Group 1 Prix de la Foret). The second dam, Charita (by Lycius), a listed 1m winner in Ireland, is a half-sister to 4 winners including the Italian Group 2 winner Stanott. (Mr Roland Alder). *"She's a nice filly, it's hard to know with her because she's only done slow canters up to now. I see her being out in mid-summer, it's a good family and they produce 2-y-o winners too".*

903. ROCKAWAY VALLEY (IRE) ★★★★

b.c. Holy Roman Emperor – Sharapova (Elusive Quality). March 21. Fourth foal. 165,000Y. Tattersalls October Book 2. BBA (Ire). Half-brother to the quite useful Irish 4-y-o 6f winner and 2-y-o Group 1 Phoenix Stakes third Lottie Dod and to the minor French 3-y-o winner Floriade (both by Invincible Spirit). The dam, a quite useful 3-y-o 7f winner, is a half-sister to 6 winners including the US stakes winner and Grade 1 placed Tamweel. The second dam, Naazeq (by Nashwan), a quite useful 10.5f winner, is a sister to the very useful 10f winner and Group 3 second Shaya and a half-sister to 9 winners. *"He's sharp and could be running in May. A medium-sized, good-moving colt with a good attitude, he has a bit of quality I think".*

904. ROCKNROLLBABY (IRE) ★★

b.f. Fastnet Rock – Jazz Baby (Fasliyev). May 8. Sixth foal. €32,000Y. Tattersalls Ireland September. BBA (Ire). Half-sister to the quite useful 2-y-o 6f winner Jazz (by Danehill Dancer) and to the fair 7f and 1m winner Combustible (by Halling). The dam is an unraced half-sister to 10 winners including the Group 1 10.5f Prix de Diane winner Rafha (the dam of 4 stakes winners including Invincible Spirit) and the Group 3 Blandford Stakes winner Chiang Mai (dam of the Group 1 Pretty Polly Stakes winner Chinese White). The second dam, Eljazzi (by Artaius), a fairly useful 2-y-o 7f winner, is a half-sister to 8 winners including the good miler Pitcairn. (Miss Kate Harrington, Mrs Gina Galvin & Mrs Yvonne Nicoll). *"She was small when we bought her but she's grown. From the look of her you'd think she'd be sharp, but being by Fastnet Rock she'll probably need a bit of time".*

905. UNNAMED ★★★

b.c. Pour Moi – Bounce (Trempolino). April 28. Seventh foal. €110,000Y. Goffs Orby. BBA (Ire). Half-brother to the French listed 13f winner Bernieres (by Montjeu) and the Swedish listed winner Hurricane Red (by Hurricane Run). The dam won 2 minor races at 3 yrs in France and is a half-sister to the French listed winner and Group 1 Criterium de Saint-Cloud second Simplex. The second dam, Russyskia (by Green Dancer), won once at 3 yrs in France and is a half-sister to 6 winners including the very smart Group 1 15.5f Prix Royal-Oak and Group 2 15f Prix Kergorlay winner Top Sunrise. (Favourite Racing Ltd). *"Very nice, but being by Pour Moi you wouldn't expect him to be out until July or August. A fine, big horse".*

906. UNNAMED ★★

b.f. Rip Van Winkle – Ermena (Dalakhani). March 24. Second foal. 24,000Y. Tattersalls October Book 2. BBA (Ire). The dam is an unraced half-sister to 3 minor winners. The second dam, Fairy Queen (by Fairy King), won 5 races including the Group 2 12f Ribblesdale Stakes and the Group 2 12.5f Prix de la Royallieu and is a half-sister to 4 winners including the smart Group 2 1m Falmouth Stakes winner Tashawak and the listed 10f winner and Prix de l'Arc de Triomphe fourth Acropolis. (Commonstown Racing Stables). *"She's coming on well but it's hard to know how long she'll take, considering her pedigree. She could take a bit of time but she's a fine, strong filly".*

907. UNNAMED ★★★

b.f. Canford Cliffs – Renashaan (Darshaan). January 12. Thirteenth foal. €90,000Y. Goffs Orby. BBA (Ire). Half-sister to 6 winners including the top-class multiple Group 1 winner Alexander Goldrun (by Gold Away), the Group 3 Prix de la Jonchere winner and Group 1 placed Medicis, the fair 1m winner

(on his only start) Shadowy Figure (both by Machiavellian), the French 10.5f winner Highshaan (by Pistolet Bleu) and the French 2-y-o 9f winner Renaleon (by Generous). The dam, a listed winner in France, was third in the Group 3 9f Prix Vanteaux and is a half-sister to 4 minor winners. The second dam, Gerbera (by Lyphard), a minor winner in France, is a half-sister to 5 winners. (Sir Peter Vela). *"A well-grown filly, I'd say she'll be out by July or maybe a bit sooner. She was an early foal and she looks it".*

BARRY HILLS

I'm grateful to Barry's Assistant, Owen Burrows, for going through the two-year-olds with me.

908. BASMA ★★★

b.f. Exceed And Excel – Miss Chicane (Refuse To Bend). March 9. First foal. €140,000Y. Goffs Orby. Shadwell Estate Co. The dam, a fair 9f winner, is a half-sister to 3 winners including the 2-y-o Group 2 6f Lowther Stakes winner Best Terms and the Italian Group 3 placed Sunsemperchi. The second dam, Sharp Terms (by Kris), is an unraced half-sister to 9 winners including the Group 2 winners First Charter and Anton Chekhov. (Hamdan Al Maktoum). *"A neat little filly, she looks quite sharp and should be one of our first 2-y-o runners. We've only cantered her so it's hard to say what trip she'd be best at, but she should be racing in May".*

909. BROADWAY MELODY ★★★★

b.f. Arcano – Oriental Melody (Sakhee). February 2. Third foal. The dam, an Irish 2-y-o 7f winner, is a half-sister to 5 winners including the useful dual 1m winner (including at 2 yrs) and Group 3 Irish 2,000 Guineas third Famous Warrior and the useful 7f and UAE 1m winner Green Coast and Group 2 second. The second dam, Oriental Fashion (by Marju), won 3 races including the Group 2 1m Premio Ribot and is a half-sister to 5 winners including the US Grade 2 winner Makderah. (Hadi Al Tajir). *"She's a lovely, quality, athletic filly that carries herself well. On looks she's not as sharp as some, but she does have a lot of quality and is probably one for seven furlongs and a mile this year".*

910. DHEYAA (IRE) ★★★
b.f. Dream Ahead – Lady Livius (Titus Livius).
March 11. Fifth foal. 210,000Y. Tattersalls
October Book 2. Shadwell Estate Co. Half-
sister to the smart 2014 2-y-o Group 3 7f
Sirenia Stakes winner Burnt Sugar (by Lope
De Vega), to the 2-y-o Group 3 5f Molecomb
Stakes and Sirenia Stakes winner Brown Sugar
(by Tamayuz), the quite useful 6f (at 2 yrs) and
7f winner Elle Woods and the minor French
4-y-o winner Widyaan (both by Lawman). The
dam, a fairly useful 5f winner of 3 races from 2
to 4 yrs, is a half-sister to 5 winners including
the Group 2 6f Mill Reef Stakes winner and
Group 1 placed Galeota. The second dam,
Refined (by Statoblest), a fairly useful dual 5f
winner, is a half-sister to 6 winners including
Pipe Major (Group 3 7f Criterion Stakes).
(Hamdan Al Maktoum). *"She's related to a
couple of smart 2-y-o's but actually she's a bit
leggy and unfurnished at the minute. If the
weather improves it may help to bring her
on, but she needs to strengthen a bit and she
doesn't look like a sprinter".*

911. EHTIRAAS ★★★★
b.c. Oasis Dream – Kareemah (Peintre Celebre).
March 24. Third foal. The dam, a French
listed 10f winner, is a half-sister to 4 winners
including the French listed 9f and subsequent
US Grade 1 10f and Grade 1 11f winner
Lahudood. The second dam, Rahayeb (by
Arazi), a fair 12.3f winner, is a full or half-sister
to 4 winners. (Hamdan Al Maktoum). *"A lovely,
quality colt that's just had a minor hold up but
nothing serious. We'll take things easy with him
for a bit, but he's a very nice colt".*

912. FAWAAREQ (IRE) ★★
b.c. Invincible Spirit – Ghandoorah (Forestry).
February 24. First foal. The dam is an unraced
half-sister to 7 winners including the 1,000
Guineas and Coronation Stakes winner
Ghanaati and the Group 3 12f Cumberland
Lodge Stakes winner and Group 1 Champions
Stakes second Mawatheeq. The second dam,
Sarayir (by Mr Prospector), a listed 1m winner,
is closely related to the top-class Champion
Stakes winner Nayef and a half-sister to the
2,000 Guineas, Eclipse, Derby and King George
winner Nashwan. (Hamdan Al Maktoum). *"He's
a little on the backward side and needs time,*

*partly because he had a touch of sore shins a
while ago. He's back cantering now although
still hanging onto his coat, so he needs a bit of
sun on his back like a lot of 2-y-o's at this time
of the year. One for later in the season, he's a
good size and once he fills out he'll be OK".*

913. JABBAAR ★★
ch.c. Medicean – Echelon (Danehill). April 7.
Fifth foal. 400,000Y. Tattersalls October Book
1. Shadwell Estate Co. Half-brother to the
Group 1 Falmouth Stakes and Group 2 Duke
Of Cambridge Stakes winner Integral (by
Dalakhani), to the useful listed-placed 7f and
1m winner Provenance and the modest 12f
winner Elysian (both by Galileo). The dam won
the Group 1 1m Matron Stakes, the Group
2 Celebration Mile and four Group 3 events
and is a half-sister to the dual Group 2 1m
Celebration Mile winner Chic. The second
dam, Exclusive (Polar Falcon), won the Group
1 1m Coronation Stakes and is a half-sister
to 9 winners including the 2,000 Guineas
winner Entrepreneur. (Hamdan Al Maktoum).
*"He's cantering away at the minute and doing
everything right. One for later in the season, he
has a good attitude and needs to strengthen. I
would have thought he'd be starting at around
a mile and he's much more of a 3-y-o type
really".*

914. KHAMEELA ★★
b.f. Equiano – Mina (Selkirk). January 31.
Fifth foal. 75,000Y. Tattersalls October Book
2. Shadwell Estate Co. Closely related to the
quite useful 2-y-o 5f winner Miss Diva and
half-sister to the listed 6f winner of 5 races
Minalisa and the quite useful 5f and 6f winner
of 7 races Peace Seeker (both by Oasis Dream).
The dam, a modest 6f winner at 4 yrs, is a half-
sister to 5 winners including the Group 3 5f
Ballyogan Stakes winner Miss Anabaa and the
smart 5f and 6f winner of 6 races Out After
Dark. The second dam, Midnight Shift (by
Night Shift), a fair dual 6f winner at 3 yrs, is a
half-sister to 8 winners including the Group
1 6f July Cup winner Owington. (Hamdan Al
Maktoum). *"She's a big, scopey filly and she's
got a few niggles at the minute so we're taking
our time. She's bred to be quite sharp and she's
got that sort of physique but she'll be a mid-to-
late season 2-y-o".*

915. MAKANAH (IRE) ★★★
b.c. New Approach – Kitty Kiernan (Pivotal).
January 19. Second foal. 320,000foal.
Tattersalls December. Shadwell Estate Co.
Brother to the 2014 Irish 2-y-o 6f winner
Ice Lady. The dam, a very useful 6f (at 2 yrs)
and 7f winner, was second in the Group 3
Coolmore Stud Sprint Stakes and third in the
Group 3 Silver Flash Stakes and is a half-sister
to one winner. The second dam, Alstemeria
(by Danehill), a useful Irish 6f winner, is a sister
to the Group 1 1m Gran Criterium winner
Spartacus and to the Group 2 10f Gallinule
Stakes and Hong Kong Derby winner Johan
Cruyff. (Hamdan Al Maktoum). *"A lovely,
quality looking colt that wants a bit of time,
but he's a lovely looking horse. A good mover,
he's one for a bit later in the season over seven
furlongs".*

916. MASARZAIN (IRE) ★★★
br.c. Kodiac – Cache Creek (Marju).
March 29. Sixth foal. 220,000Y. Tattersalls
October Book 1. Shadwell Estate Co. Half-
brother to the 7f listed-placed 2-y-o Hudson's
Bay (by Teofilo) and to the fair Irish 2-y-o 6f
winner Ballycahill (by Barathea). The dam, a
listed 9.5f winner of 6 races in Ireland, was
second in the Group 3 Blue Wind Stakes
and third in the Group 3 Meld Stakes. The
second dam, Tongue River (by Riverman), is an
unraced half-sister to 7 winners including the
Group 3 winners Lady Roberta and Tursanah.
(Hamdan Al Maktoum). *"He looks quite a
sharp, mature 2-y-o and all being well he'll
be a May/June 2-y-o. He's a good size and
everything is in proportion".*

917. MIDHMAAR ★★★★
b.c. Iffraaj – Merayaat (Darshaan). May 3.
Seventh foal. Half-brother to the smart
1m (at 2 yrs) and Group 3 12f Cumberland
Lodge Stakes winner Hawaafez (by Nayef)
and to the fair 14f and 15f winner Nateeja
(by Shamardal). The dam was a quite useful
14f winner. The second dam, Maddelina (by
Sadler's Wells), is an unplaced half-sister to 2
winners. (Hamdan Al Maktoum). *"A lovely colt
that does everything well. Even though he's a
May foal he's mature-looking and has a good,
athletic action. He'll be a 2-y-o at the back-end
of the summer".*

918. MITHQAAL (USA) ★★★
ch.c. Speightstown – Bestowal (Unbridled's
Song). March 15. Third foal. The dam is an
unraced half-sister to the 1,000 Guineas
winner Hatoof, to the Grade 1 Breeders Cup
winner Irish Prize and the dual listed winner
Insijaam. The second dam, Cadeaux d'Amie
(by Lyphard), a French 1m (at 2 yrs) and 10f
winner and third in the Group 3 1m Prix
d'Aumale, is a half-sister to Mrs Penny (Prix
Vermeille and Prix de Diane). (Hamdan Al
Maktoum). *"He's just come in from Dubai so
he needs to acclimatise but he's a neat-looking
colt that looks quite mature. We haven't been
able to assess him yet but what we see we like".*

919. MUBAJAL ★★★
br.c. Dubawi – Jadhwah (Nayef). February
19. First foal. The dam, unplaced on her only
start, is a sister to the 2,000 Guineas and
Prix Jacques le Marois winner Makfi. The
second dam, Dhelaal (by Green Desert), is
an unraced half-sister to 7 winners including
the champion 2-y-o Alhaarth (Dewhurst
Stakes, Laurent Perrier Champagne Stakes
etc.,) and the very useful 2-y-o Group 3 7f
Prix du Calvados winner Green Pola. (Hamdan
Al Maktoum). *"Cantering away, he's a nice-
looking colt and very uncomplicated. He looks
one to start off in mid-summer".*

920. MUNTAZAH ★★★
b.c. Dubawi – Rumoush (Rahy). February 2.
Second foal. The dam, a very useful 1m (at
2 yrs) and listed 9f winner, was third in the
Oaks and is a half-sister to numerous winners
including the 1,000 Guineas and Coronation
Stakes winner Ghanaati and the Group 3 12f
Cumberland Lodge Stakes winner and Group
1 Champion Stakes second Mawatheeq.
The second dam, Sarayir (by Mr Prospector),
winner of a listed 1m event, is closely related
to the Champion Stakes winner Nayef and
a half-sister to Nashwan and Unfuwain.
(Hamdan Al Maktoum). *"Just in from Dubai,
he's a big, strong-looking colt but actually he's
quite light on his feet. A nice type but we're just
getting acquainted with him".*

921. MUSTAJEER ★★★
b.c. Medicean – Qelaan (Dynaformer). April
17. Third foal. Half-brother to the fair 2014 5f
and 6f placed 2-y-o Tansfeeq (by Aqlaam) and

to the 2015 4-y-o Qatar 1m winner Makruma (by Dubawi). The dam, a quite useful 11f and 12f winner, is a half-sister to one winner. The second dam, Irtahal (by Swain), a fairly useful 1m winner, was third in the Group 3 Musidora Stakes and is a half-sister to several winners. (Hamdan Al Maktoum). *"Another one that's just come in from Dubai. From what I've seen of him so far he looks fine but he'll need time to get used to our climate".*

922. RAAQY (IRE) ★★★★ ♠
gr.f. Dubawi – Natagora (Divine Light). March 30. Fourth foal. Half-sister to the quite useful 2-y-o 6f winner Rayaheen (by Nayef). The dam, a champion 2-y-o filly and winner of the Group 1 Cheveley Park Stakes and the 1,000 Guineas, is a half-sister to 2 winners in France (including one over jumps). The second dam, Reinamixa (by Linamix), a minor French 11f winner, is a half-sister to 6 winners including the French listed winner Reinstate. (Hamdan Al Maktoum). *"A quality filly, she's just starting to grow a bit and go leggy on us but being by Dubawi she should give the dam a real chance of breeding a proper horse. This filly does look to have more quality than the dam's previous foals and she's got plenty of scope".*

923. SIRDAAL (USA) ★★
b.c. Medaglia d'Oro – Sarayir (Mr Prospector). March 16. Half-brother to 7 winners including the 1,000 Guineas and Coronation Stakes winner Ghanaati (by Giant's Causeway), the Group 3 12f Cumberland Lodge Stakes winner and Group 1 Champion Stakes second Mawatheeq, the quite useful 1m winner Itqaan (both by Danzig) and the useful 1m (at 2 yrs) and listed 9f winner Rumoush (by Rahy). The dam, a listed 1m winner, is closely related to the Champion Stakes winner Nayef and a half-sister to Nashwan and Unfuwain. The second dam, Height Of Fashion (by Bustino), won the Group 2 Princess of Wales's Stakes. (Hamdan Al Maktoum). *"A big, big horse that's just come in from Dubai. He has a great big head on him and I don't think he'll be out until the end of the season".*

924. TANASOQ (IRE) ★★
b.c. Acclamation – Alexander Youth (Exceed And Excel). February 7. Third foal. 180,000Y. Tattersalls October Book 1. Shadwell Estate Co. Half-brother to the quite useful 2014 2-y-o 6f winner Denzille Lane (by Iffraaj) and to the fairly useful 6f and 7f winner of 6 races Almargo (by Invincible Spirit). The dam, a fairly useful Group 3 placed 6f winner, is a half-sister to 8 winners including the Group 2 5f Prix du Gros-Chene and dual Group 3 5f winner Moss Vale. The second dam, Wolf Cleugh (by Last Tycoon), is an unplaced half-sister to 8 winners including the Irish listed 6f winner King's College. (Hamdan Al Maktoum). *"He's met with a setback which is a shame because he's a neat looking type. He'll be alright for the back-end of the season and he moves nicely".*

CHARLIE HILLS
Many thanks once again to Charlie's Assistant Kevin Mooney for his help in sorting out these very nicely bred two-year-olds with me.

925. ALBARAAHA (IRE) ★★★★
b.f. Iffraaj – Tolzey (Rahy). April 25. Sixth foal. £110,000Y. Doncaster Premier. Shadwell Estate Co. Half-sister to the quite useful French 7f (at 2 yrs) and 1m winner and listed-placed Game Mascot (by Kheleyf), to the quite useful 7f (at 2 yrs) and 10f winner Solicitor (by Halling) and the minor French 3-y-o winner Houlgate (by Mount Nelson). The dam, a fairly useful 2-y-o 6f winner, was listed-placed twice and is a sister to the French 2-y-o listed 7f winner Inner Temple and a half-sister to 2 winners. The second dam, Legal Opinion (by Polish Precedent), placed at 2 yrs in France, is a half-sister to 7 winners. (Hamdan Al Maktoum). *"We haven't done a lot with the 2-y-o's as we speak (in early April), but this is a nice filly. She has a good action, a good temperament and a bit of speed. She'll probably start off at six furlongs".*

926. ALEEF (IRE) ★★★
b.c. Kodiac – Okba (Diesis). March 17. Second foal. 85,000Y. Tattersalls October Book 2. Shadwell Estate Co. The dam, unplaced on her only start, is a half-sister to 3 winners including the useful 10f and 2m winner of 3 races and Group 3 2m Sagaro Stakes second Aajel. The second dam, Awtaan (by Arazi), a fair 14f winner, is a half-sister to 4 winners including the dam of the US dual Grade 1 winner Lahudood. (Hamdan Al Maktoum). *"He's just growing at the minute, but he's a nice*

horse I could see setting off at six furlongs. He'll probably be better when he gets to race over seven though".

927. AMAANY ★★
br.f. Teofilo – Almass (Elnadim). March 13. Third foal. Half-sister to Barqeyya (by Shamardal), placed fourth over 1m on her only start at 2 yrs in 2014. The dam, a smart listed 7f and listed 1m winner, is a half-sister to numerous winners including the very smart dual listed 10f winner and dual Group 1 placed Volochine and the listed winners Kahtan, Sakha and Ghataas. The second dam, Harmless Albatross (by Pas de Seul), won the Group 3 1m Prix des Chenes at 2 yrs and a 1m listed event at 3 yrs and is a half-sister to the Group 2 10f Prix d'Harcourt winner Fortune's Wheel. (Hamdan Al Maktoum). *"A big filly, she's nice but she's not going to be early. One to set off at seven furlongs in mid to late summer".*

928. A MOMENTOFMADNESS ★★★★
b.c. Elnadim – Royal Blush (Royal Applause). March 19. First foal. £72,000Y. Doncaster Premier. G Howson. The dam, a fair 2-y-o 6f winner, is a half-sister to 7 winners including the fairly useful listed 1m Masaka Stakes winner Jazz Jam. The second dam, Applaud (by Band), winner of the Group 2 6f Cherry Hinton Stakes, is a full or half-sister to 6 winners. *"I've been riding him myself and he's just growing a bit at the minute but he's got plenty of speed. He'll get a run at five furlongs, then six, and it won't be long before he's out. He's a tough little horse and I like him".*

929. ANCIENT WORLD (USA) ★★★★
ch.c. Giant's Causeway – Satulagi (Officer). April 19. Fourth foal. $235,000Y. Keeneland September. Not sold. Half-brother to the quite useful 1m (at 2 yrs) to 11f winner Teolagi (by Giant's Causeway) and to the modest 6f and 7f winner of 4 races at 2 and 3 yrs One More Roman (by Holy Roman Emperor). The dam, a useful listed 7f winner at 2 yrs, is a half-sister to 8 winners including the Grade 3 Iroquois Stakes winner Motor City. The second dam, Shawgatny (by Danzig Connection), won over 9f in Ireland and is a sister to the dual Group 3 winner Star Of Gdansk. *"A nice horse, I would say he's one to set off at six furlongs because*

he travels well and then move up to seven and a mile. He's done well, he has a nice action and a good temperament. We all like him".

930. ARCAMIST ★★
gr.f. Arcano – Good Enough (Mukaddamah). February 22. Ninth foal. 30,000Y. Tattersalls October Book 3. Jill Lamb. Closely related to the useful 7f (at 2 yrs) and listed 6f winner of 6 races Oasis Dancer (by Oasis Dream) and half-sister to 4 winners including the very useful 1m winner of 4 races and subsequent Scandinavian listed winner Smart Enough (by Cadeaux Genereux), the fair 2-y-o 5f winner Grey Street (by Royal Applause) and the fair 2-y-o 1m winner Bright Enough (by Fantastic Light). The dam won once at 3 yrs in the USA, was third in the Group 1 Prix Saint-Alary and is a half-sister to the Group 3 Molecomb Stakes winner Classic Ruler. The second dam, Viceroy Princess (by Godswalk), a modest 2-y-o 7f seller winner, is a half-sister to 7 winners. *"This filly has a bit of a knee action and I'd say she'll want seven furlongs".*

931. ARITHMETIC (IRE) ★★
b.c. Invincible Spirit – Multiplication (Marju). February 22. Third foal. 45,000Y. Tattersalls October Book 2. BBA (Ire). The dam, a quite useful 11f winner, is a half-sister to 9 winners including the very smart triple Group 3 middle-distance winner and dual Group 1 third Blue Monday and the very useful 1m to 10f winner and Italian Derby third Lundy's Lane. The second dam, Lunda (by Soviet Star), is an unplaced half-sister to 6 winners including the high-class middle-distance horses Luso (winner of the Aral-Pokal, the Italian Derby and the Hong Kong International Vase) and Warrsan (Coronation Cup and Grosser Preis von Baden). *"He's growing so we've stopped him for now. He's a big, nice horse with a good temperament, but he'll be one for a bit later on over seven furlongs because it's a family that takes time".*

932. ART STORY (IRE) ★★★★
b.f. Galileo – Impressionist Art (Giant's Causeway). February 14. First foal. The dam, a moderate 7f to 11f placed maiden, is a half-sister to 4 winners including the very useful listed 7f winner Secret Garden. The second dam, Chalamont (by Kris), a quite useful 2-y-o

dual 6f winner, is a half-sister to 5 winners including the dual Ascot Gold Cup winner Gildoran. *"This is a nice little filly, I wouldn't say she'll be early but she should be racing in mid-summer. She's not slow and she shows up well on the gallops".*

933. BURMA ROAD ★★★

b.f. Poet's Voice – Strawberry Moon (Alhaarth). January 11. Third foal. 11,000Y. Tattersalls October Book 3. Not sold. The dam, a fair 6f and 7f winner of 3 races at 2 and 3 yrs, is a half-sister to 4 winners including the Group 2 6f Cherry Hinton Stakes and listed 6f Albany Stakes winner Jewel In The Sand and the German 3-y-o listed 6f winner Davignon. The second dam, Dancing Drop (by Green Desert), a useful dual 2-y-o 6f winner, was listed-placed and is a half-sister to 9 winners. *"A strong filly, she's nice and well-grown, but she won't be sharp. Six and then seven furlongs should suit her this year".*

934. CAPTAIN JOEY (IRE) ★★★

b.c. Kodiac – Archetypal (Cape Cross). March 1. Second foal. 70,000Y. Tattersalls October Book 1. BBA (Ire). The dam is an unraced half-sister to 7 winners including the useful Italian listed 12f winner Viz and the smart 1m (at 2 yrs) to 10f winner and Group 3 placed Forbearing. The second dam, For Example (by Northern Baby), an Irish 10f placed maiden, is a half-sister to 5 winners and to the dams of the Group/Grade 1 winners Awe Inspiring, Culture Vulture, Polish Precedent and Zilzal. *"I wasn't that struck on him at first, but he's suddenly come up on the radar and he'll be one of our first runners".*

935. CLOUDY GIRL (IRE) ★★

gr.f. Lawman – Vespetta (Vespone). February 11. First foal. £40,000Y. Doncaster Premier. Sackville/Donald. The dam is an unraced half-sister to 4 winners and to the placed Spinamix (the dam of four stakes winners). The second dam, Vadsagreya (by Linamix), a French 7f (at 2 yrs) and 1m winner, was listed-placed and is a half-sister to 12 winners including the dams of the French 1,000 Guineas winner Vahorimix and the Breeders Cup Mile winner Val Royal. *"Not very big, but being by Lawman I think she'll need seven furlongs, so she's just ticking away for now".*

936. DARK CRESCENT (IRE) ★★★★★

b.c. Elnadim – Zenella (Kyllachy). February 6. First foal. 35,000Y. Tattersalls October Book 2. Sackville/Donald. The dam, a fairly useful 2-y-o listed 1m winner, is a half-sister to 2 minor winners. The second dam, West One (by Gone West), ran twice unplaced and is closely related to the US stakes-placed winner Go Baby Go and a half-sister to a winner in Italy. *"Everybody likes this horse. He was a bit babyish, but the more he's does the more he's growing up and the better he gets. He'll be a 2-y-o and he'll have speed too, he hasn't done a lot yet but he takes his work well and gives you a good feel. He'll set off at six furlongs and might get to Royal Ascot".*

937. DIAMONDSARETRUMPS (IRE) ★★★

b.f. Dick Turpin – Serial Sinner (High Chaparral). February 5. First foal. £25,000Y. Doncaster Premier. Sackville/Donald. The dam, a moderate 6f and 1m placed maiden, is a half-sister to 4 winners including Palanca (2-y-o Group 3 Premio Primi Passi). The second dam, Putout (by Dowsing), a fair 3-y-o 5f winner, is a half-sister to 3 winners including the Group 2 Sun Chariot Stakes winner Danceabout and the Group 3 6f Prix de Meautry winner Pole Position. *"A big filly with plenty of scope, she has a good action and a good temperament. She wouldn't be a five furlong 2-y-o but she'll be a mid-season type and she's a nice filly with a good action and a good temperament".*

938. DOUBLY MOTIVATED (IRE) ★★★

ch.f. Iffraaj – Chicane (Motivator). February 3. Second foal. 65,000Y. Tattersalls October Book 2. Sackville/Donald. The dam, a modest 12f winner, is a half-sister to 5 winners including the useful 7f (at 2 yrs), listed 1m and Italian Group 3 1m winner Whazzis and the useful 2-y-o listed 7f Chesham Stakes winner Whazzat. The second dam, Wosaita (by Generous), a fair 12.3f placed maiden, is a half-sister to 9 winners including the Group 1 10.5f Prix de Diane winner Rafha (the dam of four stakes winners including Invincible Spirit) and the Group 3 12f Blandford Stakes winner Chiang Mai (dam of the Group 1 Pretty Polly Stakes winner Chinese Water). *"She's done a couple of little bits of work but she's a big filly and not quite ready yet. So we'll give her a bit more time".*

939. DR DREY (IRE) ★★★
ch.c. Bahamian Bounty – Mount Lavinia (Montjeu). March 28. Second foal. 35,000Y. Tattersalls October Book 2. BBA (Ire). The dam, a quite useful 11.5f and 14f winner of 3 races, is a half-sister to 4 winners including the US listed stakes winner and French Group 2 Prix Dollar second Lord Cromby. The second dam, Havinia (by Habitat), a French 3-y-o winner, is a half-sister to 3 other minor winners. *"He's quite a nice horse that's done well and he's straightforward. Probably a seven furlong type 2-y-o".*

940. ELRONAQ ★★★ ♠
b.c. Invincible Spirit – Cartimandua (Medicean). April 3. Fourth foal. 90,000foal. Tattersalls December. Shadwell Estate Co. The dam, a dual listed 6f winner and third in the Group 3 Ballyogan Stakes, is a half-sister to 3 winners. The second dam, Agrippina (by Timeless Times), a useful 2-y-o listed 7f winner, is a half-sister to 2 winners. (Hamdan Al Maktoum). *"He's not very big, but he can go a bit. He's showing enough to say that he'll have something for you when you want him. We've given him a little break to grow and he's a nice horse".*

941. EXOTERIC ★★★
b.c. Champs Elysees – Short Dance (Hennessy). February 22. Sixth foal. Brother to the quite useful 7f (at 2 yrs) and 1m winner Fray and half-brother to the quite useful 7f winner Plover (by Oasis Dream). The dam, a very useful 6f, listed 7f (both at 2 yrs) and listed 1m winner, is a half-sister to the very useful 2-y-o 7f winner Yankadi. The second dam, Clog Dance (by Pursuit Of Love), a useful maiden, was second in the Group 3 7f Rockfel Stakes and the listed 10f Pretty Polly Stakes and is a half-sister to the smart 14f Ebor Handicap winner Tuning. (Khalid Abdulla). *"We had the dam Short Dance and we've just given this horse a break because he got very keen. We don't know if that's just cheap speed or not, but everybody who rode him liked him. He's a nice horse but he's a bit nervy and the dam was a witch but she had ability. Probably a mid-season 2-y-o".*

942. FRENCHMAN (FR) ★★★ ♠
b.c. Le Havre – Como (Cozzene). April 27.

Ninth foal. 45,000Y. Tattersalls October Book 2. G Howson. Half-brother to the useful Irish 2-y-o listed 5f winner of 5 races Pencil Hill (by Acclamation), to the quite useful 2-y-o 7f winner Hot Diggity (by Librettist) and the modest 6f winner Arzaag (by Bertolini). The dam, a quite useful dual 6f winner, is a half-sister to 4 winners and to the unraced dam of the champion sprinter Sole Power. The second dam, Merida (by Warning), a 1m winner in France and the USA, is a full or half-sister to 8 winners including the dual US Grade 2 1m winner Tychonic. *"He's a good mover with a good action. He's only cantering away at the minute because he'll take time. One to make his debut in late summer I'd say".*

943. GARTER (IRE) ★★
b.f. Fastnet Rock – Princess Iris (Desert Prince). April 28. Third living foal. €110,000Y. Goffs Orby. John Warren. Half-sister to Deemah (by Iffraaj), placed fourth over 7f on her only start at 2 yrs in 2014. The dam, a 2-y-o Group 3 6f Firth Of Clyde Stakes winner, is a half-sister to 6 winners. The second dam, Athlumney Lady (by Lycius), won 3 races at 2 yrs in Ireland including the Group 3 7f Killavullen Stakes and is a half-sister to 4 winners. *"We haven't worked out the Fastnet Rock's yet but we're not on our own. This is a well put together filly but she has seven furlongs written all over her, so she'll take a bit of time".*

944. HIGH SPEED (IRE) ★★★
b.f. Kodiac – Scarlet Empress (Second Empire). April 17. Sixth foal. 65,000Y. Tattersalls October Book 2. BBA (Ire). Half-sister to the fairly useful 2-y-o 5.5f winner and dual Group 3 placed Mary Fildes (by Chineur) and to the quite useful dual 5f winner (including at 2 yrs) Titus Andronicus (by Danetime). The dam, a fair 2-y-o 6f winner, is out of the unraced Daltak (by Night Shift), herself a half-sister to 7 winners including the Group 1 Nunthorpe Stakes winner Ya Malak. *"We're getting on with her, she's on the small side, has loads of speed and goes well. Certainly a 2-y-o and she has the right stallion for the job, she's not 'buzzy' and I'd say she'll be out in April".*

945. IBN MALIK (IRE) ★★★
ch.c. Raven's Pass – Moon's Whisper (Storm Cat). February 23. Eighth foal. Half-brother

to 5 winners including the fair 2014 2-y-o 8.5f winner Atnab (by New Approach), the useful dual 1m winner Yazamaan (by Galileo), the quite useful 5f and 6f winner of 5 races Mutafaakir (by Oasis Dream) and the fair 2m winner Hamsat Elqamar (by Nayef). The dam is an unraced half-sister to the 2-y-o Group 3 5.5f Prix d'Arenburg winner Moon Driver and the US winner and Grade 2 second Mojave Moon. The second dam, East Of The Moon (by Private Account), won the French 1,000 Guineas, Prix de Diane and Prix Jacques le Marois and is a half-sister to the top class miler and sire Kingmambo. *"He's a big, laidback horse but I think he's definitely got something in him. I like him, he'll take time and seven furlongs should be his trip this year".*

946. IMPERIOUS ONE (IRE) ★★★
b.c. Royal Applause – Never A Doubt (Night Shift). April 20. Eighth foal. 48,000Y. Tattersalls October Book 2. Not sold. Brother to the useful 5f ,7f (both at 2 yrs) and listed 7f winner and Group 2 7f Rockfel Stakes third Royal Confidence and half-brother to the quite useful 1m winner Rougette (by Red Ransom) and the quite useful 7f winner Doctor Sardonicus (by Medicean). The dam, a very useful 2-y-o winner of the Group 2 5.5f Prix Robert Papin, is a half-sister to 3 winners including the Group 3 5f third Jonny Mudball. The second dam, Waypoint (by Cadeaux Genereux), a fairly useful 6f and 7f winner of 4 races, is a half-sister to 5 winners including the Group 2 6f Diadem Stakes winner and sire Acclamation. *"He was all shapes and sizes when he came in, but he's grown and he's got a bit of speed. He's got sore shins so he's doing nothing at the moment and he'll be a six/seven furlong colt".*

947. IRISH ECLARE (IRE) ★★★
br.c. Equiano – Delitme (Val Royal). March 23. 20,000Y. Tattersalls October Book 2. Sackville/ Donald. Half-brother to the modest 6f and 7f winner Art Dzeko (by Acclamation). The dam, a winner of 4 races in Italy at 2 and 3 yrs, is a half-sister to 7 winners including the very useful 6f (at 2 yrs) and Group 3 7f Nell Gwyn Stakes winner Reunion. The second dam, Phylella (by Persian Bold), a winner in France (over 10f) and the USA, is a sister to the US stakes winner Karman Girl and a half-sister to

4 winners. *"He's done really well. He's not quite there yet but it's too early for him anyway. You couldn't get a better stamp of a horse for 20 Grand, because he's a good-looking specimen. Could be worth looking out for later in the season".* ***TRAINERS' BARGAIN BUY***

948. HIGH GROUNDS ★★★
b.c. High Chaparral – Civility Cat (Tale Of The Cat). April 9. Sixth foal. €115,000Y. Goffs Orby. BBA (Ire). Brother to the 2014 2-y-o Group 1 Racing Post Trophy fourth Jacobean and half-brother to the fair Irish 2-y-o 7f winner Rogue Element (by Holy Roman Emperor). The dam, a stakes-placed winner at 2 and 3 yrs USA, is a half-sister to 7 winners including the dam of the 2-y-o dual Group 2 winner Flashy Wings. The second dam, Civility (by Shirley Heights), a very useful 12f winner, was second in the listed Galtres Stakes and is a half-sister to 4 winners including the smart 2-y-o Piney Ridge. *"A big horse, he's been difficult to handle but he's a very good actioned horse that'll want seven furlongs in late summer. Barry Hills likes him, so you can't discount him".*

949. JOULES ★★★★
b.c. Oasis Dream – Frappe (Inchinor). March 28. Thirteenth foal. 215,000Y. Tattersalls October Book 1. Stephen Hillen. Brother to the Group 1 Irish 2,000 Guineas, Group 1 7f National Stakes and Group 2 6f Coventry Stakes winner Power and half-brother to the 7f (at 2 yrs) and Group 2 12f Ribblesdale Stakes winner Thakafaat (by Unfuwain), the fairly useful 10f winner Quantum (by Alhaarth) and the quite useful 2-y-o 7f winner Applauded (by Royal Applause). The dam, a fairly useful 2-y-o 6f winner, is a half-sister to the 2,000 Guineas winner Footstepsinthesand and the Group 1 Phoenix Stakes winner Pedro The Great. The second dam, Glatisant (by Rainbow Quest), winner of the Group 3 7f Prestige Stakes, is a half-sister to 8 winners. *"He looked like being one of our early types but he had a little setback. He's back going again now, he's a bit 'buzzy' but he's definitely got speed. He'll be quite early and could be running in May, and he's done well lately. I like him".*

950. KAFOOR (IRE) ★★
b.c. Dubawi – Tahrir (Linamix). March 20. Half-brother to the 2014 2-y-o Group 2

6f Gimcrack Stakes winner and Group 1 Middle Park Stakes third Muhaarar (by Oasis Dream), to the very useful 2-y-o 7f winner and subsequent UAE Group 3 1m second Tamaathul (by Tiger Hill), the useful 2-y-o listed 6f winner Sajwah (by Exceed And Excel), the fairly useful listed-placed 1m winner Raasekha (by Pivotal) and the fair dual 7f winner Rufoof (by Zamindar). The dam, a useful dual 7f winner, is a sister to the listed winners Mister Charm and Green Channel and a half-sister to the Group 3 Prix de Guiche winner Mister Sacha. The second dam, Miss Sacha (by Last Tycoon), a listed sprint winner, is a half-sister to 6 winners. (Hamdan Al Maktoum). *"A great big horse, he's going to want a lot of time and we might not see him out until the back-end".*

951. KEY ON KODIAC ★★

b.c. Kodiac – Kilakey (Key Of Luck). April 8. First foal. 42,000Y. Tattersalls October Book 2. Sackville/Donald. The dam is an unraced half-sister to 2 winners. The second dam, Amankila (by Revoque), a modest 9.5f winner, is a half-sister to 6 winners including the dual Group 2 winner Batshoof. *"He's quite nice and he's done well lately. He's only cantering for now but he's quite a nice horse".*

952. KOMEDY (IRE) ★★★★

b.f. Kodiac – Dancing Jest (Averti). March 16. Second foal. €70,000Y. Goffs Orby. BBA (Ire). Half-sister to the 2014 French 2-y-o 5f winner and Group 3 Prix du Bois second Jane's Memory (by Captain Rio). The dam, a modest 1m and 10f winner of 3 races, is a half-sister to 5 winners including the Group 2 6f Duke Of York Stakes winner The Kiddykid. The second dam, Mezzanine (by Sadler's Wells), is an unraced half-sister to 3 winners here and abroad. *"Not very big, we're getting on with her now and she's certainly a 2-y-o type. Very forward, it won't be long before she wins".*

953. KYLLUKEY ★★★

b.c. Kyllachy – Money Note (Librettist). January 30. First foal. 50,000Y. Tattersalls October Book 2. Sackville/Donald. The dam is an unplaced half-sister to 6 winners including the very smart Group 1 1m Gran Criterium winner and 2,000 Guineas second Lend A Hand. The second dam, Janaat (by Kris), a fair

12f winner, is a sister to the French 3-y-o listed 10.5f winner Trefoil and a half-sister to 11 winners including the smart middle-distance winners Maysoon, Richard of York, Third Watch and Three Tails (the dam of 3 Group winners). *"A great big horse, he's a nice horse in the making but he isn't going to be sharp. Much more of a seven furlong horse for later on".*

954. LAKE PLACID ★★

b.c. Champs Elysees – Phantom Wind (Storm Cat). April 12. Eighth foal. The dam, a very useful 6f (at 2 yrs) and Group 3 7f Oak Tree Stakes winner, was third in the Group 1 1m Matron Stakes. The second dam, Ryafan (by Lear Fan), was a high-class winner of the Group 1 Prix Marcel Boussac, the Grade 1 Queen Elizabeth II Challenge Cup, the Grade 1 Yellow Ribbon Stakes, the Grade 1 Flower Bowl Invitational and the Group 2 Nassau Stakes. (Khalid Abdulla). *"A plain looking horse, he's had a couple of minor issues so we've not been asking him any questions. A straightforward horse and a good mover, he's quite nice".*

955. LITTLE VOICE ★★★ ♠

b.f. Scat Daddy – Excelente (Exceed And Excel). March 28. Second foal. €160,000Y. Goffs Orby. Sackville/Donald. The dam, a fairly useful listed-placed Irish 2-y-o 7f winner, subsequently won twice in the USA and is a half-sister to 3 winners including the useful 1m and listed 15f winner Anousa and the useful 7f (at 2 yrs) and 11f winner Prince Nureyev. The second dam, Annaletta (by Belmez), a minor French 12f winner and listed-placed in Germany, is a half-sister to 7 winners including the dam of the Grade 1 E P Taylor Stakes winner Fraulein. *"He's one to be getting on with, he's got a bit of speed and he won't be long away. I see him being out in May".*

956. LORD TOPPER ★★★ ♠

b.c. Sir Percy – Fugnina (Hurricane Run). April 23. First foal. 30,000Y. Tattersalls October Book 2. Not sold. The dam, a quite useful Italian 9f and 10f winner, is a half-sister to 3 winners including the Group 2 Summer Mile and Group 3 Diomed Stakes winner Fanunalter. The second dam, Step Danzer (by Desert Prince), a listed winner in Italy and second in the Group 1 Italian Oaks, is a half-sister to 6 winners including the Italian Group 3 winner Baila Salsa. *"He goes alright and Barry likes the Sir Percy's. This one is a good mover and a good goer but he's not going to be sharp. He'll start off at seven furlongs I should think".*

957. LOVE ON THE ROCKS (IRE) ★★★★ ♠
ch.f. Exceed And Excel – My Love Thomas (Cadeaux Genereux). February 8. Third foal. 90,000Y. Tattersalls October Book 1. BBA (Ire). Sister to the fair 6f winner Double Up and half-sister to the fair 5f (at 2 yrs) to 1m winner Full Support (by Acclamation). The dam, a fair 2-y-o 6f winner, is a half-sister to 8 winners including the US Grade 3 Miesque Stakes winner Louvain. The second dam, Flanders (by Common Grounds), a very useful sprint winner of 6 races including the listed Scarbrough Stakes, was second in the Group 2 Kings Stand Stakes and is a half-sister to 8 winners. *"She's not over-big and everyone likes her although she is a bit temperamental. He'll be running in April or May, she's nice, straightforward and has a good action. Possibly one for Royal Ascot".*

958. MARBOOH (IRE) ★★★★
b.c. Dark Angel – Muluk (Rainbow Quest). April 25. Fourth foal. 120,000Y. Tattersalls October Book 2. Shadwell Estate Co. Half-brother to the quite useful 2014 2-y-o 7f winner Intiwin (by Intikhab) and to the modest 8.5f and 10f winner Daisy Boy (by Cape Cross). The dam, a fairly useful Irish 1m winner, is a half-sister to 5 minor winners. The second dam, Messina (by Sadler's Wells), is a placed half-sister to 9 winners including Enthused (Group 2 6f Lowther Stakes and Group 3 6f Princess Margaret Stakes). (Hamdan Al Maktoum). *"Everybody likes this colt. He's got a bit of speed, he gives you a good feel and he has a good action. He'll be a six furlong colt, we haven't done much with him yet but he'll be running in May".*

959. MENAI (IRE) ★★★★
b.c. Dark Angel – Glisten (Oasis Dream). February 7. Second foal. 100,000Y. Tattersalls October Book 1. B W Hills. Brother to the fairly useful 2014 2-y-o 7f to 8.5f winner Black Granite. The dam, a fairly useful Irish 2-y-o 7f winner, was listed-placed and is a half-sister

to 2 winners. The second dam, Jackie's Opera (by Indian Ridge), is an unraced half-sister to 5 winners including the dual French listed winner Arabian King. *"Barry Hills bought this colt and he likes him. He's a big horse, he's done well and although he's not the best mover in the world I'm sure he'll be alright. He's got a good temperament for a Dark Angel and is possibly one for Royal Ascot".*

960. MISS PIMPERNEL (IRE) ★★★
b.f. Clodovil – Mrs Seek (Unfuwain). March 31. Seventh foal. 60,000Y. Tattersalls October Book 2. BBA (Ire). Half-sister to the French listed 12f winner of 3 races Change The World (by Sakhee), to the fair 1m winner Mamma Rosa (by Footstepsinthesand), the fair 9.5f winner L'Avenue (by Champs Elysees) and the Italian 2-y-o winner Floral Art (by Excellent Art). The dam, an Italian winner of 3 races and listed-placed, is a half-sister to 3 minor winners. The second dam, Night Over Day (by Most Welcome), was unplaced. *"She's going to want time but she's done well. She's a very close coupled filly and she'll definitely be alright later on over seven furlongs".*

961. MONDRIAN JONES ★★
b.c. Dutch Art – Akhira (Emperor Jones). February 25. Seventh living foal. 65,000Y. Tattersalls October Book 2. Sackville/Donald. Half-brother to the fairly useful triple 5f winner (including at 2 yrs) and listed-placed Empress Jain (by Lujain), to the fair 6f winner Another Decree (by Diktat) and the modest 2-y-o 5f winner Empress Royal (by Royal Applause). The dam, a modest 4-y-o 7f winner, is a half-sister to one winner. The second dam, Fakhira (by Jareer), a quite useful 2-y-o 5f winner, is a half-sister to 6 winners including Danehill Dancer. *"He's done well lately but he's not speedy and needs time. A seven furlong 2-y-o".*

962. MOORSIDE ★★★
b.f. Champs Elysees – Marching West (Gone West). April 30. Half-sister to the fairly useful 7f (including at 2 yrs) and 1m winner of 4 races Marching Time (by Sadler's Wells), to the modest 1m winner Hint Of Promise (by Beat Hollow) and the modest 13f and 14f winner Giovanni Jack (by Three Valleys). The dam, a 2-y-o 6f winner in France, is a half-sister to the

champion 2-y-o and 3-y-o and sire Zafonic and to the smart Group 3 6f Prix de Cabourg winner and sire Zamindar. The second dam, Zaizafon (by The Minstrel), won twice over 7f at 2 yrs, was placed in the Group 1 1m Queen Elizabeth II Stakes and is a half-sister to the unraced Modena, herself dam of the Eclipse Stakes and Phoenix Champion Stakes winner Elmaamul. (Khalid Abdulla). *"She's a nice, big filly with a good temperament and a good action. Everybody likes her, she had a slight injury so she won't be early, but she's a nice filly".*

963. MUSTALLIB (IRE) ★★★

b.c. Iffraaj – Rocking (Oasis Dream). March 27. Fourth foal. 100,000foal. Goffs November. Shadwell Estate Co. Half-brother to the fair 2014 2-y-o 5f winner Rocking The Boast (by Zebedee), to the fairly useful 2-y-o 5f winner and 3-y-o Group 3 6f Ballyogan Stakes second Boston Rocker (by Acclamation) and the modest 2-y-o 5f winner Sleepy Joe (by Jeremy). The dam, a quite useful 2-y-o 5f winner, is a half-sister to 10 winners including the very smart Group 2 5f Flying Childers Stakes winner Superstar Leo (herself the dam of two stakes winners). The second dam, Council Rock (by General Assembly), a fair 9f and 10f placed 3-y-o, is a half-sister to 9 winners including the dam of the 2,000 Guineas winner Footstepsinthesand. (Hamdan Al Maktoum). *"He's quite a nice little horse, he's straightforward but not a five furlong type. I'd say he's one for six furlongs".*

964. PICKAPOCKET ★★★

b.c. Fast Company – Ann's Annie (Alzao). March 23. Ninth foal. £85,000Y. Doncaster Premier. BBA (Ire). Half-brother to the fairly useful 10f and 12f winner of 8 races Sgt Schultz (by In The Wings), to the fair 12f to 2m and hurdles winner Galianna (by Galileo), the fair 7f winner Devonelli (by Mujadil), the modest dual 1m winner including at 2 yrs Leitzu (by Barathea) and the modest 14f winner Red River Rock (by Spectrum). The dam, a quite useful 2-y-o 1m winner in Ireland, is a half-sister to 6 winners including the very smart Group 3 7f Criterion Stakes winner Pipe Major. The second dam, Annsfield Lady (by Red Sunset), a winner of 3 races in

Ireland between 9f and 10f, is a half-sister to 4 winners including the Group 2 and dual Group 3 winner Insatiable. *"He'll be running in April over five furlongs because he's showing he's ready to have a go, but he'll want six furlongs and will probably get seven. He's a very strong, straightforward colt that does everything well".*

965. PRIVATE JET ★★★

b.c. Paco Boy – Sheer Indulgence (Pivotal). May 19. Third foal. €72,000Y. Goffs Orby. Sackville/Donald. Half-brother to the fair 2014 2-y-o 6f winner Sawaahel (by Pastoral Pursuits) and to the very useful dual 5f (at 2 yrs) and listed 6f winner Mick's Yer Man (by Bahamian Bounty). The dam is an unraced half-sister to 2 winners including the listed-placed Clear Impression. The second dam, Shining Hour (by Red Ransom), won the Group 3 5f Queen Mary Stakes and is a sister to the Group 1 Moyglare Stud Stakes third Titian Time and a half-sister to 6 winners. *"A great big horse and a late foal. Everyone liked him as a yearling but he's had sore shins so we've had to back off him. He's going to want time but he's a nice horse and he could be anything".*

966. RAVELIN (USA) ★★★★

ch.f. Congrats – Rouwaki (Miswaki). February 21. Half-sister to the smart 7f (at 2 yrs) and listed 1m winner Critical Moment (by Aptitude), to the smart 2-y-o 6f and Group 3 7f Somerville Tattersall Stakes winner Rerouted (by Stormy Atlantic), the quite useful 1m winner Rattan (by Royal Anthem) and the fair dual 1m winner Cornish Castle (by Mizzen Mast). The dam is an unplaced half-sister to the Grade 1 Kentucky Oaks winner Flute. The second dam, Rougeur (by Blushing Groom), won over 10f and 12f in the USA. The sire, Congrats, won a Grade 2 stakes at Santa Anita over 8.5f. To date he's sired three Grade 1 winners from 5 crops including Turbulent Descent (four Grade 1 wins in the USA). (Khalid Abdulla). *"I like this filly, she's got a lovely way of going, quite laid-back and she hasn't come in her coat yet. I think she's got a bit of something about her and she should make a 2-y-o by the time the seven furlong races come along".*

967. SAHREEJ (IRE) ★★★★
gr.c. Zebedee – Petite Boulangere (Namid). March 13. Fifth foal. 160,000Y. Tattersalls October Book 2. Shadwell Estate Co. Half-brother to the quite useful 2014 2-y-o 5f winner She's A Worldie (by Kodiac) and to the modest dual 6f winner Ficelle (by Chineur).The dam is an unplaced half-sister to 6 winners including the smart 2-y-o Group 3 6f Sirenia Stakes winner and Group 1 Cheveley Park Stakes second Dhanyata. The second dam, Preponderance (by Cyrano de Bergerac), a quite useful 2-y-o dual 5f winner, is a half-sister to 6 winners. *"He's ready to run now. He's done all his prep work and everybody likes him. Well put together, he's got plenty of speed and he may well be our first 2-y-o winner".*

968. SEPAL (USA) ★★★★
b.f. Afleet Alex – Faraway Flower (Distant View). February 14. The dam, a useful 2-y-o 6f winner, is a half-sister to a winner. The second dam, Silver Star (by Zafonic), won over 1m at 2 yrs in France, was listed-placed over 1m at 3 yrs and is a sister to the champion European 2-y-o Xaar (winner of the Group 1 Dewhurst Stakes and the Group 1 Prix de la Salamandre) and a half-sister to the Group 3 10.5f Prix Corrida winner Diese and the Group 3 1m Prix Quincey winner Masterclass. (Khalid Abdulla). *"This is a really nice filly. She'll be a six/seven furlong 2-y-o, just needs to strengthen up a bit, but she's a lovely filly".*

969. SERRADURA (IRE) ★★★
b.f. Acclamation – Days Of Summer (Bachelor Duke). February 14. First foal. €100,000Y. Goffs Orby. Sackville/Donald. The dam, a fair 2-y-o 6f winner, is a half-sister to 6 winners including the Irish 2-y-o listed 6f winner Pharmacist (herself dam of the Grade 1 Breeders Cup Turf winner Red Rocks). The second dam, Pharaoh's Delight (by Fairy King), won the Group 1 5f Phoenix Stakes, was Group 1 placed four times and is a half-sister to 8 winners. *"She won't be slow, she's a nice size and I think she's got the speed for five furlongs".*

970. SHANGHAI GLORY (IRE) ★★★ ♠
ch.c. Exceed And Excel – Hecuba (Hector Protector). March 7. Seventh foal. €115,000Y. Goffs Orby. Sackville/Donald. Half-brother to 4 winners including the very useful listed 7f winner of 4 races Choose Me (by Choisir), the fairly useful Irish dual 10f winner Spirit Of Cuba (by Invincible Spirit), the quite useful 7f (at 2 yrs) and 1m winner of 4 races Aeronwyn Bryn (by Dylan Thomas) and the minor French 2-y-o winner Avril Rose (by Xaar). The dam, a fairly useful 10f winner, is a half-sister to 7 winners including the German Group 2 winner Bad Bertrich Again and the Group 3 Scottish Classic winner Prolix. The second dam, Ajuga (by The Minstrel), a useful 6f and 7f winner, is a half-sister to 5 winners. *"He's working now, he's taking it well and he's quite nice. He's got a lovely action and a big stride, but perhaps he'll want further than five furlongs".*

971. SIR ROGER MOORE (IRE) ★★★
b.c. Kodiac – Truly Magnificent (Elusive Quality). April 1. Second foal. €260,000Y. Goffs Orby. BBA (Ire). The dam, a modest 12f placed maiden, is a half-sister to a winner in Russia. The second dam, Magnificent Honour (by A P Indy), is an unraced sister to the US multiple Grade 1 winner Rags To Riches and a half-sister to the Grade 1 Belmont Stakes winner Jazil and the US Grade 2 winner Casino Drive. *"We're getting on with him and he was expensive but Kodiac yearlings fetch those sort of prices these days. It's a middle-distance family though, so we'll have to see whether five furlongs is too sharp for him or not".*

972. SKARA MAE (IRE) ★★★★
b.f. Canford Cliffs – Winged Valkyrie (Hawk Wing). January 29. First foal. 22,000Y. Tattersalls October Book 2. BBA (Ire). The dam, a modest 9f winner, is a half-sister to 5 winners including the Group 3 Classic Trial winner Above Average and the 2-y-o Group 3 7f Prestige Stakes winner Sent From Heaven. The second dam, Crystal Valkyrie (by Danehill), a fair 10f winner, is a half-sister to 3 minor winners. *"As tough as old boots, she's got a bit of fire in her belly, she's done well and she's a good mover. I'd say she's one for seven furlongs this year, she's growing at the minute and she's a nice, deep-bodied filly. I like her".*

973. SWILLY SUNSET ★★★★
b.c. Kyllachy – Spanish Springs (Xaar). February 8. Third foal. €80,000Y. Goffs Orby. BBA (Ire). Half-brother to the minor Italian 3-y-o winner Farmacista (by Key Of Luck).

The dam, placed once over 7f at 2 yrs, is a half-sister to 6 winners including the UAE dual Group 3 6f winner of 7 races Conroy. The second dam, Crystal Gazing (by El Gran Senor), winner of the Group 3 7f Nell Gwyn Stakes, was third in the 1,000 Guineas and is a half-sister to 3 winners. *"He was probably the pick of the yearlings, he really looked the part. But he's grown and I think he may want seven furlongs. A nice, big horse, he's good-looking with a great action".*

974. TAKATUL (USA)
b.c. Smart Strike – Torrestrella (Orpen). April 23. Half-brother to the 2014 7f placed 2-y-o (on his only start) Intilaaq (by Dynaformer) and to the Italian Group 3 6f and French listed 5.5f winner Farmah (by Speightstown). The dam, a winner of 3 races including the French 1,000 Guineas, is a half-sister to numerous winners out of Sea Ring (by Bering). (Hamdan Al-Maktoum). *"He's just arrived from Dubai so we're still learning about him. He's a nice size for a 2-y-o though and could be anything".*

975. TALLOIRE (USA) ★★★
b.br.c. Congrats – Intercontinental (Danehill). May 16. Fifth foal. Half-brother to the fairly useful 1m and 8.5f winner Abseil (by First Defence), to the fair triple 9f winner So Wise (by Elusive Quality) and the fair 2-y-o 6f winner Continental Drift (by Smart Strike). The dam, winner of Grade 1 Matriarch Stakes and the Grade 1 Filly & Mare Turf, is a sister to the triple Group/Grade 1 winners Banks Hill and Champs Elysees, the dual Group 1 winner Cacique and the Group 2 winner and high-class sire Dansili and closely related to the Grade 1 Matriarch Stakes and Grade 1 Beverly D Stakes winner Heat Haze. The second dam, Hasili (by Kahyasi), won over 5f at 2 yrs and stayed a mile. The sire, Congrats, won a Grade 2 stakes at Santa Anita over 8.5f. To date he's sired three Grade 1 winners from 5 crops including Turbulent Descent (four Grade 1 wins in the USA). (Khalid Abdulla). *"He's not very big and he's a late foal. One for seven furlongs, he's a nice little colt".*

976. TURAATHY (IRE) ★★★★
b.f. Lilbourne Lad – Key Girl (Key Of Luck). March 5. Fifth foal. £65,000Y. Doncaster Premier. Shadwell Estate Co. Closely related to the useful 2-y-o 6f and 7f winner and

Group 3 Solario Stakes third Music Theory (by Acclamation). The dam is an unplaced half-sister to 9 winners including the smart Irish 5f and listed 6f winner Rolo Tomasi and the Group 2 German 1,000 Guineas second Elegant Ridge. The second dam, Elegant Bloom (by Be My Guest), a quite useful Irish 2-y-o 6f winner, stayed 7f and is a full or half-sister to 12 winners. *"Everybody who rides her likes this filly and they all say she can go. We haven't done anything fast with her yet, but you can tell she won't take long to get ready. She's a strong-bodied filly, she's got everything and she won't be slow either".*

977. WINK AND WIN (IRE) ★★★
b.f. Rip Van Winkle – Windmill (Ezzoud). May 18. Ninth living foal. 45,000Y. Tattersalls October Book 1. Sackville/Donald. Half-brother to 5 winners including the 1m to 14f winner Deddeddeb (by Teofilo), the 2-y-o 6f winner and subsequent US and Canadian winner Winds Of Time (by Danehill), the 1m and 13f winner The Baronet (by Sir Percy) – all 3 quite useful – and the fair 9f winner Inis Boffin (by Danehill Dancer). The dam, a fair 13.8f winner, is a half-sister to 8 winners including the Group 2 12f Ribblesdale Stakes winner Gull Nook (dam of the top-class colt Pentire) and the Group 3 winners Banket and Mr Pintips. The second dam, Bempton (by Blakeney), placed three times at up to 11f, is a half-sister to Shirley Heights. *"This filly has done well, she's a short coupled filly and a late foal that'll need seven furlongs but she'll be nice".*

978. ZAAKHIR (IRE) ★★★
b.f. Raven's Pass – Zahoo (Nayef). February 21. Second foal. Half-sister to the very useful 2014 Irish 2-y-o listed 7.5f winner Convergence (by Cape Cross). The dam, a fairly useful 1m (at 2 yrs) and 10f winner and listed 10f second, is a half-sister to the smart Group 3 14f winner Tactic. The second dam, Tanaghum (by Darshaan), a useful listed-placed 10f winner, is a half-sister to 7 winners including the smart Group 2 10f Premio Lydia Tesio winner Najah. *"A very big filly, she's highly strung and we're treating her with kid gloves at the minute. One for the late summer, she has a lot to like about her but she'll take time".*

979. UNNAMED ★★
b.c. Canford Cliffs – Basanti (Galileo). March 3.
Fourth foal. 40,000Y. Tattersalls October Book
2. Not sold. Half-brother to the modest 14f
and 2m winner Man From Seville (by Duke Of
Marmalade). The dam, a fair 10f winner, is a
half-sister to 5 winners including the Group 3
5f Prix du Bois winner Ozone Layer, the very
useful dual 1m winner and Group 2 Dante
Stakes third Musalsal and the French Group 3
third Amusing Time. The second dam, Ozone
Friendly (by Green Forest), a useful 2-y-o
winner of the Group 1 5.5f Prix Robert Papin,
is a half-sister to 5 winners including the US
2-y-o stakes winner Storm Flight. *"A great big
horse, he'll be alright later on and he has a
good temperament. We'll set him off at seven
furlongs".*

980. UNNAMED ★★
b.f. Iffraaj – Burren Rose (Storm Cat). March
30. Fifth foal. €100,000Y. Goffs Orby. David
Redvers. Half-sister to the Qatar 1m and
French 12f winner Burren Quality (by Elusive
Quality) and to the fair 2014 Irish 2-y-o 8.5f
winner Bleu Ciel Et Rouge (by Manduro).
The dam, a useful Irish 1m, 10f and listed
12f winner, is a half-sister to 2 winners. The
second dam, Lisieux Rose (by Generous), won
the Group 2 11f Blandford Stakes and two
US Grade 2 events and is a half-sister to 9
winners. *"Very immature when she came in,
she's grown and matured now but she's not
going to be speedy".*

981. UNNAMED ★★★
b.f. Sakhee's Secret – Dimakya (Dayjur).
February 27. Half-sister to 6 winners including
the French 2-y-o 5.5f winner and Group 2
7f Prix du Calvados third Mpumalanga (by
Observatory), the quite useful 10f all-weather
winner Over The Rainbow (by Rainbow Quest),
the quite useful 10f and 12f winner Golano
(by Linamix) and the fair 2-y-o 6f winner
Tereed Elhawa (by Cadeaux Genereux). The
dam, a fair 7.5f winner in France, is a half-sister
to 6 winners including the listed winners
Loyalize and Remuria. The second dam, Reloy
(by Liloy), won two Grade 1 events in the USA.
*"This is a nice filly, she's had one piece of work
and she'll be ready to run over five furlongs,
but she'll improve for six I think. Should have a
bit of speed".*

982. UNNAMED ★★★
ch.c. Dutch Art – Endless Love (Dubai
Destination). April 6. Third foal. Brother to the
fairly useful 2-y-o 7f winner and listed-placed
Dutch Romance. The dam is an unraced half-
sister to one winner. The second dam, La Vita
E Bella (by Definite Article), a 2-y-o listed 1m
winner and second in the Group 3 Prix Saint-
Roman, is a half-sister to 3 winners including
the useful 2-y-o dual listed 5f winner and
Group 2 third Bella Tusa. *"He'll definitely make
a 2-y-o and he's quite a nice horse. One for six
/seven furlongs in mid-season".*

983. UNNAMED ★★
b.c. Rip Van Winkle – Faraday Light (Rainbow
Quest). March 31. Fifth foal. €420,000foal.
Goffs November. David Redvers. Half-brother
to the Group 1 Irish 1,000 Guineas and Grade
1 E P Taylor Stakes winner Just The Judge,
to the fair 1m winner Amber Silk (both by
Lawman) and the useful 2-y-o 1m winner
and 3-y-o listed 9f second Obliterator (by
Oratorio). The dam ran twice unplaced and is
a half-sister to 3 winners including the Group
3 St Simon Stakes winner and dual Group
1 placed High Heeled. The second dam,
Uncharted Haven (by Turtle Island), won two
Grade 2 events in the USA and is a half-sister
to 6 winners. *"He's backward and weak at
present, but even his half-sister Just The Judge
didn't set off until late summer over seven
furlongs".*

984. UNNAMED ★★★
b.c. Sir Percy – Half Sister (Oratorio). April 13.
Second foal. £30,000Y. Doncaster Premier. BBA
(Ire). The dam, a moderate 10f and 12f placed
maiden, is a half-sister to 3 minor winners
abroad. The second dam, Fifty Five (by Lake
Coniston), a minor French 3-y-o winner, is a
half-sister to 8 winners including the multiple
Group 1 winners and champions Grandera
and George Washington. *"Barry Hills bought
her at Doncaster, he's not over-big but he'll be
tough. One for seven furlongs later on".*

985. UNNAMED ★★★
ch.f. Dream Ahead – Khibraat (Alhaarth).
March 26. Fifth foal. 55,000Y. Tattersalls
October Book 2. Rabbah Bloodstock. Half-filly
to the fairly useful 2-y-o dual 1m winner and
Group 3 Derby Trial third Cavaleiro (by Sir

Percy) and to the quite useful 10.5f winner Westpieser (by Azamour). The dam is an unplaced half-sister to 10 winners including the smart Group 2 14.6f Park Hill Stakes winner Ranin. The second dam, Nafhaat (by Roberto), a fairly useful 12f winner, was listed-placed and stayed 15f. *"She's a nice filly but she's just cantering away because her joints are immature, but she'll be fine by mid-season".*

986. UNNAMED ★★★★
b.f. Invincible Spirit – Laywaan (Fantastic Light). April 26. Fifth foal. 67,000Y. Tattersalls October Book 2. David Redvers. Half-sister to the quite useful 2-y-o 7f winner Madmoonah (by Invincible Spirit) and to the fair 11f winner Nabat Ali (by Nayef). The dam, a fairly useful 1m and 10f winner of 4 races, is a half-sister to 5 winners including the US Grade 3 placed Run Alex Run. The second dam, Electrostat (by Dynaformer), a minor winner in the USA, is a half-sister to 8 winners including the Grade 1 Beldame Stakes winner Weber City Miss, herself dam of the dual Grade 1 winner Slew City Slew. *"This is quite a nice filly. She's got a bit about her and is probably the best of the Qatar Racing horses here. She's looks really nice and probably wants seven furlongs, so it'll be mid-season before she's ready. She's done really well, has a good action and everyone likes her".*

987. UNNAMED ★★★
ch.f. Teofilo – Queen Of Lyons (Dubai Destination). April 14. Third foal. 65,000Y. Tattersalls October Book 2. Not sold. Sister to the fair 2014 Irish 7f placed 2-y-o Perfect Fit. The dam ran twice unplaced and is a half-sister to 6 winners including Benbaun (Group 1 Prix de l'Abbaye). The second dam, Escape To Victory (by Salse), won twice at 2 yrs in Italy and is a half-sister to 6 winners including the US triple Grade 2 winner Hawksley Hill. *"For one by Teofilo this filly isn't too big and she's not backward. A few of the girls have been riding her, she's very straightforward and they like her. She's a nice filly with a good action and a good temperament".*

988. UNNAMED ★★★
b.f. Teofilo – Towards (Fusaichi Pegasus). March 21. Third foal. 55,000Y. Tattersalls October Book 1. Rabbah Bloodstock. Half-

sister to the fairly useful dual 5f winner at 2 and 3 yrs and Group 2 Queen Mary Stakes third One Chance (by Invincible Spirit). The dam is an unplaced half-sister to the multiple Group 1 winner Spinning World and the listed winner Visions Of Clarity (dam of the Group 1 National Stakes winner Pathfork). The second dam, Imperfect Circle (by Riverman), winner of the 2-y-o listed 6f Firth of Clyde Stakes and second in the Group 1 Cheveley Park Stakes, is a half-sister to the Group/Grade 1 winners Denon and Chimes of Freedom (herself the dam of two Grade 1 winners). *"This is a nice big filly with a lovely action and a good temperament. She's back cantering again after a little setback and she's going to want seven furlongs. A good-looking filly".*

WILLIAM JARVIS

989. GOLDEN KINGDOM ★★★
b.c. Elusive City – Sea Paint (Peintre Celebre). March 2. Fourth foal. 30,000Y. Tattersalls October Book 3. Blandford Bloodstock. Brother to the French 2015 3-y-o 9.5f winner Cubist (by Fastnet Rock). The dam is an unraced sister to the French multiple listed winner Celebrissime and a half-sister to 9 winners including the US dual Grade 1 winner Special Ring. The second dam, Ring Beaune (by Bering), won two minor races at 3 yrs in France and is a half-sister to 12 winners including the Group 1 Criterium de Saint-Cloud winner Poliglote. (Wee Hui Hui). *"We like this little horse and we'll be aiming him at the Tattersalls Book 3 Sales race. A well-made, well-balanced, good-looking colt, he goes OK".*

990. HIGHWAY DREAM ★★★
b.f. Dick Turpin – Just Dreams (Salse). February 19. 10,000Y. Tattersalls October Book 3. W Jarvis. Half-sister to the fair 2014 2-y-o 6f winner Mighty Warrior (by Bahamian Bounty), to the 2-y-o 7f winner (from two starts) Perfect Persuasion (by Myboycharlie), the UAE 6f and 7f winner and Group 3 second Bounty Quest (by Fasliyev), the fair Irish 7f winner Lucid Moment (by Haafhd) and the modest 12f to 2m winner Dramatic Solo (by Nayef). The dam, a modest 12f winner, is a sister the Group 1 St Leger and Group 1 Ascot Gold Cup winner Classic Cliche and a half-sister to 5 winners including the Group 1 Prix Vermeille winner My Emma. The second dam,

Pato (by High Top), a fairly useful 2-y-o 7f and triple 4-y-o 10f winner, is a sister to the very smart sprinter Crews Hill. (G B Turnbull). *"She's showing a fair bit of speed at the moment, certainly enough for five furlongs and she should be racing in April or May. A speedy little filly, we like her".* **TRAINERS' BARGAIN BUY**

991. LADY LLOYD ★★
b.f. Paco Boy – Carafe (Selkirk). February 5. Sixth living foal. 10,000Y. Tattersalls October Book 2. Blandford Bloodstock. Half-sister to a winner in Qatar by Oasis Dream. The dam, a quite useful 7f winner, is a half-sister to the fairly useful 1m winner and listed-placed Coyote (herself the dam of two stakes winners). The second dam, Caramba (by Belmez), a smart winner of the Group 2 1m Falmouth Stakes and the Group 2 10f Nassau Stakes, is a half-sister to 7 winners including the Moyglare Stud Stakes and Falmouth Stakes winner Lemon Souffle. (Robert Lloyd & Partners). *"Another cheapish filly, she's quite sharp and fairly straightforward. I should think she'll be out by June and six furlongs will be her bag".*

992. ORGAN SCHOLAR ★★★★
b.c. Nayef – Palatial (Green Desert). March 12. Ninth foal. 50,000Y. Tattersalls October Book 1. William Jarvis. Brother to 2 winners including the Group 2 1m May Hill Stakes (at 2 yrs) and Group 2 1m Windsor Forest Stakes winner and 1,000 Guineas second Spacious (by Nayef) and half-brother to the Canadian Grade 2 7f winner Dimension, the useful 7f (at 2 yrs) and 1m winner Artimino (both by Medicean) and the fair 6f winner Spice Run (by Zafonic). The dam, a useful 7f winner of 4 races at 2 and 3 yrs, is a half-sister to 6 winners including the listed 10f winners Portal and Ice Palace. The second dam, White Palace (by Shirley Heights), was a quite useful 3-y-o 8.2f winner. (Mr C A Washbourn). *"A lovely, big, well-bred horse and a half-brother to a Group 1 winner. He's one for the second half of the season but from what we've seen so far we like him. Seven furlongs is likely to be his starting point".*

993. PORT PARADISE ★★★ ♠
gr.g. Paco Boy – Yacht Woman (Mizzen Mast). March 10. Third foal. 32,000Y. Tattersalls

October Book 3. Will Edmeades. Half-brother to the French 2-y-o winner Yachtclubgenoa (by Teofilo). The dam won 4 races in Italy including a listed 5f event at 2 yrs and is a half-sister to one winner. The second dam, Yacht Club (by Sea Hero), won 3 minor races in the USA at 2 and 3 yrs and is a half-sister to 5 winners. (A N Verrier). *"We gelded him because he was a bit fiery. He's had a touch of sore shins but he seems quite a nice little horse. Strong and robust, I think once we get him rolling he'll be tough and one that can run regularly. He goes well and we like him".*

994. QUICK LOOK ★★
b.g. Kheleyf – Weqaar (Red Ransom). March 4. Eighth foal. 5,000Y. Tattersalls October Book 2. Not sold. Half-sister to the quite useful 9f winner Fadhaa (by Bahri), to the quite useful 2-y-o 10f winner Cherry Street (by Alhaarth) and the modest 2-y-o 7f winner Roving Bunny (by Aqlaam). The dam, a quite useful 10.2f winner, is a half-sister to 5 winners including Sakhee (Prix de l'Arc de Triomphe and Juddmonte International) and the listed winner Nasheed. The second dam, Thawakib (by Sadler's Wells), won twice over 7f (at 2 yrs) and the Group 2 12f Ribblesdale Stakes and is a half-sister to 9 winners including the Group 2 Princess of Wales's Stakes winner Celestial Storm. (M C Banks). *"Despite his low price tag he's a very nice horse, very willing, well-balanced and a bit 'on the leg' at the moment. We like him".*

995. TIBIBIT ★★★
br.f. Kyllachy – Cat Hunter (One Cool Cat). March 4. First foal. The dam, a modest 7f (at 2 yrs) and 1m winner, is a half-sister to a French middle-distance winner. The second dam, Eoz (by Sadler's Wells), was a quite useful 12f winner. (Mr David Cohen). *"She's a first foal and a bit small but these Kyllachy's can all run a bit and there's no reason why she won't either. A sweet, good-natured filly and she's definitely got a chance".*

996. WIMPOLE HALL ★★★★
b.c. Canford Cliffs – Sparkling Eyes (Lujain). April 17. Fourth foal. 65,000Y. Tattersalls October Book 2. William Jarvis. Half-brother to the quite useful 6f winner Blurred Vision (by Royal Applause) and to the quite useful

5.5f (at 2 yrs) and 6f winner Pea Shooter (by Piccolo). The dam, a fairly useful dual 5f winner (including at 2 yrs), was fourth in the Group 2 5f Queen Mary Stakes, is a half-sister to 3 winners here and abroad. The second dam, Lady Georgia (by Arazi), was a useful 3-y-o 7.8f winner. (Mr C A Washbourn & Nigel Gadsby). *"He's a nice horse by the first season sire Canford Cliffs and a half-brother to Blurred Vision who we trained and then sold to Hong Kong. He's got a lovely temperament just like his half-brother and he's a good mover. He should be a fast horse and a mile would be the furthest he's likely to go".*

997. UNNAMED ★★
b.br.f. Le Havre – La Chapelle (Holy Roman Emperor). January 16. First foal. 24,000Y. Tattersalls October Book 3. William Jarvis. The dam is an unplaced half-sister to the listed-placed winner Sleeping Beauty. The second dam, Nightime (by Galileo), won 2 races at 3 yrs including the Irish 1,000 Guineas and is a half-sister to 7 winners. (G B Turnbull & Mrs Susan Davis). *"I like the sire, the grandam was a classic winner and this is a strong, well-made filly. I haven't done a lot with her yet because her knees are slightly immature, but from what we've seen she's absolutely fine. She'll be a summer 2-y-o but she may need seven furlongs to start with".*

998. UNNAMED ★★★
b.c. Dick Turpin – Right Rave (Soviet Star). February 9. First foal. The dam, a fair 5f (at 2 yrs) to 9f winner of 3 races, is a half-sister to 3 winners. The second dam, Genuinely (by Groom Dancer), is a placed half-sister to 2 winners. (Rent Right). *"A big, strong, hardy looking horse out of a tough racemare, he's enthusiastic in his work and he could well be OK. He'll need six furlongs to start with".*

EVE JOHNSON HOUGHTON
999. BECCA CAMPBELL (IRE) ★★★
b.f. Roderic O'Connor – Scottendale (Zilzal). April 10. Fifth foal. €15,000Y. Tattersalls Ireland September. Eve Johnson-Houghton. Half-sister to the modest 6f winner Bush Beauty (by Bushranger). The dam is an unplaced half-sister to 6 winners including the Group 3 10f Gordon Richards Stakes winner Compton Ace. The second dam, Mountain Lodge (by

Blakeney), won the Irish St Leger and is a half-sister to 3 winners. *"A sweet filly, she won't be too long away and hopefully she'll be out by the beginning of May. She goes nicely, I'm happy with her and the pedigree has improved a bit since I bought because there's been another winner. I think she'll be alright, not a world beater but she'll win races.*

1000. CANFORD LILLI (IRE) ★★★
b.f. Canford Cliffs – Aine (Danehill Dancer). February 22. Second foal. €22,000Y. Tattersalls Ireland September. Eve Johnson Houghton. The dam, a useful listed 6f winner of 3 races, is a half-sister to 2 winners abroad. The second dam, Antinnaz (by Thatching), won the listed Cecil Frail Stakes and is a half-sister to 3 winners. (Peter Wollaston & Peter Johnson). *"She's lovely. She'll take a bit of time because she's big and quite backward, but she's very nice. We haven't put a gun to her head at all and she's one for mid-season onwards, probably over six/seven furlongs".*

1001. CARA'S MUSE (IRE) ★★★★
b.f. Zoffany – Shenkara (Night Shift). February 3. Seventh foal. €26,000Y. Goffs Orby. Eve Johnson Houghton. Half-sister to the quite useful listed-placed 5f and 7f winner You Da One (by Footstepsinthesand), to the fair 5f (at 2 yrs) to 8.5f winner of 9 races and listed-placed Crocodile Bay (by Spectrum), to the 2-y-o 5f winner (on his only start) Metal Soldier (by Antonius Pius) and a winner in Greece by Invincible Spirit. The dam, placed fourth once over 1m at 2 yrs in Ireland, is a half-sister to 3 minor winners. The second dam, Sheriyna (by Darshaan), a listed winner in France at 3 yrs, is a half-sister to 5 winners including the Prix de Diane winner and useful broodmare Shemaka. (Swanee River Partnership). *"She's got bags of pace and is probably one of the most forward I've got. Depending on the weather she may be out in April. I love her, she's switched on and very professional". TRAINERS' BARGAIN BUY*

1002. COARSE CUT (IRE) ★★★
b.c. Duke Of Marmalade – Keladora (Crafty Prospector). March 2. Fourth foal. 16,000Y. Tattersalls October Book 3. Eve Johnson Houghton. Half-brother to the fair 12f and 14f winner Kelamita (by Pivotal). The dam, a

French listed-placed winner of 3 races, is a half-sister to 3 winners including the Group 1 Prix Marcel Boussac second On Verra. The second dam, Karmifira (by Always Fair), winner of the listed Prix Finlande and second in the French 1,000 Guineas, is a half-sister to 5 winners including the listed 1m Prix Coronation winner Kart Star. (Equi ex Incertis Partners). *"He's going to take a bit of time, being by Duke Of Marmalade. A lovely, big horse with a real long stride on him, he's going to be one for the back-end, starting at seven furlongs, but he does everything easily".*

1003. CUSTODIAL (IRE) ★★★
b.f. Lawman – Chervil (Dansili). March 16. Sixth foal. 6,000Y. Tattersalls October Book 2. Eve Johnson Houghton. Half-sister to the 2014 7f fourth placed 2-y-o Faery Song (by Lawman), to the quite useful 2-y-o 7f winner Laurelita (by High Chaparral), the fair 5f and 6f winner of 4 races (including at 2 yrs) Mandy Layla (by Excellent Art) and the fair 1m winner Zeyran (by Galileo). The dam, a quite useful 6f winner, is closely related to the US Grade 1 winner Light Jig and a half-sister to 9 winners including the 2-y-o listed 1m winner. The second dam, Nashmeel (by Blushing Groom), winner of the Group 2 1m Prix d'Astarte, was second in three Group 1 events. *"She's sharp enough, quite switched on and she's got a good stride on her. But as with all my 2-y-o's she's just not that forward yet. I think she'll be one for the end of May and I can see her being suited by seven furlongs".*

1004. FANTASY QUEEN ★★
b.f. Aqlaam – Regal Curtsy (Royal Applause). March 8. Fourth foal. Half-sister to a minor 4-y-o winner abroad by Halling. The dam, a moderate 10f placed maiden, is a half-sister to several winners including the smart Group 3 10f winner Take A Bow. The second dam, Giant Nipper (by Nashwan), was unplaced on her only start and is a half-sister to 3 minor winners. (Zara Campbell-Harris). *"A nice individual and a sweet filly, she'll be out in June and does everything easily. She should win".*

1005. ICE AGE (IRE) ★★★★
b.c. Frozen Power – Incendio (Siberian Express). May 22. Twelfth foal. 21,000Y. Tattersalls October Book 3. Eve Johnson

Houghton. Half-brother to 7 winners including the fair 2014 2-y-o 5f winner Chances Are (by Dandy Man), the Group 2 6f Diadem Stakes and Group 3 5f Norfolk Stakes winner Baron's Pit (by Night Shift), the Irish 6f (at 2 yrs) and 7f winner Set Fire (by Bertolini) and the fair 5f (at 2 yrs) and 6f winner Candela Bay (by Captain Rio). The dam, an Italian winner of 9 races from 2 to 4 yrs, is a half-sister to 5 winners including the Italian listed winner of 10 races Infiel. The second dam, Indocina (by Indian King), a listed-placed winner of 4 races in Italy, is a half-sister to 7 winners including the Irish 2,000 Guineas second Sun Valley. (Eden Racing III). *"A lovely horse, he's very racy and he'll be a six furlong 2-y-o. He's a late foal and yet was giving all the signs that he might be early, but then he grew. He's catching up now though and he won't be late on the racecourse. I'd say he'll be racing in May and he's a really nice colt".*

1006. IN HASTE (IRE) ★★★
gr.c. Clodovil – Hasty Katie (Whipper). May 12. Second foal. €16,000Y. Tattersalls Ireland September. Eve Johnson Houghton. The dam, a fair 2-y-o 8.5f winner, is a half-sister to 4 winners including the Group 3 Killavullen Stakes third Takrice. The second dam, Hasanat (by Night Shift), a 7f (at 2 yrs) and 9f winner in Ireland and third in the Group 3 Concorde Stakes, is a half-sister to 5 winners. *"He'll probably be my first 2-y-o runner. I know he has a late foaling date but I don't get hung up about them too much. I go off the signs that the horse gives me as to whether he's ready or not. This horse is tough and he's got bags of pace, so he'll be a real good fun horse. I love Clodovil's because they're real trainer's horses – tough and honest. I may start him at five furlongs but I should think he'd improve for six and maybe seven".*

1007. LADY KATHERINE ★★★
b.f. Dick Turpin – Vax Star (Petong). February 3. Eleventh foal. 8,000Y. Tattersalls October Book 3. Eve Johnson Houghton. Half-sister to 7 winners including the fairly useful 2-y-o dual 6f winner Negligee (by Night Shift), the quite useful 6f (at 2 yrs) and 5f winner of 5 races Yurituni (by Bahamian Bounty) and the 2-y-o sprint winners River Crossing (by Zafonic), Trick Or Two (by Desert Style) and

Silver Shadow (by Fasliyev). The dam, a fairly useful 2-y-o 5f listed winner, is a half-sister to 4 winners. The second dam, the fairly useful listed sprint winner Vax Lady (by Millfontaine), is a half-sister to 2 winners. *"She's racy and won't be too far away if I can get her coat looking less woolly. We won the big nursery at York with her half-sister Yurituni. This is a sharp filly, a good model and she'll start off at five furlongs".*

1008. PALM AVENUE ★★★

b.c. Mount Nelson – Fascination Street (Mujadil). January 23. Sixth foal. 8,000Y. Tattersalls October Book 3. Eve Johnson Houghton. Half-brother to Amy Dorrit (by Pivotal), a minor winner of 20 races abroad from 3 to 5 yrs. The dam, a modest 7f winner at 3 yrs, is a half-sister to 6 winners including the US triple Grade 1 winner from 9f to 10f Golden Apples and the Group 3 Park Hill Stakes winner Alexander Three D. The second dam, Loon (by Kaldoun), won 4 races in France including the listed 12f Prix de la Porte de Passy and is a half-sister to 3 minor winners. (Picnic Partnership). *"He's big, but he's probably done all his growing already and he may be earlier than I thought he'd be. He's probably one for June or July and he's owned by the same partnership who own my nice 3-y-o by Mount Nelson, Room Key".*

1009. PATANJALI ★★★★

b.f. Poet's Voice – Penang (Xaar). March 10. €27,000Y. Goffs Orby. Not sold. Half-sister to the fair 1m winner of 3 races from 2 to 4 yrs Chrissycross and to the modest 1m winner Carenza (both by Cape Cross). The dam, placed fourth once over 10.5f, is a half-sister to numerous winners including the very useful 2-y-o 6f winner and Group 1 Cheveley Park Stakes third Badminton, the useful 2-y-o 7f winner and Group 3 7f Vintage Stakes third Fox and the useful 6f and 7f winner and Group 3 Nell Gwyn Stakes second Cala. The second dam, Badawi (by Diesis), was a useful 1m and 9f winner of 4 races. (Ms Kathy Phillips). *"She's nice, but she's going to take a bit longer than I thought. She's grown and gone a bit weak, so she won't come out until mid-May at the earliest over six furlongs, then we'll see how we go with her".*

1010. SCARLET DRAGON ★★

b.c. Sir Percy – Welsh Angel (Dubai Destination). March 1. Second foal. 32,000Y. Tattersalls October Book 2. Highflyer/ Shefford. The dam is an unraced half-sister to 5 winners including the listed winner and Group 2 6f Mill Reef Stakes third Nantyglo. The second dam, Bright Halo (by Bigstone), a minor French 3-y-o 9f winner, is a half-sister to 9 winners including the Group 1 Irish Oaks winner Moonstone, the Breeders Cup second L'Ancresse and the Group 1 10f Prix Saint-Alary winner Cerulean Sky (herself dam of the Group 2 Doncaster Cup winner Honolulu). (W H Ponsonby). *"He's going to take a bit of time because he's doing a lot of growing. I'll probably start him off at seven furlongs around June time. He's well put together and has a good temperament, but he's going to grow and strengthen all the time".*

MARK JOHNSTON

1011. ALEKO

b.c. Cape Cross – Monnavanna (Machiavellian). April 13. Sixth foal. 70,000Y. Tattersalls October Book 2. Mark Johnston. Brother to the fairly useful 6f (at 2 yrs) to 1m winner of 4 races Manassas, closely related to a winner in Norway by Green Desert and half-brother to Monna Valley (by Exceed And Excel), unplaced in one start at 2 yrs in 2014. The dam, a smart 6f and 7f listed winner, is a half-sister to 7 winners including the Group 2 Blandford Stakes winner Monturani. The second dam, Mezzogiorno (by Unfuwain), a very useful 7f (at 2 yrs) and 10f listed winner, was third in the Oaks is a half-sister to 3 winners. (Sheikh Hamdan bin Mohammed Al Maktoum).

1012. BURATINO

ch.c. Exceed And Excel – Bergamask (Kingmambo). March 1. Brother to the modest 8.5f winner Tayma and half-brother to the French 12f winner Ruggero (by Tiger Hill). The dam, a French listed-placed 8.5f winner, is a sister to one winner and a half-sister to 4 winners including the fairly useful 7f to 10f winner Busker. The second dam, Adonesque (by Sadler's Wells), a listed 10f winner, is a half-sister to Danehill Dancer. (Sheikh Hamdan bin Mohammed Al Maktoum). A winner at Chelmsford on his debut in late March.

1013. DELIZIA (IRE)
b.f. Dark Angel – Jo Bo Bo (Whipper). February 14. First foal. £48,000Y. Doncaster Premier. Richard Kent. The dam is an unraced half-sister to 4 winners including the Group 2 5f Kings Stand Stakes and Group 3 5f Cornwallis Stakes Dominica. The second dam, Dominio (by Dominion), a 2-y-o listed 5f winner, was second in the Group 2 5f Temple Stakes and is a half-sister to 6 winners including the very smart Group 1 5f Nunthorpe Stakes winner Ya Malak. (Lady Lonsdale).

1014. FURIANT
b.c. Invincible Spirit – Save Me The Waltz (Halling). March 10. Eighth foal. €140,000Y. Arqana Deauville August. R O'Gorman. Half-brother to 4 winners including the French listed 10f winner and US Grade 3 third Dealbata (by Dubawi) and the fairly useful 10f winner King's Warrior (by King's Best). The dam, a minor 3-y-o winner, is a half-sister to 6 winners including the Group 3 Prix Penelope winner Ombre Legere. The second dam, Flawlessly (by Rainbow Quest), is a placed half-sister to 9 winners. (Sheikh Hamdan bin Mohammed Al Maktoum).

1015. HALEY BOP (IRE)
ch.f. Dream Ahead – Hallie's Comet (One Cool Cat). May 4. Second foal. €110,000Y. Goffs Orby. Mark Johnston. Half-sister to Turakina (by Teofilo), unplaced in two starts at 2 yrs in 2014. The dam, a fairly useful 6f (at 2 yrs) and 1m winner, was third in the Group 3 C L Weld Park Stakes and is a half-sister to 5 winners including the dual listed winner Along Came Casey. The second dam, Secretariat's Tap (by Pleasant Tap), a minor US winner at 3 yrs, is a half-sister to 6 minor winners. (Abdulla Al Mansoori).

1016. HOLBROOK (IRE)
gr.c. Cape Cross – Vanishing Grey (Verglas). February 27. First foal. 125,000Y. Tattersalls October Book 2. John Ferguson. The dam, a quite useful 2-y-o 5f winner, later won and was stakes-placed in the USA and is a half-sister to the Group 1 Golden Jubilee Stakes and Group 1 Nunthorpe Stakes winner Kingsgate Native. The second dam, Native Force (Indian Ridge), a quite useful 1m winner, is a half-sister to 2 winners. (Sheikh Hamdan bin Mohammed Al Maktoum).

1017. JAAMEH (IRE)
b.c. Iffraaj – Miss Gibraltar (Rock Of Gibraltar). February 16. Fourth foal. 75,000Y. Tattersalls October Book 2. Shadwell Estate Co. Brother to the quite useful 2-y-o 6f winner Vigor and half-brother to the unplaced 2014 2-y-o Elevator Action (by Lord Shanakill) and the fairly useful 6f (at 2 yrs) to 1m winner Ewell Place (by Namid). The dam ran once unplaced and is a half-sister to 4 winners. The second dam, Photogenic (by Midyan), a fairly useful 6f and listed 7f winner at 2 yrs, is a half-sister to 6 winners including the listed winner and Group 1 placed Mona Lisa and the Italian listed winner and Group 2 1m Falmouth Stakes second Croeso Cariad. (Hamdan Al Maktoum).

1018. MARY BEALE (IRE)
ch.f. Shamardal – What A Picture (Peintre Celebre). April 30. Seventh foal. 160,000foal. Tattersalls December. John Ferguson. Half-sister to 5 winners including the French listed 1m winner of 3 races Partner Shift (by Night Shift), the useful 7f (at 2 yrs) and UAE 1m and 10f winner and UAE Group 2 second Mufarrh, the fairly useful listed-placed 11f and 12f winner Majenta (both by Marju) and the quite useful 9f to 12f winner of 5 races Art History (by Dalakhani). The dam is an unplaced half-sister to 8 winners including the Group 1 Gran Criterium winner Night Style. The second dam, Style For Life (by Law Society), won 2 races in France over middle-distances, was listed-placed and is a half-sister to 8 winners including the Irish Derby winner Grey Swallow.

1019. MINIATURIST (FR)
b.c. Shamardal – Herboriste (Hernando). February 15. Fourth foal. €180,000Y. Arqana Deauville August. R O'Gorman. The dam, a US Grade 2 12f winner, is a half-sister to 9 winners including the French listed 12f winner and subsequent Grade 1 Hollywood Derby second Fast And Furious. The second dam, Helvellyn (by Gone West), a quite useful 2-y-o 8.3f winner, is a half-sister to 6 winners. (Sheikh Hamdan bin Mohammed Al Maktoum).

1020. MUATADEL
b.c. Exceed And Excel – Rose Blossom (Pastoral Pursuits). February 21. First foal. 170,000Y. Tattersalls October Book 2. Shadwell Estate Co. The dam won 5 races including the Group 3 Summer Stakes and the listed Flying Five and is a half-sister to 3 winners. The second dam, Lamarita (by Emarati), a quite useful dual 5f winner, is a half-sister to 12 winners. (Hamdan Al Maktoum).

1021. RAH RAH
b.f. Lonhro – Rahiyah (Rahy). March 18. Fourth foal. Half-sister to the useful French 6f (at 2 yrs) and 1m winner and 2-y-o Group 3 7f second Decathlete (by Medaglia d'Oro). The dam, a very useful 2-y-o 6f winner, was second in the Group 2 Rockfel Stakes and third in the Group 1 French 1,000 Guineas and is a sister to one winner and a half-sister to another. The second dam, Meiosis (by Danzig), a useful 3-y-o 7f winner, is a half-sister to 6 winners. (Sheikh Hamdan bin Mohammed Al Maktoum). A winner at Kempton on her debut in a fillies' maiden at the end of March.

1022. RAVENHOE
ch.c. Bahamian Bounty – Breathless Kiss (Roman Ruler). March 25. First foal. £16,000Y. Doncaster Premier. M Johnston. The dam, a fairly useful 5f winner of 5 races from 2 to 4 yrs, was listed-placed and is a half-sister to 5 minor winners in the USA. The second dam, Crusading Miss Cox (by Crusader Sword), a 2-y-o winner at 2yrs in the USA and listed second at Woodbine, is a half-sister to 3 winners. (J David Abell). This colt won on his debut at Doncaster in March, but disappointed when favourite but only fourth next time out.

1023. RENFREW STREET
b.f. Iffraaj – Malpas Missile (Elusive City). March 23. First foal. 38,000Y. Tattersalls October Book 2. Mark Johnston. The dam, a fair 2-y-o listed-placed 7f winner, is a half-sister to 2 minor winners. The second dam, Second Prayer (by Singspiel), is an unraced half-sister to 6 winners including the listed Galtres Stakes winner Firecrest. (D C Livingston & M Johnston Racing).

1024. RIFLESCOPE (IRE)
b.c. Raven's Pass – Red Intrigue (Selkirk). January 25. First foal. 130,000Y. Tattersalls October Book 2. John Ferguson. The dam, a fair 10f winner, is a half-sister to 4 winners including the smart Irish dual Group 3 7f winner Redstone Dancer and the useful listed 7f winner Red Liason. The second dam, Red Affair (by Generous), an Irish listed 10f winner, is a half-sister to 6 winners. (Sheikh Hamdan bin Mohammed Al Maktoum).

1025. TAWAKKOL
b.c. Firebreak – Dayville (Dayjur). February 15. Fifteenth foal. £70,000Y. Doncaster Premier. Shadwell Estate Co. Brother to the 5f and 6f winner Daylight and half-brother to 6 winners including the listed-placed 5f and 6f winner Day By Day (by Kyllachy), the Irish 5f winner Alexander Ballet (by Mind Games and herself dam of the Group 1 Gran Criterium winner Hearts Of Fire) and the 2-y-o 1m winner Musical Day (by Singspiel) – all quite useful. The dam, a quite useful triple 6f winner, is a half-sister to the US Grade 1 winner Spanish Fern and to the unraced dams of the Group/Grade 1 winners Lord Shanakill and Heatseeker. The second dam, Chain Fern (by Blushing Groom), is an unraced sister to the dual Group 1 winner Al Bahathri (herself dam of the 2,000 Guineas and Champion Stakes winner Haafhd). (R W Huggins).

1026. WAHQA
b.c. Intikhab – Max One Two Three (Princely Heir). February 24. Second foal. £35,000Y. Doncaster Premier. Shadwell Estate Co. The dam, a 2-y-o listed 6f winner, is a sister to one winner and a half-sister to another. The second dam, Dakota Sioux (by College Chapel), a fairly useful 7f and 1m winner of 8 races from 3 to 5 yrs, is a half-sister to 5 winners including a listed winner in Italy. (Hamdan Al Maktoum).

1027. YORKEE MO SABEE (IRE)
ch.c. Teofilo – Pivotal's Princess (Pivotal). February 8. Fifth foal. 70,000Y. Tattersalls October Book 2. Mark Johnston. Half-brother to the 5f and 6f winner of 4 races Robot Boy (by Shamardal), to the fairly useful 6f (including at 2 yrs) and 7f winner of 5 races

Accession (by Acclamation) and the quite useful 6f winner Three D Alexander (by Aqlaam). The dam, a useful 5f winner of 6 races, was listed placed five times and is a half-sister to one winner. The second dam, Art Princess (by Fairy King), is an unplaced half-sister to 10 winners. (Mr P R York).

1028. UNNAMED
b.f. Royal Applause – Excellerator (Exceed And Excel). April 9. First foal. £32,000Y. Doncaster Premier. Mark Johnston. The dam, a fairly useful 2-y-o 5f winner and third in the Group 3 6f Princess Margaret Stakes, is a half-sister to 4 winners. The second dam, Amsicora (by Cadeaux Genereux), is an unraced half-sister to 3 winners. (Abdulla Al Mansoori).

1029. UNNAMED
b.c. Acclamation – Gold Bubbles (Street Cry). March 9. Second foal. €70,000Y. Goffs Orby. Mark Johnston. Half-brother to the fair 2014 7f placed 2-y-o Spiriting (by Invincible Spirit). The dam, a useful 2-y-o 6f winner and second in the Group 3 Musidora Stakes, is a half-sister to one winner. The second dam, Well Revered (by Red Ransom), is an unplaced half-sister to 5 winners including Fahal (Group 3 Rose Of Lancaster Stakes). (Kai Fai Leung).

1030. UNNAMED
gr.f. Mastercraftsman – Greta d'Argent (Great Commotion). February 24. Fifth foal. €37,000Y. Tattersalls Ireland September. Mark Johnston. Half-sister to the fairly useful 2-y-o dual 5f winners Coolminx and Baycat (both by One Cool Cat), the quite useful 6f winner of 4 races at 2 and 3 yrs Fortinbrass (by Baltic King) and a winner in Poland by Chevalier. The dam, a fairly useful 1m (at 2 yrs) to 12f winner of 4 races, is a half-sister to 6 winners including the listed winner and dual Group 2 placed Winged d'Argent. The second dam, Petite-D-Argent (by Noalto), won over 6f (at 2 yrs) and 7f and is a half-sister to one winner. (Compas Equine Columbus).

1031. UNNAMED
b.c. Poet's Voice – Ivory Gala (Galileo). May 8. Fifth foal. 72,500Y. Tattersalls October Book 2. John Ferguson. Closely related to the fairly useful 2-y-o 1m winner Red Galileo (by Dubawi) and half-brother to the fair 12f

winner Okavango (by Nayef) and the minor UAE winner Okimono (by Invincible Spirit). The dam, a fairly useful 12f winner here and listed placed in France, is a half-sister to 4 winners and to the placed dam of the dual 2-y-o Group 2 winner Approve. The second dam, Rubies From Burma (by Forty Niner), won 3 races from 5f to 6f and was listed placed and is a half-sister to 9 winners including the French 1,000 Guineas, Fillies Mile and Prix Marcel Boussac winner Culture Vulture. (Sheikh Hamdan bin Mohammed Al Maktoum).

1032. UNNAMED
b.c. Kitten's Joy – Menekineko (Kingmambo). February 22. Ninth foal. $100,000Y. Keeneland September. Mark Johnston. Half-brother to the US dual Grade 3 winner General Election (by Harlan's Holiday) and the triple Grade 1 placed Ready's Echo (by More Than Ready). The dam is an unplaced half-sister to the US stakes winner House Key. The second dam, Maison Close (by Spectacular Bid), a US stakes winner, is a half-sister to 6 winners. (Abdulla Al Mansoori).

1033. UNNAMED
b.f. Cape Cross – Million Waves (Mull Of Kintyre). February 28. Fifth living foal. 57,000Y. Tattersalls October Book 2. Mark Johnston. Half-sister to the fairly useful 1m (at 2 yrs) to 12f winner of 7 races Blue Wave (by Raven's Pass), to the fair 1m to 10f winner Waveguide (by Dubawi) and the minor French 3-y-o winner Musaadaqa (by Tamayuz). The dam, an Irish 2-y-o 7f winner, was listed-placed and is a half-sister to 5 winners including the Group 1 French 1,000 Guineas and Group 3 7f Prix du Calvados winner Elusive Wave. The second dam, Multicolour Wave (by Rainbow Quest), is a placed half-sister to 4 winners. (Paul Dean).

1034. UNNAMED
b.f. Oasis Dream – Prima Luce (Galileo). February 8. Third foal. €40,000Y. Goffs Orby. Mark Johnston. Sister to the quite useful 2014 7f placed 2-y-o Dawn Mirage. The dam, a useful Group 3 7f Athasi Stakes winner, was second in the Group 3 Solonaway Stakes and is a half-sister to 5 minor winners. The second dam, Ramona (by Desert King), is an unraced half-sister to 9 winners including

the Group 2 5f Kings Stand Stakes winner Cassandra Go (herself dam of the triple Group 1 winner Halfway To Heaven) and the smart Group 3 6f Coventry Stakes winner and Irish 2,000 Guineas second Verglas. (Abdulla Al Mansoori).

1035. UNNAMED
b.f. Invincible Spirit – White And Red (Orpen). March 4. Second foal. 85,000Y. Tattersalls October Book 1. Mark Johnston. Sister to She's Invincible, unplaced in one start at 2 yrs in 2014. The dam, a quite useful Irish dual 7f winner, is a half-sister to 4 winners including the German Group 3 winner Wild Passion. The second dam, White On Red (by Konigsstuhl), a dual winner at 2 yrs in Germany, is a half-sister to 4 winners. (A D Spence).

WILLIAM KNIGHT
1036. ARTISANDRA (FR) ★★★★ ♠
ch.f. Mastercraftsman – Kezia (Spectrum). January 27. Fourth foal. €60,000Y. Arqana Deauville August. Richard Knight. The dam, a winner at 2 and 3 yrs in France, is a half-sister to 5 winners. The second dam, Kresna (by Distant Relative), won 4 races in Greece and is a half-sister to 9 winners including the Group 1 Lockinge Stakes winner Keltos and the Group 2 winners Krataios and Loxias. (Wardley Bloodstock). *"I really like this filly, she's got lots of quality about her and I'd say she'll be ready to start off in a maiden fillies' race over seven furlongs around June/July time. She's a lovely mover with a good temperament".*

1037. AUTHOR'S DREAM ★★★
gr.c. Authorized – Spring Dream (Kalanisi). March 16. Third foal. 32,000Y. Tattersalls October Book 3. Richard Knight. Half-brother to the quite useful dual 2m winner Ballinderry Boy (by Kayf Tara) and to the modest dual 2m winner Haines (by Shirocco). The dam, a quite useful 12f to 14f and hurdles winner, is a half-sister to 4 minor winners here and abroad. The second dam, Zest (by Zilzal), is an unplaced half-sister to 5 winners. (Heseltine & Conroy). *"Despite his middle-distance pedigree he's actually going to be a more precocious type than his siblings. He's all there, he's not a weak horse and judging from what he's doing I'd say he'd have the speed for seven furlongs in August to start with, which is a very good sign".*

1038. BALLARD DOWN (IRE) ★★
b.c. Canford Cliffs – Mackenzie's Friend (Selkirk). April 6. Eighth foal. €30,000Y. Goffs Sportsmans. Richard Knight. Half-brother to the French 2-y-o 10f winner and listed-placed Sallen, to the modest 7f winner Represent Yourself (both by Oratorio), the fair 12f winner Juno The Muffinman (by Holy Roman Emperor), the fair 12f and hurdles winner Know The Law (by Danehill Dancer) and the fair 13f winner Anfield Road (by Dr Fong). The dam is an unraced half-sister to 5 winners including the Group 2 winners Allied Powers and Dane Friendly. The second dam, Always Friendly (by High Line), winner of the Group 3 12f Princess Royal Stakes, second in the Group 1 Prix Royal-Oak. (Angmering Park Thoroughbreds I). *"He's out of a Selkirk mare and he's not one to be rushing. I think he's a later-developing type and he's still got quite a lot of growing to do".*

1039. COLONEL BOSSINGTON (IRE) ★★★
b.c. Azamour – Ros The Boss (Danehill). March 27. Eighth foal. 50,000Y. Tattersalls October Book 2. Richard Knight. Half-brother to 6 winners including the useful 2014 2-y-o dual 6f winner and listed second Bossy Guest (by Medicean), to the fairly useful 2-y-o 5f winner and dual listed-placed Liberating (by Iffraaj), the quite useful Irish dual 1m winner Alsalwa (by Nayef) and the quite useful 2-y-o 5f winner Kate The Great (by Xaar). The dam, a quite useful 7f and 1m winner, is a half-sister to 8 winners including the 2-y-o listed 9f winner and Group 1 second Yehudi. The second dam, Bella Vitessa (by Thatching), is an unplaced half-sister to 6 winners including the German Group 1 winner Wind In Her Hair (dam of the Japan Cup winner Deep Impact). (The Expendables). *"A chunky, stocky 2-y-o but unfortunately he had a slight injury in February which set us back six weeks. He's back cantering now and he should be ready in June or July and he should have the speed for six/seven furlongs".*

1040. GOODWOOD ZODIAC (IRE) ★★★★
b.c. Kodiac – Insieme (Barathea). January 28. First foal. 40,000Y. Tattersalls October Book 2. R Frisby. The dam, a fair 1m winner, is a half-sister to 4 winners including the useful listed-placed Aldovrandi. The second dam,

Rasana (by Royal Academy), is an unplaced half-sister to 4 winners including the multiple Group 1 winner Rakti. *"When he arrived I thought he'd need a bit of time because he was quite weak behind, but in the last six weeks he's really started to turn himself inside out. Now I'd say he'll be ready to run around June time over seven furlongs. He's making up into a really nice looking horse".*

1041. LADY MACAPA ★★

b.f. Equiano – Brazilian Style (Exit To Nowhere). February 7. £7,000Y. Doncaster Premier. Not sold. Half-sister to the fair dual 6f winner Smidgen by Bahamian Bounty), to the fair 2-y-o 5f winner Mrs Brown's Boys (by Verglas) and the modest 7f winner Loving Thought (by Oasis Dream). The dam was placed in all three of her starts over 5f at 2 yrs and is a half-sister to 2 minor winners. The second dam, Cosmic Star (by Siberian Express), is a placed full or half-sister to 8 winners including Jubilee Song (dam of the Group 2 winners Millyant and Prince Sabo). (Fromthestables.com Racing V). *"She's got a fair bit of scope about her and a big back-end as well. I think she'll be a six furlong type in July/August and I quite like her".* **TRAINERS' BARGAIN BUY**

1042. ROBANNE ★★

b.f. Paco Boy – Arctic Song (Charnwood Forest). April 29. Sixth foal. 37,000Y. Tattersalls October Book 3. Will Edmeades. Half-sister to the very useful 6f winner (at 2 yrs) and listed placed Hartley (by Lucky Story), to the quite useful Irish dual 10f and hurdles winner Peacock's Pride (by Groom Dancer) and the fair 2-y-o 6f winner State Anthem (by Royal Applause). The dam is an unraced half-sister to the triple listed winner and Group 2 6f Gimcrack Stakes second Andronikos. The second dam, Arctic Air (by Polar Falcon), a quite useful 2-y-o 7f winner, is a sister to the listed 7f winner Arctic Char and a half-sister to the Group 2 winners Barrow Creek and Last Resort. (Mrs E C Roberts). *"She's quite weak and her knees are still immature, so we're just going to take our time with her. She's a neat, compact filly with a good back-end on her, but she's going to need a bit of time. Hopefully we'll get her out in August over seven furlongs".*

1043. SWEET SWAGGER ★★★

ch.f. Showcasing – Strawberry Leaf (Unfuwain). February 13. Fifth foal. 40,000Y. Tattersalls October Book 3. Richard Knight. Half-sister to the quite useful 2-y-o dual 6f winner Bomber Jet (by Avonbridge). The dam, a quite useful 1m and 9f winner at 3 yrs, is a half-sister to 6 winners including the very useful 6f (at 2 yrs) and 9f winner Zabaglione. The second dam, Satin Bell (by Midyan), a useful 7f winner, is a half-sister to 4 winners including the useful listed 6f winner Star Tulip. (The Oil Men Partnership). *"She's a nice, big, scopey filly and a nice moving type. Hopefully one for six/ seven furlongs in July. She's got a nice bit of size about her and is a good-looking filly. As a yearling she was one of the nicest we had and after a growing stage she's looking good again, so I'm really happy with her".*

1044. UNNAMED ★★

b.c. Champs Elysees – Blast Furnace (Sadler's Wells). February 2. Half-brother to the unplaced 2014 2-y-o Redhotraven (by Raven's Pass). The dam is an unplaced half-sister to several winners including the very smart 2-y-o Group 3 6f July Stakes and 3-y-o listed 7f winner Meshaheer and the high-class Group 1 6.5f Prix Maurice de Gheest winner King Charlemagne and the dams of the US Grade 1 winners Albertus Maximus and Here Comes Ben. The second dam, Race The Wild Wind (by Sunny's Halo), winner of the Grade 1 8.5f Santa Maria Handicap, the Grade 2 Princess Stakes and the Grade 2 Fantasy Stakes, is a half-sister to the dam of the US Grade 2 winner Mataji. (Chasemore Farm). *"A home-bred of Andrew Black's, he's a strapping individual but he's quite mature with it. We haven't pressed any buttons yet but if we can get him out around June or July he'll look like a man amongst boys in the paddock, because he's a big lad".*

1045. UNNAMED ★★★★ ♠

b.c. Lilbourne Lad – Elizabelle (Westerner). April 23. Second foal. 34,000Y. Tattersalls December. Richard Knight. Half-brother to the fairly useful 2014 2-y-o 6f, 7f and 1m winner Power Play (by Zebedee). The dam, a modest 7f placed 2-y-o, is a half-sister to the smart 2-y-o Group 2 7f Vintage Stakes winner Orizaba. The second dam, Jus'chillin' (by Efisio), was placed twice over 6f at 2 yrs and is a half-sister to 11 winners including Bay Empress (Group 3 Brownstown Stakes). (Gordon Roddick). *"He's sharp, athletic and looks every inch a 2-y-o but we've got one eye on his fairly late foaling date and we're keeping the handbrake on for the time being. If it weren't for that we'd have kicked on with him by now, he's very natural and he'll still be one of our earliest 2-y-o runners. He looks like he's got ability and six furlongs will probably suit him".*

DAN KUBLER
1046. ALASKAN PHANTOM (IRE) ★★★★
b.f. Kodiac – Alexander Phantom (Soviet Star). March 2. Sixth foal. 30,000Y. Tattersalls October Book 2. Not sold. Sister to the fairly useful 2-y-o dual 6f winner Alaskan Spirit and half-sister to the modest 2015 6f placed 3-y-o Lady In White (by Zebedee), the quite useful 7f winner Ghost (by Invincible Spirit) and a hurdles winner by Red Clubs. The dam is an unraced half-sister to 6 minor winners. The second dam, Phantom Waters (by Pharly), won twice at 3 yrs and is a full or half-sister to 9 winners including the Group 3 Solario Stakes winner Shining Water (herself dam of the Grand Criterium and Dante Stakes winner Tenby). (J-P Lim). *"She should be our first runner, she'll set off at five furlongs but she has a good stride on her and she'll end up running over six. She's got a bit of size and scope and she's very athletic".*

1047. CHUPAROSA (IRE) ★★★
ch.f. Approve – Balamiyda (Ashkalani). April 26. Eighth foal. £12,000Y. Doncaster Silver. Kubler Racing. Half-brother to 5 winners including the Irish 2-y-o 1m and subsequent Hong Kong winner Pearl Music (by Oratorio), the Italian winner of 4 races from 2 to 4 yrs and dual listed-placed Escalada (by American Post) and the minor French dual winner (including at 2 yrs) Hidden Magic (by Bering). The dam is an unraced half-sister to 6 winners including Balakheri (Group 2 10f King Edward VII Stakes). The second dam, Balanka (by Alzao), a French listed winner and third in the Group 2 9.2f Prix de l'Opera, is a half-sister to 7 winners. (Mr P J H Whitten). *"She has a fairly late foaling date and she'll take a bit of time, but she'll be a 2-y-o in the second half of the*

season. I haven't done a lot with her but she's nice and she moves well".*

1048. HILLTOP RANGER (IRE) ★★★
b.f. Bushranger – Beatrix Potter (Cadeaux Genereux). January 29. Third foal. £13,000Y. Doncaster Silver. Kubler Racing. Half-sister to the modest 2014 6f placed 2-y-o Blackfoot Brave (by Iffraaj) and to the fair 10f winner Golden Journey (by Nayef). The dam is a placed half-sister to the 2-y-o Group 2 7f Vintage Stakes and subsequent Hong Kong dual Group 1 1m winner Xtension. The second dam, Great Joy (by Grand Lodge), won at 3 yrs in Germany and was listed placed and is a half-sister to 4 winners. (Diskovery Partnership III). *"I like her, she's got a good attitude and she's very straightforward. Nothing seems to bother her, she's quite laid back and it's only when she gets on the gallops that she switches on. Possibly one to start off in June over six furlongs. There are a few shares left in the Partnership if anyone is interested".*
TRAINERS' BARGAIN BUY

1049. SILHOUETTE (IRE) ★★
ch.c. Frozen Power – Missalonghi (In The Wings). February 19. €17,000Y. Tattersalls Ireland September. Sackville/Donald. The dam, an Irish 10f placed maiden, is a half-sister to 2 minor winners. The second dam, Tropical Lass (by Ballad Rock), placed 3 times from 7f to 8.5f in Ireland, is a half-sister to 8 winners including the 5f Curragh Stakes and 6f Railway Stakes winner and smart broodmare Bermuda Classic. (Titan Assets Ltd). *"A June type 2-y-o, he doesn't have much of a page but he's quite a nice horse. I didn't think he was going to be very big but he's actually grown and filled out quite nicely. Six/seven furlongs should suit as a 2-y-o and he's a real straightforward colt. I'm sure he'll win".*

1050. UNFORESEEN ★★★
b.f. Sky Mesa – Distinctive (Tobougg). March 10. First living foal. The dam, a 2-y-o Group 3 6f Firth Of Clyde Stakes winner and third in the Group 3 Ballyogan Stakes, is a half-sister to the fairly useful dual 5f winner, including at 2 yrs, Blue Aegean. The second dam, Blue Azure (American Chance), a modest 5f placed maiden, is half-sister to 2 minor winners in the USA. (Mr & Mrs G Middlebrook). *"She's*

quite a nice filly, the mare was obviously pretty useful and this is a nice individual and very professional. One to start at six furlongs in mid-season I should think, the sire has done extremely well in America and this is definitely a 2-y-o".

1051. VIRTUOUS BELLE ★★

b.f. Virtual – Petong's Pet (Petong). March 12. Seventh foal. 2,400Y. Tattersalls October Book 4. Closely related to the fair 2-y-o 6f winner Dormer Fleet (by Kyllachy) and half-sister to the fairly useful 5f and 6f winner of 10 races Aubrietia and the quite useful 7f and 1m winner Buredyma (both by Dutch Art). The dam is an unraced sister to the Group 2 Champagne Stakes and Group 3 Coventry Stakes winner Petardia and a half-sister to 3 winners. The second dam, What A Pet (by Mummy's Pet), a minor winner at 3 yrs in France, is a sister to the US Grade 3 winner and Group 1 placed Teacher's Pet. (Denarius Consulting Ltd). *"I went to the sale and wasn't going to buy a horse but she was the only one I liked and as she wasn't expensive I decided to buy her. She's a nice individual, well put together and solid. The dam does seem to produce racehorses because they seem to do pretty well. There's quite a bit of speed in the pedigree, but she's quite big and looks like a six furlong filly".*

1052. UNNAMED ★★

b.f. Vale Of York – Irish Fountain (Irish River). April 7. Tenth living foal. Half-sister to the fairly useful 6.5f, 8.5f (both at 2 yrs) and 10f winner Rainbow Forever (by Rainbows For Life) and to the minor Italian 12f winner Batten Boom (by Mark Of Esteem). The dam, a moderate 10f fourth placed maiden, is a half-sister to one winner. The second dam, Tournelle (by Empery), is an unraced half-sister to the top-class racemare and broodmare Dahlia. (Mr M Wichser). *"We've just sent her out for a break because she needs time and will be one for seven furlongs in late summer I think. She was quite light when she came in, but she moves quite well and is straightforward".*

1053. UNNAMED ★★

b.c. Holy Roman Emperor – Love In The Mist (Silver Hawk). May 10. Seventh foal. 20,000

2-y-o. Tattersalls Craven Breeze up. Kubler Racing. Half-brother to the fair dual 7f winner Speedy Yaki (by Refuse To Bend). The dam, a modest 6f fourth laced 2-y-o, is a half-sister to 6 winners including the Irish Group 3 winner Raphane. The second dam, Fast Nellie (by Ack Ack), is an unraced sister to the US Grade 1 winner Caline and a half-sister to 4 winners. *"He was a May foal so he's still got a bit of growing to do, but he's an athletic mover and should make a cracking 2-y-o like so many by the sire. We've only just bought him and we're still looking for an owner!"*

1054. UNNAMED ★★★

b.f. Zamindar – Quiet Elegance (Fantastic Light). April 26. Second foal. Half-sister to Overage (by Medicean), unplaced in two starts at 3 yrs in 2015. The dam, a fairly useful 5f (at 2 yrs) and 6f winner, is half-sister to numerous winners including the Haydock Park Sprint Cup and Nunthorpe Stakes winner Reverence and the very useful 2-y-o listed 7f Chesham Stakes winner and 1m Britannia Handicap second Helm Bank. The second dam, Imperial Bailiwick (by Imperial Frontier), won 3 races at around 5f including the Group 2 Flying Childers Stakes and was placed in the Molecomb Stakes and the Prix du Petit-Couvert. (Mr & Mrs G Middlebrook). *"We haven't had her very long but I think she'll be fairly sharp because she's not very big. Apart from the champion sprinter Reverence I think the family tend to be on the small side. A bonny filly, she looks neat and naturally muscled up already without having done much. It's a very good family and she'll hopefully be racing by late May or early June".*

DAVID LANIGAN

1055. ACRUX ★★★

b.c. Dansili – Ikat (Pivotal). May 3. Fifth foal. Half-brother to the multiple US Grade 1 11f/12f winner and Epsom Derby second Main Sequence (by Aldebaran), to the quite useful 10f and 12f winner Ragged Robbin (by Speightstown) and the French 11f winner Achernar (by Lemon Drop Kid). The dam, a French 2-y-o 7f winner and second in the Group 3 1m Prix d'Aumale, is a half-sister to the French listed winners Zhiyi and Smoking Sun. The second dam, Burning Sunset (by Caerleon), a useful 7f and listed 1m winner, is a half-sister to the Group 1 Oaks winner Light Shift and the Group 2 winners Shiva and Limnos. (Niarchos Family). *"A very good-looking horse, he's one of the more attractive ones out of the mare. He's well-made and just cantering away at the moment. A more compact, racier looking type than his siblings but nevertheless I'll treat him as a September 2-y-o for seven furlongs and a mile".*

1056. ALASKAN BREEZE (IRE) ★★

b.f. Fastnet Rock – Arabian Mirage (Oasis Dream). February 6. Second foal. 50,000Y. Tattersalls October Book 2. Not sold. Half-sister to the unplaced 2014 2-y-o Desert Morning (by Pivotal). The dam, a fairly useful 7f (including at 2 yrs) and 6f winner, was listed placed and is a half-sister to 4 winners including the Group 1 Dubai Duty Free winner and Group 2 Dante Stakes third Al Shemali and the very useful listed 14f winner Tungsten Strike. The second dam, Bathilde (by Generous), a useful 10.4f winner, was listed placed over 12f is a half-sister to 6 winners including the Group 2 Prix du Conseil de Paris winner Crimson Quest. (Mrs Emma Capon & Mrs Jane March). *"She's still at the farm because the sire seems to be getting horses that are better with time. An attractive filly who has done very well in the last three months, she goes quite nicely".*

1057. ARMED AND READY (FR) ★★★

gr.c. Kendargent – San Sicharia (Daggers Drawn). May 8. €130,000Y. Arqana Deauville October. J Brummitt. The dam, a useful Group 3 7f Chartwell Fillies Stakes winner of 3 races, is a half-sister to 7 winners including the French listed 10f winner and subsequent Hong Kong Group 1 Hong Kong Derby second Same World, the smart dual listed 5f winner Spin Cycle and the useful listed 1m winner Spinacre. The second dam, Spinamix (by Spinning World), was placed at 2 yrs in France and is a half-sister to 4 winners. (Mr B Nielsen). *"He's a nice horse with immature knees, so we had to back off him a bit. He's going again now and hopefully he'll make a 2-y-o by mid-summer, over six furlongs to start with before stepping him up to seven".*

1058. CENERENTOLA (IRE) ★★

b.f. Shamardal – Geminiani (King Of Kings).

May 8. Eighth foal. Half-sister to the fairly useful 11f and 14f winner and Group 3 2m Queen's Vase second Amerigo (by Daylami). The dam, winner of the Group 3 7f Prestige Stakes and second in the Group 3 Musidora Stakes, is a half-sister to 4 winners including the 2-y-o Group 1 6f Phoenix Stakes and Group 2 5f Queen Mary Stakes winner Damson (herself dam of the Group 3 Molecomb Stakes winner Requinto). The second dam, Tadkiyra (by Darshaan), won over 10f at 3 yrs in France and is a half-sister to 8 winners including the Group 3 winners Tashtiya, Tassmoun and Tashkourgan. (B E Nielsen). *"She's a big filly and a bit on the weak side. She goes along nicely and is one for the end of the season. Much more of a 3-y-o type".*

1059. DANILOVNA (IRE) ★★

br.f. Dansili – Hoity Toity (Darshaan). May 10. Eighth foal. Closely related to the Group 1 1m Coronation Stakes and Group 1 1m Matron Stakes winner Lillie Langtry (by Danehill Dancer) and to the 7f (including at 2 yrs) and listed 1m winner of 4 races and dual Group 3 placed Count Of Limonade (by Duke Of Marmalade). The dam is an unraced half-sister to 5 winners. The second dam, Hiwaayati (by Shadeed), is an unraced half-sister to 6 winners including the dual Group 3 winner Great Commotion and the dual Group 2 winner Lead on Time. (Mr B Nielsen). *"A big, tall, leggy filly with a good attitude, she won't be doing anything until the end of the year because she needs to strengthen up. I think Dansili is a better fit to this mare than most the sires she's visited".*

1060. DREAM FREE ★★★★

b.c. Oasis Dream – Freedonia (Selkirk). May 27. Brother to the useful triple 6f winner and listed-placed Polybius. The dam won the Group 3 12.5f Prix de Pomone and is a half-sister to 2 minor winners. The second dam, Forest Rain (by Caerleon), won 2 minor races at 3 yrs in France and is a half-sister to 5 winners including Domedriver (Grade 1 Breeders Cup Mile). (Niarchos Family). *"An attractive horse, he's better put together than his full-brother Polybius and he goes nicely. He could make a 2-y-o despite his late foaling date. He could be nice and hopefully he'll be racing in August over six furlongs".*

1061. ENGLISH KING ★★

b.c. Sir Percy – Aqaarid (Nashwan). March 20. Half-brother to 3 winners including the quite useful 1m (at 2 yrs) and UAE 6f to 7f winner of 5 races Elmonjed (by Gulch) and the fair 7f winner Ladeena (by Dubai Millennium) and to the unraced dam of the listed Stardom Stakes winner Titus Mills. The dam, a smart winner of the Group 1 Fillies Mile and the Group 3 7.3f Fred Darling Stakes, was second in the 1,000 Guineas and is a half-sister to 2 winners. The second dam, Ashayer (by Lomond), won the Group 1 1m Prix Marcel Boussac and the Group 3 10f Prix de Psyche. (Mr B Nielsen). *"He's a big, strong, good-looking colt but one for the back-end of the season. He's done all his growing and he's got plenty of scope".*

1062. FRANK COOL ★★★★

b.c. Royal Applause – Queen Of Heaven (Mr Greeley). March 8. First foal. 22,000Y. Tattersalls October Book 3. David Lanigan. The dam, a moderate 7f fourth placed maiden, is a half-sister to a winner in Italy. The second dam, Be My Queen (by Sadler's Wells), an Irish listed-placed 1m winner, is a half-sister to 6 winners including the very smart Group 1 5f Prix de l'Abbaye winner Imperial Beauty. (Ms Liza Judd). *"Hopefully he'll make a 2-y-o because he's very uncomplicated and unassuming to look at. He just goes and does his exercise and seems bombproof. He's a nice horse, I like his sire and he'll have enough speed to start off at six furlongs and he'll probably win at seven".*
TRAINER'S BARGAIN BUY

1063. GERSHWIN ★★★★

b.c. Shamardal – Gradara (Montjeu). April 2. First foal. €100,000Y. Arqana Deauville October. J Brummitt. The dam won the listed 12f Prix Panacee at 4 yrs and is a half-sister to numerous winners including the Group 1 1m Falmouth Stakes winner Giofra. The second dam, Gracefully (by Orpen), won the 2-y-o Group 3 7f Prestige Stakes and is a sister to the listed winner Lady Grace and to the 2-y-o Group 3 third Visionist. (Mr B Nielsen). *"A nice horse, he has a real daisy-cutting action so wants top of the ground. Very straightforward, he's not top heavy like some Shamardal's can be and he goes well. I like him and he'll start off at six furlongs in the summer before stepping up to seven".*

1064. INTERCEPTED ★★★

b.c. Raven's Pass – Cape Rocker (Cape Cross). January 27. First foal. 42,000Y. Tattersalls December. J Brummitt/Kingsdown Racing. The dam is an unraced half-sister to 2 winners. The second dam, Rockerlong (by Deploy), winner of the listed Cheshire Oaks and third in the Group 1 Yorkshire Oaks, is a half-sister to 8 winners including the Group 3 Prestige Stakes winner Glatisant (herself dam of the Group 1 winners Footstepsinthesand and Pedro The Great) and to the placed dam of the very smart 2-y-o Superstar Leo. (Mr B Nielsen & Mr M Tyson). *"An attractive colt, he's big and will take a bit of time, so we'll aim to start him around September time over seven furlongs".*

1065. MIND SHIFT (USA) ★★

b.c. Arch – Light Blow (Kingmambo). February 15. First foal. $400,000Y. Keeneland September. Woodford Racing. The dam, a fair 15f winner, is a sister to 2 winners including the Oaks winner Light Shift and a half-sister to 8 winners including the Group 2 10.5f Tattersalls Gold Cup and Group 3 10f Brigadier Gerard Stakes winner Shiva and the Group 2 12f Prix Jean de Chaudenay and Group 3 12f Prix Foy winner Limnos. The second dam, Lingerie (by Shirley Heights), placed 6 times in France, is a half-sister to 7 winners and to the placed dam of two Grade 1 winners in Brazil. (Woodford Racing/Flaxman Stables). *"He's only just arrived and he's a big, tall, leggy colt. He's done nothing but grow since the day he was bought. His dam is a sister to the Oaks winner who was trained at Warren place when I was Henry Cecil's assistant. He's bigger than the rest of the family members and he'll be a back-end 2-y-o".*

1066. PALMAROLA (IRE) ★★★

b.f. Sea The Stars – Palmeraie (Lear Fan). April 18. Half-sister to 9 winners including the multiple French Group 2 middle-distance winner Policy Maker (by Sadler's Wells), the very useful listed 11f winner Place Rouge (by Desert King), the useful 1m (at 2 yrs) and listed 2m winner Pushkin (by Caerleon) and the fairly useful 1m to 10f winner Tinghir (by Dansili). The dam is a placed half-sister to the US Grade 2 12f winner Peinture Bleue (dam of the Arc winner Peintre Celebre) and to the Group/ Grade 3 winners Provins and Parme.

The second dam, Petroleuse (by Habitat), won the Group 3 8.5f Princess Elizabeth Stakes and is a half-sister to the King George VI and Queen Elizabeth Stakes, Oaks and Prix de Diane winner Pawneese. (Mr B Nielsen). *"She's done very well, strengthened up a lot and goes nicely. She's got plenty of size, she's an attractive filly and I imagine she'd start off at a mile".*

1067. TETRADRACHM ★★★★
b.c. Holy Roman Emperor – Dahlia's Krissy (Kris S). March 11. Eighth foal. 170,000Y. Tattersalls October Book 2. J Brummitt. Half-brother to the Group 1 Ascot Gold Cup winner Rite Of Passage (by Giant's Causeway) and to the fair 7f winner Bibury (by Royal Applause). The dam, a listed-placed winner of 5 races in the USA, is a half-sister to 5 winners. The second dam, Dahlia's Image (by Lyphard), is a listed-placed full or half-sister to 8 winners including the US Grade 1 winners Dahar, Delegant, Dahlia's Dreamer and Rivlia. (Mr B Nielsen). *"A nice horse, he's going very well and he should be earlier than some of his siblings. A good-sized horse, he has a good mind and is an attractive colt with a touch of quality. I think he'll start off at six furlongs and then move up to seven. Everything about him is nice".*

1068. THE LILLSTER ★★★★
b.f. Kodiac – Wind Surf (Lil's Lad). March 24. Fourth foal. 42,000Y. Tattersalls October Book 3. Charlie Gordon-Watson. Half-sister to the fair 2014 8.5f placed 2-y-o Fibre Optic (by Rip Van Winkle). The dam, a minor stakes winner in North America, is a half-sister to 3 winners. The second dam, Skirt The Wind (by Red Ransom), won 3 minor races in the USA and is a half-sister to 5 winners. (Mrs Emma Capon). "A strong filly, she's quite big but she'll be a 2-y-o alright and it looks like she could be nice. She has a lot of quality about her and I think she'll have the speed for five furlongs in May. She'd be my pick at the moment".

1069. THRILLED (IRE) ★★★★
b.f. Kodiac – Fuerta Ventura (Desert Sun). March 19. Fourth foal. 460,000Y. Tattersalls October Book 1. Flaxman Stables. Half-sister to the useful 6f and 7f winner of 4 races (including at 2 yrs) and listed-placed The Gold Cheongsam (by Red Clubs). The dam, a useful Irish 1m to 9.5f winner of 3 races, was listed-placed over 12f in Italy and is a half-sister to 3 winners including the useful 2-y-o listed 6f winner and Group 2 6f Mill Reef Stakes second Sir Xaar. The second dam, Cradle Brief (by Brief Truce), is an unraced half-sister to the Group 3 6f Greenlands Stakes winner Tiger Royal. (Flaxman Stables). *"The most expensive Kodiac ever sold, she's petite and feminine-looking, has a lovely action and is very straightforward to deal with. She has a lot of speed and should be one of the first fillies to run. One for five/six furlongs".*

1070. WAPPING (USA) ★★★★
b.c. Smart Strike – Exciting Times (Jeune Homme). May 4. Tenth foal. 90,000Y. Tattersalls October Book 2. Charlie Gordon-Watson. Half-brother to 7 winners including the US Grade 1 Beverly D Stakes and Group 2 Prix de Sandringham winner Gorella (by Grape Tree Road), the US and French listed winner and Group 1 Criterium International third Porto Santo (by Kingsalsa), the fairly useful 7f (at 2 yrs), 1m and hurdles winner Stars Over The Sea (by Sea The Stars) and the quite useful 1m (at 2 yrs) to 12f winner Jupiter Storm (by Galileo). The dam is a placed half-sister to 6 winners. The second dam, Eloura (by Top Ville), won twice in France and is a half-sister to 4 minor winners. (Lord & Lady Lloyd Webber). *"He's a lovely horse and he'll make a 2-y-o over seven furlongs although I could start him off at six. He's very straightforward and is one of the more attractive horses here. He's done very well since the sales, I'm a bit concerned that the sire's runners usually do better in America, but he's nice and I'm mad about him. A lovely horse to deal with, he has a nice temperament, he moves really well and he's a professional".*

1071. UNNAMED ★★★
b.c. Arakan – Alexander Divine (Halling). April 25. Fifth foal. 25,000Y. Tattersalls October Book 2. David Lanigan. The dam ran once unplaced and is a half-sister to 6 winners including the Group 1 Pretty Polly Stakes winner Ambivalent and the dam of the Group 1 Prix de l'Abbaye winner Total Gallery. The second dam, Darrery (by Darshaan), a listed-placed winner of 3 races at 3 and 4 yrs, is a half-sister to 3 winners. (O Bell, B Nielsen, S

Martus). *"A lovely, tall horse and a bit 'on the leg' at the moment, but he's very mature and doing everything right. I bought him because he's such a good walker, he's attractive and I thought he was cheap for what he cost".*

1072. UNNAMED ★★★★ ♠

gr.c. Kodiac – Krasotka (Soviet Star). February 28. Fifth foal. 40,000Y. Tattersalls December. J Brummitt/Kingsdown Racing. Half-brother to the modest 2014 2-y-o 6f winner Pumaflor (by Aussie Rules) and to the quite useful 5f and 6f winner The Grey Rebel (by Tagula). The dam, unplaced in five starts in Ireland, is out of the minor French placed 2-y-o Saralina (by Linamix), herself a half-sister to the French and US Group 2 winner Sayarshan. (J Connellon, E Ahearn, C McMillon). *"A very nice horse, he's compact, racy and could be one of my first runners. He's strong, easy to train and goes nicely. I can see him being out in April or May over five furlongs and he'll get six because he does have a bit of scope. Everything about him is nice".*

1073. UNNAMED ★★★★

b.c. Galileo – My Branch (Distant Relative). March 6. Half-brother to 7 winners including the Group 1 6f Haydock Sprint Cup winner Tante Rose (by Barathea), the 2-y-o listed 7f winner Bay Tree (by Daylami), the useful 1m winner and listed-placed Melodramatic (by Sadler's Wells) and the 2-y-o winners Bold Lass (by Sea The Stars), Priceless Jewel (by Selkirk) and Rosie's Posy (by Suave Dancer) – all 3 quite useful. The dam won the listed 6f Firth Of Clyde Stakes (at 2 yrs) and the listed 7f Sceptre Stakes, was third in the Irish 1,000 Guineas and is a full or half-sister to 6 winners. The second dam, Pay The Bank (by High Top), was a quite useful 2-y-o 1m winner. (Mr B Nielsen). *"This is a tall, leggy horse that's done well since the sales where he was withdrawn. I think the sales came too early for him. He could be a September 2-y-o because he's athletic and compared to the Galileo's I've had in the past he's lighter framed. He's likeable and has done very well since he got into a routine. There's too much speed in the pedigree for him to get further than a mile".*

1074. UNNAMED ★★★★

b.f. Acclamation – Rebelline (Robellino). April 27. Ninth foal. 230,000Y. Tattersalls October Book 1. Charlie Gordon-Watson. Half-sister to 6 winners including the smart Group 3 Irish 2,000 Guineas Trial winner and Group 1 10.5f Tattersalls Rogers Cup second Recharge (by Cape Cross), the useful 7f (at 2 yrs) and listed 9.5f winner I'm Yours and the quite useful Irish 2-y-o 6f winner Redoutable (both by Invincible Spirit). The dam won the Group 1 10.5f Tattersalls Gold Cup and the Group 2 Pretty Polly Stakes and is a sister to the Group 2 Blandford Stakes winner Quws and a half-sister to 5 winners. The second dam, Fleeting Rainbow (by Rainbow Quest), placed over 10f, is a half-sister to 3 winners. (Mrs Emma Capon & Lady Lloyd Webber). *"A nice filly, she goes well and should be a June 2-y-o over six furlongs. Very straightforward and one of my nicer fillies".*

GER LYONS

1075. ALDO RAINE (IRE) ★★★

b.c. Zebedee – Primo Supremo (Primo Dominie). May 16. Fifth foal. €46,000Y. Goffs Sportsmans. Ger Lyons. Half-brother to the unplaced 2014 2-y-o Primo Dynamo (by Bushranger) and to the modest 2-y-o 5f winner Sub Prime (by Danetime). The dam is an unplaced half-sister to the winner and dual listed-placed Aeroplane. The second dam, Anita At Dawn (by Anita's Prince), a modest 6f (at 2 yrs) and 7f winner, is a half-sister to 8 winners including the US Grade 3 winner Down Again and to the dam of the Irish and French 2,000 Guineas winner Bachir. (S Jones). *"A straightforward horse, he'll be a five/six furlong 2-y-o and he'll be ready to run as soon as he hits his second birthday in mid-May. I like him a lot".*

1076. ARGENTERO ★★★★ ♠

ch.c. Zoffany – Frabjous (Pivotal). February 15. Fourth foal. £50,000Y. Doncaster Premier. BBA (Ire). Half-brother to the fair 7f winner Movementneverlies (by Medicean). The dam is an unraced half-sister to 7 winners including the Group 1 Prix Maurice de Gheest winner May Ball. The second dam, Minute Waltz (by Sadler's Wells), is an unraced full or half-sister to 7 winners including the Lincoln Handicap winner King's Glory. (Jones/Spratt). *"A grand, straightforward colt, he's done everything we've asked of him and he'll be out sooner rather than later. We like him and he'll win his maiden".*

1077. BIRDCAGE ★★★★

b.f. Showcasing – Trinny (Rainbow Quest). March 27. Sixth foal. £40,000Y. Doncaster Premier. David Redvers. Half-sister to the quite useful 6f and 7f winner You're The Boss (by Royal Applause) and to the modest 6f winner of 4 races Orwellian (by Bahamian Bounty). The dam is an unraced half-sister to 2 winners. The second dam, Mall Queen (by Sheikh Albadou), won the listed Prix Yacowlef and is a half-sister to 8 winners including the listed winner Munnaya (dam of the US Grade 1 winner Alpha). (Qatar Racing). *"A lovely, sweet filly by the right sire, I like her a lot. She's ready to start but I'll wait until the ground dries up. Hopefully she'll do it on the track because we like her and she'll definitely win a maiden".*

1078. BLOOD MOON ★★★

b.g. Equiano – First Eclipse (Fayruz). February 24. Fourth foal. £28,000Y. Doncaster Premier. BBA (Ire). Half-brother to the quite useful triple 1m winner Jacob Black (by Amadeus Wolf) and to the modest Scandinavian 6f winner Ta Ajabb (by Pastoral Pursuits). The dam, a modest 2-y-o 5f winner, is a half-sister to 5 winners. The second dam, Naked Poser (by Night Shift), a quite useful 2-y-o 6f winner, is a half-sister to 4 winners including the useful sprinter Damalis. (S Jones). *"He's precocious, ready to run now, shows plenty of speed and should win his races".* A 25-1 shot, he won a median auction maiden over 5f at Dundalk on the 17th April.

1079. FISHERMAN'S BLUES ★★★

b.c. Zebedee – Southern Barfly (Southern Halo). February 18. Seventh foal. 55,000Y. Tattersalls October Book 2. BBA (Ire). Half-brother to the moderate 5f seller (at 2 yrs) and 6f winner Kano's Girl (by Kodiac) and 2 minor winners in the USA by Kitten's Joy. The dam, a minor US 3-y-o winner, is a half-sister to 4 winners including the multiple Group 3 placed One More Round. The second dam, Life Of The Party (by Pleasant Colony), is a placed half-sister to 3 winners. (S Jones). *"A quality horse, he's ready to run but probably not as mentally ready as he is physically. We'll get him out in April I should think".*

1080. MINT CHAI (IRE) ★★★

ch.c. Roderic O'Connor – Tea Chest (In The Wings). February 15. 33,000Y. Tattersalls October Book 3. BBA (Ire). Half-brother to the quite useful 7f (at 2 yrs) and 10f winner Clare Island Boy (by Strategic Prince). The dam is an unraced half-sister to one minor winner in the USA. The second dam, Tea Service (by Roi Danzig), a winner of 3 races in Ireland and the USA and listed-placed, is a half-sister to 9 winners including the US Grade 1 winner Danish and the Group 3 winners Ace and Hawkeye. (S Jones). *"He's the only one we have by this sire but I like him and he does everything we ask. He looks precocious, he'll run sooner rather than later and we like him"*

1081. RADAR O'REILLY ★★★

ch.c. Danehill Dancer – Madaen (Nureyev). April 20. Eighth foal. 38,000Y. Tattersalls October Book 2. BBA (Ire). Half-brother to the fairly useful 7.5f (at 2 yrs) to 2m winner of 7 races and dual Group 3 third Baan (by Diesis), to the fair 9.5f winner Magical Cat (by Giant's Causeway) and a winner in Russia by Gulch. The dam is an unraced half-sister to 7 winners in the USA including the Grade 2 placed Simon Pure. The second dam, Life's Magic (by Cox's Ridge), won five Grade 1 events in the USA and is a half-sister to 3 winners. (S Jones). *"A grand horse, he'll probably start off in May over six furlongs and we'll progress from there. A rock solid horse. He's named after the character from the TV series M.A.S.H".*

1082. RESTIVE ★★★★ ♠

b.c. Rip Van Winkle – I Hearyou Knocking (Danehill Dancer). May 5. Fourth living foal. £110,000Y. Doncaster Premier. David Redvers. Half-brother to the moderate 1m and 8.5f winner Let Me In (by Pivotal). The dam is an unplaced half-sister to 5 winners and to the unraced dam of the Group/Grad 1 winner Landseer. The second dam, Flood (by Riverman), a 6f winner in the USA, is a half-sister to 3 winners including the US Grade 1 winner Sabona. (Qatar Racing). *"A nice horse that's just doing a bit of growing at the minute but he has ability. He'll be out around June time over six furlongs, has a lovely temperament and we like him a lot".*

1083. SANDSTORMING (IRE) ★★★
ch.c. Zoffany – Yaky Romani (Victory Note). March 30. Fifth foal. €65,000Y. Goffs Orby. Ger Lyons. Half-brother to the moderate 10f seller winner Rock Diamond (by Rock Of Gibraltar) and to the Italian winner of 6 races Yaky Mahora (by Oratorio). The dam won 10 races from 2 to 5 yrs in Italy and is a half-sister to 6 winners including the Group 3 Phoenix Sprint Stakes winner and triple Group 2 placed Al Qasi. The second dam, Delisha (by Salse), won at 3 yrs in Germany and is a half-sister to 6 winners including the Hong Kong Mile winner Ecclesiastical. (S Jones). *"A beautiful, big horse for the second half of the season, he's a tall horse that just needs time. We like him".*

1084. SPADER (IRE) ★★★
b.c. Jeremy – Poulkovo (Sadler's Wells). March 7. Sixth foal. £42,000Y. Doncaster Premier. BBA (Ire). Half-brother to a winner in Italy by Desert Prince. The dam, a minor winner at 3 yrs in France, is a sister to the French triple listed 12f winner Pouvoir Absolu and a half-sister to 3 winners. The second dam, Pine Chip (by Nureyev), is a placed sister to the Prix de l'Arc de Triomphe, French Derby and Grand Prix de Paris winner Peintre Celebre and a half-sister to the French Group winners Pointilliste and Peinture Rare. (S Jones). *"He's sharp, straightforward and he'll running in mid-April. A nice horse, he's precocious and ready to rock and roll".*

1085. UNNAMED ★★★
b.c. Equiano – Langs Lash (Noverre). April 29. First foal. 55,000Y. Tattersalls October Book 2. BBA (Ire). The dam, winner of the 2-y-o Group 2 5f Queen Mary Stakes and third in the Group 2 Lowther Stakes, is a half-sister to 2 winners. The second dam, Temple Street (by Machiavellian), is an unraced half-sister to 4 winners and to the placed dam of the French 1,000 Guineas winner Elusive Wave. (Qatar Racing). *"He's ready to go and he's a lovely horse. He shows us enough to like him".*

1086. UNNAMED ★★
b.c. Holy Roman Emperor – Mango Groove (Unfuwain). February 11. Half-brother to the 2-y-o 1m winner and 3-y-o listed placed Cristal Fashion (by Jeremy). The dam is an unplaced half-sister to 5 winners including the Group 1 Racing Post Trophy third Feared In Flight. The second dam, Solar Crystal (Alzao), won the Group 3 1m May Hill Stakes, was third in the Group 1 1m Prix Marcel Boussac and is a half-sister to 6 winners including the Group 1 Fillies' Mile winner Crystal Spirit. (Mr Jim McDonald). *"Physically he looks a precocious type, but mentally he isn't. He had a bit of a setback, which he's recovering from now. He's a typical Holy Roman Emperor, so I'd like to think there's a race I him but we won't know that for a while yet".*

1087. UNNAMED ★★
b.c. Lilbourne Lad – Nisriyna (Intikhab). April 7. Second foal. €75,000Y. Goffs Orby. Ger Lyons. Half-brother to the quite useful 2014 2-y-o dual 6f winner Spring Loaded (by Zebedee). The dam is an unraced half-sister to 2 winners including the French dual Group 3 winner Narniyn. The second dam, Narmina (by Alhaarth), is an unraced half-sister to 4 winners including the smart Group 3 12f Princess Royal Stakes winner and smart broodmare Narwala. (S Jones). *"A lovely, big, backward type, he's only just come back from the farm where he's done a lot of growing. At the very earliest he may be out by mid-season".*

1088. UNNAMED ★★★
ch.c. Lope De Vega – Super Supreme (Zafonic). February 12. Ninth foal. €75,000Y. Goffs Orby. Ger Lyons. Half-brother to the useful 6f (at 2 yrs) and 1m winner of four races and Group 3 Desmond Stakes third Moran Gra (by Rahy), to the quite useful 7f winner Super Academy and the Irish 2-y-o 7.5f and subsequent minor US winner Vorteeva (by Bahri). The dam is an unraced sister to the listed winner Bodyguard and a half-sister to the listed winner White Gulch. The second dam, White Wisteria (by Ahonoora), is an unraced half-sister to 6 winners including the dam of the Irish 2,000 Guineas winner Bachelor Duke. (Jones/Spratt). *"He's out at the farm, I gave him a few weeks off just to grow and he'll be back in shortly. A lovely, big horse, I like him a lot, he's one for the second half of the season. He's by the right sire so you'd hope he's a nice horse".*

1089. UNNAMED ★★★★
b.c. Kodiac – Supreme Seductress (Montjeu). January 14. First foal. €52,500Y. Goffs Orby.

David Redvers. The dam is an unplaced half-sister to 3 winners including the Group 1 Italian Oaks winner Menhoubah. The second dam, Private Seductress (by Private Account), a US stakes-placed winner of 3 races, is a half-sister to 4 winners. (Qatar Racing). *"He's ready to run and has ability. A typical Kodiac, we like him a lot and he'll win his maiden all day long".*

GEORGE MARGARSON

1090. ANY GUEST (IRE) ★★★
b.c. Zoffany – Princess Speedfit (Desert Prince). March 12. Ninth foal. 45,000Y. Tattersalls October Book 2. A & E Bloodstock. Half-brother to the useful 6f and 7f winner of 6 races (including a 2-y-o listed event) Imperial Guest (by Imperial Dancer), to the fairly useful 6f (at 2 yrs) to 1m winner of 5 races Excellent Guest (by Exceed And Excel) and 2 winners abroad by Barathea Guest and Indian Haven. The dam, a fair 8.3f winner, is a half-sister to 5 winners including the French listed 12f winner and dual Group 2 placed Sibling Rival. The second dam, Perfect Sister (by Perrault), a minor French winner, is a sister to the US Grade 1 winner Frankly Perfect and a half-sister to 4 winners. (John Guest Racing Ltd). *"We've had a few out of the family who have been disappointing, but he's taken after the two brothers Imperial Guest and Excellent Guest, and especially the latter. He's very much the type to make a 2-y-o and probably progress later as a 3-y-o and 4-y-o. He's a cheeky beggar so we've given him a couple of sharpeners on the gallops. He's quite a tall, big striding, scopey horse but I won't be waiting with him and he'll be running over six furlongs in the summer. He should progress throughout the year and should be capable of winning this year, probably over seven furlongs".*

1091. OMEED ★★
b.f. Equiano – Manaaber (Medicean). February 2. First foal. 5,000Y. Tattersalls October Book 2. Robin Sharp. The dam, a fair 2-y-o 6f winner, is a half-sister to 3 winners. The second dam, Needlecraft (by Mark Of Esteem), won 4 races including the Group 3 Prix Chloe and the Group 3 Premio Sergio Cumani and is a half-sister to 6 winners including Fractional (Group 3 Prix Quincey). *"She was extremely difficult to break which apparently could be down to the sire. She's*

got a very good pedigree and we've got her cantering away now but we're keeping the lid on her. She looks every inch a 2-y-o, so it's a pity she wasn't switched on earlier really".*

1092. PEPPY MILLER ★★★
b.f. Cockney Rebel – Solar Crystal (Alzao). March 23. £1,800Y. Ascot December. Not sold. Half-sister to 4 winners including the smart 2-y-o 6f winner and Group 1 Racing Post Trophy third Feared In Flight (by Hawk Wing), the useful 2-y-o 7f winner, listed-placed and hurdles winner Lunar Crystal (by Shirley Heights) and the quite useful 10f winner Crystal (by Danehill). The dam, a smart 2-y-o, won the Group 3 1m May Hill Stakes, was third in the Group 1 1m Prix Marcel Boussac and is a half-sister to the Group 1 Fillies' Mile winner Crystal Music and the Group 3 winners Dubai Success and State Crystal. The second dam, Crystal Spray (by Beldale Flutter), a minor Irish 4-y-o 14f winner, is a half-sister to the Group 2 winner Crystal Hearted. (Mrs Mette-Campbell). *"A very well-bred filly, she's got plenty of scope and is going to grow a lot. She goes very easily and although the pedigree would suggest seven furlongs the way she's going I'm rolling her along because she's ready".*

1093. POETIC GUEST ★★★★
ch.c. Poet's Voice – Diamond Run (Hurricane Run). March 11. First foal. 80,000Y. Tattersalls October Book 2. A & E Bloodstock. The dam, a modest dual 7f winner, is a half-sister to 4 winners including the useful 5f to 1m winner of 8 races and listed-placed Alo Pura and to the placed dam of the Group 2 Gimcrack Stakes winner Approve. The second dam, Rubies From Burma (by Forty Niner), a winner of 3 races from 5f to 6f and listed placed over 5.5f in Ireland, is a half-sister to 9 winners including the French 1,000 Guineas, Fillies Mile and Prix Marcel Boussac winner Culture Vulture. (John Guest Racing Ltd). *"A really nice type and the stand-out of my 2-y-o's at the moment. I've got a lot of time for him and he's similar to one I had a few years ago called Rebellious Guest. He's very athletic and will be racing as soon as the six furlong maidens come out. Very switched on, he'll go on and improve with time. Nevertheless he should be good enough to start at six furlongs and hopefully turn up at Royal Ascot".*

1094. SHYPEN ★★★

b.f. Archipenko – Coconut Shy (Bahamian Bounty). February 6. Half-sister to the quite useful 6f and 7f winner of 6 races from 2 to 4 yrs Shyron (by Byron). The dam, a fair 2-y-o 5.5f and 6f winner, is a sister to one winner and a half-sister to another. The second dam, Lets Be Fair (by Efisio), a useful 2-y-o 5f and 6f winner, is a half-sister to 6 winners including the listed winner Miss Mirasol. (F Butler). *"She's very similar to her half-brother Shyron, but probably a better type and more of a 2-y-o than he was, although Archipenko doesn't stand out as a sire of early 2-y-o types. She looks every inch a 2-y-o and she's developed well since we started cantering her. Six/seven furlongs in mid-summer should suit her and she's very capable".*

1095. UNNAMED ★★

b.f. High Chaparral – Native Picture (Kodiac). February 21. First foal. The dam, a fair dual 6f winner at 2 and 3 yrs, is a half-sister to 4 winners including the Group 1 Golden Jubilee Stakes and Group 1 Nunthorpe Stakes winner Kingsgate Native. The second dam, Native Force (Indian Ridge), a quite useful 1m winner, is a half-sister to 2 winners. *"Just like all my 2-y-o fillies I've breezed her and she's got an engine, but being by High Chaparral I'll not rush her. Hopefully she'll be out around June time but she'll be better later in the season and will make a lovely 3-y-o. A really nice type but quite immature mentally at the moment".*

BRIAN MEEHAN

1096. ALABAALY

b.c. Tamayuz – Tatbeeq (Invincible Spirit). February 6. Fourth foal. Brother to the useful 2014 listed 1m placed Quinta Verde. The dam, a fair 1m winner, is a half-sister to 4 winners including the smart dual listed winner and multiple Group 3 placed Crosspeace. The second dam, Announcing Peace (by Danehill), is an unplaced full or half-sister to 5 minor winners.

1097. ALSHALAAL (IRE)

ch.c. Arcano – Geesala (Barathea). March 9. Second foal. Half-brother to the fair 2014 7f placed maiden Illusive Force (by Iffraaj). The dam, a fair 2-y-o listed 5f winner, is a half-sister to the fairly useful 2-y-o 5f winner and listed-placed Tomintoul Singer. The second dam, Shivaree (by Rahy), a fair 2-y-o 6f winner, is a half-sister to 2 winners.

1098. BLUE BAYOU

ch.f. Bahamian Bounty – Oshiponga (Barathea). January 26. Eleventh foal. Half-sister to the 2-y-o Group 2 7f Superlative Stakes and US Grade 3 7f winner Hatta Fort (by Cape Cross), the fair dual 1m winner Ostentation (by Dubawi), the fair 6f and 7f winner Caramack (by Danehill Dancer) and the modest 9f winner Teide Lady (by Nashwan). The dam, a fair 9f winner, is a half-sister to 8 winners including the Grade 1 E P Taylor Stakes winner Miss Keller and the Group placed Sir George Turner and Kotsi. The second dam, Ingozi (by Warning), a fairly useful winner over 7f and 1m at 3 yrs including a listed event, is a half-sister to 7 winners including the triple Group 3 7f winner Inchinor.

1099. CAPTAINTHUNDERBOLT (IRE)

br.c. Bushranger – Dream Date (Oasis Dream). March 4. Second foal. £57,000Y. Doncaster Premier. BBA (Ire). Half-brother to the Group 3 5f winner and Group 1 Nunthorpe Stakes third Extortionist (by Dandy Man). The dam, a quite useful dual 7f winner, is a half-sister to 5 winners. The second dam, Femme Fatale (by Fairy King), a useful dual 6f winner of 2 races (including a listed event at 2 yrs), is a half-sister to 4 winners including the dual listed 10f winner and smart broodmare Foodbroker Fancy (herself dam of the Group 3 winner Dalvina).

1100. EKTIFAA

b.f. Mawatheeq – Elraabeya (Seeking The Gold). February 8. First foal. The dam was a fair 1m winner. The second dam, Seattle Envoy (by Deputy Minister), is an unraced sister to the Canadian champion 2-y-o and Grade 1 winner Hello Seattle and a half-sister to 3 winners.

1101. FANG

b.c. Lawman – Desert Tigress (Storm Cat). February 22. Fifth foal. Half-brother to the useful 2014 2-y-o 6f winner and Group 2 Mill Reef Stakes second Growl (by Oasis Dream). The dam, a fair Irish 2-y-o 5f winner, is a sister to the 2-y-o Group 3 7f Horris Hill Stakes winner Hurricane Cat. The second dam, Sky Beauty (by Blushing Groom), a winner of nine Grade 1 events in the USA, is a half-sister to the quite useful 2-y-o 1m winner Ajayib. The second dam, Maplejinksy (by Nijinsky), won two Grade 1 events in the USA and is closely related to the brilliant sprinter Dayjur.

1102. FATAAWY (IRE)
b.f. Invincible Spirit – Jamaayel (Shamardal). February 7. Second foal. Half-sister to the fairly useful 2014 2-y-o 5.5f winner Rathaath (by Oasis Dream). The dam, a fairly useful Irish 2-y-o 6f and 7f winner, was listed-placed over 7f and is a half-sister to 2 winners. The second dam, Walayef (by Danzig), a listed 6f (at 2 yrs) and Group 3 7f Athasi Stakes winner, is a sister to the smart 2-y-o 6f winner Haatef, to the listed 6f winner and Group 3 Moyglare Stud Stakes second Shimah and the Irish dual listed 6f winner Ulfah. (Hamdan Al Maktoum).

1103. HARVARD MAN
b.c. Equiano – Fabulously Fast (Deputy Minister). February 22. Ninth living foal. 120,000Y. Tattersalls October Book 1. Sam Sangster. Half-brother to the fairly useful listed 1m placed Humungosaur (by Red Ransom) and to 5 winners including the quite useful 2014 2-y-o 5f winner Equally Fast (by Equiano), the fair 1m winner Fabulouslyspirited (by Selkirk) and the modest 6f winner Maria Lombardi (by Medicean). The dam won the Grade 1 Spinaway Stakes, was placed in two more Grade 1 events and is a half-sister to 5 winners. The second dam, Fabulous Notion (by Somethingfabulous), won the Grade 1 Santa Susana Stakes in the USA and is a half-sister to the Grade 1 Turf Classic winner Cacoethes. Won on his debut in a five furlong Newbury maiden on the 17th April.

1104. HORTENSIO (IRE)
b.c. Pour Moi – O'Bella Ballerina (Fusaichi Pegasus). April 3. Second foal. 100,000Y. Tattersalls October Book 1. Sam Sangster. The dam, a fair Irish 12f winner, is a half-sister to 5 winners including the Group 1 St Leger winner Millenary, the Group 3 Princess Royal Stakes winner Head In The Clouds and the Derby third Let The Lion Roar. The second dam, Ballerina (by Dancing Brave), a quite useful

2-y-o 7f winner, is a half-sister to 5 winners including the Group 3 12f Princess Royal Stakes winner Dancing Bloom and the 1,000 Guineas third River Dancer (herself dam of the Champion Stakes winner Spectrum).

1105. JOHN SPLENDID (IRE)
b.c. Acclamation – Affirmative (Pivotal). April 9. Second foal. 70,000Y. Tattersalls October Book 2. Charlie Gordon-Watson. The dam is an unraced half-sister to 2 minor winners. The second dam, Favourable Terms (by Selkirk), winner of the Group 1 Nassau Stakes and Group 2 1m Matron Stakes, is a half-sister to 3 winners.

1106. KITAABY (IRE)
b.c. Acclamation – Flower Of Kent (Diesis). April 1. Half-brother to the fair 6f and 7f winner Gravitational (by Invincible Spirit) and to the fair 10f winner Crystal Nymph (by Rock Of Gibraltar). The dam, a fair 2-y-o 1m winner, is a half-sister to the listed-placed 10f winner Imperial Pippin. The second dam, Apple Of Kent (by Kris S), winner of the Grade 2 1m Shuvee Handicap, is a sister to one winner and a half-sister to 9 winners including the US dual Grade 2 winner True Flare (the dam of three graded stakes winners) and the Group/Grade 3 winners Set Alight, Capital Secret and War Zone.

1107. MA PEEK (USA)
b.br.c. Arch – Downtown Drifter (Devil His Due). May 13. Second foal. 35,000Y. Tattersalls October Book 1. Not sold. The dam won twice at 3 yrs in the USA and is a half-sister to 6 winners including the multiple listed winner Arch Rebel and the US stakes winner On My Dime. The second dam, Sheba's Step (by Alysheba), is an unraced half-sister to 8 winners including the dam of the US Grade 1 stakes winner Archarcharch.

1108. MALAKKY (IRE)
b.c. Tamayuz – Safiya Song (Intikhab). April 23. Second foal. 170,000Y. Tattersalls October Book 2. Shadwell Estate Co. Half-brother to the fairly useful 2014 2-y-o dual 6f winner Fuwairt (by Arcano). The dam is an unraced sister to the listed-placed winner In Safe Hands and a half-sister to 5 winners including the Group 2 Flying Childers Stakes winner

Cayman Kai. The second dam, Safiya (by Riverman), is an unraced sister to the German Group 2 winner and Group 1 Premio Parioli third Sulaafah and a half-sister to 3 winners.

1109. MALMOOSA (IRE)
b.f. Shamardal – Mohafazaat (Sadler's Wells). March 9. Fourth foal. Half-sister to the quite useful 10f and 12f winner Estedaama and to the French 10.5f winner Mutebah (both by Marju). The dam, a modest 10f winner, is a half-sister to 5 winners including the US Grade 2 10f winner Makderah and the very useful 2-y-o 6f and 7f winner Oriental Fashion. The second dam, Wijdan (by Riverman), a useful 1m and 10.4f winner, is a sister to the 7f (at 2 yrs) and listed 1m winner Sarayir and a half-sister to Nashwan, Nayef and Unfuwain.

1110. MISS GILLIAN (IRE)
b.f. Canford Cliffs – Bella Bella (Sri Pekan). February 14. Fifth foal. €160,000Y. Goffs Orby. Flaxman Stables. Half-brother to the fairly useful 7f (at 2 yrs) and 6f winner and listed-placed Courageous (by Refuse To Bend) and to a bumpers winner by Kalanisi. The dam, a quite useful dual 7f winner, is a half-sister to 5 winners including the German listed winner and Group 3 third Silk Petal (herself dam of the listed winner Star Tulip) and the dam of the Group 2 winners Tashawak and Fairy Queen. The second dam, Salabella (by Sallust), is a placed half-sister to 7 winners including the Irish St Leger and the Grosser Preis von Baden winner M-Lolshan. "

1111. NAWKHATHA (USA)
ch.f. Tapit – Lear's Princess (Lear Fan). February 24. The dam, winner of the US Grade 1 9f Gazelle Stakes, is out of Pretty City (by Carson City).

1112. PACK IT IN (IRE)
br.c. Big Bad Bob – Evening Dress (Medicean). March 14. First foal. £35,000Y. Doncaster Premier. BBA (Ire). The dam is an unplaced half-sister to 2 winners including the listed Dance Design Stakes winner and Group 1 Pretty Polly Stakes second Beach Bunny. The second dam, Miss Hawai (by Peintre Celebre), is an unraced half-sister to 5 winners including the 1,000 Guineas winner Miss France.

1113. PRINCESS KODIA (IRE) ♠
b.f. Kodiac – Pixie's Blue (Hawk Wing). March 25. Third foal. £20,000Y. Doncaster Premier (private sale). Half-sister to Lady Ampthill (by Strategic Prince), unplaced in one start at 2 yrs in 2014. The dam, a fair 1m winner at 3 yrs in France, is a half-sister to 11 winners including the useful 9f, 12f and listed 2m winner Kindling and the French listed 9f winner Thattinger. The second dam, Isle Of Flame (by Shirley Heights), was unraced.

1114. QAREEN
b.c. Kyllachy – Virginia Hall (Medicean). January 31. Second foal. £70,000Y. Doncaster Premier. Shadwell Estate Co. The dam, useful 2-y-o 5f and 6f winner and second in the Group 3 Prix du Calvados, is a half-sister to 6 winners including the Group 3 6f Firth Of Clyde Stakes winner and Group 2 Rockfel Stakes second Violette and the listed 6f (at 2 yrs) and Group 3 7f Nell Gwyn Stakes winner Silca's Gift. The second dam, Odette (by Pursuit Of Love), a fair 3-y-o 5f and 5.7f winner, is a half-sister to 4 winners.

1115. RIDE THE LIGHTENING
b.c. Dalakhani – Bright Halo (Bigstone). April 5. Eleventh foal. 100,000Y. Tattersalls October Book 1. C de Moubray. Half-brother to 6 winners including the useful 6f (at 2 yrs) and listed 1m winner and Group 2 6f Mill Reef Stakes third Nantyglo (by Mark Of Esteem), the fairly useful 1m (at 2 yrs) and 12f winner Resplendent Light (by Fantastic Light), the quite useful 12f winner Saint Hilary (by Authorized) and the fair 10f and 12f winner Dalgig (by New Approach). The dam, a minor 9f winner, is a half-sister to 9 winners including Moonstone (Group 1 Irish Oaks) and Cerulean Sky (Group 1 10f Prix Saint-Alary). The second dam, Solo de Lune (by Law Society), a listed-placed 11f winner, is a half-sister to Truly A Dream (Grade 2 E P Taylor Stakes).

1116. SHARARA ♠
ch.c. Dutch Art – Tafawut (Nayef). March 29. Second foal. 100,000Y. Tattersalls October Book 2. Shadwell Estate Co. Half-brother to the moderate 2014 8.5f placed 2-y-o Politico (by Medicean). The dam, a fair 1m winner, is a half-sister to 7 winners including

the useful 5f (at 2 yrs) and listed 7f winner Kalindi (herself the dam of 3 stakes winners), the useful 6f and 7f winner (including at 2 yrs) Mahmoom and the useful French 6f and 7f winner and Group 3 6f Prix de Meautry third Tayseer. The second dam, Rohita (by Waajib), a fairly useful 2-y-o 5f and 6f winner, was third in the Group 3 6f Cherry Hinton Stakes and is a half-sister to 5 winners.

1117. TAWDHEEF (IRE)
br.c. Zebedee – Duchess Of Foxland (Medecis). March 12. First foal. £92,000Y. Doncaster Premier. Shadwell Estate Co. The dam, an Irish 6f (at 2 yrs), 7f and listed 9f winner, was dual Group 3 placed and is a half-sister to 2 winners. The second dam, Itsanothergirl (by Reprimand), a modest 7f (at 2 yrs) to 11f winner of 4 races, is a half-sister to one winner.

1118. UNNAMED
b.c. Danehill Dancer – Alchemilla (Dubai Destination). March 16. Second foal. 60,000Y. Tattersalls October Book 2. Sam Sangster. Closely related to the fair 2014 2-y-o 7f winner Stardrifter (by Rock Of Gibraltar). The dam is an unraced half-sister to 8 winners including the smart 2-y-o Group 2 July Stakes winner Strategic Prince and the listed winner and Group 2 placed Yorkshire. The second dam, Ausherra (by Diesis), won the listed 12f Lingfield Oaks Trial and is a full or half-sister to 9 winners including the Oaks, Irish Oaks and Yorkshire Oaks winner Ramruma.

1119. UNNAMED
ch.f. Sea The Stars – Altesse Imperiale (Rock Of Gibraltar). April 7. Fourth foal. 260,000Y. Tattersalls October Book 1. Hugo Merry. Half-sister to the useful 2-y-o 7f winner and Group 1 Racing Post Trophy third Altruistic (by Galileo) and to the quite useful 11.5f winner Pitchoun (by Street Cry). The dam, a fair French 10f winner, is a half-sister to the Grade 1 10f Beverly D Stakes and Grade 1 9f Diana Stakes winner Angara and the Group 2 Prix Corrida winner Actrice. The second dam, Ange Bleu (by Alleged), a French placed 3-y-o, is a half-sister to 10 winners including the Breeders Cup Classic winner Arcangues, the Group 3 Prix de Psyche winner Agathe (dam of the Grade/Group 1 winners Artiste Royale and Aquarelliste) and the dam of the 1,000 Guineas winner Cape Verdi.

1120. UNNAMED ♠
b.c. Acclamation – Fritta Mista (Linamix). April 10. Ninth foal. 47,000Y. Tattersalls October Book 2. BBA (Ire). Brother to the Irish 2-y-o 7f and subsequent Hong Kong Group 3 7f winner Montecchio and half-brother to the fairly useful 2-y-o 6f and 7f winner and Group 2 May Hill Stakes third Sans Reward (by Barathea) and the fair 5f (at 2 yrs) to 7f winner of 4 races Ursula (by Namid). The dam is a placed half-sister to one minor winner. The second dam, Sea Quest (by Rainbow Quest), is an unplaced half-sister to 9 winners including the Group 1 Yorkshire Oaks winner Hellenic (herself the dam of the Group 1 winners Islington, Greek Dance and Mountain High).

1121. UNNAMED
b.f. Oasis Dream – Liberally (Statue Of Liberty). March 17. Second foal. The dam, a quite useful 1m to 10f winner of 3 races here, was Grade 3 placed over 9f in the USA and is a half-sister to 8 winners including the 1,000 Guineas and Group 2 Rockfel Stakes winner Speciosa and the US Grade 3 stakes winner of 13 races Major Rhythm. The second dam, Specifically (by Sky Classic), won once at 2 yrs in the USA and is a half-sister to 10 winners including the Group 1 Champion Stakes, Grand Prix de Saint-Cloud and Hong Kong Cup winner Pride.

1122. UNNAMED
ch.f. Raven's Pass – Mike's Wildcat (Forest Wildcat). April 25. Eighth foal. 80,000Y. Tattersalls October Book 2. Hugo Merry. Sister to the quite useful dual 7f winner Future Reference and half-sister to 6 winners including the very useful 2014 2-y-o 6f winner and triple Group 2 placed Jungle Cat (by Iffraaj) and the US dual Grade 3 winner Texas Wildcatter. The dam, a US 2-y-o stakes winner, is a half-sister to 6 winners in North America. The second dam, Old Flame (by Black Tie Affair), was a stakes-placed winner in the USA.

1123. UNNAMED
ch.c. Monsieur Bond – Oasis Breeze (Oasis Dream). March 12. Third foal. £33,000Y. Doncaster Premier. BBA (Ire). Half-brother to the quite useful 2014 2-y-o dual 5f winner Don't Tell Annie (by Royal Applause) and to the fair 6f winner Dutch Breeze (by Dutch Art). The dam, a quite useful 2-y-o 5f and 6f

winner, is a half-sister to 8 winners including the US stakes winner Stormy Forever. The second dam, Forever Fine (by Sunshine Forever), a US stakes-placed winner at 2 yrs, is a half-sister to 7 winners.

1124. UNNAMED
b.c. Bushranger – Queen Cobra (Indian Rocket). March 21. Fifth foal. £40,000Y. Doncaster Premier. BBA (Ire). Half-brother to the fairly useful 5f winner and listed-placed City Zen (by Baltic King), to the fair 7f to 9f winner of 7 races Mr Red Clubs (by Red Clubs) and the fair 2-y-o 6f winner Red Cobra by Redback). The dam, a fair dual 5f winner at 2 yrs, is a half-sister to 4 minor winners. The second dam, Miss Sabre (by Sabrehill), is an unraced sister to a German listed winner.

1125. UNNAMED
b.f. Oasis Dream – Rainbow Springs (Selkirk). January 24. First foal. 200,000Y. Tattersalls October Book 1. Hugo Merry. The dam, a fairly useful 9f winner and third in the 2-y-o Group 1 Prix Marcel Boussac, is a sister to one winner and a half-sister to the Group 3 Prix Chloe winner Sparkling Beam. The second dam, Pearl Dance (by Nureyev), a useful 2-y-o 6f winner and third in the Group 1 Moyglare Stud Stakes, is a half-sister to 7 winners including the German listed winner and Group 1 German Derby fourth Ocean Sea and the dam of the Melbourne Cup winner Delta Blues.

1126. UNNAMED
ch.c. Fast Company – Raven One (Titus Livius). March 10. €31,000foal. Goffs November. Lynn Lodge Stud. The dam is an unplaced sister to the German Group 2 and dual Group 3 winner Sehrezad. The second dam, Trebles (by Kenmare), a minor French 3-y-o winner, is a half-sister to 5 winners.

1127. UNNAMED
ch.c. Henrythenavigator – Saintlike (Ballado). March 20. Eighth foal. €36,000Y. Goffs Orby. Brian Meehan. Half-brother to the North American stakes winner of 8 races Heart Of A King (by Lion Heart), to the US stakes-placed Nocknonheavensgate (by Grand Reward) and two minor US winners by Tapit and Tale Of The Cat. The dam won 2 minor races in the

USA and is a half-sister to 4 winners including the French listed winner Pompeyano. The second dam, Lady Lodger (by Be My Guest), a quite useful 1m and 10f winner here, won the Grade 3 Miss America Stakes and is a half-sister to 6 winners including the dual Group 1 winner Caitano.

1128. UNNAMED
b.c. Holy Roman Emperor – Sharp Relief (Galileo). February 20. First foal. 55,000Y. Tattersalls October Book 2. Sam Sangster. The dam, a fair 11f and 14f winner, is a half-sister to one winner abroad. The second dam, Jinsky's Gift (by Cadeaux Genereux), is an unraced half-sister to 8 winners including the triple listed 7f winner Modeeroch, the Group 1 1m Gran Criterium third Chinese Whisper and the Group 1 6f Cheveley Park Stakes third Danaskaya.

1129. UNNAMED
b.c. Arcano – Vestavia (Alhaarth). March 18. Fourth foal. 40,000Y. Tattersalls October Book 2. Sam Sangster. Half-brother to the fair Irish 7f winner Texas Rock (by Rock Of Gibraltar) and to the fair 6f and 7f winner Evident (by Excellent Art). The dam is an unraced half-sister to 6 winners including the Group 3 placed 2-y-o Rosabee. The second dam, Tilbrook (by Don't Forget Me), won over 1m at 3 yrs in Ireland and is a half-sister to 8 winners including the listed winner and Group 1 Phoenix Stakes second Maledetto.

ROD MILLMAN
1130. BUKLE (IRE) ★★★
b.c. Approve – Rumline (Royal Applause). February 26. Third foal. £22,000Y. Doncaster Premier. G Howson. Brother to the 2014 Irish 2-y-o 6f winner Sharaasa and half-brother to the fair 2-y-o 1m winner Raajis (by Dark Angel). The dam is an unplaced half-sister to 4 winners including very useful 2-y-o Group 2 5.5f Prix Robert Papin winner Never A Doubt. The second dam, Waypoint (by Cadeaux Genereux), a fairly useful 6f and 7f winner, is a half-sister to 5 winners including the Group 2 6f Diadem Stakes winner and sire Acclamation. (Mr C H Saunders). *"He was ready so early he could have run in February and we've been keeping the lid on him ever since! He's well put together and is a nice, early type of 2-y-o. He'll*

start his career in mid-April over five furlongs, but he'll get a mile later on. A strong, medium-sized colt, he's well-muscled and an ideal trainer's horse". **TRAINERS' BARGAIN BUY**

1131. CONCUR (IRE) ★★
ch.c. Approve – Tradmagic (Traditionally). April 20. Second foal. £24,000Y. Doncaster Premier. G Howson/R Millman. Half-brother to the unraced 2014 2-y-o Lady Mascot (by Zebedee). The dam is an unraced half-sister to the useful winner and listed-placed Magic City. The second dam, Annmarie's Magic (by Flying Spur), is a placed half-sister to 4 winners. (Miss G J Abbey). *"He's a horse with good conformation, he's tough and will probably be better over six and seven furlongs than five. Nevertheless he'll start off at five furlongs in April".*

1132. HANDYTALK (IRE) ★★★★
b.c. Lilbourne Lad – Dancing With Stars (Where Or When). April 14. Third foal. £32,000Y. Doncaster Premier. G Howson/Rod Millman. Half-brother to the modest 2014 Irish 7f placed 2-y-o Athenry Boy (by Excellent Art). The dam is an unraced half-sister to 3 winners. The second dam, Summer Dance (by Sadler's Wells), a quite useful 1m winner, is a half-sister to 6 winners including the dual Group 3 10f winner Poet and to the French 2-y-o dual 6f winner and Group 3 6f Prix Eclipse second Hothaifah. (Cantay Racing). *"A nice horse that would be quick enough for five furlongs and he should get six a bit later on. His sire only ran as a 2-y-o and I think this colt will have his highest rating as a 2-y-o as opposed to next year. He should be a pretty good 2-y-o".* This colt won on his debut on the 13th April at Windsor.

1133. JOSH PERRY ★★
b.c. Hellvelyn – Emma Peel (Emarati). March 9. Tenth foal. £16,000Y. Doncaster Silver. G Howson/Rod Millman. Half-brother to the quite useful 6f (at 2 yrs) to 8.5f winner Nameitwhatyoulike (by Trade Fair) and to the Scandinavian listed winner Females Fun (by Diktat). The useful listed 6f winner of 4 races, is a half-sister to 10 winners including the listed winner Risk Master. The second dam, Trigamy (by Tribal Chief), won 4 minor races at 2 and 3 yrs and is a half-sister to 6 winners.

(G D Thompson). *"He's quite a muscular horse but he's had a little setback and will want a bit more time than some of the others. He'll be out in mid-season and he'll be a sprinter".*

1134. O'CONNOR (IRE) ★★
ch.c. Roderic O'Connor – Fly By Magic (Indian Rocket). April 16. Second foal. £25,000Y. Doncaster Premier. G Howson/Rod Millman. Half-brother to the unplaced 2014 2-y-o Lily's Rainbow (by Intikhab). The dam, a fair dual 5f winner, is a half-sister to one winner. The second dam, Travel Tricks (by Presidium), is an unraced half-sister to 3 minor winners. (The Links Partnership). *"One for the mid-season onwards over six and seven furlongs. He'll probably go on to be a dual purpose horse".*

1135. RAJADAMRI ★★★
b.c. Hellvelyn – Crofters Ceilidh (Scottish Reel). April 4. Twelfth foal. £17,000Y. Doncaster Premier. G Howson (private sale). Brother to the fairly useful 2014 2-y-o 5f winner and Group 3 7f Prestige Stakes second Bonnie Grey and half-brother to 7 winners including the useful 2-y-o 5f and 6f winner Cop Hill Lad (by Atraf), the fairly useful listed 7f winner Clifton Dancer (by Fraam) and the fair 2-y-o winners Bahamian Ceilidh (by Bahamian Bounty) and Okikoki (by Ishiguru). The dam, a listed-placed winner of 3 races over 5f including at 2 yrs, is a half-sister to 4 winners including the Group 2 placed Lord Kintyre. The second dam, Highland Rowena (by Royben), a modest sprint winner of 4 races, is a half-sister to 2 minor winners. *"Probably the best bred of our 2-y-o's, his full sister did so well for us last year. This colt is a bigger, stronger type than her and he's also a bit cockier – she's a quiet type of filly. I've had a few out of this family and he's probably the best looking of them all. He'll be a sprinter and we'll see him out in June".*

1136. SIR RODERIC (IRE) ★★★
b.c. Roderic O'Connor – Begin The Beguine (Peintre Celebre). April 21. Seventh foal. £50,000Y. Doncaster Premier. G Howson/R Millman. Half-brother to the Italian 2-y-o winner La Grande Jatte and to the minor French 3-y-o winner Beyond Time (both by Key Of Luck). The dam, a fair 10f winner, is a half-sister to 6 winners including Group

1 Phoenix Stakes second Big Time and the Irish 2-y-o 5f and 7f winner and listed-placed Master Papa. The second dam, Beguine (by Green Dancer), is an unplaced half-sister to the champion two-year-old and high-class sire Grand Lodge and to the listed winners La Persiana and Papabile. (The Links Partnership). *"A strong, good-looking 2-y-o, he was set to run last week but he pulled a muscle. He'll make a nice 2-y-o but he's big enough to train on as well".*

1137. UNNAMED ★★★

b.c. Showcasing – Showery (Rainbow Quest). April 16. 20,000Y. Tattersalls October Book 4. Not sold. Half-brother to the useful triple 1m winner (including at 2 yrs) and listed-placed Bestam (by Selkirk), to the useful 6f and 1m winner of 7 races Tiger Reigns, the fair 10f and 11f winner Songjiang (both by Tiger Hill), the Hong Kong winner of 6 races Noble Man (by Cadeaux Genereux) and the modest 2-y-o 10f winner Louise Rayner (by Vettori). The dam, a fair 3-y-o 6f winner, is a half-sister to 5 winners including the smart Winter Derby winner Adiemus. The second dam, Anodyne (by Dominion), a useful 6f winner, is a sister to the very useful US Grade 3 winner Domynsky and a half-sister to 8 winners. *"He's has a touch of sore shins, so we're hanging on with him for now. He looks a typical sharp 2-y-o and the stallion has proved a lot of experts wrong. 18 months ago a lot of people didn't hold much hope for him, but he's done really well. Once this colt gets over his niggling problems we'll get him going again, but we've missed the first few weeks of the season".*

GARY MOORE

1138. DEGAS BRONZE ★★★

b.f. Showcasing – Local Fancy (Bahamian Bounty). February 19. 48,000Y. Doncaster November. Bobby O'Ryan. Half-sister to the quite useful triple 5f winner at 2 and 3 yrs Kyleakin Lass (by Kyllachy), to the fair 5f (at 2 yrs) to 1m winner of 4 races Local Flier (by Byron) and the fair 5f winner of 4 races including at 2 yrs Watts Up Son (by Diktat). The dam, a fair 2-y-o 5f winner, is a half-sister to one winner. The second dam, Local Abbey (by Primo Dominie), is an unraced half-sister to 3 winners including the smart 7f to 9f and subsequent US dual stakes winner Lonesome Dude. (Mr R A Green). *"She's a nice filly and quite strong but she came in late so isn't that far forward. She's backward in her coat at the moment, but I'm pleased with everything I've seen so far. She seems forward-going and very willing, she moves quite well but I haven't galloped her yet. She'll definitely be a five furlong type and I'd hope to get her out as soon as I can without rushing her".*

1139. MODELLO (IRE) ★★★★

b.f. Intikhab – Precious Citizen (Proud Citizen). April 1. Third foal. €65,000Y. Tattersalls Ireland September. Gary Moore. Half-sister to the useful 2014 2-y-o listed 5f St Hugh's Stakes winner Bronze Maquette (by Dark Angel). The dam, a moderate 9f and 10f placed maiden, is a half-sister to 3 winners. The second dam, Fasateen (by Alysheba), a winner over 1m at 2 yrs and a listed 12f event at 3 in France, is a half-sister to 8 winners including the 1,000 Guineas and Prix de l'Opera winner Hatoof and the US Grade 1 winner Irish Prize. (Mr R A Green). *"A half-sister to the good 2-y-o we had last year, Bronze Maquette, but she's a completely different type. She's bigger, stronger and more relaxed. She's been showing me stacks but I've had to back off her because she's going through a growing spurt. I'm very pleased with what I've seen so far and I'd expect her to be a six/seven furlong type from mid-season onwards".*

1140. PERSAVERANCE ★★

b.c. Sir Percy – Marliana (Mtoto). January 28. Eighth living foal. 38,000Y. Tattersalls October Book 3. G L Moore Racing. Half-brother to the quite useful 2-y-o winner The Dial House (by Tagula), to the dual 2-y-o 7f seller winner Marmite (by Vettori) and the fair 2-y-o dual 6f winner Zambach (by Namid). The dam, a French 2-y-o 6f winner, is a half-sister to 6 winners including Albisola (Group 3 Prix de Flore) and to the dam of the St James's Palace Stakes winner Much Improved. The second dam, Mahalia (by Danehill), a listed 7f winner, is a half-sister to 7 winners including the Group 3 winner Muroto. *"He's a big, backward horse and quite weak at the moment. He's a horse we like but he'll be a back-end of the season job".*

1141. UNNAMED ★★
b.g. Bahamian Bounty – Carina Ari (Imperial Ballet). March 26. Fifth foal. 25,000Y. Tattersalls October Book 2. Gary Moore/J Hinds. Half-brother to the South African winner and listed-placed Sweet Aria (by Celtic Swing). The dam was placed three times in France and is a half-sister to 7 winners including the triple US Grade 1 winner Golden Apples, the Group 3 Park Hill Stakes winner Alexander Three D and the US 1m stakes winner La Piaf. The second dam, Loon (by Kaldoun), won 4 races in France a listed 12f event and is a half-sister to 3 minor winners. (Galloping on the South Downs Partnership). *"He's a small colt and we'll try to get on with him as soon as we can, but he had a problem that meant we had to geld him. It's hard to say what trip he'll want or how soon he'll be because we just need to give him the time to catch up".*

1142. UNNAMED ★★★★
b.f. Poet's Voice – Dignify (Rainbow Quest). February 16. Ninth foal. 29,000Y. Tattersalls October Book 2. G L Moore. Half-sister to the quite useful 6f (at 2 yrs) to 10f winner of 4 races Personify (by Zafonic), to the fair 7.5f and 8.5f winner Declamation (by Shamardal) and a winner in the USA by Refuse To Bend. The dam won the Group 3 1m Prix d'Aumale at 2 yrs and is a half-sister to 7 winners. The second dam, Her Ladyship (by Polish Precedent), a French listed 10.5f winner, was second in the Group 1 10.5f Prix de Diane and is a half-sister to the Group 1 7f Prix de la Salamandre winner Lord of Men. (Galloping on the South Downs Partnership). *"She's a real nice filly and should be reasonably early. She's going well, loves to please, very solid and just a really nice filly. I couldn't be more pleased with her and I'd guess six/seven furlongs would be right for her this season".* **TRAINERS' BARGAIN BUY**

1143. UNNAMED ★★★
b.c. Shakespearean – Renascent Rahy (Rahy). March 18. Third foal. £40,0002-y-o. Ascot Breeze Up. Gary Moore Racing. The dam is an unraced half-sister to 4 winners including the US stakes winner and Grade 3 placed High Maintenance. The second dam, Speak Softly To Me (by Ogygian), is an unraced half-sister to 8 winners including Green Tune (French

2,000 Guineas) and Pas de Reponse (Cheveley Park Stakes). *"The sire is a son of Shamardal and was trained by Mark Johnston. I bought this colt at the Ascot Breeze Ups because he breezed well and it took them a while to pull him up. He's got a great way about him, so hopefully he'll be quite nice and he'll be a six/seven furlong 2-y-o".*

STAN MOORE

1144. ABBERLEY DANCER ★★★
b.br.f. Lilbourne Lad – Babberina (Danehill Dancer). February 13. Fourth foal. Half-sister to Burbanza (by Marju), a minor winner of 7 races in Italy. The dam was placed twice at 3 yrs and is a half-sister to one winner abroad. The second dam, Dos Talas (by You And I), is an unplaced half-sister to 7 winners including the Prix de l'Abbaye winner Imperial Beauty. (S A Mares, Ed Tidmarsh & J S Moore). *"A strong filly, she'll be an out-and-out 2-y-o and she goes nicely. Has a bit of an attitude, she'll be tough and hardy and should be one to follow this year".*

1145. DARK REDEEMER ★★
b.c. Dark Angel – Lush (Fasliyev). April 13. Second foal. 20,000Y. Tattersalls October Book 2. Not sold. The dam, a fair 6f (at 2 yrs) to 12f placed maiden, is a half-sister to 5 winners, two of them listed-placed. The second dam, Our Hope (by Dancing Brave), is an unraced half-sister to 5 winners including the listed winner Golden Temple. (Pineapple Stud & J S Moore). *"A lovely horse for seven furlongs a mile later in the year. He travels well and there's more to like about him than dislike".*

1146. FRENCH ENCORE ★★★★
b.g. Showcasing – French Connexion (Chineur). February 27. Second foal. 2,000Y. Ascot December. Not sold. The dam, a modest 5f placed 2-y-o, is a half-sister to 3 minor winners here and abroad. The second dam, Hunzy (by Desert King), a listed-placed winner in Italy, is a half-sister to the outstanding hurdler Hurricane Fly. *"He's also ready won his maiden – a 4.5f race in France and he won by two and a half lengths, going away. I definitely have sights on the Windsor Castle at Royal Ascot with him. I'd say he could run on any ground, he's a home-bred who didn't make his money at the sales, but never mind that because I think he's a proper 2-y-o.*

1147. HIGH SAVANNAH (IRE) ★★★
b.f. High Chaparral – Serengeti Day (Alleged).
March 14. Eleventh foal. €32,000Y. Goffs
Orby. G H Bloodstock. Half-sister to 5 winners
including the modest 11f winner Daring
Damsel (by Van Nistelrooy) and three in the
USA by Aragorn, Belong To Me and Danzig.
The dam, a minor 3-y-o winner in the USA, is
a half-sister to 11 winners including the dual
US Grade 3 winner Weekend Surprise (dam
of the top-class colts A P Indy and Summer
Squall) and the high-class sprinter Wolfhound.
The second dam, Lassie Dear (by Buckpasser),
won 5 races including the Grade 3 Villager
Stakes and is a half-sister to the high-class
middle-distance colt Gay Mecene. (Mr Donald
Kerr & J S Moore). *"More likely to make it to
the racecourse as a 2-y-o than the other High
Chaparral filly I have, I think she'll win this year
over seven furlongs or a mile and then make a
3-y-o as well".*

1148. LADY PRESIDENT ★★
b.f. Fast Company – Lovere (St Jovite). April
22. Seventh foal. €3,000Y. Goffs Open. Stan
Moore. Half-sister to the quite useful 6f (at 2
yrs) to 8.5f winner of 11 races Miami Gator
(by Titus Livius). The dam is an unplaced
half-sister 6 winners including the Group 2 6f
Lowther Stakes and Group 2 5f Queen Mary
Stakes winner Flashy Wings. The second dam,
Lovealoch (by (by Lomond), a very useful 7f
(at 2 yrs) and 9f winner here and placed in
the Group 2 Falmouth Stakes and the Group
2 Premio Lydia Tesio, subsequently won once
in the USA and is a half-sister to 7 winners.
(The Petticoat Government). *"She's owned by
a syndicate of ladies (hence the name of the
horse and the syndicate!) This is a nice filly
with plenty of size about her and I would say
she'll come to fore at six and seven furlongs".*

1149. MARY PARMENTER (IRE) ★★
b.br.f. Dick Turpin – Umniya (Bluebird).
January 22. Seventh foal. Half-sister to the
modest 2014 2-y-o 7f winner Pat Mustard (by
Royal Applause). The dam, a quite useful 2-y-
o 6f winner, was third in the Group 3 Premio
Dormello and is a half-sister to 5 winners
including the dual listed 6f winner Lady Links
(herself dam of the dual listed winner Selinka).
The second dam, Sparky's Song (by Electric), a
moderate 10.2f and 12f winner, is a half-sister

to the Group 1 6.5f winner Bold Edge and
the listed winner and Group 2 second Brave
Edge. (Mrs J S Moore). *"She's not over-big but
she'll be tough and hardy. One that could win
a couple of races, she came in late so we're a
bit behind with her, but she'll run plenty at two.
She's named after Dick Turpin's mother!"*

1150. SKY ISLAND (IRE) ★★
b.f. High Chaparral – Nasanice (Nashwan).
May 2. Thirteenth foal. 50,000Y. Tattersalls
October Book 1. Stephen Hillen. Half-sister
to 8 winners including the Group 2 12f
Hardwicke Stakes winner Maraahel, the useful
2-y-o 7f winner and Group 3 third Huja (both
by Alzao), the smart 1m Britannia Handicap
winner Mostashaar (by Intikhab), the 9f winner
Almuktahem (by Green Desert) and the dual
10f winner Sharedah (by Pivotal), both quite
useful. The dam, a fairly useful Irish 9f winner,
is a half-sister to 4 winners. The second dam,
Mathaayl (by Shadeed), a quite useful 6f and
10f winner, is a half-sister to the Group 3
Princess Margaret Stakes winner Muhbubh
(dam of the US Grade 2 winner Kayrawan). (Mr
Donald Kerr & J S Moore). *"A big filly, she
has a real good page and will probably be one
for the middle to back-end. She's one of those
that could have just have a couple of runs this
year, win or be second, and then wait for next
year".*

1151. THE BURNHAM MARE ★★
b.f. Kodiac – Courte Paille (Common Grounds).
April 1. Fifth foal. €8,000Y. Tattersalls Ireland
September. Stan Moore. The dam, a winner
over 1m and 8.5f at 3 yrs in France, is a
half-sister to 6 winners including the fairly
useful 2-y-o dual 5f winner and subsequent
US stakes-placed winner Inca Tern. The
second dam, No Hard Feelings (by Alzao), a
quite useful 5f (at 2 yrs) and 12f winner of 7
races, is a half-sister to 4 winners. (The Swan
Partnership). *"She's sharp, she's just started
working and she'll win a race, but we'll just
have to see what level she reaches".*

1152. THREEBAGSUE ★★★
ch.f. Lord Shanakill – Feet Of Flame
(Theatrical). March 24. Eighth foal. £10,000Y.
Doncaster Premier. Stan Moore. Half-sister to
the fairly useful 2-y-o 8.7f winner Fullback (by
Redback), to the fairly useful 7f to 10f winner

and Group 3 third Kinky Afro (by Modigliani) and the fair 2-y-o 7f winner Orpen Fire (by Orpen). The dam is a placed half-sister to one winner in the USA. The second dam, Red Hot Dancer (by Seattle Dancer), is a US placed half-sister to 5 winners including the minor US stakes winner at around 1m Madame Secretary (herself dam of the French 1,000 Guineas winner Ta Rib) and the Stewards Cup winner Green Ruby. (The Moore The Merrier). *"When she walks in the paddock she'll catch everyone's eye because of the strange pigmentations in her skin. She'll be sharp and I think she's got a bit of quality. I've trained a couple of her winning siblings and I'd say six furlongs will be her trip".* **TRAINERS' BARGAIN BUY**

1153. REPEAT OFFENDER (IRE) ★★★
b.c. Thewayyouare – Dame Rochelle (Danehill Dancer). April 4. Fourth foal. £15,000Y. Doncaster Premier. Not sold. Half-brother to the minor 5f to 7f winner La Canaada (by Antonius Pius) and to a minor winner abroad by Ad Valorem. The dam, a poor Irish 4-y-o 6f winner, is a half-sister to 3 minor winners. The second dam, New Rochelle (by Lafontaine), won over 14f in Ireland and is a half-sister to the triple Group 2 winner Shambo. (Mr D Kerr). *"He seems to have pace and the family are all five or six furlong winners, so he'll be a sprinter rather than a galloper. He'll be a 2-y-o alright and he should be running by early May".*

1154. ROMANCINGTHESTONE ★★★
b.f. Bertolini – Diamond Vanessa (Distinctly North). May 2. Seventh foal. 800Y. Doncaster October Book 4. Not sold. Half-sister to the moderate 5f (at 2 yrs) to 1m winner Wizby (by Wizard King) and to a winner of 16 minor races in Italy by Puissance. The dam is an unplaced half-sister to 2 winners abroad. The second dam, Elegant Act (by Shecky Greene), won 5 races from 2 to 5 yrs in the USA and is a half-sister to 8 winners. (Mr R Viney & Miss D Wisbey). *"She came in a bit late but seems to be quite professional. A little filly that could progress and win a few races this year, so I think she'll be well worth following".*

1155. WHERE IT BEGAN (IRE) ★★★
ch.f. Strategic Prince – Easy Going (Hamas).

March 15. Ninth foal. €5,500Y. Tattersalls Ireland. Stan Moore. Half-sister to the fairly useful 2-y-o 5f winner and listed-placed Going Straight (by Princely Heir), to the modest 2-y-o 5f winner Pressure Drop (by Desert Style), the modest dual 6f winner Going French (by Frenchman's Bay) and a 2-y-o winner in Italy by Byron. The dam is an unraced half-sister to 5 winners including the Flying Childers, Richmond and Cornwallis Stakes winner Easycall. The second dam, Up And Going (by Never So Bold), is an unraced half-sister to 9 winners including the Group 3 Cornwallis Stakes winner Up And At 'Em. (Mr K Badger & Mr J S Moore). *"She would have been one of my first runners if it weren't for a slight setback. She goes well and the main aim with this filly is to get her to the Tattersalls Sales race in Ireland in August".*

HUGHIE MORRISON
1156. BAHAMIAN BOY ★★★
ch.c. Paco Boy – Bahamian Babe (Bahamian Bounty). April 18. Third foal. 22,000Y. Tattersalls October Book 2. H Morrison. The dam, a 2-y-o listed 5f winner of 4 races, is a sister to 3 winners. The second dam, Baby Bunting (by Wolfhound), a modest sprint-placed maiden, is a half-sister to 7 winners including the Group 3 Cork And Orrery Stakes and US Grade 3 Jaipur Stakes winner Atraf and the Group 2 Richmond Stakes winner Son Pardo. (Paul Brockelhurst, Hugh Scott-Barrett, T Pickford). *"Yes, he's a nice little colt, there's speed on his dam's side and he's quite forward going. All being well he'll be out in May and he'll be a five/six furlong 2-y-o".* **TRAINERS' BARGAIN BUY**

1157. CATALAN (IRE) ★★★
b.f. Duke Of Marmalade – Twice The Ease (Green Desert). March 7. Ninth foal. 120,000Y. Tattersalls October Book 1. Airlie Stud. Closely related to the listed 1m winner and Group 3 third Hen Night and to the useful 2-y-o 5f winner Achilles Of Troy (both by Danehill Dancer) and half-brother to 3 winners including the US dual Grade 2 winner Amira's Prince (by Teofilo). The dam is an unplaced sister to the 2-y-o listed 6f winner Desert Ease and a half-sister to the triple Group 3 winner Two-Twenty-Two. The second dam, Easy To Copy (by Affirmed), won the Group 2 Premio

Legnano and is a sister to 3 stakes winners including Trusted Partner (1,000 Guineas winner and dam of the US Grade 1 winner Dress To Thrill). (Sonia Rogers & Sir Thomas Pilkington). *"She's only just come in and we're learning about her. She's not very big, so there's a bit of a dilemma because there are 2-y-o winners in the pedigree but this is a Duke Of Marmalade and they usually take time. She seems quite nice, but so she should do for what she cost".*

1158. CINDERS (IRE) ★★★★
b.f. Lilbourne Lad – The Fairies Did It (Elusive Quality). January 28. Second foal. €150,000Y. Goffs Orby. Sackville/Donald. Half-sister to the fair 2014 7f placed 2-y-o Tohfa (by Dutch Art). The dam is an unraced half-sister to 9 winners including the US dual listed winner and Grade 1 Kentucky Oaks third Sneaky Quiet. The second dam, No More Ironing (by Slew O'Gold), a minor 2-y-o winner in the USA, is a half-sister to 5 winners including the dam of Zanzibar (Group 1 Italian Oaks). (M Kerr-Dineen, M Hughes, W Eason & G Rothwell). *"She goes quite well, she's got a bit of size to her and we quite like the look of her. She'll be our sharpest filly and should be racing by May or June. A speedy filly, I doubt her getting further than six furlongs".*

1159. EXCELLENT SOUNDS ★★★
b.f. Exceed And Excel – Siren Sound (Singspiel). May 4. Fourth foal. 60,000Y. Tattersalls October Book 1. Not sold. Half-sister to the modest 2014 5f and 6f placed 2-y-o Siren's Cove (by Sir Percy), to the French 2-y-o 7f and 7.5f winner and 1m listed-placed Passion Blanche (by Dutch Art) and the fair 4-y-o 1m winner Aomen Rock (by Rock Of Gibraltar). The dam, a modest 7f winner, is a half-sister to 4 winners. The second dam, Warning Belle (by Warning), is an unraced half-sister to 7 winners including the Group 2 10f Prince of Wales's Stakes and Group 3 10f Brigadier Gerard Stakes winner Stagecraft, the Group 3 winner Mullins Bay and the listed winners Balalaika and Hyabella. (Helena Springfield Ltd). *"One for much later on, she only arrived yesterday so I couldn't comment on her really".*

1160. FUMATA BIANCA (IRE) ★★★
b.f. Acclamation – Divine Authority (Holy Roman Emperor). April 22. Second foal. €70,000Y. Goffs Orby. Sackville/Donald. The dam is an unraced half-sister to 4 winners including the very useful 2-y-o Group 2 6f Richmond Stakes winner Carizzo Creek. The second dam, Violet Spring (by Exactly Sharp), a 5-y-o 2m winner in Ireland, is a half-sister to 3 other minor winners. (M Hughes & M Kerr-Dineen). *"A nice, racy type, she'll hopefully make a mid-summer 2-y-o. On present thinking she'll need six furlongs, but she may speed up as we work her. She's coping, has a nice attitude and her pedigree suggests she'll be sharp. I think she was well-named!"*

1161. MACHO MAC ★★★
ch.c. Pastoral Pursuits – Clarice Orsini (Common Grounds). April 18. Ninth foal. 40,000Y. Tattersalls October Book 3. H Morrison. Brother to the quite useful 5f and 6f winner of 7 races Equitania and half-brother to 6 winners including Johnny Jumpup (by Pivotal), a winner of 3 races at 2 yrs from 5f to 7.6f and second in a German Group 2 1m event, the quite useful 5f and 6f winner Lenjawi Pride (by Elusive City), the fair 6f (at 2 yrs) and 7f winner Tiber Tilly (by King Charlemagne) and the fair 6f winner Here Comes Danny (by Kyllachy). The dam was placed over 1m in France and is a half-sister to 6 minor winners. The second dam, Be My Everything (by Be My Guest), won once at 3 yrs and is a half-sister to 9 winners including the Irish 1,000 Guineas winner Nicer. (A McAlpine, H Scott-Barrett & A J Struthers). *"He'll hopefully be a July type 2-y-o, he's forward-going and seems to have an engine. A wiry type of Pastoral Pursuits rather than a strong, heavy one. I quite like him and he'll find his level".*

1162. MAESTRO MAC ★★★
b.c. Roderic O'Connor – Union City Blues (Encosta De Lago). March 21. First foal. 44,000Y. Tattersalls October Book 2. H Morrison. The dam is an unplaced half-sister to 5 winners. The second dam, Child Prodigy (by Ballad Rock), a quite useful 2-y-o 6f winner, is a half-sister to 5 winners including the triple Group 1 winner Kutub. (A McAlpine, S De Zoete & C Hill). *"We quite like the look of him, he's quite 'together' and is probably one for seven furlongs in July. I've got two by*

the sire and I like them both. If I had a mare in Ireland I'd definitely use him".

1163. PASTORAL STAR ★★★
ch.f. Pastoral Pursuits – Movie Star (Barathea). February 3. Eleventh foal. £19,000Y. Doncaster Premier. H Morrison/A Stroud. Half-sister to 6 winners including the French listed third Golden Accolade (by Highest Honor), the quite useful 9f to 12f winner Demolition (by Starborough), the minor French 2-y-o winner Dame Helen (by Royal Applause) and the dam of the stakes winning 2-y-o's Bogart and Blaine. The dam is an unplaced full or half-sister to 3 winners including the French listed winner Kilometre Neuf. The second dam, Mary Astor (by Groom Dancer), a French 3-y-o winner of 5 races, is a half-sister to 11 winners including the Group 3 winner and high-class broodmare Kanmary. (G Swire, Mr & Mrs R Lloyd, Richard Wright). *"She's got quite a nice 2-y-o pedigree but perhaps the Barathea part has put a bit more 'time' into it. She's grown a lot, but always easily, and like all Pastoral Pursuits fillies one day she looks good and the next she doesn't. She could be alright by July time, probably starting off at six furlongs. Seven should be her best trip though".*

1164. RAVENS QUEST ★★
ch.c. Raven's Pass – Seradim (Elnadim). March 13. Second foal. 150,000Y. Tattersalls October Book 1. Not sold. Half-brother to Excellent Team (by Teofilo), unplaced in one start at 2 yrs in 2014. The dam, a fairly useful 2-y-o 7f and 1m winner, was third in two listed events and is a half-sister to 3 winners including the useful 2-y-o Group 3 1m Prix Thomas Bryon winner Circumvent. The second dam, Seren Devious (by Dr Devious), is an unraced half-sister to 7 winners including the smart Group 3 11.5f Lingfield Derby Trial winner Saddler's Quest and the French listed winners Seren Hill and Quiz Mistress. (The Fairy Story Partnership). *"Only just arrived here, he's a big, strong horse and you'd be surprised to see him out before the autumn. He has a nice character by the look of things, but he'll need plenty of quiet work to build him up slowly".*

1165. REMEMBER ME ★★★ ♠
b.f. Acclamation – Forgotten Me (Holy Roman Emperor). February 12. First foal. 55,000Y.

Tattersalls October Book 2. Will Edmeades. The dam is an unraced half-sister to 7 winners including the listed 6f winner Master Fay and the listed 6f winner and Irish 1,000 Guineas second Dimenticata. The second dam, Non Dimenticar Me (by Don't Forget Me), a modest 3-y-o 5f winner, stayed 7f and is a half-sister to 7 winners. (Thurloe Thoroughbreds). *"You would hope she'd make a mid-summer 2-y-o over six furlongs. She's a similar type to the other Acclamation 2-y-o we have. Forward-going, there's a bit of speed in the pedigree and she has a sharp action".*

1166. SCARLET PIMPERNEL ★★★★
b.f. Sir Percy – Sweet Pea (Persian Bold). March 1. Ninth foal. Half-sister to the 2-y-o Group 3 6f Princess Margaret Stakes and Group 3 Nell Gwyn Stakes winner Scarlet Runner (by Night Shift), to the fairly useful 7f (including at 2 yrs) and 1m winner Bronze Prince (by Oasis Dream) and the minor Irish 12f winner Scent (by Groom Dancer). The dam, a fairly useful winner of 4 races at around 1m, is a half-sister to 4 winners including the useful listed 6f winner Star Tulip. The second dam, Silk Petal (by Petorius), a useful German listed 1m winner and third in the Group 3 10.5f Prix de Flore, is a half-sister to 5 winners including the good broodmare Dedicated Lady (dam of the Group 2 winners Fairy Queen and Tashawak). (Nicholas Jones). *"She's got a nice, sharp pedigree and Sir Percy was a top 2-y-o. She's quite fine, so she could be a mid-summer 2-y-o if she doesn't start to grow. A forward-going filly that moves nicely, she should be suited by six/seven furlongs".*

1167. SENZA UNA DONNA ★★★
b.c. Sir Percy – Sensationally (Montjeu). April 4. Second foal. Half-brother to the quite useful 2014 2-y-o 1m and 8.5f winner of 3 races and 3-y-o 1m winner Greatest Journey (by Raven's Pass). The dam, a fair 9f winner, is a half-sister to the US Grade 2 winner Sun Boat. The second dam, One So Wonderful (by Nashwan), won the Group 1 Juddmonte International and is a half-sister to 8 winners including the Group 2 Dante Stakes winner Alnasr Alwasheek. (Castle Down Racing). *"He hasn't been here long but he looks quite 'together' and I think he'll be a September 2-y-o".*

1168. SUNSCAPE (IRE) ★★★

ch.f. Roderic O'Connor – Opatja (Nashwan). February 12. Second foal. 14,000Y. Tattersalls October Book 2. H Morrison. The dam, a listed-placed winner of 6 races on the flat from 9f to 11f in Italy and one over hurdles, is a half-sister to 4 winners. The second dam, Thundercloud (by Electric), is a placed half-sister to 9 winners including the St Leger winner Julio Mariner, the Oaks winner Scintillate and the Irish Oaks winner Juliette Marny. (Fiona Trenchard, The Hon Miss M Morrison & Declan Morrison). *"We like her, she's much more 'together' than you'd expect for 2-y-o out of a staying family at this time of the year. Hopefully she'll be out in mile maidens in August or September".*

1169. TOP BEAK (IRE) ★★

b.c. Lawman – Tree Tops (Grand Lodge). February 13. Seventh foal. 80,000Y. Tattersalls October Book 1. Sackville/Donald. Half-brother to 3 winners including the French 1m (at 2 yrs) and 15f winner and listed-placed Martial Law and the fairly useful dual 10.5f winner Snowmane (both by Galileo). The dam, a fair 1m to 10f placed maiden, is a half-sister to 3 winners including the US Grade 1 and multiple Grade 2 winner Tuscan Evening and the listed winner Barbican. The second dam, The Faraway Tree (by Suave Dancer), a very useful 6f and 14f winner, was second in the Group 3 Park Hill Stakes and is a half-sister to 12 winners including Sasuru (Group 1 Prix d'Ispahan). (Michael Kerr-Dineen & Martin Hughes). *"A big, heavy, scopey horse that might run once or twice in the autumn".*

1170. UNNAMED ★★★

ch.f. Pivotal – Passiflora (Night Shift). April 19. Tenth foal. 40,000Y. Tattersalls October Book 2. Charlie Gordon-Watson. Half-sister to 6 winners including the 2-y-o 6f and subsequent US Grade 2 winner Passified (by Compton Place), the fairly useful 6f winner of 3 races (including at 2 yrs) Zomerlust, the fair 2-y-o dual 6f winner Bond Royale (by Piccolo) and the fair 6f (at 2 yrs) and 1m winner Farang Kondiew (by Selkirk). The dam, a fair 2-y-o 6f winner, is a half-sister to the Group 2 6f Cork And Orrery Stakes winner Harmonic Way. The second dam, Pineapple (by Superlative), a fair 12f winner, is a half-sister to 6 winners

including the top-class filly In The Groove. (The End-R-Ways Partnership). *"A nice sort of filly, she looks like a Pivotal and you'd hope that she'd be out by September time over seven furlongs. She's quite nice".*

1171. UNNAMED ★★★

b.f. Invincible Spirit – Salsa Steps (Giant's Causeway). March 11. Fourth foal. Half-sister to the quite useful 1m winner and listed 10f second Spicy Dal and to the quite useful 10f winner Salmon Sushi (both by Dalakhani). The dam, a fairly useful dual 6f winner, is a half-sister to 3 winners. The second dam, Dance Design (by Sadler's Wells), won the Irish Oaks, the Group 2 Tattersalls Gold Cup and the Group 2 Pretty Polly Stakes (twice) and is a half-sister to 5 winners. (Ben & Sir Martyn Arbib). *"A really strong type, she's only just be broken in but she looks the part and might make a really nice, speedy, end of season 2-y-o".*

WILLIE MUIR

1172. ARGYLE (IRE) ★★

gr.c. Lawman – All Hallows (Dalakhani). February 4. First foal. €90,000Y. Arqana Deauville August. W Muir. The dam is an unraced half-sister to 4 winners including the Group 1 Prix Royal-Oak winner Allegretto. The second dam, Alleluia (by Caerleon), won the Group 3 Doncaster Cup and is a half-sister to 7 winners including the Nassau Stakes and Sun Chariot Stakes winner Last Second (dam of the French 2,000 Guineas winner Aussie Rules) and to the dams of the Group 1 winners Alborada, Albanova, Yesterday and Quarter Moon. The second dam, Alruccaba (by Crystal Palace), was a quite useful 2-y-o 6f winner. (C L A Edginton). *"A big colt, he has a really nice pedigree and it's a staying family but he's got natural ability. I really like him, but he's not going to be out before the late summer or autumn. I think these are the best bunch of two-year-olds I've ever had".*

1173. CALVADOS SPIRIT ★★★★

b.c. Invincible Spirit – Putois Peace (Pivotal). February 5. First foal. €220,000Y. Arqana Deauville August. Willie Muir. The dam is an unraced half-sister to 7 winners including the Group 2 12f Lancashire Oaks winner Pongee, the listed 12f and listed 14f winner

Lion Sands and the dam of the French Group 3 winner Pacifique. The second dam, Puce (by Darshaan), a very useful listed 12f winner, is a half-sister to 10 winners including the dam of the dual Oaks winner Alexandrova and the Cheveley Park Stakes winner Magical Romance. (Muir Racing Partnership – Deauville). *"He's a big, strong colt but being by Invincible Spirit that's not to say he won't be a 2-y-o type by the mid-summer. He moves well, I haven't worked him yet but I really like him. He's beautiful to look at".*

1174. ENTERTAINING BEN ★★★

b.c. Equiano – Fatal Attraction (Oasis Dream). April 14. Third foal. 36,000Y. Tattersalls October Book 2. Willie Muir. Closely related to the fair 5f (at 2 yrs) and 6f winner Minley (by Acclamation). The dam, a moderate dual 5f placed maiden, is a sister to the Group 3 Prix du Petit Couvert winner Mirza and a half-sister to 5 winners. The second dam, Millyant (by Primo Dominie), winner of the Group 2 5f Prix du Gros-Chene, is a half-sister to 5 winners including the Group 2 5f Flying Childers winner and sire Prince Sabo and the Irish listed winner Bold Jessie (herself dam of the Gimcrack Stakes winner Abou Zouz). (Berkeley, Edginton, Niven). *"Very sharp in his ways, so he's showing he'll be precocious and I think he'll be out in April. I like him and he'll be a 2-y-o winner I think".*

1175. FINE BLEND (IRE) ★★★★

br.f. Sakhee's Secret – Coffee Time (Efisio). February 15. €10,0002-y-o. Goffs February. W Muir. Sister to the fairly useful 2014 2-y-o dual 6f winner Caffeine and half-sister to the fair triple 5f winner (including at 2 yrs) Cuppacocoa (by Bertolini), the modest dual 5f winner at 2 and 3 yrs Compton Ford (by Compton Place) and a 2-y-o winner abroad by Cadeaux Genereux. The dam was placed 19 times at 2 to 4 years, including in the listed Hilary Needler Stakes at 2 yrs and is a half-sister to 7 winners. The second dam, Petula (by Petong), won the listed St Hugh's Stakes at 2 yrs and is a half-sister to 6 winners including the Group 3 Ballycorus Stakes winner Naahy. (Muir Racing Partnership – Windsor). *"A filly that'll need a bit of time. I've only just bought her and broke her in and yet she's already up cantering with the rest of them. She's a sister*

to a nice 2-y-o we had called Caffeine, she's beautiful and she's developing really well. I could see her being out in mid-summer". **TRAINERS' BARGAIN BUY**

1176. FLORENCIO ★★

b.c. Equiano – Mary Pekan (Sri Pekan). May 6. Fifth living foal. 10,000Y. Tattersalls October Book 3. Four Star Thoroughbreds. Half-brother to the Italian listed 1m winner Mantissa (by Oratorio) and to two minor winners in Italy by Duke Of Marmalade (at 2 yrs) and Rock Of Gibraltar. The dam, a winner of 6 races at 2 to 4 yrs in Italy and third in the Group 3 Premio Carlo Chiesa, is a half-sister to the Italian listed winner and Group 1 Gran Premio de Milano second Wild Wolf. The second dam, Mary Rose (by Royal Academy), won 6 races at 3 and 4 yrs in Italy and is a half-sister to 2 winners including the dam of the Middle Park Stakes winner Amadeus Wolf. (Excel Racing). *"I bought him from Newsells Park after the sale. I'll take a look at this colt soon to see where we go with him but he's a May foal and one for later in the season".*

1177. HIT MAN ★★

b.c. Canford Cliffs – Ballymore Celebre (Peintre Celebre). February 23. Half-brother to the smart 2-y-o Group 2 6f July Stakes winner Anjaal (by Bahamian Bounty), to the fair 2m winner No Time To Lose (by Authorized), the fair 10f and 12f winner Pintrada (by Tiger Hill) and the modest 10f winner Sweet Secret (by Singspiel). The dam won twice at 3 yrs in France and is a half-sister to 10 winners including the Irish multiple Group 3 winner Nysaean. The second dam, Irish Arms (by Irish River), won once in France and is a half-sister to 9 winners including the US Grade 2 winner Morold. (Mr & Mrs P Morgan). *"He came in late but he's a horse that's showing he's got talent. We'll just bring him along slowly because he'll take a bit of time. I like him and he's a half-brother to a 2-y-o Group 2 winner in Anjaal".*

1178. KING OF SPIN ★★★

b.c. Pivotal – Regina (Green Desert). April 1. Sixth foal. 30,000Y. Tattersalls October Book 2. Willie Muir. Brother to the unplaced 2014 2-yo Houdini, closely related to the fairly useful 2-y-o 5f winner and 6f listed-placed Survived (by Kyllachy) and half-brother to the quite useful 5f and 6f winner of 10 races from 2 to 7 yrs Six Wives (by Kingsalsa). The dam, a fairly useful 2-y-o dual 5f winner, is a half-sister to 5 winners. The second dam, Dazzle (by Gone West), winner of the Group 3 6f Cherry Hinton Stakes and placed in the Cheveley Park Stakes and the 1,000 Guineas, is a half-sister to 3 listed winners including Hypnotize (dam of the Group 1 Cheveley Park Stakes winner Hooray) and to the placed dam of the Group 2 winner Danehurst. (Muir Racing Partnership – Nottingham). *"He's very nice, a typical Pivotal, goes really well and I really like him. He could be a good 2-y-o because he's not too big, he's just a real solid, chunk of a horse".*

1179. KITTY FOR ME ★★★

b.f. Pour Moi – Purring (Mountain Cat). February 26. Eighth foal. 87,000foal. Tattersalls December. Foursome Thoroughbreds. Half-sister to 6 winners including the Group 3 7f Prix du Calvados and Group 3 1m Lanwades Stud Stakes winner Purr Along (by Mount Nelson), to the fairly useful 9f and subsequent US winner and dual listed-placed Lady Francesca (by Montjeu), the fairly useful dual 6f winner Katawi (by Dubawi) and the quite useful 10f and 12f winner of 8 races Jeer (by Selkirk). The dam, a quite useful 7f winner, is a half-sister to the Group 2 1m Falmouth Stakes and Group 3 1m Prix de Sandringham winner Ronda (herself dam of a Group 3 winner). The second dam, Memory's Gold (by Java Gold), a modest 3-y-o 7.6f winner, is a half-sister to 5 winners. (Edginton, Morgan, Jeffrey, Muir). *"We bought her as a foal and if we'd re-entered her as a yearling we'd have made good money. I've had three other horses from this family and they were all quite angular and narrow. This filly is stronger and quite heavy. Although she does everything well I wouldn't be looking to get her going early, she has a great temperament and I like her".*

1180. MIKMAK ★★

b.c. Makfi – Rakata (Quiet American). March 5. Fourth foal. 14,000Y. Tattersalls October Book 2. Willie Muir. Half-brother to the unplaced 2014 2-y-o Kipuka (by Authorized) and to the fair dual 1m and subsequent US winner Magma (by Singspiel). The dam, a fair winner of 4 races over 7f and 1m, was listed-placed

and is a half-sister to 4 winners. The second dam, Haleakala (by Kris), a useful 13.3f winner, is a half-sister to 5 winners including the dual US Grade 1 placed Blue Burner. (Muir Racing Partnership – Leicester). *"He was cheap this horse, but he shows he's got ability already. He does everything easily but he's big (16 hands) and still growing so I wouldn't rush him, especially because of the sire. But he's a natural and for that sort of money he was for nothing. A good-looking and correct individual".*

1181. POLISH EMPRESS ★★

b.f. Equiano – Polish Belle (Polish Precedent). March 29. Eleventh foal. 14,000Y. Tattersalls October Book 2. Not sold. Half-sister to 5 winners including the quite useful 2-y-o 6f winner and US Grade 2 placed Jairzihno (by Royal Applause), the fairly useful 2-y-o dual 6f winner and dual listed-placed Misty Conquest (by Mujadil) and the fair 1m and 9f winner Tijori (by Kyllachy). The dam is an unraced half-sister to 7 winners including the Group 2 5f winner Danehurst and the Group 3 10.5f winner Humouresque. The second dam, Miswaki Belle (by Miswaki), second over 7f on her only start, is a half-sister to 9 winners including the 1,000 Guineas third Dazzle. (Newsells Park Stud). *"She was going nicely but we've sent her home for a little holiday. She's quite narrow and backward but she moves well and has a great temperament. One for the back-end of the season I would say".*

1182. RED SPECTRE ★★★★

b.c. Kyllachy – Just Devine (Montjeu). April 2. Fifth foal. 280,000Y. Tattersalls October Book 2. Willie Muir. Half-brother to the useful 2014 2-y-o listed 6f winner Code Red (by Bahamian Bounty), to the fairly useful 2-y-o 7f winner and 3-y-o listed-placed End Of Line (by Pastoral Pursuits), the triple 6f winner Magic Secret (by Trade Fair) and the 6f winner Secret Weapon (by Choisir) – both quite useful. The dam, a modest 10f placed maiden, is a half-sister to 4 winners including the Group 3 Prix du Lys winner Airmail Special. The second dam, Shirley Blue (by Shirley Heights), placed once at 3 yrs in France, is a half-sister to 10 winners. (Muir Racing Partnership – Longchamp). *"The most expensive yearling I bought, I loved him at the sales, he's a half-brother to a nice 3-y-o we have called Code*

Red and he's by one of my favourite sires in Kyllachy. He shows all the right signs at this stage but I wouldn't be looking to race him before June. Potentially he'd be one of my star horses I would think".

1183. ROYAL RESERVE ★★★
b.c. Duke Of Marmalade – Lady Hawkfield (Hawk King). April 20. Second foal. 30,000Y. Tattersalls October Book 3. Willie Muir. Half-brother to the fairly useful 2-y-o 8.5f winner Master Apprentice (by Mastercraftsman). The dam ran once unplaced and is a half-sister to the Group 1 1m Coronation Stakes and Group 1 1m Matron Stakes winner Lillie Langtry and to the listed 7f winner and Group 3 third Count Of Limonade (by Duke Of Marmalade). The second dam, Hoity Toity (by Darshaan), is an unraced half-sister to 5 winners. (Muir Racing Partnership – Chester). *"He's got a really good page and if he hadn't been by Duke Of Marmalade I don't think I could have afforded him. He's very correct, big, tall and does everything nicely".*

1184. SENSE OF SNOW (IRE) ★★★
ch.c. Kyllachy – Miss Smilla (Red Ransom). April 19. Third foal. £72,000Y. Doncaster Premier. Willie Muir. Half-brother to the modest 2014 2-y-o 6f winner Smart Stepper (by Acclamation). The dam, a fair 2-y-o 6f winner, is a half-sister to 4 winners including the Group 2 and dual Group 3 sprint winner The Trader. The second dam, Snowing (by Tate Gallery), a quite useful dual 5f winner at 3 yrs, is a half-sister to 2 minor winners. (Mr J O'Mulloy & Mr J Collenette). *"He cost a fair bit and he looks sharp although Kyllachy's tend to make you think that way. I wouldn't rush him, he's neat, tidy and will be a 2-y-o by mid-season".*

1185. WILLYTHECONQUEROR (IRE) ★★★★
b.c. Kodiac – Jazzie (Zilzal). February 27. Eighth foal. 48,000Y. Tattersalls October Book 2. Willie Muir. Half-brother to the useful Irish listed 6f winner of 6 races Bold Thady Quill (by Tale Of The Cat), to the fairly useful dual 7f winner (including at 2 yrs) Georgian Bay (by Oratorio), the modest 6.5f and 7.5f winner Jappeli (by Selkirk) and two minor winners in France by Kingsalsa and Della Francesca. The dam, a minor French 3-y-o winner, is

a half-sister to 3 winners. The second dam, Field Dancer (by Northfields), a listed winner and Group 3 placed twice in Ireland, is a half-sister to 6 winners including So Factual (Nunthorpe Stakes) and Bold Fact (July Stakes). (Perspicacious Punters Racing Club). *"He's smart, he'll be my first runner and he's working really good. He works well with the older horses, he does everything right and he has a good temperament. I love him and I think he could be better than average".*

1186. YORK MINSTER (IRE) ★★
b.c. Vale Of York – Tintern (Diktat). February 20. Fifth foal. 24,000Y. Tattersalls October Book 3. Willie Muir. Half-brother to the fair 1m and 8.5f winner of 7 races Siouxperhero (by Sleeping Indian). The dam is an unraced half-sister to 7 winners including the dual 10f and subsequent US stakes winner and Grade 2 placed Solva. The second dam, Annapurna (by Brief Truce), a useful 2-y-o 7f winner, was listed placed over 9f and 10f and is a half-sister to 5 winners including the 2-y-o Group 3 7f Rockfel Stakes and listed 7f winner Name Of Love. (Clive Washbourn). *"He's a man of a horse, very unlike his half-brother Siouxperhero who was soft. He's a tough colt and he's just starting to go a bit quicker now. So I like him, he's pretty nice".*

1187. UNNAMED ★★
b.c. Dark Angel – Dawn Chorus (Mukaddamah). February 24. Eleventh foal. 60,000Y. Tattersalls October Book 2. Willie Muir. Half-brother to 9 winners including the Irish 7f (at 2 yrs) to 10f and subsequent Hong Kong stakes winner Solid Approach (by Definite Article), the useful Irish 7f winner and listed-placed Dangle (by Desert Style), the useful 5f to 7f winner of 5 races Zero Money (by Bachelor Duke), the quite useful 2-y-o 6f winner Bahati (by Intikhab) and the 2-y-o dual 6f winner La Campanella (by Tagula) - all four quite useful. The dam is an unraced half-sister to 6 winners including the Group 3 second Barrier Reef. The second dam, Singing Millie (by Millfontaine), won twice in Ireland at 3 yrs and is a half-sister to 7 winners. (Mr S P Hussain). *"A lovely, big horse. I'll take my time with him, he's been bought for a Hong Kong owner but he may still run here first. He's tall, he's got grace and presence. He could be anything".*

1188. UNNAMED ★★★★
b.c. Royal Applause – Good Girl (College
Chapel). February 10. Seventh foal. 42,000Y.
Tattersalls October Book 2. Willie Muir. Half-
brother to the fairly useful 6f (at 2 yrs) to
1m winner of 4 races Good Again (by Dubai
Destination), to the quite useful 6f (at 2 yrs)
to 8.5f winner Cruiser (by Oasis Dream) and
the quite useful 7f winner Ink Spot (by Diktat).
The dam, a useful 2-y-o listed 5f winner and
third in the Group 1 6f Cheveley Park Stakes,
is a half-sister to 6 winners. The second dam,
Indian Honey (by Indian King), is an unraced
half-sister to 7 winners. (Appoo, Quaintance,
Clark & Moore). *"I'm not a fan of Royal
Applause but this horse really took my eye and
he's nicer looking than his half-brother Cruiser
who we did well with. He's one I can be getting
on with because he's going really well".*

1189. UNNAMED ★★
b.f. Fastnet Rock – Highwater Dancer (Sadler's
Wells). April 5. Fifth living foal. 30,000Y.
Tattersalls December. Ric Wylie. Half-sister to
Spanish Danser (by Lord Shanakill), unplaced
in one start at 2 yrs in 2014. The dam is an
unraced half-sister to 4 winners including
the multiple Group 1 winner St Nicholas
Abbey and to the US dual Grade 2 winner
Grammarian. The second dam, Leaping Water
(by Sure Blade), is an unraced half-sister to
6 winners including the Group 1 winners
Aristotle, Ballingarry and Starborough. (Mr A
Osburg). *"She's probably one for the back-end
of the season, I couldn't say anything bad
about her because she's nice-looking, but both
the way she looks and her pedigree suggest she
needs time".*

1190. UNNAMED ★★★
b.c. Poet's Voice – Khubza (Green Desert).
April 18. Fourteenth foal. 45,000Y. Tattersalls
October Book 2. Willie Muir. Half-brother
to 9 winners including the Group 2 1m Prix
du Rond-Point and Group 3 8.5f Diomed
Stakes winner Trans Island, the Italian Group
3 winner Welsh Diva, the useful 2-y-o 7f
winner Nothing Daunted (all by Selkirk), the
useful dual 1m and jumps winner Creekside
(by Dubai Destination) and the fairly useful
Irish 7f (at 2 yrs) and 9f winner Mujaazef (by
Dubawi). The dam, a quite useful 7f winner, is
a half-sister to 7 winners including the Group

2 winners Barrow Creek and Last Resort. The
second dam, Breadcrumb (by Final Straw), a
very useful winner of 3 races over 6f and 7f, is
a half-sister to the high-class sprinter College
Chapel. (Mr K Kok). *"He's really taking the eye
at the moment. He may go to Hong Kong, but
if I think he's good his owner will let me run
him. He's doing things well".*

1191. UNNAMED ★★
b.c. Makfi – Likeable (Dalakhani). February 28.
Fourth foal. 10,000Y. Tattersalls October Book
2. Willie Muir. Half-brother to the 2014 9.5f
placed 2-y-o Inexes (by Exceed And Excel).
The dam is an unraced half-sister to 4 winners
including the UAE Grade 2 and Group 3 Select
Stakes winner Alkaadhem. The second dam,
Balalaika (by Sadler's Wells), a useful 4-y-o
listed 9f winner, is a sister to the high-class
Group 2 10f Prince of Wales's Stakes and dual
US Grade 2 winner Stagecraft and a half-sister
to 5 winners including the Group 3 Strensall
Stakes winner Mullins Bay and the very useful
dual 1m listed winner Hyabella. (Mr S P
Hussain). *"The sire is unfashionable, which is
why I got this colt so cheap, but I don't think
he'll be unfashionable by the end of the year.
His 3-y-o's are really starting to look the part
now. This is a big horse, he's really nice and just
starting to get going. I couldn't say anything
against him but he's one that'll take time and is
much more of a 3-y-o type".*

1192. UNNAMED ★★
b.f. Exceed And Excel – Nantyglo (Mark
Of Esteem). March 22. Sixth foal. 65,000Y.
Tattersalls October Book 1. Not sold. Half-
sister to the modest dual 9f winner Valley
Tiger (by Tiger Hill). The dam, a useful 6f (at
2 yrs) and listed 1m winner, was third in the
Group 2 6f Mill Reef Stakes and is a half-sister
to 4 winners. The second dam, Bright Halo (by
Bigstone), a minor French 3-y-o 9f winner, is
a half-sister to 9 winners including the Group
1 Irish Oaks winner Moonstone, the Breeders
Cup second L'Ancresse and the Group 1 10f
Prix Saint-Alary winner Cerulean Sky (herself
dam of the Group 2 Doncaster Cup winner
Honolulu). (Usk Valley Stud). *"She's never
been a problem, but the dam has been a bit
disappointing because she was such a good
racemare. This filly does everything fine and I
like her".*

1193. UNNAMED ★★
b.c. Manduro – Ornellaia (Mujadil). April 28.
Sixth foal. Brother to the fairly useful 1m (at
2 yrs) to 10.5f winner Black Schnapps and
half-brother to the fairly useful 7.5f, 1m (both
at 2 yrs) and 10f winner of 5 races Hi There,
to the modest 2-y-o 5f winner Slipstream
Angel (both by Dark Angel) and the fair
2-y-o 5f winner Super Tuscan (by Fath). The
dam, placed fourth once over 6f at 2 yrs, is a
half-sister to 5 winners including the useful
2-y-o 6f and listed 1m winner Henri Lebasque.
The second dam, Almost A Lady (by Entitled),
placed over 7f and 1m at 2 yrs, is a half-
sister to 5 winners including the dual Group
2 winner Insatiable. (O'Mulloy, Collenette &
Clark). *"He's exactly the same as his brother
Black Schnapps, which means he'll take time
and is one for seven furlongs or a mile at the
back-end of the season".*

1194. UNNAMED ★★★
b.f. Mount Nelson – Sassari (Darshaan).
April 17. Seventh foal. 18,000Y. Tattersalls
October Book 3. Willie Muir. Half-sister to 4
winners including the quite useful 2-y-o 6f
winner Chicago Cop (by Fasliyev), the fair
5f to 7f winner Sassaway (by Bertolini) and
the fair 7f (at 2 yrs), 10f and hurdles winner
Janet's Pearl (by Refuse To Bend). The dam,
a fair 10f placed maiden, is a half-sister to 8
minor winners. The second dam, Alwiyda (by
Trempolino), won once at 3 yrs in France and
is a half-sister to 6 winners. (Mr J M O'Mulloy).
*"I bought her because she's the spitting image
of Purr Along, a lovely filly I trained who was
by the same sire, Mount Nelson. She goes
well and does everything nicely. I think she
was cheap, I don't know how good she is yet
because she's just cantering, but everyone
seems to like her. One for seven furlongs I'd
say".*

1195. UNNAMED ★★
ch.c. Rip Van Winkle – Starbound (Captain
Rio). March 10. First foal. 55,000Y. Tattersalls
October Book 2. Willie Muir. The dam, a
fair 1m winner, is a half-sister to the 2-y-o
Group 1 Phoenix Stakes and Group 2 Railway
Stakes winner Alfred Nobel. The second dam,
Glinting Desert (by Desert Prince), a fair 2-y-o
7f winner, is a half-sister to 4 minor winners.
(Wayfoong Syndicate). *"He was bought to go*
*to Hong Kong, so we'll have to see how good
he is before I'll be allowed to run him. He's a
nice-looking individual that just needs a bit of
time".*

JEREMY NOSEDA
1196. BROADWAY ICON ★★★
b.c. Sixties Icon – Funny Girl (Darshaan).
January 29. Tenth foal. Brother to the modest
14f winner Hattie Jacques and half-brother
to 6 winners including the Group 2 1m Prix
de Sandringham winner of 4 races Laugh Out
Loud (by Clodovil), the useful 6f (at 2 yrs), 10f
and listed 12f winner of 6 races Suzi's Decision
(by Act One), the fairly useful 10f and 12f
winner of 4 races Pippa Greene (by Galileo)
and the fair 5f winner of 3 races Brynfa Boy
(by Namid). The dam was placed from 7f
to 9f and is a half-sister to 2 winners out of
the minor German winner Just For Fun (by
Lead On Time), herself a sister to the listed
winner Judge Decision. *"A bonny horse, he's
straightforward, has a good attitude and I'm
just about to start breezing him along. He's
quite mature and although he'll get seven
furlongs this year I think he's got a bit of toe".*

1197. DONNELLY'S RAINBOW (IRE) ★★★
b.c. Lilbourne Lad – Donnelly's Hollow
(Docksider). March 29. Fifth foal. 80,000Y.
Tattersalls October Book 2. Kerri Radcliffe.
Half-brother to the 2014 2-y-o 6f winner Puck
Fair (by Paco Boy) and to the 10f and 12f
winner Headline News (by Peintre Celebre)
– both quite useful. The dam, a modest 1m
placed maiden, is a half-sister to the Group 1
Italian Derby winner White Muzzle, the Group
2 German St Leger winner Fair Question and
the listed winner Elfaslah (dam of the Dubai
World Cup winner Almutawakel). The second
dam, Fair of the Furze (by Ela-Mana-Mou),
won the Group 2 Tattersalls Rogers Gold Cup
and is a half-sister to three listed winners. *"A
very good mover, but he's grown quite a lot
and gone a little bit weak. I like him but he's
not going to make a 2-y-o until July time. He'll
definitely do a job at two and we'll start him at
six furlongs".*

1198. DUTCH DREAM ★★★
ch.f. Dutch Art – Starry Sky (Oasis Dream).
March 18. Fourth foal. 45,000Y. Tattersalls
October Book 2. S Burns. Half-sister to

the fairly useful 2014 Irish 2-y-o 6f winner Blackbriar (by Kyllachy) and to the Irish 2-y-o 6f winner Tarn (by Royal Applause). The dam, a fair 2-y-o 7f winner, is a half-sister to 2 winners. The second dam, Succinct (by Hector Protector), a useful listed 10f winner, is a half-sister to 4 winners including the German listed winner Succession. *"She's just started doing half-speeds, I think she can do a job for us and she should be running by the middle to the end of May. I'm happy enough with her and the penny's beginning to drop".*

1199. EGYPTIAN (USA) ★★
b.c. Eskendereya – Street Talk (Street Cry). February 3. Second foal. $170,000Y. Keeneland September. Kerri Radcliffe. The dam, a minor US 4-y-o winner, is a half-sister to four US stakes winners including the Grade 1 Gazelle Handicap winner Buy The Sport. The second dam, Final Accord (by D'Accord), a minor US 3-y-o winner, is a half-sister to 7 winners. *"He's still in America but he arrives in late April. A backward horse, but one that I like, he's big, scopey and a good mover. One for the back end over seven furlongs and a mile. The sire wasn't a great 2-y-o himself but he was a real good 3-y-o and judging by his first crop of runners they seem to be following the same pattern. This colt should be a 2-y-o from August onwards but we'll see him at his best next year".*

1200. ELECTRIFY (IRE) ★★
b.f. Invincible Spirit – Elopa (Tiger Hill). April 29. Fifth foal. €52,000Y. Goffs Orby. Brian Grassick Bloodstock. Half-sister to the listed 10f winner and Group 2 Ribblesdale Stakes third Elik and to the useful 2-y-o 1m winner and Group 1 Prix Marcel Boussac fourth Wedding March (both by Dalakhani). The dam, winner of the Group 2 Prix Corrida and the Group 3 Prix Allez France, was third in the Group 1 Pretty Polly Stakes and is a half-sister to the Group 1 Singapore Airlines International winner Epalo. The second dam, Evening Kiss (by Kris), winner of the Group 3 Premio Bagutta, is a half-sister to 8 winners including the Group 3 winning 2-y-o's Grand Chelem and Splendid Moment. *"She's out having a spring break now, she's a good-moving filly, quite backward and I don't see her being out until the back end of the season*

because she's going to grow a lot even now. She has a good temperament and moves well, but being a rather late foal and out of a Tiger Hill mare she'll change a lot over the next six months".

1201. FASTLADY (IRE) ★★
ch.f. Fast Company – Brave Madam (Invincible Spirit). January 25 Fifth foal. €12,000Y. Tattersalls Ireland September. B Grassick Bloodstock. Half-sister to the quite useful 6f (at 2 yrs) and 7f winner Azagal and to the quite useful Irish 3-y-o 10f winner Azamata (both by Azamour). The dam is an unraced half-sister to 4 winners including the US listed stakes winner Insan Mala. The second dam, Madame Claude (by Paris House), a fair 2-y-o 6f winner, is a half-sister to 4 winners including the Irish dual listed winner Nashcash. *"A backward type for the back-end of July at the earliest, I'm happy enough with her because she moves well and has size and scope".*

1202. GRIZZLY BEAR ★★★★
b.c. Kodiac – Pearl Magic (Speightstown). January 24. First foal. 70,000Y. Tattersalls October Book 2. Kerri Radcliffe. The dam is an unraced half-sister to 10 winners including the very smart 7f (at 2 yrs) and Group 3 1m winner and Group 2 1m Queen Anne Stakes third Tough Speed. The second dam, Nature's Magic (by Nijinsky), is a placed half-sister to the US dual Grade 3 9f winner Stalwars and the French listed 7f winner and German Group 2 second Joy Of Glory. *"He'll most probably be our first 2-y-o runner. He's quite lazy, laid back and has a good attitude. I think he'll win races and going off his attitude I can see him improving once he gets one or two races under his belt. I think he's a progressive type that'll more than pay his way this year".*

1203. HEARTY (IRE) ★★
b.c. Big Bad Bob – Ulanova (Noverre). March 15. Third foal. €75,000Y. Goffs Orby. B Grassick Bloodstock. Brother to the unplaced 2013 2-y-o Buzz Off Barroso and half-brother to the Italian 2-y-o winner and dual listed placed Avomcic (by Avonbridge). The dam is an unraced half-sister to 5 winners including the smart Irish Group 3 7f and Group 3 1m winner Cheyenne Star and to the unraced dam of the triple Group 1 winner Gordon Lord Byron. The

second dam, Charita (by Lycius), a listed 1m winner in Ireland, is a half-sister to 4 winners including the Italian Group 2 winner Stanott. *"An July/August type 2-y-o, he's got some size and scope, I'm happy enough with him and he's done everything right so far. I haven't pushed him at all but he shows enough to suggest he can win at two".*

1204. SIXTIES GROOVE (IRE) ★★★

b.c. Sixties Icon – Gift Dancer (Imperial Dancer). February 14. First foal. 80,000Y. Tattersalls October Book 2. Hugo Merry. The dam is an unraced half-sister to 6 winners including the Group 1 Irish 1,000 Guineas winner Samitar and the 2-y-o Group 3 Albany Stakes winner Nijoom Dubai. The second dam, Aileen's Gift (by Rainbow Quest), is an unraced half-sister to 5 winners including the dam of the Group 2 Gimcrack Stakes winner Shameel. *"He was going really well but he's grown and gone up behind, so he's looking more scopey now. A horse that I like, but definitely one for the second half of the season".*

1205. TEARS IN MY EYES (IRE) ★★★

b.f. Lilbourne Lad – Genuine Charm (Sadler's Wells). March 5. Seventh foal. 130,000Y. Tattersalls October Book 1. Jeremy Noseda. Half-sister to the US Grade 1 6f and UAE Group 3 winner and Grade 1 second Rich Tapestry (by Danehill Dancer), to the fairly useful 2-y-o 7f winner Hazy Glow (by Invincible Spirit), the quite useful Irish 1m winner Anywaysmile (by Indian Ridge) and the Italian winner of 7 races from 2 to 5 yrs Genarmoly (by Holy Roman Emperor). The dam is a placed sister to the top-class winner of four Group 1 races from 7f (at 2 yrs) to 10f Refuse To Bend and a half-sister to the Melbourne Cup winner Media Puzzle. The second dam, Market Slide (by Gulch), an Irish 6f (at 2 yrs) and 6.5f winner, is a half-sister to the Breeders Cup Classic second Twilight Agenda. *"She's just doing some swinging canters now, it looks like she's got some speed and she has a straightforward attitude. One to start off in the middle of May, over five/six furlongs".*

1206. UNNAMED ★★★

br.f. More Than Ready – Alina (Came Home). March 25. Third foal. $170,000 2-y-o. OBS

Breeze Up. The dam, a winner of 4 races in the USA from 2 to 4 yrs, was second in the Grade 2 Fantasy Stakes and third in the Grade 3 Iowa Oaks and is a half-sister to 3 minor winners. The second dam, Lady Heroine (by Sea Hero), won 2 minor races at 3 yrs in the USA and is a half-sister to 3 winners. *"I bought her at the breeze-up sale in America where she breezed very well. She's had a bit of a break but is back in pre-training over there now and arrives here in late April. I'm expecting her to be ready to run at the back end of May. It looks like there's plenty of speed in the pedigree and she reminded me a bit of La Chunga who I bought at the Calder breeze up a few years ago".*

1207. UNNAMED ★★

b.c. Giant's Causeway – Cassis (Red Ransom). April 12. Half-brother to the quite useful 2014 6f and 7f placed 2-y-o Commandaria (by Smart Strike), to the fair 7f winner (his only start) Cassini Flight and the minor US 4-y-o winner Kir (both by Bernardini). The dam, winner of the Group 3 Musidora Stakes, was placed in the Group 2 Cherry Hinton Stakes and Mill Reef Stakes and is a half-sister to 7 winners including the dam of the champion US 2-y-o filly Storm Song. The second dam, Minstress (by The Minstrel), was a stakes winner and Grade 3 placed in the USA. *"He's arriving from America soon but he's quite backward and will take a bit of time. One for the autumn and much more of a 3-y-o type".*

1208. UNNAMED ★★

b.f. Hard Spun – Imiloa (Kingmambo). April 20. Fourth foal. Half-sister to the fairly useful 12f and 14f winner Wakea (by Cape Cross) and to the fair 2-y-o 7f winner Intrepid (by Invincible Spirit). The dam is an unraced half-sister to 3 winners including the 2-y-o Group 1 6f Middle Park Stakes and Group 2 6f Gimcrack Stakes winner Balmont and the US Grade 1 Wood Memorial Stakes winner Eskendereya (by Giant's Causeway). The second dam, Aldebaran Light (by Seattle Slew), a winner of 3 races at around 1m in the USA, is a half-sister to 3 winners including the 2-y-o 5.2f and subsequent US Grade 2 winner Blazonry. *"Soon to arrive from America, she'll take a bit of time. I have her half-brother here, Wakea, who stays well. So it's too early for me to pass judgement on her".*

1209. UNNAMED ★★★
b.c. Holy Roman Emperor – School Holidays (Harlan's Holidays). February 5. First foal. 55,000Y. Tattersalls October Book 2. Global Equine Group. The dam, a fair Irish 7f winner, is a half-sister to 4 winners including the Irish triple Group 3 winner One More Round. The second dam, Life Of The Party (by Pleasant Colony), placed twice in the USA, is a half-sister to 3 minor winners. *"A good-looking horse, he should come to himself in mid-summer. He looks a 2-y-o type and should have a decent 2-y-o campaign".*

1210. UNNAMED ★★
b.f. Canford Cliffs – Sentimental (Galileo). March 26. Third foal. The dam is an unraced half-sister to 5 winners including the French listed winners Bermuda Grass and Bermuda Rye. The second dam, Alleluia Tree (by Royal Academy), a French 2-y-o winner, is a half-sister to 7 winners and to the unraced dam of the triple Group 1 winner Scorpion. *"A very backward filly, even at this point you can see she's going to grow a lot. A good-moving, athletic type, but she's very much one for the autumn and for next season".*

1211. UNNAMED ★★★
b.c. Discreet Cat – Truly Blushed (Yes It's True). April 21. Third foal. $230,000 2-y-o. OBS Breeze-Up. Thoroughbred Management. Half-brother to the US stakes-placed winner of 4 races Truly Marie (by Hard Spun). The dam was a stakes-placed winner at 2 yrs in Canada and won 5 races at 3 and 4 yrs in North America. She is a half-sister to the US stakes winner Fishin Frank. The second dam, Easy To Blush (by Blushing John), was placed at 3 yrs. *"I bought him in America where he breezed really quickly, but despite that he's immature and not an obvious 2-y-o because he's going to grow a fair bit this year. I think he'll come out at the back-end and he'll win. I really like him".*

1212. UNNAMED ★★★
b.f. Showcasing – Vive Les Rouges (Acclamation). April 3. Third foal. 68,000Y. Tattersalls December. Grangebarry. Half-sister to the useful 6f winner Speedfiend (by Bahamian Bounty). The dam, a fairly useful 2-y-o 6f winner, was second in the listed Dick Poole Stakes and is a half-sister to 4 winners including the useful dual listed 6f winner of 6 races (including at 2 yrs) Bounty Box. The second dam, Bible Box (by Bin Ajwaad), was a quite useful 7f to 9f winner of 3 races from 3 to 5 yrs. *"A filly I like, I've only done one piece of work with her but I like what I see. She's a good mover and a forward-going filly I'd like to get out at the back-end of May, but she'll improve a lot as the year goes on. So although we may just have Royal Ascot in our minds after she's had her first run I don't want to mess her up if she needs longer. She's got scope and I see her as a six furlong 2-y-o rather than five".*

1213. UNNAMED ★★
b.c. Canford Cliffs – Western Sky (Barathea). April 29. Sixth foal. 65,000foal. Tattersalls December. Hugo Merry. Half-brother to the German dual Group 3 1m winner (including at 2 yrs) and Group 1 11f German Oaks second Djumama (by Aussie Rules) and to two minor winners abroad by Dark Angel and Namid. The dam, placed fourth once over 6f at 3 yrs from two starts, is a sister to the Group 3 Greenham Stakes winner and triple Group 1 placed Barathea Guest and a half-sister to 5 winners. The second dam, Western Heights (by Shirley Heights), is an unraced half-sister to 6 winners including the listed Galtres Stakes winner Startino. *"A good-looking horse and a good mover for the second half of the season. He had a little hold up before he came to me so he was late coming in, but he's a lovely looking horse. I haven't done enough with him to be able to gauge his ability but to my eye I don't see him being out until August. He was quite a late foal and is out of a middle distance family".*

AIDAN O'BRIEN
1214. ABSOLUTE RULER
b.c. Oasis Dream – Ideal (Galileo). March 10. First foal. The dam, a quite useful 10f winner, is closely related to the Racing Post Trophy (at 2 yrs), 2,000 Guineas, Derby and Irish Derby winner Camelot. The second dam, Tarfah (by Kingmambo), a useful winner of 5 races over 1m and 9f including the Group 3 Dahlia Stakes and the listed Rosemary Stakes, is a half-sister to one winner.

1215. AIR FORCE BLUE (USA)
b.br.c. War Front – Chatham (Maria's Mon).
May 2. Fifth foal. $490,000Y. Keeneland
September. M V Magnier. Half-brother to
a winner in Japan by Arch. The dam, a US
stakes-placed winner of 3 races, is a half-sister
to 2 winners. The second dam, Circle Of Gold
(by Seeking The Gold), is an unraced sister to
the US champion 2-y-o filly and dual Grade 1
winner and good broodmare Flanders.

1216. BIG BEN
b.c. Galileo – Flirtation (Pursuit Of Love).
March 1. Ninth foal. 750,000Y. Tattersalls
October Book 1. M V Magnier. Half-brother
to 5 winners including the 1,000 Guineas,
Irish 1,000 Guineas, Coronation Stakes,
Matron Stakes and Sun Chariot Stakes winner
Attraction (by Efisio), to the fairly useful dual
1m winner (including at 2 yrs) Racketeer
(by Cape Cross), the quite useful winner of
4 races and US Grade 3 second Federation
(by Motivator) and the quite useful 2-y-o 5f
winner Aunty Mary (by Common Grounds).
The dam is an unplaced half-sister to 4
winners including the Group 2 placed Carmita.
The second dam, Eastern Shore (by Sun
Prince), is a placed half-sister to 7 winners.

1217. BRAVERY
b.c. Galileo – Lady Icarus (Rainbow Quest).
February 1. Tenth foal. 400,000Y. Tattersalls
October Book 1. Charlie Gordon-Watson. Half-
brother to the Group 3 1m Irish 2,000 Guineas
Trial winner Furner's Green (by Dylan Thomas),
to the Irish listed 1m winner and Group 1 Irish
Oaks third Lady Lupus (by High Chaparral)
and the Irish listed 1m winners Palace (by
Fastnet Rock) and Mystical Lady (by Halling).
The dam is an unraced three-parts sister to
the Group 3 Supreme Stakes winner Hazaam
and the Group 3 1m Prix de la Jonchere
winner Sharman. The second dam, Sonic Lady
(by Nureyev), won the Irish 1,000 Guineas, the
Coronation Stakes, the Sussex Stakes and the
Prix du Moulin.

1218. CALIFORNIADREAMING (IRE)
b.f. Fastnet Rock – Descant (Nureyev).
January 14. Sister to the smart 6f winner
Cougar Mountain and half-sister to the fairly
useful 7f (at 2 yrs) and 1m winner of 4 races
Roaring Forte (by Cape Cross), the fair 6f

winner Climate Control (by Mt Livermore)
and the modest 5f and 6f winner Far Note (by
Distant View). The dam is an unraced half-
sister to numerous winners including Zafonic
and Zamindar. The second dam, Zaizafon
(by The Minstrel), a dual 2-y-o 7f winner, was
placed in the Group 1 1m Queen Elizabeth
II Stakes and the Group 3 1m Child Stakes
and is a half-sister to the dam of the Eclipse
Stakes and Phoenix Champion Stakes winner
Elmaamul.

1219. COOLMORE
b.f. Galileo – You'resothrilling (Storm Cat).
January 16. Third foal. Sister to the 2014 2-y-o
Group 1 National Stakes winner Gleneagles
and to the 1m (at 2 yrs) and Group 1 Irish
1,000 Guineas winner Marvellous. The dam,
winner of the Group 2 Cherry Hinton Stakes,
is a sister to several winners and a half-
sister to the top-class and genuine Giant's
Causeway, winner of the Group 1 7f Prix de
la Salamandre (at 2 yrs), the St James's Palace
Stakes, Eclipse Stakes, Irish Champion Stakes,
Sussex Stakes and Juddmonte International.
The second dam, Mariah's Storm (by Rahy),
a winner of 10 races in the USA including six
Graded stakes events from 1m to 9f, is closely
related to the Group 2 Prix d'Harcourt winner
Panoramic.

1220. DEAUVILLE
b.c. Galileo – Walklikeanegyptian (Danehill).
March 2. Brother to the quite useful 2014
2-y-o 1m winner Heatstroke and to the useful
10f to 12f winner The Corsican. The dam,
a fair 2-y-o 5f and subsequent US winner,
was Grade 3 placed and is closely related to
numerous winners including the Canadian
Grade 2 Nassau Stakes winner Callwood
Dancer and the Group 2 Italian Oaks winner
Contredanse. The second dam, Ahdaab (by
Rahy), placed once over 10f, is a half-sister to
8 winners including the Group 1 1m Queen
Elizabeth II Stakes winner Maroof and to the
placed dam of the Irish Derby winner Desert
King.

1221. GENERAL MACARTHUR
b.c. War Front – Imagine (Sadler's Wells).
March 19. Half-brother to the 2-y-o Group
1 7f Prix Jean Luc Lagardere winner Horatio
Nelson (by Danehill), to 3 winners by Giant's

Causeway including the Irish listed 7f winner and Group 2 Champagne Stakes second Viscount Nelson, the 2-y-o Group 2 7f Rockfel Stakes winner Kitty Matcham and the Irish 10f winner and Group 1 placed Red Rock Canyon (both by Rock Of Gibraltar). The dam, winner of the Irish 1,000 Guineas and Epsom Oaks, is a half-sister to Generous, winner of the Derby, Irish Derby, King George VI and the Dewhurst Stakes. The second dam, Doff The Derby (by Master Derby), is an unraced half-sister to the Prix Ganay winner Trillion (herself dam of the outstanding racemare Triptych).

1222. LIEUTENANT GENERAL

b.c. Fastnet Rock – Lady Lupus (High Chaparral). January 23. Brother to the unplaced 2014 2-y-o Shark Island. The dam, a useful Irish listed 1m winner, was third in the Group 1 Irish Oaks and is closely related to the 7f (at 2 yrs) and Group 3 1m Irish 2,000 Guineas Trial winner Furner's Green (by Dylan Thomas) and a half-sister to the useful Irish listed 1m winner Mystical Lady. The second dam, Lady Icarus (by Rainbow Quest), is an unraced three-parts sister to the very useful Hazaam, winner of four races from 7f to 1m at 3 yrs including the Group 3 Supreme Stakes and to the very useful Group 3 1m Prix de la Jonchere winner Sharman.

1223. MONARCH

b.c. Galileo – Tarbela (Grand Lodge). March 31. Eighth foal. Half-brother to the smart 2-y-o listed 7f and listed 1m winner Big Audio (by Oratorio), to the modest 6f winner Spiritual Healing (by Invincible Spirit) and a minor winner abroad by Kheleyf. The dam, a moderate 7f placed 2-y-o in Ireland, is a half-sister to 3 winners and to the dams of the Group 1 winners Arcano and Gilt Edge Girl. The second dam, Tarwiya (by Dominion), won the Group 3 7f C L Weld Park Stakes, was third in the Irish 1,000 Guineas and is a half-sister to 5 winners including the Group 3 Norfolk Stakes winner Blue Dakota.

1224. SHOGUN

b.c. Fastnet Rock – Perihelion (Galileo). April 28. Fourth foal. €400,000Y. Goffs Orby. Blandford Bloodstock. Brother to the 2-y-o 7f Group 3 7f C.L & M.F Weld Park Stakes winner Qualify and closely related to the fairly useful

10f winner Satellite (by Danehill Dancer). The dam, a useful 14.7f winner and second in the Group 2 Park Hill Stakes, is a half-sister to 5 winners. The second dam, Medicosma (by The Minstrel), a quite useful 12f and 2m winner, is a half-sister to 5 winners including the Park Hill Stakes winner Eva Luna (the dam of four stakes winners) and the dam of the US Grade 1 winner Flute.

1225. PAINTED CLIFFS

b.c. Canford Cliffs – Lulawin (Kyllachy). January 25. Second foal. €200,000Y. Goffs Orby. M V Magnier. Half-brother to the fair 2014 2-y-o 7f winner Rockaroundtheclock (by Starspangledbanner). The dam is an unraced half-sister to 6 winners including the Group 1 St James's Palace Stakes and Group 2 Mill Reef Stakes winner and Grade 1 Breeders Cup Mile second Excellent Art and the smart 7f (at 2 yrs), 12f and 2m 4f Ascot Stakes winner Double Obsession. The second dam, Obsessive (by Seeking The Gold), a useful 2-y-o 6f winner and third in the Group 3 10.4f Musidora Stakes, is a half-sister to 7 winners.

1226. WASHINGTON DC

b.c. Zoffany – How's She Cuttin' (Shinko Forest). March 10. Second living foal. €340,000Y. Goffs Orby. BBA (Ire). The dam, a quite useful 5f winner of 7 races, was listed-placed and is a half-sister to 3 winners. The second dam, Magic Annemarie (by Dancing Dissident), a fair 5f and 6f winner of 3 races, is a half-sister to 3 winners. This colt was second in a five furlong median auction maiden on his debut on the 17th April.

1227. WATERLOO BRIDGE

b.c. Zoffany – Miss Childrey (Dr Fong). March 12. Sixth foal. 350,000Y. Tattersalls October Book 1. Peter & Ross Doyle. Half-brother to the 1m (at 2 yrs) and Group 3 12.5f Prix Minerve winner and Group 1 Prix Saint-Alary third Forces Of Darkness, to the moderate 10.5f winner Tetard (both by Lawman) and the fair Irish 7f winner Independent Girl (by Bachelor Duke). The dam, an Irish 2-y-o listed 6f winner, was third in the Group 3 Irish 1,000 Guineas Trial and is a half-sister to 6 winners. The second dam, Blazing Glory (by Glow), won 3 races over 5f and is a full or half-sister to 6 winners.

1228. ZIG ZAG
br.c. Zoffany – Le Montrachet (Nashwan).
May 3. Half-brother to the fairly useful 8.5f
and 10f winner Daredevil Day (by Holy Roman
Emperor), to the quite useful 2-y-o 6f winner
Barzan (by Danehill Dancer), the fair 2-y-o 1m
winner Fly By White (by Hawk Wing), the quite
useful 12f winner Baba Ganouge (by Desert
Prince) and a minor winner in New Zealand
by Green Desert. The dam is an unraced
half-sister to the Group 1 Coronation Stakes
and Group 1 Prix Marcel Boussac winner
Gold Splash and to Born Gold (dam of the
outstanding Goldikova). The second dam,
Riviere d'Or (by Lyphard), won the Group 1
10f Prix Saint-Alary.

1229. UNNAMED
b.c. Galileo – Airwave (Air Express).
April 8. Brother to the useful Irish Group 3
9f winner of 3 races Aloof and to the French
listed 1m winner Orator and half-brother to
the useful 2-y-o listed 5f winner and Group
2 5f Queen Mary Stakes second Meow (by
Storm Cat). The dam, a champion 2-y-o filly
and winner of 6 races including the Group 1
6f Cheveley Park Stakes, is a half-sister to 6
winners. The second dam, Kangra Valley (by
Indian Ridge), a moderate 2-y-o 5f winner, is a
half-sister to 7 minor winners.

1230. UNNAMED
ch.f. Galileo – Aleagueoftheirown (Danehill
Dancer). May 4. Fourth foal. 550,000Y.
Tattersalls October Book 1. M V Magnier. Sister
to the 12f winner and Group 2 12f Ribblesdale
Stakes third Criteria and to the useful Irish
2-y-o 7f winner and Group 3 Tyros Stakes
third Kingston Jamaica. The dam, a useful Irish
9f winner, was listed-placed and is a half-sister
to 2 winners. The second dam, Golden Coral
(by Slew O'Gold), is an unplaced sister to the
Group 1 Coronation Stakes and Group 3 Prix
du Rond Point winner Golden Opinion and a
half-sister to 7 winners.

1231. UNNAMED
b.f. Oasis Dream – All For Glory (Giant's
Causeway). January 22. Second foal. Sister to
the useful 2014 2-y-o 6f winner and Group
2 Debutante Stakes third Toogoodtobetrue.
The dam is an unraced half-sister to 3 winners
including the very smart listed 11f winner,

Group 1 Oaks second and Group 1 Irish Oaks
third Wonder Of Wonders (by Kingmambo).
The second dam, All Too Beautiful (by Sadler's
Wells), a Group 3 10.5f Middleton Stakes
and listed 10f winner, is a sister to the Derby,
Irish Derby and King George VI and Queen
Elizabeth Diamond Stakes winner Galileo and
the dual Group 1 winner Black Sam Bellamy
and a half-sister to four stakes winners notably
the outstanding colt Sea The Stars.

1232. UNNAMED
b.c. Galileo – Another Storm (Gone West).
April 18. Eighth foal. 875,000Y. Tattersalls
October Book 1. China Horse Club/M Wallace.
Brother to the useful 2014 2-y-o 1m winner
and listed placed Order Of St George and half-
brother to 4 winners including the 2-y-o 1m
and subsequent French Group 3 1m winner
Asperity (by War Chant), the US Grade 3 9f
winner Angel Terrace (by Ghostzapper) and
the listed 12f winner Sehoy (by Menifee). The
dam, a minor US 2-y-o winner, is a half-sister
to 3 winners. The second dam, Storm Song (by
Summer Squall), was a dual Grade 1 winner
and champion 2-y-o filly.

1233. UNNAMED
b.c. Galileo – Chintz (Danehill Dancer).
March 31. Third foal. Brother to the 2014 2-y-
o 7f winner (on her only start) Queen Nefertiti
and to the 2-y-o 7f winner (on his only start)
Illinois. The dam was a useful winner of the
2-y-o Group 3 7f C L Weld Park Stakes and
is a half-sister to 3 winners. The second dam,
Gold Dodger (by Slew O'Gold), a listed 10f
winner of 2 races in France, is a half-sister to 9
winners including the French Group winners
Prospect Wells and Prospect Park.

1234. UNNAMED
b.c. Galileo – Christmas Kid (Lemon Drop Kid).
May 6. Third foal. Half-brother to the 2-y-o
5f winner and Group 3 7f Killavullan Stakes
second Michaelmas (by Elusive Quality).
The dam won 4 races including the Grade
1 Ashland Stakes and the Grade 2 Davona
Dale Stakes and is a half-sister to the US
stakes winner Elusive Gift. The second dam,
Christmas Gift (by Green Desert), won two
Grade 3 events in the USA and is a half-sister
to 10 winners.

1235. UNNAMED

b.c. Galileo – Circle Of Life (Belong To Me). May 8. Half-brother to the US Grade 1 7f Hopeful Stakes (at 2 yrs) and dual Grade 2 winner Circular Quay (by Thunder Gulch) and the US winner of 6 races and triple Grade 2 placed The Roundhouse (by Fusaichi Pegasus). The dam won the Grade 1 7f Spinaway Stakes at 2 yrs in the USA and is a half-sister to 6 winners. The second dam, Concentric (by Shadeed), was placed at 2 yrs in the USA.

1236. UNNAMED

b.c. Galileo – Devoted To You (Danehill Dancer). February 28. Second foal. The dam, an Irish 2-y-o 7f winner, was second in the Group 2 7f Debutante Stakes and is a half-sister to 8 winners including the US Grade 3 8.5f Honeybee Handicap winner Humble Eight and the Irish listed winners Royal Devotion, Thady Quill and April Starlight. The second dam, Alleged Devotion (by Alleged), is an unraced half-sister to 10 winners including the top-class Irish Derby and Epsom Oaks winner Balanchine and the Group 2 winners Romanov and Red Slippers.

1237. UNNAMED

gr.c. Galileo – Famous (Danehill Dancer). January 16. Second foal. 600,000Y. Tattersalls October Book 1. Blandford Bloodstock. The dam, a useful Irish 2-y-o 7f winner, was second in the Group 1 7f Moyglare Stud Stakes and is a sister to the Group 1 Phoenix Stakes, National Stakes and Irish 2,000 Guineas winner Mastercraftsman and closely related to the US Grade 3 winner Genuine Devotion. The second dam, Starlight Dreams (by Black Tie Affair), won twice at 3 yrs in the USA and is a half-sister to 5 winners including the listed Zetland Stakes winner Matahif and the dam of the dual Group 1 winner Pressing.

1238. UNNAMED

b.c. War Front – Gold Vault (Arch). February 6. Fifth foal. $2,200,000Y. Keeneland September. M V Magnier. Half-brother to 3 winners including the US Grade 1 1m Test Stakes and Grade 1 7f Acorn Stakes winner Contested (by Ghostzapper). The dam, a minor winner of 3 races in the USA at 4 yrs, is a half-sister to the US dual Grade 1 winner Pomeroy. The second dam, Questress (by Seeking The Gold), was a minor winner in the USA at 2 and 3 yrs.

1239. UNNAMED

ch.c. Galileo – Halland Park Lass (Spectrum). April 10. Seventh foal. Brother to the 2014 2-y-o 6f winner (on her only start) Lap Of Luxury and to the Group 2 10f Blandford Stakes and Group 3 9f winner Up and half-brother to the 2-y-o Group 1 Middle Park Stakes and Group 1 Prix Morny winner and sire Dutch Art (by Medicean). The dam ran 3 times unplaced and is a half-sister to 4 winners including the Scandinavian Group 3 winner King Quantas. The second dam, Palacegate Episode (by Drumalis), won 11 races including the Group 3 Premio Omenoni and the listed St Hugh's Stakes and is a half-sister to the listed winners Palacegate Jack and Another Episode.

1240. UNNAMED

b.c. Montjeu – Honorlina (Linamix). February 19. Third foal. 675,000Y. Tattersalls October Book 1. M V Magnier. The dam, a French 2-y-o 1m winner, is a sister to the French 2,000 Guineas winner Vahorimix and to the French listed winner Vadalix and a half-sister to 4 winners. The second dam, Vadsa Honor (by Highest Honor), won the listed Prix de Thiberville and is a half-sister to 12 winners including the dam of the Breeders Cup Mile winner Val Royal.

1241. UNNAMED

b.c. Galileo – Hveger (Danehill). March 14. Fifth foal. 750,000Y. Tattersalls October Book 1. M V Magnier. Brother to the 2-y-o Group 2 7f Vintage Stakes winner Highland Reel and half-brother to the Australian 3-y-o winner and dual Group 1 second Valdemoro (by Encosta De Lago). The dam won once in Australia and was Group 1 placed and is a sister to the multiple Group 1 winner Elvstroem and a half-sister to the Group 1 Queen Anne Stakes and dual Australian Group 1 winner Hardasun. The second dam, Circles Of Gold (by Marscay), won the Group 1 AJC Oaks in Australia and is a half-sister to 5 winners including the Australian Group 2 winner Gold Wells.

1242. UNNAMED

b.c. Galileo – Inca Princess (Holy Roman Emperor). April 20. First foal. €300,000Y. Goffs Orby. BBA (Ire). The dam, a quite useful Irish 2-y-o 6f winner, is a half-sister to 2 winners including the smart Irish 10f and 13f winner Changingoftheguard. The second dam, Miletrian (by Marju), a smart Group 2 Ribblesdale Stakes and Group 3 Park Hill Stakes winner, is a sister to one winner and a half-sister to the Group 2 Geoffrey Freer Stakes winner Mr Combustible.

1243. UNNAMED

b.f. Galileo – Jacqueline Quest (Rock Of Gibraltar). January 17. First foal. 625,000Y. Tattersalls October Book 1. M V Magnier. The dam, a smart 2-y-o 7f winner, Group 1 1,000 Guineas second and Group 1 Coronation Stakes third, is a half-sister to 3 winners. The second dam, Coquette Rouge (by Croco Rouge), a quite useful Irish 12f and 17f winner, is a half-sister to 5 winners including the Group 3 Classic Trial winner Regime and the 2-y-o 5f listed winner and Group 2 Cherry Hinton second Salut d'Amour.

1244. UNNAMED

b.c. Galileo – Lahinch (Danehill Dancer). March 15. Seventh foal. Brother to the very useful 10.5f winner and Group 2 9f Kilboy Estate Stakes second Lahinch Classics and half-brother to the Irish 7.5f (at 2 yrs) and Group 3 10f Kilternan Stakes winner and dual Group 2 placed The Bogberry (by Hawk Wing), to the Irish 2-y-o Group 3 6f Ballyogan Stakes winner Liscanna (by Sadler's Wells) and the fair 9f winner Quarante Deux (by Fusaichi Pegasus). The dam, a useful listed 5f (at 2 yrs) and listed 6f winner, is a half-sister to 7 winners including the smart 2-y-o 5f and subsequent US stakes winner Perugino Bay. The second dam, Dublah (by Private Account), is an unraced half-sister to 5 minor winners.

1245. UNNAMED

b.f. Galileo – Like A Dame (Danehill). March 14. Fourth foal. 400,000Y. Tattersalls October Book 1. Charlie Gordon-Watson. Half-sister to the Group 3 1m Atalanta Stakes and listed 1m winner Ladys First (by Dutch Art). The dam, a minor 3-y-o winner in France, is a half-sister to 5 other minor winners. The second dam, Anysheba (by Alysheba), a French listed-placed 3-y-o winner, is a half-sister to 8 winners including the Sadler's Flag (Group 3 Prix de Royaumont).

1246. UNNAMED

b.c. War Front – Liscanna (Sadler's Wells). February 20. Third foal. The dam, an Irish 2-y-o Group 3 6f Ballyogan Stakes winner, is a half-sister to the Irish 7.5f (at 2 yrs) and Group 3 10f Kilternan Stakes winner and dual Group 2 placed The Bogberry. The second dam, Lahinch (by Danehill Dancer), a useful listed 5f (at 2 yrs) and listed 6f winner, was second in the Group 2 Rockfel Stakes and is a half-sister to 7 winners including the smart 2-y-o 5f and subsequent US stakes winner Perugino Bay.

1247. UNNAMED

b.c. Pour Moi – Marjalina (Marju). March 20. First foal. 210,000Y. Tattersalls October Book 1. M V Magnier. The dam, winner of the Group 3 Park Express Stakes, is a half-sister to 4 winners including the useful Irish 7f (at 2 yrs) and listed 12f winner What A Charm. The second dam, Atalina (by Linamix), won once over 12.5f in France and is a half-sister to 4 winners including the French listed winner Paix Blanche (the dam of two stakes winners).

1248. UNNAMED

b.c. Galileo – Moonstone (Dalakhani). February 28. Fourth foal. Half-brother to the 2014 2-y-o 7f winner, on her only start, Words, to the useful 1m (at 2 yrs) and listed 11f winner Nevis (both by Dansili) and the useful 2-y-o listed 6f winner Stubbs (by Danehill Dancer). The dam, winner of the Group 1 Irish Oaks, is closely related to the Breeders Cup second L'Ancresse, to the Group 1 10f Prix Saint-Alary winner Cerulean Sky (herself dam of the Group 2 Doncaster Cup winner Honolulu) and the useful 10f winner and Group 3 placed Qaatef. The second dam, Solo de Lune (by Law Society), a French 11f winner, is a half-sister to 6 winners including the Grade 2 E P Taylor Stakes winner Truly A Dream and the French Group 2 winner Wareed.

1249. UNNAMED

b.c. Galileo – Penang Pearl (Bering). March 9. Eleventh foal. 2,600,000Y. Tattersalls October Book 1. M V Magnier. Half-brother to the Group 1 12f King George VI Queen Elizabeth Stakes and Group 2 12f Hardwicke Stakes winner Harbinger (by Dansili), to the fair 7f to 12f winner of 12 races Penang Cinta (by

Halling), the fair 12f winner Penangdouble O One (by Starcraft), the modest 2-y-o 5f winner Penang Sapphire (by Spectrum) and a winner in France by Sakhee. The dam was a very useful 3-y-o listed 1m winner of 3 races. The second dam, Guapa (by Shareef Dancer), won twice over 1m and is a half-sister to 7 winners including the Group 2 winners Dusty Dollar and Kind Of Hush.

1250. UNNAMED
b.c. Galileo – Rags To Riches (A P Indy). April 24. The dam, a winner of four Grade 1 stakes in the USA from 1m to 12f, is a half-sister to several winners including the Grade 1 12f Belmont Stakes winner Jazil and the US Grade 2 winner Casino Drive. The second dam, Better Than Honour (by Deputy Minister), won the Grade 2 9f Demoiselle Stakes and is a sister to the Group 2 1m Beresford Stakes winner Turnberry Isle and a half-sister to the Group 1 Fillies' Mile second and good broodmare Maryinski and the Group 2 1m Prix d'Astarte winner Smolensk.

1251. UNNAMED
ch.c. Galileo – Remember When (Danehill Dancer). February 18. Second foal. Brother to the promising 2015 3-y-o 10f placed Wedding Vow. The dam was second in the Oaks and is closely related to the top-class middle-distance winner of six Group 1 events Dylan Thomas and a half-sister to the champion 2-y-o filly and Group 1 6f Cheveley Park Stakes winner Queen's Logic. The second dam, Lagrion (by Diesis), was placed 5 times in Ireland and stayed 12f and is a sister to the Group 1 Middle Park Stakes second Pure Genius.

1252. UNNAMED
b.c. Galileo – Rimth (Oasis Dream). February 17. First foal. The dam won the Group 3 Fred Darling Stakes and was second in the Group 1 Cheveley Park Stakes. The second dam, Dorelia (by Efisio), a fair 1m winner, is a half-sister to 3 winners including the smart Group 2 5f Kings Stand Stakes and Group 3 5f Cornwallis Stakes winner Dominica.

1253. UNNAMED
b.c. Galileo – Rumplestiltskin (Danehill). February 17. Brother to the 2014 2-y-o Group

3 1m winner John F Kennedy, to the 2-y-o Group 2 7f Debutante Stakes and Group 1 Yorkshire Oaks winner Tapestry and to the fairly useful Irish 2-y-o 7f winners Theatre and Why. The dam won the Group 1 Prix Marcel Boussac and the Group 1 Moyglare Stud Stakes and is a full or half-sister to 5 winners including the Group 2 second Tower Rock. The second dam, Monevassia (by Mr Prospector), is a placed sister to the triple Group 1 1m winner Kingmambo and to the smart Group 3 6f winner Miesque's Son and a half-sister to the high-class triple Group 1 winner East of the Moon.

1254. UNNAMED
b.c. Galileo – Secret Garden (Danehill). May 8. Ninth foal. Brother to the Group 1 1m Criterium International (at 2 yrs) and Group 1 Irish 2,000 Guineas winner Roderic O'Connor and to the useful 1m (at 2 yrs) and listed 10f winner Dazzling and half-brother to 3 winners including the fairly useful 2-y-o 6f winner and Group 3 6f Sirenia Stakes third Weatherstaff (by Elusive Quality) and the quite useful 2-y-o 1m winner Burnett (by Dynaformer). The dam, a listed 7f winner, is a full or half-sister to 4 winners. The second dam, Chalamont (by Kris), a quite useful 2-y-o dual 6f winner, is a half-sister to the dual Ascot Gold Cup winner Gildoran.

1255. UNNAMED
b.f. Pour Moi – Sistine (Dubai Destination). January 28. First foal. 350,000Y. Tattersalls October Book 2. John Warren. The dam, a modest 4-y-o 14f winner, is a half-sister to 4 winners including the useful Group 3 Dahlia Stakes winner Tarfah (herself dam of the dual Derby and 2,000 Guineas winner Camelot. The second dam, Fickle (by Danehill), a fairly useful 1m and listed 10f winner, is a half-sister to 7 winners including the listed winners Birdie and Faru.

1256. UNNAMED
b.c. Galileo – Sumora (Danehill). April 28. Seventh foal. Brother to the 2-y-o Group 1 7f Moyglare Stud Stakes winner and 1,000 Guineas third Maybe. The dam, a 2-y-o listed 5f St Hugh's Stakes winner, is a sister to the useful Irish 7f winner Fleeting Shadow and a half-sister to the Oaks and German Oaks

winner Dancing Rain. The second dam, Rain Flower (by Indian Ridge), is an unraced three-parts sister to the Epsom Derby, Irish Champion Stakes and Dewhurst Stakes winner Dr Devious and a half-sister to 5 winners including the Japanese listed winner Shinko King and the Group 3 winners Royal Court and Archway.

1257. UNNAMED
b.c. War Front – Treasure Trail (Pulpit). February 2. Second foal. $800,000 foal. Keeneland November. Aisling Duignan. The dam is an unraced half-sister to the outstanding racemare Zenyatta and the triple US Grade 1 winner Balance. The second dam, Vertigineux (by Kris S), won 2 minor races at 4 yrs in the USA and is a half-sister to the Grand Prix de Lyon winner Restrained.

1258. UNNAMED
b.c. Oasis Dream – Wonder Of Wonders (Kingmambo). January 14. First foal. The dam, a very smart listed 11f winner, was second in the Oaks and third in the Irish Oaks. The second dam, All Too Beautiful (by Sadler's Wells), a Group 3 10.5f Middleton Stakes and listed 10f winner, is a sister to the Derby, Irish Derby and King George VI and Queen Elizabeth Diamond Stakes winner Galileo and the dual Group 1 winner Black Sam Bellamy and a half-sister to four stakes winners notably the outstanding colt Sea The Stars.

JAMIE OSBORNE
1259. CANFORD CHIMES (IRE) ★★
b.c. Canford Cliffs – Appleblossom Pearl (Peintre Celebre). April 4. Fourth foal. 60,000Y. Tattersalls October Book 1. F Barberini. Half-brother to the fair 2-y-o 6f winner Silent Footsteps (by Footstepsinthesand). The dam, a minor 4-y-o Irish 7f winner, is a half-sister to 6 winners including the Group 3 placed Rabi and Kawagino. The second dam, Sharakawa (by Darshaan), is an unraced half-sister to 4 winners including the Group 3 placed Mempari. (Apple Tree Stud). *"A big, good-looking horse with a good action, but he's very much a 3-y-o type. There's a bit more of the damsire Peintre Celebre about him than Canford Cliffs I'd say, so he's one we wouldn't maximise until next year".*

1260. DALAVAND (IRE) ★★
ch.c. Tamayuz – Kirunavaara (Galileo). March 29. Third foal. 28,000foal. Tattersalls December. Kitty Cowhey. Half-brother to the quite useful 2014 2-y-o 7f winner Bartel (by Aussie Rules) and to the minor German 3-y-o winner Kelida Dancer (by Clodovil). The dam, placed at 2 and 3 yrs in Germany, is a half-sister to 2 winners. The second dam, Kimbajar (by Royal Abjar), won three listed races from 7f to 1m at 3 and 4 yrs in Germany and is a half-sister to 4 winners including the 1,000 Guineas and Oaks winner Kazzia (herself dam of the UAE Group 1 winner Eastern Anthem). (Apple Tree Stud). *"He's strong and could be a 2-y-o from the mid-summer onwards. A good actioned horse, he's nice but we haven't done much with him yet. Has the look of a horse for the second half of the season".*

1261. DREAM DANA (IRE) ★★★
b.f. Dream Ahead – Lidanna (Nicholas). February 2. Tenth foal. 100,000Y. Tattersalls October Book 1. F Barberini. Half-sister to 6 winners including the smart listed 7f winner Yaa Wayl, the fairly useful 6f (at 2 yrs) to 8.5f winner Robert The Painter (both by Whipper), the 2-y-o 5f and subsequent Hong Kong listed second Prince Monalulu (by Intikhab), the fairly useful Irish 7f winner and listed-placed Lidanski (by Soviet Star and herself dam of the Group 1 winning sprinter Wizz Kid) and the quite useful Irish dual 6f winner Capall An Ibre (by Traditionally). The dam, a dual Group 3 winner in Ireland over 5f and 6f, is a half-sister to 5 winners. The second dam, Shapely Test (by Elocutionist), a 1m winner, is a half-sister to a listed winner in Australia. (Apple Tree Stud). *"I like the Dream Ahead's and this one has a good pedigree, it's a fast family and she's nice. Not the most precocious of the three I have by this sire, but she will be a 2-y-o from the mid-summer onwards".*

1262. DREAM DREAMER ★★★
b.f. Dream Ahead – Moonlit Garden (Exceed And Excel). January 14. First foal. £35,000Y. Doncaster Premier. Federico Barberini. The dam, a fairly useful 2-y-o 6f winner, was listed-placed three times and is a half-sister to one winner. The second dam, Fingal Nights (by Night Shift), was a fair 6f and 7f winner at 2 and 3 yrs. (Ian Barratt, Stephen Short, Adam

Signy). *"She's the most forward of the Dream Ahead 2-y-o's I have, she shows plenty of speed and hopefully she'll be out very soon. A five furlong 2-y-o, she probably won't go beyond that".*

1263. DREAM POWER (IRE) ★★★

b.c. Frozen Power – Karaliyfa (Kahyasi). February 9. Eighth foal. €48,000Y. Goffs Sportsmans. F Barberini. Half-sister to the fairly useful 1m (at 2 yrs) to 12f winner of 3 races Mighty Yar (by Teofilo), to the fairly useful Irish 1m and 10f winner Karawana (by King's Best), the moderate 12f winner Ocean Bluff (by Dalakhani) and a hurdles by Kalanisi. The dam, a quite useful 9f winner, is a half-sister to 7 winners including Karasta (2-y-o Group 3 1m May Hill Stakes), Kasthari (Group 2 2m 2f Doncaster Cup in a dead-heat) and Kargali (Group 3 Gladness Stakes). The second dam, Karliyka (by Last Tycoon), a French 3-y-o winner of 4 races, was listed placed over 1m and 10f and is a half-sister to 4 winners. *"He's a nice horse that's going to take a bit of time. Very good-looking and from the first crop of Frozen Power, he's more of a second half of the season 2-y-o with a nice bit of scope and a good action".*

1264. HUNGARIAN RHAPSODY ★★★★

b.c. Showcasing – Rockburst (Xaar). February 13. Fourth foal. 85,000Y. Tattersalls October Book 2. Jamie Osborne. Half-brother to the unplaced 2014 2-y-o Don't Tell Bertie (by Bertolini), to the useful dual 5f (at 2 yrs) and dual 6f winner and listed-placed Annunciation and the fair 5f winner Proclamationofwar (both by Proclamation). The dam, a fair 2-y-o dual 6f winner, is a half-sister to 4 winners. The second dam, Topwinder (by Topsider), is an unplaced half-sister to 5 winners. (M Buckley, Mrs S Ricci, Mrs P Shanahan). *"A nice, good-looking colt with a good action, I'm a big fan of the stallion and his yearlings were very hard to buy. I don't think this colt was too expensive for what he is, he has a lot of quality and he's mature and well-grown. Hopefully he'll run in May, although he's probably more of a six furlong horse than five".*

1265. ILLEGALLY BLONDE (IRE) ★★★

b.f. Lawman – Kayak (Singspiel). March 19.

Eighth foal. 14,000Y. Tattersalls October Book 2. F Barberini. Half-sister to the quite useful 2014 2-y-o 5f and 6.5f winner of 3 races Midterm Break (by Intense Focus), to the quite useful 2-y-o 7f winner Goodwood Atlantis (by Elusive City) and to 3 winners abroad by Bachelor Duke, Shantou and Traditionally. The dam, a listed-placed winner of two races in Italy, is a half-sister to 6 winners. The second dam, Kelang (by Kris), is an unplaced half-sister to 8 minor winners. (Mr & Mrs I Barratt). *"She's a nice filly that seems very straightforward and with a good action. She was quite a small yearling and I think that made her quite cheap, but she's grown a fair bit without getting weak. She's a good sized filly now, I wouldn't be getting her ready to run over five furlongs but she's one for the middle of the summer onwards over six or seven furlongs".*

1266. INHERENT VICE (IRE) ★★★

b.c. Kodiac – Ting A Greeley (Mr Greeley). April 27. Sixth foal. €55,000Y. Goffs Orby. F Barberini. Half-brother to 4 winners including the fair 1m winner Dalmarella Dancer (by Mastercraftsman) and the minor US winner of 3 races King Ting (by Holy Roman Emperor). The dam is an unraced half-sister to 3 winners. The second dam, Ting A Folie (by Careafolie), a dual Group 2 winner in Argentina, is a sister to Campesino (a triple Group 1 winner in Argentina). (Mrs S Ricci, M Buckley, Mrs P Shanahan). *"He's quite forward and although he looks to me more like a six furlong 2-y-o than five I may be brave enough to start him over the minimum trip. He's not small but he's strong and well-grown. He lifts his knees a little bit but he gets from A to B quite well".*

1267. LEITRIM TRAVELLER (USA) ★★

b.c. Henrythenavigator – Purple (Royal Academy). March 24. Fourth foal. 20,000Y. Tattersalls October Book 2. F Barberini. Half-brother to the quite useful Irish 10f winner Violet Lashes (by Badge Of Silver) and to a minor winner at 4 yrs in the USA by Artie Schiller. The dam, a minor US 3-y-o winner, is a half-sister to 4 winners. The second dam, Royal Beluga (by Soviet Star), is an unraced half-sister to 4 winners including the listed winner Hawait Al Barr. (David Watkins & David N Reynolds). *"Not the biggest, but he's doing plenty of work at the moment. I'll probably wait for the six furlong races with him, but he's a 2-y-o".*

1268. LONG JOHN SILVER (IRE) ★★

b.c. Canford Cliffs – Billet (Danehill). April 14. Fifth foal. €105,000Y. Goffs Orby. F Barberini. Half-brother to the fair 12f to 2m and hurdles winner Star Power (by Galileo). The dam, placed second once over 6f at 2 yrs, is a half-sister to 3 minor winners. The second dam, Tathkara (by Alydar), is an unraced sister to the US Grade 1 winner Talinum and a half-sister to 7 winners. (M Buckley, Mrs S Ricci, Mrs P Shanahan). *"We don't know about these Canford Cliffs yet and this isn't a precocious horse, he's more of a 2-y-o for the second half of the season. I wouldn't be thinking about trying to get him ready to run over five furlongs, but he's a good-looking horse with a good action".*

1269. MIA TESORO (IRE) ★★★★

b.f. Danehill Dancer – Souter's Sister (Desert Style). April 14. Second foal. Half-sister to Rocky Desert (by Rock Of Gibraltar), placed fourth once over 7f from four runs at 2 yrs in 2014. The dam, a useful 2-y-o Group 3 7f Oh So Sharp Stakes winner, is a half-sister to several winners including the fairly useful 5f (at 2 yrs) to 7f winner of 3 races Premier Fantasy. The second dam, Hemaca (Distinctly North), was unraced. (Mr Deron Pearson). *"I love this filly, she's got a beautiful action and I hope she'll be a good work companion to another lovely 2-y-o of ours, Sante. Hopefully she'll be a Royal Ascot filly, she does everything easily and has a beautiful action. So she has a chance of being a stakes filly and her pedigree is good enough to give us plenty of encouragement".*

1270. PACKING (IRE) ★★★

b.c. Lilbourne Lad – Elegant Ridge (Indian Ridge). March 25. Ninth foal. 32,000Y. Tattersalls October Book 2. Barberini Bloodstock. Half-brother to the very smart Group 3 and dual listed winner and dual Group 2 second Montiridge (by Ramonti) and to the minor winner of 3 races in the USA Woodward Park (by High Yield). The dam, a useful German 6.5f winner and second in the German Group 2 1,000 Guineas, subsequently

won in the USA and is a half-sister to 8 winners including the smart Irish 5f and listed 6f winner Rolo Tomasi. The second dam, Elegant Bloom (by Be My Guest), a quite useful Irish 2-y-o 6f winner, stayed 7f and is a full or half-sister to 12 winners. (Mr & Mrs I Barrett). *"He had a little setback and missed a couple of weeks but he's back working now. Strong and racy looking, he's just a bit behind where I should be with him, but I like him and he looks like he could be quick".*

1271. PACKING EMPIRE (IRE) ★★★

b.c. Holy Roman Emperor – Ceoil An Aith (Accordion). March 21. Second foal. 45,000Y. Tattersalls December. Barberini Bloodstock. The dam, a fair 12f winner, is a sister to the German Group 1 and French Group 2 winner of 16 races Yavana's Pace and the listed winner Littlepacepaddocks. The second dam, Lady In Pace (by Burslem), a dual 5f winner in Ireland, is a half-sister to 2 winners. (Edmund Lee & Mr Fra Ma). *"He was a bit on the small side when we bought him, like a lot by the sire, but I'm pleased to say he's grown quote a lot and he's not that small anymore. A nice type, he's very well-balanced, but because he's been growing I haven't pushed him yet. One for the second half of the season".*

1272. RAMPERS ★★★

b.c. Thewayyouare – Korresia (Elnadim). January 21. First foal. $15,000Y. Tattersalls Ireland September. F Barberini. The dam is an unraced half-sister to 2 winners in Italy. The second dam, Joud (by Dancing Brave), a quite useful 2-y-o 6f winner, is a half-sister to 5 winners. *"He's not typical of the sire and looks more like the damsire Elnadim. Very butty, strong and sharp-looking. He's a bit lazy so I'm piling the work into him now and he's taking it. He could run in May and unusually for one by Thewayyouare he could run over five furlongs. He's named after the cricketer Ramprakash because he's a member of the syndicate that owns him".*

1273. REDMANE ★★★★

b.c. Bahamian Bounty – Miss Villefranche (Danehill Dancer). April 5. First foal. 48,000Y. Tattersalls October Book 2. Barberini Bloodstock. The dam, a modest dual 9f winner, is a half-sister to 3 winners including the very useful 1m winner and listed-placed Moyenne Corniche. The second dam, Miss Corniche (Hernando), a 7f (at 2 yrs) and listed 10f winner, is a full or half-sister to 10 winners including the listed winner Miss Riviera Golf. *"He's showing me lots of speed, he has a very good action and could be one of the more forward colts. I'll hopefully be running him in May and we like him. He looks quick and what he's doing at the moment he does it well".*

1274. RUE RIVOLI (IRE) ★★

b.c. Champs Elysees – Rondo Alla Turca (Noverre). April 6. First foal. 120,000Y. Tattersalls October Book 2. F Barberini. The dam is an unplaced half-sister to 5 winners including the Group 3 12f and listed 1m winner and Group 2 Blandford Stakes second Sina Cova and the dual listed winner Blessyourpinksox. The second dam, Kumta (by Priolo), is an unraced half-sister to 7 winners including the dams of the Derby winner Kahyasi and the Group 1 Yorkshire Oaks winner Key Change. (Mrs S Ricci, M Buckley & Mrs P Shanahan). *"A backward colt with a good action, he's growing so I wouldn't be training him very hard at the moment. Definitely one for the second half of the season".*

1275. SANTE (IRE) ★★★★ ♠

b.f. Dream Ahead – Zeiting (Zieten). March 16. Tenth foal. €220,000Y. Goffs Orby. Anthony Stroud. Half-brother to 7 winners including the Group 3 Geoffrey Freer Stakes winner Royal Empire (by Teofilo), the useful 2-y-o 7f winner and triple Group 3 placed Bikini Babe (by Montjeu), the German Group 2 winner Combat Zone (by Refuse To Bend), the French 2-y-o 6f winner and Group 3 third Zut Alors (by Pivotal) and the useful 2-y-o 6f winner Mutawajid (by Zafonic). The dam, a 2-y-o listed 6f winner, later won minor stakes events in the USA and is a half-sister to 6 winners out of the Irish 13f winner Belle de Cadix (by Law Society). (Mr & Mrs R Kelvin-Hughes). *"A good horse! She's the most expensive filly we've ever bought and looks like a 3-y-o already. Very mature, well-grown and with a great attitude, she has a load of scope so I hope she'll keep progressing. She shows us a very good level of ability now but it is early days, so I'm still pondering whether or not to get her ready early to see if she's Royal Ascot*

material. It would be nice to get a good one for these owners and I think this filly could be the one".*

1276. SCHOOLBOY ERROR (IRE) ★★

ch.c. Roderic O'Connor – La Grande Zoa (Fantastic Light). April 19. Fifth foal. 18,000Y. Tattersalls October Book 3. Not sold. Half-brother to the quite useful 7f (at 2 yrs) and 12f winner Trip To Paris (by Champs Elysees). The dam is an unraced half-sister to a winner in Greece. The second dam, Majestic Sister (by Last Tycoon), is an unraced sister to Ezzoud (Juddmonte International Stakes, Eclipse Stakes, etc) and a half-sister to Distant Relative (Sussex Stakes, Prix du Moulin, etc). (Dunkley, Gumienny & Signy). *"A horse with a beautiful action, he's very good-looking but he doesn't have five furlong pace. He's a nice horse and he's not backward, but he's a galloper and will want seven furlongs to start with".*

1277. SECRET TALE (IRE) ★★★

b.f. Zoffany – Intimate Secret (Invincible Spirit). April 27. Third foal. $7,000Y. Goffs Sportsmans. F Barberini. Half-sister to Invincible Missile (by Majestic Missile), unplaced in two starts at 2 yrs in 2014. The dam, a fair Irish 6f placed maiden, is a half-sister to 4 minor winners. The second dam, Habaza (by Shernazar), is an unplaced half-sister to 7 winners. (Bo Derek's 10). *"She's quick and she didn't cost much, but she could be our first runner. A sharp filly, not very big, but a ball of muscle".* ***TRAINERS' BARGAIN BUY***

1278. SONNET (IRE) ★★

b.f. Kyllachy – Poetical (Croco Rouge). March 27. Fourth foal. €100,000Y. Goffs Orby. Anthony Stroud. Sister to the smart Dragon Pulse, winner of the 2-y-o Group 2 7f Futurity Stakes and the Group 3 Prix de Fontainebleau and second in the Group 1 7f National Stakes. The dam, a useful Group 3 placed 1m winner in Ireland, was third in the Group 3 7f Concorde Stakes and is a half-sister to 3 winners. The second dam, Abyat (by Shadeed), is an unraced half-sister to 9 winners including Hayil (Group 1 Middle Park Stakes). (Mr & Mrs R Kelvin-Hughes). *"A good-looking filly, she's done well having been a bit small and weak in the autumn. She's bulking up and putting condition on, but still looks a bit wintry in her coat so I'm not going to rush her. I'm not as far forward with her as some of the other fillies, so we'll have to see, but she's nice".*

1279. TURN ON THE TEARS (USA) ★★★
ch.f. Cape Blanco – Down The Well (Mujadil). April 6. First foal. $20,000Y. Keeneland September. F Barberini. The dam, a fair 2-y-o dual 5f winner, is a half-sister to 6 winners including the French Group 3 placed Speedfriend. The second dam, Batchelor's Button (by Kenmare), a minor French 3-y-o winner, is a half-sister to 6 other minor winners. (D Durkan). *"Yes, she's alright and she won't take long. I trained her mother who we sold her to America and then Federico bought this filly at Keeneland. She goes alright, she's not the biggest but her mother wasn't either and she could run. She should be up to winning a maiden and then we'll see where we go after that. She should give us a bit of fun".*

1280. WAYFARING STRANGER (IRE) ★★
b.c. Lope De Vega – Portelet (Night Shift). February 28. Thirteenth living foal. €90,000Y. Goffs Orby. F Barberini. Half-brother to 7 winners including the very smart 2-y-o Group 2 7f Champagne Stakes winner and Group 1 6f July Cup third Etlaala, the useful 7f and 1m winner and listed-placed Selective, the fairly useful dual 1m winner Splendorinthegrass (all by Selkirk), the useful 6f and 7f winner Overspect (by Spectrum) and the quite useful 6f winner and listed-placed Button Moon (by Compton Place). The dam, a fairly useful 5f winner of 4 races, is a half-sister to 4 winners. The second dam, Noirmont (by Dominion), is an unraced half-sister to the Group winners Braashee, Adam Smith and Ghariba. *"A big, backward horse, he's tall and quite typical of the sire. He has a good action but is a 3-y-o type and a long term project".*

1281. UNNAMED ★★★
b.f. Oasis Dream – Applauded (Royal Applause). March 1. Fourth foal. 150,000Y. Tattersalls October Book 1. Blandford Bloodstock. Half-sister to the quite useful 2-y-o 6f winner (here) and subsequent minor US stakes winner Amnesia (by Invincible Spirit) and to the French 10f winner Arthur The King (by Medicean). The dam, a quite useful 2-y-o 7f winner, is a half-sister to 3 winners including the Group 1 National Stakes winner

Power and the Group 2 12f Ribblesdale Stakes winner Thakafaat. The second dam, Frappe (by Inchinor), a fairly useful 2-y-o 6f winner, is a half-sister to 4 winners including the Footstepsinthesand (2,000 Guineas) and Pedro The Great (Phoenix Stakes). (Mrs P Shanahan, Mrs H Lascelles, Mr T Hyde). *"She's not over big and hasn't done as well as I thought, but she's still wintry in her coat and is just starting to come now. Probably one for the mid-summer onwards".*

1282. UNNAMED ★★
b.f. Dark Angel – Border Minstral (Sri Pekan). April 27. Seventh foal. 38,000Y. Tattersalls October Book 2. Not sold. Half-sister to the useful 5f winner of 9 races including at 2 yrs, Oldjoesaid (by Royal Applause), to the fair dual 5f winner including at 2 yrs Felsham (by Kyllachy) and the fair 1m winner Cultural Desert (by Footstepsinthesand). The dam, a fair 2-y-o 6f winner, is a full or half-sister to 7 winners including Please Sing (Group 2 Cherry Hinton Stakes) and the Group 1 National Stakes third Mountain Song. The second dam, Persian Song (by Persian Bold), is an unplaced sister to the Solario Stakes winner Bold Arrangement (placed in seven Group/Grade 1 races including the Kentucky Derby) and a half-sister to 4 winners. (Charlie Nelson & Partners). *"She's not as far forward as I'd hoped she'd be at this point. A nice filly, she's looking better all the time but she's only cantered. Seems pretty straightforward".*

1283. UNNAMED ★★
b.f. Clodovil – Elouges (Dalakhani). February 5. Fifth foal. £23,000Y. Doncaster Premier. F Barberini. Half-sister to the fair 2-y-o 8.5f winner Dragoon Guard (by Jeremy) and to a minor winner in France by Indian Haven. The dam was placed in France and is a half-sister to 9 winners including the very smart Group 2 1m Royal Lodge Stakes winner Mons and the smart 10f winner and Irish Oaks third Inforapenny. The second dam, Morina (by Lyphard), won over 11f in France and is a half-sister to 10 winners. (Bo Derek's 10). *"She's a funny one, because she looks very precocious, she's strong and taking everything I'm giving her, but I don't think she's got the speed for five furlongs. I think I'll wait for six furlongs and she'll probably get further later on".*

- Won the **G1 Dewhurst Stakes** in a faster time than **Frankel**
- Won the **G2 Coventry Stakes** by 6 lengths
- Won the **G2 Galileo Futurity Stakes** by 3 lengths

NEW

NEW SIRES IN EUROPE IN 2015
(by European 2YO Thoroughbred Rankings)

1	WAR COMMAND	119
-	NO NAY NEVER	119
3	KINGSBARNS	118
4	AUSTRALIA	117
-	Olympic Glory	117
6	Moohaajim	116
-	Xtension	116
8	Gale Force Ten	115
9	Toronado	114
10	Charm Spirit	113
-	Joshua Tree	113
12	Battle of Marengo	111
-	Kingman	111
14	Bungle Inthejungle	110

WAR COMMAND

- By **DANZIG**'s brilliant young sire son **WAR FRONT** (13% SW/Rnrs)
- Out of E.P. Taylor Stakes-Gr.2 winner **WANDERING STAR**
- From the family of leading sire **SILVER HAWK** (10% SW/Rnrs)

COOLMORE

Fee: €15,000
(Stg. £11,250)

ontact: **Coolmore Stud**, Fethard, Clonmel, Co. Tipperary, Ireland. Tel: 353-52-6131298. Fax: 353-52-6131382. **Christy Grassick, David O'Loughlin, Eddie Fitzpatrick, Tim Corballis, Maurice Moloney, Gerry Aherne, Mathieu Legars** or **Jason Walsh. Tom Gaffney, David Magnier, Joe Hernon** or **Cathal Murphy**: 353-25-31966/31689. **Kevin Buckley** (UK Rep.) 44-7827-795156.
E-mail: **sales@coolmore.ie** Web site: **www.coolmore.com** All stallions nominated to EBF.

BET

AND

WATCH
ANYWHERE

LIVE HORSE RACING NOW AVAILABLE ON THE APP

Simply place a bet of £1 or more to watch the live action.

THE LIVING LEGEND RACING PARTNERSHIP

For an inexpensive way to enjoy the benefits of being a racehorse owner, join us in 2015.

Call Steve Taplin on 07754 094204 or e-mail stevetaplin@blueyonder.co.uk

Kickboxer at Ripon, June 2014

SOMETIMES WE ALL NEED A REMINDER

With the Horse Tracker feature on the Racing Post iPad app you can follow, make notes on and receive alerts for horses that catch your eye.

FREE 30-DAY TRIAL. ON THE APP STORE NOW

1284. UNNAMED ★★★
b.f. Kodiac – Good Shot Noreen (Sleeping Indian). February 2. First foal. £12,000Y. Doncaster Premier. F Barberini. Homecroft Wealth Racing. The dam, a fair Irish 7f winner, is a half-sister to several winners including the US Grade 2 winner Prize Giving and to the dam of the dual US Grade 1 winner Alpride. The second dam, Glowing With Pride (by Ile de Bourbon), a 7f and 10.5f winner, was second in the Park Hill Stakes. *"Yes, she's OK and she'll be a 2-y-o. She's round and 'butty', had a little setback otherwise I'd have been more forward with her than I am, but I can see her running in May".*

1285. UNNAMED ★★★
b.f. Lawman – Mamela (GER) (Protektor). April 17. Fourth foal. €25,000Y. Goffs Orby. F Barberini. Sister to the fair 2-y-o 5f winner Boom And Bloom. The dam, winner of a Group 3 1m event in Italy at 2 yrs and a listed event in France over 1m at 3 yrs, s out of My Rita (by Brief Truce). (Bo Derek's 10). *"She's nice, clearly not that precocious but beautifully balanced, a good mover and she goes very well. Developing all the time, she may be marginally more of a 3-y-o type, but a nice filly".*

1286. UNNAMED ★★★
b.f. Lilbourne Lad – Mary Spring Rice (Saffron Walden). March 27. Second foal. 23,000Y. Tattersalls December. Not sold. The dam, a poor 12f placed maiden, is a half-sister to 7 winners including the German 10f Group winners Fight Club and Flambo. The second dam, Flaming Song (by Darshaan), a 2-y-o winner in France, is a half-sister to two other minor winners. *"She's quite forward, could be running in April or May, she's quite wiry and she wants to please you. She's not slow, so there's a chance for her early in the season".*

1287. UNNAMED ★★
ch.f. Excellent Art – Savignano (Polish Precedent). May 13. Eleventh foal. Half-sister to 4 winners including the Group 2 1m Premio Ribot winner Saint Bernard (by Three Valleys), the Italian listed winner Momix (by Selkirk) and the fairly useful 7f (at 2 yrs) and Hong Kong winner Easy Ahead (by Hawk Wing). The dam, a French 3-y-o winner, is a half-sister to 7 winners including the Group 1 Prix de la Foret winner and smart broodmare Field Of Hope. The second dam, Fracci (by Raise A Cup), an Italian listed winner, was Group 3 placed twice. *"A month ago I thought she'd be too backward to push on with, but she's turned the corner and is doing alright. A nice-actioned filly, she's about to do her first proper bit of work".*

1288. UNNAMED ★★
b.f. High Chaparral – Summerhill Parkes (Zafonic). February 7. Sixth foal. 20,000Y. Tattersalls October Book 1. F Barberini. Sister to the fair 10f winner Stampede and half-sister to the fair 7f winner Lucky Meadows (by Noverre), the fair 8.5f and subsequent minor Italian winner Seleet (by Sakhee) and a winner over hurdles by Haafhd. The dam, a useful listed 6f winner, is a half-sister to 7 winners including the 2-y-o 5f and 6f winner Ace Of Parkes, the useful dual 5f winner and Moyglare, Lowther and Queen Mary Stakes placed My Melody Parkes and the useful winner of 17 races over 5f Lucky Parkes. The second dam, Summerhill Spruce (by Windjammer), a fair 3-y-o 6f seller winner, is a half-sister to the German Group 2 winner Jimmy Barnie. (Bo Derek's 10). *"She's one for the second half of the season, especially as she's by High Chaparral. I've had a few by the sire before and they're a bit 'busy' in their brains so you have to keep the lid on them a bit. She has a good action and she's a nice type, but I haven't thought about working her yet".*

JOHN OXX
1289. ALPHONSUS ★★★
b.c. Invincible Spirit – Ela Athena (Ezzoud). March 24. Eighth foal. 175,000Y. Tattersalls October Book 1. BBA (Ire). Half-brother to 3 winners including the useful listed winner of 5 races from 10f to 2m Pallasator (by Motivator) and the fairly useful 2-y-o 1m winner and listed placed Elas Diamond (by Danehill Dancer). The dam, a winner of 3 races including the Group 3 Lancashire Oaks, was placed in seven Group/Grade 1 events and is a half-sister to 5 winners. The second dam, Crodelle (by Formidable), a French 3-y-o 9.5f winner, is a half-sister to 7 winners. *"He's a nice horse out of a good mare and of course Invincible Spirit's generally show something at two. He's growing a bit at the moment so he'll*

take a bit of time, but he's a nice colt and we expect him to run from mid-season onwards. He's a sharp looking Invincible Spirit but the pedigree tells you he's probably going to need seven furlongs".

1290. AULD BRIG ★★★★

b.c. Holy Roman Emperor – Romie's Kastett (Halling). April 4. Second foal. 85,000Y. Tattersalls October Book 1. BBA (Ire). The dam, a quite useful Irish 9f winner, is a sister to the Group 3 Earl Of Sefton Stakes and Group 3 Sovereign Stakes winner and multiple Group 1 placed Norse Dancer and a half-sister to 7 winners. The second dam, River Patrol (by Rousillon), a fairly useful 10.2f winner, is a half-sister to 3 winners including the smart middle-distance stayer Dry Dock and to the dams of the Group/Grade 1 winners Mail The Desert and Good Faith. *"He's quite a bit bigger than a lot by the sire but he's been doing a bit of fast work already and goes nicely. Hopefully he'll be racing in June and he's a nice colt. I trained the dam and she was useful. This colt finds his work quite easy so I'm hopeful he'll win at two".*

1291. CHAMPAGNE TIME ★★★

b.f. Oasis Dream – Roses For The Lady (Sadler's Wells). March 1. The dam, a smart Irish listed 13f winner, was second in the Group 1 Irish Oaks, is a half-sister to 2 winners. The second dam, Head In The Clouds (by Rainbow Quest), won the Group 3 12f Princess Royal Stakes and is a sister to the high-class St Leger, Chester Vase and Jockey Club Stakes winner Millenary and a half-sister to the very smart 1m (at 2 yrs) and 10f winner and Derby third Let The Lion Roar. *"There's a bit of a clash of distances in the pedigree because on the one hand you have Oasis Dream which suggests speed and on the other a Sadler's Wells mare who won over a mile and five. Having said that, she looks sharpish and even though the dam's side is going to have an effect on her precocity she's got a bit of the Oasis Dream sharpness about her too. She's quite sharp, clever and a lovely mover. A nice filly, I think she'll be out in mid-season".*

1292. CORSTORPHINE ★★★

b.c. Sir Percy – Misplace (Green Desert). February 26. Ninth foal. €65,000Y. Goffs Orby.

John Oxx. Brother to the fair dual 12f winner Miss Blakeney and half-brother to 3 winners including the French 1m to 10f winner of 6 races and Group 3 third Mayweather (by Nayef) and the French 1m winner of 3 races (including at 2 yrs) Mistaken Identity (by Vettori). The dam won once at 3 yrs in France and is a half-sister to 6 winners including the French Group 3 winner Not Just Swing and to the unraced dam of the Group 1 1m Falmouth Stakes winner Nahoodh. The second dam, Misbegotten (by Baillamont), a French listed 1m winner and second in the Group 2 Prix de l'Opera, is a half-sister to 4 winners. *"A very sharp, good-looking colt, he's done a couple of bits of work and hopefully he'll be out in June. From what I'm told he looks different to some other members of the family who needed a bit of a trip".*

1293. GLAMOUR BOY ★★★

b.c. Sea The Stars – Angel Of The Gwaun (Sadler's Wells). January 28. Half-brother to the 7f (at 2 yrs) and Group 3 10f Blue Wind Stakes winner Beauty O'Gwaun (by Rainbow Quest), to the Japanese Grade 3 2m winner Cosmo Meadow, the fairly useful 2-y-o 7f winner Angelonmyshoulder, the quite useful 12f winner Whitey O'Gwaun (by Dalakhani) and the fair Irish 12f winner Missy O'Gwaun (all by King's Best). The dam is an unraced sister to 3 winners including the Derby third Let The Lion Roar and a half-sister to the St Leger winner Millenary and the Group 3 Princess Royal Stakes winner Head In The Clouds. The second dam, Ballerina (by Dancing Brave), a quite useful 2-y-o 7f winner, is a half-sister to the Group 3 12f Princess Royal Stakes winner Dancing Bloom and the good French 2-y-o 5f winner and 1,000 Guineas third River Dancer (herself dam of the Champion Stakes winner Spectrum). *"A very nice colt, obviously he'll be for later in the year, but he's a very good-looking, correct and lovely moving colt. He has a good, sensible temperament like all of them by Sea The Stars and he's a very nice horse for the autumn".*

1294. LEAVING FOR GOOD ★★

b.f. Pivotal – Leavingonajetplane (Danehill). March 10. Third foal. Half-brother to Ashridge Lad (by Invincible Spirit), unplaced in two starts at 2 yrs in 2014 and to Jetonamand (by

Manduro), a minor winner at 2 and 3 yrs in Italy. The dam, placed over 7f at 2 yrs from two starts, is a half-sister to 2 minor winners in France and Japan. The second dam, the Irish listed winner Peach Out Of Reach, is a sister to the listed 10f Trigo Stakes winner and Group 3 12f Princess Royal Stakes second Briolette and a half-sister to 6 winners including the multiple Group 1 winner Pilsudski and the champion Japanese filly Fine Motion. *"A very big filly, she's a nice mover and has a lovely, free action. But like a lot of Pivotal's she'll take time".*

1295. POCKET OF STARS ★★★
b.f. Sea The Stars – Hidden Silver (Anabaa). March 14. Seventh foal. Half-sister to the Group 1 French 2,000 Guineas winner Silver Frost, to the French 1m to 10f winner Blazon (both by Verglas), the French listed 13f winner Spiritjim (by Galileo) and the French 12f winner Rock Climber (by Poliglote). The dam won once at 3 yrs in France and is a half-sister to 8 winners including the French Group 3 winners Homeland and High Rock. The second dam, Hint Of Silver (by Alysheba), won once at 2 yrs in France and is a sister to one listed winner and a half-sister to another. *"A fine, big filly, he's not an early one and she'll take a bit of time, but she has a lovely temperament and is a good mover. One of her half-brothers Silver Frost won a Group One and another one, Spiritjim, also won a Group One only to be disqualified. So this filly is very well-related and she'll be a very nice filly come the autumn".*

1296. SEA OF MYSTERY ★★★
b.c. Sea The Stars – Sassenach (Night Shift). April 30. Eleventh foal. Half-brother to the US Grade 3 and Irish listed winner Dress Rehearsal , the fair 1m winner Newton's Night (both by Galileo), the Irish listed 7f winner Fairy Of The Night, to the minor Irish 10f winner Night Fairy (both by Danehill) and the useful dual 1m winner Gold Sovereign (by King's Best). The dam, a winner over 13f at 4 yrs in Ireland, is a half-sister to 5 winners including the Group 3 2m 2f Doncaster Cup winner Far Cry. The second dam, Darabaka (by Doyoun), is an unraced half-sister to 5 stakes winners including the Group 3 Prix Minerve winner Daralinsha. *"A lovely colt and a beautiful mover, he'll take a little bit of time but he's*

likeable and will be out in the second half of the year".*

1297. SEA OF WONDERS ★★★
b.f. Fastnet Rock – Mer De Corail (Sadler's Wells). May 1. Sixth foal. €250,000Y. Arqana Deauville August. Mandore International. Half-sister to the useful 1m, 9f and listed 10f winner of 5 races Alsace Lorraine (by Giant's Causeway), to the quite useful 2-y-o 1m winner Hot Bed (by Dashing Blade) and the minor French triple 10f winner Travertine. The dam, winner of the listed 10f Prix d'Automne, is a sister to the winner and listed-placed Maximum Security. The second dam, Miss Tahiti (by Tirol), won the Group 1 1m Prix Marcel Boussac at 2 yrs and was placed in the Prix de Diane, the Prix Vermeille and the Prix Saint-Alary. *"She's was a May foal and Fastnet Rock's are not precocious, contrary to what people were expecting, but she is a nice looking filly for the autumn".*

1298. SEA THE SUN ★★
ch.f. Sea The Stars – Sanwa (Monsun). April 14. Sister to the Group 1 German Derby winner Sea The Moon and half-sister to the French listed-placed dual 1m winner Sansiwa (by Dansili). The dam is an unraced sister to the German Group 1 winners Samum, Schiaparelli and Salve Regina and a half-sister to 6 winners. The second dam, Sacarina (by Old Vic), is an unraced half-sister to 6 winners. *"A full sister to last year's German Derby winner, she's backward and needs to mature a bit yet. She's a beautiful mover and I'll be aiming her at her 3-y-o career".*

1299. SKY KINGDOM ★★★
b.c. Montjeu – We Can Say It Now (Starcraft). February 3. The dam, a Group 1 1m winner in New Zealand, is out of We Can't Say That (by Generous). *"He's a beautiful colt. A terrific mover with a very good temperament and he'll be a nice horse for the autumn. A striking sort of horse".*

1300. STAR GLITTER ★★★
ch.c. Sea The Stars – Gadalka (Giant's Causeway). February 6. Third foal. €150,000Y. Arqana Deauville August. Mandore International. The dam is a placed half-sister to 4 winners including the smart UAE listed

7f winner and Group 2 placed Ibn Battuta. The second dam, Sulk (by Selkirk), winner of the Group 1 1m Prix Marcel Boussac and second in the Group 1 10f Nassau Stakes, is a half-sister to 4 winners including the Group 1 Hong Kong Cup and Group 2 Beresford Stakes winner Eagle Mountain. *"A very nice colt, he's a beautiful mover and is quite sharp-looking actually. He was trying to do things too early, so with respect to the sire we didn't press on, but he's a nice colt and a quick learner, so I think he'll show some precocity at two".*

1301. STAR OF KINGS ★★★★
b.f. Sea The Stars – Kocooning (King's Best). January 31. Half-sister to the fairly useful dual 6f winner Golden Steps (by Footstepsinthesand). The dam, a French 5f winner, is a half-sister to numerous winners including the Group 2 Prix du Gros-Chene winner Beauty Is Truth. The second dam, Zelding (by Warning), a Group 3 5f Prix du Bois and listed 1m winner, is a half-sister to 6 winners including Zipping (Group 2 5.5f Prix Robert Papin) and Nipping (Group 3 5f Prix du Petit Couvert). *"A particularly nice filly, she'll make a 2-y-o and she comes from quite a fast family. A lovely looker, she's lengthy, a beautiful mover and a perfect representative of the sire's stock. She looks quite precocious, quite mature and will definitely be out in June all being well".*

1302. STAR WAVES ★★
br.f. Sea The Stars – Photophore (Clodovil). April 19. Fourth foal. €300,000Y. Goffs Orby. Sunderland Holding Inc. Half-sister to the 2-y-o 5f and listed 6f winner City Image (by Elusive City) and to the fairly useful Irish 6f (at 2 yrs) and 8.5f winner Tahaany (by Raven's Pass). The dam, a French 10f winner, is a half-sister to 5 winners including the Group 1 French 1,000 Guineas winner Elusive Wave. The second dam, Multicolour Wave (by Rainbow Quest), is a placed half-sister to 4 winners. *"She's grown a lot since we bought her, so that's going to slow things down. We'll take our time and she'll be better next year".*

1303. UNNAMED ★★★
b.c. Sir Percy – Conciliatory (Medicean). February 2. First foal. €44,000Y. Tattersalls Ireland September. John Oxx. The dam, a quite useful 1m winner of 3 races, is a half-sister to a minor winner. The second dam, Condoleezza (by Cozzene), was a fair 14f winner. *"A particularly nice looking colt, we bought him at Fairyhouse and he's a well-balanced horse and a good mover. He's started doing some fast work and I expect him to run well and do well at two".*

1304. UNNAMED ★★
gr.c. Dalakhani – Barring Order (Barathea). March 9. Seventh foal. Brother to the useful 10f and 11f winner and multiple listed-placed Barring Decree and half-brother to the fair Irish 2-y-o 1m winner and subsequent US Grade 3 second Bogie (by Pivotal). The dam, a listed 7f Loughbrown Stakes winner, is a half-sister to 4 winners including the very smart 2-y-o Group 1 7f National Stakes winner Beckett. The second dam, Groom Order (by Groom Dancer), is an unraced half-sister to 3 minor winners. *"A nice colt, a bit backward but a good mover. An autumn type 2-y-o, but he's had no problems and he's done plenty of cantering so far. I didn't have him too early in the winter but he's making up for lost time".*

1305. UNNAMED ★★★
b.f. Acclamation – Helen Of Sparta (Barathea). February 5. Second foal. Half-sister to the fair 2014 6f and 7f placed Looper (by Lope De Vega). The dam is an unplaced sister to 2 winners including the useful listed 1m winner Hymn Of Love and a half-sister to 4 winners. The second dam, Perils Of Joy (by Rainbow Quest), a 3-y-o 1m winner in Ireland, is a half-sister to 5 winners including the Italian Group 3 winner Sweetened Offer. *"A sharp little filly, she's not too big and might have a run towards the end of May. She's 'on the ball' and a typically sharp Acclamation that could start at six furlongs"*

HUGO PALMER
1306. ARCHITECTURE (IRE) ★★★
b.f. Zoffany – Brigayev (Fasliyev). February 23. Second foal. £26,000Y. Doncaster Premier. Amanda Skiffington. Half-sister to the Italian 3-y-o winner of 3 races Norbanus (by Footstepsinthesand). The dam, placed at 2 yrs in Italy, is a half-sister to 3 winners. The second dam, Brighella (by Sadler's Wells), placed at 3 yrs in France, is a half-sister to 6 winners. (Mr C M Humber). *"Probably the best moving*

of my 2-y-o fillies, she's athletic, goes along extremely nicely and I like her a lot. She'll be ready from the middle of May onwards and is probably a six furlong type to begin with".

1306. EDIYE ★★★★

b.f. Fast Company – Sweet Home Alabama (Desert Prince). March 30. Seventh foal. £29,000Y. Doncaster Premier. Rob Speers. Half-sister to the 2014 6f placed 2-y-o Rahmah (by Vale Of York) and to 3 winners including the useful 2-y-o 1m winner and dual Group 3 third Havana Beat (by Teofilo) and the modest 1m and hurdles winner King's Realm (by King's Best). The dam, placed fourth over 7f and 1m, is a half-sister to the Group 1 1m Sussex Stakes winner Proclamation and to the German dual listed winner No Refuge. The second dam, Shamarra (by Zayyani), is an unraced half-sister to the smart middle-distance performer Shantaroun and to the dams of the Group winners Sardaniya and Shaiybara. (Mr V I Araci). "I think she's quite forward and I think Fast Company is an underrated sire. Quite speedy, she's not very big and looks like a real 2-y-o so it wouldn't surprise me to see her start at five furlongs, but she'll certainly run over six as well. I see her as being one of the more forward ones".

1307. FIFTYSHADESOFPINK (IRE) ★★

b.f. Pour Moi – Maakrah (Dubai Destination). March 18. Second foal. 68,000Y. Tattersalls October Book 2. Not sold. Half-sister to the fair 7f and 1m winner Matravers (by Oasis Dream). The dam is an unraced sister to 2 winners including the Group 3 Winter Derby winner and Grade 1 Breeders Cup Juvenile third Farraaj and a half-sister to 9 winners including the triple Group 2 winner and sire Iffraaj and the useful 2-y-o Group 3 7f Prix du Calvados winner Kareymah. The second dam, Pastorale (by Nureyev), a fairly useful 3-y-o 7f winner, is a half-sister to 8 winners including the Group 1 Lockinge Stakes winner and high-class sire Cape Cross. (Mrs M Bryce). "Just as her name suggests she's all sorts of pinky colours! Her riders love her but she's just a frame at present and if she's nice you'd hope she'd be an Oaks filly rather than a 2-y-o. A filly with a lovely pedigree, I think she's really nice and I guess she'll be starting off in September".

1308. FULL EXTENSION (IRE) ★★

br.c. Big Bad Bob – Fire Up (Motivator). March 19. Second foal. €87,000Y. Goffs Orby. Amanda Skiffington. Half-brother to the 2014 Irish 1m placed 2-y-o B Cosmos (by Avonbridge). The dam, placed at 3 yrs in France, is a half-sister to 3 winners including the Group 1 Tattersalls Gold Cup, Prince Of Wales's Stakes and Eclipse Stakes winner Al Kazeem. The second dam, Kazeem (by Darshaan), is an unplaced sister to the winner and subsequent US Grade 2 third Treasurer and a half-sister to 6 minor winners. (Westward Bloodstock). "One of my more experienced lads says he wouldn't swap him for anything else in the yard. Quite a light-framed horse, he has a real air of quality about him and he'll be an autumn type 2-y-o. He has a Derby entry, he's found his work easy from the word go and he's a very nice, well-balanced horse".

1309. GASPIRALI ★★★★

b.c. Oasis Dream – Lion Forest (Forestry). March 5. Third foal. The dam is an unraced sister to the US Grade 1 Hollywood Starlet Stakes winner Diplomat Lady and a half-sister to 9 winners including the US Grade 2 Comely Stakes winner Dream Play. The second dam, Playcaller (by Saratoga Six), a winner of 3 stakes races at 2 and 3 yrs in the USA, is a half-sister to 8 winners. (Mr V I Araci). "The first of two horses I have here that Mr Araci has bred. He's a strong, muscular colt that finds his work easy and he's certainly a nice colt. Just how good, time will tell. He's a bit more robust looking than the Oasis Dream 3-y-o we have, Aktabantay, and he has a similar stride. Hopefully the owner has bred a really good one here and all being well he should be out in May".

1310. GIFTED MASTER (IRE) ★★★★

b.c. Kodiac – Shobobb (Shamardal). April 3. Second foal. 75,000Y. Tattersalls October Book 1. Rabbah Bloodstock. Half-brother to the unplaced 2014 2-y-o Mary Ann Blugg (by Bushranger). The dam is an unraced half-sister to 5 winners including Alzerra (Group 3 Cornwallis Stakes). The second dam, Belle Argentine (by Fijar Tango), a listed winner in France and third in the French 1,000 Guineas, is a half-sister to one winner. (Dr A Ridha). "I *think he might be very smart. He's one of those horses who, from the word go, has given the impression he's done it all before. He'll start in fast work very soon and I'll be disappointed if he's not better than average".* Gifted Master won on his debut in a Newmarket maiden on the 15th April.

1311. GIMLET ★★★

b.c. Poet's Voice – Poppo's Song (Polish Navy). March 31. Sixth foal. 45,000Y. Tattersalls October Book 2. Sackville/Donald. Half-brother to the French 7.5f (at 2 yrs) to 9.5f winner of 3 races and listed-placed Nabbaash (by Aqlaam), to the moderate 5f winner Talqaa (by Exceed And Excel), the fair 2m 1f winner Petaluma (by Teofilo) and the Italian winner of 5 races at 3 and 4 yrs Pretium Sceleris (by Johannesburg). The dam, a Canadian listed stakes winner of 2 races at 3 and 4 yrs, is a half-sister to 2 winners. The second dam, Bridled Song (by Seattle Slew), is a placed half-sister to 4 winners. (De La Warr). *"A mid-summer type 2-y-o, I loved him at the sales and I still do. A very attractive, well-balanced colt, he hasn't done as much as some of the others but he'll make a 2-y-o alright".*

1312. HARRY CHAMPION ★★★

b.c. Cockney Rebel – Nine Red (Royal Applause). April 25. Fourth living foal. The dam, a moderate 7f placed maiden, is a half-sister to the smart listed 6f winner and Group 3 placed Snow Kid and to the useful 2-y-o 5f winner and Group 2 6f Richmond Stakes second Sarson. The second dam, Sarcita (by Primo Dominie), a very useful sprint winner of 6 races including the Portland Handicap, is a half-sister to 6 winners including the Group 2 5f Flying Childers Stakes winner Mrs P. (R C Tooth). *"A strong, muscular, forward colt, he's nearly ready for working and he finds everything very easy. I think he'll be one for six furlongs but he may even be one for five. He does everything right and I think he'll be a really nice, first half of the season horse. I didn't like him initially but at the moment I like everything I see about him".*

1313. HAWKSMOOR (IRE) ★★★★ ♠

b.f. Azamour – Bridal Dance (Danehill Dancer). March 14. Third foal. €80,000Y. Tattersalls Ireland September. Amanda Skiffington.

The dam is an unplaced half-sister to 5 winners including the listed 7f King Charles II Stakes and subsequent US Grade 3 winner Millennium Dragon. The second dam, Feather Bride (by Groom Dancer), a minor 10.5f winner at 3 yrs in France, is a half-sister to 5 winners. (Mr C M Humber). *"She's something of a standout and wasn't cheap for her sire or pedigree. She's strong and athletic, she moves well and nothing is difficult for her. She's growing at the moment and it'll be sometime before we start to press any buttons but it looks like she's very nice".*

1314. INDIA ★★

ch.f. Paco Boy – Friendlier (Zafonic). March 24. Eighth foal. Half-sister to the fairly useful 2-y-o 1m winner and 3-y-o listed 10f placed Madame Defarge (by Motivator), to the fairly useful 7f (at 2 yrs) and 1m winner Foolin Myself (by Montjeu), the fairly useful 7f (at 2 yrs) and 1m winner Unex El Greco, the quite useful 2-y-o 7f winner Gender Agenda (both by Holy Roman Emperor) and the fair 2-y-o 1m and subsequent UAE 7f winner Comradeship (by Dubawi). The dam is an unraced half-sister to User Friendly, winner of the Oaks, the St Leger, the Irish Oaks and the Yorkshire Oaks. The second dam, Rostova (by Blakeney), a fairly useful winner of 4 races from 12f to 14f, is a half-sister to 7 winners. (W J & T C O Gredley). *"She hasn't arrived here yet but the reports from her pre-training yard are excellent".*

1315. MAGICAL PATH (IRE) ★★★★ ♠

gr.f. Zebedee – Road To Reality (Indian Danehill). April 26. Third foal. €20,000Y. Tattersalls Ireland September. Amanda Skiffington. Brother to the modest 2014 1m placed 2-y-o Joshua Potman. The dam is an unraced half-sister to 2 winners. The second dam, Home To Reality (by Imperial Frontier), is an unraced half-sister to one winner. (Anglia Bloodstock Syndicate VI). *"I see her as a June type 2-y-o. She's grown quite a lot and is staggeringly athletic, really strong and I like everything I've seen of her".*

1316. NIDNOD ★★★

b.f. Myboycharlie – Littlemisstutti (Noverre). February 4. Second foal. 30,000Y. Tattersalls October Book 3. Amanda Skiffington. The dam is an unraced half-sister to 6 winners including the 2-y-o Group 3 Sirenia Stakes winner and Group 1 placed Dhanyata. The second dam, Preponderance (by Cyrano de Bergerac), a quite useful 2-y-o dual 5f winner, is a half-sister to 6 winners. (Anglia Bloodstock Syndicate VI). *"An early type 2-y-o. She cost a bit more than I wanted to spend, but I've been second in two of the Sales races and I want a winner! I love her, she's really coping with her work well and if I've got one or two I can race in April she's one of them".*

1317. PARIS MAGIC ★★★
b.c. Champs Elysees – Belgooree (Haafhd). February 15. Second foal. 20,000Y. Tattersalls October Book 2. Rabbah Bloodstock. The dam is an unplaced half-sister to 2 minor winners. The second dam, Ziggy Zaggy (by Diktat), is an unraced half-sister to 7 winners to the Group 1 Premio Roma winner Imperial Dancer. (Mr A Al Mansoori). *"He should be racing in the second half of the season and he finds his work so easy that I'd be disappointed if he didn't win races this year".*

1318. PASS THE MOON (IRE) ★★★★
ch.f. Raven's Pass – Dubai Moon (Malibu Moon). March 12. First foal. Tattersalls October Book 2. C McCormack. The dam, third over 7f on her only 2-y-o start, is a sister to the US Grade 1 CCA Oaks winner Funny Moon and a half-sister to 5 winners including the US stakes winner Throng. The second dam, Fun Crowd (by Easy Goer), is an unraced half-sister to 10 winners including the US triple Grade 1 winner Vanlandingham. (S Manana). *"A real 2-y-o type. I've got three by this sire and they're all completely different to each other. This filly is ready for fast work, she has a fabulous stride, a real fast ground action and she looks like a 2-y-o".*

1319. SHERIFF (IRE) ★★
b.c. Lawman – Dievotchkina (Bluebird). April 14. Tenth foal. 65,000Y. Tattersalls October Book 2. W J Gredley. Half-brother to the fairly useful 1m (at 2 yrs) and 10f winner Stormardal (by Shamardal), to the useful triple 6f (at 2 yrs) and 7f winner of 5 races Khor Dubai (by Kheleyf) and a 2-y-o winner in Greece by Choisir. The dam won twice at 3 yrs in France and is a half-sister to 9 winners including the

French Group winners Esoterique, Russian Cross, Russian Hope and Archange D'or. The second dam, Dievotchka (by Dancing Brave), is an unraced half-sister to 7 winners. (W J & T C O Gredley). *"Very much one for the back-end of the season and for next year. He's a big, strong horse who strikes me as wanting at least a mile but he's a very good mover and an attractive horse".*

1320. THE PARIS SHRUG ★★
b.f. Manduro – Miss Brown To You (Fasliyev). March 2. Sister to the modest 9f winner Empowermentofwomen and half-sister to the dual listed 14f winner Big Orange (by Duke Of Marmalade). The dam, a fair 1m winner, is a half-sister to numerous winners including the dual Group 3 5f winner Almaty and the very useful triple 1m and subsequent Hong Kong Group 1 winner Race (renamed Military Attack). The second dam, Almaaseh (by Dancing Brave), placed once over 6f at 3 yrs, is a half-sister to 8 winners including the 2,000 Guineas and Champion Stakes winner Haafhd. (W J & T C O Gredley). *"More of a 3-y-o type than a 2-y-o, but she'll run this year alright. She hasn't been here that long because she was difficult to break, probably due to the bad temperament of the stallion coming out. Quite a strong character but a lovely mover and she finds her work easy. So if we can get her right I'd say there's definitely something there".*

1321. THEY SEEK HIM HERE ★★★
b.br.c. Elusive Pimpernel – Spiritville (Invincible Spirit). March 20. Fourth foal. €50,000Y. Tattersalls Ireland September. Amanda Skiffington. Half-brother to the fair 12f winner Officer Drivel (by Captain Rio). The dam, a moderate 6f (at 2 yrs) and 6.5f placed maiden, is a half-sister to 4 minor winners. The second dam, Woodville (by Deploy), is an unraced half-sister to 3 winners. (MPH Racing). *"He's the image of his Dad, an extraordinarily good-looking horse, and I wasn't leaving Tattersalls Ireland without him. I love him just as much now, he's a good mover with quite a knee action and I would hope he'll be ready for a seven furlong maiden in July".*

1322. ZODIAKOS (IRE) ★★★
b.c. Kodiac – Zonic (Zafonic). February 9. Fifth foal. 15,000Y. Tattersalls October Book 2.

Sackville/Donald. Half-brother to the fair 2-y-o 5f winner Tarita (by Bahamian Bounty) and to a minor winner in Hong Kong by Marju. The dam, a modest 6f placed 2-y-o, is half-sister to 3 winners including the dam of the Group 2 July Stakes winner Nevisian Lad. The second dam, Ferber's Follies (by Saratoga Six), a winning 2-y-o sprinter, was third in the Grade 2 6f Adirondack Stakes and is a half-sister to 11 winners including the US 2-y-o Grade 2 6f winner Blue Jean Baby. (Seventh Lap Racing). *"Not a very typical Kodiac, he's a big horse and much more like the damsire Zafonic. But he's quite mature and I suggest he'll be starting over six furlongs. I'd be disappointed if he didn't win races this year".*

1323. UNNAMED ★★
b.c. Dutch Art – Bay Of Pearls (Rock Of Gibraltar). March 25. First foal. 40,000Y. Tattersalls October Book 2. BBA (Ire). The dam, unplaced in one start, is half-sister to 6 winners including the French listed winner Danehill's Pearl. The second dam, Mother Of Pearl (by Sadler's Wells), winner of both her starts at 2 yrs including the Group 3 1m Prix Saint-Roman, was second in the Group 3 Musidora Stakes and is a closely related to the high-class colt Turtle Island, winner of the Group 1 6f Phoenix Stakes and the Irish 2,000 Guineas. *"A big, tall colt that moves nicely and will be one for the second half of the season".*

1324. UNNAMED ★★★ ♠
b.f. Mastercraftsman – Dama'a (Green Desert). February 20. Sixth foal. 35,000Y. Tattersalls October Book 2. Not sold. Sister to the fair 2014 Irish 7f fourth placed 2-y-o Pantomime and half-sister to the quite useful 2-y-o 6f and 7f winner Art Official (by Excellent Art) and the quite useful 2-y-o 7f winner Darkening (by Shamardal). The dam, a quite useful 6f winner at 3 yrs, is a half-sister to 2 winners including the Group 2 placed Himalya. The second dam, Lady Miletrian (by Barathea), a useful 1m winner and second in the listed Princess Elizabeth Stakes, is a sister to the listed winning 2-y-o Duty Paid and a half-sister to 3 winners. *"She came in quite late so although she's not backward she's quite a bit behind some of the others. A strong, athletic, good-moving filly, she's just cantering at the moment. I would have thought she'd be a July*

type 2-y-o and as she's a good size she'll have a real 3-y-o career ahead of her as well".

1325. UNNAMED ★★★★★
b.c. Lope De Vega – Danielli (Danehill). February 18. Sixth foal. 150,000Y. Tattersalls October Book 1. Rob Speers. Brother to the 2014 2-y-o 6f winner (from two starts) Very Special (by Lope De Vega) and half-brother to 3 winners including the 2-y-o Group 1 6f Cheveley Park Stakes and Grade 1 Breeders Cup Juvenile Fillies Turf winner Chriselliam (by Iffraaj) and the fair 2-y-o 7f winner and subsequent US Grade 3 9f third Janicellaine (by Beat Hollow). The dam, placed at up to 13f in Ireland, is a half-sister to 8 winners including Priory Belle (Group 1 7f Moyglare Stud Stakes), Eva's Request (Group 3 C L Weld Park Stakes) and Wild Bluebell (Group 3 7f Concorde Stakes). The second dam, Ingabelle (by Taufan), won the Group 3 Phoenix Sprint Stakes. (Mr V I Araci). *"I've loved this horse ever since I first saw him. He's got an enormous head, which is a trait of the stallion I think, and he finds his work extraordinarily easy despite the fact he's the biggest of my 2-y-o's. So far he seems to be very clean-limbed and to be coping very well. He's bulking out and getting stronger all the time and is definitely a 2-y-o for the second half of the year. We're a long way off knowing how good he is, but if you told me he'll be the champion 2-y-o I wouldn't argue with you. Everything he's shown me indicates he's a real star horse".*

1326. UNNAMED ★★
b.c. Teofilo – Eclaircie (Thunder Gulch). April 11. Fourth foal. Half-brother to the useful 2-y-o 6f winner Ginger Goose (by Royal Applause). The dam, a minor French 3-y-o 10f winner, is a half-sister to 5 winners including the 2-y-o Group 1 Racing Post Trophy third Skanky Biscuit. The second dam, Blushing Gleam (by Caerleon), won the Group 3 Prix du Calvados and the listed Prix de Saint-Cyr and is a half-sister to 8 winners including Gold Away (four Group wins in France) and the Group 3 winner Danzigaway (herself dam of the US Grade 2 winner Silent Name). (Sheikh J D Al Maktoum). *"He's a very nice home-bred of Sheikh Juma's and I believe they were going to give up on the mare until they saw how attractive this one is. He's a long way from doing anything more*

than cantering because he's a big horse, but he has a lovely fast ground action and I like what I've seen so far".

1327. UNNAMED ★★★

br.f. Dark Angel – Embassy Pearl (Invincible Spirit). March 30. Second foal. 20,000Y. Tattersalls October Book 3. Amanda Skiffington. Half-sister to the unplaced 2014 2-y-o Mr Christopher (by Bahamian Bounty). The dam, a fair 7f winner, is a half-sister to one winner. The second dam, Embassy Belle (by Marju), a fair Irish 7f and 1m winner of 3 races at 4 yrs, was Grade 2 placed in the USA and is a half-sister to 6 winners. *"If Nidnod doesn't win the Sales race this one will! She's virtually got no page but the dam, after winning her first race by eight lengths, was retired after her second race. After work on Warren Hill this morning the rider of this filly said it was like the hill wasn't there, and she's been like that from the word go. She's quite a good size, so she'll have a 3-y-o career as well. Both her sire and damsire have reputations for breeding horses that can be tricky and although this filly is very willing in her work she'd kick you as soon as look at you. I quite like that in a filly though. She's very attractive and I'm very pleased with her".* **TRAINERS' BARGAIN BUY**

1328. UNNAMED ★★★★

b.f. Elusive Quality – Fashion Insider (Indian Charlie). January 23. First foal. $150,000Y. Keeneland September. Blandford Bloodstock. The dam, placed over 1m at 2 yrs from two starts here, won minor races at 3 and 4 yrs in the USA and is a half-sister to 5 winners including the US Grade 2 Amsterdam Stakes winner Bwana Charlie, the US Grade 2 Super Derby winner My Pal Charlie (both by Indian Charlie), the US Grade 3 winner Bwana Bull (by Holy Bull) and the US stakes-placed winner Ten Halos (by Marquetry). The second dam, Shahalo (by Halo), was unplaced in 2 starts. (Sheikh Juma Dalmook Al Maktoum). *"She'll be a 2-y-o. She's a muscular, good-moving filly and her riders all say she's nice. I don't think she's going to be an Ascot type, but it wouldn't surprise me if she was ticking all the right boxes from July onwards. I think she's lovely and she appears to go very well".*

1329. UNNAMED ★★

ch.f. Mount Nelson – Fidelio's Miracle (Mountain Cat). May 13. Eighth foal. €40,000Y. Goffs Orby. Amanda Skiffington. Sister to the useful listed 6f winner of 4 races Ninjago and half-sister to the quite useful 6f winner Florestans Match (by Medicean). The dam won 3 races from 7f to 10f including a French listed event, was second in the Group 3 Prix de la Grotte and is a half-sister to 3 winners. The second dam, Flurry (by Groom Dancer), a winner in France and the USA and listed-placed twice, is a half-sister to 6 winners and to the dams of the Group/Grade 1 winners Myboycharlie and Snowland. *"This filly is getting stronger and stronger. She finds her work easy but she was a May foal so I'd like to think she'll make an August/September 2-y-o with a lovely 3-y-o career ahead of her. Very athletic, she moves well and carries quite a lot of natural muscle about her which I always think is attractive in a filly because they look naturally strong".*

1330. UNNAMED ★★

ch.c. Paco Boy – Galicuix (Galileo). January 31. First foal. €33,000Y. Tattersalls Ireland September. Amanda Skiffington. The dam ran twice unplaced and is a half-sister to one winner. The second dam, Clizia (by Machiavellian), is an unraced half-sister to 3 winners including the multiple listed winner and Group 2 placed Mont Rocher. *"I love him, to look at he's probably more like Galileo than Paco Boy because he's finer than most Paco Boy's – they tend to be muscular. I think he'll be a lovely 2-y-o in the second half of the season and a real 3-y-o as well. It's a young family because this is a first foal and the dam was as well.*

1331. UNNAMED ★★

ch.c. Pivotal – Invitee (Medicean). March 11. Second foal. €65,000Y. Arqana Deauville August. Flemington Bloodstock. The dam, placed fourth three times over 10f and 12f, is a half-sister to 11 winners including the Group 2 6.5f Criterium des 2 Ans and Group 2 5f Prix du Gros-Chene winner and sire Titus Livius and the Group 2 German 1,000 Guineas winner Briseida. The second dam, Party Doll (by Be My Guest), a very useful winner of 4 races in France including 3 listed events from 5f to 1m, was Group 3 placed twice and is a half-sister to 10 winners. (Flemington Bloodstock Partnership 2). *"He's a colt that finds everything easy. He won't be early but he's very strong, growing and changing all the time, but doing everything right".*

1332. UNNAMED ★★

ch.c. Mastercraftsman – Jacquelin Jag (Fayruz). April 26. Second foal. 15,000Y. Tattersalls December. BBA (Ire). Half-brother to the fair 2014 2-y-o 6f winner Jaganory (by Dylan Thomas). The dam is an unraced sister to the very smart sprinter and Group 1 Golden Jubilee Stakes winner Fayr Jag and a half-sister to 2 winners. The second dam, Lominda (by Lomitas), a quite useful 2-y-o 6f winner, is a half-sister to 8 winners. (Decadent Racing). *"He's just having a little break at the moment. I've seen enough to know that I like him very much but he's one for the autumn".*

1333. UNNAMED ★★★

b.f. Fastnet Rock – Jewel In The Sand (Bluebird). February 20. Fifth foal. 70,000Y. Tattersalls October Book 2. Hugo Palmer. Closely related to the fair 2-y-o 5f winner Dansili Dual (by Dansili) and half-sister to the quite useful 10f winner Falkirk and the fair 2-y-o 5f winner The Rising (by Pivotal). The dam, a winner of 4 races including the Group 2 6f Cherry Hinton Stakes and the Albany Stakes, is a half-sister to 4 winners including the German 3-y-o listed 6f winner Davignon. The second dam, Dancing Drop (by Green Desert), a useful dual 2-y-o 6f winner, was listed-placed and is a half-sister to 9 winners. (Mr M V Magnier & Partners/T Hyde). *"I don't think anyone in the country has worked out the Fastnet Rock's yet, but I'm still in the camp that believes he's too good a sire to fail. I think they need to be bred to speed and this filly is a case in point. She's on the small side but won't be very early, she's muscular and strong and goes very well. Hopefully she'll be winning by the end of June".*

1334. UNNAMED ★★

b.c. Raven's Pass – Lady Elgar (Sadler's Wells). March 16. Twelfth foal. €110,000Y. Arqana Deauville August. RCB Speers. Half-brother to the US Grade 1 12f Sword Dancer Handicap

and Grade 1 Turf Classic winner Grand Couturier (by Grand Lodge), to the listed 12f winner Alainmaar (by Johar), the listed 10f winner Yaqeen (by Green Desert), the useful triple 1m winner Ascription (by Dansili) and the quite useful 10f winner Sir Edward Elgar (by King's Best). The dam, unplaced in one start, is a sister to the Sha Tin Trophy winner and Irish Derby third Desert Fox and a half-sister to the US Grade 3 winners Poolesta and Home Of The Free. The second dam, Radiant (by Foolish Pleasure), won at 3 yrs and is a half-sister to the multiple German Group 1 winner Gold And Ivory. (Mr V I Araci). *"I think he may run at two, but he's no 2-y-o. A very attractive colt, his half-brother Ascription is with us and he's not quite as solid as that horse, but he goes nicely and is a back-end 2-y-o".*

1335. UNNAMED ★★★★

ch.c. Arcano – Manuelita Rose (Desert Style). January 22. First foal. 37,000Y. Tattersalls October Book 2. A C Elliott. The dam is an unraced half-sister to 5 winners including the Irish listed winner and dual Group 3 third Rose Hip. The second dam, Rose Tint (by Salse), is an unplaced half-sister to 8 winners. (M P H Racing). *"He's very mature, very forward and with a fast ground action. A real 2-y-o, but big enough to go on at 3, he's definitely one for the first half of this season. He has a cracking attitude and I'm sure he'll be winning races, certainly over six furlongs, and he might just win a maiden over five".*

1336. UNNAMED ★★

b.f. Cape Blanco – Moon Giant (Giant's Causeway). January 5. First foal. €150,000Y. Arqana Deauville August. RCB Speers. The dam is an unraced half-sister to 2 winners including the Group 3 Dee Stakes winner and Derby third Astrology. The second dam, Ask For The Moon (by Dr Fong), won the Group 1 Prix de Saint-Alary and the Group 3 Prix Penelope. (Mr V I Araci). *"I have a feeling this will be a very nice filly come the back-end of the season. She's growing a lot, which is great because she needed to, and she's going to end up a lovely size but at the moment she's quite weak. I'd be surprised if she ran before August but hopefully she will run at two".*

1337. UNNAMED ★★
b.f. Royal Applause – Nahab (Selkirk). April 15. First foal. The dam, quite useful 1m and 8.5f winner, is a half-sister to 4 winners including the listed Masaka Stakes second Song Of Silence. The second dam, State Secret (by Green Desert), a winner over 6.5f at 2 yrs in France, is a half-sister to 8 winners including the 2-y-o Group 2 Criterium de Maisons-Laffitte winner Bitooh and the dams of the Group/Grade 1 winners Storming Home, Music Note and Musical Chimes. (S Ali). *"She's very small but is growing. If she puts her best foot forward she'll hopefully prove able to win a race".*

1338. UNNAMED ★★★
ch.f. Shamardal – Neshla (Singspiel). March 21. Fourth foal. 45,000Y. Tattersalls October Book 2. Not sold. Sister to the quite useful 2-y-o 6f winner Wahylah and to the quite useful UAE dual 1m winner Muhtaram and half-sister to the fair 2014 2-y-o dual 7f winner Faraajh (by Iffraaj). The dam, a poor 11f placed maiden, is a half-sister to 9 winners including the Group 3 7.3f Fred Darling Stakes winner and Group 2 10f Nassau Stakes third Sueboog (herself dam of the Group 1 winner Best Of The Bests) and the listed winners Sell Out and Marika. The dam, Nordica (by Northfields), a useful 6f and 1m winner, is a half-sister to 2 winners. (S Manana). *"There's really something about this filly. Shamardal is such a good stallion and this is the first one I've had. She's a lovely mover, puts a smile on her rider's face every morning which in turn makes me happy and I'd expect her to be a June/July type over seven furlongs".*

1339. UNNAMED ★★
ch.c. Compton Place – Setting Forth (Daggers Drawn). February 27. First foal. 35,000Y. Tattersalls October Book 2. Sackville/Donald. The dam is an unraced half-sister to 4 winners including the listed winner Our Little Secret (herself dam of the smart dual listed winner Pearl Secret). The second dam, Sports Post Lady (by M Double M), a fair 5f winner of 4 races, is a half-sister to 5 winners including the useful sprinter Palacegate Episode (a winner of 11 races here and abroad including a Group 3 race in Italy and numerous listed events). *"A little bit like his three-parts brother Pearl Secret he looks speedy and forward but actually I think he'll get better and better with time. He's very good-looking and has a real sprinter's action, he's doing well, isn't that forward and I think he'll make a really nice 3-y-o. Fingers crossed he'll make the track this year as well".*

1340. UNNAMED ★★★★
b.c. Rock Of Gibraltar – Splashdown (Falbrav). March 21. Third foal. 85,000Y. Tattersalls October Book 2. Rob Speers. Half-brother to the 2014 2-y-o Group 3 7f Solario Stakes winner and Group 2 Superlative Stakes second Aktabantay (by Oasis Dream) and to the quite useful 7f winner Synergise (by Danehill Dancer). The dam, a listed 10f winner and listed-placed another four times, is a half-sister to 4 winners including listed 10f winner Cosmodrome. The second dam, Space Time (by Bering) was placed over 7f at 2 yrs in France and is a half-sister to 5 minor winners. (Mr V I Araci). *"This colt is no less nice in any way than his half-brother Aktabantay was at this stage. He's every bit as athletic, forward-going and willing. His riders say he's a joy to ride and gives them a feeling of real class. He's taller than Aktabantay, slightly light-framed and doesn't have as much bone – I suppose that's the difference between Rock Of Gibraltar and Oasis Dream. I see him as a second half of the season horse and I like everything I've seen so far".*

1341. UNNAMED ★★★
b.f. Lope De Vega – Takizada (Sendawar). January 26. First foal. 65,000Y. Tattersalls October Book 2. Blandford Bloodstock. The dam, placed from 1m to 10.5f, is a half-sister to 7 winners including the US dual Grade 2 and Group 3 12f Meld Stakes winner Takarian, the listed 12f Galtres Stakes winner and dual Group 2 third Tanoura, the Group 2 Royal Whip Stakes Takali and the Group 3 Minstrel Stakes winner Takar. The second dam, Takarouna (by Green Dancer), won the Group 2 12f Pretty Polly Stakes and is a sister to the smart Group 2 Dante Stakes winner Torjoun and a half-sister to 4 winners. (Al Asayl). *"She hasn't been here that long but she's a gorgeous mover and by a sensational stallion. She strikes me as being a filly with huge potential, probably more for the second half of the season, but she's lovely".*

1342. UNNAMED ★★★
b.f. Acclamation – Turning Light (Fantastic Light). May 9. Sixth foal. 35,000Y. Tattersalls October Book 2. John Murphy. Sister to the moderate 9f winner Quadriga and half-sister to the useful 2-y-o 7f winner, dual Group 3 7f placed and subsequent US stakes winner Surrey Star (by Dubawi). The dam won a Group 3 and a listed event in Germany and is a half-sister to 4 winners. The second dam, Turning Leaf (by Last Tycoon), a German 2-y-o winner and third in the Group 2 German 1,000 Guineas, is a half-sister to 6 winners. (Seventh Lap Racing). *"Quite a late foal but she's done nothing but improve. She's coping, muscling and looking more and more like a smart 2-y-o type. Because she's a May foal she probably wouldn't run until she's at least two, but I've been really impressed with her. I own a small share in her and I'm glad to do so".*

1343. UNNAMED ★★
b.c. Sea The Stars – Unity (Sadler's Wells). March 24. First foal. 180,000Y. Tattersalls October. BBA (Ire). The dam, a useful 12f winner and third in the Group 3 12f Noblesse Stakes, is closely related to 2 winners including the Group 3 Give Thanks Stakes third Eternal Beauty. The second dam, Moments Of Joy (by Darshaan), a smart 12f and listed 14f winner, is a half-sister to 5 winners. (Mr V I Araci). *"All the Sea The Stars look like they're going to take a bit of time. This lad doesn't look terribly backward but I don't want to be deceived by him. A really nice colt for the back-end of the season and next year".*

AMANDA PERRETT
1344. BALANCING TIME ★★
b.c. Pivotal – Time On (Sadler's Wells). May 19. Second living foal. 140,000Y. Tattersalls October Book 1. Peter & Ross Doyle. Half-brother to the quite useful 2-y-o 1m winner Moontime (by Sea The Stars). The dam, a Group 2 Prix de Malleret and listed Cheshire Oaks winner, is a sister to the winner Time Control (herself dam of the 2-y-o Group 1 Moyglare winner Cursory Glance). The second dam, Time Away (by Darshaan), won the Group 3 10.4f Musidora Stakes, was third in the Group 1 Prix de Diane and the Group 1 Nassau Stakes and is a half-sister to 6 winners including the 10f winner and Prix de Diane

second Time Ahead. (John Connolly & Odile Griffith). *"He's a big horse, 16.2, so when you also consider his late foaling date he's clearly going to need some time. He has a wonderful pedigree, but we'll be looking at seven furlongs to a mile at the back-end of the season".*

1345. CAMERAMAN ★★★
b.c. Rail Link – Photographic (Oasis Dream). February 17. First foal. The dam, a fairly useful dual 1m winner, is a half-sister to numerous winners including the Australian triple Group 1 winner Foreteller, the Group 2 1m Prix de Sandringham winner Modern Look and useful listed 6f winner Arabesque. The second dam, Prophecy (by Warning), a useful winner of the Group 1 6f Cheveley Park Stakes, was second in the Group 3 7f Nell Gwyn Stakes. (Khalid Abdulla). *"A compact, well-made colt, I imagine we'll be looking for seven furlongs with him from mid-season, as his pedigree would suggest. He's not a big strapping colt, rather he looks like a racy individual and he's doing some sensible work aimed at seven furlongs in June/July".*

1346. CANFORD BELLE ★★★
b.f. Canford Cliffs – Ballyea (Acclamation). February 12. First foal. 20,000Y. Tattersalls October Book 2. Amanda Perrett/Peter & Ross Doyle. The dam, a fair 2-y-o 6f winner, is a half-sister to 2 winners including the Group 2 Coventry Stakes third Rakaan. The second dam, Petite Spectre (by Spectrum), a fair 2-y-o 6f winner, is a half-sister to 8 winners including the useful 2-y-o Group 3 7f C L Weld Park Stakes winner Rag Top. (Coombelands Racing Syndicate 3). *"The first three dams have all won over 6f as 2-y-o's and I should think this filly will be our first 2-y-o runner. She'll have the speed to win over five furlongs and she'll be racing in the first couple of weeks in May. She's not over-big but she's quick and has a good attitude".*

1347. CATCHMENT ★★★★
b.f. Oasis Dream – Mirror Lake (Dubai Destination). February 14. First foal. The dam, a dual listed 10f winner, was second in the Group 3 10f Select Stakes and is a half-sister to 3 winners. The second dam, Reflections (by Sadler's Wells), ran once unplaced and is a half-sister to the smart Group 3 12f Prix de

Minerve and dual 10f listed winner Danefair, to the Group 3 9f Prix Chloe winner Prove, the smart multiple 7f to 8.5f winner Vortex and the listed 12f Prix Joubert winner Erudite. (Khalid Abdulla). *"A lovely filly and the first foal of Mirror Lake who we trained. We were really chuffed to get her. She looks a 2-y-o runner and is doing some nice work at the moment, so hopefully we'll see her out in May. She's a lovely individual and a five/six furlong 2-y-o".*

1348. COMBATIVE ★★★
b.c. Sinndar – Intense (Dansili). April 1. Third foal. Half-brother to the quite useful 2015 3-y-o 11f and 12f winner Process (by Nayef). The dam, a fairly useful 7f (at 2 yrs) and 1m winner, is a sister to one winner and a half-sister to the very useful 10f and 12f winner and Group 3 Chester Vase second Model Pupil. The second dam, Modesta (by Sadler's Wells), a useful 11.5f and listed 14f winner, is closely related to the Oaks, Fillies Mile, Musidora Stakes and May Hill Stakes winner Reams of Verse and to the smart 2-y-o 1m winner and Group-placed High Walden and a half-sister to the high-class Group 1 10f Coral Eclipse Stakes and Group 1 10f Phoenix Champion Stakes winner Elmaamul. (Khalid Abdulla). *"A beautifully bred, neat individual, the dam won over 7f and a mile and it's a lovely family. He has a Derby entry and he's doing his work nicely enough to expect him to be out over seven furlongs in June".*

1349. EQUINETTE ★★★
b.f. Equiano – Rougette (Red Ransom). March 31. First foal. The dam, a quite useful 1m winner, is a half-sister to 2 winners including the useful 5f ,7f (both at 2 yrs) and listed 7f winner and Group 2 7f Rockfel Stakes third Royal Confidence. The second dam, Never A Doubt (by Night Shift), a very useful 2-y-o winner of the Group 2 5.5f Prix Robert Papin, is a half-sister to 3 winners including the Group 3 5f third Jonny Mudball. (D M James). *"She's just been a bit immature over the last six weeks but she's coming back into work now and she zips along. There's a lot of speed in the pedigree, she was bred by her owner and it would be great if she came good. She's really racy and I'm very pleased with her".*

1350. GALES POINT ★★★
b.c. Zamindar – Disclose (Dansili). February 5. The dam, a French listed-placed 1m winner, is a sister to two winners including the useful French 7f (at 2 yrs) and 1m winner and listed placed World Ruler and closely related to the useful French 2-y-o dual 6f winner and Group 3 1m third Grand Vista. The second dam, Revealing (by Halling), a very useful 2-y-o 1m winner, is a half-sister to the useful 12f winner and dual Group 3 placed Singleton and the useful 6f winner Brevity. (Khalid Abdulla). *"Quite a tall individual, both the dam and the second dam won over a mile but I think this horse has enough speed to win over six furlongs. He's quite a mature, athletic horse with a lovely attitude to his work".*

1351. LADY ROCKA ★★
ch.f. Rock Of Gibraltar – Tap Dance Way (Azamour). March 25. First foal. 7,500Y. Tattersalls October Book 3. Amanda Perrett/ Peter & Ross Doyle. The dam, a modest 1m winner, is a half-sister to the Japanese 1m stakes winner Live Concert and the fairly useful 1m (at 2 yrs) and listed 13f winner Charleston Lady. The second dam, Dance Lively (by Kingmambo), is an unraced half-sister to 9 winners including 3 stakes winners in the USA. (Coombelands Racing Syndicate). *"There looks to be plenty of stamina in the dam's side, but she does her work really easily for a cheap filly. She just might be alright and we'll start her at seven furlongs".* **TRAINERS' BARGAIN BUY**

1352. MAQUEDA (USA) ★★
b.f. Rock Hard Ten – Proud Fact (Known Fact). April 15. Sister to the US 3-y-o Grade 3 9f fourth Tattenham and half-sister to 4 winners including the quite useful dual 7f winner (including at 2 yrs) Alzanti (by Arch), the quite useful 1m to 12f winner of 6 races Evident Pride (by Chester House) and the quite useful 10f and 12f winner Direct Answer (by Dynaformer). The dam, a French listed 7f winner, is a sister to the fairly useful 10f winner Modus Operandi and a half-sister to the French 1,000 Guineas winner Houseproud. The second dam, Proud Lou (by Proud Clarion), won the 2-y-o Grade 1 1m Frizette Stakes and is a half-sister to 5 winners. The second dam, Baby Louise (by Exclusive Native), won a 2-y-o

stakes event in the USA. (Khalid Abdulla). *"She's quite a big filly and I would say she's just going to need a bit of time to mature. We've trained two of her siblings and her half-sister Alzanti won as a 2-y-o but that was in November. I see this filly as being a back-end type as well".*

1353. MISCHIEF MAISY (IRE) ★★★
gr.f. Clodovil – Maise And Blue (Distant View). April 10. Second foal. 25,000Y. Tattersalls December. A Perrett/Peter & Ross Doyle. The dam, a listed-placed winner at 3 yrs in the USA, is a half-sister to 5 winners, two of them stakes winners in the USA. The second dam, Plate Queen (by Pilgrim), a US dual Grade 3 winner, is a half-sister to 6 winners. (Cotton, Conway). *"She's a bit of a late foal but her pedigree is speed over speed. It's a good old filly family and I should think we'll see her running over six furlongs around Goodwood time".*

1354. NUTBOURNE LAD (IRE) ★★
b.c. Lilbourne Lad – Cape Sydney (Cape Cross). March 2. Fourth foal. 20,000Y. Tattersalls October Book 2. A Perrett/Peter & Ross Doyle. The dam, a moderate 7f winner, is a half-sister to 5 winners. The second dam, Lady At War (by Warning), is an unraced half-sister to 5 minor winners here and in Italy. (Coombelands Racing Syndicate 2). *"The sire has just had his first winner and this colt has quite a speedy pedigree and it's a tough, hard running family. I like what I see of him, he's a bit immature at the moment because he's been growing. Once he levels out I should think he'll be running over six furlongs".*

1355. ROYAL HERO ★★★
b.c. Royal Applause – Heronetta (Halling). February 6. Fifth foal. 48,000Y. Tattersalls October Book 2. A Perrett/Peter & Ross Doyle. Half-brother to the fairly useful triple 10f winner Ask The Butler (by Dansili) and to the German 7f and 1m winner Beagle Boy (by American Post). The dam, a fair 12f winner, is a half-sister to the Group 3 Prix de Meautry winner and triple Group 1 placed Three Points. The second dam, Trazl (by Zilzal), a fair 13f to 15f winner, is a half-sister to 7 winners including the Group 2 Sun Chariot Stakes winner Talented. (Harwood Racing Syndicate). *"He's a bonny horse, he was an early foal and*

his knees are closed so he's ready to go really. The dam's had two winners from two runners and they've won 15 races between them. There's a bit of a mixture of speed and stamina in this colt's pedigree, but I'm not seeing blinding speed from him at the moment, so I should think he'll start over six furlongs and we'll step up to seven afterwards. His target is to run in May".

1356. YOU'RE HIRED ★★
b.c. Dalakhani – Heaven Sent (Pivotal). April 8. Third foal. 130,000Y. Tattersalls October Book 1. A Perrett/Peter & Ross Doyle. Half-brother to the quite useful 2014 2-y-o 1m winner Firmament (by Cape Cross). The dam, a winner of 6 races including the Group 3 Dahlia Stakes (twice), was Group 1 placed three times and is a sister to the US dual Grade 1 winner Megahertz and the fairly useful dual 1m winner and listed-placed Heavenly Dawn. The second dam, Heavenly Ray (by Rahy), a fairly useful 7f and 1m winner, is a half-sister to 3 winners. (G D P Materna). *"He was bought as a staying horse for next year, his sire has a good record with his stayers and this is a wonderful Cheveley Park family. He's quite a tall colt, he's going to want a bit of time and I should imagine we're looking at seven furlongs from the end of July onwards with him".*

1357. ZHUI FENG (IRE) ★★★★ ♠
b.c. Invincible Spirit – Es Que (Inchinor). February 5. Fifth foal. 340,000Y. Tattersalls October Book 1. Peter & Ross Doyle. Half-brother to the fair 2014 2-y-o 8.5f winner Stoked (by Fast Company), to the very useful 7f (at 2 yrs) and 10f winner, Group 2 10.5f York Stakes third and subsequent Hong Kong Vase winner Dominant (by Cacique) and to the smart Group 2 7f Lennox Stakes winner Es Que Love (by Clodovil). The dam, a minor winner at 3 yrs in France, is a half-sister to one winner abroad. The second dam, Bellona (by Bering), a listed 11f winner in France, is a half-sister to 7 winners including the Group 2 Prix de Flore winner In Clover. (John Connolly & Odile Griffith). *"He's a really nice, classy individual to match his sale price. It's a good family and I would hope to be giving him a run in June. He has a wonderful pedigree and should be able to run fast with a bit of luck. If he proves good enough to take to Royal Ascot*

the Coventry Stakes would be the obvious target. His name is Chinese for 'the Emperor's Favourite Horse'".

1358. UNNAMED ★★

ch.c. Frozen Power – La Mere Germaine (Indian Ridge). February 3. First foal. 52,000Y. Tattersalls October Book 2. Amanda Perrett. The dam, a fair 1m winner, is a half-sister to 4 minor winners. The second dam, Champs Elysees (by Distant Relative), a listed stakes winner of 5 races in the USA, is a half-sister to 3 winners including the Group 3 Supreme Stakes and US Grade 2 winner Anshan. (A D Spence). *"He's going to take a bit of time I think, he's quite immature and I should think the sun on his back would do him good. But he's a nice, free-walking individual and is cantering away quite happily at the moment".*

JONATHAN PORTMAN

1359. BELLOTTA ★★

ch.f. Nayef – Ela Paparouna (Vettori). April 11. £5,000Y. Doncaster Premier. Johnny Portman. Half-sister to the quite useful 6f and 7f winner of 7 races Take A Note (by Singspiel) and to the modest 6f winner Pomeroy (by Green Desert). The dam, a quite useful 7f winner, is a half-sister to 10 winners including the top-class Group 1 5f Nunthorpe Stakes winner and sire Kyllachy and the very useful triple 5f winner Borders. The second dam, Pretty Poppy (by Song), a modest 2-y-o 5f winner, stayed 7.6f and is a half-sister to 4 winners including the Criterium de Maisons-Laffitte winner Corviglia. (P Afia). *"More of a 3-y-o type, not only because she's by Nayef but because she's grown a fair bit. But she's got a bit of quality and I think she'll be running later this season".*

1360. ELEGANT ANNIE ★★★

b.f. Lawman – An Ghalanta (Holy Roman Emperor). March 6. First foal. 22,000Y. Tattersalls October Book 2. Not sold. The dam, a useful Irish 2-y-o listed 5f winner, was third in the Group 3 Round Tower Stakes and is a half-sister to 4 winners. The second dam, Alamanta (by Ali-Royal), is an unraced half-sister to one winner. (Tom Edwards & Partners). *"She's just taking a bit of time. She's a bit lazy so it's quite hard to judge her on the gallops, but I've liked what I've seen and I'll take my time with her. She's one for June/July and I like her".*

1361. INTIMATELY ★★★

b.c. Intense Focus – Midnight Fling (Groom Dancer). March 20. Third foal. £10,000Y. Doncaster Silver. Jon Portman. Half-brother to the quite useful 2-y-o dual 5f and subsequent US winner Bridge Night (by Avonbridge). The dam, a fair 5f, 6f (both at 2 yrs) and 7f placed maiden, is a half-sister to the dual Group 3 winning sprinter winner Definightly. The second dam, Perfect Night (by Danzig Connection), a fair 6f and 7f winner, is a half-sister to one winner. (Whitcoombe Park Racing). *"A lovely, straightforward horse. He's as tough as nails and not very big but the family tend to be that way. I was hoping he'd be my first runner but he got sore shins so I backed off him. Hopefully he'll be out in early May, he's a bonny colt and he doesn't give you any trouble, he's just very professional".*

1362. PAUSE FOR APPLAUSE ★★

b.g. Royal Applause – Zarkavean (Medicean). April 1. Second foal. 15,000Y. Tattersalls December. Kern/Lillingston. The dam is an unraced half-sister to 7 winners including the 2-y-o Group 3 1m Prix des Reservoirs winner Emily Bronte (the dam of two Group 3 winners) and the very useful listed 6f winner of 4 races Zelanda (the dam of two stakes winners). The second dam, Zafadola (by Darshaan), won the listed 11f Oaks Trial in Ireland and was third in the Group 1 Irish St Leger. (C R Lambourne, M Forbes, D Losse). *"An enormous horse for a 2-y-o, there's a lot of quality about him but it's all a game to him at the moment. A back-end/3-y-o type".*

1363. PINCH A KISS ★★★

ch.f. Sakhee's Secret – Pin Cushion (Pivotal). March 24. First foal. 7,000Y. Follow The Flag Partnership. Tattersalls October Book 4. The dam, a fair 6f winner, is a half-sister to 2 winners. The second dam, Frizzante (by Efisio), won 7 races including the Group 1 July Cup and is a half-sister to 4 winners including the Stewards Cup winner Zidane and the dual 6f listed winner Firenze. (Follow The Flag Partnership). *"She's nice, looks fairly early and I could see her starting off at five furlongs in late April/early May. She's not very big and looks a 2-y-o type".* **TRAINERS' BARGAIN BUY**

1364. POP CULTURE ★★★

ch.f. Equiano – Naizak (Medicean). March 14.

Third foal. 10,000Y. Tattersalls October Book 2. J Portman/G Howson. Half-sister to the quite useful 2014 2-y-o 6.5f winner Mujassam (by Kyllachy) and to the fair 2-y-o 6f winner Smart Salute (by Royal Applause). The dam, placed twice at 3 yrs, is a half-sister to 8 winners including the useful 6f (at 2 yrs) and subsequent Swedish listed winner Warming Trends. The second dam, Sunny Davis (by Alydar), was a fair 2-y-o 7f winner. (Mr & Mrs L J Walker). *"The agents went off Equiano last year. I think if she'd been by any other stallion she would have fetched a lot more than she did. She's well put together and a pretty filly with a bit of quality. One for the late summer".*

1365. RAVENSWOOD ★★
b.c. Lawman – Whatami (Daylami). March 30. Third foal. 47,000Y. Tattersalls October Book 2. J Portman. Half-brother to the fair 2-y-o 5f and 7f winner Constantine (by Holy Roman Emperor). The dam, a modest 12f placed maiden, is a sister to the 2-y-o listed Chesham Stakes winner Whazzat and a half-sister to 5 winners including the Italian Group 3 1m winner Whazzis. The second dam, Wosaita (by Generous), a fair 12.3f placed maiden, is a half-sister to 10 winners including the Group 1 10.5f Prix de Diane winner Rafha (dam of the Haydock Sprint Cup winner and sire Invincible Spirit) and the dam of the Group 1 Pretty Polly Stakes winner Chinese White. (Mr J T Habershon-Butcher). *"The owner doesn't like 2-y-o runners so this colt is just going through the motions at the moment, although I may be able to persuade him to run him at the back-end. He's a lovely moving horse with a lot of scope about him, but much more of a long-term project".*

1366. RUSSIAN RANGER (IRE) ★★
b.c. Bushranger – Pink Sovietstaia (Soviet Star). April 10. Eleventh foal. €13,000Y. Tattersalls Ireland September. Jon Portman. Half-brother to the fairly useful 2-y-o 6f winner and multiple listed-placed Russian Rosie (by Traditionally), to the quite useful 2-y-o 6f winners King's Icon (by King's Best) and Russian Ruby (by Vettori) and the fair 2-y-o 6f winner Observatory Star (by Observatory). The dam, awarded a race over 9f, is a half-sister to 9 winners including the listed winner Pinaflore (the dam of three Group/Graded stakes

winners). The second dam, Pink Satin (by Right Royal V), a Group 3 placed 2-y-o winner, is a half-sister to the French Group 1 winners Amber Rama and Blue Tom. (Graham Clark & Partners). *"He's grown an awful lot after looking very racy as a yearling. He's quite lazy and may not be as backward as he appears, but he'd be more the type for the second half of the season over six furlongs".*

1367. SUNNY SPIRIT (IRE) ★★★
b.f. Zebedee – Chingford (Redback). February 19. Fourth foal. £6,000 2-y-o. Ascot February. Half-sister to the moderate 5.5f winner Connaught Water (by Aussie Rules) and to the modest 2-y-o 5f winner Courtland Avenue (by Kodiac). The dam, a modest 5f placed 2-y-o, is a half-sister to a fair 2-y-o winner. The second dam, Beverley Macca (by Piccolo), a fair 5f winner of 4 races including at 2 yrs, is a half-sister to 5 winners including the 2-y-o Group 1 Cheveley Park Stakes and dual Group 2 winner Airwave. (Prof. C.D. Green). *"She goes quite well, she's small and compact and at the moment looks pretty 'set' and early. We had the half-brothers and they both won and she looks tough and early. A proper little 2-y-o".*

1368. TIZ HERSELF (IRE) ★★★
gr.f. Dandy Man – Pitullie (Rockport Harbor). March 5. First foal. £17,000Y. Doncaster Premier. G Howson/J Portman. The dam is an unraced half-sister to 2 winners including the US stakes winner Lexi's Love. The second dam, Rosehearty (by Rahy), won over 6f at 2 yrs and was second in the Group 3 Princess Margaret Stakes. (Berkeley Racing). *"A lovely-bodied filly, she was very ill during the winter but she's tough and hardy. I could see her being ready to run at the end of April, she's not big but she goes well".*

1369. UNNAMED ★★★
b.f. Excellent Art – Accede (Acclamation). April 1. Third foal. £12,000Y. Doncaster Silver. Jon Portman. Half-sister to the modest 2014 2-y-o 7f winner Miss Van Gogh (by Dutch Art). The dam, a quite useful 2-y-o 6f winner, is a half-sister to one winner. The second dam, Here To Me (by Muhtarram), a fair 3-y-o 6f winner, is a half-sister to 5 winners. (Berkeley Racing). *"I love her, but she just needs a bit of time. So she'll be a June/July type 2-y-o, we*

know the family well and we like her. She's rather dainty and still growing but there's a lot to like about her".

1370. UNNAMED ★★

ch.c. Equiano – Halfwaytoparadise (Observatory). March 31. Fourth foal. Half-brother to the modest 2014 7f to 8.5f placed maiden Edge Of Heaven (by Pastoral Pursuits). The dam, a moderate 7f winner, is a full or half-sister to 3 winners. The second dam, Always On My Mind (by Distant Relative), a quite useful 6f winner of 4 races, is a half-sister to 7 winners including the smart Group 1 6f Middle Park Stakes second Red Carpet. (Mascalls Stud). *"I stopped him because of sore shins but that's not a problem because he's too big a horse to get out early. He had an injury as a foal which is why he didn't go the sales. He looks the part and just looks like a nice colt for the second half of the season".*

1371. UNNAMED ★★

b.f. Roderic O'Connor – Nutshell (Dubai Destination). April 12. First foal. 5,000Y. Tattersalls October Book 3. A C Elliott/J Portman. The dam, a modest 10f winner, is a half-sister to 9 winners including the smart Group 2 1m Falmouth Stakes winner Macadamia, the very useful 6f (at 2 yrs) to 1m winner and Group 2 placed Azarole, the listed winner Captivator and the useful 2-y-o 5f and 6f winner Pistachio – subsequently a Group 3 winner in Scandinavia. The second dam, Cashew (by Sharrood), a quite useful 1m winner, is a half-sister to 6 winners here and abroad. *"She's tiny and she cost peanuts but I like her and she goes well. Her knees are immature, so I'll leave her until mid-season over six furlongs. I'm still looking for an owner for her".*

KEVIN PRENDERGAST

1372. AKHTAAM (IRE) ★★

b.c. Haatef – Aadaat (Dixie Union). February 23. Third foal. Half-brother to the quite useful 2013 2-y-o 7f winner Zakhm (by Marju). The dam, placed second over 7f at 2 yrs on her only start, is a half-sister to numerous winners including the smart 2-y-o Group 2 1m Royal Lodge Stakes winner Al Jadeed. The second dam, Aljawza (by Riverman), an Irish 2-y-o 6f winner, is a half-sister to 11 winners including

the smart Group 2 10f Gallinule Stakes winner Sportsworld, the smart Group 1 6f Cheveley Park Stakes winner Gay Gallanta, the useful 10.4f John Smiths Cup winner Porto Foricos and the useful 6f (at 2 yrs) and 7f winner Sundance Kid. (Hamdan Al Maktoum). *"He came in a bit later than the others so we haven't done much with him. He looks a 2-y-o and he's nice. One for six/seven furlongs from mid-season onwards".*

1373. AVA (IRE) ★★

b.f. Elnadim – Kawn (Cadeaux Genereux). March 10. Fifth foal. €24,000Y. Tattersalls Ireland September. Kevin Prendergast. Half-sister to the fairly useful 1m to 10.5f winner of 7 races Jawhar (by Halling), to the fairly useful 7f winner of 4 races Mundahesh (by Tamayuz) and the moderate 8.5f and 9.5f winner Safwaan (by Selkirk). The dam, unplaced on one start, is a half-sister to 9 winners including the Group 2 1m Prix du Rond-Point and Group 3 8.5f Diomed Stakes winner Trans Island and the Italian Group 3 winner Welsh Diva. The second dam, Khubza (by Green Desert), a quite useful 3-y-o 7f winner, is a half-sister to 7 winners including the Group 2 winners Barrow Creek and Last Resort. (Anne & Trevor McCormack). *"Owned by my daughter and her husband, this filly has entries in the Fairyhouse Sales race and the Phoenix Stakes (just in case she shows us anything). She's a half-sister to 3 winners and it's not a bad family. A nice type, she's not very big but muscular".*

1374. AWTAAD (IRE) ★★

b.c. Cape Cross – Asheerah (Shamardal). February 1. First foal. The dam, a fairly useful Irish listed-placed 7f winner, is a half-sister to the useful 2-y-o 6f winner and Group 3 7f Killavullan Stakes third Aaraas and the useful Irish 2-y-o 6f winner and Group 3 7f Silver Flash Stakes third Alshahbaa. The second dam, Adaala (by Sahm), an Irish 7f (at 2 yrs) and listed 9f winner, is a half-sister to 2 winners. (Hamdan Al Maktoum). *"It's a family that come late so he'll be more of a back-end type than early. We like him but he's backward for now".*

1375. BEBHINN (USA) ★★★★★

b.br.f. Street Boss – Passion Overflow

(Hennessy). April 18. First foal. €42,000Y. Goffs Orby. Kevin Prendergast. The dam, a 2-y-o 6f winner (from two starts), is a half-sister to 6 winners including the Group 2 6f Prix Robert Papin winner and Group 1 1m Coronation Stakes second Ocean Ridge, the smart 2-y-o listed 7f winner and Group 2 6f Gimcrack Stakes second Fokine and the listed winners Mr Redbyrd and Polar Circle. The second dam, Polar Bird (by Thatching), a very useful winner of 6 races here and in the USA including the 2-y-o Group 3 5f Debutante Stakes, is a half-sister to 6 winners. (J C Harley). *"She ran at the Curragh the other day and finished second, so she may have won a maiden before your book comes out. She has an entry in the Phoenix Stakes, she's a very strong filly and looks more like a colt. She'll get much further than five furlongs and I'd be happy with her going six or seven".* This filly won her second start easily at Navan on the 18th April.

1376. ETIDAAL (IRE) ★★★

b.c. Dark Angel – Ellasha (Shamardal). April 2. Second foal. 160,000Y. Tattersalls October Book 2. Shadwell Estate Co. Half-brother to the fair 2014 2-y-o 9.5f winner Counterproof (by Authorized). The dam, a minor winner at 3 yrs in Germany, is a half-sister to 9 winners including the listed winner and Group 2 second Smirk. The second dam, Elfin Laughter (by Alzao), a fair 2-y-o 7.5f and 1m winner, is a half-sister to 11 winners including the US Grade 2 winner Sign Of Hope. (Hamdan Al Maktoum). *"A fine, big colt he'll take a bit of time because despite being by Dark Angel he'll want at least seven furlongs. One for the second half of the season".*

1377. JAAFY (IRE) ★★

ch.c. Iffraaj – Mirabile Dictu (King's Best). January 31. Second foal. 60,000Y. Tattersalls October Book 2. Shadwell Estate Co. The dam, a fair 7f to 9.5f placed maiden, is a half-sister to 2 winners. The second dam, Miss Honorine (by Highest Honor), a winner of 4 races at 3 and 4 yrs in Ireland including three listed events from 1m to 10f, was Group 3 placed twice and is a half-sister to 8 winners including the US Grade 2 winner Mekong Melody. (Hamdan Al Maktoum). *"He arrived late after a setback he had early on, but we like him. He's just cantering away for now and we*

probably won't see him until the second half of the season".

1378. JEALOUS BEAUTY ★★★

b.f. Lawman – Jolie Jioconde (Marju). April 28. Third foal. Half-sister to the modest 2014 7f and 1m placed 2-y-o Jeune Et Jolie (by Verglas). The dam, a fairly useful 11f winner at 3 yrs, was third in the 2-y-o Group 3 7f Tyros Stakes and is a sister to the 2-y-o Group 1 6f Cheveley Park Stakes and Group 3 6f Round Tower Stakes winner Lightening Pearl. The second dam, Jioconda (by Rossini), won the listed Silken Glider Stakes and was third in the Group 3 Killavullan Stakes. (Lady O'Reilly). *"A very nice filly, she's had one run and finished second. She'll improve a good bit with better ground and six or seven furlongs will be no problem to her".*

1379. JEFFERSON DAVIS (IRE) ★★★

b.c. Duke Of Marmalade – Samorra (In The Wings). February 14. Third foal. €36,000Y. Goffs Sportsmans. Kevin Prendergast. Closely related to the fair 5f winner Rock N Rouge (by Rock Of Gibraltar) and half-brother to the fair 2-y-o 5f winner Cuisine (by Holy Roman Emperor). The dam, a fair 2-y-o 6f winner, is a half-sister to 4 winners including the Group 1 10f Nassau Stakes and Group 10.4f Musidora Stakes winner Zahrat Dubai. The second dam, Walesiana (by Star Appeal), won the German 1,000 Guineas and is a half-sister to 8 winners. (Bonnie and Tommie Hamilton). *"We gave him a run just to waken him up and he ran respectably. When he goes over 7f or a mile I think he'll be a very nice horse".*

1380. MIZAAH (IRE) ★★★

b.c. Invincible Spirit – Miss Beabea (Catrail). May 15. 140,000foal. Goffs November. Shadwell Estate Co. Half-brother to the 2-y-o Group 1 7f Moyglare Stud Stakes winner and Group 1 Phoenix Stakes third Miss Beatrix and to the fair Irish 6f winner Krivan (both by Danehill Dancer). The dam, an Irish 2-y-o 6f winner and second in the Group 1 6f Phoenix Stakes, is a half-sister to 7 winners including the very useful 5f winner Ellen's Lad. The second dam, Lady Ellen (by Horage), won 3 races in Ireland from 7f to 1m and is a half-sister to 3 winners including Indian Ridge. (Hamdan Al Maktoum). *"I trained the dam who was quite a good filly and she also bred a nice filly in Miss Beatrix. Both of them were placed in the Phoenix Stakes. He's a nice horse but a late foal and he won't be running until July or August. Six furlongs should suit him and we like him. He seems to take after his sire more than the dam".*

1381. MOGAZ (IRE) ★★★

gr.c. Sakhee's Secret – Tina's Spirit (Invincible Spirit). February 7. First foal. £70,000Y. Doncaster Premier. Shadwell Estate Co. The dam, a fair 1m winner, is a sister to on winner and a half-sister to 6 winners including the 2-y-o 6f and subsequent US stakes winner and Group 2 6f Coventry Stakes third Luck Money and the 2-y-o Group 3 7f Prix du Calvados winner Charlotte O'Fraise. The dam, a quite useful 7f winner, is a half-sister to 6 winners including the Group 3 6f winner Seltitude. The second dam, Dunoof (by Shirley Heights), a fairly useful 2-y-o 7f winner, is a sister to the Group 1 Premio Roma winner High Hawk (the dam of In the Wings) and to the dams of the Derby winner High-Rise and the Grade 1 winner Infamy. (Hamdan Al Maktoum). *"We like him and he should be racing by the end of May. He's out of an Invincible Spirit mare, so he should have a bit of toe and he's a nice horse with plenty of size and a good temperament. He might need a bit of cut in the ground".*

1382. MUNSHID (IRE) ★★★★

b.c. Dutch Art – Lightwood Lady (Anabaa). February 25. Fifth foal. €240,000Y. Goffs Orby. Shadwell Estate Co. Half-brother to the quite useful 2-y-o 5f winner (on only start) Its Alright (by King's Best), to the quite useful dual 1m winner Express Himself (by Dylan Thomas), the fair 1m winner and subsequent US winner Totheendoftheearth (by Hurricane Run) and the minor French dual 3-y-o winner Halendale (by Elusive City). The dam, a fair Irish 6f winner, is a half-sister to 6 winners. The second dam, Lyrical Dance (by Lear Fan), a minor winner at 4 yrs in the USA, is a full or half-sister to 7 winners including the Group/Grade 1 winners Black Minnaloushe, Pennekamp and Nasr El Arab. (Hamdan Al Maktoum). *"A very nice horse that cost plenty, he should be ready to run by mid-May. I'd expect him to get six furlongs plus and he should be one to follow".*

1383. MUTADAFFEQ ★★

b.c. Teofilo – Saajidah (Dynaformer). April 9. Second foal. Brother to the 2014 1m placed 2-y-o, from two starts, Taqaseem. The dam, a quite useful 10f and 11f winner, is a half-sister to numerous winners including the Irish 1,000 Guineas and Group 2 Rockfel Stakes winner Hula Angel and the minor US stakes winner Schedule. The second dam, Jode (by Danzig), a fair 2-y-o 6f winner here and in America at 3 yrs, is a sister to 2 winners and a half-sister to 9 winners including the Kentucky Derby winner Spend A Buck. (Hamdan Al Maktoum). *"He only arrived from Dubai a couple of weeks ago. I trained the dam and this is a good-moving horse for the back-end of the season. I like him".*

1384. RATHBRIDE RAVEN ★★★

b.f. Raven's Pass – Broadway Hit (Sadler's Wells). April 19. Sixth foal. 12,000Y. Tattersalls October Book 2. K Prendergast. Half-sister to the French 10f winner Coutances (by Shamardal) and to the minor French 11f winner Spiritus Hit (by Dubai Destination). The dam is an unraced half-sister to 5 winners including the smart 2-y-o Group 1 1m Prix Marcel Boussac winner and Group 1 10f Nassau Stakes second Sulk, the Group1 Hong Kong Cup winner and Epsom Derby second Eagle Mountain and the smart 1m listed winner Wallace. The second dam, Masskana (by Darshaan), a minor 9f and 10f winner in France, is a half-sister to 3 winners including Madjaristan (US Grade 3 Arcadia Handicap) and Massyar (Group 2 Gallinule Stakes). (Comerford Brothers). *"We like her a lot. She has a good pedigree but looked small at the sales, but I thought that with a pedigree like that she's surely worth more than we paid for her. She'll be running in May, probably starting at Leopardstown over six furlongs".*

1385. ROSEISAROSE ★★★

b.f. Acclamation – Red Feather (Marju). April 12. Sixth foal. Half-sister to the very useful listed 6f and listed 7f winner and dual Group 3 placed Rose Bonheur (by Danehill Dancer) and to the 2-y-o 6f winner and Group 3 7f Silver Flash Stakes third Roseraie (by Lawman). The dam, a Group 3 1m winner in Ireland, was second in the Group 1 Moyglare Stud Stakes and is a half-sister to the smart dual 10f winner and dual Group 3 12f placed Frankies Dream. The second dam, Galyph (by Lyphard), a modest Irish 10f winner at 4 yrs, is a half-sister to 2 minor winners. (Lady O'Reilly). *"A very nice filly, we like her and she should be ready to run in mid-to-late May. This filly looks very much like the family, short coupled and more sprinting-bred than staying".*

1386. RUE BONAPARTE ★★★
b.f. Dark Angel – Redoutable (Invincible Spirit). April 15. First foal. The dam, a quite useful Irish 2-y-o 6f winner, is a half-sister to several winners including the smart Group 3 Irish 2,000 Guineas Trial and listed 1m winner and Group 1 10.5f Tattersalls Rogers Cup second Recharge. The second dam, Rebelline (by Robellino), won the Group 1 10.5f Tattersalls Gold Cup and the Group 2 Pretty Polly Stakes and is a sister to the Group 2 Blandford Stakes winner Quws and a half-sister to 5 winners. (Lady O'Reilly). *"A nice filly, she's very like her dam and she'll be racing in May. She could run over five, six and maybe seven furlongs this year".*

1387. SHARRIS (IRE) ★★
b.c. Zebedee – Alshimaal (Namid). April 21. Fourth foal. £60,000Y. Doncaster Premier. Shadwell Estate Co. The dam is an unraced half-sister to 4 winners including Misty Eyed (Group 3 5f Molecomb Stakes). The second dam, Bold As Love (by Lomond), is an unraced half-sister to 3 winners. (Hamdan Al Maktoum). *"Quite a nice horse, but not as forward as you might think considering his pedigree. We haven't done a lot with him but what he has done seems to be OK".*

1388. SUFOOF (IRE) ★★★★
b.f. Acclamation – Walayef (Danzig). April 17. Half-sister to the fairly useful Irish 2-y-o 6f and 7f winner and 3-y-o listed-placed Jamaayel (by Shamardal), to the quite useful Irish 1m winner Estithmaar (by Pivotal) and the quite useful Irish 2-y-o 7f winner Reyaada (by Daylami). The dam, a listed 6f (at 2 yrs) and Group 3 7f Athasi Stakes winner, is a sister to the smart 2-y-o 6f winner Haatef, to the listed 6f winner and Group 1 Moyglare Stud Stakes second Shimah and the Irish dual listed 6f winner Ulfah. The second dam, Sayedat Alhadh (by Mr Prospector), a US 7f winner, is

a sister to the US Grade 2 7f winner Kayrawan and a half-sister to the useful winners Amaniy, Elsaamri and Mathkurh. (Hamdan Al Maktoum). *"We like her a lot and she should be racing in May over six furlongs. I've trained a lot of the family and they're better off going six than five. I think she'll make a nice 2-y-o, she's very strong and looks like a 3-y-o now. We've made a Group 1 entry for her".*

1389. WAARIF (IRE) ★★★
b.c. Arcano – Indian Belle (Indian Ridge). April 3. Eighth foal. 78,000Y. Tattersalls October Book 2. Shadwell Estate Co. Closely related to the fairly useful Irish 5f winner Sioduil (by Oasis Dream) and half-brother to 3 winners including the useful 10f winner Blue Corner (by Teofilo) and the fair 1m winner Indian Mist (by Cape Cross). The dam, a fairly useful Irish 10f winner, is a half-sister to 3 winners including the dam of the Group 2 Futurity Stakes winner Dragon Pulse. The second dam, Abyat (by Shadeed), is an unraced half-sister to 9 winners including the Group 1 Middle Park Stakes winner Hayil. (Hamdan Al Maktoum). *"A very nice horse bought in Newmarket. He seems to move well but he's the sort that could just go an extra furlong than his pedigree suggests. So seven furlongs or a mile will be his trip".*

1390. UNNAMED ★★
b.c. Lawman – Oshima (Danehill). February 11. Eleventh living foal. 27,000Y. Tattersalls October Book 2. J O'Byrne. Half-brother to the Italian winner of 6 races at 2 and 3 yrs and Group 1 Italian Oaks second Rosa Di Brema (by Lomitas and herself the dam of two stakes winners), to three minor Italian winners by Beat Of Drums, Winged Love and Singspiel and to the unraced dam of the Italian Group 2 winner Sneak A Peak. The dam won 3 minor races at 3 and 4 yrs in Italy and is a half-sister to 5 other minor winners. The second dam, Orangerie (by Gay Mecene), placed once in France, is a half-sister to Orsa Maggiore, a winner of three Group 1 events in Italy. (J P McManus). *"A nice horse for seven furlongs, he'll probably start around Galway festival time".*

1391. UNNAMED ★★★
b.f. Teofilo – Posterity (Indian Ridge). March 4. Fourth foal. €80,000Y. Goffs Orby. James

Kelly. Closely related to the fairly useful 2-y-o 7f winner and Group 3 third Rasmeyaa (by New Approach) and half-sister to the smart 6f, 7f winner and Group 3 1m Desmond Stakes winner Future Generation (by Hurricane Run). The dam is an unraced half-sister to 9 winners including the Group 3 6f Prix de Meautry winner Do The Honours and the listed 7f Chesham Stakes winner Seba. The second dam, Persian Secret (by Persian Heights), a fairly useful 2-y-o 6f winner here, won a listed event in France and is a half-sister to 8 winners including the Group winners Cassandra Go and Verglas. (Lady O'Reilly). *"We like her a lot, she's one for seven furlongs plus and she's from a good family".*

SIR MARK PRESCOTT

1392. ABBEYLEIX ★★
gr.c. Sir Percy – Alvarita (Selkirk). April 30. Seventh foal. €55,000Y. Goffs Orby. J Brummitt. Brother to the useful Irish 1m (at 2 yrs) and Group 3 10f Kilternan Stakes winner Alla Speranza and half-brother to the fairly useful 10f to 14f winner of 6 races Alcaeus and the quite useful 12f and 13f winner Albert Bridge (both by Hernando). The dam, a French listed 10.5f winner, is a sister to one winner and a half-sister to the 10f winner and Group 2 10f Prix Greffulhe second Albion. The second dam, Alborada (by Alzao), won the Champion Stakes (twice), the Nassau Stakes and Pretty Polly Stakes and is a sister to the German triple Group 1 winner Albanova and a half-sister to 7 winners. (Mr T J Rooney). *"He's quite a nice horse and having a spring break at the moment. We won't see him out until the autumn because he's quite a tall horse and all the family stay".*

1393. ALAKAZAM ★★★
b.c. Archipenko – Alakananda (Hernando). April 20. Eighth foal. 45,000Y. Tattersalls October Book 2. Sir Mark Prescott. Half-brother to 5 winners including the listed winner, Epsom Derby second and Irish Derby fourth Dragon Dancer (by Sadler's Wells), the useful 2-y-o 1m winner Ajaan (by Machiavellian) and the quite useful 1m (at 2 yrs), 10.5f and hurdles winner Rigidity (by Indian Ridge). The dam, a fairly useful dual 11.5f winner, is a half-sister to the dual Champion Stakes winner Alborada and the

triple German Group 1 winner Albanova. The second dam, Alouette (by Darshaan), a useful 1m (at 2 yrs) and listed 12f winner, is a sister to the placed dam of the Group 1 winners Yesterday and Quarter Moon and a half-sister to the Group winners Last Second (dam of the French 2,000 Guineas winner Aussie Rules) and Alleluia (dam of the Prix Royal-Oak winner Allegretto). (Mr R P Fry). *"Obviously a well-bred horse, he'll be running by July or August. He had a hiccup a few weeks ago but he's back with us now. One for seven furlongs to a mile, he's a tall horse with plenty of scope".*

1394. ALINSTANTE ★★★
b.f. Archipenko – Algarade (Green Desert). April 22. Second foal. Half-sister to the modest 13f and 2m winner of 3 races Alba Verde (by Verglas). The dam, a quite useful 1m (at 2 yrs) and 10f winner, is a half-sister to numerous winners including the fairly useful listed-placed Alambic. The second dam, Alexandrine (by Nashwan), a fair 10f to 13f winner of 4 races, is a half-sister to the Nassau Stakes and Sun Chariot Stakes winner Last Second (dam of the French 2,000 Guineas winner Aussie Rules), the Doncaster Cup winner Alleluia (dam of the Prix Royal-Oak winner Allegretto) and the Moyglare Stud Stakes third Alouette (dam of the dual Champion Stakes winner Alborada and the triple German Group 1 winner Albanova) and to the placed dam of the Group 1 winners Yesterday and Quarter Moon. (Miss K Rausing). *"She's a big filly from a big family. They've been multiple winners for us, including the half-sister who won three last year. This one might not take as much time as the others, she'll run at two and should start off at seven furlongs".*

1395. ALSACIENNE ★★
gr.f. Dalakhani – Alabastrine (Green Desert). March 1. Eighth foal. €35,000Y. Goffs Orby. R Frisby. Half-sister to the useful Irish 7.5f (at 2 yrs) and 9f winner Hail Caesar (by Montjeu), to the quite useful 2-y-o 7f winner Albaspina (by Selkirk) and the fair 12f winner Callistan (by Galileo). The dam, placed over 7f at 2 yrs, is a half-sister to 8 winners including the Nassau Stakes and Sun Chariot Stakes winner Last Second (dam of the French 2,000 Guineas winner Aussie Rules) and the dams of the Group 1 winners Alborada, Albanova,

Allegretto, Yesterday and Quarter Moon. The second dam, Alruccaba (by Crystal Palace), was a quite useful 2-y-o 6f winner. (Miss K Rausing). *"Turned out at the moment having a break, she's very much a 3-y-o filly in the making. A good-actioned filly, she looks like a firm ground horse".*

1396. BEAR FACED ★★★
b.c. Intikhab – Hulcote Rose (Rock Of Gibraltar). January 16. First foal. 40,000Y. Tattersalls October Book 2. Sir Mark Prescott. The dam, a fair 6f (at 2 yrs) to 8.5f winner of 5 races, is a half-sister to 2 minor winners. The second dam, Siksikawa (by Mark Of Esteem), ran once unplaced and is a half-sister to 7 winners including the Group/Graded stakes winners Labeeb, Fanmore and Alrassaam. (The Barkers & Chris Jenkins). *"He was a January foal and we'd be looking to start him in work very shortly. He'll be 'speed or bust' I should think and is one of our earlier 2-y-o's".*

1397. CAPE CRYSTAL (IRE) ★★★
b.f. Cape Cross – Lady Rockfield (Rock Of Gibraltar). April 24. Third foal. 30,000Y. Tattersalls October Book 2. Axom. Half-sister to the unplaced 2014 2-y-o Belle Dormant (by Rip Van Winkle). The dam, a modest 1m placed maiden, is a half-sister to 4 winners including the 2-y-o Group 3 7f C L Weld Park Stakes and 3-y-o listed 6f winner and Group 1 7f Moyglare Stud Stakes second Ugo Fire. The second dam, Quiet Mouse (by Quiet American), is an unraced half-sister to 7 winners including the smart broodmare Witch Of Fife (the dam of 3 stakes winners). (Axom LVII). *"A tall, straightforward filly, she's growing at the moment but will be running around July time. A good goer, it looks like she'd go on firm ground".*

1398. CLINE ★★
ch.f. Pivotal – Graduation (Lomitas). April 5. Fifth foal. Half-sister to the fair 2015 3-y-o 9.5f winner Marma's Boy (by Duke Of Marmalade), to the quite useful 8.5f winner Certificate (by Pivotal) and a winner in Sweden by Sakhee. The dam, a fairly useful 1m winner, was listed-placed. The second dam, Ceremonial (by Lion Cavern), a fair 1m winner, is a half-sister to 6 winners including the Group 2 Great Voltigeur Stakes and Group 2 Prix Jean de Chaudenay

winner Sacrament. (Cheveley Park Stud). *"She was quite poorly in the spring but she's coming back to us next week. She's a July/August type 2-y-o, a good mover and a pleasant filly but I don't know more than that at the moment".*

1399. COLOMBE BLEU ★★★
b.f. Manduro – Blue Dream (Cadeaux Genereux). March 12. Fifth foal. Half-sister to the fair 2-y-o 7f winner Medicoe (by Medicean). The dam, a useful 6f winner, was listed-placed and is a half-sister to 5 winners including the 1m (at 2 yrs) and 9.2f winner and listed-placed Equity Princess. The second dam, Hawait Al Barr (by Green Desert), a useful 12f to 2m winner, is a half-sister to 3 winners. (Mr J B Haggas). *"We had her half-brother who won for us but the mare's been basically disappointing. She'll run as soon as the six/seven furlong races start and so seems to take after the dam rather more than Manduro".*

1400. COTE D'AZUR ★★★★
ch.c. Champs Elysees – Florentia (Medicean). February 25. Second foal. Half-brother to the fair 2-y-o 6f to 7.f winner of 3 races Flora Medici (by Sir Percy). The dam, a modest 1m and 10f winner, is a half-sister to 9 winners including the useful 6f and 7f winner of 4 races Flying Officer. The second dam, Area Girl (by Jareer), a fair 2-y-o 5f winner, is a half-sister to 3 minor winners. (Mr N Greig). *"It's a very prolific family – they win a stack of races. Between the grandam and the dam I think I've trained their offspring to win 40 races! They all go on firm ground, they're generally willing and straightforward and this colt will be a mid-season 2-y-o".*

1401. DUSTY RAVEN ★★★★
ch.c. Raven's Pass – Dust Dancer (Suave Dancer). April 30. Half-brother to 6 winners including the listed 1m and subsequent US Grade 2 winner Spotlight, the quite useful 2-y-o 7f winner Dusty Moon (both by Dr Fong), the fairly useful dual 7f winner Tyranny (by Machiavellian and herself dam of the Group 1 Phoenix Stakes winner Zoffany), the quite useful 2-y-o 7f winner and listed 1m placed Dusty Answer (by Zafonic) and the fair 2-y-o 7f winner Dusty Moon (by Dr Fong). The dam won 4 races including the Group 3 10f Prix

de la Nonette and is a half-sister to 6 winners including the Group 3 7.3f Fred Darling Stakes winner Bulaxie (dam of the Group 2 winner Claxon). The second dam, Galaxie Dust (by Blushing Groom), a quite useful 2-y-o 6f winner, is a half-sister to 2 minor winners. (Bluehills Racing Ltd). *"Not over-big, he's a light framed, firm ground horse. He'll be starting work in May and looks a mid-season 2-y-o for six/seven furlongs".*

1402. DUTCH HEIRESS ★★★★

b.f. Dutch Art – Regal Heiress (Pivotal). February 7. First foal. The dam, a fair 7f to 8.5f placed maiden, is a half-sister to 4 winners. The second dam, Regal Rose (by Danehill), won both her starts including the Group 1 6f Cheveley Park Stakes and is a sister to the Japanese 10f stakes winner Generalist and a half-sister to 8 winners. (Cheveley Park Stud). *"A tall filly, but she's more precocious than you'd think. She's always cantered nicely, she's grown since she came here and looks a 2-y-o".*

1403. LATE SHOW ★★★

br.f. Authorized– Hydro Calido (Nureyev). February 24. Half-sister to the French listed 7f winner Esperero (by Forty Niner), to the fair 10f winner Best Intent (by King's Best) and the moderate 9f winner Lady Calido (by El Prado). The dam, a very useful filly and winner of the Group 2 1m Prix d'Astarte, was second in the French 1,000 Guineas and is a half-sister to the champion European 2-y-o and 2,000 Guineas second Machiavellian, to the Group 1 Prix Morny and Group 1 Prix de la Salamandre winner Coup de Genie and the Group 1 Prix Jacques le Marois winner Exit to Nowhere (by Irish River). The second dam, Coup de Folie (by Halo), won four races from 6f to 10f including the Group 3 1m Prix d'Aumale. (Lordship Stud). *"A nice-enough filly, she went home for a break in January and comes back in May. She'll be a seven furlong 2-y-o in June or July".*

1404. LUGANO ★★★ ♠

b.c. Galileo – Swiss Lake (Indian Ridge). March 2. Eighth foal. 250,000Y. Tattersalls October Book 1. J Brummitt. Half-brother to 6 winners including the Group 3 6f Prix de Meautry and Group 3 5f Prix de Petit Couvert winner Swiss Diva (by Pivotal), the very useful

6f (at 2 yrs) and Group 3 5f winner Swiss Spirit (by Invincible Spirit), the useful triple listed 6f winner Swiss Dream (by Oasis Dream) and the smart 2-y-o 5f winner and triple Group 2 placed Swiss Franc (by Mr Greeley). The dam, a dual listed 5f winner (including at 2 yrs), is a half-sister to 4 winners. The second dam, Blue Iris (by Petong), was a useful winner of 5 races over 5f and 6f. (Mr J L C Pearce). *"A very tall horse, he's a very good mover and he has a very pleasant nature. You wouldn't know when he'd come to hand because he's a Galileo but there's a lot of pace in the family as well. For his pedigree he wasn't over expensive, but that could be because he's a big colt".*

1405. MARSHA (IRE) ★★★★

b.f. Acclamation – Marlinka (Marju). March 16. Second foal. Half-sister to the quite useful 2014 2-y-o triple 5f winner Judicial (by Iffraaj). The dam, a fairly useful 2-y-o listed 5f winner of 3 races, is a sister to one winner and a half-sister to 2 winners. The second dam, Baralinka (by Barathea), a useful 5f (at 2 yrs) and triple 6f winner, is a half-sister to the Group 1 Fillies Mile, Falmouth Stakes, Sussex Stakes and Matron Stakes winner Soviet Song (by Marju). (Elite Racing Club). *"A very nice filly with a very pleasant nature, she canters very nicely. She's having a break at present and won't be ready to run until September time because she's done plenty of growing".*

1406. MEDDLESOME ★★★★

b.c. Medicean – Meddle (Diktat). March 5. Fifth foal. 20,000Y. Tattersalls October Book 1. Sir Mark Prescott. Half-brother to the fair 2014 2-y-o dual 6f winner Anastazia (by Kyllachy), to the fair 6f (at 2 yrs) to 1m winner of 7 races Darnathean (by Librettist), the modest 9.5f and 11.5f winner Little Jazz (by Doyen) and the moderate 9f and 10f winner Entrapping (by Tiger Hill). The dam is an unplaced half-sister to 4 winners including the very useful Group 3 6.3f Anglesey Stakes winner Pan Jammer. The second dam, Ingerence (by Akarad), was placed three times in France and is a half-sister to 6 winners including the Group 3 10.5f Prix Penelope winner La Monalisa. (Mr N Greig – Osborne House). *"I think he was the cheapest horse from the Book 1 catalogue, but he's an elegant horse and he canters nicely. A sound, pleasant natured horse with a firm ground action, he looks like making a 2-y-o over six/seven furlongs in July".*

1407. MOCKINBIRD (IRE) ★★★
b.f. Makfi – Littlefeather (Indian Ridge). March 27. Ninth foal. €55,000Y. Goffs Orby. Not sold. Half-sister to 7 winners including the useful 2-y-o 6.5f winner and Group 3 third Expedition (by Oasis Dream), the listed-placed 6f winner of 4 races Bee Eater (by Green Desert), the quite useful dual 9f winner Rare Tern (by Pivotal) and the fair 2-y-o 5f winner Rock Dove (by Danehill). The dam, a 5f (at 2 yrs) and 6f winner of 4 races, was third in the Group 1 7f Moyglare Stakes and is a half-sister to the multiple Group 1 winner Marling and the multiple Group 1 placed Caerwent. The second dam, Marwell (by Habitat), a champion sprinter, won four Group 1 events. (Sir Edmund Loder). *"A filly from a great family, we trained the mother and one of the half-sisters called Bee Eater. She's done a bit of growing now but you'd think she'd be a June type 2-y-o because most of the family come in mid-season".*

1408. MONJENI ★★★
b.c. Montjeu – Polly's Mark (Mark Of Esteem). February 7. First foal. 650,000Y. Tattersalls October Book 1. Sir Mark Prescott. The dam, a useful dual listed 12f winner, was second in the Group 2 Lancashire Oaks and third in the Group 2 Park Hill Stakes and is a half-sister to 2 winners. The second dam, Kotdiji (Mtoto), is an unraced half-sister to 4 winners including the 1,000 Guineas winner Ameerat. (Fergus Anstock & Alice Mills). *"A colt with a high price tag at the sales, he was retained by his breeder and he's a very good-looking horse. He canters very nicely and he's out having a break now but he'll be back in May. He'll start off in September time".*

1409. OCEAN READY (USA) ★★★★
b.c. More Than Ready – Tjinouska (Cozzene). March 4. Ninth foal. $110,000Y. Keeneland September. Oliver St Lawrence. Brother to the fairly useful 2-y-o 7f and 1m winner and subsequent US Grade 2 placed In The Slips and half-brother to 5 winners including the fair 10f winner Straits Of Hormuz (by War Chant) and the fair 2-y-o 7f winner Delta Diva (by Victory Gallop). The dam, a

quite useful 12f winner, is a half-sister to 7 winners including the useful 2-y-o 6f winner and Group 1 Moyglare Stud Stakes third Pearl Dance. The second dam, Ocean Jewel (by Alleged), was unraced. (Messrs Baxter, Gregson, Jenkins & Warman). *"A tough, burly, early type of 2-y-o, he'll be running earlier than the pedigree would indicate. I think he'd be a horse to run in June/July over six/seven furlongs. He's a strong colt".*

1410. O'CONNOR'S GIRL ★★★
b.f. Roderic O'Connor – Dollar Bird (Kris). February 15. Eighth foal. 32,000Y. Tattersalls December. Not sold. Half-sister to 4 winners including the useful 9.7f winner and listed-placed Higher Love (by Sadler's Wells), the fairly useful 6f (at 2 yrs) to 11f winner Buckland (by Oratorio) and the quite useful 7f (at 2 yrs) and 9f winner Dollar Chick (by Dansili). The dam, a useful 2-y-o 8.2f winner and second in the listed 11.5f Oaks Trial, is a half-sister to 7 winners including the Group 2 12f King Edward VII Stakes winner Amfortas and the Group 3 10.5f Prix de Royaumont winner Legend Maker (dam of the 1,000 Guineas winner Virginia Waters). The second dam, High Spirited (by Shirley Heights), a quite useful winner of two races over 14f and 2m, is a sister to the Premio Roma winner High Hawk (dam of the Breeders Cup Turf winner In The Wings) and a half-sister to 8 winners . (Biddestone Racing Partnership). *"She was broken in late after failing to reach her reserve at the sales and she's now having a spring break. A good mover, she's done a lot of growing and hopefully she'll come back a bit stronger".*

1411. PALISADE ★★
b.c. Fastnet Rock – Portal (Hernando). April 12. Fourth foal. Half-brother to the smart 1m (at 2 yrs) to 12f winner and Group 3 placed Windshear (by Hurricane Run) and to the fair 12f to 2m winner of 5 races Porcini (by Azamour). The dam, useful listed 10f winner, was second in the Group 2 Lancashire Oaks and is a half-sister to 6 winners including the listed 10f winner Ice Palace and the dam of the dual Group 2 winner Spacious. The second dam, White Palace (by Shirley Heights), a quite useful 8.2f winner, is a half-brother to one winner abroad. (Cheveley Park Stud).

"A cheery soul! He's a strong, burly, good-natured horse and we won't know how much ability he's got until we ask him to go. He might be a nice horse but you just wouldn't know until you work him".

1412. RED BOX ★★
b.f. Exceed And Excel – Confidential Lady (Singspiel). March 31. Fifth foal. The dam, winner of the Group 3 7f Prix du Calvados (at 2 yrs) and the Group 1 10.5f Prix de Diane, is a half-sister to 5 winners. The second dam, Confidante (by Dayjur), a fairly useful 3-y-o dual 7f winner, is a half-sister to 6 winners including the 2-y-o 6f winner Wind Cheetah, the Group 3 7f Solario Stakes winner White Crown and the 11.8f winner Zuboon – all useful. (Cheveley Park Stud). *"The mare has been basically disappointing up to date for such a good racemare, so Cheveley Park tried a change and went to a fast stallion. This filly will be ready to work around July time, she's not over-big so if she was any good you'd expect her to show it this year".*

1413. SILAS R (IRE) ★★★
b.c. Pour Moi – Playwithmyheart (Diktat). April 9. Second foal. €85,000Y. Goffs Orby. J Brummitt. Half-brother to the moderate 2014 7f placed 2-y-o Candle Of The Sea (by Makfi). The dam, a 2-y-o 1m winner in France, is a half-sister to 7 winners including the Group 1 7f Prix de la Foret winner of 16 races Toylsome and the 2-y-o Group 3 winner Coral Mist. The second dam, Treasure Trove (by The Minstrel), a modest 5f to 7f placed 2-y-o, is a half-sister to 4 winners including the US Grade 3 winner Ocean Queen and the Queen Mary Stakes and Fred Darling Stakes winner Dance Parade – subsequently a Grade 2 winner in the USA. (Mr T J Rooney). *"A good-topped, solid horse, he'll be a July type 2-y-o over seven furlongs I should think".*

1414. SOUND OF THE SEA ★★
b.f. Acclamation – Summer Night (Nashwan). March 4. Half-sister to 7 winners including the 2-y-o Group 3 1m Prix des Reservoirs winner Songerie, the fairly useful 2-y-o 7.2f winner and Group 3 1m Prix des Reservoirs third Souvenance (both by Hernando), the useful listed 9.5f winner of 3 races Soft Morning

(by Pivotal) and the fairly useful 7f (at 2 yrs) and Scandinavian listed 8.5f winner Sourire (by Domedriver). The dam, a fairly useful 6f winner, is a half-sister to 7 winners including the Group 3 Prix d'Arenburg winner Starlit Sands and the listed 6f winner Sea Dane. The second dam, Shimmering Sea (by Slip Anchor), a fairly useful Irish 2-y-o 5f winner and third in the Group 3 Silken Glider Stakes, is a half-sister to 5 winners including the King George VI and Queen Elizabeth Stakes winner Petoski. (Miss K Rausing). *"She came in late due to an injury at stud. She's been fine since, but she's behind the others and won't be able to run much earlier than September".*

1415. STATUS QUO (IRE) ★★
br.c. Thewayyouare – Again Royale (Royal Academy). April 8. Ninth foal. €28,000Y. Goffs Orby. J Brummitt. Half-brother to the listed 5f winner Sacred Aspect (by Haatef) and to the 1m to 11f winner of 5 races and listed third Super Say (by Intikhab) – both fairly useful. The dam is an unraced sister to the Group 3 6f Greenlands Stakes winner Tiger Royal and to the dam of the Group 2 placed Sir Xaar. The second dam, Lady Redford (by Bold Lad), ran once unplaced and is a half-sister to 5 winners. (Mr G Moore – Osborne House II). *"A gorgeous looking horse, but very big. Whatever he does this year he'll be much better as a 3-y-o".*

1416. ST MICHEL ★★★
b.c. Sea The Stars – Miss Provence (Hernando). February 25. Sixth foal. Half-brother to the fairly useful 2-y-o dual 7f winner and dual 1m listed placed Oasis Cannes (by Oasis Dream), to the quite useful 10f to 12f winner Miss Aix (by Selkirk) and the fair 2015 3-y-o 8.5f and 10f winner Miss Minuty (by Verglas). The dam, a quite useful 9f winner, is a sister to 2 winners including the 7f (at 2 yrs) and listed 10f winner Miss Corniche and a half-sister to 5 winners. The second dam, Miss Beaulieu (by Northfields), was a useful 6f and 10f winner. (J L C Pierce). *"A good-natured horse that could make a 2-y-o at some stage. I trained two out of the mare – one was as slow as a hearse and one was the useful Oasis Cannes. A very pleasant horse and a good goer, he's not a backward type and he might be a bit earlier than a lot by the sire".*

1417. TENZING NORGAY ★★
gr.c. Aussie Rules – Miss Katmandu (Rainbow Quest). May 13. Half-brother to the quite useful 13f to 2m winner Kashgar (by Hernando). The dam, unplaced in one start, is a half-sister to the very smart 7f (at 2 yrs), Group 3 12f September Stakes and Group 3 13.4f Ormonde Stakes winner Asian Heights (by Hernando)and to the smart 10f winner St Expedit. The second dam, Miss Rinjani (by Shirley Heights), a fair 2-y-o 7f winner, was placed over 12f at 3 yrs and is a half-sister to several winners. (Mr J L C Pearce). *"A nice horse that canters well and he's by a sire that gets lots of winners without being very fashionable. The mare has been slightly disappointing to date but for a late foal he canters well. This is the best named horse in the yard and his owner is 96, so when you're that age if your brain is as sharp as his you'll be happy!"*

1418. TIME WARP ★★★
ch.c. Archipenko – Here To Eternity (Stormy Atlantic). January 28. First foal. €37,000Y. Tattersalls Ireland September. J Brummitt. The dam, a modest 7f winner, is a half-sister to one winner. The second dam, Heat Of The Night (by Lear Fan), a dual 9f winner here, subsequently won a listed 1m event in Germany and is a half-sister to one winner. (Mr W E Sturt). *"A big horse, he'll be a six/seven furlong 2-y-o in July".*

1419. UNNAMED ★★
b.f. Jeremy – Rising Wind (Shirocco). February 14. First foal. €29,000Y. Goffs Sportsmans. Not sold. The dam, an Irish 2-y-o 1m winner , was listed placed over 1m. The second dam, Right Key (by Key Of Luck), a very useful Irish 7f (at 2 yrs) and dual Group 3 winner over 10f and 12f, is a sister to several winners including the Irish dual 7f (at 2 yrs) and listed 1m winner and dual Group 2 placed Wrong Key. (Lady O'Reilly). *"A nice filly, she's tall and from one of Lady O'Reilly's good families – they always do something at some stage. She's done too much growing to know at the moment".*

1420. UNNAMED ★★
b.c. Galileo – Turning Top (Pivotal). February 10. First foal. The dam, a fair 7f and 8.5f winner here, later won a Grade 3 over 10f in the USA. The second dam, Pietra Dura (by Cadeaux Genereux), an Irish 2-y-o 7f winner, was listed-placed and is a half-sister to 3 winners. (Michael Tabor). *"He's not as big as a lot of the Galileo's and he's a very good natured horse. You wouldn't know how good he was until you pressed the button, but we may be able to get him out in late summer".*

NOEL QUINLAN
1421. AIZU ★★★
b.g. Sakhee's Secret – Lemon Rock (Green Desert). January 27. First foal. £14,000Y. Doncaster Premier. Not sold. The dam, a fair 5f and 6f placed 2-y-o, is a half-sister to the useful listed 6f (at 2 yrs) and listed 7f winner Selinka. The second dam, Lady Links (Bahamian Bounty), a dual listed 6f winner (including at 2 yrs), is a half-sister to 5 winners including the quite useful 2-y-o 6f winner and Group 3 placed Umniya. (Mr Tommy Cummins). *"We trained the dam who didn't win but she was placed a couple of times as a 2-y-o before she got injured. A nice, early foal. he's almost ready to run".*

1422. FOLLOW THE RULES ★★
b.c. Kheleyf – It's The War (Consolidator). March 14. First foal. The dam is an unraced daughter of the unplaced Shine A Light (by Diesis), herself a half-sister to 3 minor winners. *"I'm not saying he's top-class but he'll definitely win his races. He's improving all the time"".*

1423. LIL'S JOY ★★★
b.f. Lilbourne Lad – Eman's Joy (Lion Cavern). January 27. Closely related to the modest 1m and 8.5f winner Joyful Sound (by Acclamation) and half-sister to the 2-y-o Group 3 1m Autumn Stakes winner Blitzkrieg, to the quite useful 1m and 10f winner Summer Gold (both by Barathea) and the fair 2-y-o 6f winner Toledo Gold (by Needwood Blade). The dam, a modest 3-y-o 6f winner, is a half-sister to 8 winners including the Group 3 Diomed Stakes winner Eton Lad. The second dam, Carolside (by Music Maestro), a very useful 2-y-o 5f winner, was second in the Cherry Hinton Stakes and is a half-sister to 6 winners. *"She's very sharp and may have won before your book comes out. At first she was quite fiery and I was a bit concerned, but the more she's worked the more she's calmed down".*

1424. UNNAMED ★★★
b.f. Equiano – Bible Box (Bin Ajwaad).
February 22. Seventh foal. 26,000foal.
Tattersalls December. D McGreavy. Half-
sister to the useful dual listed 6f winner of
6 races (including at 2 yrs) Bounty Box, to
the French 2-y-o 9f listed-placed Bahamian
Box, the fair 5f winner Blessing Box (all by
Bahamian Bounty), the fairly useful 2-y-o 6f
winner and listed-placed Vive Les Rouges
(by Acclamation) and the fair 7f winner
Charity Box (by Haafhd). The dam, a quite
useful 7f to 9f winner of 3 races, is out of the
2-y-o 1m seller winner Addie Pray (by Great
Commotion), herself a half-sister to 7 winners.
(Mr G Wilding). *"The dam breeds nothing but
winners and although the sire hasn't set the
world on fire yet this is a nice filly and certainly
a 2-y-o".*

1425. UNNAMED ★★
br.f. Captain Rio – Five Sisters (Mujahid). April
16. Third foal. €7,200Y. Goffs Open. Noel
Quinlan. Half-sister to the quite useful 2-y-o 6f
winner Mr Matthews (by Diamond Green). The
dam is an unraced half-sister to one winner.
The second dam, Quite Happy (by Statoblest),
a modest dual 5f winner, is a half-sister to 6
winners. *"She'll prove to be a bargain I think
and she'll be racing from April onwards. She's
not been here long but she's working nicely".*
TRAINERS' BARGAIN BUY

1426. UNNAMED ★★
b.f. Kheleyf – Haiti Dancer (Josr Algharoud).
March 22. Fifth foal. 2,500Y. Tattersalls
October Book 3. Not sold. The dam, a modest
2-y-o 7f winner, is a half-sister to 9 winners.
The second dam, Haitienne (by Green Dancer),
won once at 3 yrs in France and is a half-sister
to 7 winners. *"The dam hasn't bred a winner
yet but there are fairly good reports about two
of them. The sire gets plenty of winners, they're
not great but they win. She might not be one
of my better 2-y-o's but she'll be racing by the
end of May I'd say".*

1427. UNNAMED ★★
ch.f. Approve – Mairead Anne (Elusive Quality).
January 24. Third foal. 16,000Y. Tattersalls
October Book 3. Noel Quinlan. Half-sister to
the Italian winner of 9 races from 2 to 5 yrs
Grey Arrow (by Verglas). The dam, a minor

winner at 3 yrs in the USA, is a half-sister to 6
winners. The second dam, Quarrel Over Halo
(by Halo), won 2 minor races at 3 yrs in the
USA and is a half-sister to 9 winners including
Suvi (Grade 2 Del Mar Oaks). (Shane Long).
*"She's nice but quite big so I gave her a month
off, she's got a huge stride and I think a lot
of her. She'll be quite useful over six/seven
furlongs and she's owned by the footballer
Shane Long".*

1428. UNNAMED ★★★ ♠
b.f. Acclamation – Musical Bar (Barathea).
March 21. Third foal. Sister to the quite useful
2-y-o 6f winner Chord Chart. The dam, a fairly
useful 7f winner and second in a listed event
over 1m (both her starts), is a half-sister to 4
winners including the Prix Marcel Boussac,
1,000 Guineas and Irish 1,000 Guineas winner
Finsceal Beo and the Group 2 German 2,000
Guineas winner Frozen Power. The second
dam, Musical Treat (by Royal Academy), a
useful 7f winner and listed-placed twice, won
at 4 yrs in Canada and the USA and is a half-
sister to 6 winners. *"She'll be making her debut
at Newmarket in the six furlongs fillies' maiden
in May. She's very strong, does her work really
good, has a great constitution and just gives
you the feeling that there's a huge amount
under the bonnet".*

JOHN QUINN
1429. AL ZUBARAH ★★★
b.f. Exceed And Excel – Tropical Paradise
(Verglas). March 5. First foal. £120,000Y.
Doncaster Premier. Mandore International.
The dam won 6 races including the Group 3
7f Oak Tree and Group 3 7f Supreme Stakes
and is a half-sister to 3 winners. The second
dam, Ladylishandra (by Mujadil), an Irish 2-y-o
6f winner, is a half-sister to 7 winners. (Qatar
Racing). *"She shouldn't be too long in running,
possibly late April/early May, we like her and
she looks quite quick. She shouldn't have a
problem winning a maiden and she's a five/six
furlong 2-y-o".*

1430. ANCIENT ASTRONAUT ★★★★ ♠
b.c. Kodiac – Tatora (Selkirk). April 23. Tenth
foal. 100,000Y. Tattersalls October Book 1.
Not sold. Half-brother to the Group 2 Betfair
Lennox Stakes and Group 3 Jersey Stakes
winner Tariq, to the quite useful 7f winner

of 5 races including at 2 yrs Tariq Too (both by Kyllachy) and the French 2-y-o winner Duniatty (by Green Desert). The dam is an unraced half-sister to 3 winners and to the placed dam of the Group 2 Flying Childers Stakes winner Wi Dud. The second dam, Tatouma (by The Minstrel), won twice at 2 yrs and is a half-sister to 4 winners. (Harlen Ltd). *"A horse bought privately outside the ring at Tatts after he was led out unsold. His half-brother Tariq was a good winner for Peter Chapple-Hyam and this horse wouldn't be dissimilar to him. He'll come into his own over six and seven furlongs in mid-summer. Should be one to follow".*

1431. FROZEN VENTURE (IRE) ★★
b.c. Frozen Power – Taqarub (Marju). April 9. Third foal. £48,000Y. Doncaster Premier. Richard Knight/Quinn. The dam, a minor French 3-y-o winner, is a half-sister to 8 winners including the very useful 2-y-o listed 5f winner and subsequent French 3-y-o 5f listed winner Khasayl and the useful listed 2-y-o 7f winner Muklah. The second dam, Maraatib (by Green Desert), a quite useful 5f and 6f winner, is a half-sister to 6 winners. (Racing Ventures 2014). *"A horse for the mid-summer, we haven't done a lot with him so I couldn't tell you too much at this point, other than he's got a good attitude and is a nice mover. Probably one for six/seven furlongs".*

1432. INDIAN PURSUIT (IRE) ★★★
b.c. Compton Place – Church Melody (Oasis Dream). April 12. Third foal. £60,000Y. Doncaster Premier. Richard Knight/Quinn. Half-brother to the quite useful 2014 2-y-o dual 5f winner Al Ghuwariyah (by Acclamation). The dam is an unraced half-sister to 4 winners including the dual Group 2 winning stayer Gospel Choir. The second dam, Chorist (by Pivotal), won the Group 1 10f Curragh Pretty Polly Stakes and two Group 3 events and is a half-sister to 9 winners including the very useful 2-y-o 7f winner and Group 3 7f Prestige Stakes second Choirgirl. (Mr M Walker). *"A nice horse, he looks a five/six furlong type, he's showing up nicely and has done plenty of work on grass. He'll be out by late April/early May, he's pleasing us at home and has a brilliant attitude".*

1433. LEARNING CURVE (IRE) ★★★ ♠
b.g. Monsieur Bond – Existentialist (Exceed And Excel). March 30. First living foal. £65,000Y. Doncaster Premier. Richard Knight/Quinn. The dam, a fair 2-y-o 5f and 6f winner, is a half-sister to 6 winners including the smart Group 3 5.2f and 6f Wokingham Handicap winner Ratio and to the dam of the multiple Group 3 winner Ladies Are Forever and the smart sprinter Hoof It. The second dam, Owdbetts (by High Estate), a fair 7f to 10.2f winner of 4 races from 2 to 4 yrs, is a half-sister to 5 minor winners. (Racing Ventures 2014). *"We've gelded him just because he was a bit active, but we're happy with him. He's probably going to be a six furlong horse, hasn't really come into himself fully yet, but I'd be surprised if he doesn't have an engine under the bonnet because he's a brilliant mover. One of the things that attracted us to the pedigree was that two good sprinters, Ladies Are Forever and Hoof It, are in the family and they're both by Monsieur Bond".*

1434. REPUTATION ★★★★ ♠
b.c. Royal Applause – Semaphore (Zamindar). April 7. Fifth foal. £70,000Y. Doncaster Premier. John & Jake Warren. Half-brother to the 2014 6f placed 2-y-o Deep Blue Sea (by Rip Van Winkle), to the useful 2-y-o 7f winner and Group 3 7f Oh So Sharp Stakes third Annie's Fortune (by Montjeu) and the modest 10f winner Kalahari (by Halling). The dam is an unraced half-sister to 3 winners including the dam of the Group 3 winners Fantasia and Pink Symphony. The second dam, Blue Duster (by Danzig), winner of the Group 1 6f Cheveley Park Stakes, is a sister to the smart Group 1 6f Middle Park Stakes winner Zieten and a half-sister to 9 winners. (Highclere Thoroughbred Racing, Applause). *"A really nice horse, he's done a couple of pieces of work on grass but nothing serious yet. I imagine he'll be a six furlong 2-y-o, he's quite big and scopey and he'll be one we should see out from the mid-season onwards. A nice horse".*

1435. SAFE VOYAGE (IRE) ★★★
b.c. Fast Company – Shishangaan (Mujadil). April 15. Fourth foal. £52,000Y. Doncaster Premier. Richard Knight/Quinn. Half-brother to the fair 2014 Irish 5f and 6f placed 2-y-o Sauanna Belle (by Acclamation). The dam won

over 6f at 2 yrs in Italy and was listed-placed twice and is a half-sister to 2 winners. The second dam, Irish Flower (by Zieten), a listed-placed winner of 4 races in France, is a half-sister to 9 winners. (Mr R Harmon). *"He wasn't showing a huge amount until a month ago and he's really come to life now. He's done a couple of pieces on grass and I'd be surprised if he wasn't up to winning a maiden. Everything he's done is good and he's a real compact, ball of a horse. A proper 2-y-o type".*

1436. SMART MOVER (IRE) ★★★
b.f. Fast Company – Alltherightmoves (Namid). February 2. First foal. €35,000Y. Tattersalls Ireland September. Richard Knight/Sean Quinn. The dam, a moderate 5f fourth placed 2-y-o, is a half-sister to 10 winners including the listed winners and Group 1 placed Crown Of Light and Alboostan. The second dam, Russian Countess (by Nureyev), a useful French 2-y-o 1m winner and listed-placed, is a half-sister to 5 winners. (Racing Ventures 2014). *"She ran well on her debut when a bit of inexperience and a slightly rough passage cost her from getting placed. She's a nice filly and I think she can win a maiden and maybe sneak a bit of black type".*

1437. SPEED COMPANY (IRE) ★★★
b.c. Fast Company – Trentini (Singspiel). February 13. Second foal. £48,000Y. Doncaster Premier. Richard Knight/Quinn. The dam, a minor French 3-y-o winner, is a sister to one winner. The second dam, Nawadi (by Machiavellian), a quite useful 10f winner, is a sister to the very smart Group 2 Celebration Mile and Group 2 Queen Anne Stakes winner No Excuse Needed and to the useful 2-y-o 5f winner and Group 3 Norfolk Stakes third Skywards and a half-sister to the UAE Group 1 winner Capponi. (Racing Ventures 2014). *"He's one for mid-season, he hasn't worked yet but he's a big, strong horse and the type to go on. When the penny does drop he'll be OK and I think he'll be a seven furlong/mile horse later in the year".*

1438. SPIRIT OF ZEBEDEE (IRE) ★★★ ♠
b.c. Zebedee – Sampers (Exceed And Excel). March 29. Second foal. €60,000Y. Tattersalls Ireland September. Richard Knight/Sean Quinn. Half-brother to the 2014 5f and

6.5f placed 2-y-o Spirit Of Wedza (by Footstepsinthesand). The dam, a quite useful 5f and 6f winner, is a half-sister to one winner. The second dam, Gujarat (by Distant View), is an unraced half-sister to 6 winners. (Mr M Walker). *"He's a sharp type, he moves very well and I'd imagine he'd want top of the ground. He's very easy to deal with – he just does his work and sleeps. We like him and the Fairyhouse Sales race would be in the back of our minds for later in the year. He was one of the nicest lots at that sale".*

1439. WOWCHA (IRE) ★★★
b.f. Zoffany – Muravka (High Chaparral). March 21. Second foal. £150,000Y. Doncaster Premier. Chasemore Farm. Half-sister to the 2014 2-y-o Group 1 6f Prix Morny and Group 2 6f Coventry Stakes winner The Wow Signal (by Starspangledbanner). The dam is an unraced half-sister to 5 winners including the dual listed winner Tolpuddle. The second dam, Tabdea (by Topsider), won the listed Firth Of Clyde Stakes and listed Sceptre Stakes and is a half-sister to 8 winners including the French 1,000 Guineas winner Ta Rib. (Chasemore Farm). *"She came to us late having been prepped at home and as a result she's a bit behind the other fillies and hasn't done a piece of work yet. Obviously with her pedigree it's exciting to have her and she does remind us of her half-brother The Wow Factor. He's a very big horse and she's very big and strong for a filly and she has the same head as him. So there's a family resemblance in terms of looks anyway. The middle of the summer should be her starting point".*

1440. UNNAMED ★★★★
b.f. Kodiac – Atishoo (Revoque). March 26. Sixth foal. £42,000Y. Doncaster Premier. Richard Knight/Quinn. Half-sister to the fairly useful 6f, 7f (both at 2 yrs) and 10f winner and listed-placed Sonoran Sands (by Footstepsinthesand), to the fair 2-y-o 5f winner Kodatish (by Kodiac) and the modest 6f winner Point At Issue (by One Cool Cat). The dam, a modest Irish 1m placed maiden, is a half-sister to 4 winners including the listed winner and Group 2 Pretty Polly Stakes second Snippets. The second dam, Sniffle (by Shernazar), is an unplaced half-sister to the Grade 1 12f Hollywood Turf Cup winner

Frenchpark and the Group 1 Prix Vermeille winner Pearly Shells. (Harlen Ltd). *"A sharp type, she should be out in May and she looks a runner. Five furlongs will suite her, it's a real 2-y-o family and she looks to have followed suit".*

1441. UNNAMED ★★★★ ♠
b.c. Approve – Miznapp (Pennekamp). April 28. Tenth foal. €47,000Y. Goffs Orby. Richard Knight. Half-brother to 4 winners including the quite useful 1m to 10f winner and subsequent Qatar listed-placed Clean Bowled (by Footstepsinthesand), to the minor US winner of 2 races at 3 and 4 yrs Violet Sky (by Montjeu) and the moderate dual 5f (including at 2 yrs) and 7f winner Boga (by Invincible Spirit). The dam is an unraced half-sister to 4 winners including the Group 3 Ballycorus Stakes winner Al Tadh. The second dam, Tithcar (by Cadeaux Genereux), is a placed half-sister to 7 winners including the dual Group 2 winner Zindabad. (Harlen Ltd). *"A nice horse, he's strong and a lot more forward than you'd think by just looking at him. He'll be out in May and could be quite decent. Definitely a 2-y-o".*

1442. UNNAMED ★★
br.f. Kheleyf – Perino (Speightstown). February 1. First foal. €35,000Y. Tattersalls Ireland September. Richard Knight/Sean Quinn. The dam, a fair 5f winner at 3 yrs, is a half-sister to 4 winners including the Irish listed winner and Group 3 third Adaala. The second dam, Alshoowg (by Riverman), is an unraced half-sister to 4 winners. (Mr T G S Wood). *"A very straightforward filly, she hasn't done a piece of work yet but she's a good mover and we like her but she just hasn't done as much as some of the others. I imagine she'll be a five/six furlong filly".*

KEVIN RYAN
1443. AHLAN BIL EMARATI (IRE)
ch.c. Fast Company – Law Review (Case Law). April 12. Tenth foal. €72,000Y. Goffs Orby. Stephen Hillen. Half-brother to 6 winners including the useful 6f (at 2 yrs) and 9f winner Layazaal (by Mujadil), the fairly useful 5f (at 2 yrs) and 6f winner of 5 races Falasteen, the quite useful 2-y-o 5f and 6f winner Latin Review (both by Titus Livius), the quite useful

2-y-o 6f winner Grecian and the 2-y-o 6f winner, on his only start, Integrity (both by Dark Angel). The dam, placed once over 1m, is a half-sister to 10 winners including the Group 1 July Cup winner and sire Lake Coniston. The second dam, Persian Polly (by Persian Bold), a useful Irish 2-y-o 7f winner, was third in the Group 3 Park Stakes. (Ahmad Abdulla Al Shaikh & Co).

1444. CAPTAIN DION
gr.c. Equiano – Bandanna (Bandmaster). March 25. Ninth foal. £35,000Y. Doncaster Premier. Hillen & Ryan. Half-brother to the fairly useful Group 3 6f placed 2-y-o Slope (by Acclamation), to the fairly useful 2-y-o 5.5f and subsequent Hong Kong winner Art Sale, the fair dual 5f winner Mandy's Hero (both by Compton Place), the fairly useful 2-y-o 7f winner Markazzi (by Dansili) and the quite useful 2-y-o 5f winner Rowayton (by Lujain). The dam, a fairly useful 5f and 6f winner of 6 races (including at 2 yrs), was third in the Group 3 Princess Margaret Stakes and is a half-sister to 5 winners including the Group 3 July Stakes winner Rich Ground. The second dam, Gratclo (by Belfort), a modest winner of 5 races from 2 to 4 yrs, is a half-sister to 3 winners. (Mr T A Rahman).

1445. DREAMING VOICE (IRE)
ch.c. Poet's Voice – North East Bay (Prospect Bay). March 5. Eighth foal. 60,000Y. Tattersalls October Book 1. Rabbah Bloodstock. Closely related to the UAE Group 1 10f, Group 2 Prix du Conseil de Paris and Group 3 10f Prix du Prince d'Orange winner Prince Bishop (by Dubawi) and half-sister to 4 winners including the fairly useful 1m (at 2 yrs) and 10f winner Strategic Mission (by Red Ransom) and the quite useful 2-y-o 6f winner Acquiesced (by Refuse To Bend). The dam, unplaced on her only start, is a half-sister to 8 winners including the listed winner Hold To Ransom. The second dam, Wassifa (by Sure Blade), a fairly useful 11f winner here, subsequently won 3 minor races in the USA and was stakes-placed. (Mr Sultan Ali).

1446. GLORIOUS TIMES (IRE)
b.f. Galileo – Quiet Mouse (Quiet American). March 25. Sister to the fair 12f and hurdles winner Bohemian Rhapsody and half-sister to

3 winners including the 2-y-o Group 3 7f C L Weld Park Stakes and 3-y-o listed 6f winner and Group 1 7f Moyglare Stud Stakes second Ugo Fire. The dam is an unraced half-sister to 7 winners including the smart broodmare Witch Of Fife (the dam of 3 stakes winners). The second dam, Fife (by Lomond), a fairly useful 1m winner, is a half-sister to 5 winners including Piffle (dam of the Group 1 winners Frenchpark and Pearly Shells). (Ahmad Abdulla Al Shaikh & Co).

1447. GOODKNIGHT PERCY (IRE)
ch.c. Sir Percy – Ekhraaj (El Prado). February 8. First foal. £30,000Y. Doncaster Premier. Hillen & Ryan. The dam ran once unplaced and is a half-sister to 2 winners including the 2-y-o 7f and UAE listed winner Nawwaar. The second dam, Mostaqeleh (by Rahy), a very useful 2-y-o 6f and 7f winner, was second in the Group 2 1m Prix de Sandringham and is a half-sister to 3 winners including the very smart listed 7f (at 2 yrs) and listed 10f winner Muqbil. (The Better Together Partnership).

1448. KAJAKI (IRE)
b.c. Mastercraftsman – No Quest (Rainbow Quest). May 8. Fourteenth foal. €85,000Y. Tattersalls Ireland September. Hillen & Ryan. Half-brother to 6 winners including the useful 1m to 10f and subsequent US Grade 3 winner and dual Grade 1 second Macaw (by Bluebird), the quite useful 2-y-o 1m winner Prince Desire (by Fasliyev), the fair 14f and 2m winner Irish Quest (by Galileo), the fair 1m (at 2 yrs) and 11f winner Rutters Rebel (by Entrepreneur) and the fair 1m and 12f winner Quest For More (by Teofilo). The dam is a placed half-sister to 9 winners including the French 2,000 Guineas winner No Pass No Sale. The second dam, No Disgrace (by Djakao), a French 2-y-o 7.5f winner, was fourth in three Group 3 events and is a half-sister to 3 winners. (Mr F Gillespie).

1449. LAGENDA
b.c. Dick Turpin – Whirly Dancer (Danehill Dancer). February 28. First foal. £32,000Y. Doncaster Premier. Hillen & Ryan. The dam, a quite useful dual 7f winner, is a half-sister to 2 winners. The second dam, Whirly Bird (by Nashwan), a useful 9.5f to 11f winner, is a half-

sister to 4 winners including the very useful 12f listed Galtres Stakes winner Inchiri. (Mr T A Rahman).

1450. MJNOON (IRE)
b.c. Roderic O'Connor – Elshamms (Zafonic). April 6. Eleventh foal. €65,000Y. Goffs Orby. Stephen Hillen. Half-brother to 10 winners including the 2014 2-y-o 6f winner Flaming Spear (by Lope De Vega), the 2-y-o 7f winner and Group 2 Rockfel Stakes third Desert Blossom (by Shamardal) and the useful triple 6f (including at 2 yrs) and UAE listed 5f winner Taqseem (by Fantastic Light). The dam, a fairly useful 2-y-o 7f winner and third in the Group 3 Prestige Stakes, is a half-sister to 10 winners. The second dam, Gharam (by Green Dancer), a 2-y-o 6f winner and third in French 1,000 Guineas, is a half-sister to the US Grade 1 winner Talinum. (Mr Hussain Alabbas Lootah).

1451. NEW HOPE (IRE) ♠
b.c. Exceed And Excel – Great Hope (Halling). April 5. Sixth foal. €375,000Y. Goffs Orby. David Redvers. Closely related to the fairly useful 2-y-o 1m winner and triple listed placed Reckoning (by Danehill Dancer) and half-brother to the quite useful 2-y-o 7f winner Stylish One (by Invincible Spirit). The dam, a quite useful Irish dual 1m winner, is a half-sister to 5 winners including the dual Group 3 placed Chivalrous. The second dam, Aspiration (by Sadler's Wells), a 10f winner in Ireland, is a sister to the Group 1 1m Gran Criterium winner Sholokhov and a half-sister the listed winners Zavaleta, Napper Tandy and Affianced (dam of the Irish Derby winner Soldier Of Fortune). (Qatar Racing).

1452. TAKING LIBERTYS
b.c. Makfi – Liberty Chery (Statue Of Liberty). April 14. £18,000Y. Doncaster Premier. Stephen Hillen. Brother to the modest 2014 6f placed 2-y-o Songye. The dam, a French 1m winner, was listed-placed twice and is a half-sister to 2 winners including the 2-y-o 7f winner and Group 1 Criterium de Saint-Cloud second Fauvelia. The second dam, Marion (by Doyoun), a minor French dual winner at 3 yrs, is a half-sister to 5 winners. (Hambleton Racing Ltd). This colt won on his debut at Beverley on the 15th April.

1453. UNNAMED
b.c. Distorted Humor – Wile Cat (Storm Cat).
March 18. Fourth foal. $260,000Y. Keeneland
September. David Redvers. Half-brother to the
2-y-o Group 3 Sirenia Stakes winner Shumoos
(by Distorted Humor). The dam is an unraced
sister to the Grade 2 La Canada Stakes winner
Cat Fighter and a half-sister to the Group 3
winner and sire Ishiguru. The second dam,
Strategic Maneuver (by Cryptoclearance),
winner of the Grade 1 6f Spinaway Stakes,
the Grade 1 7f Matron Stakes and two Grade
2 events at 2 yrs in the USA, is a half-sister to
10 winners including the US stakes winners
Ashford Castle and Missionary. (Qatar Racing).

DAVID SIMCOCK
1454. AL NASSER ALWASHIK ★★★
b.c. Intikhab – Crystal Moments (Haafhd).
March 17. Third foal. The dam, a quite useful
5f, 6f (both at 2 yrs) and 7f winner, is a half-
sister to 3 minor winners. The second dam,
Celestial Choir (by Celestial Storm), a quite
useful 7f to 12f winner of 9 races on the flat,
also won 7 races over jumps and is a half-sister
to 5 winners. *"He's not the biggest but he's an
enthusiastic goer and one we should push on
with earlier. He has a nice way of going and
shows a bit of speed".*

1455. CHINOISERIES ★★
b.f. Archipenko – Robe Chinoise (Robellino).
February 4. Sixth foal. Sister to the very smart
Group 1 12f British Champions Fillies and
Mares Stakes and Group 3 Musidora Stakes
winner Madame Chiang and half-sister to the
quite useful 1m winner of 4 races Oriental
Scot and the fair 1m (at 2 yrs) and 12f winner
Mannlichen (both by Selkirk). The dam, a quite
useful 10f and 12f winner, is a half-sister to 3
winners. The second dam, Kiliniski (by Niniski),
winner of the Group 3 12f Lingfield Oaks Trial,
was second in the Yorkshire Oaks and fourth
in the Epsom Oaks and is a half-sister to 5
winners including the dam of the US triple
Grade 1 winner Bienamado. *"A full sister to
Madame Chiang, she's similar to her in looks
although possibly not as big as her at this stage.
She trains well and she's straightforward but it's
difficult at this stage to gauge her ability".*

1456. COSMIC STORM ★★★★
br.f. Sea The Stars – Riotous Applause (Royal

Applause). March 18. Fifth foal. 200,000foal.
Tattersalls December. Eclipse Partnership.
Half-sister to the useful 2-y-o listed 6f winner
Invincible Warrior (by Invincible Spirit), to
the quite useful 7f winner Riot Of Colour (by
Excellent Art) and the quite useful 7f to 8.5f
winner of 4 races Crowdmania (by Shamardal).
The dam, a fairly useful dual 6f winner
(including at 2 yrs), was listed-placed and is
a sister to one winner and a half-sister to 6
winners including the high-class 2-y-o Group
1 1m Racing Post Trophy winner Crowded
House and to the placed dam of the US dual
Grade 1 winner Ticker Tape. The second dam,
Wiener Wald (Woodman), is an unplaced
half-sister to 6 minor winners abroad. *"A lovely
big filly, she's a good goer and one we admire
every morning. If you stood her up you'd think
she needs plenty of time, but when you watch
her at exercise she looks far more forward than
you would have imagined. In my opinion she
has a real chance".*

1457. CROSS EXAMINE ★★★★
b.c. Roderic O'Connor – Red Vale (Halling).
March 12. Seventh foal. 42,000Y. Tattersalls
October Book 2. Rabbah Bloodstock. Half-
brother to the 2-y-o Grade 1 8.5f Breeders
Cup Juvenile and listed 7f Stardom Stakes
winner Vale Of York and to the quite useful
8.5f winner Iffraaj Pink (by Iffraaj). The dam is
an unraced half-sister to 9 winners including
the fairly useful 10f and subsequent US Grade
3 winner Uraib. The second dam, Hamsaat
(by Sadler's Wells), a quite useful winner over
1m at 3 yrs on her only outing, is a sister to
2 winners including the dual Group 2 winner
Batshoof and a half-sister to 4 winners. *"He
goes well, he's very natural, shows plenty of
speed and looks like being our first 2-y-o colt
runner of the year. One with a nice way of
going, he's really surprised me with how well
he's done".*

1458. ELECTORAL (IRE) ★★★
b.c. Rip Van Winkle – Sumingasefa (Danehill).
April 24. Seventh living foal. €22,000Y.
Tattersalls Ireland September. BBA (Ire).
Half-brother to the quite useful 2-y-o dual 7f
winner Famcred (by Inchinor), to the Italian
winner of 7 races at 3 to 5 yrs Fagutela (by Dr
Fong) and the modest 6f winner Summersault
(by Footstepsinthesand). The dam, a listed-

placed winner of 5 races in Italy, is a half-sister to 7 winners. The second dam, Svanzega (by Sharpen Up), winner of the Group 3 Premio Baggio, was third in the Group 2 Premio Lydia Tesio and is a half-sister to 8 winners. *"A big horse with a lot of size and scope, he canters well and is a nice natured colt. Not one for the first half of the season though".*

1459. GOLDMEMBER ★★★

ch.c. New Approach – Sister Act (Marju). January 25. Third foal. 300,000Y. Tattersalls October Book 1. David Redvers. Half-brother to the Group 1 10f Prix Jean Romanet winner and Group 1 10f Prix de l'Opera second Ribbons (by Manduro). The dam, a fair 1m winner, is a sister to the Group 1 Fillies Mile, Falmouth Stakes, Sussex Stakes and Matron Stakes winner Soviet Song, and a half-sister to 3 winners including the useful 5f (at 2 yrs) and triple 6f winner Baralinka. The second dam, Kalinka (by Soviet Star), a quite useful 2-y-o 7f winner, is a half-sister to 2 winners. *"A flashy, attractive looking horse, not the biggest but he's well-related. His half-sister Ribbons was a late developer but I'd like to think he's a bit more forward than that. He has a very likeable attitude and way of going".*

1460. HOLY BOY (IRE) ★★★

b.c. Holy Roman Emperor – Sister Golightly (Mtoto). April 1. Sixth foal. €70,000Y. Goffs Orby. Blandford Bloodstock. Half-brother to the 2014 2-y-o 6f winner and Group 3 6f Balanchine Stakes second Jeanne Girl (by Rip Van Winkle), to the French and Italian listed-placed winner of 7 races Jack Boy (by Hawk Wing) and two minor 3-y-o winners in Italy by Redback and Oratorio. The dam is an unraced half-sister to the Group 1 Falmouth Stakes winner Rajeem. The second dam, Magic Sister (by Cadeaux Genereux), a modest 3-y-o 7f placed maiden, is a sister to the very smart 2-y-o Group 1 6f Prix Morny and Group 3 5f Molecomb Stakes winner Hoh Magic and a half-sister to 5 winners. *"A fine looking horse with a good action, he's cantering away but hasn't done anything fast. An impressive horse to look at, he would have a bit more size than some by the sire".*

1461. KING OF DREAMS ★★★★

ch.c. Dream Ahead – Complexion (Hurricane Run). February 9. First foal. 240,000Y. Tattersalls October Book 2. Mark Crossman. The dam, a quite useful 1m winner, is a half-sister to the high-class 7f (at 2 yrs) and Group 2 Celebration Mile winner and Group 1 Queen Elizabeth II Stakes second Zacinto. The second dam, Ithaca (by Distant View), a useful 2-y-o 7f winner and second in the Group 3 7f Prestige Stakes, is a half-sister to 5 winners including the Canadian Grade 3 14f winner Eagle Poise. *"A lovely horse, he's very straightforward and really wants to get on with everything in a nice, professional way. A very likeable horse, we should see him in high summer and I'm very pleased with him at the moment. He's very similar to his sire in the way he carries himself and the way he stands up".*

1462. MS GILLARD ★★★ ♠

b.f. Aussie Rules – Oval Office (Pursuit Of Love). January 31. Fifth foal. Half-sister to the smart 2-y-o Group 3 6f Sirenia Stakes winner Glass Office (by Verglas) and to the quite useful 9.5f and 12.5f winner Captain Morley (by Hernando). The dam, a fairly useful dual 1m winner, is a half-sister to 12 winners including the smart 6f (at 2 yrs) and Nell Gwyn Stakes winner Myself and the smart 2-y-o 6f Princess Margaret Stakes and 3-y-o 6f Prix de Seine et Oise winner Bluebook. The second dam, Pushy (by Sharpen Up), won the Queen Mary Stakes and is a half-sister to 10 winners including the good winners Precocious and Jupiter Island. *"We have two of her relations, Glass Office is a speed horse and Captain Morley is a middle-distance horse. She's more like Glass Office. She has a good attitude, is a good goer and there's plenty of her. An earlyish type, I should imagine she'll start at six or seven furlongs and she's doing everything right".*

1463. NAMOOSE (USA) ★★★★

b.c. Blame – Petition The Lady (Petionville). February 19. First foal. $105,000Y. Keeneland September. Blandford Bloodstock. The dam, a US stakes winner of 6 races, is a half-sister to the US winner and Grade 1 third Saucey Evening. The second dam, Jeweled Lady (by General Meeting), is an unraced sister to the US Grade 1 winners General Challenge and Notable Career. *"A lovely horse. The sire is new to me but I know he stayed very well. There's lots of speed on the mare's side though and this is a very natural horse with a good way of going and he's a neat individual, not over-big but you wouldn't call him small. I'm very pleased with him and he'll be one to start over seven furlongs in high summer. I like him".*

1464. PROSECUTE (FR) ★★★ ♠

b.c. Lawman – Dissitation (Spectrum). February 23. €50,000Y. Arqana Deauville August. R Pritchard Gordon. Half-brother to a bumpers winner by Diamond Green. The dam, a fair 7f and 1m placed maiden, is a sister to the Group 3 7f Ballycorus Stakes winner Rum Charger (herself dam of the US multiple Grade 1 winner Winchester) and a half-sister to 5 winners. The second dam, Park Charger (by Tirol), a useful winner over 1m and 10f at 3 yrs in Ireland, was listed-placed four times and is a half-sister to 9 winners. *"He has a nice way of going, he's a big horse and I haven't been disappointed with anything he's done yet. You could have looked at him at first and thought 'big and backward' but he's actually trained very well and surprisingly showed good ability. He'll start over seven furlongs around July time".*

1465. SING YOUR SONG (IRE) ★★

b.f. Aqlaam – Dhan Dhana (Dubawi). February 1. Second foal. The dam, a fair dual 10f winner, is a half-sister to 4 winners including the fairly useful 2-y-o 7f winner and listed UAE 1,000 Guineas third Purple Sage and the very useful listed 1m winner and dual Group 3 placed Annabelle's Charm. The second dam, Kylemore (by Sadler's Wells), is an unplaced full or half-sister to the Group 1 winner Ballingarry, Aristotle and Starborough and to the unraced dam of the multiple Group 1 winner St Nicholas Abbey. *"A straightforward filly, she'll take a little bit of time and is cantering away. She's done very little wrong".*

1466. VEENA (FR) ★★★

b.f. Elusive City – Kensita (Soviet Star). February 19. Third foal. €40,000Y. Arqana Deauville August. Blandford Bloodstock. The dam is an unraced half-sister to 3 winners including Keraka (Group 3 Anglesey Stakes). The second dam, Kerita (by Formidable), winner of the Group 3 7f Supreme Stakes and third in the Group 2 Challenge Stakes, is

a half-sister to 3 winners. *"A filly that's grown plenty, so she's a good size now and has a nice attitude. She won't be particularly early but she has a nice way of going".*

1467. UNNAMED ★★★

b.f. Mastercraftsman – Abbeyleix Lady (Montjeu). February 10. Fourth foal. £44,000Y. Doncaster Premier. Blandford Bloodstock. Half-sister to the modest 5f winner Meebo (by Captain Rio). The dam is an unraced half-sister to 8 winners including the dam of the Group winners Pomellato and Parivash. The second dam, Premier Amour (by Salmon Leap), a German Group 3 winner and third in the Group 1 French Oaks, is a half-sister to 9 winners. *"A filly that's grown plenty. She was very untypical of a horse from the Doncaster Sales in that you can see plenty of Montjeu in her. She has a good, fluent action and a good attitude. A filly for later in the year".*

1468. UNNAMED ★★★

b.f. Kodiac – Admire The View (Dubawi). March 2. Second foal. £18,000Y. Doncaster Premier. David Redvers. The dam, a quite useful 7f (including at 2 yrs) and 1m winner, is a half-sister to one winner. The second dam, Miss Honorine (by Highest Honor), a winner of 4 races at 3 and 4 yrs in Ireland including three listed events from 1m to 10f, was Group 3 placed twice and is a half-sister to 8 winners. *"A small, nippy filly, she has a good attitude and will be one of our earliest runners. She could start over five, or more likely six furlongs".*

1469. UNNAMED ★★★ ♠

gr.c. Archipenko – Albanova (Alzao). April 9. Seventh foal. 140,000Y. Tattersalls October Book 1. BBA (Ire). Half-brother to the listed 10.5f winner All At Sea (by Sea The Stars), to the quite useful 2-y-o 9f winner and listed-placed Albamara (by Galileo), the fair 1m (at 2 yrs) to 14f winner and listed-placed Alwilda (by Hernando) and the fair 10f winner Albertus Pictor (by Selkirk). The dam, a triple Group 1 12f winner in Germany, is a sister to the dual Champion Stakes winner Alborada and a half-sister to 7 winners. The second dam, Alouette (by Darshaan), a 1m (at 2 yrs) and listed 12f winner, is a half-sister to the Group 2 Nassau Stakes winner Last

Second (dam of the Group 1 winner Aussie Rules) and the dams of the Group 1 winners Yesterday, Quarter Moon and Allegretto. *"A nice individual from a good family, he shows surprisingly natural ability and is by a sire that's doing very well. He's a colt we'll see later in the year, but I'm very pleased with what he's done so for".*

1470. UNNAMED ★★

gr.f. Sir Percy – Altitude (Green Desert). April 20. Third foal. 28,000Y. Tattersalls October Book 2. Blandford Bloodstock. Half-sister to the fair 1m winner Alegra (by Galileo). The dam, a fair 12f winner, is a half-sister to 8 winners including the Group 1 winners Alborada and Albanova. The second dam, Alouette (by Darshaan), a useful 1m (at 2 yrs) and listed 12f winner, is a sister to the listed winner Arrikala and a half-sister to the Nassau Stakes and Sun Chariot Stakes winner Last Second (dam of the French 2,000 Guineas winner Aussie Rules), the Doncaster Cup winner Alleluia (dam of the Prix Royal-Oak winner Allegretto) and the placed dam of the Group 1 winners Quarter Moon and Yesterday. *"She was quite well-bought I think, but she was late coming in so she hasn't done a great deal. She was quite small at the sales and she's grown and done well since then. On pedigree you'd say she'd want a mile to start with".* **TRAINERS' BARGAIN BUY**

1471. UNNAMED ★★★★

b.f. Sir Percy – Artistic Blue (Diesis). March 27. Eleventh foal. 52,000Y. Tattersalls October Book 3. Blandford Bloodstock. Half-sister to 5 winners including the dual 2014 2-y-o dual 6f winner Heartbreak Hero (by Exceed And Excel), the useful 7f to 10f winner of 5 races here and in Hong Kong, Indigo Way (by Encosta De Lago) and the quite useful 12f winner Wandle (by Galileo). The dam, winner of the listed 7f Tyros Stakes, was second in the Group 3 7f Boland Stakes and is a half-sister to 6 winners including the Irish listed winners Queen Of Palms and Cool Clarity. The second dam, Tapolite (by Tap On Wood), winner of the listed Tyros Stakes, is a sister to the 2-y-o Group 3 1m Killavullen Stakes winner Sedulous. *"A strong filly that shows good natural ability, she's not over-big and she looks like a speed filly. You'd love to think she'd be out in May".*

1472. UNNAMED ★★★

b.f. Dubawi – Diary (Green Desert). April 1. Sixth foal. Half-sister to the Group 1 5f Prix de l'Abbaye and dual listed 6f winner Total Gallery (by Namid), to the 5f winner (at 2 yrs) and Group 1 Fillies' Mile second Lady Darshaan, the useful listed 13f winner Tempest Fugit (both by High Chaparral) and a winner abroad by Lujain. The dam won 3 races in Greece over 7f at 3 yrs and is a half-sister to 4 winners including the Group 1 Gran Criterium third Al Waffi and the Triumph Hurdle winner Made In Japan. The second dam, Darrery (by Darshaan), won 3 races at 3 and 4 yrs, was listed-placed and is a half-sister to 3 winners. *"A very attractive looking filly with a nice way of going. She's probably not going to be as precocious as one or two of her siblings and we're looking at the second half of the season for her over seven furlongs".*

1473. UNNAMED ★★★

b.c. Vale Of York – Dubai Power (Cadeaux Genereux). March 29. Third foal. Brother to the fair 2014 2-y-o 5f winner Escrick and half-brother to the fairly useful 2-y-o 1m winner and listed-placed Power Of Light (by Echo Of Light). The dam, a quite useful 6f and 1m winner, is a half-sister to the fairly useful 7f and 1m winner of 3 races and listed-placed Vanguard Dream. The second dam, Garmoucheh (by Silver Hawk), a fairly useful 7f (at 2 yrs) and 10.3f winner, was listed-placed and is a half-sister to 4 winners the Irish listed-placed Lady Shannon. *"Totally opposite to his full sister Escrick who won over five furlongs at two. He's a good-sized colt with a nice way of going and has a good action. There's plenty of him and he's a colt that's doing well, so I'd like to think he's one for the high summer".*

1474. UNNAMED ★★

gr.f. Mastercraftsman – Duchess Dee (Bachelor Duke). April 16. First foal. €40,000Y. Arqana Deauville August. Not sold. The dam is an unplaced half-sister to 6 winners including the listed 9f winner and subsequent Canadian Grade 2 third Cayman Sunset. The second dam, Robinia (by Roberto), a fairly useful 2-y-o 7f winner, is a half-sister to 5 winners here and abroad. *"She wasn't terribly expensive but she has plenty of size and scope. Quite a natural filly, she's very full of herself and playful all the time, but has a nice way of going".*

1475. UNNAMED ★★★
b.f. Invincible Spirit – Elle Galante (Galileo).
March 20. Fifth foal. Half-sister to the 2014
2-y-o 1m winner, on his only start, Balios (by
Shamardal). The dam, a German listed-placed
11f winner of 3 races, is a sister to the German
listed winner Elle Gala and a half-sister to the
German Group 3 1m second Elle Shadow and
the German listed 10f winner El Comodin. The
second dam, Elle Danzig (Roi Danzig), won the
Group 1 Premio Roma (twice) and the Group
1 10f Grosser Preis Bayerisches Zuchtrennen
and is a half-sister to 10 winners. *"She's not
the biggest but she's shaping quite nicely. The
more she's done the more she's learned and
she's actually getting quicker as her training
develops. I'd love to think she's a six/seven
furlong filly and she should be ready to run
around June time".*

1476. UNNAMED ★★★
ch.g. New Approach – Frivolity (Pivotal).
March 25. Third foal. Half-brother to the fair
5.5f winner Ashkari (by Dutch Art). The dam
is an unraced half-sister to numerous winners
including the smart 2-y-o Group 2 6f Mill Reef
Stakes winner Byron and the useful 1m and
10.3f winner Gallant Hero. The second dam,
Gay Gallanta (by Woodman), a very smart
winner of the Group 1 6f Cheveley Park Stakes
and the Group 3 5f Queen Mary Stakes, was
second in the 1m Falmouth Stakes and is a
half-sister to the smart Group 2 10f Gallinule
Stakes winner Sportsworld. *"He's trained very
well and shown more speed than I thought he
would but his half-sister was speedy too. He's
quite natural in everything he does and ambles
up there very innocuously if you didn't know
him, but when asked he comes to life. He's
quite likeable".*

1477. UNNAMED ★★★
ch.c. Medicean – Hymnsheet (Pivotal).
February 28. Second foal. 48,000Y. Tattersalls
October Book 2. Blandford Bloodstock. The
dam, a quite useful 2-y-o 1m winner, is a
sister to 2 winners including the Group 1 10f
Curragh Pretty Polly Stakes and dual Group 3
winner Chorist and a half-sister to 7 winners.
The second dam, Choir Mistress (by Chief
Singer), is an unraced half-sister to 7 winners
including the smart Group 2 11.9f Great
Voltigeur Stakes winner Sacrament. *"A colt that
came in late but has caught up very quickly. He*

*has a nice way of going and is quite a natural
horse. I'm very pleased with him and he's
surprised me at how well he's taken to training
considering he was late in".*

1478. UNNAMED ★★★
b.c. Bahamian Bounty – Kerrys Requiem
(King's Best). February 4. First foal. 70,000Y.
Tattersalls October Book 2. Blandford
Bloodstock. The dam, a fairly useful listed-
placed 5f (at 2 yrs) and 6f winner, is a
half-sister to 3 minor winners. The dam is
an unraced full or half-sister to 7 winners
including Group 1 Dewhurst Stakes second
Fencing Master and the Group 1 Prix de Diane
second Millionaia. *"A horse that's grown plenty
since the sale, he's a nice goer, hasn't missed a
day and he's improved with training. He's got a
big knee action so I'm pretty sure he'll enjoy a
little bit of cut".*

1479. UNNAMED ★★
b.c. Galileo – Looking Back (Stravinsky).
January 15. Brother to the Sussex Stakes,
Queen Elizabeth II Stakes and Juddmonte
International winner Rip Van Winkle, to the
quite useful 9f winner Illusive and the fair 1m
winner A Star Is Born and half-brother to the
Italian Group 3 1m winner Le Vie Infinite (by
La Vie Dei Colori). The dam, an Italian winner
of 2 races at 2 and 3 yrs and listed-placed, is
a half-sister to 2 winners. The second dam,
Mustique Dream (by Don't Forget Me), a quite
useful dual 1m winner, is a half-sister to 6
winners. *"A fine looking horse, he will need a
bit of time but he's a good actioned horse that
won't be rushed".*

1480. UNNAMED ★★★
b.c. Galileo – Looking Lovely (Storm Cat). April
17. Second foal. Brother to Gran Paradiso,
unplaced over 7f on his only start at 2 yrs
in 2014. The dam, a quite useful 2-y-o 6f
winner, is a half-sister to the Derby winner
Ruler Of The World (by Galileo) and to the
multiple Group 1 10f to 12f winner Duke Of
Marmalade. The second dam, Love Me True
(by Kingmambo), an Irish 1m winner, was third
in the Group 3 Killavullan Stakes and is a half-
sister to the Grade 2 Sanford Stakes winner
Bite The Bullet and the smart listed 10f winner
Shuailaan. *"A much more forward colt than my
other Galileo 2-y-o, he's a good size but much*

more natural and he's shown a little more, so I quite like him".

1481. UNNAMED ★★★

ch.c. Poet's Voice – O Fourlunda (Halling). February 14. Fifth foal. 26,000Y. Tattersalls October Book 3. Not sold. Half-brother to a minor winner abroad by Green Desert. The dam, a modest triple 6f placed maiden, is a half-sister to 10 winners including the triple Group 3 winner and Group 1 placed Blue Monday. The second dam, Lunda (by Soviet Star), is an unplaced half-sister to 6 winners including the high-class middle-distance horses and multiple Group 1 winners Luso and Warrsan, the smart Group 3 winners Cloud Castle and Needle Gun. *"A different type of Poet's Voice than the other two I have. He's taller, attractive, quite well-bought and one for the second part of the season but with a nice way of going".*

1482. UNNAMED ★★

gr.c. Starspangledbanner – Ultimate Best (King's Best). February 6. First foal. £230,000Y. Doncaster Premier. David Redvers. The dam, a moderate 12f placed maiden, is a half-sister to 6 winners including the useful 10f and 12f listed winner Film Script (herself dam of the listed winner Free Agent), the Group 3 Chipchase Stakes winner Barney McGrew and the fairly useful 6f and 7f and subsequent US stakes winner National Park. The second dam, Success Story (by Sharrood), a modest dual 10f winner, is a half-sister to 7 winners including the Group 2 13.5f Prix de Pomone winner Interlude. *"A great big horse, every time we try to push on with him he seems to grow and get a bit weak. He has a likeable way of going but he'll be one for the second half of the year".*

TOMMY STACK

1483. ASPAR (IRE) ★★★★

b.c. Holy Roman Emperor – Lisa Gherardini (Barathea). February 6. First foal. £47,000Y. Doncaster Premier. Margaret O'Toole. The dam is an unplaced half-sister to 3 winners including the Group 2 Coventry Stakes third Rakaan. The second dam, Petite Spectre (by Spectrum), a fair 2-y-o 6f winner, is a half-sister to 8 winners including the useful 2-y-o Group 3 7f C L Weld Park Stakes winner Rag

Top. *"He seems sharp and he should be out in May over six furlongs. Like most Holy Roman Emperor's he's not very big, but he's a nice early 2-y-o type".*

1484. CIAVENNA (IRE) ★★

b.f. Canford Cliffs – Chantarella (Royal Academy). April 14. Half-sister to the fairly useful 2-y-o 5f winner, listed-placed and Group 2 6f Railway Stakes fourth Another Express, to the fairly useful listed-placed triple 5f winner Celerina (both by Choisir), the US 2-y-o triple 1m winner Clenor (by Oratorio) and the moderate Irish 6f winner Candy Kiss (by Mull Of Kintyre). The dam is an unplaced half-sister to several winners including the listed 5f Rous Stakes winner My-O-My. The second dam, Maimiti (by Goldhill), is an unplaced half-sister to the useful Irish sprinter Title Roll, winner of the Group 3 King George Stakes and to the listed sprint winner Northern Express. *"A light framed filly we don't know much about yet because we haven't done much with her. In terms of her siblings she's more in line with her half-sister Celerina (who only came into her own as a 4-y-o) than the others".*

1485. CRY ME A RIVER (IRE) ★★★★

b.f. Danehill Dancer – River Flow (Affirmed). April 8. Tenth foal. £50,000Y. Doncaster Premier. Fozzy Stack. Sister to the fairly useful Irish 2-y-o 5f winner Danehill Brook and half-sister to the Australian dual listed winner Skiddaw Peak and to a minor winner in New Zealand (both by Generous). The dam is an unraced half-sister to 5 winners including the Group 1 placed King Sound and to the unraced dam of the French 2,000 Guineas and US Grade 1 winner Landseer. The second dam, Flood (by Riverman), won once over 6f in the USA and is a half-sister to 3 winners including the Grade 1 Californian Stakes winner Sabona. *"She goes nicely, we'll probably set her off at six furlongs and she's a big, strong mature filly. She goes well".*

1486. DIAMOND FIELDS (IRE) ★★

b.f. Fastnet Rock – Question Times (Shamardal). January 11. First foal. €28,000Y. Goffs Orby. Form Bloodstock. The dam, a fairly useful listed 6f placed 2-y-o and 6f 3-y-o winner, is a half-sister to the smart

Group 3 Sceptre Stakes winner and Group 1 6f Cheveley Park Stakes second Sunday Times. The second dam, Forever Times (by So Factual), a fairly useful 5f (at 2 yrs) to 7f winner, is half-sister to 7 winners including Welsh Emperor (Group 2 7f Hungerford Stakes) and the listed 5f winner Majestic Times. *"The Fastnet Rock horses take a bit of time. This is a big, strong filly but she's definitely one for the second half of the year".*

1487. DR DORO (IRE) ★★★
b.f. Holy Roman Emperor – Stellarina (Night Shift). March 31. Second foal. The dam, a modest 6f winner, is a half-sister to the useful 1m, 10f and Australian Group 3 10f winner Fanjura. The second dam, Accelerating (by Lear Fan), was a quite useful 2-y-o 7f winner. *"She looks like being quite early, she's strong, has a bit of pace and is typical of the sire in that she's not over-big. She's all there and is one for five and six furlongs".*

1488. GOLD CROWN (IRE) ★★
b.f. Holy Roman Emperor – Medicean Star (Galileo). May 10. Half-sister to the fair Irish dual 10f winner Equity Swap (by Strategic Prince) and to 2 minor winners abroad by Aussie Rules and Oratorio. The dam ran once unplaced and is a half-sister to 3 winners. The second dam, Fear And Greed (by Brief Truce), an Irish 2-y-o 6f winner and second in the Group 1 7f Moyglare Stud Stakes, is a half-sister to 4 winners. *"She was a late foal but seems very mature, so she's one for us to crack on with and see what sort of trip she'll want. A good, strong filly, she's out of a Galileo mare so it's hard to predict".*

1489. LADY OAK (IRE) ★★★★
b.f. Arcano – Lady Of Kildare (Mujadil). April 2. Ninth foal. €40,000Y. Goffs Orby. C McCormack. Half-sister to the quite useful dual 1m winner Katherine Lee, to the fair 12f winner Morning Watch (both by Azamour), the quite useful Irish 2-y-o 6f winner El Soprano (by Noverre) and a minor winner abroad by Exceed And Excel. The dam, a fairly useful 2-y-o listed 6f winner, is a half-sister to one winner. The second dam, Dancing Sunset (by Red Sunset), a smart winner of the Group 3 10f Royal Whip Stakes, is a full or half-sister to 5 winners including the US stakes winner

Truly. *"A good strong filly, she seems to move well and hopefully she'll be running from mid-to-late May. I should imagine she'll start at six furlongs and then we'll see where we go from there".*

1490. SHORT STACKED ★★★
b.c. Dutch Art – Rotunda (Pivotal). March 15. Fourth foal. £40,000Y. Doncaster Premier. C McCormack. Brother to the fair 2014 2-y-o 7f winner Finial and to the quite useful 2-y-o 5f winner Dutch Interior. The dam is an unraced half-sister to 5 winners including the Group 2 1m May Hill Stakes (at 2 yrs) and Group 2 1m Windsor Forest Stakes winner and 1,000 Guineas second Spacious. The second dam, Palatial (by Green Desert), a useful winner of 4 races over 7f (including at 2 yrs), is a half-sister to 6 winners including the useful listed 10f winners Portal and Ice Palace. *"A big horse, he goes quite nicely. We'll see him out in late June over six furlongs".*

1491. VICTORIOUS SECRET (IRE) ★★★
b.f. Holy Roman Emperor – Highindi (Montjeu). March 3. Fifth foal. €85,000Y. Goffs Orby. C McCormack. Half-sister to the 2014 Irish 6f placed 2-y-o Windsor Beach (by Starspangledbanner) and to the modest Irish 10f winner Salacious Sally (by Excellent Art). The dam ran once unplaced and is a half-sister to the Grade 2 La Prevoyante Handicap winner and Group 1 10f Prix Saint-Alary third Arvada and to the Group 3 7f Craven Stakes winner Adagio. The second dam, Lalindi (by Cadeaux Genereux), a fair middle-distance winner of 7 races, is a half-sister to 5 winners including the dam of the Group 1 winners Summoner and Compton Admiral. *"She goes well and five/six furlongs will be her trip. She had a little setback, nothing serious, which held us up a little bit otherwise she'd have been almost ready to run by now. We're possibly looking at mid-season for her now".*

1492. UNNAMED ★★
b.f. Cape Blanco – Alabaq (Riverman). April 12. Half-sister to the quite useful 7f and 1m winner Alraased (by Exchange Rate), to the fairly useful 7f and 1m winner of 5 races Aamaaq (by Danehill), the fair dual 10f winner Asaateel (by Unfuwain) and he fair 9.5f winner Salariaq (by Daaher). The dam, a smart winner

of the Group 3 1m Premio Bagutta and listed 10f Pretty Polly Stakes, is a half-sister to the Group 3 Rockfel Stakes winner Bint Salsabil and to the very useful 2-y-o 6f and 7f winner Sahm. The second dam, Salsabil (by Sadler's Wells), won the Prix Marcel Boussac, the 1,000 Guineas, the Irish Derby, the Epsom Oaks and the Prix Vermeille - all Group 1 events. She is a half-sister to the high-class colt Marju, winner of the St James's Palace Stakes. *"She's definitely more of a 3-y-o type. There's plenty of size and scope about her and although it's a good family it's not the most precocious. She moves well but I wouldn't know much more about her yet".*

1493. UNNAMED ★★★

b.f. Champs Elysees – Looby Loo (Kyllachy). February 9. Third foal. €115,000Y. Arqana Deauville August. James Stack. The dam, placed once over 5f at 2 yrs, is a half-sister to the 2-y-o Group 1 Middle Park Stakes and Group 1 Prix Morny winner Dutch Art and to the Group 2 10f Blandford Stakes winner Up. The second dam, Halland Park Lass (by Spectrum), ran 3 times unplaced and is a half-sister to 4 winners including the Scandinavian Group 3 winner King Quantas. *"She seems to go OK and she should be out in late May over six furlongs".*

1494. UNNAMED ★★★

b.c. High Chaparral – Miss Beatrix (Danehill Dancer). May 8. Fifth foal. €140,000Y. Goffs Orby. C McCormack. Half-brother to the French 5.5f (at 2 yrs) to 1m winner of 4 races and Group 3 Prix de Cabourg third Jally (by Tamayuz). The dam won 3 races at 2 yrs including the Group 1 7f Moyglare Stud Stakes and was third in the Group 1 Phoenix Stakes. The second dam, Miss Beabea (by Catrail), an Irish 2-y-o listed 6f winner and second in the Group 1 6f Phoenix Stakes, is a half-sister to 9 winners including the very useful 5f winner Ellen's Lad. *"A good, hardy sort, he shouldn't take too long but being by High Chaparral I imagine he'll want seven furlongs to begin with. A June/July type 2-y-o that'll improve with time".*

1495. UNNAMED ★★

b.c. Approve – Reign Of Fire (Perugino). April 20. Sixth foal. 42,000Y. Tattersalls October

Book 2. C McCormack. Half-brother to the quite useful 2-y-o 6f winner King Dragon (by Iffraaj), to the fair 2-y-o 7f winner Not Bad For A Boy (by Elusive City) and the multiple Italian winners Canarina (by Amadeus Wolf) Very Glamour (by Pyrus). The dam was placed at 2 yrs and is a half-sister to 4 winners including the US Grade 3 winner and Group 3 July Stakes second Media Mogul. The second dam, White Heat (by Last Tycoon), was placed at 2 yrs and is a half-sister to 5 winners including the dual listed winner Watching. *"Quite a big horse, he moves well but he's not an early type and definitely one for mid-summer onwards".*

1496. UNNAMED ★★★

b.c. Arcano – Sassy Gal (King's Best). February 18. Third foal. 60,000Y. Tattersalls October Book 2. C McCormack. Half-brother to the fairly useful 5f (at 2 yrs) and 6f winner Ben Hall (by Bushranger). The dam, a quite useful 1m (at 2 yrs) and 7f winner, is a half-sister to 9 winners including the very useful 6f (at 2 yrs) to 10f winner and Group 3 placed Firebet and the useful 10f winner Dancing Phantom. The second dam, Dancing Prize (by Sadler's Wells), a useful maiden and third in the listed Lingfield Oaks Trial, is a sister to 3 winners including the Group 1 Fillies Mile second and good broodmare Dance To The Top and a half-sister to 5 winners. *"Quite a big horse, he seems to go well and we've done a few little bits of work with him but backed off because he's growing. He'll be out around July time and he's quite a nice horse".*

1497. UNNAMED ★★

b.c. Henrythenavigator – Tashawak (Night Shift). April 27. Eighth foal. €52,000Y. Goffs Orby. C McCormack. Closely related to the quite useful 7f and 1m winner Nadawat (by Kingmambo) and half-brother to 4 winners including the fairly useful 7f (including at 2 yrs) and 1m winner Shebebi (by Mr Greeley) and the fair 2-y-o 7f winner Afnoon (by Street Cry). The dam, a smart 6f (at 2 yrs) and Group 2 1m Falmouth Stakes winner, is a sister to one winner and a half-sister to 4 winners including the Group 1 1m Criterium International third Acropolis and the dual Group 2 winner Fairy Queen. The second dam, Dedicated Lady (by Pennine Walk), a 2-y-o 5f and 6f winner, is a half-sister to 5 winners. *"Quite a late foal, he moves OK and does everything we've asked. He won't take long to come to hand unless he suddenly starts to grow".*

OLLY STEVENS
1498. CACCINI ★★
b.c. Authorized – Key Change (Darshaan). April 26. Half-brother to the fairly useful Irish 2m and very smart hurdles winner Pittoni (by Peintre Celebre), to the quite useful Irish 1m winner and listed-placed Sandtime, the Irish 10f winner and listed-placed Calorando (both by Green Desert) and the quite useful 12f winners Interchange (by Montjeu) and Carenage (by Alzao). The dam, a winner of 4 races including the Group 1 12f Yorkshire Oaks, is a full or half-sister to numerous minor winners. The second dam, Kashka (by The Minstrel), a winner over 12f at 3 yrs in France, is a half-sister to the Italian Group 3 winner Karkisiya and to the dams of the Derby winner Kahyasi and the Group 3 winners Kaliana and Kalajana and Kithanga. *"He's a really nice horse, a late maturing type out of a very good mare. Both physically and on his page I'm not going to get him going early. It would be lovely to think we could run him at the back-end".*

1499. GOLDENFIELD (IRE) ★★★★
b.c. Footstepsinthesand – Society Gal (Gulch). January 24. Third foal. 55,000Y. Tattersalls October Book 2. Peter & Ross Doyle. Half-brother to the quite useful 2014 2-y-o listed-placed 6f winner Red Icon (by Acclamation) and to the fair Irish 2-y-o 1m winner Bleeding Hearts (by Peintre Celebre). The dam is an unraced half-sister to the US Grade 3 winner Good Mood. The second dam, Pillars Of Society (by Caerleon), a fairly useful Irish 10f winner, was Group 3 placed and is a half-sister to 5 winners. (Mr & Mrs W W Fleming). *"A big, strong, well-made colt. I wouldn't think he'd be ready for Royal Ascot but there's plenty of quality about him. He has the right sort of temperament in that he wants to get on and do work but without being stupid. He's a lovely, capable, big-moving horse that should be wheeled out around mid-summer over six furlongs, although I think he'll get better at seven".*

1500. KEMSING (IRE) ★★★
ch.c. Footstepsinthesand – St Edith (Desert King). April 12. Ninth foal. £33,000Y. Doncaster Premier. David Redvers. Half-brother to the fair 2-y-o 6f and 1m winner That's Dangerous (by Three Valleys), to the moderate 6f (at 2 yrs) to 1m winner That's All A Game (by Sleeping Indian), the Italian listed-placed winner Furia Ceca (by Mujahid) and a hurdles winner by Haafhd. The dam, placed fourth once over 1m, is a half-sister to 7 winners. The second dam, Carnelly (by Priolo), an Irish 9f winner, was listed-placed and is a sister to the winner and Group 3 placed Wenda. (Qatar Racing Ltd). *"He wants to get on with it and isn't quite as tall as my other Footstepsinthesand 2-y-o. He could well be an earlier type and we'll try and get him out before Ascot in case he goes and does something. I think he'd have the speed for five furlongs at lower levels but ultimately as he progresses he might want further".*

1501. PLAYFUL DUDE ★★★
b.c. Drosselmeyer – Choice Play (Vindication). March 10. First foal. $82,000Y. Keeneland September. Fir Grove. The dam was a stakes-placed winner of 3 races at 4 and 6 yrs in the USA and is a half-sister to another stakes-placed winner. The second dam, Sharp Eyes (by Storm Cat), a minor US winner at 3 and 4 yrs, is a half-sister to the Group 2 Prix Chaudenay winner Celtic Celeb. The sire, a son of Distorted Humor, won the Belmont Stakes and the Breeders Cup Classic. (Pearl Bloodstock). *"This is an interesting one because I was involved with Drosselmeyer when I was working in the States and broke him in! Physically he's a bigger, back-end type but he's really capable. I've got half an eye on the fact that his sire won over a mile and half, which means he's eligible for the Chesham at Royal Ascot. I'm not going to force him to get there because he's a tall, rangy horse – but at the same time he is so capable. I can send him with the more forward 2-y-o's and he goes with them easily with his big, long stride".*

1502. SHOW AYA (IRE) ★★★★★ ♠
ch.f. Showcasing – Mimiteh (Maria's Mon). April 10. Fourth foal. £27,000Y. Doncaster Premier. Sackville/Donald. Half-sister to the quite useful 1m to 10f winner of 6 races Balmoral Castle (by Royal Applause). The dam, a fair 5f (at 2 yrs) and 6f winner, is a half-sister

to 4 winners including the Group 1 Cheveley Park Stakes winner Rosdhu Queen. The second dam, Green Minstrel (by Green Tune), won the Group 3 Prix d'Aumale at 2 yrs and is a half-sister to 4 winners. (S Al Ansari). *"A very fast filly. Physically she's incredibly forward and my aim with her is to get her to Royal Ascot. We took her for a gallop at Lingfield and although mentally she's very green, physically she's capable. Having Showcasing as her sire and Rosdhu Queen as her dam's half-sister gives us further encouragement. I'd say she looks to be the best 2-y-o we've had so far".* **TRAINERS' BARGAIN BUY**

1503. WARRIOR SONG (USA) ★★★★
b.f. Harlan's Holiday – More Oats Please (Smart Strike). May 18. Third foal. $145,000Y. Keeneland September. David Redvers. Half-sister to the 2014 2-y-o Grade 1 8.5f Alcibiades Stakes winner Peace And War (by War Front). The dam, a minor US 3-y-o winner of 2 races, is a half-sister to 3 winners including the US stakes winner and Grade 3 second Miss Valentine. The second dam, Miss Yiayia (by Gilded Time), a US stakes-placed winner of 7 races, is a half-sister to the US dual Grade 3 winner Stoneleigh's Hope. (Qatar Racing Ltd & Sheikh Suhaim Al Thani). *"A half-sister to our 2-y-o Grade 1 winner from last year Peace And War and she's very similar to her. I really like her, she's got bags of quality and if she broke her maiden on polytrack well I could see myself taking her over to the States to do something similar to Peace And War".*

1504. UNNAMED ★★
b.c. Dandy Man – Masakira (Royal Academy). February 21. Eighth foal. £30,000Y. Doncaster Premier. David Redvers. Half-brother to the moderate Irish 13f and hurdles winner Priest Field (by Daggers Drawn) and to two minor winners in Germany and Sweden by Clodovil. The dam, a modest 7.5f placed maiden, is a half-sister to 4 winners. The second dam, Masafiya (by Shernazar), is a placed half-sister to Group/Graded stakes winners Massyar and Madjaristan and to Masskana (dam of the Group/Grade 1 winners Dank, Eagle Mountain and Sulk). (Qatar Racing Ltd). *"He goes well enough and I'm happy with him. I hope we'll have in out in late May or early June and he'll be a sprinter".*

1505. UNNAMED ★★★
b.f. Fast Company – Tawaafur (Fantastic Light). March 27. Fourth foal. £82,000Y. Doncaster Premier. David Redvers. Sister to the 2014 2-y-o Group 2 Norfolk Stakes winner Baitha Alga and half-sister to two winners abroad by Atraf and Clodovil. The dam, a quite useful Irish 1m winner, is a half-sister to 7 winners including the US Grade 2 winner Elhayq and the Group 3 Minstrel Stakes winner Shibl. The second dam, Mahasin (by Danzig), a quite useful 7f and 1m winner, is a half-sister to 4 stakes winners including Al Hareb (2-y-o Group 1 William Hill Futurity Stakes). (Qatar Racing Ltd). *"A nice filly, but still a bit immature physically so we've not pushed her too much and we've had to slightly ignore what her full brother Baitha Alga did last year. She's perfectly nice, but just not forward enough for me to push on with".*

SIR MICHAEL STOUTE
1506. ACROSS THE STARS ♠
b.c. Sea The Stars – Victoria Cross (Mark Of Esteem). March 28. Ninth foal. 600,000Y. Tattersalls October Book 1. Charlie Gordon-Watson. Half-brother to 6 winners including the dual Group 2 12f winner Bronze Cannon, the US Grade 3 winner Valiant Girl (both by Lemon Drop Kid), the useful 2-y-o dual 7f winner Elusive Award (by Elusive Quality) and the fairly useful listed-placed 2-y-o 7f winner Valiance (by Horse Chestnut). The dam, a listed-placed 7f winner, is a half-sister to the US Grade 2 winner Prize Giving and to the dam of the dual US Grade 1 winner Alpride. The second dam, Glowing With Pride (by Ile de Bourbon), a 7f and 10.5f winner, was second in the Park Hill Stakes.

1507. ATONE
b.f. Oasis Dream – Midsummer (Kingmambo). April 29. Eighth foal. Sister to the high-class racemare Midday, a winner of six Group 1 races (Breeders Cup Filly & Mare Turf, Prix Vermeille, Yorkshire Oaks and Nassau Stakes (three times)) and to the fair 10f winner Popular and half-sister to the smart 1m (at 2 yrs) and Group 3 7f winner and Group 1 Nassau Stakes third Hot Snap (by Pivotal) and the useful listed-placed 10f and 12f winner Midsummer Sun (by Monsun). The dam, a quite useful listed-placed 11f winner, is a

half-sister to the Oaks and Fillies Mile winner Reams of Verse and the Eclipse Stakes and Phoenix Champion Stakes winner Elmaamul. The second dam, Modena (by Roberto), is an unraced half-sister to the dam of Zafonic. (Khalid Abdulla).

1508. BALLET CONCERTO ♠
b.c. Dansili – Ballet Ballon (Rahy). April 13. Sixth foal. 300,000Y. Tattersalls October Book 1. Charlie Gordon-Watson. Half-brother to the useful French 2-y-o 6f to 1m winner of 4 races and French 2,000 Guineas second Havane Smoker (by Dubawi), to the fair 7f (at 2 yrs) and 1m winner Halling Dancer (by Halling) and the fair 9.5f and 12f winner Maxie T (by Danehill Dancer). The dam, a fair 10f winner, is a half-sister to the useful listed-placed 10f winner Design Perfection. The second dam, Bella Ballerina (by Sadler's Wells), a quite useful 9f winner, is a full or half-sister to 6 winners including the Group 2 10f Prince of Wales's Stakes winner Stagecraft, the Group 3 Strensall Stakes winner Mullins Bay and the dual 1m listed winner Hyabella.

1509. COMMODITY ♠
ch.c. Dutch Art – Royale Danehill (Danehill). March 18. Third living foal. 190,000Y. Tattersalls October Book 1. John Warren. Half-brother to the quite useful dual 6f winner at 2 and 3 yrs Souville (by Dalakhani) and to the quite useful 2-y-o 6f winner Bircham (by Dubawi). The dam won 2 minor races at 4 yrs in France and is a half-sister to 6 winners. The second dam, Royal Ballerina (by Sadler's Wells), winner of the Group 2 12f Blandford Stakes and second in the Oaks, is a half-sister to 7 winners including the dual Group 2 10f Sun Chariot Stakes winner Free Guest (herself dam of the Group 1 Fillies Mile winner and Oaks second Shamshir).

1510. ENGAGE (IRE)
b.f. Pour Moi – Brooklyn's Storm (Storm Cat). April 28. Eighth foal. 160,000Y. Tattersalls October Book 1. John Warren. Half-sister to 3 winners including the French 1m and US triple stakes winner and Group 2 1m Prix de Sandringham third Stormina (by Gulch and herself dam of the dual Group 1 winner Silasol) and the French 10f winner Propulsion (by Pulpit). The dam won 2 minor races at

2 and 4 yrs in France and the USA and is a half-sister to 11 winners including the French Group winners Prospect Wells, Solemia and Prospect Park. The second dam, Brooklyn's Dance (by Shirley Heights), won the Group 3 Prix Cleopatre and is a half-sister to 8 winners and to the unraced dam of Authorized.

1511. ESTIDRAAK (IRE)
ch.c. Iffraaj – Gold Hush (Seeking The Gold). March 5. Fourth foal. 130,000Y. Tattersalls October Book 2. Shadwell Estate Co. Half-brother to the fairly useful triple 10f winner Elhaame (by Acclamation) and to a minor winner in Italy by Tiger Hill. The dam, a quite useful 1m and 10f winner, is a half-sister to 3 winners including the useful 2-y-o 1m winner and Group 3 1m Autumn Stakes second Menokee. The second dam, Meniatarra (by Zilzal), unplaced in one run at 2 yrs, is a sister to the smart 1m to 10f winner Kammtarra and the useful 10f winner Haltarra and a half-sister to Lammtarra, winner of the Derby, the King George and the Prix de l'Arc de Triomphe.

1512. FORGE
b.c. Dubawi – Heat Haze ((Green Desert). February 18. Fourth foal. Brother to the useful 2-y-o 7f winner and listed-placed Radiator. The dam, winner of the Grade 1 Matriarch Stakes and the Grade 1 Beverly D Stakes, is closely related to the Coronation Stakes, Prix Jacques Le Marois and Breeders Cup Filly & Mare Turf winner Banks Hill, to the Grade 1 Matriarch Stakes winner Intercontinental, the US dual Grade 1 winner Cacique, the North American triple Group 1 winner Champs Elysees and the Group 2 winner and high-class sire Dansili. The second dam, Hasili (by Kahyasi), won over 5f at 2 yrs and stayed a mile. (Khalid Abdulla).

1513. IDYLLIC (IRE)
b.f. Rip Van Winkle – Cilium (War Chant). April 24. Second foal. 50,000Y. Tattersalls October Book 1. John Warren. The dam, a quite useful Irish 1m and 11f winner, was listed-placed over 10f and is a half-sister to 3 winners. The second dam, Venturi (by Danehill Dancer), winner of the Group 3 7f C L Weld Park Stakes, was subsequently second in two US Grade 3 events and is a sister to the French listed winner and Group 1 Criterium de Saint-Cloud third Feels All Right.

1514. KOKONI (IRE)
b.c. Acclamation – Belgique (Compton Place). March 27. Second foal. 75,000Y. Tattersalls October Book 2. John Warren. Half-brother to the fair 2014 7f placed 2-y-o Zylan (by Kyllachy). The dam, a quite useful 7f and 1m winner, is a half-sister to 3 winners including the useful Irish 2-y-o 6f and listed 7f winner Bruges. The second dam, Liege (by Night Shift), is an unraced half-sister to 2 winners including the dam of the multiple Group 1 winner Moonlight Cloud.

1515. LABRYNTH (IRE)
b.f. Lawman – Kerry Gal (Galileo). February 27. First foal. 260,000Y. Tattersalls October Book 2. John Warren. The dam is an unraced half-sister to 8 winners including the 2-y-o 7f winner and French and Irish 1,000 Guineas placed La Nuit Rose (herself dam of the US Grade 2 winner Tam Lin). The second dam, Caerlina (Caerleon), won over 5.5f (at 2 yrs), the Group 1 10.5f Prix de Diane and the Group 3 10f Prix de la Nonette and is a full or half-sister to 8 winners.

1516. LOLWAH ♠
ch.f. Pivotal – Palace Affair (Pursuit Of Love). March 20. Eighth foal. 220,000Y. Tattersalls October Book 1. John Warren. Sister the fair 7f to 9f winner of 15 races April Fool and half-sister to the useful 2-y-o listed 6f winner Queen's Grace, to the modest 2-y-o 6f winner Black Rodded (both by Bahamian Bounty) and the modest 2-y-o 5f winner Dubai Affair (by Dubawi). The dam, a multiple listed winner from 5f to 7f, is a sister to one winner and a half-sister to 9 winners including Sakhee's Secret (Group 1 6f July Cup). The second dam, Palace Street (by Secreto), a dual listed winner including the Cammidge Trophy, is a half-sister to 7 winners including the dual listed winner Indian Trail.

1517. MIDTERM
b.c. Galileo – Midday (Oasis Dream). January 16. First foal. The dam was a high-class racemare and a winner of six Group 1 races (Breeders Cup Filly & Mare Turf, Prix Vermeille, Yorkshire Oaks and Nassau Stakes (three times) and is a full or half-sister to several winners including the smart 1m (at 2 yrs) and Group 3 7f winner and Group 1 Nassau Stakes third Hot Snap. The second dam, Midsummer (by Kingmambo), a quite useful listed-placed 11f winner, is a half-sister to the Oaks and Fillies Mile winner Reams of Verse and the Eclipse Stakes and Phoenix Champion Stakes winner Elmaamul. (Khalid Abdulla).

1518. MOKHALAD
ch.c. Dubawi – Model Queen (Kingmambo). March 11. Tenth foal. 500,000Y. Tattersalls October Book 1. Shadwell Estate Co. Half-brother to 7 winners including the Group 1 Haydock Sprint Cup and Group 1 Prix Maurice de Gheest winner Regal Parade (by Pivotal), the Group 3 7f Acomb Stakes winner and Group 2 7f Champagne Stakes third Entifaadha (by Dansili), the useful 1m (at 2 yrs) and 10f winner and triple Group 3 placed Hot Prospect (by Motivator) and the French 11f and 12f winner and listed third Mount Helicon. The dam, a fair 7f winner, is a half-sister to 5 winners. The second dam, Model Bride (by Blushing Groom), is an unraced half-sister to the Group 3 winner Zaizafon (the dam of Zafonic and Zamindar) and to the unraced dam of Elmaamul and Reams Of Verse.

1519. POET'S WORD (IRE) ♠
b.c. Poet's Voice – Whirly Bird (Nashwan). April 5. Sixth foal. 300,000Y. Tattersalls October Book 2. Charlie Gordon-Watson. Half-brother to the smart 2014 2-y-o Group 3 7f winner Malabar (by Raven's Pass), to the fairly useful 10f and 11f winner Clowance Estate (by Teofilo), the quite useful dual 7f winner Whirly Dancer (by Danehill Dancer) and the quite useful 12f and 13f winner Royal Signaller (by Dylan Thomas). The dam, a useful 9.5f to 11f winner, is a half-sister to 4 winners including the very useful listed Galtres Stakes winner Inchiri. The second dam, Inchyre (by Shirley Heights), a useful listed-placed 1m winner, is a half-sister to 7 winners including the triple Group 3 7f winner Inchinor and the dam of the Canadian Grade 1 winner Miss Keller.

1520. QUEEN'S TRUST ♠
b.f. Dansili – Queen's Best (King's Best). March 4. Fourth foal. The dam, a smart winner of the Group 3 10f Winter Hill Stakes and the listed 12f Chalice Stakes, was second in the

Group 2 Blandford Stakes and is a half-sister to 4 winners including the French 12f winner and Group 3 Prix de Royaumont third Reverie Solitaire. The second dam, Cloud Castle (by In The Wings), won the Group 3 Nell Gwyn Stakes and was placed in the Group 1 Yorkshire Oaks and the Group 1 Prix Vermeille. She is a half-sister to the high-class middle-distance horses and multiple Group 1 winners Warrsan and Luso, and the dam of the Group 3 winners Tastahil, Hattan, Blue Monday and Laaheb. (Cheveley Park Stud).

1521. SHABBAH (IRE)
br.c. Sea The Stars – Alizaya (Highest Honor). April 8. Fifth foal. 200,000Y. Tattersalls October Book 1. John Warren. Half-brother to the quite useful 7f (at 2 yrs) to 10f winner of 5 races Ingleby Symphony and to the minor French 3-y-o winner Oratello (both by Oratorio). The dam is an unraced half-sister to 5 winners including the Group 1 Irish St Leger and Group 1 Prix du Cadran winner Alandi and the Irish 1m (at 2 yrs) and listed 12f winner Aliyfa. The second dam, Aliya (by Darshaan), a dual 12f winner in Ireland, is a sister to the high-class Group 3 12f Lingfield Oaks Trial winner and disqualified Epsom Oaks winner Aliysa and a half-sister to 7 winners.

1522. SIDLE (IRE)
b.f. Lawman – Slink (Selkirk). March 14. Fifth foal. 170,000Y. Tattersalls October Book 1. Cheveley Park Stud. Half-sister to the Irish 2-y-o Group 3 6f winner Bye Bye Birdie and to the modest 7f winner Sleek (both by Oasis Dream). The dam is an unraced sister to the 2-y-o Group 1 1m Prix Marcel Boussac winner and triple Group 1 placed Sulk and a half-sister to 4 winners including the Group 1 10f Hong Kong Cup and dual Group 2 winner Eagle Mountain and dual US Grade 1 winner Dank. The second dam, Masskana (by Darshaan), a minor 9f and 10f winner in France, is a half-sister to 3 winners including Massyar (Group 2 Gallinule Stakes) and Madjaristan (Grade 3 Arcadia Handicap).

1523. STATUESQUE
b.f. Sea The Stars – Kahara (Sadler's Wells). February 24. Fourth foal. 375,000Y. Tattersalls October Book 1. Cheveley Park Stud. Half-sister to a winner in Germany by Danehill

Dancer. The dam, a fairly useful 12f winner, is a sister to 2 winners including the St Leger and Great Voltigeur Stakes winner Milan and a half-sister to 6 winners including the Irish 2-y-o 7f winner and Group 2 Great Voltigeur Stakes third Go For Gold. The second dam, Kithanga (by Darshaan), was a smart winner of 3 races including the Group 3 12f St Simon Stakes and the listed 12f Galtres Stakes.

1524. ULYSSES (IRE)
ch.c. Galileo – Light Shift (Kingmambo). March 20. Second foal. Half-sister to the useful dual 12f winner Dr Yes (by Dansili). The dam won the Group 1 12f Oaks and is a full or half-sister to 6 winners including the Group 2 10.5f Tattersalls Gold Cup and Group 3 10f Brigadier Gerard Stakes winner Shiva and the high-class Group 2 12f Prix Jean de Chaudenay and Group 3 12f Prix Foy winner Limnos. The second dam, Lingerie (by Shirley Heights), placed 7 times in France, is a half-sister to 4 winners including the French listed placed Evocatrice. (Niarchos Family).

1525. VOLITION (IRE)
gr.f. Dark Angel – Warshah (Shamardal). January 23. First foal. 300,000Y. Tattersalls October Book 2. Cheveley Park Stud. The dam is an unraced half-sister to 3 winners including Group 1 Prix de l'Opera and Group 2 1m May Hill Stakes winner Kinnaird (herself dam of the 2-y-o Group 2 Royal Lodge Stakes winner Berkshire) and the Group 3 Chester Vase winner Mickdaam. The second dam, Ribot's Guest (by Be My Guest), ran unplaced in Italy and is a half-sister to 6 winners including the Italian listed winner Raysiza.

JAMES TATE
1526. ADHAM (IRE) ★★★ ♠
b.c. Dream Ahead – Leopard Creek (Weldnaas). April 14. Fifth foal. €75,000Y. Goffs Orby. Rabbah Bloodstock. Half-brother to the 2014 6f fourth placed 2-y-o Fayreway (by Strategic Prince), to the 2-y-o Group 3 5f Cornwallis Stakes winner Ponty Acclaim (by Acclamation) and a winner in Greece by One Cool Cat. The dam, a modest 5f placed 3-y-o, is a sister to the listed winning sprinter Astonished and a half-sister to 5 winners including the Group 3 Prix du Petit Couvert winner Bishops Court. The second dam, Indigo

(by Primo Dominie), a quite useful 2-y-o dual 5f winner, is a half-sister to 5 winners. (Sheikh R D Al Maktoum). *"This colt is frustrating because he looked good early on but he had a minor setback about a month ago. He should still be mentioned because he's a strong colt who has shown plenty and will be expected to be a good 2-y-o this year. He goes well".*

1527. AMAZEMENT ★★★★★ ♠
ch.c. Lope De Vega – Aglow (Spinning World). March 25. Seventh foal. 48,000Y. Tattersalls December. Rabbah Bloodstock. Half-brother to the German listed winner and Group 3 second Altair Star (by Kris Kin), to the French and German winner of 8 races and listed-placed Aden Gulf (by Medicean) and 2 minor winners by Hurricane Run. The dam, a quite useful 2-y-o 1m winner, is a half-sister to 3 minor winners. The second dam, Flame Valley (by Gulch), a smart listed 10f winner, was placed in the Group 2 10f Sun Chariot Stakes and in the Grade 1 10f E P Taylor Stakes and is a half-sister to 3 winners including the US Grade 2 winner Beyrouth. (Sheikh J D Al Maktoum). *"He's very, very nice. A big colt that's working well despite not being bred for shorter distances. Hopefully he's a proper horse. You'd have thought he'd be a seven furlongs/mile 2-y-o, but we may even give him a run over six furlongs when the time comes"*

1528. DREAM ISLAND (IRE) ★★★
b.f. Kheleyf – Takawiri (Danehill). February 18. Sixth foal. 12,000Y. Tattersalls October Book 3. Rabbah Bloodstock. Half-sister to the fairly useful triple 6f winner at 2 and 3 yrs Midnight Flower (by Haafhd) and to 3 minor winners in Italy and Greece by Dilshaan, Iffraaj and Refuse To Bend. The dam is an unraced half-sister to 2 winners including the French 2-y-o Group 2 second Ascot Glory. The second dam, Lake Victoria (by Lake Coniston), was listed-placed in Ireland and is a half-sister to 5 winners including the US Grade 1 winner Delighter and the Oaks third Oakmead. *"A small, very strong, 2-y-o type, she's showing up well on the grass and will be an early sort".*

1529. HILLSIDE DREAM ★★★★
b.f. Dream Ahead – Knapton Hill (Zamindar). March 12. Fourth foal. 82,000Y. Tattersalls October Book 1. Rabbah Bloodstock. Half-

sister to the fairly useful Irish 2-y-o 6f winner Pitlochry (by Chineur), to the Irish 2-y-o 6f and 6.5f winner Vallado (by Clodovil) and the fair dual 6f winner The Dark Wizard (by Dark Angel). The dam, a quite useful 7f winner at 3 yrs, is a half-sister to 2 winners. The second dam, Torgau (by Zieten), a Group 2 6f Cherry Hinton Stakes winner, was second in the Group 1 6f Cheveley Park Stakes and the Group 1 7f Moyglare Stud Stakes and is a half-sister to 9 winners. (S Ali). *"She wants a few stars adding to her name, she goes very nicely and will probably make her debut at the Craven meeting. A medium-sized, strong, imposing filly who is working well".*

1530. LONE ANGEL ★★★
gr.f. Dark Angel – The Hermitage (Kheleyf). March 16. Second foal. 9,000Y. Tattersalls October Book 2. Rabbah Bloodstock. Sister to the fair 2015 3-y-o 6f winner Where's Sue. The dam, a quite useful listed-placed 2-y-o 5f winner, is a half-sister to 9 winners including the listed winners and Group 1 placed Crown Of Light and Alboostan. The second dam, Russian Countess (by Nureyev), a useful French 2-y-o 1m winner and listed-placed, is a half-sister to 5 winners. (S Manana). *"She'll be our first runner and she's very small but quite speedy and certainly a 2-y-o type. I remember the dam because I was at Mark Johnston's when she was there. She was second in the Hilary Needler when it was still a listed race and that's the sort of thing that this filly will be going for".* **TRAINERS' BARGAIN BUY**

1531. MAYASA (IRE) ★★
ch.f. Iffraaj – Lanzana (Kalanisi). March 23. Fifth foal. €90,000Y. Goffs Orby. Rabbah Bloodstock. Half-sister to the winner of 11 races abroad Heyaaraat (by Lawman). The dam is an unraced half-sister to 8 winners, notably the top-class broodmare Ebaziya, a triple listed winner from 7f (at 2 yrs) to 12f in Ireland and dam of the Group 1 winners Edabiya, Ebadiyla, Estimate and Enzeli. The second dam, Ezana (by Ela-Mana-Mou), a winner in France at 3 yrs over 11.5f, is a half-sister to 5 winners including the Group 3 10.5f Prix de Flore and Group 3 10.5f Prix Penelope winner Demia. (Sheikh R D Al Maktoum). *"A strong Iffraaj filly who is doing nothing wrong and will be expected to make her debut in a six furlong maiden".*

1532. RATEEL (IRE) ★★★
b.c. Arcano – Spanish Pride (Night Shift). March 25. First foal. 38,000Y. Tattersalls October Book 2. Rabbah Bloodstock. The dam, a modest 7f winner, is a half-sister to 3 winners including the Italian listed winner Spanish Hidalgo. The second dam, Spanish Lady (by Bering), placed fourth once over 12f, is a half-sister to 4 winners. (Sheikh R D Al Maktoum). *"A very attractive, nearly black colt who goes very nicely. I think we'll wait for the six furlong races with him, but he's nice and he goes very well".*

1533. ROMANTIC COMEDY ★★★
ch.f. Equiano – Gay Romance (Singspiel). April 27. 10,000Y. Tattersalls October Book 3. Half-sister to the useful 7f (including at 2 yrs) and 1m winner of 6 races and Group 3 1m Prix Quincey second Belgian Bill (by Exceed And Excel) and to the moderate 12f winner Layla's Boy (by Sakhee). The dam, a fair 7f winner, is a half-sister to 6 winners including the Hawksley Hill (by Rahy), winner of the Arcadia Handicap, El Rincon Handicap and San Francisco Mile (all US Grade 2 events) and the dam of the Group 1 Prix de l'Abbaye winner Benbaun. The second dam, Gaijin (by Caerleon), a useful 2-y-o 6f winner, is a full or half-sister to 6 winners. (S Manana). *"Not a big filly, she's an early 2-y-o type and showing plenty of speed. She'll be out in May and I'd be surprised if she didn't win this year".*

1534. TEAJAN (IRE) ★★★
gr.c. Dandy Man – Red Riddle (Verglas). April 11. First foal. £50,000Y. Doncaster Premier. Rabbah Bloodstock. The dam is an unplaced half-sister to 2 winners including the Group placed Eleval. The second dam, Penny Rouge (by Pennekamp), is an unplaced half-sister to 5 winners including the Irish dual Group 3 winner Redstone Dancer. (Sheikh R D Al Maktoum). *"A strong, nearly white colt, he's working nicely. Mentally I think he may need a race or two before he realises what he's doing, but I would expect him to be out sooner rather than later. A 2-y-o type".*

1535. WAY AHEAD ★★★
b.c. Kyllachy – On Her Way (Medicean). February 5. First foal. 47,000Y. Tattersalls October Book 3. Rabbah Bloodstock. The dam,

a quite useful 10f and 11f winner of 3 races, is a half-sister to the useful 2-y-o dual 1m winner and Group 2 1m Royal Lodge Stakes third On Our Way. The second dam, Singed (by Zamindar), won once at around 1m in France and is a half-sister to the French listed winner and Group 3 placed Inhabitant. (S Ali). *"A small, speedy Kyllachy colt. He has a bit of a temperament about him, as did his dam, but he's got a bit of ability. He'll probably make his debut in May".*

1536. WEATHER FRONT (USA) ★★★
ch.c. Stormy Atlantic – Kiswahili (Selkirk). January 19. Fourth living foal. 40,000Y. Tattersalls October Book 1. Rabbah Bloodstock. Brother to the 2-y-o listed 7f winner and dual Group 3 third Kinetica and half-brother to the fair 12f and 14f winner Slip Of The Tongue (by Zamindar) and the fair 10f winner Four Nations (by Langfuhr). The dam won 4 races including a listed 14f event in Germany and is a half-sister to 3 winners. The second dam, Kiliniski (by Niniski), a very smart winner of the Group 3 12f Lingfield Oaks Trial, was second in the Yorkshire Oaks and fourth in the Epsom Oaks and is a half-sister to 5 winners including the dam of the US triple Grade 1 winner Bienamado. (S Ali). *"I'm not sure when he'll be ready to run, because on the one hand his full sister was a listed winner as a 2-y-o, but he's a big colt. He goes very nicely and would be one to follow whenever he makes his debut".*

1537. UNNAMED ★★★★
ch.f. Exceed And Excel – Fashionable (Nashwan). May 5. Sixth foal. €150,000Y. Goffs Orby. Rabbah Bloodstock. Half-sister to the 2014 2-y-o Group 3 Silver Flash Stakes and listed 1m winner Jack Naylor (by Champs Elysees), to the quite useful 10f winner Seamless (by Beat Hollow), the fair 12f and 13f winner Linkable (by Rail Link) and a 2-y-o winner abroad by Rail Link. The dam, a useful listed 10f winner, is a half-sister to 6 winners. The second dam, Fine Detail (by Shirley Heights), a fairly useful 12f winner, is a half-sister to the dual US Grade 1 winner Wandesta, to the Group 2 12f winner De Quest and the listed winners Source of Light and Turners Hill. (Sheikh J D Al Maktoum). *"She's a medium-sized, very good-moving*

Exceed And Excel filly with a good pedigree. She goes very well, will probably make her debut sometime in May and she's nice".

1538. UNNAMED ★★★
ch.f. Iffraaj – Funday (Daylami). January 28. Second foal. 27,000Y. Tattersalls October Book 1. Rabbah Bloodstock. Half-sister to Miss Giler (by High Chaparral), unplaced in one start at 2 yrs in 2014. The dam, a quite useful listed-placed 10f and 12f winner, is a half-sister to 8 winners including the very smart Group 2 1m Royal Lodge Stakes winner Mons and the smart 10f winner and Irish Oaks third Inforapenny. The second dam, Morina (by Lyphard), won over 11f in France and is a half-sister to 10 winners. (S Ali). *"An early foal but out of a Daylami mare, she goes nicely and will be starting off in early May".*

1539. UNNAMED ★★★
b.f. Iffraaj – Lysandra (Danehill). January 22. Fifth foal. £30,000Y. Doncaster Premier. Rabbah Bloodstock. Half-sister to the quite useful 2-y-o 7.5f winner Annina (by Singspiel). The dam, a quite useful 1m to 10f winner of 4 races, is a half-sister to 6 winners including the Irish 1m winner and Group 2 12f King Edward VII Stakes third Barati. The second dam, Oriane (by Nashwan), won over 1m and was listed-placed three times in Ireland and is a half-sister to 6 winners including the smart 8.2f winner Killer Instinct and the very useful 2-y-o 7f winner and Group 2 second Pick of the Pops. (Sheikh J D Al Maktoum). *"A medium-sized filly from a proven Iffraaj x Danehill cross, she's working nicely and will be expected to run in April or May".*

1540. UNNAMED ★★★
b.c. Dark Angel – Miss Windley (Oratorio). February 16. First foal. 50,000Y. Tattersalls October Book 3. Rabbah Bloodstock. The dam, a minor Italian 3-y-o winner, is a half-sister to 7 winners including the useful 7f (at 2 yrs) to 12f winner Our Teddy. The second dam, Lady Windley (by Baillamont), an 11f winner of 3 races in France, is a half-sister to 6 winners and to the placed Lingerie (herself dam of the Oaks winner Light Shift, the Group 1 Tattersalls Gold Cup winner Shiva and the Group 2 Prix Jean du Chaudenay winner Limnos). (S Manana). *"He had a minor problem that held*

him back, but he's working well now and he should be a nice 2-y-o this year. Definitely a sprinting type".

1541. UNNAMED ★★★
br.f. Dick Turpin – Misty Eyed (Paris House). February 16. Fifth foal. 32,000Y. Tattersalls October Book 3. Rabbah Bloodstock. Half-sister to the fair 5f and 6f (at 2 yrs) and 1m winner of 5 races Mister Musicmaster (by Amadeus Wolf) and to the fair Irish 7f winner Sirikoi (by Myboycharlie). The dam, a smart 2-y-o winner of 4 races including the Group 3 5f Molecomb Stakes, was second in the Group 2 Flying Childers Stakes and the Group 2 King's Stand Stakes and is a half-sister to 3 minor winners. The second dam, Bold As Love (by Lomond), is an unraced half-sister to 3 winners. (S Manana). *"A big, strong filly, she's showing up nicely but probably won't be ready until May or June. The dam was a five furlong flyer but this filly looks like a six/seven furlong type".*

1542. UNNAMED ★★★★
b.c. Iffraaj – Musical Sands (Green Desert). March 1. First foal. 50,000Y. Tattersalls October Book 1. Rabbah Bloodstock. The dam is an unraced sister to the UAE Grade 2 and Group 3 Select Stakes winner Alkaadhem and a half-sister to 3 winners. The second dam, Balalaika (by Sadler's Wells), a useful 4-y-o listed 9f winner, is a half-sister to the high-class Group 2 10f Prince of Wales's Stakes and dual US Grade 2 winner Stagecraft and a half-sister to 5 winners including the Group 3 Strensall Stakes winner Mullins Bay and the very useful dual 1m listed winner Hyabella. (S Ali). *"He goes well. A big, strong colt and one that's likely to contest six furlong races. He's one we like".*

1543. UNNAMED ★★★
b.f. Poet's Voice – Peaceful Soul (Dynaformer). March 14. First foal. 30,000Y. Tattersalls October Book 3. Rabbah Bloodstock. The dam is an unplaced half-sister to 7 winners, two of them stakes-placed in the USA. The second dam, Serenity Jane (by Affirmed), is an unplaced half-sister to 10 winners including the US Grade 1 and dual Grade 2 winner Include. *"A filly for the second half of the season, but she really does catch the eye in her everyday canters, so she could be nice".*

1544. UNNAMED ★★★★

b.f. Iffraaj – Peace Signal (Time For A Change). March 29. Eleventh foal. 70,000Y. Tattersalls October Book 2. Rabbah Bloodstock. Half-sister to the South African listed winner Painter's Dream (by Sadler's Wells), to the French 2-y-o dual 9f winner Plume Rose (by Marchand De Sable), the French 2-y-o 6f winner Pertinence (by Fasliyev) and 2 minor French winners by Dalakhani and Spinning World. The dam is an unraced half-sister to 6 winners including the Prix de l'Arc de Triomphe, French Derby and Grand Prix de Paris winner Peintre Celebre and the French Group winners Peinture Rare and Pointilliste. The second dam, Peinture Bleue (by Alydar), a French listed and US Grade 2 12f winner, is a half-sister to the Group/Grade 3 winners Parme and Provins. (Sheikh J D Al Maktoum). *"She's very nice. A good-moving filly, she's done a couple of pieces of work on the grass and it appears she'll be a six/seven furlong 2-y-o. She's nice and has a lot of quality about her".*

1545. UNNAMED ★★★

b.f. Kodiac – Sheila Blige (Zamindar). February 21. Eighth foal. £62,000Y. Doncaster Premier. Rabbah Bloodstock. Half-sister to Lady Lily (by Desert Sun), a quite useful 2-y-o 5f and 6f winner of 4 races here and a listed-placed winner of 6 races in Scandinavia, to the Italian 2-y-o winner World All Fruit (by Refuse To Bend) and the fair Irish 9f winner Apt (by Danetime). The dam, a quite useful 2-y-o 5f winner, is a half-sister to 6 winners including the very useful 1m (at 2 yrs) to 12f winner and Group 3 Gordon Richards Stakes third Naked Welcome. The second dam, Stripanoora (by Ahonoora), was placed once at 3 yrs and stayed 1m and is a full or half-sister to 5 minor winners. (Sheikh J D Al Maktoum). *"She's a 2-y-o type and a filly with a huge backside. She hasn't done any work on the grass yet because she had a small setback in the spring. On everything we know about her she should be a nice 2-y-o type but we don't know enough yet".*

1546. UNNAMED ★★

b.f. Teofilo – Sunset Avenue (Street Cry). February 3. First foal. 80,000Y. Tattersalls October Book 2. Anthony Stroud. The dam, a fair 2-y-o 7f winner on her only start, is a

half-sister to 5 winners including the listed winner subsequent US Grade 2 second True Cause. The second dam, Dearly (by Rahy), won the Group 3 Blandford Stakes and is a half-sister to 4 winners including Balletto (Grade 1 Frizette Stakes in the USA). (S Ali). *"She's going to be better next year, but she'll start in seven furlong maiden fillies' races this year. Just cantering now, she's a good mover and looks a nice filly".*

1547. UNNAMED ★★★

b.c. Sir Percy – Whole Grain (Polish Precedent). March 20. Fifth living foal. 65,000Y. Tattersalls October Book 2. Rabbah Bloodstock. Half-brother to the modest 2014 7f placed Swaheen (by Lawman) and to the smart 6f and 7f winner of 7 races and Group 3 third Louis The Pious (by Holy Roman Emperor). The dam, last of 3 runners twice over 12f and 2m in France, is a sister to 2 winners including the Group 1 12f Irish Oaks and Group 1 12f Yorkshire Oaks winner Pure Grain and a half-sister to 7 winners. The second dam, Mill Line (by Mill Reef), a fair 14.6f winner at 3 yrs, is a half-sister to 6 winners. (S Manana). *"A nice, big colt, his pedigree gives mixed messages so it's hard to assess what trip he'll be best at. He's quite a big colt and babyish, so I'd say he's one for the second half of the season".*

MARK TOMPKINS

1548. ASTROSECRET ★★

b.f. Halling – Optimistic (Reprimand). March 8. Tenth foal. Sister to the fair 2-y-o 7f winner Rayvin Black and half-sister to 4 winners including the quite useful 2-y-o 7f winner Such Optimism, to the moderate dual 10f and hurdles winner Astrolibra (both by Sakhee) and the quite useful 2-y-o 7f winner Astrobella (by Medicean). The dam, a fairly useful 2-y-o dual 7f winner, is a half-sister to several winners including the fairly useful 3-y-o dual 7f winner Woodbeck (dam of the Group 2 Yorkshire Cup winner Franklins Gardens). The second dam, Arminda (by Blakeney), is an unraced half-sister to the Group 1 Prix de Diane winner Madam Gay. (Mystic Meg Ltd). *"She's quite a delicate but nice-looking filly. Being by Halling she'll be more of a 3-y-o type but hopefully she'll be running from the late summer onwards".*

1549. MARKTIME ★★★

b.f. Royal Applause – Nice Time (Tagula). April 26. Third foal. Half-sister to the modest 2015 3-y-o 1m winner Prayer Time (by Pastoral Pursuits). The dam, a fair 2-y-o 1m winner, is a half-sister to 3 winners including the useful 2-y-o 7f winner Prose, subsequently a winner in the USA. The second dam, Nicea (by Dominion), a fairly useful Irish 2-y-o 7f winner from 2 starts, is a half-sister to 2 winners. (Sarabex). *"A fairly late foal, she's growing now and she's 'up behind' but she'll be alright from the middle of the season onwards and I do like the sire".*

1550. MR TURNER ★★★★

b.c. Nayef – Seasonal Blossom (Fairy King). March 14. Half-brother to 5 winners including the very useful 6f to 12f winner of 4 races (including the listed Galtres Stakes) Brushing (by Medicean), the fair 10f to 14f winner of 6 races Wee Charlie Castle (by Sinndar) and the fair 1m winner of 4 races Seasonal Cross (by Cape Cross). The dam is an unplaced half-sister to 7 winners including the US Grade 2 winner Wait Till Monday and the Irish Group 3 winner Token Gesture (dam of the Grade 1 winner Relaxed Gesture). The second dam, Temporary Lull (by Super Concorde), is an unraced sister to the Group 3 Nell Gwyn Stakes winner Martha Stevens. (Sarabex). *"This is the nicest colt the dam's ever bred and he's a proper racehorse. He's doing so well, so I'm very happy with him. We called him Mr Turner after the recent film about the artist – bearing in mind that the half-sister to this colt is called Brushing!"*

1551. SWEEPING BEAUTY ★★★

b.f. Authorized – Brushing (Medicean). February 5. First foal. The dam, a very useful 6f to 12f winner of 4 races (including the listed Galtres Stakes), is a half-sister to 4 winners. The second dam, Seasonal Blossom (by Fairy King), is an unplaced half-sister to 7 winners including the US Grade 2 winner Wait Till Monday and the Irish Group 3 winner Token Gesture (dam of the Grade 1 winner Relaxed Gesture). (J Brenchley). *"The first foal of the Galtres winner Brushing, she's strong, well-grown and will want decent ground. I like her a lot, she's a very nice first foal with the right attitude and she could well be alright from mid-season onwards".*

1552. TOPALOVA ★★★

ch.f. Champs Elysees – Topatori (Topanoora). February 11. Half-sister to the Group 3 10.3f Middleton Stakes winner Topatoo (by Bahamian Bounty), the quite useful 1m to 14f winner Toparudi (by Rudimentary), the fair 1m (at 2 yrs) to 10.5f winner Topamichi (by Beat Hollow) and the fair 1m winner Top Shot (by College Chapel) and Top Tiger (by Mtoto), and the modest 12f and 14f winner Topaling (by Halling). The dam, a quite useful 7f to 11f winner of 4 races, is a half-sister to one winner. The second dam, Partygoer (by Cadeaux Genereux), was unplaced. (M P Bowring). *"We love her and think she's one of the nicest out of the dam. All her foals win and this filly moves well, she's straightforward and has a great temperament. She'll be one for the middle of the season onwards".*

1553. UNNAMED ★★★

b.f. Equiano – Amanda Carter (Tobougg). March 16. Second foal. 45,000Y. Tattersalls October Book 3. Not sold. Half-sister to the useful 2014 2-y-o dual 7f winner and Group 2 1m Royal Lodge Stakes third Salateen (by Dutch Art). The dam, a fair 9f to 13f winner of 6 races on the Flat and one over hurdles, is a half-sister to 7 winners here and abroad. The second dam, Al Guswa (by Shernazar), a dual 1m (at 2 yrs) and 10f winner in Ireland, is a half-sister to 5 winners. (Mrs Janis MacPherson). *"A great-moving filly, she's strong and should be racing soon enough, although people tell me that Equiano's flatter to deceive in that they look early and then they're not. She's strong and compact and doing everything right at the moment".*

1554. UNNAMED ★★★

ch.c. Medicean – Astrodonna (Carnival Dancer). January 31. Second foal. 18,000Y. Tattersalls October Book 3. K MacPherson. Half-brother to the unplaced 2014 2-y-o Bahamian Art (by Bahamian Bounty). The dam, a fair 9f (at 2 yrs) and 1m winner of 4 races, is a half-sister to 3 winners. The second dam, Mega (by Petardia), is an unplaced half-sister to 7 winners including the listed winners Bolino Star and Don Fayruz. (Kenneth MacPherson). *"We really like him, he's a strong, good-going colt and a perfect size for being a 2-y-o. The mare was good, she won four races and this colt has been showing us plenty at home. He's got the right attitude and we're hoping he'll be out in May".*

1555. UNNAMED ★★★
b.f. Royal Applause – Astromancer (Silver Hawk). March 22. Seventh foal. 2,000Y. Tattersalls October Book 2. M Tompkins. Half-sister to the modest 11f winner Cotton Grass (by Medicean). The dam, a moderate 4-y-o 14f winner, is a half-sister to one winner. The second dam, Colour Dance (by Rainbow Quest), is an unplaced full or half-sister to 4 winners including the very useful French 1m listed winner and Group 1 Prix Morny third Barricade. (Dahab Racing). *"I only paid two grand for her but she's a certain winner. She's a well-made, attractive filly, goes well and she's a racehorse all right. She's qualified for maiden auctions where she'll get weight concessions which will help of course - but she's better than that".* **TRAINERS' BARGAIN BUY**

1556. UNNAMED ★★
b.f. Sir Percy – Four Miracles (Vettori). April 13. Second foal. Half-sister to the moderate 2015 3-y-o 8.5f winner Hold Firm (by Refuse To Bend). The dam, a quite useful 10f to 2m 2f winner, is a half-sister to a winner. The second dam, North Kildare (by Northjet), is a half-sister to 7 winners including the Grade 1 9f Hollywood Derby winner Labeeb, the Group/Grade 2 winners Fanmore and Alrassaam. (Raceworld). *"She'll be an early runner. She's compact, strong, has a bit of an attitude about her and she'll be tough. I like her".*

1557. UNNAMED ★★★
b.f. Lawman – Katajan (Halling). February 1. Second foal. 25,000Y. Tattersalls October Book 2. Not sold. The dam is an unraced half-sister to 4 winners including the French listed 12f placed Flow Chart. The second dam, Kartajana (by Shernazar), won the Group 1 10.5f Prix Ganay, the Group 1 10f Grosser Preis Bayerisches Zuchtrennen, the Group 2 10f Nassau Stakes and the Group 2 10f Sun Chariot Stakes and is a sister to a French listed winner and a half-sister to 3 winners including the dual Australian Group 1 placed Karasi. (Dahab Racing). *"A filly with a good pedigree and by a good sire, she's doing everything right but she's going to grow a bit now so we'll wait until the mid-season and seven furlongs for her. We like her quite a lot".*

MARCUS TREGONING

1558. ALAMODE ♠
ch.f. Sir Percy – Almamia (Hernando). March 27. Fourth foal. €35,000Y. Goffs Sportsmans. Not sold. Half-brother to Alguazil (by Selkirk), unplaced in one start at 2 yrs in 2014 and to the fair 11f winner Aloha (by With Approval). The dam, a fair 1m and 9f placed maiden, is a half-sister to 3 winners including the French 10f winner and Group 2 second Albion and the listed 11f winner Alvarita. The second dam, Alborada (by Alzao), won the Group 1 Champion Stakes (twice) and is a sister to the triple German Group 1 winner Albanova. (Miss K Rausing).

1559. DANCE THE DREAM
b.f. Sir Percy – Shadow Dancing (Unfuwain). April 26. Sixth foal. 70,000Y. Tattersalls October Book 1. Not sold. Half-sister to the useful 2-y-o 1m winner and Group 3 10.3f Dee Stakes third Rasmy (by Red Ransom), to the fairly useful 11f winner Black Shadow (by New Approach) and the fair 2-y-o 1m winner Hazy Dancer (by Oasis Dream). The dam, winner of the listed Cheshire Oaks, was third in the Oaks and second in the Group 2 Ribblesdale Stakes and in the Group 2 Prix de Pomone and is a half-sister to 6 winners. The second dam, Salchow (by Niniski), won the listed Cheshire Oaks, was second in the Group 2 Park Hill Stakes and is a half-sister to 7 winners. (Mrs M A Dalgety).

1560. DAWREYA (IRE)
b.f. Acclamation – Darajaat (Elusive Quality). January 31. First foal. The dam, a useful 2-y-o 6f winner, was Group 3 placed and is a half-sister to the useful listed 1m winner and Group 3 7f Oak Tree Stakes third Shabiba. The second dam, Misterah (by Alhaarth), a very useful listed 6f (at 2 yrs) and Group 3 7f Nell Gwyn Stakes winner, is a full or half-sister to 4 winners. (Hamdan Al Maktoum).

1561. SUMOU (IRE)
b.c. Arcano – Three Times (Bahamian Bounty). March 27. Second living foal. £70,000Y. Doncaster Premier. Shadwell Estate Co. The dam ran twice unplaced and is a half-sister to 9 winners including the listed 10.5f winner and Group 3 Prix de la Nonette second Trinity Joy. The second dam, Triple Joy (by Most

Welcome), a useful 6f and 7f winner and second in the listed Abernant Stakes, is a half-sister to 7 winners including the Sun Chariot Stakes winner Talented (dam of the Group 2 Dante Stakes winner Carlton House). (Hamdan Al Maktoum).

1562. TAZAAYUD
b.c. Kodiac – Esteemed Lady (Mark Of Esteem). April 27. Seventh foal. £90,000Y. Doncaster Premier. Shadwell Estate Co. Half-brother to the quite useful dual 6f (at 2 yrs) and 1m winner Edgewater (by Bahamian Bounty), to the quite useful 6f winner Mutawathea (by Exceed And Excel), the fair 5f and 6f winner of 11 races Sleepy Blue Ocean (by Oasis Dream) and a winner abroad by Refuse To Bend. The dam, placed once over 6f at 2 yrs, is a half-sister to 6 winners including the 2-y-o Group 2 6f Richmond Stakes winner Revenue. The second dam, Bareilly (by Lyphard), is an unraced three-parts sister to the Group 3 1m Prix de la Grotte winner Baya and the Italian Group 2 winner Narrative. (Hamdan Al Maktoum).

1563. THAQAFFA (IRE)
b.c. Kodiac – Incense (Unfuwain). April 17. Sixth foal. 80,000Y. Tattersalls October Book 2. Shadwell Estate Co. Half-brother to the fair triple 1m winner Green Zone (by Bushranger), to the 1m winner Petit Chou (by Captain Rio) and the moderate 8.5f winner Inffiraaj (by Iffraaj). The dam, a modest dual 1m placed maiden, is a half-sister to 6 winners including the useful Group 3 7f Prestige Stakes winner Icicle. The second dam, Blessed Honour (by Ahonoora), a quite useful 2-y-o 7f winner, is a half-sister to 6 winners including the smart Group 2 11.9f Great Voltigeur Stakes winner Sacrament and to the unraced dam of the Group 1 winner Chorist. (Hamdan Al Maktoum).

1564. TUKHOOM (IRE)
b.c. Acclamation – Carioca (Rakti). February 16. Second foal. 100,000Y. Tattersalls October Book 2. Shadwell Estate Co. Half-brother to the useful 2-y-o 7f winner and Group 2 7fVintage Stakes second Tupi (by Tamayuz). The dam, a useful Italian listed 1m winner, is a half-sister to 3 winners including the 5f Windsor Castle Stakes winner and Group 2

6f Mill Reef Stakes second Irony. The second dam, Cidaris (by Persian Bold), ran once unplaced and is a half-sister to 3 winners including the dam of the South African dual Grade 1 winner Rabiya. (Hamdan Al Maktoum).

ROGER VARIAN

1565. ABSOLUTE ZERO (IRE) ★★★
b.c. Cape Cross – Emsiyah (Bernardini). February 3. First foal. €55,000Y. Goffs Orby. A & E Bloodstock. The dam ran twice unplaced and is a half-sister to one winner. The second dam, Menhoubah (by Dixieland Band), won the Group 1 Italian Oaks, was third in the 2-y-o Group 1 Moyglare Stud Stakes and is a half-sister to 2 winners. (Jon Collins, Chris Fahy & Mrs H Varian). *"He moves alright, he won't be early but should be out by mid-summer over seven furlongs. A good-looking colt".*

1566. AGHAANY ★★★★★
gr.f. Dubawi – Hathrah (Linamix). April 26. Fifth foal. Half-sister to the smart listed 10f winner and Group 1 Prix de l'Opera third Hadaatha (by Sea The Stars) and to the fairly useful dual 10f and 2m winner Itlaak (by Alhaarth). The dam, winner of the listed 1m Masaka Stakes and third in the 1,000 Guineas, is a half-sister to 5 winners including the smart Group 2 12f Premio Ellington winner Ivan Luis and the French/German listed winners Amathia and Zero Problemo. The second dam, Zivania (by Shernazar), a useful Irish winner of 4 races from 1m to 9.5f, is a half-sister to the Group 3 Prix Gontaut Biron winner Muroto. (Hamdan Al Maktoum). *"She's lovely. A very good type that moves well, there's a lot to like about her and I should imagine she'd start off at seven furlongs. Looks like a five star 2-y-o to me".*

1567. ALQUFFAAL ★★★★
br.c. Dansili – Cuis Ghaire (Galileo). April 4. The dam, a smart 2-y-o dual Group 3 6f winner and second in the 1,000 Guineas, is a sister to the Irish 2-y-o 7f winner and Coronation Stakes second Gile Na Greine, to the Group 3 9f winner Scintillula and the very useful Irish 1m winner and dual Group 3 placed Claiomh Solais. The second dam, Scribonia (by Danehill), is an unraced half-sister to 6 winners including the 2-y-o listed 6f winner and dual Group 1 placed Luminata. (Hamdan

Al Maktoum). *"He's a nice colt and he's got a lot of quality. A big, scopey horse and a nice prospect, he's one for the late summer onwards I should think".*

1568. ANEESAH ★★★
b.f. Canford Cliffs – Decorative (Danehill Dancer). January 31. First foal. £180,000Y. Doncaster Premier. Tony Nerses. The dam, a fairly useful 6f (at 2 yrs) and 1m winner, is a full sister to one winner and a half-sister to another. The second dam, Source Of Life (by Fasliyev), is an unraced half-sister to 9 winners including the Group 3 winners Australie and Forgotten Voice. (Saleh Al Homaizi & Imad Al Sagar). *"She moves nicely and will be a mid-summer 2-y-o. She has a good action and a good temperament".*

1569. ASKARI ★★
b.c. Sea The Stars – Loulwa (Montjeu). March 15. Fourth foal. Half-brother to the very useful 6f (at 2 yrs) and listed 5f winner of 4 races and Group 2 5f King George Stakes third Justineo (by Oasis Dream) and to the modest 6f winner Elhaam (by Shamardal). The dam, a fairly useful 11f and listed 13f winner, is a half-sister to 5 winners including the Group 2 6f Mill Reef Stakes winner and Group 1 placed Galeota and the fairly useful 2-y-o 5f Weatherbys Supersprint winner Lady Livius. The second dam, Refined (by Statoblest), a fairly useful dual 5f winner, is a half-sister to 6 winners including the very smart Group 3 7f Criterion Stakes winner Pipe Major. (Saleh Al Homaizi & Imad Al Sagar). *"A good-balanced colt, he's not early but there's nothing wrong with him and he carries himself nicely".*

1570. CLIFF EDGE (IRE) ★★★ ♠
b.c. Canford Cliffs – That's My Style (Dalakhani). March 24. First foal. £65,000Y. Doncaster Premier. Will Edmeades. The dam, a minor winner at 4 yrs in Germany, is a half-sister to 4 winners including Sparkling Beam (Group 3 Prix Chloe) and the 2-y-o Group 1 Prix Marcel Boussac third Rainbow Springs. The second dam, Pearl Dance (by Nureyev), a useful 2-y-o 6f winner and third in the Group 1 Moyglare Stud Stakes, is a half-sister to 7 winners including the dam of the Melbourne Cup winner Delta Blues. (Thurloe Thoroughbreds XXXVI). *"He moves alright, he could be a summer 2-y-o and he's not the*

biggest but there's a bit of length to him and he has a good action".

1571. COMPEL (FR) ★★★
ch.f. Exceed And Excel – Good Hope (GER) (Seattle Dancer). March 31. Second foal. €45,000Y. Tattersalls Ireland September. B Grassick Bloodstock. The dam, a winner at 2 yrs in Germany, was listed placed in France and Germany and is a half-sister to 4 winners. The second dam, Giralda (by Tenby), a listed-placed 3-y-o winner in Germany, is a half-sister to 2 winners. (Miss Y M G Jacques). *"A sharp, sprinting type filly and she could be out early doors, perhaps in May over five furlongs on fast ground".*

1572. DALALAH ★★★
b.f. Exceed And Excel – Bashasha (Kingmambo). February 16. Half-sister to the fair 9.5f to 12f and jumps winner Muntami (by Dansili). The dam, a minor Irish 12f winner, is a half-sister to numerous winners including the very useful Irish listed 10f winner Nafisah and the very useful Irish 1m and 9f winner Bawaader. The second dam, Alyakkh (by Sadler's Wells), a fair 3-y-o 1m winner, is a half-sister to the very useful Irish 3-y-o 1m listed stakes winner and Group 1 Coronation Stakes second Hasbah. (Hamdan Al Maktoum). *"She's goes alright and she'll be a summer 2-y-o. A filly with a good action, it's too early to know about her ability though".*

1573. DANCE BAND (IRE) ★★★
b.f. Danehill Dancer – Maidin Maith (Montjeu). April 16. Second foal. €150,000Y. Goffs Orby. Cheveley Park Stud. Half-sister to Mezajy (by Makfi), placed fourth over 7f and 1m on both his starts at 2 yrs in 2014. The dam, an Irish 2-y-o 7f winner, is a sister to the winner and Group 1 Gran Criterium third Chinese Whisper and a half-sister to 6 winners including the useful triple listed 7f winner (including at 2 yrs) Modeeroch and the useful Irish 2-y-o 6f winner and Group 1 6f Cheveley Park Stakes third Danaskaya. The second dam, Majinskaya (by Marignan), winner of the listed 12f Prix des Tuileries, is a half-sister to 6 winners including the dam of the Group 1 5f Prix de l'Abbaye winner Kistena. (Cheveley Park Stud). *"A filly with a good action and a decent pedigree, it's a bit too early to tell but she should be a summer 2-y-o".*

1574. DAWN OF HOPE (IRE) ★★★
ch.f. Mastercraftsman – Sweet Firebird (Sadler's Wells). February 10. Sixth foal. €220,000Y. Goffs Orby. Tony Nerses. Half-sister to 4 winners including the useful listed-placed 8.5f winner Ayrad (by Dalakhani), the fair 6f winner Alsium (by Invincible Spirit) and the modest 6f and 7f winner But Beautiful (by Pivotal). The dam, a 10f winner and third in the Group 3 Blue Wind Stakes, is a sister to the Group 2 1m Royal Lodge Stakes second Moscow Ballet and a half-sister to 6 winners including Stravinsky (Group 1 July Cup and Group 1 Nunthorpe Stakes). The second dam, Fire The Groom (by Blushing Groom), won the Grade 1 Beverly D Stakes and is a half-sister to the Group 1 Vernons Sprint Cup winner Dowsing. (Saleh Al Homaizi & Imad Al Sagar). *"A nice filly with a good action. She's not precocious but she could run at two and I like her".*

1575. FASHAAR ★★★
b.c. Showcasing – Avessia (Averti). March 23. Seventh foal. 75,000Y. Tattersalls October Book 2. Roger Varian. Half-brother to the fairly useful 2-y-o 6f and 7f winner Trading Profit (by Kheleyf) and to the quite useful 5f to 7.5f winner Avertor (by Oasis Dream). The dam, placed fourth once over 6f from two starts, is a sister to 2 winners including the Group 1 5f Prix de l'Abbaye winner and sire Avonbridge and a half-sister to the Prix de l'Abbaye winner Patavellian. The second dam, Alessia (by Caerleon), a quite useful 2-y-o 7f winner, is a sister to the Group 2 14.6f Park Hill Stakes winner Casey and a half-sister to 4 winners. (Sheikh Ahmed Al Maktoum). *"He's alright, he doesn't lack speed, he moves nicely and should be a summer 2-y-o over six furlongs".*

1576. FIRST RATE ★★★★
b.c. Kyllachy – Hooray (Invincible Spirit). April 13. First foal. The dam, a smart winner of 5 races including the Group 1 6f Cheveley Park Stakes and the Group 2 6f Lowther Stakes, is a half-sister to 4 winners including the useful 2-y-o listed 8.3f winner of 7 races Hypnotic. The second dam, Hypnotize (by Machiavellian), a useful 2-y-o dual 7f winner, is closely related to 2 winners including Dazzle (Group 3 6f Cherry Hinton Stakes) and a half-sister to 5 winners including the listed 1m winner Fantasize and to the placed dam

of the Group 2 winning sprinter Danehurst. (Cheveley Park Stud). *"This colt goes well. It's obviously a good pedigree and he could be a summer 2-y-o. A strong, well-matured horse that should be out in May or June over six furlongs".*

1577. FOOL TO CRY (IRE) ★★★
ch.f. Fast Company – Islandagore (Indian Ridge). March 25. 17,000Y. Tattersalls December. J Shack. Half-sister to the fairly useful 7f (at 2 yrs) to 10f winner of 5 races Island Sunset (by Trans Island), to the listed-placed 6f (at 2 yrs) and 7f winner of 6 races Alice's Dancer, the 2-y-o 6f winner (from two starts) Iron Range, the Irish 2-y-o 7f winner Tintean (all by Clodovil) - all three quite useful, and the fair 2-y-o winners Right Ted and Toby's Dream (both by Mujadil). The dam, a listed-placed 7f winner in Ireland, is a half-sister to the 2-y-o listed 6f winner Lady Of Kildare. The second dam, Dancing Sunset (by Red Sunset), winner of the Group 3 10f Royal Whip Stakes, is a full or half-sister to 5 winners. (J Shack & G Barnard). *"She moves well enough, it's too early to judge her ability but she'll be racing by mid-summer".*

1578. GO PACO ★★★
b.c. Paco Boy – Russian Rhapsody (Cosmonaut). April 12. Fifth foal. 32,000Y. Tattersalls October Book 3. Roger Varian. Half-brother to the fairly useful listed 6f winner Russian Spirit (by Falbrav) and to the fair 7f (at 2 yrs), 1m and jumps winner Russian Epic (by Diktat) and a winner in Germany by Haafhd. The dam, a fairly useful listed-placed 7f and 1m winner, is a half-sister to 3 winners. The second dam, Hannah's Music (by Music Boy), a fairly useful dual 5f winner, is a half-sister to 3 winners. (The Go Paco Partnership). *"He moves alright, he's a 2-y-o type and although he's not the biggest there's a bit of strength to him. He'll make a summer 2-y-o".*

1579. GWENDOLYN (GER) ★★★ ♠
b.f. Invincible Spirit – Golden Whip (Seattle Dancer). January 10. First foal. 60,000Y. Tattersalls October Book 2. David Redvers. The dam, a German dual listed 7f winner, is a half-sister to 8 minor winners. The second dam, Genevra (by Danehill), a German listed 1m winner, is a half-sister to 10 winners.

(Sheikh Khalifa, Sheikh Suhaim and Qatar Racing Ltd). *"There's a good bit of strength to her and she'll be one of the more precocious ones. She's moves alright and should be a May type runner".*

1580. HAALICK ★★★★
ch.c. Roderic O'Connor – Lucky Pipit (Key Of Luck). April 14. Seventh living foal. 170,000Y. Tattersalls October Book 2. Shadwell Estate Co. Half-brother to 4 minor winners in North America by Mr Greeley (2), Rahy and Student Council. The dam, a useful 2-y-o 7f listed winner, is a half-sister to 5 winners. The second dam, Meadow Pipit (by Meadowlake), a smart winner of 4 races at 4 yrs from 7f to 10f including a listed event, is a half-sister to 9 winners. (Sheikh Ahmed Al Maktoum). *"He's a very athletic, likeable horse that does everything in his stride. A good type and one you can give four stars to I think".*

1581. HEART SPRINKLED (IRE) ★★★
b.f. Galileo – Heart Shaped (Storm Cat). April 15. Third foal. $145,000Y. Keeneland September. Not sold. The dam, a useful Irish 2-y-o listed 5f Marble Hill Stakes winner, was second in the Group 3 Irish 1,000 Guineas Trial and is a sister to the fairly useful Irish 2-y-o 5f winner and listed-placed Facchetti and a half-sister to the US Grade 1 Champagne Stakes winner and Preakness Stakes second A P Valentine (by A P Indy) and the minor US stakes winner of 10 races Summer Bet. The second dam, Twenty Eight Carat (by Alydar), a minor US 4-y-o winner of 2 races over 6f and 1m, is a half-sister to 6 winners including the stakes winner Pulling Punches. (Teruya Yoshida). *"She's a nice type, I don't think she'll be early though. One for the back-end of the season".*

1582. IDEALIST ★★★
b.f. Rip Van Winkle – Illusion (Anabaa). May 7. Fourth foal. Half-sister to the quite useful 2014 7f and 1m placed 2-y-o and 3-y-o 7f winner Ventriloquist (by New Approach). The dam, a fairly useful 1m winner, was listed-placed and is a half-sister to 2 winners. The second dam, Fantasize (by Groom Dancer), a useful 7f (at 2 yrs) and listed 1m winner, is a half-sister to the Group 3 6f Cherry Hinton Stakes winner and 1,000 Guineas third Dazzle

and to the useful 2-y-o listed 7f winner Hypnotize. (Cheveley Park Stud). *"A filly for July or August, she's a nice type that moves well and she's good-looking".*

1583. IKRAAMM ★★★
b.c. Street Cry – Red Dune (Red Ransom). April 18. Brother to the fairly useful 2-y-o 7f and 1m winner and 3-y-o UAE Group 3 9.5f third Feedyah. The dam, a useful 7f and 1m winner, was listed-placed and is a full or half-sister to 4 winners. The second dam, Desert Beauty (Green Desert), a useful 7f and 1m winner, is a half-sister to the Yorkshire Oaks and Nassau Stakes winner Islington, to the smart stayer Election Day and the smart 10f performer Greek Dance. (Sheikh Ahmed Al Maktoum). *"He's alright, a bit backward and he'll take a bit of time, but he's not a bad type and he has a good action".*

1584. ISTANBUL BEY ★★★
ch.c. Exceed And Excel – Starfala (Galileo). February 6. Second foal. 85,000Y. Tattersalls October Book 1. Highflyer Bloodstock. The dam, a useful dual 12f winner and second in the Group 2 Park Hill Stakes, is a half-sister to 5 winners including the 2-y-o listed 10f Zetland Stakes winner and Group 2 12f Lancashire Oaks second Under The Rainbow. The second dam, Farfala (by Linamix), a French listed 12f winner, is a sister to the Group 1 Grand Prix de Saint-Cloud winner Fragrant Mix and the Group 3 Prix d'Hedouville winner Fracassant. (Simon Munir & Isaac Souede). *"A nice colt, he's scopey for an Exceed And Excel so he's not an early type, but there's every chance he'll be a summer 2-y-o. Moves well".*

1585. KARAKOZ ★★★
b.f. Danehill Dancer – Card Shop (Chester House). January 31. Third foal. Half-sister to the Group 3 7f Prestige Stakes winner Ollie Olga (by Stormy Atlantic). The dam, placed at 2 and 3yrs in France, is a half-sister to the Group 2 Hardwicke Stakes winner and Group 1 Juddmonte International Stakes third Await The Dawn and to the French listed winner and Group 1 Criterium de Saint-Cloud third Putney Bridge (by Mizzen Mast). The second dam, Valentine Band (by Dixieland Band), a listed-placed 3-y-o winner, is a half-sister to 8 winners including the Group 3 winners

Memorise and Multiplex. (N Bizakov). *"A filly with a good action, she's a medium-sized, late summer type 2-y-o".*

1586. MAJDOOL (IRE) ★★★

b.c. Acclamation – Maany (Mr Greeley). February 6. First foal. The dam, placed third once over 6f from 3 starts, half-sister to several wines including the US Grade 2 9f Wood Memorial Stakes winner and dual Grade 1 second Adonis. The second dam, Dixie Card (by Dixieland Band), a minor US stakes winner, won from 6f (including at 2 yrs) to 8.5f. (Hamdan Al Maktoum). *"Quite a mature horse that moves nicely, hopefully he'll be a summer 2-y-o and he has a good action".*

1587. MEGHWAR (IRE) ★★★

gr.c. Zebedee – Champion Tipster (Pursuit Of Love). April 1. Sixth foal. 90,000Y. Tattersalls October Book 2. Roger Varian. Half-brother to the quite useful 2-y-o 5f and 6f winner and listed-placed All On Red (by Red Clubs), to the quite useful 6f winner Shearman (by Elusive City) and the fair 5f to 1m winner Shadow Bay (by Deportivo). The dam is an unraced half-sister to 3 winners. The second dam, Halloa (by Wolfhound), a fairly useful listed-placed 2-y-o 6f winner, is a half-sister to 4 winners. (Sheikh Ahmed Al Maktoum). *"He's precocious, so he's one of our earlier sorts. He shows a bit of speed and there's a bit of strength to him, so he could start over five furlongs in May".*

1588. MURINA EYES (USA) ★★★

ch.c. Cape Blanco – Desert Sky (Green Desert). March 9. Sixth foal. 78,000Y. Tattersalls October Book 2. Roger Varian. Half-brother to the US Grade 2 1m winner No Jet Lag (by Johar) and to the French 2-y-o dual 6f winner and Group 3 6f Prix de Cabourg third Optari (by Diesis). The dam, a 2-y-o listed 6f Silver Flash Stakes winner, is a sister to the 6f winner and UAE listed placed Moonis and a half-sister to 3 winners. The second dam, Badrah (by Private Account), is a placed half-sister to 5 winners including the Group 3 Brigadier Gerard Stakes winner Husyan. (Mr M Almutairi). *"He moves nicely this horse. I like him, he goes well and could be quite sharp".*

1589. MUTARAJJIL (IRE) ★★★

b.c. Acclamation – Rouge Noir (Saint Ballado).

April 8. Eighth foal. 105,000Y. Tattersalls October Book 2. Shadwell Estate Co. Half-brother to 5 winners including the useful 2-y-o listed 5f winner Light The Fire (by Invincible Spirit), the useful 2-y-o 7f winner and listed-placed Cadley Road (by Elusive City), the fair 2-y-o 7f winner Joohaina (by New Approach) and the Italian winner of 7 races from 2 to 4 yrs Crazy Duck (by Kheleyf). The dam, a minor winner at 3 yrs in the USA, is a half-sister to 6 winners in Japan. The second dam, Ardana (by Danehill), won the Group 3 Premio Bagutta and is a half-sister to 5 winners. (Hamdan Al Maktoum). *"He's a straightforward horse with a reasonable action and there's a bit of strength to him. He should be a summer 2-y-o".*

1590. OPEN 'N SHUT ★★★

ch.c. Kyllachy – Our Faye (College Chapel). April 16. Third foal. £40,000Y. Doncaster Premier. Armando Duarte. Half-brother to the 2014 5f placed 2-y-o Effectual (by Exceed And Excel). The dam, a fairly useful winner of 7 races from 6f to 1m including the Group 3 Summer Stakes, is a half-sister to 3 winners. The second dam, Tamara (by Marju), a fairly useful 2-y-o 5f winner, is a half-sister to 2 winners. *"He moves nicely and although he's not that precocious he could be a June/July horse and it's a speedy pedigree".*

1591. PAPER FACES (USA) ★★★

ch.f. Lemon Drop Kid – Liffey Dancer (Sadler's Wells). February 1. Third foal. Half-sister to the fair Melbourne Shuffle (by Street Cry), placed over 1m at 2 yrs (in 2014) and 3 yrs. The dam is an unraced sister to 4 winners including the Group 1 7f Moyglare Stud Stakes winner Sequoyah (herself dam of the multiple Group 1 winner Henrythenavigator) and the 2-y-o Group 1 Fillies' Mile winner Listen and a half-sister to the listed 5.6f winner and Group 3 placed Oyster Catcher (by Bluebird). The second dam, Brigid (by Irish River), a minor French 1m winner, is a sister to the French listed 7f winner Or Vision (dam of the Group/Grade 1 winners Dolphin Street, Insight and Saffron Walden). (Merry Fox Stud Ltd). *"A 2-y-o type with a good action, she could be a summer filly, possibly with the speed for six furlongs".*

1592. PHILADELPHIA (IRE) ★★★
b.c. Roderic O'Connor – Harvest Joy (Daggers Drawn). February 26. Third foal. €52,000Y. Goffs Orby. A & E Bloodstock. Half-brother to the quite useful 2014 2-y-o 6f winner Don Sigfredo (by Majestic Missile) and to the fairly useful 2-y-o 5f to 7f winner and listed-placed Andysontherun (by Captain Rio). The dam, a fairly useful listed-placed 6f (at 2 yrs) and 10f winner, is a half-sister to 2 winners. The second dam, Windomen (by Forest Wind), is an unraced half-sister to 4 winners including the Italian Group 1 third and smart broodmare Super Bobbina. (The Philadelphia Partnership). *"He's alright, I quite like him and he moves well. A summer 2-y-o".*

1593. PLANTATION (IRE) ★★★ ♠
b.c. Invincible Spirit – Matula (Halling). April 10. First foal. €110,000Y. Goffs Orby. John Warren. The dam, a quite useful 2-y-o 1m winner, is a half-sister to the fairly useful 2-y-o 7f winner Diala. The second dam, Quaich (by Danehill), a fair 7f winner, is a half-sister to 2 winners. (Highclere Thoroughbred Racing, Rosebery). *"He goes well and is one of the earlier types. Hopefully he'll be running in May".*

1594. RASHAAQA ★★★★
b.f. Oasis Dream – Shimah (Storm Cat). April 19. Third foal. Sister to the useful 2-y-o listed 6f winner Mushir and half-sister to the 2014 unplaced 2-y-o in two starts, Estikhraaj (by Dansili). The dam, a listed 6f winner and second in the Group 1 Moyglare Stud Stakes, is a half-sister to the listed 6f (at 2 yrs) and Group 3 7f Athasi Stakes winner Walayef, the Group 2 6f Diomed Stakes winner Haatef and the Irish dual listed 6f winner Ulfah. The second dam, Sayedat Alhadh (by Mr Prospector), a US 7f winner, is a sister to the US Grade 2 7f winner Kayrawan and a half-sister to the useful winners Amaniy, Elsaamri and Mathkurh. (Hamdan Al Maktoum). *"A nice type of filly, she's strong and mature, not early but more likely a summer 2-y-o. She moves nicely and I like her".*

1595. SAIDDAA (USA) ★★★
b.f. Hard Spun – My Dubai (Dubai Millennium). January 25. Half-sister to the quite useful 6f to 1m winner Mishaal (by Kheleyf), to

the quite useful dual 7f winner Mizwaaj (by Invincible Spirit) and the fair 7f and 9f winner Naddwah (by Pivotal). The dam, placed over 7f on her only start, is a half-sister to 7 winners including the very smart triple Group 2 7f winner Iffraaj, the useful 2-y-o Group 3 7f Prix du Calvados winner Kareymah and the useful dual 1m winner Jathaabeh. The second dam, Pastorale (by Nureyev), a fairly useful 3-y-o 7f winner, ran only twice more including in a walk-over. (Sheikh Ahmed Al Maktoum). *"She's a likeable filly that moves well enough. She'll make a 2-y-o by mid-summer I should think".*

1596. SEA THE BLUE (IRE) ★★★
b.c. Dark Angel – Bowness (Efisio). April 6. Fourth foal. 55,000Y. Tattersalls October Book 2. Rabbah Bloodstock. Half-brother to the fair 2014 2-y-o 6f winner Luna Mission (by Acclamation). The dam, a quite useful 5f and 6f winner, was third in the listed 5f Land O'Burns Stakes and is a half-sister to 3 winners including the Group 2 5f Kings Stand Stakes and Group 3 5f Cornwallis Stakes Dominica. The second dam, Dominio (by Dominion), a 2-y-o listed 5f winner, was second in the Group 2 5f Temple Stakes and is a half-sister to 6 winners including the very smart Group 1 5f Nunthorpe Stakes winner Ya Malak. (Sheikh R D Al Maktoum). *"A sharp sort of horse with a bit of strength to him. He moves well and should be out in May. I like him and his pedigree is all speed so hopefully he'll have a bit of boot".*

1597. SHANYRRAK ★★★
b.c. Medicean – Shabyt (Sadler's Wells). January 29. First foal. The dam is an unraced half-sister to the listed 11f winner and Group 1 Oaks second Secret Gesture. The second dam, Shastye (by Danehill), a useful 12f and 13f winner, was listed-placed and is a half-sister to 8 winners including the Prix de l'Arc de Triomphe winner Sagamix, the Group 1 Criterium de Saint-Cloud winner Sagacity and the Group 2 Prix de Malleret winner Sage Et Jolie (herself dam of the Group 1 winner Sageburg). (N Bizakov). *"He moves well and has a 2-y-o frame with a bit of strength to him. Not an early horse, but a seven furlong July type 2-y-o".*

1598. TAILWIND ★★★★ ♠
b.c. Dubawi – Time Saved (Green Desert).
February 4. Ninth foal. 550,000Y. Tattersalls
October Book 1. Not sold. Half-brother to
6 winners including the Group 2 12f King
Edward VII Stakes winner Plea Bargain (by
Machiavellian), the Group 3 10f Winter Hill
Stakes winner Lay Time (by Galileo) and the
useful listed 6f winner Jira (by Medicean).
The dam, a fairly useful 10f winner, is a full or
half-sister to 6 winners including Zinaad and
Time Allowed (both winners of the Group 2
12f Jockey Club Stakes). The second dam,
Time Charter (by Saritamer), won the Oaks,
the King George VI and Queen Elizabeth
Diamond Stakes, the Champion Stakes and
the Coronation Cup. (R Barnett). *"He's a nice
colt, he moves well, he's very good-looking and
very uncomplicated with a good attitude. He
could be a July type 2-y-o".*

1599. TARSEEKH ★★
b.c. Kyllachy – Constitute (Gone West).
February 25. Ninth foal. 320,000Y. Tattersalls
October Book 2. Shadwell Estate Co. Brother
to 3 winners including the fairly useful listed-
placed dual 6f winner (including at 2 yrs)
Enact and the fair 2-y-o 6f winner Assembly
and closely related to two winners by Pivotal
including the fairly useful 6f and 7f winner
and listed-placed Enrol. The dam, a quite
useful 1m winner, is a half-sister to 7 winners
including the smart Group 3 second Battle
Chant. The second dam, Appointed One (by
Danzig), a Grade 3 placed US stakes winner, is
a sister to 3 winners including Emperor Jones
(Group 2 1m Lockinge Stakes) and a half-sister
to the Group 1 1m William Hill Futurity Stakes
winner Bakharoff. (Hamdan Al Maktoum). *"A
big horse, he's grown since the sale so he's not
a precocious Kyllachy. One for the second half
of the season and although he should have the
zip for six furlongs it's too early to tell".*

1600. TAWWAAQ (IRE) ★★★
gr.f. Zebedee – Killinallan (Vettori).
March 24. Fourth foal. £120,000Y. Doncaster
Premier. Shadwell Estate Co. Half-sister to the
smart dual listed 5f winner of 8 races Steps
(by Verglas). The dam ran once unplaced and
is a half-sister to 6 winners including the dual
Group 3 winning sprinter Deep Finesse and to
the placed dam of the dual Group 1 winner

Dick Turpin. The second dam, Babycham
Sparkle (by So Blessed), a quite useful 5f
and 6f winner, is a half-sister to 6 winners.
(Hamdan Al Maktoum). *"A half-sister to our
good older sprinter Steps, she moves nicely, has
a bit of strength to her and could be one of our
more precocious ones. I'd like to think we could
get her out in May and we like what we've
seen of her so far".*

1601. TESTIMONY ★★★★
b.f. Lawman – Macleya (Winged Love).
February 10. Fourth foal. The dam won 7 races
including the Group 2 12.5f Prix de Pomone
and the Group 3 10f Prix Allez France and is
a half-sister to 4 winners. The second dam,
Minaccia (by Platini), won a listed event in
Germany over 7f at 3 yrs and is a half-sister to
4 winners. (Cheveley Park Stud). *"She's a lovely
filly and stands out a bit at the moment. She's
not going to be early but she's very natural and
could be a July/August 2-y-o".*

1602. TIERCEL ★★★
b.c. Olden Times – Sharp Mode (Diesis).
April 14. Seventh foal. Half-brother to the
2014 French 2-y-o 1m winner Eternal (by
New Approach), to the quite useful 7f (at 2
yrs) and 12f winner Amralah (by Teofilo), the
fair 2-y-o 6f winner Homestretch (by Holy
Roman Emperor) and the modest 2-y-o 5f
winner Midget (by Invincible Spirit). The dam
is an unraced half-sister to 2 minor winners.
The second dam, A La Mode (by Known Fact),
placed at 2 yrs and subsequently a minor
winner at 5 yrs in the USA, is a sister to the US
Grade 3 winner Modernise and a half-sister
to five Group winners including the Group
1 winners Elmaamul and Reams Of Verse.
(Prince A A Faisal). *"A big horse, he's very good-
looking but won't be doing much until the
second half of the season. He could be alright".*

1603. TIFL ★★★
ch.c. Approve – Isobel Rose (Royal Applause).
February 15. Fourth foal. £38,000Y. Doncaster
Premier. Shadwell Estate. Half-brother to the
modest 2-y-o 6f winner Sakhee's Rose (by
Sakhee's Secret) and to a minor winner in
Italy by Piccolo. The dam was a modest 6f
winner at 4 yrs. The second dam, Total Love
(by Cadeaux Genereux), a useful 2-y-o 6f
winner and third in the Group 3 7f Rockfel

Stakes, is a half-sister to 8 winners. (Hamdan Al Maktoum). *"He's a sharp horse that moves nicely. There's a bit of strength to him and he should be out in May over five furlongs. I quite like him".*

1604. TREBLE STRIKE (USA) ★★★

b.c. Hat Trick – Lady Simpson (Yankee Victor). April 2. Third foal. 27,000Y. Tattersalls October Book 2. Roger Varian. The dam is an unplaced half-sister to 8 winners including the Group 1 Racing Post Trophy winner Palace Episode and the dam of the Group 2 winner and Group 1 second Laughing Lashes. The second dam, Palace Weekend (by Seattle Dancer), is an unraced half-sister to the US Grade 2 winners More Royal and Tejano Run. (S Hassiakos, M Mannaseh & H Varian). *"He moves well, isn't precocious but he's a likeable colt with a good action. The sire hasn't had many runners over here but he did have the champion European 2-y-o Dabirsim a few years ago".*

1605. VIZIER ★★★

b.c. Pivotal – Rare Ransom (Oasis Dream). February 1. Third foal. 290,000Y. Tattersalls October Book 1. Not sold. Half-brother to the quite useful 1m (at 2 yrs) and 10f winner Alex Vino (by High Chaparral). The dam, a fairly useful Irish 7f (at 2 yrs) and 1m winner and third in the Group 3 7f Debutante Stakes, is a full or half-sister to 5 winners. The second dam, Rapid Ransom (by Red Ransom), a quite useful Irish 10f winner, was Grade 3 placed in the USA and is a half-sister to the Irish 2-y-o listed winner Warrior Queen (dam of the US Grade 2 winner and Grade 1 placed A P Warrior). (N Bizakov). *"He's not a bad type but he'll take time. Like a lot of Pivotal's he's not precocious, but he moves fine and is one for the back-end of the season".*

1606. UNNAMED ★★★

ch.c. Danehill Dancer – Alsace Lorraine (Giant's Causeway). March 4. Second foal. 330,000Y. Tattersalls October Book 2. Paul Smith. The dam, a very useful 1m, 9f and listed 10f winner, is a half-sister to 2 winners. The second dam, Mer de Corail (by Sadler's Wells), winner of the listed 10f Prix d'Automne, is a sister to the listed-placed winner Maximum Security and a half-sister to the French 1,000 Guineas winner Miss France. (Mr P D Smith). *"A nice*

type of horse with a good action and a bit of quality about him. He'll make a 2-y-o by August but he's not a sprinter and will probably want seven furlongs to begin with".

1607. UNNAMED ★★★

b.c. Dream Ahead – Anna's Rock (Rock Of Gibraltar). May 14. Fourth foal. 70,000Y. Tattersalls October Book 1. Roger Varian. Half-brother to the listed winner and Group 3 John Of Gaunt Stakes second Breton Rock (by Bahamian Bounty). The dam, a useful Irish 7f (at 2 yrs) and listed 7.5f winner, is a half-sister to 3 winners. The second dam, Anna Karenina (by Atticus), is an unraced half-sister to 10 winners including Agathe (Group 3 Prix de Psyche and herself dam of the Grade/Group 1 winners Artiste Royale and Aquarelliste), the Breeders Cup Classic winner Arcangues and the dams of the Group/Grade 1 winners Cape Verdi and Angara. (Mr S Rashid). *"A nice type, she moves nicely and is well-balanced. Should be racing by July or August".*

1608. UNNAMED ★★★

ch.c. Exceed And Excel – Annabelle's Charm (Indian Ridge). January 30. Second foal. Half-brother to the 2014 2-y-o Group 16f Middle Park Stakes winner Charming Thought (by Oasis Dream). The dam, a very useful listed 1m winner, was Group 3 placed twice over 1m and is a half-sister to 4 winners including the fairly useful 2-y-o 7f winner and listed UAE 1,000 Guineas third Purple Sage. The second dam, Kylemore (by Sadler's Wells), ran twice unplaced and is a sister to the dual Group 1 winner Ballingarry and to the Racing Post Trophy winner Aristotle and a half-sister to the St James's Palace Stakes and Prix Jean Prat winner Starborough. (Merry Fox Stud Ltd). *"This horse is alright, he has a good pedigree and a good shape to him. Not early, but he'll make a 2-y-o".*

1609. UNNAMED ★★

gr.c. Rip Van Winkle – Bali Breeze (Common Grounds). February 28. Sixth foal. 80,000Y. Tattersalls October Book 2. Roger Varian. Half-brother to the modest 2014 2-y-o 6f winner Thewaythewindblows (by Thewayyouare), to the useful dual 10f winner and Group 3 10f second Alkimos (by High Chaparral), the French winner of 4 races Soulside (by

Whipper) and the modest 2-y-o 1m winner Storm (by Excellent Art). The dam, a quite useful 10f, 12f and hurdles winner, is a full or half-sister to 4 winners. The second dam, Bahia Laura (by Bellypha), a minor winner over 10.5f at 4 yrs in France, is a half-sister to 7 winners including the Group 3 10.5f Prix de Flore winner Benicia. (A D Spence). *"He moves well enough and should be racing by July or August over seven furlongs. It's too early to tell on ability but he'll be alright".*

1610. UNNAMED ★★★
b.c. Rip Van Winkle – Cawett (Danehill Dancer). April 21. Second foal. €170,000Y. Goffs Orby. China Horse Club/Michael Wallace. The dam is an unraced half-sister to 6 winners including the listed winners Asawer and Chercheuse (herself dam of the Group 3 winner and US Grade 1 placed Questing). The second dam, Sassy Bird (by Storm Bird), is a placed sister to the Group 2 winner Mukaddamah and a half-sister to 8 winners including the Group 2 winner Tatami. (China Horse Club, HK). *"A scopey horse so he won't be early, but he's a good-looking colt with a good action. He'll make a 2-y-o by July or August I should think".*

1611. UNNAMED ★★★★
ch.c. Sea The Stars – Evensong (Waky Nao). March 1. Fourth living foal. €850,000Y. Goffs Orby. China Horse Club/Michael Wallace. Half-sister to the quite useful 9f and 10f winner Night And Dance (by Danehill Dancer) and to a minor winner abroad by Holy Roman Emperor. The dam won 4 races in France and Germany including a French listed event over 9f and is a half-sister to 5 winners including the German Group 2 winners Eye Of The Tiger and Eagle Rise and the French listed winner Echoes Rock. The second dam, Evening Breeze (by Surumu), a German listed winner of 6 races, is a half-sister to the Singapore Group 1 winner Epalo and the French Group 2 winner Elopa. (China Horse Club, HK). *"A lovely horse with a lot of quality to him and he moves well. He's a nice horse that'll just run once or twice this year I should think, but he's a belter".*

1612. UNNAMED ★★★
gr.c. Mastercraftsman – Gold Charm (Key Of Luck). May 5. Seventh foal. 100,000Y.

Tattersalls October Book 2. Roger Varian. Half-brother to the 9.5f winner (at 2 yrs in 2014) and 3-y-o listed 10f winner Princess Charm (by Rip Van Winkle) and to two minor winners in France by Kingsalsa and Lando. The dam, a French 6f (at 2 yrs) and 3-y-o listed 7f winner, is a half-sister to 9 minor winners in France and Germany. The second dam, Goldkatze (by Czarevich), won 4 minor races in Germany and is a half-sister to 6 winners in Europe. (Mr P D Smith). *"A nice, very straightforward horse, he gets on with the job and has a good action. It's too early to tell on ability but there's plenty to like about him".*

1613. UNNAMED ★★★
b.c. Cape Blanco – Keepers Hill (Danehill). January 27. Seventh foal. 150,000Y. Tattersalls October Book 2. Charlie Gordon-Watson. Half-brother to the fairly useful 6f and 6.5f winner at 2 and 3 yrs Swilly Ferry (by Wiseman's Ferry) and to 3 minor winners in North America by Sir Shackleton, Toccet and Bernstein). The dam, an Irish listed-placed 5f winner, is a half-sister to 8 winners including the Group 3 winners Forgotten Voice and Australie. The second dam, Asnieres (by Spend A Buck), a French 4-y-o winner, is a half-sister to the Breeders Cup Classic and Prix d'Ispahan winner Arcangues, to the Group 3 Prix de Psyche winner Agathe (dam of the triple Group 1 winner Aquarelliste) and the dam of the 1,000 Guineas winner Cape Verdi. (Mr P D Smith). *"A good-looking horse, well-balanced and with good action. He's one for the second half of the season and he's not a bad type".*

1614. UNNAMED ★★★
gr.c. Galileo – Laddies Poker Two (Choisir). January 14. First foal. The dam, a useful triple 6f winner at 3 and 5 yrs, is a half-sister to 4 winners. The second dam, Break Of Day (by Favorite Trick), is an unraced half-sister to 5 winners including the Group 2 Gimcrack Stakes second Ma Yoram. (Mr P D Smith). *"He's a nice colt that moves well, there's a good shape to him and I like him. He could be a mid-summer horse, which for Galileo would be plenty early enough".*

1615. UNNAMED ★★★
b.c. Deep Impact – Listen (Sadler's Wells). March 11. Third foal. The dam won the Group

1 Fillies' Mile at 2 yrs and is a sister to 3 winners including the Group 1 7f Moyglare Stud Stakes winner Sequoyah (the dam of Henrythenavigator) and a half-sister to the Irish listed 5.6f winner and Group 3 7f placed Oyster Catcher. The second dam, Brigid (by Irish River), a minor French 3-y-o 1m winner, is a sister to the French listed 7f winner Or Vision (herself dam of the Group/Grade 1 winners Dolphin Street, Insight and Saffron Walden) and a half-sister to 6 winners. (Qatar Racing Ltd). *"It's exciting to have a horse in the yard by Deep Impact who is going great guns in Japan. This is a tall horse, narrow and very athletic. We like what we've seen of him so far but he's not going to be an early type".*

1616. UNNAMED ★★★
b.c. Equiano – Nouvelle Amie (Noverre). April 20. Third foal. 16,000Y. Tattersalls October Book 2. Roger Varian. The dam won 5 races at 4 yrs in Germany and is a half-sister to 2 winners including the Italian Group 3 winner Nouvelle Noblesse. The second dam, Nouvelle Perle (by Lando), won at 2 yrs in Germany and is a half-sister to 10 winners. (Holylay & Co. Ltd & Mrs H Varian). *"He's a likeable horse with a good attitude and he moves well. We haven't done much with him yet but hopefully he'll be able to go a bit when we do".* **TRAINERS' BARGAIN BUY**

1617. UNNAMED ★★★
b.f. Acclamation – Roo (Rudimentary). February 21. Ninth living foal. 300,000Y. Half-sister to 6 winners including the very smart 6f (at 2 yrs) and 7f winner and Group 2 Prix Morny second Gallagher (by Bahamian Bounty), the very useful 7f (including at 2 yrs) to 10f winner and listed-placed Quick Wit (by Oasis Dream), the useful 5f (at 2 yrs) and 7f winner and listed-placed Roodeye (by Inchinor) and the quite useful 2-y-o winners Cockney Dancer (by Cockney Rebel) and Roodolph (by Primo Valentino). The dam, a quite useful 2-y-o 5f and 6f winner, was listed-placed and is a half-sister to the Group 2 6f Gimcrack Stakes winner Bannister. The second dam, Shall We Run (by Hotfoot), placed once over 5f at 2 yrs, is a half-sister to the Group 1 6f Cheveley Park Stakes winner Dead Certain. (China Horse Club HK). *"She moves alright and although she's not that precocious she could*

be a summer 2-y-o. A fairly sharp filly and speedily-bred".

1618. UNNAMED ★★★
b.f. Lawman – Solar Event (Galileo). February 20. First foal. 170,000foal. Tattersalls December. David Redvers. The dam, a modest 12f placed maiden, is a half-sister to the Group 2 Prix de Malleret and listed Cheshire Oaks winner Time On. The second dam, Time Away (by Darshaan), won the Group 3 10.4f Musidora Stakes, was third in the Group 1 Prix de Diane and the Group 1 Nassau Stakes and is a half-sister to 6 winners including the 10f winner and Prix de Diane second Time Ahead. (Qatar Racing Ltd). *"She's a nice filly that'll take a bit of time but she has a good balance to her and a nice way of going. She's likeable".*

1619. UNNAMED ★★★
b.f. Iffraaj – Spiritual Air (Royal Applause). May 6. Seventh foal. £78,000Y. Doncaster Premier. David Redvers. Sister to the quite useful 7f winner Perfect Step and half-sister the fair 2-y-o 7f winner Andean Margin (by Giant's Causeway) and the modest 7f and 1m winner of 4 races Emeralds Spirit (by Rock Of Gibraltar). The dam, a fairly useful 2-y-o 6f winner, subsequently won at 4 yrs in the USA and is a half-sister to 3 winners including the Group 2 6f Mill Reef Stakes second Mystical Land. The second dam, Samsung Spirit (by Statoblest), a fair dual 6f winner (including at 2 yrs), is a half-sister to 7 winners and to the dam of the Mill Reef Stakes winner Indian Rocket. (Qatar Racing Ltd). *"She moves alright, not precocious, but she could be a summer 2-y-o and there's nothing wrong with her".*

1620. UNNAMED ★★★
b.c. Dream Ahead – Tiger Spice (Royal Applause). April 5. Fourth foal. 110,000Y. Goffs Orby. China Horse Club/Michael Wallace. Half-brother to the quite useful triple 7f (including at 2 yrs) winner Azrur (by Sir Percy) and to the fair 6f (at 2 yrs) and 7.5f winner Spiceupyourlife (by Sakhee's Secret). The dam, a modest 2-y-o 9f winner, is a half-sister to 5 winners including the dam of the Group 3 Oak Tree Stakes winner Summer Fete and to the unplaced dam of the US Grade 2 and Grade 3 winner Up In Time. The second dam, Up And About (by Barathea), a fair 14.8f winner, is a

half-sister to 9 winners including the listed winner and Group 1 placed Musicanna and the dam of the champion European 3-y-o sprinter Overdose. (China Horse Club, HK). *"I like him, he moves well, has a bit of size, scope and strength. A nice type for the mid-summer".*

1621. UNNAMED ★★★★
b.f. Montjeu – Vital Statistics (Indian Ridge). January 30. Half-sister to Caelica (by Sea The Stars), unplaced in two starts at 2 yrs in 2014 and to the useful 6f (at 2 yrs) and 7f winner Ashaadd (by Dansili). The dam, listed 6f winner and second in the Group 3 Princess Margaret Stakes, is a half-sister to 5 winners. The second dam, Emerald Peace (by Green Desert), a useful listed 5f winner of 4 races and second in the Group 2 5f Flying Childers Stakes, is a half-sister to 5 winners. (Mr Mitaab Abdullah). *"A nice filly with a bit of strength and a good mind to her for a Montjeu. She has a good action and is a nice type of filly".*

ED VAUGHAN
1622. BONNEFIO ★★
b.f. Teofilo – Crimson Ribbon (Lemon Drop Kid). March 11. The dam, a quite useful 12f winner, is a sister to the very smart Group 2 12f Hardwicke Stakes and Group 2 12f Jockey Club Stakes winner of 8 races Bronze Cannon and a half-sister to 4 winners including the useful Irish 2-y-o dual 7f winner Elusive Award. The second dam, Victoria Cross (by Mark Of Esteem), a useful 7f winner here and listed-placed in France, is a half-sister to 6 winners including the Grade 2 San Marcos Handicap winner Prize Giving and to the placed dam of the dual US Grade 1 winner Alpride. (Mr A Oppenheimer). *"A nice filly that only came to us just recently. She's more of a back-end of the season type, as you would imagine given her pedigree. I like her, she's a good-actioned filly and Malcolm Bastard had her in pre-training and he liked her also. I would expect her to start off at seven furlongs or a mile".*

1623. MISS FRIDAYTHORPE ★★★★
b.f. Pastoral Pursuits – Cosmic Destiny (Soviet Star). March 29. Third foal. Sister to the fairly useful 5f and 6f winner of 6 races at 2 (in 2014) and 3 yrs Primrose Valley and to the fair 6f winner Costa Filey. The dam, a modest but tough winner of 6 races over 5f and from 3 to

6yrs, is a half-sister to 3 winners. The second dam, Cruelle (by Irish River), was placed at up to 7.5f in France at 2 and 3 yrs and is a half-sister to 5 winners. (Alan Pickering). *"She might well follow in the footsteps of her full sister last year and be our first 2-y-o runner. She seems a nice, forward-going filly, on pedigree she should be quick enough for five furlongs and I can imagine her starting off in late April. Mentally the family can be a bit tricky but the 3-y-o Primrose Valley seems to be just like the dam – as tough as you like. I'd be high on her, she canters very well and I'd say she's quick enough for five furlongs".*

1624. UNNAMED ★★
b.f. Royal Applause – Caldy Dancer (Soviet Star). January 21. Seventh foal. Half-sister to the smart 7f to 9f winner of 7 races and dual Group 3 placed Dance And Dance (by Royal Applause), to the Hong Kong 7f and 1m winner and Group 1 third Rewarding Hero (by Exceed And Excel) and the fair 9f winner On With The Dance (by Byron). The dam, a useful 2-y-o dual 5f winner and second in the Group 3 7f Debutante Stakes, is a half-sister to 4 winners. The second dam, Smile Awhile (by Woodman), ran once unplaced and is a full or half-sister to 3 winners. (Mohammed Rashid). *"She's a lot bigger than the other members of the family I've trained and looks more of a seven furlong type for towards the back-end of the season. Quite a rangy filly, she came in quite late and is still playing catch-up".*

1625. UNNAMED ★★
b.c. Vale Of York – Finnmark (Halling). March 5. Sixth foal. 19,000Y. Tattersalls October Book 3. Not sold. Brother to the 2014 1m placed 2-y-o, from two starts, Niblawi and half-brother to the fair 2-y-o 7f winner of 4 races Finn Class (by Exceed And Excel) and to the fair 1m to 14f winner Cape Safari (by Cape Cross). The dam is an unraced half-sister to 8 winners including the very smart Group 2 15f Prix Hubert de Chaudenay winner Affadavit, the French listed 12f winner Nalani, the 10f and 12f listed winner Altamura and the Italian listed winner Tea Garden. The second dam, Narwala (by Darshaan), won the Group 3 12f Princess Royal Stakes and was second in the Grade 2 12f Long Island Handicap. (Abdulla Al Mansoori). *"A big, strong colt, he shows a bit*

of knee action which suggests he'll appreciate a bit of give in the ground. Coming along nicely, he's one to start off at six furlongs before stepping up to seven".

1626. UNNAMED ★★★

b.c. Acclamation – Hijab (King's Best). March 19. Third foal. 52,000Y. Tattersalls October Book 2. Oliver St Lawrence. Half-brother to the modest dual 6f winner Jimmy Elder (by Invincible Spirit). The dam is an unraced half-sister to 2 winners. The second dam, Hi Dubai (by Rahy), winner of the listed Pretty Polly Stakes and Group 1 placed twice, is a sister to the multiple Group 1 winner Fantastic Light. (Salem Rashid). *"He looks an all-out 2-y-o type. Probably one for six furlongs and he has a quick, fast ground action. He'll be doing fast work by the beginning of April and he looks like one we can crack on with".*

1627. UNNAMED ★★

b.f. Equiano – Italian Connection (Cadeaux Genereux). February 14. Third foal. 20,000Y. Tattersalls October Book 3. Jill Lamb. Half-sister to the quite useful Irish 7f winner I'vegotafeeling (by Rock Of Gibraltar). The dam is an unraced sister to the Irish 2-y-o 7f winner and listed placed Pietra Dura (herself dam of the US Grade 3 winner and Grade 1 second Turning Top) and a half-sister to 4 winners. The second dam, Bianca Nera (by Salse) won the Group 1 7f Moyglare Stud Stakes and the Group 2 6f Lowther Stakes, and is a half-sister to 4 winners including the very useful Group 1 Moyglare Stud Stakes second Hotelgenie Dot Com (dam of the dual Group 1 winner Simply Perfect). (David Thorpe). *"A very nice filly, I followed her into the ring to buy her but didn't succeed. Then by pure coincidence I got a phone call ten minutes later to ask if I wanted to train her, so of course I said I'd love to. Despite looking sharp enough for six furlongs I think she'll want seven this year, but she has a good action and is a nice type of filly".* **TRAINERS' BARGAIN BUY**

1628. UNNAMED ★★★

b.f. Exceed And Excel – Madam Ninette (Mark Of Esteem). March 26. Ninth foal. 80,000Y. Tattersalls October Book 2. Oliver St Lawrence. Sister to the useful dual 5f (at 2 yrs) and 3-y-o listed 5f winner Excelette and half-sister to

the very useful 2014 Irish 2-y-o 6f winner and dual Group 3 placed Rapid Applause (by Royal Applause), the quite useful 2-y-o 6f winner Blessington (by Kheleyf) and the modest 9f to 12f winner of 5 races Waahej (by Haafhd). The dam is an unraced half-sister to 9 winners including the King's Stand Stakes winner Bolshoi and the useful sprinters Mariinsky, Great Chaddington and Tod. The second dam, Mainly Dry (by The Brianstan), is an unraced half-sister to 4 winners. (Hamed Rashid bin Ghadayer). *"A filly from a nice, fast family, I thought she was well-bought because she has a lovely pedigree. Despite being a filly that looks quick enough she's going to take time because she's quite tall and I won't rush her".*

1629. UNNAMED ★★★★

b.f. Exceed And Excel – Wild Gardenia (Alhaarth). February 25. Third foal. 50,000Y. Tattersalls October Book 2. Not sold. Half-sister to the fair 8.5f and 9f winner Raheeba (by Invincible Spirit). The dam, placed fourth once over 12f, is a half-sister to 4 winners including Power (Group 1 Irish 2,000 Guineas and Group 1 National Stakes) and Thakafaat (Group 2 Ribblesdale Stakes). The second dam, Frappe (by Inchinor), a fairly useful 2-y-o 6f winner, is a half-sister to 4 winners including the 2,000 Guineas winner Footstepsinthesand and the Group 1 Phoenix Stakes winner Pedro The Great. (L & V Bloodstock). *"A very nice filly, I saw her at the sales and loved her. I was delighted to get her to train because she's a nice, sharp filly with a great brain, a lovely pedigree and a great attitude. She has a fast ground action, should be racing by the end of April and should be suited by six furlongs".*

ED WALKER

1630. ATLANTEIA (IRE) ★★★

ch.f. Duke Of Marmalade – Teide Lady (Nashwan). April 13. Sixth foal. 20,000Y. Tattersalls October Book 2. Sackville/Donald. Closely related to the useful 2-y-o Group 3 7f winner of 4 races Ayaar (by Rock Of Gibraltar) and half-sister to the quite useful 5f (including at 2 yrs) and 6f winner of 4 races Albany Rose (by Noverre) and the modest 9.5f to 12f winner Teide Peak (by Cape Cross). The dam, a modest 9f winner, is a half-sister to 3 winners including the 2-y-o Group 2 7f Superlative Stakes and US Grade 3 7f winner Hatta Fort.

The second dam, Oshiponga (by Barathea), a fair 9f winner, is a half-sister to 8 winners including the Group 2 second Kotsi and the Group 3 second Sir George Turner. (Mr M J Cottis). *"I quite like her, she wasn't very big at the sales but she's grown a lot and maintained her strength. A very athletic, good-natured filly, the sire has generally done better with his fillies than colts and the dam's three runners have all won. This filly will make a 2-y-o in the second half of the season, probably starting at seven furlongs and she'll progress next year, so she's a nice sort".* **TRAINERS' BARGAIN BUY**

1631. BRYGHT BOY ★★★★

b.c. Paco Boy – Bright Moll (Mind Games). March 21. Fifth foal. Half-brother to the useful listed 6f winner of 3 races (including at 2 yrs), Aeolus (by Araafa), to the fairly useful listed-placed 7f (at 2 yrs) and 6f winner Hezmah (by Oasis Dream), the quite useful 6f (at 2yrs) and 7f winner Tartiflette (by Dr Fong) and the fair 6f winner Lochan Mor (by Kyllachy). The dam, a fairly useful 2-y-o 5f and 6f winner, is a half-sister to 4 winners including the Group 2 Mill Reef Stakes second Doctor Brown (by Dr Fong). The second dam, Molly Brown (by Rudimentary), a fairly useful 5f (at 2 yrs) and 6f winner, is a half-sister to 4 winners. (Mr Andrew Buxton). *"Quite a big lad, so he's certainly one for the second half of the season, but he does everything extremely well and the family have had a number of 2-y-o winners. He's a lovely big colt and the dam has done very well despite not always having visited the best stallions. One to keep an eye on".*

1632. DARK SIEGE ★★★ ♠

b.c. Iffraaj – Green Poppy (Green Desert). February 7. Second foal. 115,000Y. Tattersalls October Book 2. Sackville/Donald. Half-brother to the quite useful 2014 2-y-o 5f winner Burtonwood (by Acclamation). The dam, a moderate 6f winner, is a half-sister to one winner in France. The second dam, Vimy Ridge (by Indian Ridge), is an unraced half-sister to 9 winners including the very smart Group 1 7f Prix de la Foret winner Septieme Ciel, the Group 1 1m Prix Marcel Boussac winner Macoumba and the dam of the Grade 1 winner Riviera. (Mr C U F Ma). *"He looks a 2-y-o, he's done very well and is a strong, solid,*

good-looking colt. The pedigree is a bit weak so his high purchase price is down to his good looks. He's done everything very nicely so far and I'd like to think he'll be out by June. He's bred to be speedy and although we haven't asked him any big questions yet from what we've seen of him so far he will be".*

1633. DREAM GLORY (IRE) ★★

b.c. Dream Ahead – Do The Honours (Highest Honor). February 5. Ninth foal. 200,000Y. Tattersalls October Book 1. Sackville/Donald. Half-brother to 4 winners including the French 1m winner and Group 3 Prix de la Grotte second Woven Lace (by Hard Spun) and the French 7f listed-placed Waitress (by Kingmambo). The dam, a French 5.5f (at 2 yrs) and Group 3 6f Prix de Meautry winner, is a half-sister to 8 winners including Seba (Chesham Stakes). The second dam, Persian Secret (by Persian Heights), a fairly useful 2-y-o 6f winner here and a listed winner in France, is a half-sister to the dual Group 2 winning sprinter and smart broodmare Cassandra Go and the Group 3 Coventry Stakes winner and sire Verglas. (Ms A A Yap & Mr F Ma). *"He's grown and done very well, but he's not going to be that early – probably an August 2-y-o. A very good mover and very likeable, I'll think he'll end up being a miler".*

1634. DULJANAH ★★★

ch.f. Dream Ahead – Centreofattention (Danehill). February 17. Fourth foal. 45,000Y. Tattersalls October Book 2. Sackville/Donald. Half-sister to Lifting Me Higher (by Sea The Stars), unplaced on her first start at 3 yrs in 2015. The dam, placed at 3 yrs in Australia, is a sister to the dual Group 1 winner Holy Roman Emperor and to the Australian Group 3 winner Milanova and a half-sister to 5 winners. The second dam, L'On Vite (by Secretariat), is an unraced sister to the Canadian 2-y-o Grade 1 winner Medaille d'Or and the Grade 2 winner D'Accord and a half-sister to the Grade 1 winners La Voyageuse and L'Enjoleur. (Mrs D A Shah). *"A very nice filly, she was very well bought because if she wins she'll be worth an awful lot considering her excellent pedigree. She's very athletic, a little bit hot, but she's settled down very well. A June/July 2-y-o, she's doing everything well at the moment".*

1635. EXCEL QUEST ★★★

b.c. Exceed And Excel – Rayyana (Rainbow Quest). May 16. Seventh foal. 80,000Y. Tattersalls October Book 2. Sackville/Donald. Half-brother to the Group 3 7f Killavullan Stakes (at 2 yrs) and listed 6f winner and Irish 2,000 Guineas second Rayeni (by Indian Ridge), to the fair Irish 12f winner Rayina (by Sinndar) and the modest 2m and hurdles winner Rayadour (by Azamour). The dam, an Irish 10f winner, is a half-sister to 4 winners out of the Group 3 Royal Whip Stakes winner Rayseka (by Dancing Brave), herself a half-sister to 5 winners. (Mr M H Lui). *"A late foal but a really nice colt and I think he was inexpensive for what he is. Maybe people were put off because he was a late foal, and looked it, at the Sales. But although I haven't done a lot with him, just letting him catch up with the others, he's done really well. He moves very well and his temperament is bomb proof. We'll probably set him off at six furlongs in the second half of the season. A nice colt".*

1636. GALE SONG ★★★★ ♠

b.f. Invincible Spirit – Please Sing (Royal Applause). February 10. Second foal. 120,000foal. Tattersalls December. One Agency. Half-sister to the 6f, 7f (including at 2 yrs in 2014) and 1m winner of 5 races Four Seasons (by Dubawi). The dam, winner of the Group 2 6f Cherry Hinton Stakes and third in the Group 3 Oak Tree Stakes and the Group 3 Chartwell Stakes, is a half-sister to 8 winners including the very useful 7f (at 2 yrs) to 10f winner and Group 1 National Stakes third Mountain Song and the 2-y-o 6f winner and Group 3 6f Princess Margaret Stakes third Raindancing. The second dam, Persian Song (by Persian Bold), is an unplaced sister to the Solario Stakes winner Bold Arrangement (placed in seven Group/Grade 1 races including the Kentucky Derby). (Lordship Stud). *"A very nice filly, hugely athletic and does everything easy at this stage. She's grown a lot and got a little bit leggy, so she needs to fill out but will certainly be a 2-y-o. A very likeable filly from a good family, she's got plenty of speed".*

1637. HOPE COVE ★★★

b.c. Shamardal – Deveron (Cozzene). April 28. Sixth foal. 100,000Y. Tattersalls October Book 2. Sackville/Donald. Brother to True Respect, placed fourth over 7f on his only outing at 2 yrs in 2014 and to the quite useful 2-y-o 7f winner Dffar and half-brother to the fairly useful 2-y-o 6f winner and triple listed-placed Lamar (by Cape Cross) and the modest 2-y-o 1m winner Open Letter (by New Approach). The dam, a very useful 2-y-o 7f winner and third in the Group 1 1m Prix Marcel Boussac, is a sister to the Canadian dual Grade 2 winner Windward Islands and a half-sister to 5 winners. The second dam, Cruisie (by Assert), won 3 minor races at 3 yrs in the USA and is a half-sister to 4 stakes winners including the dam of the US Grade 1 winner Capote Belle. (Mr M H Lui). *"He's not very big, but he's built like a bull. Very solid and well-made, the dam's done well and this colt will make a 2-y-o. He lacks an inch or two but he looks great at the moment and I certainly think he'll be out and winning races in the second half of the season".*

1638. JUDICIAL ENQUIRY ★★

br.c. Lawman – Koniya (Doyoun). March 26. Tenth foal. 45,000Y. Tattersalls October Book 2. Sackville/Donald. Half-brother to the unplaced 2014 2-y-o Artesana (by Mastercraftsman), to the fairly useful 9f and 10f winner and Group 3 9f Dahlia Stakes second Casilda (by Cape Cross), the fairly useful dual 10f winner King Of Dreams (by Sadler's Wells) and the minor French 14f winner Kekova (by Montjeu). The dam, a minor French 15f winner, is a half-sister to 7 winners including the Irish 1,000 Guineas Trial winners Khanata and Kotama and to the unraced dam of High Chaparral. The second dam, Kozana (by Kris), won the Group 2 Prix de Malleret and was third in the Prix de l'Arc de Triomphe. (E C D Walker). *"He'll be a mid-summer 2-y-o, he's not very big but he's a bonny, racy-looking colt and straightforward".*

1639. SMILEY BAGEL ★★★

b.c. Kyllachy – Epistoliere (Alzao). April 27. Eighth foal. €90,000Y. Goffs Orby. Sackville/Donald (private sale). Half-brother to 4 winners including the smart 7f (at 2 yrs) to 2m 5f winner and Group 1 Ascot Gold Cup second Simenon (by Marju), the useful listed-placed 10f to 13f winner of 5 races and Vivacious Vivienne (by Dubai Destination) and the French 2-y-o 1m winner and listed-placed Kyurem (by Verglas). The dam is a placed sister to the Group 2 Grand Prix de Deauville winner Epistolaire and a half-sister to the Group 2 Prix Hubert de Chaudenay winner Epitre. The second dam, Epistolienne (by Law Society), is a listed-placed half-sister to 10 winners including Acclimatise (Group 2 Nassau Stakes). (L A Bellman). *"I love this colt, but I'm a bit biased because I'm a big fan of the sire – Kyllachy has been quite lucky for me in the past. This guy will probably do like his half-brother Simenon did and improve with age, he's got a great stride on him and does everything easily. Likely to be a second half-of the season 2-y-o over seven furlongs, but he'll be better at three".*

1640. THORNADO ★★★★

b.c. Scat Daddy – Oui Say Oui (Royal Applause). February 28. Second foal. €280,000Y. Goffs Orby. Fiona Shaw. The dam, a useful 2-y-o 6f winner and second in the Group 2 7f Debutante Stakes, is a half-sister to 5 winners including the smart 2-y-o Group 3 6f Sirenia Stakes and Group 3 1m Joel Stakes winner Satchem and the listed 12f and listed 2m winner Eye Of The Storm. The second dam, Mohican Princess (by Shirley Heights), fourth over 10f on her only start, is a half-sister to 5 winners. (Mark Keller). *A classy-looking 2-y-o type, he looks one of my more forward types and should be out in May. He does everything great, the stallion seems to be setting the world alight and I think he's quite exciting".*

1641. TOGETHERNESS (IRE) ★★★

b.c. Pour Moi – Madeira Mist (Grand Lodge). March 3. Eighth foal. €200,000Y. Goffs Orby. Badgers Bloodstock. Closely related to Joshua Tree (by Montjeu) winner of the Group 1 Canadian International (three times) and the 2-y-o Group 2 1m Royal Lodge Stakes and half-brother to the fairly useful 12f winner Stencive (by Dansili) and a winner in Japan by Invincible Spirit. The dam won 8 races including the Grade 3 Dance Smartly Handicap and is a half-sister to 10 winners including the listed winner and Group 3 placed Misty Heights. The second dam, Mountains Of Mist (by Shirley Heights), a quite useful 10f winner, is a half-sister to 8 winners including Enthused (Group 2 Lowther Stakes). (Weston Brook Farm, Bromfield & Whitaker). *"I like the couple of Pour Moi's that*

I've got. They look classy and they have a sort of Montjeu edgy temperament about them. Certainly nothing bad or worrying, it's just that you can see the Montjeu influence. This colt is a really good mover, very athletic and a well-bred colt, so he's very exciting".

1642. TRIKINGDOM ★★★ ♠

b.c. Showcasing – Spritzeria (Bigstone). February 11. Sixth foal. 60,000Y. Tattersalls October Book 2. Sackville/Donald. Half-brother to the quite useful 6f and 7f winner of 8 races Esprit De Midas (by Namid), to the fair 5f winner Be Lucky (by Kyllachy) and a 4-y-o winner in Hong Kong by Green Desert. The dam, a quite useful 2-y-o 6f winner, is a half-sister to 8 winners including the smart 2-y-o 6f winner and Group 1 1m Racing Post Trophy third Henrik , the useful 2-y-o 6f winner and Group 2 6f Gimcrack Stakes third Sir Reginald and the fairly useful listed 7f winner Intense Pink. The second dam, Clincher Club (by Polish Patriot), a fair 5f (at 2 yrs) and 7.5f winner, is a half-sister to 9 winners. (F Ma, R Cheung, S Tung). *"The sire obviously did very well last year and this is a nice colt that probably looked sharper two months ago than he does now. He's grown a lot and I see him as being a mid-summer sprinting 2-y-o, he does everything nicely and I like him".*

1643. VALENTINE GLORY ★★

b.f. Kyllachy – Time Crystal (Sadler's Wells). February 8. Seventh foal. 70,000Y. Tattersalls October Book 2. Sackville/Donald. Half-sister to 4 winners including the useful 1m (at 2 yrs) and listed 11f winner Sparkling Portrait (by Excellent Art), the fairly useful 9f (at 2 yrs) and dual 1m winner and UAE Group 3 third Start Right (by Footstepsinthesand) and the modest 12f winner Loving Your Work (by Royal Applause). The dam, a quite useful 12f winner, is a half-sister to 8 winners. The second dam, State Crystal (by High Estate), winner of the Group 3 12f Lancashire Oaks and placed in the Yorkshire Oaks and the Prix Vermeille, is a half-sister to 6 winners including the Group 1 Fillies' Mile winner Crystal Music. (Ms A A Yap & Mr F Ma). *"She's more of a back-end type 2-y-o but she's a good-looking filly from a good family. She's changed quite a lot and done quite well physically. Moves well, but is one for the late summer onwards".*

CHRIS WALL

1644. ALL FOR LOVE ★★
b.f. Giant's Causeway – Wallis (King's Best). April 15. First foal. 70,000Y. Tattersalls October Book 1. C Wall. The dam, a quite useful 6f and 1m winner here, subsequently won and was stakes-placed in the USA. She is a half-sister to 4 winners including the Grade 1 Northern Dancer Turf and dual Grade 2 Sky Classic winner Forte Dei Marmi (by Selkirk) and the very useful 12f and listed 14f winner Savarain (by Rainbow Quest). The second dam, Frangy (by Sadler's Wells), a fair dual 12f winner, is a full or half-sister to 8 winners including the German 1m to 9.5f winner of 7 races and listed-placed Flying Heights. (Ms A Fustoq). *"A big filly bred by Luca Cumani, it's a pedigree that does better when they're three and four-year-olds and as she's done a lot of growing this spring I would have thought this filly will follow that mode".*

1645. ALWAYS A DREAM ★★
b.f. Oasis Dream – Always Remembered (Galileo). January 19. First foal. The unraced dam is closely related to the Derby, Racing Post Trophy and Dante Stakes winner Motivator and to the Group 2 12f Hardwicke Stakes winner Macarthur and a half-sister to the smart listed 10f winner Imperial Star. The second dam, Out West (by Gone West), a useful 7.5f (at 2 yrs) and listed 1m winner, is a half-sister to 3 winners including the US Grade 3 placed Auggies Here. (Ms A Fustoq). *"A filly out of a Galileo three-parts sister to Motivator, the dam was injured in the paddocks and didn't run. This is a nice enough filly but one with a staying pedigree so she'll probably start her career in a mile maiden towards the back-end of the season".*

1646. CAMBODIA (IRE) ★★
ch.c. Fast Company – Remarkable Story (Mark Of Esteem). April 25. Sixth foal. 45,000Y. Tattersalls October Book 2. Des Thurlby. Half-brother to the useful listed 10f winner of 6 races Grendisar, to the fair 6f winner of 6 races Alnoomaas (by Oasis Dream) and the fair dual 1m winner Bobby Benton (by Invincible Spirit). The dam ran once unplaced and is a half-sister to 3 winners including the 2-y-o Group 1 7f Moyglare Stud Stakes winner and US Grade 1 placed Necklace. The second dam, Spinning

The Yarn (by Barathea), ran once unplaced and is closely related to the top-class King George VI winner Opera House and the Ascot Gold Cup and Irish St Leger winner Kayf Tara and a half-sister to the Group 1 Prix de l'Opera winner Zee Zee Top. (Mr D M Thurlby). *'The sire got off to a good start with his first runners last year. This colt has done a bit of growing and he was a fairly late foal, so I don't know how precocious he's going to be. He's a half-brother to a horse that did better with age, so maybe that will have an effect on his 2-y-o career. He doesn't have the physique to be a sprinting 2-y-o, but I like the look of him and I'll probably aim him for seven furlongs with a bit of ease in the ground. Given his good pedigree and the strength of the market I think we were lucky to get him for what he cost".*

1647. EAGLE FALLS ★★★
b.c. Paco Boy – Miss Excel (Exceed And Excel). January 26. First foal. 18,000Y. Tattersalls October Book 4. The dam, a moderate maiden, was placed fourth four times from 1m to 10f and is a half-sister to 3 winners. The second dam, Shaiybara (by Kahyasi), won the Group 3 15f Prix du Lutece and is a half-sister to 3 winners. (Follow The Flag Partnership). *"He's relatively sharp, but if we learned anything about Paco Boy's stock last year it was that they seemed to get better as the season went on. This horse will be the same and the longer we leave him the better he'll be. Having said that, he should be a 2-y-o by mid-season. His dam's side has a fair bit of stamina but he doesn't look a staying type, so I expect him to be suited by six/seven furlongs".*

1648. LUANG PRABANG (IRE) ★★★★
b.f. Invincible Spirit – Sauvage (Sri Pekan). February 12. Fourth foal. 48,000Y. Tattersalls October Book 2. Des Thurlby. Half-sister to the quite useful triple 1m winner Bassara (by Oasis Dream) and to the modest 10f and 11f winner Posh Boy (by Duke Of Marmalade). The dam won 5 races at 2 to 5 yrs in France and the USA including the Grade 2 Sheepshead Bay Handicap and is a half-sister to 4 winners including the German Group 3 winner Eyeq. The second dam, Sans Prix (by Caerleon), won over 9f in Ireland and is a half-sister to 3 winners. (Mr D M Thurlby). *"A nice filly, I like her and we've had all three of her siblings.*

With the exception of Posh Boy who wasn't particularly tall the rest of them are quite well grown and the mare is big too. This filly is much taller now than at the sales, but having said that she's an athletic filly and she should be a summer 2-y-o over seven furlongs. She's one I have a bit of time for".

1649. LUDI LU ★★★★

b.f. New Approach – Sunspear (Montjeu). March 31. Third foal. 180,000Y. Tattersalls October Book 1. Not sold. The dam is an unraced sister to the Derby winner Motivator and the Group 2 Hardwicke Stakes winner Macarthur and a half-sister to the listed 10f winner Imperial Star. The second dam, Out West (by Gone West), a useful 7.5f (at 2 yrs) and listed 1m winner, is a half-sister to 3 winners. (Ms A Fustoq). *"As you'd expect from a New Approach this is quite a big filly with plenty of scope. It's a family that improves with age and a trip, I like her but she's one for the back-end I would have thought. A nice, scopey filly that's done everything easily so far, so hopefully she's got quite a bit of ability".*

1650. MATILDA'S LAW ★★★

b.f. Aussie Rules – Oatey (Master Willie). April 3. Twelfth living foal. 5,500Y. Tattersalls Book 4. C Wall. Half-sister to 6 winners including the quite useful 2-y-o 5f winner Alternative (by Dr Fong), the fair dual 6f (at 2 yrs) to 12f and hurdles winner Spiritual Art (by Invincible Spirit), the modest dual 1m winner Jomus (by Soviet Star) and the moderate 2-y-o 7f winner Cat Queen. The dam, a modest dual 5f winner at 3 yrs, is a half-sister to 10 winners including the smart Group 3 Lingfield Derby Trial winner Munwar and the smart Irish middle-distance listed winner Hateel. The second dam, Oatfield (by Great Nephew), was placed at 2 yrs. *"A racy little filly, I already know the family a little bit in that we've already had one out of the dam who won a little race for us. A nice, bonny filly, the family want to stay a bit but Aussie Rules has probably sharpened things up to some extent. I would have thought she'd be a summer 2-y-o over seven furlongs, I like her and she's got plenty of character – a cheeky little thing with a bit of something about her".* (Archangels 2).

1651. MIX AND MINGLE (IRE) ★★

ch.f. Exceed And Excel – Mango Lady (Dalakhani). February 25. Third foal. 50,000Y. Tattersalls October Book 2. Not sold. Sister to a minor 4-y-o winner in Germany and half-sister to the modest 9.5f winner May Queen (by Shamardal). The dam, a fair 12f winner, is a half-sister to 4 winners including the Group 2 12f King Edward VII Stakes and dual Group 3 winner High Accolade and the dual listed-placed Oasis Knight. The second dam, Generous Lady (by Generous), a middle-distance winner of 4 races in Ireland and listed-placed, is a half-sister to 6 winners including the Group 2 Premio Guido Beradelli and Group 3 St Leger Italiano winner Jape. (Ms A Fustoq). *"The dam won over a mile and a half and she's from a staying family. They put her to Exceed And Excel to try and sharpen her up a bit, but she still strikes me as being typical of the female line. Not a speedster, she's another one for the back-end of the season".*

1652. SONG OF PARADISE ★★★

ch.f. Kyllachy – Merry Diva (Bahamian Bounty). February 13. Third foal. 18,000Y. Tattersalls October Book 2. Chris Wall. Half-sister to the 2014 2-y-o 6f winner, from two starts, Belvoir Diva (by Exceed And Excel) and to the fair 7f winner Concrete Mac (by Machiavellian). The dam, a fair 2-y-o 6f winner, is sister to the dual listed winner and Group 3 third Paradise Isle and a half-sister to 8 winners. The second dam, Merry Rous (by Rousillon), won once at 2 yrs and is a half-sister to 5 winners including the dual Group 3 winning sprinter Tina's Pet. (The Equema Partners). *"Like most of the family she's not very big, but she's sturdy and strong which is what you'd expect from a Kyllachy. If I've got a sharp, speedy 2-y-o this is it, but I haven't done much with her yet because she was off colour for a few weeks. Six furlongs with a bit of cut in the ground should suit, but the family don't want extremes. They wouldn't go on fast or heavy ground. If she's as sharp as most of the others in the family we'll have some fun with her".* **TRAINERS' BARGAIN BUY**

1653. UNNAMED ★★

b.f. Bahri – Lark In The Park (Grand Lodge). March 17. Fifth foal. Half-sister to the fairly useful dual 7f (at 2 yrs) and 6f winner Secretinthepark (by Sakhee's Secret), to the quite useful 1m and 10.5f winner of 5 races Dolphin Rock (by Mark Of Esteem) and the modest triple 5f winner at 2 and 3 yrs Passionada (by Avonbridge). The dam, a moderate 1m winner at 3 yrs, is a half-sister to several winners including the quite useful 1m to 12f winner of 8 races Invasian. The second dam, Jarrayan (by Machiavellian), is an unplaced half-sister to several winners including the 2-y-o listed 6f Silver Flash Stakes winner, is a sister to the 6f winner and listed placed Moonis. (Mia Racing). *"She's a well-grown filly but seems to do everything nicely. One for seven furlongs or a mile in the second half of the season and she could be OK."*

1654. UNNAMED ★★★
b.c. Iffraaj – Maine Rose (Red Ransom). March 19. Third foal. 80,000Y. Tattersalls October Book 1. Rabbah Bloodstock. Half-brother to two minor winners in France by Footstepsinthesand and Muhtathir. The dam won two minor races in France at 3 yrs and is a half-sister to the listed-placed winner Sunley Peace. The second dam, Messila Rose (by Darshaan), is an unraced half-sister to 4 winners. (Sheikh Rashid Dalmook Al Maktoum). *"I suppose he's fairly typical of what you might expect for an Iffraaj really. He wouldn't be the most precocious in the world but he should be a 2-y-o for the summer over six/seven furlongs".*

DERMOT WELD
1655. AASHEQ (IRE) ★★★★
b.c. Dubawi – Beach Bunny (High Chaparral). February 18. Third foal. Half-brother to the useful 2014 2-y-o listed 6f winner Beach Belle (by Invincible Spirit) and to the very useful 7f (at 2 yrs) and dual listed 6f winner Naadirr (by Oasis Dream). The dam won 3 races including the listed Dance Design Stakes, was second in the Group 1 Pretty Polly Stakes and is a half-sister to one winner. The second dam, Miss Hawai (by Peintre Celebre), is an unraced half-sister to 4 winners including the French dual listed winner Mer de Corail. (Hamdan Al Maktoum). *"A lovely colt, we like him a lot. One for July/August over seven furlongs, he's a strong, powerful horse".*

1656. A LIKELY STORY (IRE) ★★★
b.c. Exceed And Excel – Where We Left Off (Dr Devious). April 10. Half-brother to the useful Irish 1m and 8.5f winner Stay De Night (by Shamardal), to the 7f and 11f winner Encrypted Message (by Dansili) the 1m (at 2 yrs) and 10f winner Late Day Sun (by Montjeu), the 10f and hurdles winner Polished Rock (by Rock Of Gibraltar) and the 11f winner Walk Beside Me (by Theatrical) – all quite useful. The dam, a US Grade 3 9f winner, is a half-sister to the Australian Group 2 10f winner Rekindled Interest and the French listed 11f winner Porticcio. The second dam, Rekindled Affair (by Rainbow Quest), is an unraced half-sister to 4 winners and to the unraced smart broodmare Summer Trysting (the dam of two Group winners). (Moyglare Stud Farms Ltd). *"He's a sharp colt and I'd hope to have him out in May over six furlongs".*

1657. ALMANAARA (IRE) ★★★
gr.c. Shamardal – Midnight Angel (Machiavellian). March 29. 370,000Y. Tattersalls October Book 1. Shadwell Estate Co. Half-brother to the 2-y-o Group 1 6f Middle Park Stakes and Group 2 Mill Reef Stakes winner Dark Angel (by Acclamation), to the smart 2-y-o 5f and 6f winner and Group 2 6f Mill Reef Stakes second Angel's Pursuit (by Pastoral Pursuits), the fair 4-y-o 12f winner Colleton River (by Croco Rouge) and 2 winners abroad by Entrepreneur and Ashkalani. The dam is an unraced half-sister to 9 winners. The second dam, Night At Sea (by Night Shift), a sprint winner of 3 races including the listed Trafalgar House Stakes, is a half-sister to 6 winners. (Hamdan Al Maktoum). *"A big, active colt, he's growing so he just needs to develop a lot more. A good mover, I see him as being one for September".*

1658. ALSINAAFY (IRE) ★★★
b.c. Oasis Dream – Bethrah (Marju). January 23. Second foal. The dam won 3 races at 3 yrs including the Group 1 Irish 1,000 Guineas and the Group 3 1m Irish 1,000 Guineas Trial. The second dam, Reve d'Iman (by Highest Honor), a minor 3-y-o 9f winner in France, is a sister to the Group 1 Prix Saint-Alary winner Reve d'Oscar, the Group 2 Prix Hocquart winner Numide and the listed French 3-y-o winner Sir Eric. (Hamdan Al Maktoum). *"A very*

well-balanced colt, he's quite sharp and I can see him being ready for June/July. The dam was my classic winner for Sheikh Hamdan and I'd like to think this colt would get a mile next year".

1659. BREVET ★★★

b.c. Zamindar – Prove (Danehill). February 27. Half-brother to the 7f (including at 2 yrs) and Group 3 7.5f Fairy Bridge Stakes winner Tested (by Selkirk), to the fairly useful 10f and 14f winner and listed-placed Track Record (by Montjeu) and the fair French 1m winner Trajectory (by Dubai Destination). The dam, winner of the Group 3 9f Prix Chloe, is a sister to the Group 3 12f Prix de Minerve winner Danefair and the smart multiple 7f to 8.5f winner Vortex. The second dam, Roupala (by Vaguely Noble), a fair 3-y-o 1m winner, is a half-sister to 4 winners and the dams of the German Group 2 winner Bad Bertrich Again, the Group 3 Scottish Classic winner Prolix and the US Grade 2 winner Daros. (Khalid Abdulla). *"It's a family that's done well for me with his half-sister Tested. He's a nice colt for seven furlongs in July/August".*

1660. BURMA STAR ★★★★

ch.f. Shamardal – Shamayel (Pivotal). April 26. Fourth foal. €85,000Y. Goffs Sportsmans. Bobby O'Ryan/D K Weld. Sister to the quite useful 7f (at 2 yrs) to 10f winner of 5 races Mushaakis. The dam, a quite useful 2-y-o 7f winner, is a half-sister to 4 winners. The second dam, Maori Moon (by Green Desert), won 4 races including the listed Oak Tree Stakes and is a half-sister to 5 winners including the Singapore Derby winner Kimbridge Knight. (Mr D K Weld). *"A very nice filly, it's an interesting Shamardal x Pivotal cross and I see her as one for July/August. A quality filly".*

1661. CARIBBEAN SPRING (IRE) ★★★

b.c. Dark Angel – Bogini (Holy Roman Emperor). March 14. First foal. €110,000Y. Tattersalls Ireland September. Bobby O'Ryan/D K Weld. The dam, a quite useful 5f (including at 2 yrs) and 6f winner of 4 races, is a half-brother to 3 winners including the listed Tetrarch Stakes winner Alkasser. The second dam, Alexander Queen (by King's Best), a fairly useful 2-y-o 5f winner, is a half-sister to 5 winners including the Group 3 Palace House

Stakes winner and Group 1 placed Dandy Man. (Dr R Lambe). *"He's precocious and should be running in May over six furlongs".*

1662. COLOUR BRIGHT (IRE) ★★★★

b.f. Dream Ahead – Flashing Green (Green Desert). April 3. Eleventh foal. €350,000Y. Goffs Orby. Moyglare Stud. Half-sister to 6 winners including the very useful 2-y-o listed 7f Chesham Stakes winner and Group 2 Champagne Stakes third Tha'Ir (by New Approach), the German listed winner and Group 3 placed Flashing Colour (by Pivotal) and the French/German listed-placed Flash Dance (by Monsun). The dam, a German 3-y-o winner, is a half-sister to 6 winners including the Group 2 1m Falmouth Stakes second Croeso Cariad and the triple Group 1 placed Mona Lisa. The second dam, Colorsnap (by Shirley Heights), is an unraced half-sister to the Group 1 winners Cezanne and Colorspin. (Moyglare Stud Farms Ltd). *"A quality, sweet, good-moving filly, she looks to be a 2-y-o and should be out around May/June".*

1663. DALTON HIGHWAY (IRE) ★★★★

b.c. Zoffany – Poinsettia (Galileo). March 9. First foal. 125,000Y. Tattersalls October Book 2. Aidan O'Ryan/D K Weld. The dam, placed twice over 1m at 2 yrs in Ireland, is out of the Irish 2-y-o 1m winner and listed-placed Mermaid Island (by Mujadil), herself a half-sister to 7 winners including the Group 1 1,000 Guineas winner Nightime. (Dr R Lambe). *"This is a very nice, well-balanced, quality colt, I like him a lot and I would hope to have him out in July or August. He's named after one of the longest roads in the world that leads to the oil fields in Alaska".*

1664. EBEDIYIN (IRE) ★★★

b.c. Raven's Pass – Ebadiyla (Sadler's Wells). April 15. Half-brother to 8 winners including the smart 7f winner and Group 3 10f third Ebanoran (by Oasis Dream), the useful 1m winner and Group 1 National Stakes third Eyshal (by Green Desert) and the useful Irish 10f winner Ehsan (by Sinndar). The dam won the Group 1 Irish Oaks and the Group 1 Prix Royal-Oak and is a half-sister to Group 1 winners Edabiya (Moyglare Stud Stakes), Estimate and Enzeli (both Ascot Gold Cup). The second dam, Ebaziya (by Darshaan), won from 7f (at 2 yrs) to 12f including three listed races and was third in the Group 2 12f Blandford Stakes. (H H Aga Khan). *"A nice, balanced colt and I'd hope to have him out around August/September".*

1665. EZANAK (IRE) ★★★
b.c. Sea The Stars – Ebaza (Sinndar). March 19. Half-brother to the very useful Group 3 7f Athasi Stakes winner Emiyna (by Maria's Mon), to the useful 10f winner Emerita (by Mizzen Mast), the fairly useful 10f winner Ebazan (by Lemon Drop Kid) and the quite useful 11f and 2m winner Emrani (by Rahy). The dam is an unplaced half-sister to the Group 1 winners Ebadiyla, Edabiya and Enzeli. The second dam, Ebaziya (by Darshaan), won from 7f (at 2 yrs) to 12f including three listed races and was third in the Group 2 12f Blandford Stakes. (H H Aga Khan). *"He's typical of the sire in that he'll take a bit of time but he's nice. One for September/October".*

1666. FLAGSTAFF ★★★
b.f. Dansili – Etoile Montante (Miswaki). April 12. Half-sister to the US Grade 2 10f and triple Grade 3 winner Starformer (by Dynaformer). The dam won the Group 1 7f Prix de la Foret and is a half-sister to the listed-placed winner Starfan and to the dam of the French Group 3 winner Glaswegian. The second dam, Willstar (by Nureyev), won over 1m in France and is a half-sister to the US Grade 2 winner Revasser. (Khalid Abdulla). *"Very much a quality filly and a very nice moving 2-y-o for seven furlongs in September/ October".*

1667. FOOTBRIDGE ★★★
ch.c. Zamindar – Tates Creek (Rahy). March 30. Fifth foal. The dam won 11 races from 6f to 10f in the USA including the Grade 1 Gamely Breeders Cup Handicap and the Grade 1 Yellow Ribbon Stakes and is a half-sister to Sightseek, a winner of seven Grade 1 events in the USA from 7f to 9f. The second dam, Viviana (by Nureyev), a French listed winner, is a half-sister to Hometown Queen, a stakes winner of 5 races in the USA and Grade 1 placed on four occasions and to the US Grade 2 winner Revasser. (Khalid Abdulla). *"An interesting colt, he's an extremely good mover and I can see him making a nice 2-y-o in July/ August".*

1668. HARZAND (IRE) ★★★
br.c. Sea The Stars – Hazariya (Xaar). March 6. Fifth foal. Half-brother to the 2-y-o Group 3 7f Silver Flash Stakes winner Harasiya (by Pivotal), to the useful dual 10f winner and Group 3 second Haziyna (by Halling) and the useful listed 12f winner Hazarafa (by Daylami). The dam, winner of the Group 3 7f Athasi Stakes and a listed event over 7f, is a half-sister to the Group 3 Blue Wind Stakes winner Hazarista and a half-sister to numerous minor winners. The second dam, Hazaradjat (by Darshaan), won twice at 2 and 3 yrs and is a half-sister to 10 winners including the Group 1 Flying Childers Stakes winner Hittite Glory. (H H Aga Khan). *"Another of those Sea The Stars that I like, but he'll be a seven furlongs/ mile horse from September onwards".*

1669. HEARTFUL (IRE) ★★★
b.f. Shamardal – Mad About You (Indian Ridge). March 29. Second foal. The dam, a smart Irish Group 3 7f Gladness Stakes winner and placed in four Group 1 events, is a half-sister to the Group 2 Ribblesdale Stakes winner Princess Highway and the Group 1 Irish St Leger winner Royal Diamond. The second dam, Irresistible Jewel (by Danehill), won the Group 2 12f Ribblesdale Stakes and the Group 3 10f Blandford Stakes and is a half-sister to numerous winners including the listed 12f winner Diamond Trim. (Moyglare Stud Farms Ltd). *"She's a very taking, quality filly and I trained her dam who was very good. I'd love to have her starting off in July/August".*

1670. JULIETTE FAIR (IRE) ★★★
gr.f. Dark Angel – Capulet Monteque (Camacho). February 17. First foal. €240,000Y. Goffs Orby. Moyglare Stud. The dam, a quite useful 5f and 6f placed maiden in Ireland, won at 3 yrs in Qatar and is a half-sister to 8 winners including the listed Scarborough Stakes winner and Group 2 Kings Stand Stakes second Flanders. The second dam, Family at War (by Explodent), a fair 2-y-o 5f winner, is a half-sister to 4 minor winners in the USA. (Moyglare Stud Farms Ltd). *"A nice filly for July/August over seven furlongs".*

1671. KIDD MALIBU (USA) ★★★
ch.c. Malibu Moon – Kiddari (Smarty Jones). January 20. Second foal. $550,000Y. Keeneland

September. Shadwell Estate Co. The dam, a minor stakes winner of 5 races in the USA, is a half-sister to 7 winners including the US Graded stakes winners Mission Impazible, Forest Camp and Spanish Empire. The second dam, La Paz (by Hold Your Peace), a US stakes winner of 8 races, is a half-sister to two other stakes winners. (Hamdan Al Maktoum). *"A big, powerful, American bred colt. There's a lot of quality to him and I'd hope to have him out in July".*

1672. LOOK CLOSER (IRE) ★★★
ch.c. Danehill Dancer – Key Secure (Sadler's Wells). February 10. Second foal. The dam, placed second over 9f on her only start, is a sister to 3 winners including Refuse To Bend, a top-class winner of four Group 1 races from 7f (at 2 yrs) to 10f and the very useful 2-y-o 7f winner and Group 2 Beresford Stakes second Domestic Fund and a half-sister to the Melbourne Cup winner Media Puzzle. The second dam, Market Slide (by Gulch), an Irish 6f (at 2 yrs) and 6.5f winner, is closely related to the minor Irish 7f winner First Breeze and a half-sister to the Breeders Cup Classic second Twilight Agenda. (Moyglare Stud Farms Ltd). *"He goes well. He's by Danehill Dancer and they usually like a bit of cut in the ground, but I can see him coming out in mid-summer".*

1673. LOVE IN THE SUN (IRE) ★★★
b.f. Kodiac – Summer Trysting (Alleged). February 1. Closely related to the Irish 2-y-o 7f listed and subsequent US Grade 2 9.5f Arlington Derby winner Simple Exchange (by Danehill) and half-sister to numerous winners including the Irish 7f (at 2 yrs), Group 3 Brigadier Gerard Stakes and Group 3 Newbury Dubai Duty Free 'Arc' Trial winner Sights On Gold (by Indian Ridge) and the Group 1 National Stakes second Designs On Rome (by Holy Roman Emperor). The dam was placed at up to 12f in Ireland and is a half-sister to the smart performer at up to 10f Smooth Performance. The second dam, Seasonal Pickup (by The Minstrel), won four listed races in Ireland and is a half-sister to the dam of Grey Swallow. (Moyglare Stud Farms Ltd). *"She's a nice filly out of an older mare. I like her well and she's a good moving, balanced 2-y-o. I would say July/August will be her starting point. Hopefully Kodiac will have put a bit of zip into her".*

1674. LUNE DE SABLE (IRE) ★★★
b.f. Medicean – Token Gesture (Alzao). January 24. Half-sister to numerous winners including the 7f (at 2 yrs in Ireland) and Grade 1 Canadian International winner Relaxed Gesture, the useful 10f winner and Group 3 10f Gallinule Stakes third Central Station (both by Indian Ridge), the quite useful 2-y-o 1m winner Hit The Jackpot (by Pivotal), the US Grade 2 American Derby winner Evolving Tactics (by Machiavellian) and the fairly useful 2-y-o 7f winner Braveheart Move (by Cape Cross). The dam won the Group 3 7f C L Weld Park Stakes and is a half-sister to the US Grade 2 winner Wait Till Monday. The second dam, Temporary Lull (by Super Concorde), is an unraced sister to the Nell Gwyn Stakes winner Martha Stevens. (Moyglare Stud Farms Ltd). *"A lovely, big filly with a lot of quality to her, but she's unlikely to be ready before the autumn I'd say".*

1675. MIDST ★★★
b.f. Oasis Dream – Jibboom (Mizzen Mast). May 5. Third foal. Sister to the Group 3 7f Athasi Stakes winner Flying Jib. The dam, a US Grade 2 7f and dual Grade 3 winner over 7f and 1m, was second in the Grade 1 Santa Monica Handicap and is a half-sister to 2 winners. The second dam, Palisade (by Gone West), a quite useful 2-y-o 7f winner, is a half-sister to the useful 3-y-o 1m winner Emplane and to the useful 2-y-o 1m winner Boatman. (Khalid Abdulla). *"She's a nice filly and I trained her good sister last year, Flying Jib. One for August/September".*

1676. MOUNIRA (IRE) ★★★★
ch.f. Raven's Pass – Mouramara (Kahyasi). April 21. Half-sister to 5 winners including the very smart 2-y-o listed 9f winner and Irish Derby third Mourayan (by Alhaarth), the very smart listed 14f winner and Melbourne Cup third Mourilyan (by Desert Prince) and the useful 12f, 13f and hurdles winner Mourad (by Sinndar). The dam, winner of the Group 2 12.5f Prix de Royallieu, is a half-sister to several winners in France and Germany. The second dam, Mamoura (by Lomond), won over 10f and 12f in Ireland and is a half-sister to 5 winners including the Group 3 12f Meld Stakes third Mirana (herself dam of the Group 3 Prix de Flore winner Miliana). (H H

Aga Khan). *"This filly has a lot of quality, she's lengthy and I see her wanting seven furlongs or a mile in September/October".*

1677. MUNAASHID (USA) ★★★★
b.br.c. Lonhro – Freefourracing (French Deputy). January 28. Eighth foal. €450,000Y. Goffs Orby. Shadwell Racing. Half-brother to 5 winners in the USA including the stakes winners Speedway (by Forest Wildcat) and Ready Racer (by More Than Ready) and the stakes-placed Free Brave (by Cherokee Run). The dam won 6 races including the 2-y-o Group 3 Prestige Stakes and is a half-sister to 8 winners including the US dual Grade 2 placed Kamsack. The second dam, Gerri N Jo Go (by Top Command), a dual listed stakes winner in the USA, was Grade 3 placed and is a half-sister to 12 winners. (Hamdan Al Maktoum). *"A very nice colt that came from Goffs Sales. I appreciate the sire won Group One races in Australia at up to ten furlongs, but this colt looks a 2-y-o and he'll be out around June/July I'd say. I like this horse".*

1678. MURRAQIB (USA) ★★★
ch.c. Summer Bird – Golden Party (Seeking The Gold). February 19. Eighth living foal. €200,000Y. Goffs Orby. Shadwell Estate Co. Half-brother to the Group 3 Prix Exbury winner Polytechnicien and to 3 minor winners in France and the USA by Alhaarth, Lomitas and Include. The dam is a placed half-sister to 10 winners including the US Grade 1 winners Dare And Go and Go Deputy. The second dam, Partygoer (by Secretariat), a minor US winner, is a half-sister to 7 winners including the US Graded stakes winners Virilify and Agacerie. (Hamdan Al Maktoum). *"The sire won three Grade 1's in America over 10f and 12f as a 3-y-o, including the Belmont Stakes. A good-looking, quality colt for July/August".*

1679. ORANGEY RED ★★★
b.f. Lawman – Triple Try (Sadler's Wells). March 13. Half-sister to 5 winners including the useful 1m (at 2 yrs) and 10f winner and Group 3 10f Ballysax Stakes third Unwritten Rule (by Dalakhani), the useful 7f (at 2 yrs) and listed 1m winner Go For Goal (by Verglas) and the fairly useful dual 7f winner (including at 2 yrs) Offbeat Fashion (by Rock Of Gibraltar). The dam, a quite useful Irish dual 10f winner,

is a sister to the Irish Oaks and Tattersalls Gold Cup winner Dance Design. The second dam, Elegance In Design (by Habitat), a useful Irish listed 6f winner, is a sister to the high-class Coronation Stakes winner Chalon (herself dam of the Prix Ganay winner Creator). (Moyglare Stud Farms Ltd). *"A nice filly, I'd say she'll come in June or July over six/seven furlongs".*

1680. PIAZZINI (IRE) ★★★
b.f. Kyllachy – Polite Reply (Be My Guest). March 15. Half-sister to the fairly useful 2-y-o dual 5f winner Hidden Charm (by Big Shuffle) and to the quite useful dual 7f winners In A Rush (by Hernando) and Flic Flac (by Bahamian Bounty). The dam, a quite useful 7f and 1m winner, is closely related to the Irish winner and listed-placed Dance Pass and a half-sister to 3 winners including the Group 3 Ballyroan Stakes winner Sense Of Purpose. The second dam, Super Gift (by Darshaan), won twice over 1m at 2 yrs and was second in the Group 3 7f C.L. Weld Park Stakes. (Moyglare Stud Farms Ltd). *"A strong, powerful filly that should be ready to run in June or July".*

1681. SHAMREEN (IRE) ★★★★
b.f. Dubawi – Shareen (Bahri). February 24. Second foal. The dam, a useful Irish Group 3 9.5f winner, is a half-sister to the smart listed 1m and listed 10f winner Sharestan and the useful 6f (at 2 yrs) and 7f winner and listed-placed Sharleez. The second dam, Sharesha (by Ashkalani), a fairly useful Irish 10f winner, is a half-sister to 4 winners out of the 1m placed Sharemata (by Doyoun). (H H Aga Khan). *"She's a nice Dubawi filly that should be racing in July or August".*

1682. SMOKEY QUARTZ (IRE) ★★★
gr.f. Dark Angel – Instant Sparkle (Danehill) April 3. The dam, a quite useful Irish 12f winner, is a sister to the Group 2 12f Ribblesdale Stakes winner Irresistible Jewel (herself dam of the Group 3 winner Mad About You) and a half-sister to 5 winners including the listed 12f winner Diamond Trim (herself dam of the Group 3 winner Profound Beauty) and the useful Irish 1m winner and Group 3 placed Legal Jousting. The second dam, In Anticipation (by Sadler's Wells), won over 12f and 14f in Ireland and is a half-sister to 6 winners. (Moyglare Stud Farms Ltd).

"A big, lengthy filly, she's nice, goes well and I see her wanting six or seven furlongs in August/September".

1683. TARAYEF (IRE) ★★★★
b.f. Teofilo – Grecian Bride (Groom Dancer). February 25. Eleventh foal. €950,000Y. Goffs Orby. Shadwell Estate Co. Sister to Group 3 Blue Wind Stakes winner and Group 1 Oaks second Tarfasha, closely related to the 2-y-o 1m winner, Irish Derby second and Epsom Derby third Galileo Rock (by Galileo) and half-sister to 5 winners including the dual Group 2 winning stayer Saddler's Rock, (by Sadler's Wells). The dam is an unraced sister to the listed 10f winner Athens Belle and a half-sister to the Group 1 Grand Prix de Saint-Cloud winner Gamut. The second dam, the French 10f and 12f winner Greektown (by Ela-Mana-Mou) is a half-sister to the high-class stayer Sought Out (dam of the Derby winner North Light). (Hamdan Al Maktoum). *"A very nice filly. She was expensive and she's a full sister of course to Tarfasha. I think she'll make a lovely filly in the second half of the season. Like her sister she should be one for seven furlongs to a mile as a 2-y-o. We'll see her out in September or October".*

1684. TRUE SOLITAIRE (IRE) ★★★★★
b.c. Oasis Dream – Majestic Silver (Linamix). April 21. Third foal. Half-brother to the 2015 3-y-o 1m winner Joailliere (by Dubawi), to the very useful Group 3 9f Dance Design Stakes winner of 4 races Carla Bianca (by Dansili). The dam is an unraced half-sister to the Irish Group 3 12f and Group 3 14f winner Profound Beauty and to the useful 7f to 10f winner Rock Critic. The second dam, Diamond Trim (by Highest Honor), a winner of 5 races from 1m to 12f including a listed event, is a half-sister to 5 winners including the Group 2 12f Ribblesdale Stakes winner Irresistible Jewel. (Moyglare Stud Farms Ltd). *"A very nice colt, he's going to be a racehorse! I would hope to get him out in July or August over six/seven furlongs. His 3-y-o half-sister Joailliere is very good, as was the year older Carla Bianca, so it looks like the dam is a good one".*

1685. YASOOD (IRE) ★★★
b.c. Acclamation – Lucina (Machiavellian). April 18. Seventh foal. 300,000Y. Tattersalls

October Book 1. Shadwell Estate Co. Half-brother to the quite useful 12f winner Parvana (by Galileo), to the fair 2-y-o 6f and 7f winner My One Weakness (by Bertolini) and the modest 6f winner Rapscallion Deep (by Danehill Dancer). The dam is an unraced half-sister to 8 winners including the triple Group 3 winner and dual Group 1 third Blue Monday and the Group 1 Italian Derby third Lundy's Lane. The second dam, Lunda (by Soviet Star), is an unplaced half-sister to Luso (winner of the Aral-Pokal, the Italian Derby and the Hong Kong International Vase), Warrsan (Coronation Cup and Grosser Preis von Baden) and the Group 3 winners Cloud Castle and Needle Gun. (Hamdan Al Maktoum). *"A big colt, he's lengthy and goes nicely. Six or seven furlongs in July/August should be fine for him".*

1686. UNNAMED ★★★★
b.f. High Chaparral – Agnetha (Big Shuffle). February 2. Ninth foal. 210,000Y. Tattersalls October Book 1. Armando Duarte. Closely related to the US dual Grade 3 winner Starstruck, to the quite useful Irish 1m and 9f winner Anaverna (both by Galileo) and the quite useful Irish 7f winner Scarlet O'Hara (by Sadler's Wells) and half-sister to 3 winners including the quite useful 10f to 12f winner Der Meister (by Mastercraftsman). The dam won the listed Silver Flash Stakes (at 2 yrs) and the Group 3 5f King George Stakes and is a sister to the German Group 2 sprint winner Areion and to the Irish listed winner Anna Frid. The second dam, Aerleona (by Caerleon), a German 2-y-o 6f winner, is a half-sister to 5 winners including the Fillies' Mile winner Nepula. (Calumet Farm). *"She's a very taking filly out of a champion sprinter who has bred a very good filly in America called Starstruck. I would say this is a very quality filly for August/ September".*

1687. UNNAMED ★★★
b.f. Galileo – Lesson In Humility (Mujadil). April 29. Third foal. Half-sister to the very useful 2-y-o listed 5f winner and Group 2 5f Norfolk Stakes second Coach House (by Oasis Dream). The dam, a winner of 6 races including the Group 3 6f Ballyogan Stakes, was third in the Group 1 Golden Jubilee Stakes and the Group 1 Prix Maurice de Gheest and is a half-sister to 4 winners including the listed

1m winner Boastful. The second dam, Vanity (by Thatching), is a placed half-sister to 5 winners including the listed winner and smart broodmare Ffestiniog. (Mrs J Magnier). *"A very nice filly for the autumn".*

1688. UNNAMED ★★★★
b.c. Canford Cliffs – Zanzibar Girl (Johannesburg). March 8. First foal. €90,000Y. Goffs Orby. D K Weld. The dam is an unraced half-sister to 7 winners including the Group 3 Gordon Stakes and listed winner Rabah. The second dam, The Perfect Life (by Try My Best), won the Group 3 5f Prix du Bois, was second in the Group 2 Prix Robert Papin and is a sister to the triple Group 1 winner Last Tycoon and a half-sister to 9 winners including the dams of the Group 1 winners Immortal Verse, Sense Of Style, Tie Black and Valentine Waltz. (Calumet Farm). *"A very nice colt, he's one for seven furlongs in June/July. A grand horse and a racehorse".*

Sires Reference

This section deals with those sires represented by three or more two-year-olds in the book. All the top British and Irish sires are represented and you will also see some of the best sires standing in America such as Distorted Humor, Elusive Quality, Giant's Causeway, Kitten's Joy, Medaglia d'Oro, Smart Strike, Street Cry and War Front.

Amongst the first-season sires, I think there'll be plenty of winners sired by Poet's Voice, Canford Cliffs, Lilbourne Lad, Roderic O'Connor, Zoffany and Dream Ahead.

Please note that the reference numbers given with each sire correspond with their two-year-olds in the book.

ACCLAMATION (2000) Royal Applause – Princess Athena (Ahonoora). *Racing record:* Won 6 times, including Diadem Stakes. Also placed in King's Stand and Nunthorpe. *Stud record:* This is his Ninth crop and his Group winners to date are Dark Angel (G1 Middle Park Stakes), Equiano (G1 King's Stand Stakes), Harbour Watch, Saayerr (both winners of the G2 Richmond Stakes), Lilbourne Lad (G2 Railway Stakes), Angels Will Fall (G3 Princess Margaret Stakes), Alsindi (G3 Oh So Sharp Stakes), Hitchens (G3 Greenlands Stakes), Ponty Acclaim (G3 Cornwallis Stakes), Talwar (G3 Solario Stakes) and Sparkling Power (G3 in Hong Kong). He also has numerous listed winners to his name. Standing at Rathbarry Stud, Ireland. *2015 fee:* €35,000.

APPROVE (2008) Oasis Dream – Wyola (Sadler's Wells). *Racing record:* Won three races at 2 yrs including the Group 2 5f Norfolk Stakes and the Group 2 6f Gimcrack Stakes and third in the Group 1 6f Middle Park Stakes. Unraced after his 2-y-o career. *Stud record:* His first runners appeared last season and to date he has the winners of around 40 races including the Irish listed winner and Group 2 Flying Childers Stakes third Accepted. Standing at Morristown Lattin Stud in Ireland. *2015 fee:* €5,000.

AQLAAM (2005) Oasis Dream – Bourbonella (Rainbow Quest). *Racing record:* Won the Group 1 Prix de Moulin and the Group 2 Jersey Stakes. *Stud record:* With two crops racing he has sired the winners of around 40 races including Moonee Valley (Group 3 Prix des Reservoirs) and Aqlaam Vision (listed Radley Stakes). Standing at Nunnery Stud. Died in 2013.

ARAKAN (2000) Nureyev – Far Across (Common Grounds). *Racing record:* Won 6 races including the Group 3 Criterion Stakes, the Group 3 Supreme Stakes (both 7f), the listed Abernant Stakes and the City Of York Stakes (both 6f). *Stud record:* His best winners to date are the dual Group 1 winner Dick Turpin, the Group 1 National Stakes winner Toormore, the dual Group 2 winner Trumpet Major and the Irish Group 3 winner Sruthan. Standing at Ballyhane Stud. *2015 fee:* €4,000.

ARCANO (2007) Oasis Dream – Tariysha (Daylami). *Racing record:* Won three races at 2 yrs including the Group 1 6f Prix Morny and the Group 2 6f July Stakes. *Stud record:* His first crop were racing last season and to date they've won 35 races between them, including the Italian Group 3 winner Misterious Boy. Standing at Derrinstown Stud, Ireland. *2015 fee:* €5,000.

ARCH (1995) Kris S – Aurora (Danzig). *Racing record:* 5 wins including the Super Derby and the Fayette Stakes. *Stud record:* Best winners so far include Arravale (Grade 1 Del Mar Oaks), Archarcharch (Grade 1 Arkansas Derby), Hymn Book (Grade 1 Donn Handicap), Blame (three US Grade 1 wins), Les Arcs (Golden Jubilee Stakes and July Cup), Love Theway Youare (Grade 1 Vanity Handicap), Overarching (South African dual Group 1 winner), Pine Island (dual US Grade 1 winner), Prince Arch (US Grade 1 winner), Montgomery's Arch (Group 2 Richmond Stakes), Waterway Run (Group 3 Oh So Sharp Stakes) and the Hong Kong Group 3 winner Art Trader. Standing at Claiborne Farm, Kentucky. *2015 fee:* $40,000.

ARCHIPENKO (2004) Kingmambo – Bound (Nijinsky). *Racing record:* Won the Group 1 10f Audemars Piguet Queen Elizabeth II Cup at Sha Tin and five other Group races including the Group 2 Summer Mile. *Stud record:* His second crop appeared in 2014 and his best winners to date are Madame Chiang (Group 1 British Champions Fillies/Mare Stakes), the South African Group 2 winner Kingston Mines and the listed winners Lady Penko and Russian Punch. Standing at Lanwades Stud, Newmarket. *2015 fee:* £10,000.

ATLANTIC SPORT (2005) Machiavellian – Shy Lady (Kaldoun). *Racing record:* Won four races over 6f (at 2 yrs) and 7f including a Listed event. *Stud record:* A half-brother to the St James's Palace Stakes winner Zafeen, his first crop are 2-y-o's this year. Now standing abroad.

AUSSIE RULES (2003) Danehill – Last Second (Alzao). *Racing record:* Won four races including the US Grade 1 Shadwell Turf Mile and the Group 1 French 2,000 Guineas. *Stud record:* His best winners to date are Fiesolana (Group 1 Matron Stakes), Djumama (two Group 3 wins in Germany), Duck Feet (Group 3 Premio Guido Berardelli), the Australian Group 3 winner Hard Ball Get and 12 listed winners including the Group placed Aussie Reigns, Bertinoro, Boomerang Bob, Cazals, Chinese Wall, Dinkum Diamond, Grand Treasure, Kramulkie and Private Jet. Standing at Lanwades Stud. *2015 fee:* £7,000.

AUTHORIZED (2004) Montjeu – Funsie (Saumarez). *Racing record:* Won four races including the Group 1 Racing Post Trophy, Epsom Derby, Juddmonte International (all Group 1 events). *Stud record:* The sire of four Group 1 winners to date – Ambivalent (Pretty Polly Stakes), Complacent, Hartnell (both in Australia) and Seal Of Approval (Qipco British Champions Fillies/Mare Stakes). His other stakes performers include the Australian Group 2 winner Maygrove and six Group 3 winners including Hartnell, Rehn's Nest and Sugar Boy. Standing at Haras Du Logis. *2015 fee:* €10,000.

AZAMOUR (2001) Night Shift – Asmara (Lear Fan). *Racing record:* Won the St James's Palace Stakes, Irish Champion Stakes, Prince of Wales's Stakes and King George VI and Queen Elizabeth Diamond Stakes. *Stud record:* First runners in 2009. Best winners to date include Valyra (Group 1 Prix de Diane), the Group 2 winners Dolniya, Eleonora Duse, Shankardeh and Wade Giles and seven Group 3 winners including Azmeel, Colombian, Liber Nauticus, Native Khan and Colombian. Died in 2014.

BAHAMIAN BOUNTY (1994) Cadeaux Genereux – Clarentia (Ballad Rock). *Racing record:* Winner of 3 races at 2 yrs, notably the Prix Morny and the Middle Park Stakes. *Stud record:* Sire of the Group 1 winners Pastoral Pursuits (July Cup) and Goodricke (Sprint Cup), the US Grade 2 winner Mister Napper Tandy, the Group 2 Hungerford Stakes winner Breton Rock, the 2-y-o Group 2 winners Anjaal and Sendmylovetorose and the Group 3 winners Cay Verde, Coral Mist, Life's A Bounty, Naahy, New Providence and Topatoo. Standing at the National Stud, Newmarket. *2015 fee:* £8,500.

BALTIC KING (2000) Danetime – Lindfield Belle (Fairy King). *Racing record:* Won 8 races including two listed events and the Wokingham Handicap. *Stud record:* His first runners appeared in 2011. To date his best runners have been the listed 1m winner Baltic Knight and the useful 5f to 7f winner and listed-placed Factory Time. Standing at Tally Ho Stud. *2015 fee:* €2,500.

BIG BAD BOB (2000) Bob Back – Fantasy Girl (Marju). *Racing record:* Won 8 races including a Group 3 10f event in Germany and listed races at Ascot (1m) and Deauville (10f). *Stud record:* Has done very well from limited chances and now getting better quality mares. To date he's had three Group 3 winners in Ireland (Berg Bahn, Bible Belt and Brendan Brackan), three Irish listed winners (Backbench Blues, Bible Black and Bob Le Beau), the Italian listed winner Cherie Good. Standing at the Irish National Stud. *2015 fee:* €9,000.

BLAME (2006) Arch – Liable (Seeking The Gold). *Racing record:* Won three Grade 1 events over 9f and 10f (Stephen Foster Handicap, Whitney Handicap and Breeders Cup Classic) and three other Graded stakes. *Stud record:* His first crop of runners appeared last year and they included the US Grade 3 winner Far From Over and three Graded stakes placed horses. Standing at Claiborne Farm, Kentucky. *2014 fee:* $20,000.

BUSHRANGER (2006) Danetime – Danz Danz (Efisio). *Race record:* Won the Group 1 Prix Morny and the Group 1 Middle Park Stakes, both at 2 yrs. *Stud record:* From two crops racing he's had plenty of minor winners including a listed winner in Turkey, plus six listed-placed horses here and abroad. Standing at Tally Ho Stud, Ireland. *2015 fee:* €2,500.

CACIQUE (2001) Danehill – Hasili (Kahyasi). Race record: Won 18 races from 3 to 5 yrs including the Grade 1 11f Man O'War Stakes, Grade 1 10f Manhattan Handicap and the Grade 2 1m Prix Daniel Wildenstein. *Stud record:* From limited books of mares he has the winners of 49 races including the Group 1 Hong Kong Vase winner Dominant, the Group 2 Prix de Chaudenay winner Canticum and the Group 3 Geoffrey Freer Stakes winner Census. Standing at Banstead Manor Stud, Newmarket. *2015 fee:* £12,500.

CANFORD CLIFFS (2007) Tagula – Mrs Marsh (Marju). *Racing record:* Won 7 races at 2 to 4 yrs and from 6f to 1m including the Irish 2,000 Guineas, St James's Palace Stakes, Sussex Stakes, Lockinge Stakes and Queen Anne Stakes (all Group 1 events). *Stud record:* His first crop are two-year-olds this year. Standing at Coolmore Stud in Ireland. *2015 fee:* €12,500.

CAPE BLANCO (2007) Galileo – Laurel Delight (Presidium). *Racing record:* Won 9 races including the Irish Derby, Irish Champion Stakes, Man O'War Stakes, Arlington Million and Turf Classic (all Group/Grade 1 events). *Stud record:* His first crop are now two-year-olds. Now standing in Japan.

CAPE CROSS (1994) Green Desert – Park Appeal (Ahonoora). *Racing record:* Won 4 races including the Lockinge Stakes, Queen Anne Stakes and Celebration Mile. *Stud record:* First runners in 2003. Sire of ten Group 1 winners including the outstanding colt Sea The Stars (2,000 Guineas, Derby, Prix de l'Arc de Triomphe etc,), the top-class Ouija Board (7 Group 1 wins including the Oaks & the Breeders' Cup Filly and Mare Turf), Behkabad (Grand Prix de Paris), Nayarra (Group 1 Gran

Criterium) and the Australasian horses Gaze, I'm Your Man, Kindacross, Mikki Street and Seachange. His 19 Group 2 winners include Cape Dollar, Crystal Capella, Halicarnassus, Hatta Fort, Joviality, Moohaajim, Russian Cross, Sabana Perdida and Treat Gently. Standing at Kildangan Stud, Ireland. *2015 fee:* €20,000.

CAPTAIN RIO (2000) Pivotal – Beloved Visitor (Miswaki). *Racing record:* Won 4 times including the Criterium de Maisons-Laffitte at 2 yrs. *Stud record:* His best progeny to date include the Australian triple Group 1 winner Terravista, the New Zealand Group 1 winner Il Quello Veloce, the Australian Group 1 winner Brazilian Pulse, the New Zealand Group 2 winner Riomoral and the Group 3 winners Art Beat, Capt Chaos, Energised, Philario and Red Badge.

CHAMPS ELYSEES (2003) Danehill – Hasili (Kahyasi). *Racing record:* Won the Canadian International, the Hollywood Turf Cup and the Northern Dancer Turf Stakes (all Grade 1). *Stud record:* With two crops to have raced so far he's the sire of the winners of over 70 races including the Group 3 Silver Flash Stakes winner Jack Naylor, the Group 3 winner and French 1,000 Guineas third Xcellence and the listed winners and Group placed Avenue Gabriel, Lustrous and Regardez. Standing at Banstead Manor Stud, Newmarket. *2015 fee:* £10,000.

CLODOVIL (2001) Danehill – Clodora (Linamix). *Racing record:* Won 5 races including the French 2,000 Guineas. *Stud record:* His first crop were two-year-olds in 2007 and his best winners to date are Nahoodh (Group 1 Falmouth Stakes), Moriarty (Group 1 and three Group 2's in Australia), the Group 2 winners Es Que Love, Gregorian and Laugh Out Loud, the dual Group 3 winner Beacon Lodge and eleven listed winners. Standing at Rathasker Stud, Ireland. *2015 fee:* €10,000.

COMPTON PLACE (1994) Indian Ridge – Nosey (Nebbiolo). *Racing record:* Won 3 races, notably the July Cup. *Stud record:* First runners in 2002. Sire of 11 Group winners and 13 listed winners, notably the dual Group 1 Nunthorpe Stakes winner Borderlescott, the Group 2 and multiple Group 3 winner

Deacon Blues, the smart Boogie Street and Intrepid Jack, US Grade 2 winner Passified, the Group 2 winners Godfrey Street and Prolific, the Italian Group 3 winners Pleasure Place, Champion Place and Shifting Place, and numerous useful performers including Angus News, Compton's Eleven, If Paradise, Judd Street, Hunter Street, Master Of War, Pacific Pride and Pearl Secret. Standing at Whitsbury Manor Stud, Hampshire. *2015 fee:* £5,500.

DALAKHANI (2001) Darshaan – Daltawa (Miswaki). *Racing record:* Won 8 of his 9 starts, including the Prix du Jockey Club and the Arc. *Stud record:* First crop were two-year-olds in 2007. *Stud record:* To date he's bred the Group 1 winners Conduit (St Leger, Breeders Cup Turf (twice), King George VI & Queen Elizabeth Stakes), Integral (Sun Chariot and Falmouth Stakes), Moonstone (Irish Oaks), Chinese White (Pretty Polly Stakes), Reliable Man (Prix du Jockey Club), Duncan (Irish St Leger) and Seismos (Grosser Preis von Bayen). His six Group 2 winners are Centennial, Armure, Silk Sari, Terrubi, Vadamar and Democratie, and there are 11 Group 3 winners to his name. Standing at Gilltown Stud, Ireland. *2015 fee:* €17,000.

DANDY MAN (2003) Mozart – Lady Alexander (Night Shift). *Racing record:* Won 6 races including the Group 3 5f Palace House Stakes and two listed events. *Stud record:* Gets plenty of 2-y-o winners. His best runners to date are the Hong Kong Group 1 winner Peniaphobia, the Group 3 and listed winner Extortionist and the triple Group 2 placed Parbold. Standing at Ballyhane Stud. *2015 fee:* €6,500.

DANEHILL DANCER (1993) Danehill – Mira Adonde (Sharpen Up). *Racing record:* Winner of 4 races, including the Phoenix Stakes and National Stakes at 2 yrs and the Greenham at 3. *Stud record:* Sire of numerous Group 1 winners including Again, Alexander Tango, Atomic Force, Choisir, Dancing Rain, Lillie Langtry, Mastercraftsman, Planteur, Private Steer, Speciosa and Where Or When. Standing at Coolmore Stud, Ireland. Retired from stud.

DANSILI (1996) Danehill – Hasili (Kahyasi). *Racing record:* Won 5 races in France and placed in six Group/Grade 1 events including Sussex Stakes and Breeders' Cup Mile.

Stud record: First runners in 2004. Sire of 18 Group/Grade 1 winners including Rail Link (Arc, Grand Prix de Paris), Harbinger (King George VI), Emulous (Matron Stakes), Giofra (Falmouth Stakes), Miss France (1,000 Guineas), Passage of Time (Criterium de Saint-Cloud), The Fugue (four Group 1's), We Are (Prix de l'Opera), Winsili (Nassau Stakes), Zoffany (Phoenix Stakes), Zambezi Sun (Grand Prix de Paris) and in the USA Dank, Laughing, Price Tag and Proviso. Standing at Banstead Manor Stud, Newmarket. *2015 fee:* £100,000.

DARK ANGEL (2005) Acclamation – Midnight Angel (Machiavellian). *Racing record:* Won four races at 2 yrs including the Group 1 Middle Park Stakes. *Stud Record:* First runners 2011. His best winners to date are Lethal Force (Group 1 July Cup & Group 1 Diamond Jubilee Stakes), Alhebayeb (Group 2 July Stakes), Estidhkaar (Group 2 Champagne Stakes & Group 2 Superlative Stakes), the Group 3 winners Exogenesis, Heeraat Lily's Angel and Mecca's Angel, and five listed winners. Stands at Morristown Lattin Stud, Ireland. *2015 fee:* €27,500.

DICK TURPIN (2007) Arakan – Merrily (Sharrood). *Racing record:* Won 9 races from 6f to a mile and from 2 to 4 yrs including the Group 1 Prix Jean Prat and the Group 1 Premio Vittorio de Capua. *Stud record:* His first crop are now two-year-olds. Standing at the National Stud in Newmarket. 2015 stud fee: £4,000.

DISTORTED HUMOR (1993) Forty Niner – Danzig's Beauty (Danzig). *Racing record:* Won 11 races in the USA including the Champagne Stakes, Futurity Stakes, Haskell Invitational and Travers Stakes (all Grade 1). Champion 2-y-o. *Stud record:* Sire of fifteen Grade 1 winners – Aesop's Fables, Any Given Saturday, Awesome Humor, Bit Of Whimsy, Boisterous, Commentator, Cursory Glance, Drosselmeyer, Flower Alley, Fourty Niner's Son, Funny Cide, Hystericalady, Jimmy Creed, Pathfork and Rinky Dink. Standing at Win Star Farm, Kentucky. *2015 fee:* $100,000.

DREAM AHEAD (2008) Diktat – Land Of Dreams (Cadeaux Genereux). *Racing record:* Won five Group 1 races from 6f to 7f, at 2 and 3 yrs (Prix Morny, Middle Park Stakes, July Cup, Haydock Park Sprint Cup and Prix de la Foret). *Stud record:* His first crop are now two-year-olds. Standing at Ballylinch Stud in Ireland. 2015 stud fee: €15,000.

DUBAWI (2002) Dubai Millennium – Zomaradah (Deploy). *Racing record:* Won the National Stakes at 2 and the Irish 2,000 Guineas and Prix Jacques le Marois at 3. Third in the Derby. *Stud record:* Sire of 56 Group winners including 17 Group 1 scorers. They include Akeed Mofeed (in Hong Kong), Al Kazeem (three Group 1's), Dubawi Heights (Gamely Stakes, Yellow Ribbon Stakes), Happy Archer (two Group 1's in Australia), Hunters Light (Premio Roma), Lucky Nine (Hong Kong Sprint), Makfi (2,000 Guineas, Prix Jacques le Marois), Monterosso, Prince Bishop (both Dubai World Cup winners), Night Of Thunder (2,000 Guineas), Poet's Voice (Queen Elizabeth II Stakes), Secret Admirer (two Group 1's in Australia), Sheikhzayedroad (Northern Dancer Turf Stakes), Waldpark (German Derby) and Willow Magic (in South Africa). Standing at Dalham Hall Stud, Newmarket. *2015 fee:* £125,000.

DUKE OF MARMALADE (2004) Danehill – Love Me True (Kingmambo). *Racing record:* Won 6 races including the Juddmonte International Stakes, King George VI and Queen Elizabeth Stakes, Prince of Wales's Stakes, Tattersalls Gold Cup and Prix Ganay. *Stud record:* His first two year olds appeared in 2012. His 9 Group winners to date include Big Memory (Group 2 in Australia) and the Group 3 winners Venus De Milo, Hall Of Mirrors and Wannabe Better (all in Ireland). Now standing in South Africa.

DUTCH ART (2004) Medicean – Halland Park Lass (Spectrum). *Racing record:* Won four races at 2 yrs including the Group 1 Prix Morny and the Group 1 Middle Park Stakes. *Stud record:* Leading first crop sire in 2011 and a consistently good sire ever since. His best winners to date include Slade Power (dual Group 1 6f winner), Garswood (Group 1 Prix Maurice de Gheest), Caspar Netscher (Group 2 Mill Reef Stakes and Group 2 Gimcrack Stakes), Van Der Neer (Group 1 Racing Post Trophy second), Producer (Group 2 in Turkey and the Group 3 Supreme Stakes) and Dutch Masterpiece (Group 3 Flying Five). Standing at Cheveley Park Stud. *2015 fee:* £40,000.

ELNADIM (1994) Danzig – Elle Seule (Exclusive Native). *Racing record:* Won 5 races, notably the July Cup and the Diadem Stakes. *Stud record:* Sire of the New Zealand Group 1 winner Culminate, the smart performers Al Qasi (Group 3 Phoenix Stakes), Caldra (Group 3 Autumn Stakes), Elletelle (Group 2 Queen Mary Stakes), Elnawin (Group 3 Sirenia Stakes), Wi Dud (Group 2 Flying Childers Stakes), Soraaya (Group 3 Princess Margaret Stakes), New Zealand Group 3 winners Accardo, Elblitzem and Pendragon, the US Grade 3 winner Pasar Silbano and the dual listed winner Almass. *2014 fee:* €4,000. Died January 2015.

ELUSIVE CITY (2000) Elusive Quality – Star Of Paris (Dayjur). *Racing record:* Won the 2-y-o Group 1 6f Prix Morny and third in the 2-y-o Group 1 6f Middle Park Stakes. *Stud record:* Sire of 14 Group winners including Elusive Wave (French 2,000 Guineas), three Group 1 winners in New Zealand and the 2-y-o Group 2 Criterium de Maisons Laffitte winner Kiram. Standing at Haras d'Etreham. *2015 fee:* €10,000.

ELUSIVE PIMPERNEL (2007) Elusive Quality – Cara Fantasy (Sadler's Wells). *Racing record:* Won the Group 3 7f Acomb Stakes (at 2 yrs) and the Group 3 1m Craven Stakes. Second in the Group 1 Racing Post Trophy. *Stud record:* His first crop are now two-year-olds. Standing at the Irish National Stud. 2015 stud fee: €1,000.

ELUSIVE QUALITY (1993) Gone West – Touch of Greatness (Hero's Honor). *Racing record:* Won 9 races in USA including Grade 3 events at 7f/1m. *Stud record:* Sire of top-class Kentucky Derby/Preakness Stakes winner Smarty Jones, Breeders Cup Classic and Queen Elizabeth II Stakes winner Raven's Pass, Prix Morny winner Elusive City, dual Group 1 winner Elusive Kate, Australian multiple Group 1 winner Sepoy, the US Grade 1 winners Quality Road and Maryfield, the Group winning two-year-olds Certify, Elusive Pimpernel and Evasive, numerous US graded stakes winners including Chimichurri, Elusive Diva, Girl Warrior, Omega Code, Royal Michele and True Quality, the Group 2 and triple Group 3 winner Shuruq and the smart dual listed winner Baharah. Standing at Jonabell Farm, Kentucky. *2015 fee:* $40,000.

EQUIANO (2005) Acclamation – Entente Cordiale (Ela-Mana-Mou). *Racing record:* Won 7 races starting with two wins as a 2-y-o over 7f in Spain, before maturing into a high-class sprinter and twice capturing the Group 1 5f King's Stand Stakes. *Stud record:* His first crop of 2-y-o's appeared last year and they included the Group 3 Firth Of Clyde Stakes winner Dark Reckoning, the Group 2 Prix Robert Papin second Strath Burn, the Irish Group 3 second Lola Beaux and the useful Tattersalls Millions Fillies' winner Lacing. Standing at Newsells Park Stud. *2015 fee:* £8,000.

EXCEED AND EXCEL (2000) Danehill – Patrona (Lomond). *Racing record:* Champion sprinter in Australia, won 7 races including the Grade 1 Newmarket H'cap, the Grade 1 Dubai Racing Club Cup and the Grade 2 Todman Stakes. *Stud record:* His best winners include Excelebration (Queen Elizabeth II Stakes, Prix du Moulin, Prix Jacques le Marois), Margot Did (Nunthorpe Stakes), Outstrip (Breeders Cup Juvenile Turf), Amber Sky (Group 1 Al Quoz Sprint), the Group 2 winners Fulbright, Heavy Metal, Best Terms, Infamous Angel and Masamah, and the 2-y-o Group 3 winner Bungleinthejungle. His Australasian winners include the Group 1 winners Guelph, Helmet, Overreach, Reward For Effort and Sidestep, Group 2 winner Wilander and the Group 3 winners Exceedingly Good, Sugar Babe and Believe 'n' Succeed. Standing at Kildangan Stud, Ireland. *2015 fee:* £40,000.

EXCELLENT ART (2004) Pivotal – Obsessive (Seeking The Gold). *Racing record:* Won 4 races including the Group 1 St James's Palace Stakes and the Group 2 Mill Reef Stakes. *Stud record:* First runners 2011. Winners include Experience (Group 3 Grangecon Stud Stakes), Hazel Lavery (Group 3 St Simon Stakes), Graphic (Group 3 Prix Messidor) and the listed winners Artistic Jewel, Lady Lara, Sparkling Portrait, Tropaios and Nimohe. Now standing in India.

FAST COMPANY (2005) Danehill Dancer – Sheezalady (Zafonic). *Racing record:* Ran only three times, all at 2 yrs, winning the Group 3 7f Acomb Stakes and finishing second in the Group 1 7f Dewhurst Stakes. *Stud record:* Sired 26 individual winners from his first crop in 2014, notably the Group 2 Norfolk

Stakes winner Baitha Alga and the Group 3 Molecomb Stakes second Fast Act. Standing at Rathasker Stud, Ireland. *2015 fee:* €7,500.

FASTNET ROCK (2001) Danehill – Piccadilly Circus (Royal Academy). *Racing record:* Raced in Australia and won two Grade 1's, two Grade 2's and two Grade 3 events over 5f and 6f. *Stud record:* A champion sire in Australia where he's produced 18 Group 1 winners including Atlante, Atlantic Jewel, Foxwedge, Irish Lights, Lone Rock, Mosheen, Nechita, Planet Rock, Rock 'N' Pop, Rock Classic, Sea Siren, Super Cool, Wanted and Your Song. Now in Ireland, he hasn't had the same sort of impact here yet although he has had the Irish Group 3 winners Fascinating Rock and Qualify. Standing at Coolmore Stud in Ireland. *2015 fee:* Private.

FIREBREAK (1999) Charnwood Forest – Breakaway (Song). *Racing record:* Won the Godolphin Mile in Dubai (twice), Challenge Stakes and Hong Kong Mile. *Stud record:* From seven crops racing his best winners to date are Hearts Of Fire (Group 1 Gran Criterium), Caledonia Lady (Group 3 Sandown Sprint Stakes), Fire Ship (Group 3 Prix Quincey) and the listed Radley Stakes winner Electric Feel. Standing at Bearstone Stud. *2015 fee:* £4,500.

FIRST DEFENCE (2004) Unbridled's Song – Honest Lady (Seattle Slew). *Racing record:* Won the Grade 1 7f Forego Handicap and the Grade 3 6f Jaipur Stakes. *Stud record:* With three crops racing he is the sire of the winners of 159 races. His best runners have been the US multiple Grade 1 winner Close Hatches and the Group 3 Acomb Stakes winner Dundonnell. Standing at Juddmonte Farms, Kentucky. *2015 fee:* $10,000.

FOOTSTEPSINTHESAND (2002) Giant's Causeway – Glatisant (Rainbow Quest). *Racing record:* Won all 3 of his starts, notably the 2,000 Guineas. *Stud record:* His best winners include the Chachamaidee (Group 1 Matron Stakes), the Italian and Argentine Group 1 winners Infiltrada, Sand Bijou and Shamalgan, Canadian Grade 1 winner Steinbeck, the Group 2 winners Barefoot Lady, Formosina, Giant Sandman, Living The Life, Minakshi and, in Argentina, King Kon, Sagitariana and Sand Puce, plus six Group 3 winners. Standing at Coolmore Stud, Ireland. *2015 fee:* €10,000.

FROZEN POWER (2007) Oasis Dream – Musical Treat (Royal Academy). *Racing record:* Won five races from 6f to a mile including the Group 2 German 2,000 Guineas. *Stud record:* His first crop are now two-year-olds. Standing at Ballyhane Stud in Ireland. 2015 stud fee: €4,000.

GALILEO (1998) Sadler's Wells – Urban Sea (Miswaki). *Racing record:* Won 6 races including the Derby, Irish Derby and King George VI and Queen Elizabeth Stakes. *Stud record:* First runners in 2005. Sire of 46 Group 1 winners, notably the outstanding champion Frankel, champion 2-y-o's Teofilo and New Approach (subsequent Derby, Champion Stakes and Irish Champion Stakes winner), Derby, Irish Derby and Juddmonte International winner Australia, the triple Group 1 winner Rip Van Winkle, Sixties Icon (St Leger), triple Group 1 winner Noble Mission, Red Rocks (Breeders' Cup Turf), Allegretto (Prix Royal-Oak), Lush Lashes (three Group 1 wins), Soldier Of Fortune (Irish Derby & Coronation Cup), Nightime (Irish 1000 Guineas), Roderic O'Connor (Criterium International, Irish 2,000 Guineas), Cape Blanco (five Group 1 wins), Nathaniel (King George VI & Queen Elizabeth Stakes), Ruler Of The World (Epsom Derby), Treasure Beach (Irish Derby, Secretariat Stakes), Golden Lilac (French 1,000 Guineas, Prix d'Ispahan and Prix de Diane), Was (Oaks), Misty For Me (four Group 1 wins), Maybe (Moyglare Stud Stakes) and Galikova (Prix Vermeille). Standing at Coolmore Stud, Ireland. *2015 fee:* Private.

GIANT'S CAUSEWAY (1997) Storm Cat – Mariah's Storm (Rahy). *Racing record:* Won 9 races, 6 of them Group 1 events, including the Prix de la Salamandre, Juddmonte International and Sussex Stakes. *Stud record:* First runners in 2004. The sire of the 30 Group/Grade 1 winners including Shamardal (Dewhurst Stakes, St James's Palace Stakes and Prix du Jockey Club), Footstepsinthesand (2,000 Guineas), Ghanaati (1,000 Guineas and Coronation Stakes), Aragorn (dual US Grade 1 winner), Eishin Apollon (Group 1 miler in Japan), Heatseeker (Santa Anita Handicap), Maids Causeway (Coronation Stakes), Intense Focus (Dewhurst Stakes), Eskendereya, First

Samurai, My Typhoon, Swift Temper (US Grade 1 winners), Dalkala (Prix de l'Opera) and Rite of Passage (Ascot Gold Cup). Standing at Ashford Stud, Kentucky. *2015 fee:* Private (was $85,000 in 2014).

HALLING (1991) Diesis – Dance Machine (Green Dancer). *Racing record:* Won 12 races including Coral-Eclipse Stakes (twice), Juddmonte International (twice) and Prix d'Ispahan. *Stud record:* First runners in 2000. Sire of the Group 1 Grand Prix de Paris winner Cavalryman, the high-class Norse Dancer, Group 1 Prix Ganay winner Cutlass Bay, Group 2 winners Boscobel, Opinion Poll, Coastal Path, Dandoun, Eastern Aria, Fisich, Franklins Gardens, Giovani Imperatore, Harland, Nordhal, Pinson and Vanderlin, plus numerous other smart performers including Bauer, Chancellor, Foodbroker Fancy, Hala Bek, Hattan, Hero's Journey, Mkuzi, Parasol, Romsdal and The Geezer.

HARD SPUN (2004) Danzig – Turkish Tryst (Turkoman). *Racing record:* Won 4 races in the USA from 7f to 9f at 3 yrs including the Grade 1 King's Bishop Stakes, the Grade 2 Kentucky Classic and the Grade 2 Lane's End Stakes. *Stud record:* Sire of 36 stakes winners including the Grade 1 winner Hard Not To Like (turf), Wicked Strong (turf), Hardest Core, Questing, the US Grade 2 winner Big John B and the Group 2 5f King George V winner Moviestar. Standing at Jonabell Farm, Kentucky. *2015 fee:* $35,000.

HELLVELYN (2004) Ishiguru – Cumbrian Melody (Petong). *Racing record:* Won five races over 5f and 6f including the Group 2 Coventry Stakes (at 2 yrs) and the listed Beverley Bullet Sprint and second in the Group 1 Phoenix Stakes. *Stud record:* His first crop appeared on the racecourse last year and yielded a sprinkling of 2-y-o winners including the Group 3 Prestige Stakes second Bonny Grey. Standing at Bucklands Farm & Stud. *2015 fee:* £3,000.

HENRYTHENAVIGATOR (2005) Kingmambo – Sequoyah (Sadler's Wells) *Racing record:* Won the Sussex Stakes, St James's Palace Stakes, 2000 Guineas and Irish 2,000 Guineas. *Stud record:* His first two year olds appeared in 2012 and to date he's had 3 individual Group 1 winners – George Vancouver

(Grade 1 Breeders Cup Juvenile Turf), Pedro The Great (Group 1 Phoenix Stakes) and Sudirman (Group 1 Phoenix Stakes). He also has three listed winners and the Group 2 placed Cristoforo Colombo, Zhiyi, Amerigo Vespucci, Samuel Dechamplain and Sir John Hawkins. Standing at: Coolmore Stud. *2015 fee:* €15,000.

HIGH CHAPARRAL (2000) Sadler's Wells – Kasora (Darshaan). *Racing record:* Won 10 races, including the Derby, Irish Champion Stakes and Breeders' Cup Turf (twice). *Stud record:* First crop were two-year-olds in 2007. Best performers to date include the multiple Group 1 winner So You Think, Group 1 Sussex Stakes and Queen Anne Stakes winner Toronado, Australian Group 1 winners Dundeel (six Group 1 wins), Descarado, Monaco Consul and Shoot Out, German Group 1 winner Lucky Lion, Grade 1 Northern Dancer Turf Stakes winners Redwood and Wigmore Hall, Grade 1 Breeders Cup Turf winner Wrote, High Jinx (Group 1 Prix du Cadran), eight Group 2 winners including The Miniver Rose and Joanna, and 16 Group 3 winners. Died in 2014.

HOLY ROMAN EMPEROR (2004) Danehill – L'On Vite (Secretariat). *Racing record:* Won 4 races at 2 yrs including the Group 1 7f Prix Jean-Luc Lagardere, the Group 1 6f Waterford Phoenix Stakes and Group 2 6f Railway Stakes. *Stud record:* His best winners so far include Homecoming Queen (1,000 Guineas), Morandi (Group 1 Criterium de Saint Cloud), Hong Kong triple Group 1 winner Designs On Rome, New Zealand Group 1 winners Rollout The Carpet and Mongolian Khan, Grade 1 Santa Anita Sprint winner Rich Tapestry 18 other Group winners including Angelic Light, Banimpire, Charles The Great, Mango Diva (all Group 2 winners) and the Group 1 placed Amarillo, Honorius, Ishvana, Leitir Mor and Princess Noor. Standing at Coolmore Stud, Ireland. *2015 fee:* €20,000.

IFFRAAJ (2001) Zafonic – Pastorale (Nureyev). *Racing record:* Won 7 races including the Group 2 7f Park Stakes (twice), the Group 2 7f Betfair Cup (Lennox St) and the 6f Wokingham Stakes. *Stud record:* First runners came in 2010 when he had more winners (38) than any first-crop European sire ever. His best to date are Chriselliam (Group 1 Fillies'

Mile and Grade 1 Breeders Cup Juvenile Fillies), Wootton Bassett (Group 1 Prix Jean-Luc Lagardere), Rizeena (Group 1 Moyglare Stud Stakes), the New Zealand Group 1 winner Turn Me Loose and nine other Group winners including the New Zealand Group 2 winner Fix and the Group 1 Middle Park Stakes third Hot Streak. Standing at Dalham Hall Stud, Newmarket. *2015 fee:* €22,500.

INTENSE FOCUS (2006) Giant's Causeway – Daneleta (Danehill). *Racing record:* Won the 2-y-o Group 1 7f Dewhurst Stakes. *Stud record:* From two crops racing he's the sire of the winners of over 100 races, notably the Group 1 Middle Park Stakes winner Astaire and the Group 3 placed Heart Focus and Home School. Standing at Ballylinch Stud, Ireland. *2015 fee:* €7,000.

INTIKHAB (1994) Red Ransom – Crafty Example (Crafty Prospector). *Racing record:* 8 wins including the Diomed Stakes and the Queen Anne Stakes. *Stud record:* Sire of the outstanding racemare and multiple Group 1 winner Snow Fairy, the Group 1 Lockinge Stakes & Group 1 Matron Stakes winner Red Evie, the Group 1 Criterium de Saint-Cloud winner Paita, the Group 2 Yorkshire Cup winner Glen's Diamond and the Group 3 winners Ascertain, Hoh Mike, Moon Unit, Toupie and Tell Dad. Standing at Derrinstown Stud, Ireland. *2015 fee:* €6,000.

INVINCIBLE SPIRIT (1997) Green Desert – Rafha (Kris). *Racing record:* 7 wins, notably the Group 1 Sprint Cup at 5 yrs. *Stud record:* First runners in 2006. High-class sire of ten Group 1 winners – Charm Spirit (QE II Stakes, Prix Jean Prat & Prix du Moulin), Kingman – four Group 1's including the Sussex Stakes and St James's Palace Stakes), Lawman (French Derby & Prix Jean Prat), Fleeting Spirit (July Cup), Vale Of York (Breeders Cup Juvenile), Moonlight Cloud (six Group 1's in France), Yosai (three Group 1 wins in Australia), Mayson (July Cup), Hooray & Rosdhu Queen (both Cheveley Park Stakes) and ten Group 2 winners - Allied Powers, Campfire Glow, Captain Marvelous, Conquest, Our Jonathan, Madame Trop Vite, Speaking Of Which (in the USA), Zebedee, Spirit Quartz and Spirit Song. Standing at the Irish National Stud. *2015 fee:* €100,000.

JEREMY (2003) Danehill Dancer – Glint in Her Eye (Arazi). *Racing record:* Won 4 races including the Group 2 Betfred Mile at Sandown and the Group 3 7f Jersey Stakes. *Stud record:* First runners 2011. His best runners to date are the dual Group 2 winning 2-y-o Kool Kompany, Yellow Rosebud (Group 3 Concorde Stakes and Group 3 1,000 Guineas Trial), the listed winner Pearl Of Africa and the Irish 1,000 Guineas third Princess Sinead. Died in 2014.

KHELEYF (2001) Green Desert – Society Lady (Mr Prospector). *Racing record:* Won 3 races including the Group 3 Jersey Stakes. *Stud record:* A good source of two-year-old winners, his best so far are Sayif (Group 2 Diadem Stakes), Penny's Picnic (Group 2 Criterium de Maisons Laffitte), Percolator (Group 3 Prix du Bois), Group 1 Phoenix Stakes second Big Time, Group 3 Ballyogan Stakes winner Majestic Queen, US Grade 3 winner Charlie 'Em and twelve listed winners including Captain Ramius, Playfellow (third in the Group 2 Champagne Stakes) and Vladimir (third in the Group 1 Prix Morny). Standing at Dalham Hall Stud, Newmarket. *2015 fee:* £3,000.

KITTEN'S JOY (2001) El Prado – Kitten's First (Lear Fan). *Racing record:* Won 9 races including the Grade 1 10f Secretariat Stakes and the Grade 1 12f Turf Classic. *Stud record:* A leading turf sire in the USA. Sire of 20 Graded stakes winners including the US Grade 1 winners Admiral's Kitten, Bobby's Kitten, Big Blue Kitten, Kitten's Dumplings, Real Solution and Stephanie's Kitten. Standing at Ramsay Fram in the USA. *2015 fee:* $100,000.

KODIAC (2001) Danehill – Rafha (Kris). *Racing record:* Won 4 races here and in the UAE over 6f and 7f including the Datel Trophy and Group 3 placed. *Stud record:* His first runners appeared in 2010 and he's a reliable source of decent class winners including the champion 2-y-o filly Tiggy Wiggy (Group 1 Cheveley Park Stakes), the Group 3 winners Coulsty and Jamesie, and eleven listed winners including Bathwick (Ripon Champion Two Year old Trophy), Indigo River (Grade 2 placed in US), Kodi Bear (Group 1 Dewhurst Stakes second), Kohala (St Hugh's Stakes), Riskit For a Biskit (Prix de Cercle), Sweet Cecily (Bosra Sham Stakes), Indigo River (Sweet Life Stakes

in the USA), Star Kodiac and Ileny Princess (both in Italy) and the Group placed Elleval, Haikbidiac, Stone Of Folca and Eastern Sun. Standing at Tally Ho Stud, Ireland. *2015 fee:* €25,000.

KYLLACHY (1998) Pivotal – Pretty Poppy (Song). *Racing record:* Winner of 6 races including the Group 1 Nunthorpe Stakes at 4 yrs. *Stud record:* First runners in 2006. Sire of the dual Group 1 Nunthorpe Stakes and dual Group 1 King's Stand Stakes winner Sole Power, the Group 1 6f Golden Shaheen winner Krypton Factor, Hong Kong Group 1 winner Dim Sum, the Group 2 winners Arabian Gleam, Dragon Pulse, Penitent, Supplicant and Tariq and numerous smart performers including Awinnersgame, Befortyfour, Mood Music, Gracia Directa and Noble Hachy. Standing at Cheveley Park Stud, Newmarket. *2015 fee:* £15,000.

LAWMAN (2004) Invincible Spirit – Laramie (Gulch). *Racing record:* Won four races including the Group 1 Prix du Jockey Club and the Group Prix Jean Prat. *Stud record:* First runners 2011. He's had a good start at stud with three Group 1 winners in his first two years – Just The Judge (Group 1 Irish 1,000 Guineas, E P Taylor Stakes), Most Improved (Group 1 St James's Palace Stakes) and Law Enforcement (Group 1 Premio Gran Criterium) and the Group winners Agnes Stewart (Group 2 May Hill Stakes), Forces of Darkness (Group 3 Prix Minerve), Loi (Group 3 Prix de Conde), Lady Wingshot (Group 3 Fairy Bridge Stakes), Nargys (Group 3 Sceptre Stakes) and US Law (Group 3 Prix Thomas Bryon). Ballylinch Stud, Ireland. *2015 fee:* €25,000.

LE HAVRE (2006) Noverre – Marie Rheinberg (Surako). *Racing record:* Won 4 races including the Group 1 10.5f French Derby. *Stud record:* Sire of the winners of 100 races including the dual Group1 and classic winner Avenir Certain (French 1,000 Guineas and French Oaks), the Group 2 Prix Chaudenay winner Auvray, the 2-y-o Group 3 Prix du Calvados winner Queen Bee and four French listed winners. Standing at Haras de la Cauviniere in France. *2015 fee:* €20,000.

LEMON DROP KID (1996) Kingmambo – Charming Lassie (Seattle Slew). *Racing record:*

Won the Belmont Stakes, Whitney Handicap and Woodward Stakes (all Grade 1 events). *Stud record:* Best performers to date include the US Grade 1 winners Richard's Kid, Santa Teresita, Christmas Kid, Cittronade, Somali Lemonade and Lemon's Forever and eleven Group/Grade 2 winners (Bronze Cannon, Balance The Books, Bear's Kid, Charitable Man, Dreamy Kid, Hangover Kid, It's A Knockout, Juniper Pass, Pisco Sour, Sparkling Review and Wilkinson). Standing at Lane's End Farm, Kentucky. *2015 fee:* $40,000.

LILBOURNE LAD (2009) Acclamation – Sogno Verde (Green Desert). *Racing record:* Won 3 races including the Group 2 Railway Stakes. Raced only at 2 yrs. *Stud record:* His first crop are now two-year-olds. Standing at Rathbarry Stud in Ireland. *2015 fee:* €7,500.

LOPE DE VEGA (2007) Shamardal – Lady Vettori (Vettori). *Racing record:* Won four races from 7f (at 2 yrs) to 11f including the Group 1 French Derby and the Group 1 French 2,000 Guineas. *Stud record:* His first crop were 2-y-o's in 2014. He had an excellent start at stud with the winners of 38 races, notably the Group 1 Dewhurst Stakes winner Belardo and the Group winners Burnt Sugar and Hero Look. Standing at Ballylinch Stud, Ireland. *2015 fee:* €40,000.

LORD SHANAKILL (2006) Speightstown – Green Room (Theatrical). *Racing record:* Won five races from 6f to 1m and from 2 to 4 yrs including the Group 1 Prix Jean Prat, the Group 2 Mill Reef Stakes (at 2 yrs) and the Group 2 Lennox Stakes (Betfair Cup), and second in the Group 1 Dewhurst Stakes. *Stud record:* His first runners appeared in 2014 and he had the winners of 21 races, plus a listed-placed in Italy. Standing at the Irish National Stud. *2015 fee:* €5,000.

MAKFI (2007) Dubawi – Dhelaal (Green Desert). *Racing record:* Won four races, notably the 2,000 Guineas and Prix Jacques le Marois. *Stud record:* His first runners appeared in 2014 and to date he's had the winners of 28 races including the Australian Group 3 winner Marky Mark, the French listed winner Cornwallville and the Group 3 Oh So Sharp Stakes second Astrelle. Standing at Haras de Bonneval. *2015 fee:* €17,500.

MANDURO (2002) Monsun – Mandellicht (Be My Guest). *Racing record:* Won the Group 1 1m Prix Jacques Le Marois, the Group 1 10f Prince of Wales's Stakes and Group 1 10f Prix d'Ispahan. *Stud record:* His first runners appeared in 2011. To date his best runners are Mandaean (Group 1 Criterium de Saint Cloud), Charity Line (Group 1 Premio Lydia Tesio), Bonfire (Group 2 Dante Stakes), Ribbons (Group 1 Prix Jean Romanet), Fractional (Group 2 Prix Dollar), Kolonel (Group 3 Prix de Seine-et-Oise), Trois Lunes (Group 3 Prix Vanteaux), the German Group 3 winner Meerjungfrau and eight listed winners. Standing at Haras du Logis, France. *2015 fee:* €7,000.

MASTERCRAFTSMAN (2006) Danehill Dancer – Starlight Dreams (Black Tie Affair). *Racing record:* Won 7 races, notably the Phoenix Stakes, National Stakes, St James's Palace Stakes and Irish 2,000 Guineas (all Group 1 races). *Stud record:* His first Two Year Olds appeared in 2013 and he was the leading European first-crop sire with 28 winners. The best of his winners to date are The Grey Gatsby (Group 1 French Derby and Group 1 Irish Champion Stakes), Kingston Hill (Group 1 Racing Post Trophy and Group 1 St Leger), New Zealand Group 2 winner Thunder Lady, six Group 3 winners including Amazing Maria (Prestige Stakes) and Craftsman (Killavullan Stakes), and two Listed winners. Standing at Coolmore Stud, Ireland. *2015 fee:* €40,000.

MAWATHEEQ (2005) Danzig – Sarayir (Mr Prospector). *Racing record:* Won four races 1m to 12f including the Group 3 Cumberland Lodge Stakes and second in the Group 1 Champion Stakes. *Stud record:* Had his first runners last year. Just 4 winners to date. Standing at Nunnery Stud. *2015 fee:* Private.

MEDAGLIA D'ORO (1999) El Prado – Cappucino Bay (Bailjumper). *Racing record:* Won the Travers Stakes, Jim Dandy Stakes and San Felipe Stakes. *Stud record:* Best winners include the US champion Rachel Alexandra (five Grade 1 wins) and the Group/Grade 1 winners C. S. Silk, Champagne d'Oro, Gabby's Golden Gal, Passion For Gold, Marketing Mix, Mshawish, Plum Pretty, Violence and Warrior's Reward. Standing at Jonabell Farm, Kentucky. *2015 fee:* $125,000.

MEDICEAN (1997) Machiavellian – Mystic Goddess (Storm Bird). *Racing record:* 6 wins including the Lockinge Stakes and Eclipse. *Stud record:* First runners in 2005. Sire of very smart Dutch Art (Prix Morny, Middle Park), the smart performer Nannina (Fillies' Mile, Coronation Stakes), Capponi and Al Shemali (both Dubai Group 1 winners), the very smart miler Bankable (Dubai Group 2 and Group 3 winners), Siyouma (Group 1 Sun Chariot Stakes and Group 1 E P Taylor Stakes), Almerita (Group 1 German Oaks), Chevron (Group 1 Raffles International Cup), Bayrir (Grade 1 Secretariat Stakes), Hong Kong Group 1 winner Mr Medici, the Group 2 British Champions Fillies and Mares Stakes Sapphire, the Group 2 Blandford Stakes winner Manieree and the Group 3 and triple listed winner Mince. Standing at Cheveley Park Stud. *2015 fee:* £8,000.

MONTJEU (1996) Sadler's Wells – Floripedes (Top Ville). *Racing record:* Won 11 races including the Prix de l'Arc de Triomphe and King George VI and Queen Elizabeth Diamond Stakes. *Stud record:* First runners in 2004. A top-class stallion son of Sadler's Wells. Sire of the top-class Hurricane Run (Irish Derby, Prix de l'Arc de Triomphe, Tattersalls Gold Cup and King George), Authorized (Racing Post Trophy, Derby & Juddmonte International), Motivator (Racing Post Trophy and Derby), Camelot (four Group 1's including the 2,000 Guineas and Derby), Pour Moi (Derby) and Fame And Glory (Racing Post Trophy, Irish Derby, Ascot Gold Cup), St Nicholas Abbey (five Group 1 wins), Masked Marvel (St Leger) and the high-class Alessandro Volta, Frozen Fire, Honolulu, Jan Vermeer Corre Caminos, Jukebox Jury, Macarthur, Montmartre, Papal Bull and Scorpion. Died in 2012.

MORE THAN READY (1997) Southern Halo – Woodman's Girl (Woodman). *Racing record:* Won 7 races in the USA including the Grade 1 7f King's Bishop Stakes and the 2-y-o Grade 2 6f Sanford Stakes. *Stud record:* Sire of 59 Group/Graded stakes winners including 15 Grade 1 winners – Buster's Ready, Carry On Cutie, Daredevil, Regally Ready, Room Service, Verrazano (all in North America), Benicio, Dreamaway, Gimmethegreenlight, More Joyous, More Than Sacred, Perfectly Ready, Phelan Ready, Samaready and Sebring (all in Australia/New Zealand). Standing at WinStar Farm, Kentucky. *2015 fee:* $50,000.

MOUNT NELSON (2004) Rock of Gibraltar – Independence (Selkirk). *Racing record:* Won the Group 1 1m Criterium International at 2 yrs and the Group 1 10f Eclipse Stakes. *Stud Record:* His first two-year-olds ran in 2012 and to date he's had the Group 2 Royal Lodge Stakes winner Berkshire, the Group 3 Prix du Calvados winner Purr Along, Group 3 Chartwell Stakes winner Emerald Star and the listed winners Ninjago, Mohave Princess, Special Meaning and Volume to his name. Standing at Newsells Park Stud, Herts. *2015 fee:* £6,000.

MYBOYCHARLIE (2005) Danetime – Dulceata (Rousillon). *Racing record:* Won the Group 1 6f Prix Morny and the Group 3 6f Anglesey Stakes, both at 2 yrs. *Stud record:* The Australian Group 1 winner Peggy Jean, US Grade 1 Beverly D Stakes winner Euro Charlene, Australian Group 2 6f winner Charlie Boy and the New Zealand Group 2 second Charlestown are his first major hits as a sire. In Europe with his first two-year-olds in 2013 he had the French listed 1m winner Salai. Standing at Haras du Mezeray. *2015 fee:* €5,000.

NAYEF (1999) Gulch – Height of Fashion (Bustino). *Racing record:* Won 9 races including the Champion Stakes and the Juddmonte International Stakes. *Stud record:* His first crop were two-year-olds in 2007 and his best winners so far are Tamayuz (dual Group 1 winner in France), Lady Marian (Group 1 Prix de l'Opera), Spacious (dual Group 2 winner and 1,000 Guineas second), Tasaday (Group 2 Prix de la Nonette), Valirann (Group 2 Prix Chaudenay) and the Group 3 winners Confront (Joel Stakes), Hawaafez (Cumberland Lodge Stakes), Mustajeeb (Amethyst Stakes and Jersey Stakes), Sparkling Beam (Prix Chloe), Tabassum (Oh So Sharp Stakes) and Snow Sky (Gordon Stakes). Standing at Nunnery Stud, Norfolk. *2015 fee:* £5,000.

NEW APPROACH (2005) Galileo – Park Express (Ahonoora). *Racing record:* Won five Group 1 events including the Derby, the Champion Stakes and the Irish Champion Stakes. *Stud record:* First two year olds appeared in 2012. Sire of the champion 2-y-o Dawn Approach (Dewhurst Stakes, National Stakes, 2,000 Guineas, St James's Palace Stakes), Talent (Group 1 Epsom Oaks), May's Dream (Group 1 Australasian Oaks), Sultanina (Group 1 Nassau Stakes), Libertarian (Group 2 Dante Stakes) and the Group 3 winners Cap O'Rushes (Gordon Stakes), Elliptique (Prix Chloe), Newfangled (Albany Stakes), Montsegure and Gamblin' Guru (both in Australia). Standing at: Dalham Hall Stud, Newmarket. 2014 stud fee: £80,000.

NOTNOWCATO (2002) Inchinor – Rambling Rose (Cadeaux Genereux). *Racing record:* Won 7 races including the Group 1 10f Eclipse Stakes, the Group 1 10.5f Tattersalls Gold Cup and the Group 1 Juddmonte International. *Stud record:* His first runners came in 2010. Sire of around 30 winners in four years including the Group 3 Gladness Stakes winner Custom Cut, the listed winner and Group 2 placed Chil The Kite, the listed winner Waila and the US dual Grade 3 placed Miss Cato. Standing at Knockhouse Stud in Ireland. *2015 fee:* Private.

OASIS DREAM (2001) Green Desert – Hope (Dancing Brave). *Racing record:* Won 4 races, including the Middle Park Stakes, July Cup and Nunthorpe Stakes (all Group 1 events). *Stud record:* His first crop were two-year-olds in 2007 and he's built himself an outstanding reputation. His twelve Group 1 winners are Aqlaam (Prix du Moulin), Arcano (Prix Morny), Charming Thought (Middle Park Stakes), Jwala (Nunthorpe Stakes), Lady Jane Digby (in Germany), Midday (six Group/Grade One's including the Nassau Stakes, Prix Vermeille and Breeders Cup Filly & Mare Turf), Naaqoos (Prix Jean-Luc Lagardere), Opiniong (in Australia), Power (National Stakes & Irish 2,000 Guineas), Prohibit (King's Stand Stakes), Querari (in Italy) and Tuscan Evening (US Gamely Handicap). His 13 Group 2 scorers include Approve, Frozen Power, Hard Dream, Misheer, Monitor Closely, Peace At Last, Quiet Oasis (in USA), Showcasing, Sri Putra and Welwitschia (South Africa). Standing at Banstead Manor Stud, Newmarket. *2015 fee:* £75,000.

PACO BOY (2005) Desert Style – Tappen Zee (Sandhurst Prince). *Racing record:* Won 10 races from 6f to 1m including the Group

1 Prix de la Foret, Queen Anne Stakes and Lockinge Stakes. *Stud record:* Had his first 2-y-o's in 2014 and had a good start with the Group 2 Flying Childers winner Beacon, the Group 3 Horris Hill winner Smaih and the listed winner Lexington Times. Standing at Highclere Stud. *2015 fee:* £9,000.

PASTORAL PURSUITS (2001) Bahamian Bounty – Star (Most Welcome). *Racing record:* Won 6 races including the Group 1 6f July Cup, Group 2 7f Park Stakes and Group 3 6f Sirenia Stakes. *Stud record:* His first crop appeared as 2-y-o's in 2009 and his best winners to date are Pastoral Player (Group 3 John of Gaunt Stakes), Rose Blossom (Group 3 Summer Stakes), the listed winners Angel's Pursuit, Marine Commando, Terra Di Tuffi (in Italy) and Ventura Mist, and the triple Group 3 placed Sagramor. Standing at the National Stud. *2015 fee:* £4,000.

PIVOTAL (1993) Polar Falcon – Fearless Revival (Cozzene). *Racing record:* 4 wins including the Nunthorpe Stakes and King's Stand Stakes. *Stud record:* First runners in 2000. An outstanding sire whose best winners include the Excellent Art (St James's Palace Stakes), Falco (French 2,000 Guineas), Farhh (Champion Stakes), Golden Apples (triple US Grade 1 winner), Halfway To Heaven (Irish 1,00 Guineas, Nassau Stakes and Sun Chariot Stakes), Immortal Verse (dual Group 1 winning miler), Kyllachy (Nunthorpe Stakes), Regal Parade (Haydock Sprint Cup), Sariska (Oaks and Irish Oaks) and Somnus (Sprint Cup, Prix de la Foret, Prix Maurice de Gheest). Other top performers of his include Beauty Is Truth (Group 2 Prix du Chene), Captain Rio (Group 2 Criterium des Maisons-Laffitte), Chorist (Group 1 Pretty Polly Stakes), Izzi Top (Prix Jean Romanet and Pretty Polly Stakes), Leo (Group 2 Royal Lodge Stakes), Megahertz (two US Grade 1 events), Peeress (Lockinge Stakes, Sun Chariot Stakes), Pivotal Point (Group 2 Diadem Stakes), Saoire (Irish 1000 Guineas), Silvester Lady (German Oaks), Virtual (Lockinge Stakes) and Siyouni (2-y-o Group 1 Prix Jean-Luc Lagardere). Standing at Cheveley Park Stud, Newmarket. *2015 fee:* £45,000.

POET'S VOICE (2007) Dubawi – Bright Tiara (Chief's Crown). *Racing record:* Won 4 races over 7f and a mile, and at 2 and 3 yrs, notably the Group 1 Queen Elizabeth II Stakes, the Group 2 Champagne Stakes (at 2 yrs) and the Group 2 Celebration Mile. *Stud record:* His first crop are now two-year-olds. Standing at Dalham Hall Stud in Newmarket. *2015 fee:* £12,000.

POUR MOI (2008) Montjeu – Gwynn (Darshaan). *Racing record:* Won 3 races, notably the Epsom Derby and the Group 2 10f Prix Greffulhe. *Stud record:* His first crop are now two-year-olds. Standing at Coolmore Stud in Ireland. *2015 fee:* €12,500.

RAIL LINK (2003) Dansili – Docklands (Theatrical). *Racing record:* Won seven races including the Prix de L'Arc de Triomphe, Prix Niel, Grand Prix de Paris and Prix du Lys. *Stud record:* His first runners appeared in 2011 and his best to date are Spillway (Group 1 10f in Australia), Epicuris (2-y-o Group 1 10f Criterium de Saint-Cloud), Bugie d'Amor (Group 3 Premio Dormello), Last Train (Group 3 Prix de Barbeville and second in the Group 1 Grand Prix de Paris), Sediciosa (Group 3 Prix de Royaumont), the listed winner and Group 1 Gran Premio di Milano second Wild Wolf and the listed winners Destruct and Trip To Rhodos. Standing at Haras National de Cercy La Tour. *2015 fee:* €2,800.

RAVEN'S PASS (2005) Elusive Quality – Ascutney (Lord At War). *Racing record:* Won 6 races, notably the Group 1 1m Queen Elizabeth II Stakes and the Grade 1 10f Breeders Cup Classic. *Stud record:* His first crop of two-year-olds appeared in 2012 and his best winners to date are Steeler (Group 2 Royal Lodge Stakes winner and Group 1 Racing Post Trophy second), the Group 3 Prestige Sakes winner Malabar, the Group 3 Cumberland Lodge Stakes winner Secret Number, the listed winners Alonsoa, Alta Stima, Lovely Pass, Redbrook and Richard Pankhurst, and the Group 2 placed Mutashaded. Standing at Kildangan Stud, Ireland. *2015 fee:* €20,000.

RIP VAN WINKLE (2006) Galileo – Looking Back (Stravinsky). *Racing record:* Won five races from 7f (at 2 yrs) to 10f including the Group 1 Sussex Stakes, Queen Elizabeth II Stakes and Juddmonte International. *Stud record:* His first 2-y-o's ran in 2014 and amongst them were the Group 1 Phoenix

Stakes winner Dick Whittington, the Group 3 winners I Am Beautiful and Magic Dancer (in New Zealand), the French listed winner Princess Charm and the Group 3 placed Jeanne Girl. Standing at Coolmore Stud, Ireland. *2015 fee:* €25,000.

ROCK OF GIBRALTAR (1999) Danehill – Offshore Boom (Be My Guest). *Racing record:* Won seven Group 1 races including the Dewhurst Stakes, 2,000 Guineas, St James's Palace Stakes and Sussex Stakes. *Stud record:* The sire of eleven Group 1 winners including the US dual Grade 1 winner Diamondrella, Eagle Mountain (in Hong Kong), Mount Nelson (Eclipse and Criterium International), Samitar (Irish 1,000 Guineas and Garden City Stakes), Prince Gibraltar (Criterium de Saint-Cloud), dual Group 1 winning sprinter Society Rock and Varenar (Prix de la Foret) as well as around 50 other Group winners. Standing at Coolmore Stud, Ireland. *2015 fee:* €12,500.

RODERIC O'CONNOR (2008) Galileo – Secret Garden (Danehill). *Racing record:* Won 3 races, notably the Group 1 1m Grand Criterium (at 2 yrs) and the Group 1 Irish 2,000 Guineas. *Stud record:* His first crop are now two-year-olds. Standing at Ballyhane Stud in Ireland. *2015 fee:* €7,500.

ROYAL APPLAUSE (1993) Waajib – Flying Melody (Auction Ring). *Racing record:* Winner of 9 races, including Middle Park at 2 yrs and the Haydock Park Sprint Cup at 4 yrs (both Group 1). *Stud record:* First runners in 2001. Sire of the US dual Grade 1 winner Ticker Tape, the Group/Grade 2 winners Acclamation, Battle Of Hastings, Finjaan, Lovelace, Mister Cosmi, Nevisian Lad, Please Sing and Whatsthescript and numerous other very smart performers including Crime Scene, triple Group 3 winner Majestic Missile, Peak To Creek and Prince Siegfried. Standing at The Royal Studs, Norfolk. *2015 fee:* Private.

SAKHEE'S SECRET (2004) Sakhee – Palace Street (Secreto). *Racing record:* Won 5 races over 6f notably the Group 1 July Cup. *Stud record:* His first crop of 2-y-o's appeared in 2012. Sire of the New Zealand Group 1 10f winner Sakhee's Soldier, Italian Group 3 winner Salford Secret and the listed winners Thunder Strike and Cryptic (NZ). Standing in Italy. *2015 fee:* Private.

SCAT DADDY (2004) Johannesburg – Love Style (Mr Prospector). *Racing record:* Won four Graded Stakes from 6f to 9f and at 2 and 3 yrs notably the Grade 1 Champagne Stakes (at 2 yrs) and the Grade 1 Florida Derby. *Stud record:* His best winners to date include No Nay Never (Group 1 Morny and Group 2 Norfolk Stakes), Daddy Long Legs (Group 2 Royal Lodge Stakes), US dual Grade 1 winner Lady Of Shamrock, US Grade 2 and Grade 3 winner Handsome Mike, US 2-y-o Grade 2 winner El Kabeir, US triple Grade 3 winner Daddy Nose Best and two Grade 1 winners in Chile. Standing at Ashford Stud, Kentucky. Stud fee: $35,000.

SEA THE STARS (2006) Cape Cross – Urban Sea (Miswaki). *Racing record:* Outstanding winner of 9 races including the Derby, 2,000 Guineas, Prix de L'Arc de Triomphe, Irish Champion Stakes, Juddmonte International Stakes and Eclipse Stakes. *Stud record:* His first two-year-olds appeared in 2013 and he's already had three Group 1 winners to his name – Taghrooda (Oaks and King George VI), Sea The Moon (German Derby) and Vazira (Prix Saint-Alary, along with the Group 3 winners Afternoon Sunshine, My Titania and Zarshana, five listed winners and the Group 1 French Derby second Shamkiyr. Standing at Gilltown Stud, Ireland. Stud fee: €125,000.

SHAMARDAL (2002) Giant's Causeway – Helsinki (Machiavellian). *Racing record:* Won the Dewhurst Stakes, French 2,000 Guineas, French Derby and St James's Palace Stakes (all Group 1 events). *Stud record:* Has sired 13 Group 1 winners from his first five crops – Able Friend (three Group 1's in Hong Kong), Baltic Baroness (Prix Vermeille), Casamento (Racing Post Trophy), Lope De Vega (French 2,000 Guineas and French Derby), Mukhadram (Eclipse Stakes), Sagawara (Prix Saint-Alary), Dunboyne Express (renamed 'Dan Excel' in Hong Kong), three in Australia and three in Italy. His 25 Group 2/Group 3 winners include the Group 1 placed Fintry, Ihtimal, Mukhadram, Elle Shadow (Germany), No Evidence Needed and Puissance de Lune (both in Australia). Standing at Kildangan Stud, Ireland. *2015 fee:* €70,000.

SHIROCCO (2001) Monsun – So Sedulous (The Minstrel). *Racing record:* Won 7 races including the German Derby, French Derby, Breeders Cup Turf and Coronation Cup (all Group 1, 12f events). *Stud record:* Has had five crops racing so far and his best winners include Brown Panther (Group 1 Irish St Leger), the Brazilian Group 1 winners January Jones and Calendula, Grand Vent (Group 2 Prix Noailles), Arrigo (Group 2 Oppenheim Union Rennen), Wild Coco (Group 2 Park Hill Stakes), Abu Sidra (Group 3 Prix du Ris-Orangis), Hartani (Group 3 Curragh Cup), Ibicenco (Group 3 Geelong Cup in Australia), Born To Run (German Group 3) and the Group 1 placed Shirocco Star. Now a dual-purpose stallion, standing at Glenview Stud in Ireland. *2015 fee:* Private.

SHOWCASING (2007) Oasis Dream – Arabesque (Zafonic). *Racing record:* Won 2 races at 2 yrs including the Group 2 6f Gimcrack Stakes. *Stud record:* Had an excellent start with his first runners in 2014 with 25 individual winners including Toocoolforschool (Group 2 Mill Reef Stakes), Showbay (Group 2 in New Zealand), Cappella Sansevero (Group 3 Round Tower Stakes winner and Group 1 third) and the listed winners Accipiter and Hardline (in New Zealand). Standing at Whitsbury Manor Stud. *2015 fee:* £15,000.

SIR PERCY (2003) Mark of Esteem – Percy's Lass (Blakeney). *Racing record:* Won the Derby and the Dewhurst Stakes. *Stud record:* His first runners appeared in 2011. Sire of 4 Group winners Sir Andrew (Group 2 in New Zealand), Alla Speranza (Group 3 Kilternan Stakes), Lady Pimpernel (US Grade 3) and Wake Forest (German Group 3) and 6 listed winners the Group 2 Royal Lodge Stakes second Nafaqa. Standing at Lanwades Stud, Newmarket. *2015 fee:* £7,000.

SIXTIES ICON (2003) Galileo – Love Divine (Diesis). *Racing record:* Won 8 races including the Group 1 St Leger, the Group 2 Jockey Club Cup and four Group events. *Stud Record:* His first two year olds appeared in 2012 and his best winners to date include Chilworth Icon (Group 3 Premio Primi Passi & listed Woodcote Stakes), the listed winners Audacia and Cruck Realta, and the listed-placed Effie B. Sire of the winners of 66 races to March 2015. Standing at Norman Court Stud, Wiltshire. 2014 stud fee: £6,000.

SMART STRIKE (1992) Mr Prospector – Classy 'n Smart (Smarten). *Racing record:* Won 8 races in the USA including the Grade 2 8.5f Philip H Iselin Handicap and the Grade 3 Salvator Mile. *Stud record:* 56 Group winners including the top-class colt Curlin (Preakness Stakes, Dubai World Cup, Breeders Cup Classic), the US Grade 1 winners Centre Court, English Channel, Fabulous Strike, Furthest Land, Lookin At Lucky, My Miss Aurelia, Never Retreat, Shadow Cast, Soaring Free, Square Eddie, Streaming and Swagger Jack and the Japan Cup winner Fleetstreet Dancer. Standing at Lane's End Farm, Kentucky. *2015 fee:* €100,000.

SPEIGHTSTOWN (1998) Gone West – Silken Cat (Storm Cat). *Racing record:* Won 4 races in the USA including the Grade 1 Breeders Cup Sprint (as a 6-y-o) and two Grade 2 events - all over six furlongs. *Stud record:* Sire of 27 Group/Graded stakes winners including 10 Group/Grade 1 winners - Lord Shanakill (Prix Jean Prat), Dance To Bristol, Golden Ticket, Haynesfield, Jersey Town, Lighthouse Bay, Mona de Momma, Poseidon's Warrior, Seek Again (all in the USA), Reynaldothewizard (in Dubai) and She's Happy (in Argentina). Standing at WinStar Farm, Kentucky. 2015 stud fee: $80,000Y.

STARSPANGLEDBANNER (2006) Choisir – Gold Anthem (Made Of Gold). *Racing record:* Won two Group 1's in Australia over 6f and 1m, the Group 1 6f Golden Jubilee Stakes and the Group 1 6f July Cup. *Stud record:* Had his first runners in 2014. Sire of the Group 1 Prix Morny winner The Wow Signal, the Group 2 Queen Mary winner Anthem Alexander and the Australian Group 3 winner Of The Brave. Standing at Coolmore Stud, Ireland. *2015 fee:* €25,000.

STREET CRY (1998) Machiavellian – Helen Street (Troy). *Racing record:* 5 wins including the Group 1 10f Dubai World Cup and the US Grade 1 9f Stephen Foster Handicap. *Stud record:* First runners in 2006. Sire of the outstanding multiple Grade 1 winning racemare Zenyatta and the Group/Grade 1 winners Street Sense (Breeders' Cup Juvenile, Kentucky Derby, Travers Stakes), Cry And Catch Me (Oak Leaf Stakes), Majestic Roi (Sun Chariot Stakes), Street Boss (Triple Bend Invitational, Bing Crosby Handicap), Seventh

Street (Go For Wand Handicap, Apple Blossom Handicap), Street Hero (Norfolk Stakes), Here Comes Ben (Forego Handicap), Victor's Cry (Shoemaker Mile Handicap), Street Hero (Norfolk Stakes), Zaidan (Hong Kong Classic Cup) and the Australian Group 1 winners Shocking (Melbourne Cup) and Whobegotyou (Caulfield Guineas and Yalumba Stakes). Also, the Group 2 Dante Stakes winner Carlton House, the Ribblesdale Stakes winner Princess Highway and Group 2 Champagne Stakes winner Saamidd. Died in 2014.

TAGULA (1993) Taufan – Twin Island (Standaan). *Racing record:* Won 4 races including the Group 1 6f Prix Morny (at 2 yrs) and the Group 3 7f Supreme Stakes. *Stud record:* Sires plenty of winners, amongst the best being the high-class 2-y-o and miler Canford Cliffs, the Group 2 Prix du Gros-Chene winner Tax Free, the Group 2 Royal Lodge Stakes winner Atlantis Prince, the German Group 2 winner Tagshira, the smart Group 2 placed Beaver Patrol and the listed winners Bakewell Tart, Double Vie, Drawnfromthepast, King Orchisios, Limato, Macaroon, Pure Poetry and Red Millennium. Standing at Rathbarry Stud in Ireland. *2015 fee:* €4,000.

TAMAYUZ (2005) Nayef – Al Ishq (Nureyev). *Racing record:* Won the Group 1 1m Prix Jacques Le Marois and the Group 1 Prix Jean Prat. *Stud Record:* His first two year olds appeared in 2012. He's had a very good start with winners like G Force (Group 1 Haydock Park Sprint), Sir Prancealot (Group 2 Flying Childers Stakes), Group 3 Molecomb Stakes winner Brown Sugar, Japanese Group 3 winner Meiner Eternel, Group 3 Prix de Ris-Orangis winner Thawaany and the listed winners Best Regards, Ighraa and Royal Spring. Standing at Derrinstown Stud in Ireland. *2015 fee:* €15,000.

TEOFILO (2004) Galileo – Speirbhhean (Danehill). *Racing record:* Won 5 races at 2 yrs including the Group 1 Dewhurst Stakes and the Group 1 National Stakes. *Stud record:* First runners 2011. Six Group 1 winners so far – Parish Hall (Dewhurst Stakes), Havana Gold (Prix Jean Prat), Loch Garman (Criterium International), Trading Leather (Irish Derby), Sonntag (in Australia) and Voleuse De

Coeurs (Irish St Leger), plus the US Grade 2 winner Amira's Prince, Light Heavy (Group 2 Derrinstown Stud Derby Trial), Tarfasha (Group 2 Blandford Stakes), and the Group 3 winners Amralah, Fate, Kermadec (in New Zealand), Remember Alexander, Royal Empire, Samba Brazil and Tobann. Standing at Kildangan Stud, Ireland. *2015 fee:* €50,000.

THEWAYYOUARE (2005) Kingmambo – Maryinski (Sadler's Wells). *Racing record:* Won four races in France including the Group 1 1m Criterium International and the Group 3 1m Prix Thomas Bryon. *Stud record:* Sire of the high-class Group 2 UAE Derby winner and Grade 1 Breeders Cup Classic second Toast Of New York, the Peruvian Grade 3 winner El Jader and two listed winners in New Zealand. Standing at Coolmore Stud in Ireland. *2015 fee:* €5,000.

VALE OF YORK (2007) Invincible Spirit – Red Vale (Halling). *Racing record:* Won 3 races including the Grade 1 9f Breeders Cup Juvenile and the listed 7f Stardom Stakes and second in the Group 1 1m Gran Criterium (all at 2 yrs). *Stud record:* Had his first 2-y-o runners in 2014. To date (March 2015) he's the sire of the winners of 30 races including the Italian dual Group 3 and dual listed winner Fontanelice and the fairly useful sprint winner Haxby. Standing at Kildangan Stud in Ireland. *2015 fee:* €3,000.

WAR FRONT (2003) Danzig – Starry Dreamer (Rubiano). *Racing record:* Won four races at 3 and 4 yrs including the Grade 2 6f Alfred G Vanderbilt Breeders Cup Handicap at Saratoga. *Stud record:* Had an excellent start at stud and in his first four crops he has sired six Group 1/Grade 1 winners – Data Link (Maker's 46 Mile Stakes), Declaration Of War (Juddmonte International, Queen Anne Stakes), Peace And War (Alcibiades Stakes), Summer Soiree (Del Mar Oaks), The Factor (Malibu Stakes & Pat O'Brien Stakes) and War Command (Dewhurst Stakes), along with eight Group/Grade 2 winners – Bashart, Departing, Lines Of Battle, Pontchatrain, Soldat, State Of Play, Summer Front and War Dancer. Standing at Claiborne Farm, Kentucky. *2015 fee:* $150,000.

ZAMINDAR (1994) Gone West – Zaizafon (The Minstrel). *Racing record:* Won the Group 3 6f Prix de Cabourg at 2 yrs and was placed in the Prix Morny and the Prix de la Salamandre. *Stud record:* A full-brother to the champion Zafonic. He has sired a number of very good fillies, notably the outstanding Zarkava (five Group 1 wins including the Prix de l'Arc de Triomphe), Darjina (three Group 1 wins), the Group 1 Prix Saint-Alary winner Coquerelle, the Group 1 Falmouth Stakes winner Timepiece and the Group 1 French 1,000 Guineas winner Zenda. He also has the Group 2 winners Crossharbour and Modern Look, as well as the Group 3 winners Jubilation, So Beautiful, Starboard and Zantenda. Retired from stud.

ZEBEDEE (2008) Invincible Spirit – Cozy Maria (Cozzene). *Racing record:* Won 6 races over 5f and 6f as a 2-y-o including the Group 2 Flying Childers Stakes, the Group 3 Molecomb Stakes and the listed Dragon Stakes. *Stud record:* Had his first runners last season and he had an excellent start, particularly with the dual Group 2 winner Ivawood and the Group 3 placed Parsley. Sire of the winners of 57 races to date (6th April 2015). Standing at Tally Ho Stud in Ireland. *2015 fee:* €10,000.

ZOFFANY (2008) Dansili – Tyranny (Machiavellian). *Racing record:* Won 5 races as a 2-y-o including the Group 1 6f Phoenix Stakes and the Group 3 7f Tyros Stakes. *Stud record:* His first crop are now two-year-olds. Standing at Coolmore Stud in Ireland. *2015 fee:* €12,500.

Sires Index

Champs Elysees	45, 61, 76, 152, 221, 255, 269, 271, 274, 372, 418, 575, 619, 757, 759, 846, 941, 954, 962, 1044, 1274, 1317, 1400, 1493, 1552
Clodovil	139, 306, 311, 316, 352, 597, 960, 1006, 1283, 1353
Cockney Rebel	1092, 1312
Compton Place	88, 253, 338, 455, 520, 592, 599, 600, 1339, 1432
Congrats	966, 975
Dalakhani	1115, 1304, 1356, 1395
Dalghar	78
Dandy Man	212, 267, 468, 586, 842, 1368, 1504, 1534
Danehill Dancer	43, 100, 101, 146, 336, 399, 473, 779, 1081, 1118, 1269, 1485, 1573, 1585, 1606, 1672
Dansili	96, 199, 348, 371, 422, 528, 641, 643, 645, 663, 699, 739, 789, 1055, 1059, 1508, 1520, 1567, 1666
Dark Angel	27, 87, 103, 182, 216, 242, 279, 298, 406, 445, 453, 460, 500, 517, 555, 582, 610, 670, 672, 691, 705, 799, 821, 833, 853, 863, 872, 892, 958, 959, 1013, 1145, 1187, 1282, 1327, 1376, 1386, 1525, 1530, 1540, 1596, 1661, 1670, 1682
Dashing Blade	67
Deep Impact	1615
Desert Party	624
Dick Turpin	225, 257, 402, 554, 630, 837, 851, 888, 937, 990, 998, 1007, 1149, 1449, 1541
Diktat	401
Discreet Cat	1211
Discreetly Mine	388
Distorted Humor	17, 165, 1453
Dream Ahead	80, 102, 130, 205, 230, 314, 558, 565, 716, 747, 758, 790, 804, 840, 869, 896, 910, 985, 1015, 1261, 1262, 1275, 1461, 1526, 1529, 1607, 1620, 1633, 1634, 1662
Drosselmeyer	1501
Dubawi	10, 12, 14, 22, 168, 170, 172, 178, 179, 576, 611, 649, 660, 668, 684, 729, 919, 920, 922, 950, 1472, 1512, 1518, 1566, 1598, 1655, 1681
Duke Of Marmalade	71, 136, 434, 712, 1002, 1157, 1183, 1379, 1630
Dutch Art	68, 109, 119, 125, 223, 349, 465, 525, 544, 547, 579, 589, 664, 692, 749, 782, 859, 961, 982, 1116, 1198, 1323, 1382, 1402, 1490, 1509
Dylan Thomas	75
Elnadim	400, 451, 856, 928, 936, 1373
Elusive City	635, 711, 989, 1466
Elusive Pimpernel	826, 849, 895, 1321
Elusive Quality	19, 1328
Equiano	117, 239, 250, 345, 574, 914, 947, 1041, 1078, 1085, 1091, 1103, 1174, 1176, 1181, 1349, 1364, 1370, 1424, 1444, 1533, 1553, 1616, 1627
Eskendereya	1199

Kitten's Joy	7, 24, 1032
Kodiac	90, 93, 106, 124, 127, 260, 275, 390, 407, 430, 450, 466, 501, 503, 506, 521, 561, 581, 634, 638, 657, 720, 778, 811, 814, 818, 820, 838, 891, 916, 926, 934, 944, 951, 952, 971, 1040, 1046, 1068, 1069, 1072, 1089, 1113, 1151, 1185, 1202, 1266, 1284, 1310, 1322, 1430, 1440, 1468, 1545, 1562, 1563, 1673
Kyllachy	114, 135, 148, 234, 249, 266, 340, 350, 403, 425, 486, 492, 644, 713, 714, 726, 731, 745, 843, 854, 879, 953, 973, 995, 1114, 1182, 1184, 1278, 1535, 1576, 1590, 1599, 1639, 1643, 1652, 1680
Lawman	36, 134, 209, 282, 321, 333, 343, 344, 366, 413, 831, 935, 1003, 1101, 1169, 1172, 1265, 1285, 1319, 1360, 1365, 1378, 1390, 1464, 1515, 1522, 1557, 1601, 1618, 1638, 1679
Le Havre	332, 384, 942, 997
Lemon Drop Kid	673, 1591
Lilbourne Lad	74, 210, 226, 238, 287, 383, 394, 478, 596, 618, 710, 741, 795, 802, 816, 867, 868, 976, 1045, 1087, 1132, 1144, 1158, 1197, 1205, 1270, 1286, 1354, 1423
Lonhro	1021, 1677
Lope De Vega	62, 339, 436, 662, 683, 750, 862, 901, 1088, 1280, 1325, 1341, 1527
Lord Of England	55
Lord Shanakill	159, 416, 476, 1152
Majestic Missile	519
Major Cadeaux	145
Makfi	50, 56, 81, 92, 105, 142, 228, 337, 573, 798, 1180, 1191, 1407, 1452
Malibu Moon	1671
Manduro	65, 233, 272, 771, 1193, 1320, 1399
Mastercraftsman	69, 261, 463, 507, 622, 730, 1030, 1036, 1324, 1332, 1448, 1467, 1474, 1574, 1612
Mawatheeq	1100
Medaglia d'Oro	923
Medicean	147, 256, 259, 280, 300, 331, 627, 902, 913, 921, 1406, 1477, 1554, 1597, 1674
Monsieur Bond	144, 247, 480, 541, 633, 791, 1123, 1433
Montjeu	120, 341, 1240, 1299, 1408, 1621
More Than Ready	23, 1206, 1409
Motivator	201, 303, 629
Mount Nelson	29, 510, 850, 1008, 1194, 1329
Munnings	391
Myboycharlie	1316
Nayef	175, 464, 992, 1359, 1550
New Approach	3, 4, 13, 99, 176, 177, 186, 192, 202, 214, 365, 429, 440, 471, 485, 514, 553, 564, 642, 646, 652, 721, 722, 829, 847, 915, 1459, 1476, 1649
Norse Dancer	570
Notnowcato	264, 307, 396
Oasis Dream	16, 25, 203, 224, 353, 368, 382, 420, 424, 426, 428, 433, 653, 656, 666, 703, 736, 764, 788, 807, 911, 949, 1034, 1060, 1121, 1125, 1214, 1231, 1258,

	1281, 1291, 1309, 1347, 1507, 1594, 1645, 1658, 1675, 1684
Olden Times	1602
Paco Boy	49, 70, 131, 213, 523, 524, 572, 593, 806, 835, 873, 885, 965, 991, 993, 1042, 1156, 1314, 1330, 1578, 1631, 1647
Pastoral Pursuits	158, 443, 499, 591, 1161, 1163, 1623
Phoenix Reach	59
Piccolo	548
Pivotal	193, 367, 419, 421, 432, 484, 605, 674, 785, 880, 1170, 1178, 1294, 1331, 1344, 1398, 1516, 1605
Poet's Voice	6, 40, 52, 149, 162, 169, 184, 222, 231, 232, 265, 389, 531, 532, 583, 623, 655, 669, 697, 725, 740, 887, 933, 1009, 1031, 1093, 1142, 1190, 1311, 1445, 1481, 1519, 1543
Pour Moi	46, 84, 211, 690, 905, 1104, 1179, 1247, 1255, 1307, 1413, 1510, 1641
Quality Road	51
Rail Link 569,	1345
Raven's Pass	31, 73, 89, 281, 526, 540, 702, 770, 773, 784, 945, 978, 1024, 1064, 1122, 1164, 1318, 1334, 1384, 1401, 1664, 1676
Rip Van Winkle	60, 143, 204, 219, 431, 490, 620, 687, 844, 848, 899, 906, 977, 983, 1082, 1195, 1458, 1513, 1582, 1609, 1610
Rock Hard Ten	1352
Rock Of Gibraltar	57, 66, 107, 115, 122, 155, 217, 294, 437, 439, 489, 549, 637, 1340, 1351
Roderic O'Connor	326, 454, 534, 801, 819, 999, 1080, 1134, 1136, 1162, 1168, 1276, 1371, 1410, 1450, 1457, 1580, 1592
Royal Applause	141, 328, 356, 385, 392, 487, 603, 852, 876, 946, 1028, 1062, 1188, 1337, 1355, 1362, 1434, 1549, 1555, 1624
Sakhee's Secret	72, 317, 539, 545, 566, 800, 981, 1175, 1363, 1381, 1421
Scat Daddy	387, 560, 825, 955, 1640
Sea The Stars	118, 377, 435, 477, 678, 680, 698, 737, 777, 882, 1066, 1119, 1293, 1295, 1296, 1298, 1300, 1301, 1302, 1343, 1416, 1456, 1506, 1521, 1523, 1569, 1611, 1665, 1668
Shakespearean	1143
Shamardal	1, 5, 9, 11, 32, 112, 132, 174, 188, 200, 312, 355, 505, 614, 679, 695, 696, 767, 1018, 1019, 1058, 1063, 1109, 1338, 1637, 1657, 1660, 1669
Shirocco	38, 304, 625
Showcasing	26, 108, 244, 246, 360, 408, 488, 578, 615, 752, 1043, 1077, 1137, 1138, 1146, 1212, 1264, 1502, 1575, 1642
Sinndar	1348
Sir Percy	53, 95, 151, 423, 448, 626, 956, 984, 1010, 1061, 1140, 1166, 1167, 1292, 1303, 1392, 1447, 1470, 1471, 1547, 1556, 1558, 1559
Sixties Icon	284, 285, 288, 290, 291, 296, 302, 320, 323, 324, 1196, 1204
Sky Mesa	1050
Slickly	542
Smart Strike	252, 676, 974, 1070
Speightstown	98, 481, 797, 918

Racing Trends

The following tables focus on those two-year-old races that seem to produce winners that improve the following year as three-year-olds. This type of analysis can enable us to select some of the best of this year's classic generation.

In the tables, the figure in the third column indicates the number of wins recorded as a three-year-old, with GW signifying a Group race winner at that age.

The horses listed below are the winners of the featured races in 2014. Three of them (Belardo, Dutch Connection and Tiggy Wiggy) won twice each. Anyone looking for horses to follow in the Group and Classic events of this season might well want to bear them in mind. I feel that those in bold text are particularly worthy of close scrutiny.

Adaay	Belardo (2)
Crafty Choice	**Dutch Connection (2)**
Elm Park	**Estidhkaar**
Gleneagles	**Highland Reel**
Lexington Times	**Lucida**
Maftool	**Ol' Man River**
Snoano	**Tiggy Wiggy (2)**

Lowther Stakes
York, 6 furlongs, August.

2001	Queen's Logic	1 GW
2002	Russian Rhythm	3 GW
2003	Carry On Katie	0
2004	Soar	0
2005	Flashy Wings	0
2006	Silk Blossom	0
2007	Nahoodh	1 GW
2008	Infamous Angel	0
2009	Lady of the Desert	1 GW
2010	Hooray	1
2011	Best Terms	0
2012	Rosdhu Queen	0
2013	Lucky Kristale	0
2014	Tiggy Wiggy	

You have to look back to Russian Rhythm for a filly that had a real impact on the following season's Group 1 events (although Nahoodh did win the Falmouth Stakes) but it remains of race of some importance. The first question about Tiggy Wiggy at the start of the season was "Will she stay the mile of the Guineas". Finishing third in the Fred Darling strongly suggested she won't. Surely she'll be aimed at the inaugural running of the Group 1 Commonwealth Cup over six furlongs at Royal Ascot.

Dewhurst Stakes
Newmarket, 7 furlongs, October.

2001	Rock Of Gibraltar	5 GW
2002	Tout Seul	0
2003	Milk It Mick	0
2004	Shamardal	3 GW
2005	Sir Percy	1 GW
2006	Teofilo	NR
2007	New Approach	3 GW
2008	Intense Focus	0
2009	Beethoven	1 GW
2010	Frankel	5 GW
2011	Parish Hall	0
2012	Dawn Approach	1 GW
2013	War Command	0
2014	Belardo	

The Dewhurst Stakes remains our premier race for two-year-old colts. Frankel proved himself an outstanding champion of course and Rock of Gibraltar was a real star too. Other outstanding colts to win this in the last twenty years are Shamardal, Zafonic, Dr Devious, Grand Lodge, Sir Percy and New Approach. Belardo looks unlikely to prove that good, but I hope he wins another Group race this year for trainer Roger Varian. Some cut in the ground will suit him.

Zetland Stakes
Newmarket, 10 furlongs, October/
November.

2000	Worthily	0
2001	Alexandra Three D	2 GW
2002	Forest Magic	NR
2003	Fun And Games	NR
2004	Ayam Zaman	0
2005	Under The Rainbow	0
2006	Empire Day	NR
2007	Twice Over	2 GW
2008	Heliodor	1
2009	Take It To The Max	0
2010	Indigo Way	NR
2011	Mojave	0
2012	Restraint of Trade	NR
2013	Hartnell	2 GW
2014	Crafty Choice	

Previous winners include the St Leger and Coronation Cup winner Silver Patriarch, the good four-year-olds Double Eclipse and Rock Hopper, Bob's Return (also a St Leger hero), the Ascot Gold Cup winner Double Trigger and of course Twice Over who won four Group 1's during his career with Henry Cecil including as a 6-y-o in 2011. So there's clearly an emphasis on winners of the Zetland improving with age. After winning this race Crafty Choice was fourth in the Group 1 Criterium de Saint-Cloud, but perhaps he'll need to lower his sights to win more races this season.

Cheveley Park Stakes
Newmarket, 6 furlongs, October.

2001	Queen's Logic	1 GW
2002	Airwave	1 GW
2003	Carry On Katie	0
2004	Magical Romance	0
2005	Donna Blini	1
2006	Indian Ink	1 GW
2007	Natagora	2 GW
2008	Serious Attitude	1 GW
2009	Special Duty	2GW
2010	Hooray	1
2011	Lightening Pearl	0
2012	Rosdhu Queen	0
2013	Vorda	0
2014	Tiggy Wiggy	

A number of these fillies have gone on to further Group race success. Indian Ink saved her best day for Royal Ascot, Natagora and Special Duty both went on to win the 1,000 Guineas and Serious Attitude returned to sprinting for another Group race success and the following year she won a Grade 1 sprint in Canada. Tiggy Wiggy can win more races this season over sprint distances.

Denford Stud Stakes (registered as
Washington Singer Stakes) Newbury,
7 furlongs, August.

2001	Funfair Wane	1
2002	Muqbil	1 GW
2003	Haafhd	3 GW
2004	Kings Quay	0
2005	Innocent Air	1
2006	Dubai's Touch	2
2007	Sharp Nephew	1
2008	Cry of Freedom	0
2009	Azmeel	2 GW
2010	Janood	0
2011	Fencing	0
2012	Just The Judge	1 GW
2013	Somewhat	0
2014	Belardo	

This race can often provide us with Group race or Classic pointers and in that regard the 90's winners Lammtarra and Rodrigo de Triano were outstanding and Haafhd won the 2,000 Guineas and the Champion Stakes. Azmeel trained on to win the Sandown Classic Trial and the Dee Stakes, but the race needed a pick-me-up and Just The Judge did that when winning the Irish 1,000 Guineas. Belardo disappointed in the Greenham on Good to Firm ground on his return to action this year. He seems to needs some cut in the ground to be seen at his best.

Veuve Clicquot Vintage Stakes
Goodwood, 7 furlongs, July.

2001	Naheef	1 GW
2002	Dublin	1
2003	Lucky Story	0
2004	Shamardal	3 GW
2005	Sir Percy	1 GW
2006	Strategic Prince	0
2007	Rio De La Plata	0
2008	Orizaba	0
2009	Xtension	0

2010	King Torus	2
2011	Chandlery	0
2012	Olympic Glory	2 GW
2013	Toormore	1 GW
2014	Highland Reel	

All in all this race is very informative in terms of sorting out future stars, with the classic winners Sir Percy, Shamardal, Don't Forget Me, Dr Devious and Mister Baileys, plus the King George hero Petoski being the standouts of the past twenty odd years. Olympic Glory won two more Group 1's as a 4-y-o, so he can certainly be added to that list. Highland Reel, a son of Galileo out of a Danehill mare, looks very promising and sure to win more Group races.

National Stakes, Curragh, 7f, September.		
2001	Hawk Wing	1 GW
2002	Refuse To Bend	3 GW
2003	One Cool Cat	1 GW
2004	Dubawi	2 GW
2005	George Washington	2 GW
2006	Teofilo	NR
2007	New Approach	3 GW
2008	Mastercraftsman	3 GW
2009	Kingsfort	1
2010	Pathfork	0
2011	Power	1 GW
2012	Dawn Approach	1 GW
2013	Toormore	1 GW
2014	Gleneagles	

As one can see by the list of recent winners, this race is as important as any for figuring out the following year's top performers. For instance New Approach was outstanding when winning the Derby, the Champion Stakes and the Irish Champion, Mastercraftsman managed a couple of Group One wins at 3 yrs, and both Power and Dawn Approach notched up Group 1 success as well. Gleneagles was disqualified for interference after winning the Prix Jean-Luc Lagardere, but to me he was the winner on merit. A son of Galileo out of a Storm Cat mare, he'll win more races at the highest level.

Racing Post Trophy		
Doncaster, 8 furlongs, October.		
2001	High Chapparal	5 GW
2002	Brian Boru	1 GW
2003	American Post	3 GW
2004	Motivator	2 GW
2005	Palace Episode	0
2006	Authorized	3 GW
2007	Ibn Khaldun	0
2008	Crowded House	0
2009	St Nicholas Abbey	0
2010	Casamento	1 GW
2011	Camelot	3 GW
2012	Kingsbarns	0
2013	Kingston Hill	1 GW
2014	Elm Park	

Some notable performers have won this race, including the outstanding colt High Chaparral, the Derby heroes Motivator and Authorized (both by Montjeu – also the sire of St Nicholas Abbey) and of course the 2,000 Guineas and Derby hero Camelot. Elm Park will contest the 2,000 Guineas before heading for the Epsom Derby. Middle-distances will suit him and maybe the St Leger trip. It's a long way off, but I can see him having a great chance in the season's final classic.

Haynes, Hanson and Clark Stakes		
Newbury, 8 furlongs, September.		
2001	Fight Your Corner	1 GW
2002	Saturn	0
2003	Elshadi	0
2004	Merchant	NR
2005	Winged Cupid	NR
2006	Teslin	2
2007	Centennial	2 GW
2008	Taameer	0
2009	Ameer	0
2010	Moriarty	0
2011	Cavaleiro	0
2012	Wentworth	1
2013	Pinzolo	1
2014	Snoano	

The high-class horses Rainbow Quest, Unfuwain, King's Theatre and Nayef have all won this race and indeed Shergar won it in 1980, but it's been a while since those glory days although Centennial did manage two Group race wins in 2008. Snoano, a son of Nayef, should stay ten furlongs at least. He'll win again.

Somerville Tattersall Stakes Newmarket, 7 furlongs, September/October.		
2001	Where Or When	2 GW
2002	Governor Brown	NR
2003	Milk It Mick	0
2004	Diktatorial	0
2005	Aussie Rules	2 GW
2006	Thousand Words	0
2007	River Proud	1
2008	Ashram	2
2009	Sir Parky	0
2010	Rerouted	0
2011	Crius	0
2012	Havana Gold	1 GW
2013	Miracle Of Medinah	0
2014	Maftool	

The Group winners speak for themselves but Milk It Mick also went on to win a Grade 1 in America as a five-year-old. Aussie Rules took the French 2,000 Guineas and also won a Grade 1 event in America. Both River Proud and Ashram won listed races in their 3-y-o season and Havana Gold took the Prix Jean Prat over a mile. Maftool disappointed in the Dewhurst, possibly because of the ground. He is a smart colt that should win more races up to a mile.

Rockfel Stakes, 7 furlongs, Newmarket.		
2001	Distant Valley	0
2002	Luvah Girl	1 in USA
2003	Cairns	0
2004	Maids Causeway	1 GW
2005	Speciosa	1 GW
2006	Finsceal Beo	2 GW
2007	Kitty Matcham	0
2008	Lahaleeb	2 GW
2009	Music Show	2 GW
2010	Cape Dollar	0
2011	Wading	0
2012	Just The Judge	1 GW
2013	Al Thakhira	1
2014	Lucida	

Three Newmarket 1,000 Guineas winners have hailed from the winners of this race since 1999 – Lahan, Speciosa and Finsceal Beo. For good measure Maids Causeway won the Coronation Stakes and Hula Angel won the Irish 1,000 Guineas (a race Finsceal Beo also added to her tally). Lahaleeb, Music Show and Just The Judge all went on to record Group 1 success

at 3yrs. Al Thakhira's 3-y-o win came at Listed level. Lucida, a daughter of Shamardal, was unplaced in the Fillies' Mile but she ought to stay that trip. Should win another nice race or two.

Beresford Stakes, Curragh, 1m.		
2001	Castle Gandolfo	1
2002	Alamshar	3 GW
2003	Azamour	2 GW
2004	Albert Hall	0
2005	Septimus	1 GW
2006	Eagle Mountain	1 GW
2007	Curtain Call	1
2008	Sea The Stars	6 GW
2009	St Nicholas Abbey	0
2010	Casamento	1 GW
2011	David Livingston	0
2012	Battle of Marengo	2 GW
2013	Geoffrey Chaucer	0
2014	Ol' Man River	

Aidan O'Brien has taken over from John Oxx (Sea The Stars, Alamshar and Azamour) as the trainer who dominates this race. A son of Montjeu out of the 1,000 Guineas winner Finsceal Beo, Ol' Man River has excellent prospects of winning further good races, maybe a classic, as a 3-y-o.

Acomb Stakes, York, 7 furlongs, August.		
2001	Comfy	NR
2002	Bourbonnais	0
2003	Rule Of Law	2 GW
2004	Elliots World	1
2005	Palace Episode	0
2006	Big Timer	0
2007	Fast Company	0
2008	ABANDONED	
2009	Elusive Pimpernel	1 GW
2010	Waiter's Dream	NR
2011	Entifaadha	0
2012	Dundonnell	1
2013	Treaty Of Paris	NR
2014	Dutch Connection	

There have been a few disappointing seasons since the victories in the 90's of King's Best (2,000 Guineas) and Bijou d'Inde (St James's Palace Stakes), but Rule Of Law turned things around in 2004 with his St Leger victory and Elusive Pimpernel was successful in the Group 3 Craven Stakes. Dutch Connection was third in the National Stakes at the Curragh, enhancing his prospects of winning further races this year at up to a mile.

Two-Year-Old Maiden for Colts Newbury Lockinge Meeting, 6 furlongs, May.		
2001	Amour Sans Fin	0
2002	Cap Ferrat	2
2003	Grand Reward	1
2004	Iceman	0
2005	Championship Point	1
	To Sender	0
2006	Major Cadeaux	1 GW
2007	Coasting	NR
2008	Instalment	1
	Orizaba	0
2009	Canford Cliffs	3 GW
	Meglio Ancora	0
2010	Memen (Div 1)	0
	Strong Suit (Div 11)	3 GW
2011	Wise Venture	0
2012	Sir Patrick Moore	0
2013	Championship	1
2014	Adaay	

One of the season's first six furlong 2-y-o maidens, it regularly attracts a high quality field with plenty of winners going on to future success. Richard Hannon trained winners have regularly gone on to Group success and Canford Cliffs in particular is a standout here. Adaay was unplaced in the Coventry Stakes, but he's a useful colt and can win again at Listed level.

7 furlong 2-y-o maiden at Newmarket's July Meeting (formerly the Strutt & Parker Maiden).		
2001	Dubai Destination	0
2002	Tycoon Hall	0
2003	Josephus	0
2004	Belenus	2 GW
2005	Gin Jockey	0
2006	Kalgoorlie	0
2007	Rio De La Plata	0
2008	Soul City	0

2009	Elusive Pimpernel	1 GW
2010	Native Khan	1 GW
2011	Rougemont	0
2012	Ghurair	0
2013	True Story	1
2014	Lexington Times	

Although the statistics don't look that encouraging it should be noted that six out of the last ten winners went on to group success as older horses. Most notably, Dubai Destination took the Group 1 Queen Anne as a 4-y-o and Rio De La Plata was five before he won a pair of Group One's in Italy. Lexington Times has recently won a Listed race (in March) over seven furlongs. He can win again at up to a mile.

7 Furlong 2-y-o maiden (formerly the Trundle Maiden, Glorious Goodwood.		
2001	Sweet Band	0
2002	Wahsheeq	0
2003	Psychiatrist	0
2004	Jonquil	0
2005	Opera Cape	0
2006	Kilburn	0
2007	Latin Lad	0
2008	Jukebox Jury	3 GW
2009	Stags Leap	1
2010	Pausanias	1 Listed
2011	Nawwaar	0
2012	Steeler	NR
2013	Snow Trouble	0
2014	Dutch Connection	

This was once a reliable maiden where numerous quality horses made their debuts in 70's, 80's and early 90's. The quality of winners declined markedly but there have been signs of an upturn recently. Dutch Connection, a very useful colt who was third in the National Stakes, can win again in races up to a mile.

Superlative Stakes		
Newmarket, 7 furlongs, July.		
2001	Redback	
2002	Surbiton	
2003	Kings Point	
2004	Dubawi	
2005	Horatio Nelson	
2006	Halicarnasus	
2007	Hatta Fort	
2008	Ole Ole	
2009	Silver Grecian	
2010	King Torus	
2011	Red Duke	
2012	Olympic Glory	
2013	Good Old Boy Lukey	
2014	Estidhkaar	

This race was raised to Group 2 from Group 3 in 2006. There are some very decent winners in this list, notably Dubawi and the more recent Olympic Glory who added two more Group 1's as a 4-y-o. Estidhkaar is a smart colt who disappointed in the Dewhurst, but ran really well on his return when second in the Greenham. He can win more Group races at up to a mile.

Horse Index

Electra Voice	725	Flying Pursuit	546
Electrify	1200	Flying Royal	547
Elegant Annie	1360	Flyweight	650
Elronaq	940	Fol O'Yasmine	729
Eltezam	814	Follow The Rules	1422
Emarati Bin Dubai	328	Fool To Cry	1577
Emerald Bay	726	Footbridge	1667
Emerald Loch	100	Forecaster	137
Emperor Napoleon	45	Forever A Lady	445
Endless Acres	619	Forge	1512
Engage	1510	Forgotten Wish	816
English King	1061	Formative	271
Enjoy Life	171	Foundation	651
Entertaining Ben	1174	Four's Company	469
Entsar	727	Frank Cool	1062
Epsom Day	647	Freddie Freeloader	329
Epsom Icon	288	Free Passage	256
Equinette	1349	French Encore	1146
Eshaan	769	French Legend	46
Estidraak	1511	Frenchman	942
Etidaal	1376	Fresh Arugula	470
Ettie Hart	289	Frozen Venture	1431
Evangelical	589	Full Extension	1308
Excel Quest	1635	Fumata Bianca	1160
Excellent Sounds	1159	Funny Oyster	27
Excessable	545	Furiant	1014
Executor	354	G K Chesterton	6
Exist	648	Gabriella	524
Exoteric	941	Gadwa	420
Eyeshine	649	Gale Song	1636
Ezanak	1665	Gales Point	1350
Falcon Annie	466	Galley Bay	47
Fang	1101	Gallipoli	592
Fantasy Queen	1004	Gambit	471
Farkle Minkus	444	Gamesters Boy	472
Fashaak	815	Gandvik	292
Fashaar	1575	Garcia	593
Fashionata	728	Garter	943
Fast And Furious	155	Gaspirali	1309
Fastlady	1201	Gecko	817
Fataawy	1102	Gemmulal	330
Fawaareq	912	General Hazard	138
Feel This Moment	206	General MacArthur	1221
Feelin Dicky	630	Generalship	652
Ferntina	290	Gershwin	1063
Fiftyshadesofpink	1307	Giant Shadow	139
Final Frontier	896	Gift Wrap	770
Fine Blend	1175	Gifted Master	1310
Fingertips	385	Gimlet	1311
Fire Diamond	467	Gin In The Inn	594
Firesnake	468	Ginger Joe	331
First Rate	1576	Girl With A Pearl	525
First Selection	401	Girls In A Bentley	631
First To Post	590	Gittan	818
First Victory	172	Glamour Boy	1293
Fishergate	591	Glittering	567
Fisherman's Blues	1079	Glorious Times	1446
Fisherman's Friend	239	Gloryette	526
Fiuntach	291	Go Paco	1578
Flagstaff	1666	Gold Crown	1488
Florencio	1176	Gold Faith	103

Jufn	175	Late Show	1403
Juliette Fair	1670	Lathom	599
Jumeirah Star	386	Le Tissier	53
Justice Angel	555	Learning Curve	1433
Justice Bold	556	Leaving For Good	1294
Justice Focused	557	Lee Bay	661
Justice Lady	558	Lee Lane	600
Justice Lass	559	Leitrim Traveller	1267
Justice Lucky	560	Lembit And Butler	478
Justice Pleasing	561	Lexington Law	831
Justice Rock	562	Lieutenant General	1222
Kafoo	528	Light Infantry	832
Kafoor	950	Like No Other	734
Kajaki	1448	Lil's Joy	1423
Kakashan	657	Limonata	258
Kalasadi	774	Line Sport	601
Karaama	656	Linguistic	662
Karakoz	1585	Little Voice	955
Kashtan	539	Livella Fella	447
Kassia	299	Lizzie Siddal	663
Kemsing	1500	Log Out Island	833
Kept Under Wraps	597	Logistics	775
Kesselring	829	Lohalvar	332
Key On Kodiac	951	Lolwah	1516
Khaleesy	658	Lone Angel	1530
Khameela	914	Long Island	568
Khor Al Udaid	659	Long John Silver	1268
Kidd Malibu	1671	Look Closer	1672
Kilim	422	Looks Great	176
Kindly	403	Lord Aslan	54
King Cole	387	Lord Huntingdon	55
King Of Dreams	1461	Lord Topper	956
King Of Rooks	830	Loud Applause	141
King Of Saxony	193	Love In The Sun	1673
King Of Spin	1178	Love On The Rocks	957
Kiri Sunrise	598	Loveisallaround	898
Kiss	423	Lovell	10
Kitaaby	1106	Luang Prabang	1648
Kitty For Me	1179	Lucky Lot	404
Kokoni	1514	Ludi Lu	1649
Komedy	952	Lugano	1404
Kuantan	359	Lunar Son	300
Kyllukey	953	Lune De Sable	1674
La Celebs Ville	477	Lydiate	602
La Mortola	660	Ma Peek	1107
Labrynth	1515	Macho Mac	1161
Lady Canford	157	Maestro Mac	1162
Lady Katherine	1007	Magic Mirror	664
Lady Lloyd	991	Magical Path	1315
Lady Macapa	1041	Magnificent Madiba	29
Lady Nahema	511	Majdool	1586
Lady Oak	1489	Majestique	208
Lady Perignon	52	Makanah	915
Lady President	1148	Make Fast	56
Lady Rocka	1351	Malaika	302
Lagenda	1449	Malakky	1108
Lake Hamana	9	Malmoosa	1109
Lake Placid	954	Manaafidh	834
Landlocked	194	Manshood	735
Lapilli	733	Mansoob	835
Lastmanlastround	706	Maqueda	1352

Olympic Runner	742	Playful Dude	1501
Omeed	1091	Pleasure Dome	337
Onesie	212	Pocket	572
Opal Tiara	305	Pocket Of Stars	1295
Open 'n Shut	1590	Poetic Guest	1093
Operative	499	Poet's Word	1519
Orangey Red	1679	Point Of View	429
Organ Scholar	992	Point Of Woods	108
Ornate	743	Poldark	848
Orotaveo	604	Polish Empress	1181
Orvar	842	Pop Culture	1364
Our Elton	481	Poppypiccolina	548
Out And About	744	Port Paradise	993
Out Of The Dark	843	Pouliche	541
Pacches	306	Powerallied	606
Pacharana	428	Predetermined	62
Pacific Salt	361	Predilection	671
Pack It In	1112	Premier Currency	849
Packing	1270	Prequel	672
Packing Empire	1271	Press Gang	850
Pacommand	213	Pride Of Angels	406
Paddy Power	605	Princely Sum	673
Painted Cliffs	1225	Princess Kodia	1113
Palenville	844	Private Jet	965
Paling	362	Projection	363
Palisade	1411	Prosecute	1464
Palm Avenue	1008	Protocol	778
Palmarola	1066	Proud Maria	902
Palpitation	243	Pure Art	109
Papa Luigi	845	Pure Fantasy	364
Paper Faces	1591	Pure Note	14
Papou Tony	31	Pure Vanity	365
Parafin Young	335	Qareen	1114
Paris Bound	61	Qeyaadah	530
Paris Magic	1317	Qortaaj	745
Paris Protocol	846	Queen Of Sicily	196
Party For Ever	195	Queen's Trust	1520
Pass The Moon	1318	Queensbury Odyssey	531
Past Master	261	Quick Look	994
Pastoral Star	1163	Quick March	366
Patanjali	1009	Raaqy	922
Pause For Applause	1362	Raasmaal	532
Peaceful Journey	180	Radar O'Reilly	1081
Pennerley	571	Rah Rah	1021
Penny Poet	405	Rahyah	746
Peppy Miller	1092	Rajadamri	1135
Perfect Spirit	669	Rampers	1272
Perfectly Fair	181	Rantan	90
Performer	847	Rashaaqa	1594
Pericles	336	Rateel	1532
Persaverance	1140	Rathbride Raven	1384
Persuasive	670	Raucous	747
Philadelphia	1592	Ravelin	966
Piacere	214	Ravenhoe	1022
Piazzini	1680	Ravens Quest	1164
Pickapocket	964	Ravenswood	1365
Pillar	107	Receding Waves	851
Pilot Hill	380	Recent Acquisition	381
Pinch A Kiss	1363	Reconsider	215
Pirquet	777	Recorder	748
Plantation	1593	Red Box	1412

Dams Index

Carpet Lady	612	Coffee Time	1175
Carpet Lover	27	Coh Sho No	569
Cartimandua	940	Coin Box	216
Cascata	428	Come April	258
Cassandra Go	5	Come Touch The Sun	433
Cassis	1207	Comeback Queen	812
Casual Look	649	Comic	179
Cat Hunter	995	Como	942
Catch Me Later	391	Complexion	1461
Cat's Eye Witness	825	Conciliatory	1303
Causeway Charm	536	Confidential Lady	1412
Causeway Lass	19	Constitute	1599
Causeway Queen	217	Convidada	832
Cawett	1610	Cool Kitten	182
Ceilidh House	107	Copperbeech	13
Celestial Dream	558	Copy-Cat	376
Celestial Girl	665	Corrozal	333
Celestial Welcome	241	Cosmic Destiny	1623
Centifolia	583	Cosmic Wing	386
Centreofattention	1634	Cosmodrome	10
Ceoil An Aith	1271	Costa Brava	40
Cercle D'Amour	184	Courte Paille	1151
Chameleon	817	Coy	148
Champion Tipster	1587	Cozy Maria	640
Chantarella	1484	Creative Mind	257
Chanter	683	Crimson Ribbon	1622
Chantilly Beauty	556	Crofters Ceilidh	1135
Chasing Stars	271	Cross Your Fingers	372
Chatham	1215	Crystal Gaze	77
Chatifa	597	Crystal House	185
Chehalis Sunset	687	Crystal Maze	689
Chelsea Rose	379	Crystal Moments	1454
Chervil	1003	Crystal Music	14
Chiarezza	486	Cuilaphuca	867
Chiba	430	Cuis Ghaire	1567
Chicane	938	Cyber Star	304
Chifney Rush	229	Daganya	585
Child Bride	207	Dahama	221
Chingford	1367	Dahlia's Krissy	1067
Chintz	1233	Dalvina	757
Chiosina	89	Dama'a	1324
Chocolada	59	Dame Rochelle	1153
Choice Play	1501	Dance Away	88
Choisette	546	Dance Hall Girl	682
Choose Me	670	Dancing Jest	952
Christmas Kid	1234	Dancing With Stars	1132
Christmas Tart	710	Danedrop	438
Church Melody	1432	Danehill Dreamer	176
Chushka	480	Danehill's Dream	44
Cilium	1513	Danetime Out	794
Circle Of Life	1235	Daneville	509
City Sister	688	Danielli	1325
Civility Cat	948	Danish Gem	874
Claba Di San Jore	660	Danzelline	894
Claiomh Solais	191	Darajaat	1560
Clarice Orsini	1161	Dark Missile	43
Classical Dancer	162	Dashiba	553
Clever Day	491	Date With Destiny	414
Clodilla	319	Dawn Chorus	1187
Clowance	371	Dawnus	303
Coconut Shy	1094	Days Of Summer	969

Fashion Rocks	562	Gallic Star	312
Fashionable	1537	Galvano	512
Fast Flow	46	Gamesters Lady	472
Fatal Attraction	1174	Ganga	740
Fathoming	478	Garter Star	244
Featherweight	876	Gay Mirage	359
Feelin Foxy	630	Gay Romance	1533
Feet Of Flame	1152	Gaze	737
Felin Gruvy	498	Geesala	1097
Festoso	120	Gemini Gold	632
Fictitious	364	Geminiani	1058
Fidelio's Miracle	1329	Gemma's Pearl	476
Field Of Clover	51	Genuine Charm	1205
Fillthegobletagain	616	Georgie The Fourth	26
Fine Threads	785	Germane	208
Finnmark	1625	Gertrude Bell	645
Finsceal Beo	189	Getaway Girl	240
Fire Up	1308	Ghandoorah	912
First Eclipse	1078	Ghurra	675
Firth Of Lorne	198	Gift Dancer	1204
Fiscal Policy	395	Gilded Vanity	473
Fiumicino	291	Gilt Linked	499
Five Sisters	1425	Gitane	539
Flame Of Ireland	460	Glen Rosie	690
Flanders	758	Glisten	959
Flashing Green	1662	Glitz	538
Flashy Wings	576	Gold Bubbles	1029
Fleche d'Or	759	Gold Charm	1612
Fleeting Spirit	658	Gold Hush	1511
Flirtation	1216	Gold Vault	1238
Floating	266	Goldamour	458
Florentia	1400	Golden Party	1678
Flower Of Kent	1106	Golden Whip	1579
Fly By Magic	1134	Gonfilia	781
Fly In Style	152	Good Enough	930
Folle Blanche	883	Good Girl	1188
Follow My Lead	900	Good Hope	1571
Foolish Ambition	899	Good Shot Noreen	1284
Foot Of Pride	902	Gower Song	505
Forest Crown	98	Gradara	1063
Forgotten Me	1165	Graduation	1398
Four Miracles	1556	Grain Only	410
Frabjous	1076	Grand Zafeen	603
Frappe	949	Great Hope	1451
Free Offer	256	Grecian Bride	1683
Freedonia	1060	Greek Easter	121
Freefourracing	1677	Green Poppy	1632
French Connexion	1146	Green Room	122
Friendlier	1314	Grenadia	793
Fritta Mista	1120	Greta d'Argent	1030
Frivolity	1476	Growling	15
Frosted	466	Guajira	415
Fuerta Ventura	1069	Guard Hill	500
Fugnina	956	Guessing	341
Funday	1538	Guilia	712
Funny Girl	1196	Gwynn	685
Gadalka	1300	Gypsy Carnival	644
Gala Style	604	Habaayib	529
Gale Green	857	Haigh Hall	579
Galeaza	91	Hairspray	288
Galicuix	1330	Haiti Dancer	1426

Joyfullness	127	Lady Catherine	772
Jules	622	Lady Elgar	1334
Juniper Girl	149	Lady Gray	809
Just Devine	1182	Lady Hawkfield	1183
Just Dreams	990	Lady Hen	859
Justice System	316	Lady Icarus	1217
Kahara	1523	Lady Livius	910
Kahlua Kiss	746	Lady Lupus	1222
Kalidaha	774	Lady Of Everest	420
Kalleidoscope	34	Lady Of Kildare	1489
Kaplinsky	606	Lady Rockfield	1397
Karaliyfa	1263	Lady Simpson	1604
Kareemah	911	Lady Xara	717
Kashoof	715	Lahinch	1244
Katajan	1557	Lake Toya	9
Katy Nowaitee	461	Lanark Belle	534
Kawn	1373	Land Of Dreams	194
Kayak	1265	Landela	760
Keep Dancing	750	Landmark	123
Keepers Hill	1613	Langs Lash	1085
Keladora	1002	Lanzana	1531
Kelly Nicole	655	Lark In The Park	1653
Kelowna	692	Lasso	274
Kelsey Rose	279	Lastroseofsummer	706
Kensita	1466	Lathaat	242
Kerry Gal	1515	Latte	133
Kerrys Requiem	1478	Laureldean Gale	166
Key Change	1498	Laurelei	631
Key Girl	976	Law Review	1443
Key Secure	1672	Lawyers Choice	402
Kezia	1036	Layla Jamil	582
Khatela	816	Laywaan	986
Kheleyf's Silver	628	Le Montrachet	1228
Khibraat	985	Lear's Princess	1111
Khubza	1190	Leavingonajetplane	1294
Kibara	422	Lebenstanz	282
Kiddari	1671	Lemon Rock	1421
Kilakey	951	Leopard Creek	1526
Killinallan	1600	Lesson In Humility	1687
Kilo Alpha	643	Liberally	1121
King's Siren	117	Liberty Chery	1452
Kintyre	423	Lidanna	1261
Kirunavaara	1260	Liffey Dancer	1591
Kiswahili	1536	Light Blow	1065
Kitty Kiernan	915	Light Sea	87
Kiva	881	Light Shift	1524
Knapton Hill	1529	Lighthouse	855
Kocooning	1301	Lightwood Lady	1382
Koniya	1638	Like A Dame	1245
Korresia	1272	Likeable	1191
Krasotka	1072	Lilac Moon	464
Krynica	233	Lilakiya	795
Kummel Excess	545	Lilli Marlane	885
Kyniska	134	Lion Forest	1309
La Bataille	468	Lisa Gherardini	1483
La Chapelle	997	Liscanna	1246
La Grande Zoa	1276	Liscoa	551
La Mere Germaine	1358	Lisfannon	516
Laddies Poker Two	1614	Listen	1615
Lady Avenger	275	Little Audio	853
Lady Brora	38	Little Scotland	111

Raisonable	775	Roscoff	125
Rakata	1180	Rose Blossom	1020
Rare Ransom	1605	Rose Cheval	284
Rare Virtue	360	Rose De France	209
Ras Shaikh	624	Rose Of Battle	892
Raven One	1126	Roselyn	779
Raymi Coya	56	Rose's Destination	463
Raysiza	350	Roses For The Lady	1291
Rayyana	1635	Roses From Ridey	826
Razzle	272	Rosinka	178
Razzle	567	Roskeen	842
Real Doll	82	Rosy Dudley	636
Real Sense	699	Rotunda	1490
Reality	377	Rouge Noir	1589
Rebecca Rolfe	263	Rougette	1349
Rebelline	1074	Rouwaki	966
Record Time	249	Royal Blush	928
Red Dune	1583	Royal Esteem	322
Red Feather	1385	Royal Punch	547
Red Intrigue	1024	Royale Danehill	1509
Red Red Rose	728	Roystonea	651
Red Remanso	891	Rugged Up	206
Red Riddle	1534	Rule Of Nature	369
Red Vale	1457	Rumline	1130
Redglow	637	Rumoush	920
Redoutable	1386	Rumplestiltskin	1253
Regal Curtsy	1004	Runaway Top	489
Regal Heiress	1402	Ruse	893
Regal Lustre	292	Russian Rhapsody	1578
Regency Rose	340	Russian Spirit	531
Regina	1178	Rutba	850
Reign Of Fire	1495	Saajidah	1383
Reine Violette	297	Sabria	83
Remarkable Story	1646	Sacred Love	238
Remember When	1251	Saddlers Bend	338
Renascent Rahy	1143	Safina	836
Renashaan	907	Safiya Song	1108
Resort	679	Sahara Sky	765
Rhal	234	Sainte Colombe	384
Right After Moyne	124	Saintlike	1127
Right Rave	998	Saldenaera	638
Rimth	1252	Salsa Steps	1171
Ringarooma	306	Salt Rose	799
Riotous Applause	1456	Salvia	158
Rising Wind	1419	Samorra	1379
Rivara	439	Sampers	1438
River Bounty	93	San Sicharia	1057
River Flow	1485	Sant Elena	738
Riymaisa	315	Sanwa	1298
Road To Reality	1315	Saoire	190
Robe Chinoise	1455	Sarayir	923
Robema	801	Sassari	1194
Rockburst	1264	Sassenach	1296
Rocking	963	Sassy Gal	1496
Romantic Myth	108	Satin Cape	462
Romarca	586	Sattelight	450
Romie's Kastett	1290	Satulagi	929
Rondo Alla Turca	1274	Saturday Girl	41
Roo	1617	Saturn Girl	84
Ros The Boss	1039	Sauvage	1648
Rosabee	47	Save Me The Waltz	1014